CALIFORNIA FISHING

Tom Stienstra

Foghorn
Press Inc.

ISBN 0-935701-34-6

51995>

9 780935 701340

CALIFORNIA FISHING

Foghorn Press
555 De Haro Street
The Boiler Room, # 220
San Francisco, CA 94107
Telephone: (415) 241-9550

Library of Congress Cataloging in Publication Data

Stienstra, Tom
California fishing: the complete guide / by Tom Stienstra.
    p. cm.
Includes index.
ISBN 0-935701-34-6: $19.95
1. Fishing--California--Guide-books. I. Title.
SH473.S75 1992
799.1'09794--dc20   91-43499
                                          CIP

Printed in the United States

CALIFORNIA FISHING

Tom Stienstra

Foghorn
Press Inc.

Managing Editor.....................................Ann Marie Brown

Senior Research Editor............................Robyn Schlueter

Bay Area Research Editor....................Nancy Christensen

Copy Editor ....Nina Schuyler

Book Design and Maps...............................Luke Thrasher

Dear Anglers:
We've done our best to make this the most accurate and complete guide to California fishing possible. However, if you have a suggestion, revision or addition to make this book even better, please send it to us at Foghorn Press, 555 De Haro Street, The Boiler Room, # 220, San Francisco, CA 94107. Thank you, and happy fishing!

CONTENTS

HOW TO USE THIS BOOK

■ You can search for your ideal fishing spot in two ways:

1. If you have a specific lake, stream, river or waterway in mind and want to see what CALIFORNIA FISHING has to say about it, use the index on page 744 to find it, and turn to the corresponding page.

2. If you'd like to go fishing in a general area, and want to know what that area has to offer, use the California state maps on page 9 or in the back of this book. Find the zone you'd like to fish in (such as E1 for the San Francisco Bay Area or H3 for Santa Barbara), then turn to the corresponding pages in the book.

■ The book is conveniently divided into Northern, Central and Southern California. Within these sections, the book is further divided into map sections to allow for greater detail.

Northern California, Pages 119-538
> (map sections AØ, A1, A2, A3, A4, BØ, B1, B2, B3, B4, CØ, C1, C2, C3, C4, DØ, D1, D2, D3, D4, EØ, E1, E2, E3, E4, E5)

Central California, Pages 539-654
> (map sections F1, F2, F3, F4, F5, G2, G3, G4, G5, H2, H3, H4, H5, H9)

Southern California, Pages 655-738
> (map sections I3, I4, I5, I6, I7, I9, J5, J6, J7, J8, J9)

see the bottom of every page for reference to corresponding maps

■ What the Ratings Mean

Every fishing spot in this book is designated with a fishing rating of 1 through 10. The ratings are based on three elements:

1. Quality of fish available.
2. Quantity of fish available.
3. Scenic beauty and side-trips available.

*Note that in some cases, one of the elements may be so compelling that it causes the rating to rise or fall a notch or two. Remember that many factors infuence fishing success. Many waters rated 4 and 5 can provide good fishing and a quality adventure when conditions are ideal.

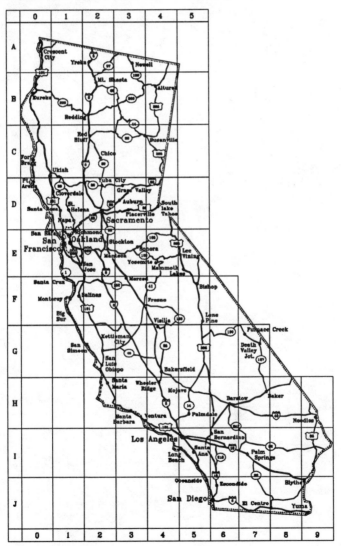

10	Can't be improved—GREAT!
9	Has three elements.
8	Has two elements, almost three.
7	Has two of the elements.
6	Has one element, almost two.
5	Has one element, parts of others.
4	Has one of the elements.
3	Almost has one of the elements.
2	Has none of the elements.
1	Hopeless.

SECRETS OF THE MASTERS

ANGLER ETHICS

1. Always keep only fish that you will eat. Never waste a fish.
2. Always bring a plastic bag along to pick up any litter you come across. Never litter.
3. Always check state fishing regulations prior to fishing any water. Never guess.
4. Always take personal responsibility to practice safe boating skills. Never hope.
5. Always have a map before venturing to hike-in streams. Never trespass.
6. Always conduct yourself quietly in campgrounds. Never disturb your neighbor.
7. Always be absolutely fire safe. Never figure "It'll be OK."
8. Always call the Fish and Game toll-free poacher hotline at 1-800-952-5400 if you see illegal activity. Never ignore it.
9. Always share information with children, particularly those new to the sport. Never be rude; you will be repaid in kind.
10. Always pick the conservation organization that best protects your favorite fishery, and support it financially. Never expect somebody else to protect it.

BLUEGILL, CRAPPIE & SUNFISH
BONDING A FAMILY FOR LIFE

Mom and Dad were taking their children fishing, and at a small lake known for some little bluegill and sunfish, a magic scene unfolded.

Dad baited his hook with a worm, clipped on a little red and white bobber a few feet above it, then tossed it out along a patch of tules. Before long, he had done so for all five of his kids, three girls and two boys, and they all sat along the shore transfixed by the sight of the bobbers floating about on the surface.

"Let's count to 25," said Dad.

"One ... two ... three ... four ... " started Mom, leading the family chant.

Suddenly, when the family had counted to 12, one of the bobbers started popping around, dancing a bit from side to side, then was pulled under the surface a few inches. The oldest boy, Bobby, grabbed his rod, and his eyes looked like they were going to pop out of his head.

"I've got one, I've got one," he shouted. He tussled away with the fish, and after a few moments, brought a four-inch bluegill to the shore.

"It's a beauty," said Mom.

"Let's put it in a bucket," added Dad.

He then dipped a big bucket in the lake, filling it with water, and the bluegill was dropped in. The two younger children, Susan and Tommy, immediately stopped fishing to watch the bluegill in the bucket. But in the next hour, Bobby had caught another, Dad caught two, and Mom and the two older girls, Nancy and Janet, shared catching one.

So after an hour, there were five bluegill swimming around the big bucket, which fascinated the kids, the little boy in particular. He picked up his rod and reeled in the line, then put the bait in the bucket, dangling it amid the five bluegill.

"I don't know why you're fishing over in the lake," he announced. "The fish are here, right in the bucket. You can see them."

I remember the episode well because that little kid was me, age 4, right about when I started to grow my beard.

An adventure like this can bond a family for life. It transcends all differences in age, size and sex for the participants, a time when big people and little people can share the exact same experience, rather than one watching, the other doing. In the many years since those weekend fishing trips, all five of us kids have turned out completely different, each leading separate, distinctive lifestyles in different parts of the western United States. But we remain bonded for life and it was the family adventures that did it.

Fishing for bluegill, crappie or sunfish can also get children fascinated by the sport, because they are apt to get their first genuine success from it. So many youngsters give up fishing simply because when they first try it, they don't catch anything. "What's the point?" they figure.

The answer comes with bluegill, crappie and sunfish, and in some cases, yellow perch or Sacramento perch. These are species that can be caught by the bucketful, where it is common to catch five or 10, and not unusual to catch 20 or 30.

My dad, Bob Stienstra Sr., always has had a remarkable knack for catching bluegill and crappie. It starts with his great natural enthusiasm, and is followed by grounded confidence that he could get a nibble at any time.

"The key is to make sure you have a good time," he advises. "The people who catch lots of bluegill and crappie always enjoy themselves tremendously, and that includes kids. I can always tell when somebody isn't going to catch much. Before they even go out, they're upset about something, complaining about something not being perfect enough for them. I believe there is a big bluegill in the sky who rewards happy people and gets revenge on unhappy people. If you are having fun, you will usually catch something."

First you must identify a pond or lake that has panfish available. Small ponds are the best for bluegill and sunfish, especially those with many tules along the shoreline. Crappie usually require a larger water base to expand to large populations, and Sacramento and yellow perch always are abundant wherever they are introduced.

Once on the water, the best spots for bluegill, sunfish and perch are always on the edge of tule berms, in the vicinity of submerged trees, or in shady areas during very hot weather. Crappie, meanwhile, prefer underwater structures, such as trees, old dock pilings, and submerged rockpiles.

"If you don't start getting nibbles within 10 or 15 minutes, then it's time to move," advises my dad. "These fish like to school up together, often in groups of 50 or more, and you should keep exploring new spots until you find them."

To help find a school of fish, my buddy Foonsky takes an unusual approach. After catching a bluegill, he puts a hook through its back, ties on 15 feet of fishing line, then ties on a small, inflated balloon. The logic is that the bluegill will swim back to the school, tugging the balloon along the surface as an indicator. "Cast to the balloon and you are casting to the school of fish," Foonsky says. Alas, it doesn't seem to work in practice as well as when he explains it.

My dad, on the other hand, keeps trying new spots until finally getting a hookup. He prefers the shallows along the left or right edge of a tule berm, or in an opening between two tule berms.

"For bluegill and sunfish, I really like to use a Colorado Spinner baited with a small worm," he says. "But it can be hard to find Colorado Spinners. It drives me nuts when I walk into a tackle shop, ask for them, and they look at me with a total blank on their faces. That's when I realize they don't know sickum about bluegill."

A Colorado Spinner is simply a hook with a small spinner blade on the shank of it. After tying it on the line, you simply place a small bobber a few feet above it, then put a small red worm on for bait. What happens is that the spinner puts out a small flash to help attract fish to your bait, imparted whenever the bobber moves around a bit, either by a light breeze, a tug by you, or by a nibbling fish. By using a bobber, it adds to the excitement because you are "sight-fishing," that is, every nibble, tug and bite on your bait is telegraphed through that little dancing bobber.

There are other options. If you fish from a float tube, small raft or boat, you can cast-catch bluegill like crazy during the beginning of summer with a one-inch Rapala, best in blue or gold, casting it right along the shoreline, tules and trees. When a flyfisher finds a school of bluegill, a fish can be caught on nearly every cast by using a woolly worm and strip retrieve.

For crappie, a different approach is required, because crappie prefer eating minnows rather than worms.

There are two species of crappie: White crappie are often abundant but small; black crappie are always fewer but larger. Either way, they are among the best tasting fish available in freshwater. When you get into a school, you can catch dozens of them.

The best technique for crappie is to fish at night, right under an intense, bright light at a dock. Cabela's, the mail-order specialist, also offers an attractor light that can be placed in the water. The light attracts gnats, which in turn attracts minnows, which in turn attracts crappie. When fishing at night with a bright light, you either offer a live minnow for bait, hooking it gently through the back, or cast small white crappie jigs across the path of the light.

During the day, instead of letting the fish come to you, you have to go to the fish. They tend to hang 15 or 20 feet deep amid submerged trees with lots of branches, or suspended near areas with rockpiles. The technique is very simple: With a white or yellow crappie jig, you let it straight down below the boat, then simply pull on your line with the rod, then let the jig settle again. Up and down, that's all there is to it. When you get a bite, stick to the spot, because crappie always hang out in schools, even the big ones.

A good fishfinder can really help in locating crappie. I use a Lowrance X-15, and their new models are also tremendous. In addition, crappie are often discovered by accident while bass fishing, because a big crappie will often hit a bass lure. When that happens, we always tie on crappie jigs, get right over the fish, and start jigging straight up and down. A good crappie bite is as exciting as anything in fishing.

When I was 11, I remember a vacation trip to Clear Lake, when we arrived close to midnight and almost couldn't find a camping spot. As the rest of my family were getting out their sleeping bags, I was getting out my fishing rod.

"What do you think you are doing, young man?" my mother asked me.

"I'm going fishing."

"In the middle of the night?" she asked.

"Yep."

My dad just grinned as I used a flashlight to find my way to the lake. At a small marina, a bright light was beaming through the darkness at the end of a little wood dock. I still can remember how excited I was. After all, I was "on my own."

I flipped a short cast across the lighted piece of water, and instantly hooked up. Next cast, same thing. By 3 a.m. I was so tired and groggy that I had turn my back on the fish.

When I returned to the camp, everybody was deep asleep. Not for long, though. I woke them up.

"Look!" I said. "Look at all the fish I caught!" I held up a stringer loaded with about 30 crappie.

"Great," said my dad, bleary-eyed. "We'll have 'em for breakfast."

Mom just smiled, her eyes only half open. "We're proud of you."

I never slept as well as I did that night.

MR. CATFISH
THE LEGEND

If you have ever heard of the legend of "Mr. Catfish," you might think the man was a myth. But he was as real as the fish he caught, some 4,000 to 5,000 catfish per year, and he did it right in the middle of the day, when catfishing is supposed to be at its ultimate worst.

His real name was George Powers, a kind but eccentric fellow right to the day he died at age 77. In his late 60s, he went scuba diving in lakes to watch catfish, and from what he learned, created a system that works like none other ever practiced. The first time I went fishing with him, we caught 27 catfish between noon and 2 p.m., and then went home because he made a cast and didn't catch a fish. Over the several years that I fished with him, it was always like this.

"If I bring my bait in even once without a fish on, I'll move or go home," he said. "I either get my bite or leave."

And what a character: He drove an ancient truck with no brakes, stopping by using the hand-powered emergency brake. He said he drank glasses of cow's blood to stay healthy, "tastes just like warm milk," and then lived 30 years after having a serious heart attack and three doctors telling him he had a terminal case of cancer. He said the faith of his wife of more than 50 years, Carrie, had more to do with his recovery than anything a doctor prescribed.

When George first started catfishing, he couldn't understand why everybody seemed so content fishing well into the night, using heavy gear, and catching three or four, rarely a few more.

"That's not good enough for me," he told me one day as we drove to a launch ramp at Clear Lake, his left hand poised on the hand brake. "Three or four in a night? I knew there had to be a better way so I told my wife I was going to find it."

So at age 63, this small, friendly man borrowed some scuba gear and went diving in Clear Lake.

"I couldn't believe what I saw," he said. "The catfish were right on the bottom all right, but every one of them was lying perfectly still on the shady side of the little mud dobs, the little hills on the bottom of the lake. I never saw a fish on the sunny side of those mud dobs. That told me something. That is when I started to figure it all out."

You see, Powers explained, at night catfish spread out "all over creation," searching for something to eat. That's why so many people fish for catfish only at night. As a result, "You never really know where to fish, and you are just picking up strays." But in the day, you know where the catfish will be—on the bottom on the shaded side of those hills.

"Since I knew where the catfish were, I figured if I could figure out a way to get my bait right in front of them, I could catch 'em all day long," Powers said.

It took a few months of experimenting, but soon he had developed a system that had confounding results: 5,000 catfish in a single year, an 18-pounder on six-pound line, a fish per cast for hours. That is how legends are made.

We launched his little 11-foot boat near Rodman Slough at the north end of Clear Lake, cruised out several hundred yards offshore, then anchored. I was surprised at his light equipment—ultra-light spinning tackle and an unusual rigging for catfish: two small No. 10 Kahle hooks, with a 1/32-ounce splitshot placed on the line 12 inches above the hooks. Next he put on his bait: two dead minnows that had their stomachs slit and were hooked through their backs, opposite each other.

This is far from the traditional method. Most people who fish for catfish use standard surf leaders with two large hooks and a sinker, then use clams, anchovies, sardines or chicken livers for bait. They fish at night, waiting, waiting and waiting. Not Mr. Catfish.

He cast out his offering about 40 feet, and then did absolutely nothing, setting his rod down and allowing the line to settle limply on the water.

"It takes about two minutes to let it sink to the bottom," George announced. "Remember that we know exactly where the catfish are, on the shady side of those mud dobs. That's why I cast directly into the sun."

When the bait reached the bottom, Mr. Catfish went to work. He took his fishing line between his thumb and forefinger and began to pull it toward him at the rate of about seven or eight inches per minute. After three minutes, he had retrieved about two feet of line, when the light tip of his rod began to pull down about an inch.

"Look! See that!" George said. "See how the rod tip is pulling down just a bit? That is because the bait is being dragged uphill on one of those mud dobs. Because I casted right into the sun, it's now on the sunny side."

He pulled the line two more inches, and the rod tip bent down a bit more. He pulled one more inch, and the rod tip sprang straight, the pressure relieved.

"Watch this!" he exclaimed. "The bait just tumbled toward me on the shady side of that mud dob!"

An instant later, the fishing line moved in the water about three inches. "I'm getting my bite," Powers said, and then with a mighty tug, he set the hook. The little rod bent down like a croquet hoop, and George tussled away with the fish. Five minutes later, a five-pounder was in the net. A beauty.

Seeing was believing, and now I understood the logic behind his passion. The angler should always cast directly toward the sun and retrieve slowly, so the bait tumbles over these hills on the lake bottom and falls gently into the shady side, right into the lair of a catfish. Hungry or not, the fish cannot resist your bait.

The method works perfectly at natural lakes, ponds, and up the arms of reservoirs, spots where the bottom has natural ledges, hills and holes. At reservoirs where the banks are very steeply sloped, you either use the traditional prisoner-of-hope technique, or head to the warm water in protected coves far up the lake arms.

Over the years, I fished with George several times, and as long as it was sunny, we caught fish after fish. But stray even a bit from the Mr. Catfish Method, and I would catch nothing. One time, as an experiment during a day when we were catching a catfish on every cast, I attempted to do the exact opposite—casting with my back to the sun. My beloved companion shook his head in exasperation, wondering how I could possibly try anything different from what had been proven.

In this unscientific test, I didn't get a bite for 30 minutes while Mr. Catfish, casting directly into the sun, continued to fill the stringer. I finally turned around, started casting into the sun again, letting the bait tumble into the shady side of those mud dobs, and immediately began catching fish.

"You're a stubborn one," said George, a bit irked. "A lot of people are like that. Dang it, I try. A lot of people listen but they don't practice what they're listenin' to."

LARGEMOUTH BASS
TO CATCH A WORLD RECORD

On a magic spring day at Otay Lake, Jack Neu caught five largemouth bass that weighed a total of 53 pounds, 12 ounces, likely the largest five-fish bass limit ever caught on Planet Earth. I was with Jack on that special day, and as the day evolved, it was like everyone at Otay had been launched into a different orbit than that of the rest of the world. In a two-hour span at the dock scale, there were 30 bass checked that weighed eight pounds or more. Out on the water, though, Jack and I were still at it. He'd caught four that weighed 45 pounds, topped by a 16-pounder. One more and he'd have a place in history.

But when it comes to bass, history is being lived in California, not just looked up in record books. In the past few years, there have been several line-class world records for largemouth bass (see the record listings in the appendix), including the most famous of all, the 22-pound bass caught and released at Lake Castaic by Bob Crupi, which was just four ounces shy of the all-time world record. Because so many anglers spend so much effort searching for big bass, the world record has become a legend among legends. It weighed 22 pounds, four ounces, and was caught in 1932 in Georgia by a postal worker named George Perry, who after documenting its weight, took it home, cut it up, cooked it, and then with the help of his family, ate it.

The pursuit of a new world record bass has turned many California lakes into intense, sometimes maniacal scenes: Guns have even been drawn (see text on Lake Casitas in Zone H3). You often have to reserve your bait in advance. In the choice between bass or spouse, some anglers have chosen bass. At lakes that are open only on Wednesdays and weekends, some anglers will pay college kids to sit/sleep/eat in their trucks with trailered boats so come Saturday morning, they will have a good place in the line at the boat ramp. Crazy? You bet it is. But the possibility of catching a 15 or 20-pound bass can do strange things to the afflicted.

Before you start your search, however, you need to choose between one of two strategies. Do you want maximum excitement and catch rates, but virtually no chance at a monster-sized bass? Or do you want that monster, and are you willing to have long periods of dead time in the process?

Jack Neu and I chose the latter, and in the amazing script that followed, Jack caught four bass that weighed 45 pounds. One more and he'd make history, so we cruised off to a cove at Otay Lake in search of No. 5. It was a clear, warm spring day. The hills were still green, and after a cold winter, the bass were coming to life with the warming water temperatures. Jack reached an old favorite spot, slowed the boat to a crawl, and with a switch, flipped on his paper depth graph.

"The new electronic fishfinders are outstanding," Neu said. "They show bottom contour, depth, water temperature, and mark fish. But I really prefer the paper graphs, even though they are more expensive because you have to keep buying paper scrolls for them. They not only are more detailed, even showing the size of individual fish, but because it is all recorded on paper, you can take it home, lay it out on a table, and study the lake bottom. After doing this for a while, you can get to know the bottom of a lake as well as the layout of your own home."

For 10 or 15 minutes, Jack motored his boat around the cove at the pace of a slow walk, and while doing so, studied the marks on the graph. Suddenly, his shoulders tightened, his moustache scrunched up, and he pointed at the graph.

"Look! Look!" Neu exclaimed, like a safecracker who had just heard the right click on the dial. "There's a big one down there." He pointed to the mark on the paper where a large inverted "U" had been marked, indicating a large fish.

Jack immediately tossed out a small buoy, which spun around as a rope weighted with a sinker unrolled to the lake bottom. The buoy then floated in place, secure, and Jack pointed at it. "That marks the spot," he said. "That is where the big one is."

He slowly motored the boat off to the side, threw out an anchor, then turned off the engine. His breathing was shallow and short, his speech edgy but excited. It was like sparks were shooting from him. For a moment, I thought Jack might become the first exploding fisherman in history.

Then he pulled out a cardboard flat, the kind that will hold two 12-packs of Budweiser, but instead of beer it contained about 15 live crawdads. Jack waved his hands over the top of the crawdads as if he was a sorcerer applying a magic spell.

"First one that moves gets elected," Jack said. Gets elected as bait, that is. By waving your hand over the top, you can find the liveliest bait. One squiggled a bit, and Jack grabbed it. "You're elected," he told the crawdad.

Jack held the crawdad on its side with a thumb and forefinger, positioned so the little bugger couldn't nail him with a pincher, then hooked it right between the eyes with the No. 8 hook that was tied to his fishing line. Jack uses no sinker, no leader. Just a small hook.

"That way the crawdad will swim around most naturally," Jack said. "When a big bass starts to chase it, the crawdad will swim off trying to escape. Nothing gets a big bass more excited than what appears to be a good meal about to escape."

With his rod and reel in hand, Jack tossed the bait out toward the buoy, then let the crawdad swim to the bottom. For bass fishing tackle, Neu believes in a rod and reel which is comfortable for the angler, regardless of whether it is a spinning outfit or revolving spool reel. "What is more important," he explained, "is knowing what to do, then doing it exactly right."

For 20 minutes, knowing what to do was to do nothing. We waited and watched, staring at where our lines entered the lake. Then suddenly, his line twitched in the water a bit.

"I'm getting bit," Jack said. His eyes looked like they were about to pop out of his head. Jack stood with his rod, careful not to pull or twitch it, and pointed it at the water. As he did so, his line gained a bit of slack, and it settled limply in the water. Jack's stare burrowed in on that limp line, and for 20 seconds, nothing happened.

"I know a big bass is down there," Jack said, almost panting now. "I know my crawdad is down there. And I know that something made it move."

Five seconds later, the slack line began to draw tight.

"He's picking it up, he's picking it up," Jack said. The line tightened further, then tightened a lot, and Jack Neu set the hook hard, and it was whoo-ya time; the rod bent down like he'd hooked Moby Bass. He'd hooked it! The fish never jumped, but instead it bulldogged in short thrusts of power near the lake bottom, just as the big ones so often like to do. The runs were very short bursts, and Jack had trouble turning the fish toward the boat. Finally, though, he started to do so, and soon after that, the fish was alongside, then in the net. Jack Neu had caught that magic bass No. 5, and it was another beauty.

Well, it turned out to weigh an even eight pounds, bringing Jack's five-bass limit to 53 pounds, 12 ounces. It is one of the most extraordinary angling accomplishments in history, and Jack's strategies and techniques provide an excellent fishing lesson that anyone can learn from.

But just don't think that all you have to do is show up, use electronics to find a big bass, and then toss your bait out to catch it. "It sure doesn't work that way most of the time," Jack said with a laugh.

For example, I have had the opportunity to "pre-fish" many of the great bass lakes in Southern California. That is where one has the chance to fish a lake that has been closed for many months before being opened to the public. Sounds like a can't-miss deal, right? Wrong. I've had times where electronic fishfinders marked hundreds and hundreds of fish, yet not one of them would bite.

"The first day I started using electronics to locate fish, I couldn't believe how many bass were down there," Jack said. "Then after I didn't catch any, I was ready to throw the thing overboard. I started to wish I didn't know how many fish there were. Electronics can provide an edge, not a guarantee. To catch these big bass, everything from start to finish needs to be working for you."

On that magic day at Otay, everything was.

■ Another Way To Do It ... Larry Brower Shows How

If Larry Brower's fishing boat looks like a miniature tackle shop, it's because it is. Larry actually owns a small tackle shop, and as different lures designed for largemouth bass become available, he is one of the first anglers able to obtain them and test them. Thus, over the years he has tried just about everything, and as one who fishes bass tournaments throughout the west, he has also fished every premium bass water in California. Larry has been able to put it all together and not only win a lot of tournaments, but also develop skills that anyone who wants to catch bass can learn from.

For my fishing lesson, we ventured to Shasta Lake, which with 365 miles of shoreline is the largest reservoir in California. It is also Larry's home water. "I love the place because each of the lake arms is like a completely different lake," Larry said, putting his boat in gear, and cruising out of Bridge Bay.

Like all anglers who fish bass tournaments, Larry never uses bait and tries never to kill a fish. Instead, only lures are used, and fish are kept in a live well until weigh-in, then released. The results are higher catch rates than for those who use bait, with days of 15 to 20 bass common during good bites on warm spring days. Alas, you often have to wade through many dinks to hook a few in the 14 or 15-inch class, rarely bigger.

So bass anglers who only use lures can get more action, try more varieties of strategy, and cover a lot more water than anglers who use bait. The trade-off, however, is a trend toward smaller fish. It is an attractive deal because instead of waiting for the fish, you are pursuing them. To do it, though, requires the approach of a detective.

"You have to take several key factors into consideration," Larry said as he slowed his boat and pulled into a cove. "Time of year, water temperature, water clarity, weather, depth of fish and whether they are in pre-spawn, spawn or post-spawn periods . . . each of these can have a tremendous influence on your approach at any lake or reservoir. Then there is the lake itself, and you must have the ability to find habitat that will hold bass. You have to be able to do these things."

That can be very easy at times. One of the best ways to introduce a newcomer to fishing is to take them to a small lake or farm pond in the spring, when the first warm weather of the year gets the bass hungry, active, and inspired to move into the shallows and carve out spawning territory. From bank or boat, you cast out small lures along the shore, and there are times when the bass often seem to smack the lure almost as soon as it hits the water. Over the years, I have gained permission from private landowners to fish many farm ponds. I just search out the name and address of the owners through the respective county's assessor offices.

Sometime from March through May, my bass buddy Ed Ow and I will take a trip to these ponds, fishing out of float tubes, or even a small little raft I've got. We'll paddle around, then cast along the shoreline, using either spinning gear or fly tackle. Floating or shallow diving lures, such as the one-inch Rapala, or small poppers can attract large numbers of surface strikes. We've had many days where we've caught 50 to 100 fish, although only rarely will one be larger than 14 or 15 inches. Regardless, it is one of the best ways to clear a bad case of brain cobwebs.

Then there are times when it isn't so easy, and that is when Larry Brower can provide some assistance. "One of the first orders of business is to determine how deep the bass are and what seasonal influences are affecting them," he said. You then divide the year into a series of periods: Pre-spawn, spawn, post-spawn, and winter.

To do these things, Larry explained, you start by coordinating time of year with water temperature and recent weather trends. As spring arrives, for instance, when the first warm weather of the year is starting to show and the water temperature climbs from the high 40s to the low 60s, the bass change their behavior. They begin to emerge from the winter slowdown, and start to think about eating something. This is called the pre-spawn. During this period, most of the bass are 15 to 25 feet deep, deeper if the water is cold, shallower if it is warm. The best way to entice them is using quarter-ounce jigs with a pork-rind trailer, which is called "pig & jig" in the lingo of bassers, Salt & Pepper Grubs, Gits-Its, large spinnerbaits, and diving plugs.

"Each lake has a different set of factors, of course," Larry explained, "but as the water starts to warm up, the bass will usually go from being very deep and suspended (often along underwater drop-offs), to moving up a bit off submerged rockpiles, near creek inlets, and off shoreline points."

During the pre-spawn period, the water temperature can fluctuate up and down for months, just as the weather always seems to have trouble making its mind up whether it wants to be hot or cold, dry or wet, windy or calm. In turn, that affects the depth of the fish.

But as spring arrives in force, the first warm weather of the year comes and the water temperature will then rise to 62 to 66 degrees. This is when the bass change their behavior for a second time. They rise up to the shallows, in the backs of coves, along stretches of shoreline with tules, submerged trees, or overhanging bushes. When this occurs, the bass are getting ready to spawn, marking out some territory. It can provide some of the most exciting fishing of the year, although all fish should be released so they can spawn successfully.

You approach the coves quietly, then make precise casts right along the shoreline in as little as two inches of water. One trick when using a mouse (imitation), spinnerbait, or plastic worm, is to cast it right on the shoreline, then twitch it so it plops in the water. It looks just like something alive, and the bass, now territorial and defending the nest, will often attack like a German shepherd police dog biting into a burglar's butt.

Many lures are effective during this period. Plastic lures that imitate shad are called "hard baits" or "crank baits" and many work well, since to the bass it appears an invading minnow might want to nibble on their nest. The following are worth using: Shad Rap, Rattletrap, Countdown Rapala, Fat Rap, Hula Popper, Jitterbug, Rebel minnow, Crawdad, Rebel Pop-R, and Chugger. Spinnerbaits, buzzbaits, and even plastic worms fished shallow also can entice strikes.

After the spawn, usually in early summer, the fish will move "off the beds", leaving the shallows and moving into areas where there is good underwater structure, usually about eight to 15 feet deep. By this time, the water temperature is usually from 68 to 74 degrees, and this "post-spawn" period extends from early summer through fall.

"This is where knowing a lake really pays off," Brower said. "You can spend a lot of time looking for the fish and not finding them if you don't know where to find traditional structure that will hold the bass during the summer. Shade becomes very important. I've caught some tournament-winning fish by casting right along boat docks, because the fish will often hang under the dock to catch some shade."

In addition to docks, other excellent habitat for bass during the post-spawn are submerged trees ("stickups") and bushes, areas around old dock pilings, deep coves where shoreline vegetation provides shade, and large rockpiles. Although some surface action occurs at dawn and dusk, the best results come when fishing deeper. And while some hard baits can attract bass (Shad Rap and

Rattletrap are good examples), the best results are on "plastics," or plastic worms and grubs. The best is the Green Weenie, especially the small one with the red head, but several varieties of worms are the best offering you can provide during the summer for bass. The best colors are motor oil, purple and black, or the grubs that are flecked with salt and pepper.

"Worming" takes a lot of skill to do it right. "Most people cast the worm out and reel it back in way too fast," Larry said. "Consider how it looks to the bass. It must appear as natural as possible, and that means working it very slowly."

The favored technique is to "walk it" down shoreline ledges into structure. "Walking it" simply means retrieving it slow enough along the lake bottom so it slithers along, right into the intended destination, right where a bass is hanging out for the day.

As the summer progresses and the water temperature continues to climb, the bass become more and more difficult to catch. This is compounded at reservoirs with dropping water levels, which force the bass to move to different areas. This combination is rough on anglers, because they have to approach a familiar lake that has had a dropping water level as a completely new water. Add intense waterskiing pressure, where the wake from speeding boats slaps against the shoreline and makes the bass especially jittery, and you face a very challenging scenario. Challenging? By late August, it can seem like you need a Jaws of Life to get their mouths to open.

Finally in winter, the cold weather returns, the bass metabolism slows down, and they head deep to find the warmest water in the lake. Few anglers even try for bass during this period because conventional methods rarely work. It can seem like there isn't a single bass in the entire lake. What to do? The answer is to drift your boat over an underwater ledge, drop-off or hole that is 35 to 50 feet deep, then simply vertically jig straight up and down. This technique also can take fish during the pre-spawn period, when a cold weather snap returns the fish to winter tendencies.

"Regardless of the time of year, I like using revolving spool reels with conventional bass rods," Larry said. "When casting hard baits, plastics or jigs, you need to be in close touch with your bait. You don't get that with a spinning outfit."

He also mentioned that water clarity can cause problems for some anglers.

"If the water is clear, the bass can be spooked off from biting by being able to see your line," he explained. "At lakes or reservoirs with clear water, anything heavier than eight-pound line can get you in trouble." Sometimes the water can be so clear that six-pound line is required. Other times, it is not even a factor. In any case, if you feel you are doing everything right, yet still are not getting bit, then switch to a lighter, low-visibility line. My personal favorite is the Maxima ultra-green.

"When you start fishing a lot, these things become almost automatic, and you start catching a lot of bass," Larry said.

He was a living testimonial to that. On our trip to Lake Shasta, he deduced in a matter of minutes that the fish were in late pre-spawn, adding up a series of factors: Time of year (spring), the weather (hot for three straight days), water temperature (up three degrees to 59), and water clarity (fair from recent rain runoff). Larry tied on a spinnerbait, and I used a diving Rattletrap lure.

"The bass are bound to be 12 to 18 feet deep off rockpiles," he announced.

Using a foot pedal to control an electric motor, Larry navigated the boat along a series of coves, and we casted as we went. Our lures would sink quickly, then we'd crank the reel and give the rod a twitch so they would come to life, the lures appearing alive as they bumped off the rockpiles and through the adjacent water. Bang! Larry had one. Wham! So did I. Doubleheader. Both were about 13 or 14 inches long, and they disappeared into the green water after being released.

"You have to be something of a detective to fish for bass," Larry said. He smiled, pushed the foot pedal for the electric motor to move the boat onward, and then pointed at a little creek inlet where a trickle of water was flowing into the lake.

"This looks like a good spot," he said. And he smiled again as he let fly with his lure, always thinking, always hoping, happy in a sport where all you need is just one more bass to cast to.

TROUT FISHING
A CHALLENGE AND AN ANSWER

Trout fishing in California is like religion: many paths, one truth. Trout are found in more habitats than any other fish, from the lonely creeks in the South Warner Mountains of Modoc County to the urban ponds in the Bay Area and L.A. Basin, from the large reservoirs in the foothills to the gem-like lakes in high wilderness. They come in a variety of sizes and species, and the methods used to try and entice them vary just as much. You can troll for them or baitdunk for them, sneak up on a pool in a stream like a Mi-Wok Indian, or spend an evening wading hip-deep with a fly rod. Many paths, one truth. No fish inspires more dreams, fulfills more good times, or takes people off on more adventures of greatness than the trout. Many paths, one truth.

■ Trolling For Trout . . . Ed "The Dunk" Dunckel

The Dunk was a great baseball pitcher in the 1940s, painting the corners of the plate with a variety of fastball, curveball and knuckleball brushes. Lefty O'Doul, a two-time .400 hitter with the Yankees and a legend in the old California league, spotted The Dunk one day, and after a tryout, was ready to sign him to a professional contract. But the next week, Uncle Sam got The Dunk first, drafting him into the U.S. Army.

Well, the years flow by, and now The Dunk crafts his artwork with a fishing rod instead of a baseball. He fishes for everything, and drives damn near everywhere in this pursuit, but his specialty is trolling for trout, where he consistently catches more and bigger trout than anybody I have ever fished with.

On one April trip with Ed Dunckel, we were heading to a mountain lake where the access road had just been snowplowed the week before. We met a pair of Caltrans plow drivers while buying some goodies for the trip.

"Gonna try Beardsley out?" one of them asked me.

I nodded while The Dunk just listened.

"Heard it's plenty tough," answered the other. "But there was this one guy who caught a limit the other day with a couple of 25-inchers."

"Well, we'll just have to try a little," said The Dunk.

A moment later, we were in my truck, driving down the highway, and The Dunk had a grin like a Cheshire cat.

"You know the guy they were talking about who caught the 25-inchers?" he asked me.

"You know who it was?" I asked.

"Sure," said The Dunk. "Me." Then he paused, still with the grin. "Except they got it wrong. They were 20-inchers, not 25. That's OK. Let 'em dream."

More people troll for trout than try any other method across California's hundreds of lakes and reservoirs, and the Dunckel method can help any of them catch more and larger fish. The keys are basic but the application is not: proper rigging, trolling speed, finding holding areas, and getting the depth exactly right. Here is a capsule account:

■ Proper Rigging

You just plain have to get it right. The standard technique is to trail a nightcrawler behind a set of flashers. The problem is that most of the flashers are too big, too heavy or too long, and can make catching a small trout about as exciting as reeling in a weed.

Dunckel always uses Cousin Carl's Half-Fast flashers with the two half-brass and half-silver blades in the flat (not dimpled) finish. I also like the Sep's Mini Flashers, because of their minimal drag. Many other types can work, and the most famous are the Luhr Jensen Ford Fenders. In any case, be sure you follow the directions on the back of the container and have the exact amount of leader the manufacturer recommends.

There are a few tricks, however. "I always use a half of a nightcrawler and work it on the hook so it lies perfectly straight in the water, with a small piece running free behind the hook," advises The Dunk. If you don't have the patience to work a hook through the center of a nightcrawler, it can be done quickly with a worm threader.

For those unfamiliar, you do not use sewing thread. You don't use any thread at all. Instead you skewer the nightcrawler with the threader, which is just a small diameter piece of metal tubing, and place your hook on one end of the tubing. Then work the nightcrawler from the tubing to your hook and line. Thus, the worm lies perfectly flat in the water.

If you get short strikes, where trout consistently bite off the end of the nightcrawler, resist the urge to shorten the nightcrawler, as this will reduce its action in the water. "Instead," says The Dunk, "add a stinger hook." To accomplish this, when you tie on a hook, do not trim off the excess line. Tie on an additional hook to the line, then hook the end of the nightcrawler with it as a trailer or stinger.

When using lures, always test them with and without snap swivels. The lures must look perfect as they are trolled, or a trout will no more hit it than a chicken will sit on a duck egg.

The following lures are excellent for trout in lakes: Triple Teaser (white with red head), Z-Ray (gold with red dots), Rainbow Runner (red), Needlefish (in rainbow or gold with flecked dots), Roostertail (yellow with silver spinner), Little Cleo (gold), Kastmaster (gold), Mepps Lightning, Bingo Bug, Speedy Shiner (gold), Rapala, and Wee Wart. In addition, trolling a black or dark green woolly worm fly either naked or behind flashers also can work well. You may have your own preferences, but these are our favorites for California lakes.

Dunckel prefers using a long, light graphite rod set up with a small level-wind reel over spinning tackle. "You don't get the line twist you sometimes get with spinning reels," he says, "and it seems a lot easier to set the hook quick."

One wildcard option is drift-jigging. Instead of trolling, you turn the engine off and let the boat drift slowly over prime areas that have been identified as holding trout. You let a lure descend straight down from the boat, then when satisfied with the depth (often best right off the bottom), you simply jerk the rod up, then let the lure settle back down. You repeat this over and over. Crazy? Give it a try, especially in late winter. Many huge trout can be caught with this method when nothing else will work. The best lures for drift-jigging for trout are a white crappie jig, Gits-It and Krocadile spoon.

■ Trolling Speed

Most anglers yearn for a flat calm day when even a large lake looks like an Oregon mill pond. Not The Dunk. "A little breeze can often help," he said. "The trout often come up shallower when there is a riffle on the water from a little wind, and if it blows enough, it can provide the perfect trolling speed."

That's right. Dunckel likes to turn his engine off, then let the late afternoon breeze push his boat over the best spots. "It is the perfect drift, because nature and the wind are in control, not you or me. Almost everybody trolls too fast, even most of the people who know better and point out others who are trolling too fast." By using this method on several windy late April trout openers, we have limited several times even though just about everybody else was having trouble. Many thought we had a secret bait. Wrong. It was the wind.

If the wind isn't strong enough to push the boat along, then The Dunk advises adding a trolling plate to any motor larger than two horsepower in order to be able to slow the boat down. If you are renting a boat, and the motor does not have a trolling plate, then bring a five-gallon bucket with a rope along so that you can tie it to the side or drag it behind to slow down the boat. "When you are trolling with flashers and a nightcrawler, you want the blades to just barely tumble. That's what gets 'em."

When using lures, you can go a bit faster, a tiny bit. The natural way to select trolling speed with lures, of course, is to trail the lure alongside the boat and watch to see if the action is exactly right. A tip is to let it trail about 10 feet behind the boat, then check it out, because many lures behave differently with more line in the water. When using Rapalas for brown trout, it is important to troll slower than when using flashy metal lures for rainbow trout.

Another trick when trolling is to zigzag your course, run in figure eights over a hot spot, or to stop the boat completely, then give it a surge. Why? Each of these actions makes the lure drop in the water, fluttering as it goes, as if it is wounded, then when it gets straightened out again by the line, it will swim as if trying to escape. We discovered this by accident years ago when my engine ran out of gas one day, stopping the boat (causing the lure to drop in the water). When The Dunk and I both started to reel in, big trout immediately hammered both of our lures.

■ **Finding Holding Areas**

Every habitat has areas that hold larger numbers of trout than others. In many lakes, particularly lakes with little underwater structure, reefs, or drop-offs, the rule is that 10 percent of the water will hold 90 percent of the trout. A lot of people think the central purpose of electronic fishfinders is finding the little blips that indicate fish, but actually they are best used to examine the bottom contours of the lake. My Lowrance X-15 is suited perfectly for this.

Any time there is a dramatic change in the habitat, you will find fish along the edge of that change. Long, straight, bare stretches of shoreline do not hold fish. On the other hand, jagged points, coves, rockpiles, drop-offs, submerged boulders and trees do. Look for the change. It might be where a tiny feeder stream is trickling into the lake or the late afternoon shade line crosses the water. You must locate and then fish these areas.

One tip The Dunk discovered is that during periods of drought, when lake drawdowns can be significant, you can take a hard look at the dry lakebed and memorize the areas that will attract trout during high water. "I always get out of my boat and hike along these areas, even with my bad legs," said The Dunk. "It is amazing how many lures you can find. People snag them and lose them during high water, and then in low water, you can go out on a fortune hunt, hiking around on the dry lakebed. Over the years I've found hundreds and hundreds of lures."

■ **Getting The Depth Right**

Earlier I mentioned that 90 percent of the trout are usually found in 10 percent of the water. That is true not only horizontally (at key habitat areas), but vertically as well. You must troll at the precise depth, especially if you want to catch big trout.

In the spring, the trout are often near the surface, roaming around in the top 10 to 15 feet of water, picking off the first insect hatches of the year and snaring misled minnows. As summer arrives, the warm water on top drives the trout deeper to a layer known as the thermocline, where the water is cool, and rich in oxygen and food. In the fall, usually around the third week of October, lakes will "turn over", as the stratified temperature zones do a flip-flop, bringing the trout again to the surface for several weeks. Finally, winter sets in and the trout again go deep, this time finding warmer water.

So right off, the spring and fall are the best times to troll for trout because the fish are near the surface and no specialized deep-water techniques are required. In the summer, though, when most people fish, the trout are buried in the thermocline except for brief periods at dawn and dusk, when they come up to the surface for the evening rise. By that time, however, many people have already left without getting a bite. The problem is that they troll too shallow, right over the top of the trout.

Many methods are available to troll deeper: downriggers, plastic planers, lead-core line, or just adding weight. Whatever you choose, just make sure you do it. I like using either downriggers or lead-core. With downriggers, no heavy weight is required on your line, so using very light tackle is necessary even when fishing deep (see text on salmon trolling). With lead-core, I like to tie on 30 feet of leader and then troll a Triple Teaser.

Always test different depths until you find the fish, starting deep, then testing more shallow. Downriggers and lead-core trolling line are excellent because downriggers provide exact readouts of how deep the line is, and lead-core line is color coded. Therefore, when you find the fish, you can return to the same depth every drop. Trout will stay in an ideal temperature zone as if they are locked in jail.

Besides mastering technique, though, there is something special about The Dunk when he feels he's catching on to a lake. He glows with energy.

On one trip we took to Canada, Dunk caught a five-pound rainbow trout and a bystander who saw the entire affair was amazed. "It was like he knew that trout was going to bite . . . like he thought it right onto his hook."

In a way, he does just that. It's a combination of knowing his craft mixed with a natural sense of enthusiasm. The latter is the best lesson of all.

■ Shoreline Baitdunking . . . An Old-timer Shows How

The first time I saw Dave Lyons, I thought he looked kind of like a statue. He appeared to be about 60 years old, sitting motionless with his line trailing out in the water, as if he had been sitting there for 20 years.

"Catch anything?" I asked.

"A few," he said, and I instantly noticed the deep kindness in his eyes, a look not many people have. Then he hoisted up a stringer with four of the most beautiful rainbow trout you could imagine.

Before I could say another word, he suddenly dropped the fish, picked up his little spinning rod and slashed it back, setting the hook. The little rod bent down, and Dave just smiled that real kind smile of his, and worked the fish to the boat. It was another beauty, about 15 inches, and he had his limit.

"I'm not used to 'em this big," he said with a grin. "The first one scared me because it was bigger than I usually get. Usually I just get the little ones."

Back at the dock, it turned out that Dave Lyons was hardly a statue, but more like a fish-catching machine; he had caught trout limits 46 times in a 50-day span. It also turned out that he wasn't 60, but more like 73. As for the kindness in his eyes, well, I was right about that. In my career as a journalist, I have met an entire spectrum of people who fish, from the governor to the garbage man, from scientists to Hells Angels, but the kindest gent of them all is Dave Lyons. He freely gives to strangers what most people are so protective of: friendship, time and knowledge.

It wasn't long before I arranged a fishing trip with Mr. Lyons. I was fascinated with the guy. After all, it doesn't seem to be too tough to toss out some bait in a lake and catch trout, but 46 limits in 50 days? Well, it turns out that the old-timer puts his own spin on it that makes it quite easy. His techniques are applicable when baitfishing for trout at any urban lake or mountain reservoir, and they work.

Dave insisted on rowing a boat to his chosen spot, a quiet little cove, where we tied up. He was using very light spinning gear, an ultra-light graphite rod with a micro spinning reel, and light line. "Never anything heavier than four-pound test," he said. "Don't want the fish to see it."

He took his fishing line in hand and slipped a little, clear red bead on it, then tied on a snap swivel. "Got to give them something to look at," he said, explaining the red bead. To the snap swivel, he tied on a Lyons Leader, which consists of a loop (which is attached to the snap swivel), with 18 inches of leader to a No. 8 bait hook on one side, then eight inches of leader to a No. 8 egg hook on the other side. He uses four-pound Maxima line.

"OK, OK," Dave announced, "time to feed 'em. You have to feed the trout, you know, try a little of everything, get 'em excited and hungry."

Dave then proceeded to put a half of a nightcrawler on the bait hook. "I don't use any weight," he said, "just the nightcrawler. It's enough to get the bait down." On the other hook, he popped on a salmon egg, working it up to the eye of the hook, then molded a small piece of yellow Power Bait over the shank and hook. With a careful flip, he tossed it out 35 or 40 feet, and watched the bait disappear into the lake.

"I like to bring lots of different kinds of bait," said the old-timer. "I use everything at one time or another, sometimes on the same hook." Other baits include Power Wigglers, Zeke's Floating Cheese, Targhee's cheese, Pautzke's salmon eggs, and small garlic marshmallows. He has even used canned corn.

I had also tossed out my bait, and after about 15 seconds, it too settled to the bottom.

"What happens down there is that the nightcrawler sinks to the bottom, but the Power Bait and egg float up a bit, just above any weeds down there, right where the trout are swimming," Dave said. "Now I'll show you a little trick."

He laid his rod down, leaving the bail of his spinning reel open, then took the line from the reel and placed it under the light plastic lid of a worm tub.

"There's virtually no resistance so when a fish picks up the bait, he doesn't get spooked," he explained. "But when the line gets pulled out from under that lid, I know darn well there's something going on down there."

Just as he said so, his line was pulled from the worm tub lid, exactly as he said it would. "Now it's time to get ready," he said. The line tightened just an inch or two, and he reared back on the tiny rod to set the hook.

"Got him!" Dave said, then playing it lightly, let the trout scurry around, eventually persuading it alongside, where I netted it.

The entire time, the old master had that special kind look on his face, a look that cannot be faked, that comes only from a life lived without anger or bitterness over the strange cards that are sometimes dealt and then must be played.

There are other ways to rig, of course. The most simple is a single-hook rig. You start by slipping a small barrel sinker (for casting weight) over your line, then tying a snap swivel to the line. Add 14 inches of leader and a No. 8 hook.

A key with this set-up is making sure your bait floats up off the bottom a few inches. That can be done by using Power Bait, Zeke's Floating Cheese, or a marshmallow. If you use a nightcrawler for bait, you can use a worm inflater to pump it up like a little balloon to make it float. A worm inflater is actually just a small empty plastic bottle with a hollow needle. You jab the needle into the nightcrawler, give the bottle a squeeze, and the little guy looks like a little brown balloon.

Suddenly, my line started to move a bit in the water. It tightened a few inches and I set the hook, and instantly felt the weight of a trout bending the rod. Meanwhile, the master was also getting a bite, his line having been tugged from under the plastic lid. Dave then set the hook and had a trout of his own. After a few minutes, both trout were alongside the boat, 14 and 15-inchers.

"You better net 'em both," Lyons said with that kind smile of his. "These are awful big. I'm afraid of fish this big. I better get the paddles out in case they attack the boat."

We both just laughed, a winner's laugh.

■ Fishing Streams ... Living In A Time Machine

He wears moccasins, and walks softly, but doesn't carry a big stick; more like a magic wand when he does his thing in the mountain streams of California. It's my older brother, Bob Stienstra Jr., the best stream fisherman around, who's a mix of Davy Crockett and a Mi-Wok chief when he stalks the evening rise.

To fish trout streams, you have to be willing to hike, and hike a lot. You have to hike into remote areas, then hike some more up and down the stream, then hike back to camp. Ol' Bob is such a gutsy but stubborn hiker that he's been tagged with nicknames like Rambob and Mr. Steelhead. But when he returns to camp, he's the one with the awesome stringer of trout. Every time.

The people who say it takes patience to catch fish have not met Rambob. Even when he was Rambobby, the guy never had any patience. On the stream, he does not wait around for the fish to bite. Instead, he chases them down like a river hunter who would fit a part in a Louis L'Amour western.

There is nothing complicated about it, even though the results always confound our longtime camping companions, Jeff "Foonsky" Patty and Michael "Furnai" Furniss. After hiking all day, Rambob slips off his pack and slips on his moccasins. While the rest of us are complaining about how sore and tired we are, Rambob just smiles and quickly puts his six-piece Daiwa pack rod together, fastens on his micro Sigma spinning reel, puts his tiny tackle box in his shirt pocket and slinks off toward the nearest river.

He sneaks up along the stream, walking softly and low, keeping his shadow off the water, then zips short casts into the headwaters of pools, the edges of riffles, tailouts, and the pockets along boulders. Rambob doesn't wait long for an answer. He either gets his bite or moves on, spending only a few casts at each hole, and therein lies his secret. He covers a tremendous amount of water in a short time.

If you ever take a look at the underwater world of a trout stream, you would be stunned to see the number of small fish in every pool, often as many as 75 to 150. Among those are a sprinkling of bigger fellows, and maybe even a few reaching 14 inches or larger. When your lure hits the water, every trout in the pool sees it almost immediately, and responds by twitching a bit in the water. After five or six casts, they even start to get used to it. The lesson? If you haven't caught one by then, you are not going to—time to move on.

Rambob has the stamina to carry out this strategy. He covers about a mile of river per hour, walking almost as much as fishing, but in the process he gets a fresh look at a new hole every few minutes. When we walked the entire John Muir Trail together, about a 225-mile trip, Rambob added another 50 miles to his total simply by fishing each night. He's in his 40s and there is scarcely a 20-year-old around these days who can keep up with him. But after all, he's a Stienstra. Heh, heh, heh.

His tackle is simple, and so is his tackle box. He specializes in small metal lures and pinpoint casts, and occasionally uses the fly-and-bubble combination, especially in the eastern Sierra. The lure that works best is the gold Met-L Fly, which has been out of production now for 20 years—but we still have a stash of about

15 remaining. The inventor's son, Jim Douglas Jr., said he plans to re-introduce the lure to the market sometime in the 90s. Other lures that work well are the Panther Martin spinner (black body and yellow spots), Z-Ray (black with red spots, or gold with red spots), yellow Roostertail, or Kastmaster (gold).

Ed "The Dunk" Dunckel invented a lure we call the Mr. Dunckel Special, which works particularly well in clear-water conditions, when many lures frighten the fish instead of attract them. It is a 1/16-ounce Dardevle spoon which is painted flat black, then dabbed with five tiny spots of red paint.

When Rambob is on the prowl, he looks something like a burglar sneaking out of Fort Knox with an armful of gold. With those moccasins on, he moves quickly and silently, stopping at the good-looking spots to make short but precise casts, then moving on again.

I've never seen him so happy as when he's in his moccasins in the wilderness, then comes around a bend and spots a deep river hole, the kind where the water flows through a chute at the head of it like a miniature waterfall. He knows what's ahead, and the vision is enough to inspire him onward.

It's like being in a time machine, back in the days of Joe Walker and Liver-Eatin' Johnson, and who knows, maybe Rambob has some reincarnated roots from that era.

■ Flyfishing . . . California's Trout Legend

The world's best angler, a bear, was in the middle of the stream, waiting and pouncing, thrashing and crawling, trying to catch a trout. But alas, the bear was zilched, and it finally hopped away, empty-pawed, when it spotted us.

"You know there's fish in that pool," said Ted Fay, nodding at me. "The bear wouldn't be there otherwise. We'll have to try it later."

I thought Ted had to be kidding. I mean, if a bear can't catch a fish, how are we supposed to? Later that day, however, we did return. Ted sneaked up on the spot, flycast his line so the fly landed lightly at the head of the pool, and looked as stoic as a cigar store Indian as the fly drifted without a hit. Next cast, nothing again.

"C'mon Ted," I said, "let's move on and . . ." —but right then, Ted struck, and his fly rod suddenly bent practically in half. He had a big trout on, and in the shallows, it skittered across the top, raising hell and splashing water. It ended up being a six-pounder, 27 inches long, a magnificent fish, and as we left, that same bear appeared from the forest, wondering just how Ted Fay did it.

A lot of people have wondered the same thing. Ted has since passed away, but his unique method of flyfishing remains a force in California angling, as well as his legendary accomplishments. Ted is the only person I have ever seen catch 10 trout on five casts with a fly rod, or who could take fish in water just previously worked, unsuccessfully, by other anglers. A legend? After I wrote a story on him in *Western Outdoors* magazine, he received 22,000 orders in three weeks for his unique weighted nymphs.

When he was ill and near his death, I asked him what he considered his greatest angling accomplishment. "It would have to be the salmon," he said, smiling. "In one day in Alaska, I caught 63 salmon on the fly. Nobody else was catching anything." But actually, Ted's greatest accomplishment was introducing flyfishing to anglers who had always been scared off by the possibility, making them realize it isn't a casting nightmare with a lot of snagged bushes and few hooked trout.

His true passion was for trout, where he invented the system of using weighted nymphs, two at a time with a dropper, and fishing pocket water with short casts.

It always bothered Ted Fay that many people considered flyfishing an elitist sport that required special skills. He maintained that some of that was due to sportsman's shows where casting experts flail the line back and forth before delivering long, perfect casts.

"That gives people the wrong idea," Ted said. "Newcomers think they have to do all that back-and-forth stuff with the line to cast and catch fish. I teach the opposite, with a minimum of back-and-forth, short casts, and a lot of fishing time, not casting time. If you are going back-and-forth with the fly line too much, you're not fishing, and you're bound to get yourself into trouble."

The advantage of flyfishing is that you have the opportunity to fish more, not less, than with other methods. Ted Fay taught me how. With hip waders and a wading staff, you wade near the center of a fair-running stream, then zip those short casts to the little spots that hold trout. The fly should land just upstream of the spot, then be allowed to drift past the spot. Then, pick the fly up, backcast once to dry it off, and zip the cast to the next spot on the river. With a spinning rod, you have to retrieve the lure all the way back through unproductive water, so you can spend much more time actually fishing promising spots by wading and flyfishing.

Flyfishing is not only productive, but you learn tremendous lessons about insects, water temperatures, feed patterns, and cycles of the seasons. For newcomers, it is best to fill your fly box with a selection of major patterns: Caddis, Cahill, Mayfly, Paraduns, Mosquito, Woolly, Parachute, Wulff, and some weighted nymphs, Bomber, Stonefly, and Hare's Ear. Buy a fly reel with interchangeable spools, loading a floating line on one, sink-tip line on another. Use three by nine-foot leaders. Many quality fly rods are available, but I am particularly impressed with the renovated line of Fenwicks, especially the IronFeathers. For newcomers, I suggest getting a No. 6, eight-foot length, and then when more experienced, getting an 8 1/2-footer for longer casts.

Ted Fay was a master at getting the perfect drift out of his fly and knowing precisely when to strike. He would make short casts, not long ones, then mend his line, or flip it to the outside, so the fly would drift straight with the current, as if no line was attached. If the fly skids instead of drifts, not only will no trout hit it, but you may even spook the hole.

"I believe in following my fly with the rod," Fay explained, demonstrating this on the river. "I do that by keeping my rod in the direction of the fly, and then I watch my line ever so carefully on the drift. Often the trout are just sitting in the pockets, moving just an inch or two either way to pick off insects as they come floating past. Remember, you don't need much line out. If you are fishing a nymph (wet), all you will see when a trout grabs it is that the downstream flow of your line stops. You have to strike, like right now. You'll never feel a thing. It's all in the watching."

In fishing cold, freestone streams, Ted designed a system using two flies simultaneously, usually both weighted nymphs, a Stonefly and a Bomber. It was a fantastic display that early summer day when he caught 10 trout on his first five casts, and then just grinned at me as if he did it all the time. Turns out, it wasn't that unusual.

"I've heard of him doing that many times and I have seen him do it several times myself," confirmed John Reginato, a close friend of Ted Fay, and as the longtime general manager of Shasta

Cascade, also a legendary figure in the outdoors history of California.

Flyfishing is a fun, exciting sport that provides the maximum intimacy with your river surroundings. You get more than fishing; you get an experience that touches all of the senses.

"A lot of people look at flyfishing like it's an art form, but remember, it's supposed to be fun," Ted told me. "It's possible to make it both. Remember that."

MACKINAW TROUT
TAHOE'S BEST BET

Fishing and gambling have a lot in common. The number of big trout, like the poker chips, never seem to equal the demand.

But fishing is always a gamble, and at daybreak, I was ready to place my bet at Lake Tahoe, cruising out on the giant lake with guide Dan Hannum in his 21-footer, then pulling up about a mile offshore of the casinos at South Shore. In the casinos, haggard all-nighters were still looking for an edge. On the water, we were doing the same, plowing the boat along slowly, studying the screen of the electronic depthfinder in order to analyze the contours of the lake bottom.

"Look at that," said Hannum, alert even at 5 a.m., pointing at the screen. "The bottom is coming up."

In the space of about 100 yards, the lake bottom of Tahoe went from 750 feet deep to only 160 feet deep, then moving inshore, it fell off again to 265 feet. We had discovered an underwater dome that is about 50 yards across. Beneath the flat, dark blue surface of Tahoe, this dome rises high above the surrounding lake bottom like an underwater mountain top.

"That dome has about 10 feet of grass growing on top of it and the big trout lay in it, swimming around, feeding," Hannum said. "Not many fish are caught here, but most of them are big."

When I gamble, I like to go for the big win, so at first light we were at the dome, fishing for mackinaw trout.

Mackinaws can get big and strong, and when they do, they can provide a fight that is like being grabbed by the hair on your head and being lifted right off the ground. They are not a well-known fish in California, living only in high mountain lakes that are deep and cold. Lake Tahoe is the most famous of the mackinaw lakes in the West, and some people think that no other lake in California even has mackinaws. Not so. Several other mountain lakes do as well: Bear River Reservoir, Caples Lake, Donner Lake, Gilmore

Lake, Gold Lake, Hell Hole Reservoir, Silver Lake, Stampede Lake and Weaver Lake.

The big mackinaws are called "lakers," as in lake trout, and are better known as the king of lakes in the Arctic. My life-best catch is a 42-pounder that measured 47 inches long, taken on 10-pound line in 15 feet of water, and landed after a 45-minute fight. Although no laker that big has ever been landed at Lake Tahoe—the state record is a 38-pounder at Tahoe—there are legends of 50 and 60-pounders roaming even now.

"I am sure there is a 60-pounder in this lake," said guide Hannum. "In fact, this lake is so big and so deep that there are a lot of things in here that nobody has any idea about."

Mackinaw trout inhabit only cold water, preferring water that is no warmer than 50 degrees. That is why they often roam hundreds of feet deep during the summer months, but emerge to shallower areas during the coldest days of the year in late winter. They are also especially light-sensitive, and can be driven to darker and deeper depths during days with flat water and bright sun and nights with a bright moon.

So for my trip with Hannum, I picked an early spring day when the moon was in the dark, and a gray overcast was shielding the sun by day. A 12-knot wind was chopping the water, another plus. Everything seemed perfect, and we were on the water before dawn.

"There is usually a good bite from dawn to 7:30 a.m., then it gets spotty to about 9 a.m., and then you might as well quit," Hannum said. "There are a lot of days when we've limited for all aboard and are back by 8:30 or nine in the morning."

In nearby casinos, gamblers were putting their cards on the table. But on our boat, we were the ones doing the dealing.

By using digital Lake Systems downriggers that provide precise depth counts, we were able to troll Flatfish lures exactly 140 feet deep, just above the thicket of grass covering the under-water dome. A downrigger is a separate reel of wire line that is heavily weighted—your fishing line is attached to the wire line by a clip. Then when a fish strikes, your fishing line pops free, and you fight only the fish, not any weight. That is why downriggers are so perfect for trolling deep.

Dark cumulus clouds buried the ridgeline that surrounds Tahoe and a cold north wind raised a few goose pimples. Then, just 30 seconds after dropping the lure down, the rod suddenly started dancing. I set the hook and the trout responded like an Alaskan salmon, shaking and jerking.

"It's a good one," Hannum said, a reliable judge from having spent 200 days on Tahoe per year since 1983. Because the water at Tahoe is so pure and clear, we could see the flashing sides of the big trout more than 40 feet down. Right then, though, as we saw the fish, the fish also saw the boat. It hurtled off on a 160-foot power dive, all the way back to the bottom. I just held on and watched my line disappear off the reel. It took 15 minutes of give-and-take to compel the trout near the surface, and in the clear water, we could see that the hook was hanging from the fish's mouth by only a thin membrane. One more flip of the tail and it may have pulled loose, but Hannum made a quick, knife-like swipe with the net, and the fish was ours. It measured 32 inches long and weighed 11 pounds, the kind of fish that makes mackinaw trout a special prize for anyone who has ever tangled with a big one.

Even though the fish come big, and they often go deep, you don't need particularly heavy tackle for them. Most of the prime mackinaw water is not loaded with bottom structure, so you usually don't have to fear the fish winding the line around a submerged tree stump or other snag and breaking it. In addition, it is the downrigger that takes the strain of the lead needed to get deep, not the rod.

A good set-up is a six or 6 1/2-foot graphite composite rod rated for 15-pound line, and a level-wind reel that will hold 200 yards of line, filled with fresh 10 to 15-pound line. The exact setup Hannum uses on his guided trips is a six-foot Fenwick Eagle graphite rod, rated at 10 to 20-pound test, an Abu-Garcia Ambassadeur 6000 level-wind, and 16-pound test line, green DuPont Magna-Thin. The latter is ultra-clear in the water, which makes a big difference in the ultra-clear water of Tahoe, and also very small in diameter, which means it cuts through the water instead of creating a large bow. That means light hits are more easily detected.

For terminal tackle, Hannum says the day-in, day-out winner is called a dodger-and-minnow combination. For bait, you use a large Tahoe redside minnow—the only minnow legal to use at Tahoe. Hannum "threads" a treble hook through the minnow. To

SECRETS OF THE MASTERS

do that, take a needle and your line, and start a six-inch taxidermy needle through the anal opening. Pass the needle through the minnow's mouth, then tie the treble hook to the line so the shaft of the hook is entering the fish. It looks just like a lure, only better, because when the big mackinaws come up to nibble it, they taste fish, not plastic.

To make it even better, the minnow is best trolled 18 inches behind a No. 00 solid chrome Dodger made by Luhr Jensen. The dodger-and-minnow combo provides perfect action, attraction, and smell, especially during the summer months, when the mackinaws sometimes have to be teased into striking. When the bite is tougher, a shorter leader, 12 to 14 inches, which can provide more back-and-forth action, is a good insurance policy to remember.

In the cold months from November through May, you can get a hookup by simply trolling an ivory-colored, M-2 Flatfish lure—your line being clipped to the downrigger line to get it to the proper depth, of course.

If you are fishing a lake for the first time for mackinaws, you need a good depthfinder to locate the deep bottom ledges. At Tahoe, the fish are often suspended just off the underwater ledge, symbolic of the situation at all mackinaw lakes. Long, sloping bottoms will not hold fish. They like the sudden drop-off. On a trip in the Northwest Territories at Great Bear Lake, my pal Trevor Slaymaker and I spent two days searching for such a spot, camping out along the shore for a few hours each night while en route. We finally found it in a large bay, where an eight-foot bottom was cut by a 15-foot to 25-foot canyon down the center of the bay. We then trolled that canyon and in four hours caught six huge mackinaws—42, 38, 32, 26, 22 and 20 pounds—one of the most remarkable sessions of fishing I have ever had.

On the trip with Hannum at Lake Tahoe, we used a similar principal to find a good spot: Scan the bottom for the dramatic drop-off. This it how it is at the dome, and we had been there less than 15 minutes and had the 11-pounder.

"The fish hang out in the grass that grows on top of the dome," Hannum said. "By trolling our lure right across the top of it, we're trying to entice them to come up and take a look."

In the next hour, three more were hooked, all in the more common three to five-pound range. Then, my rod started dancing again, I set the hook, and felt the power of another big one. I looked at Hannum and he just smiled.

This fish immediately ripped off on a 20-yard burst, but then the line went completely limp.

Gone? Maybe. Maybe not. I started reeling as fast as possible—sometimes a big fish will turn and swim straight for the boat to get slack in the line—and sure enough, after five seconds, I had caught up to him. In response, the trout turned around and went full steam back to the bottom. Whoo-ya! If I'd been thumbing the reel, it would have snapped the line for sure.

Ten minutes later, I had the fish back up, and this time we could see its sides flashing below the boat, about 40 feet deep.

"Is he ready?" Hannum asked me.

The fish answered for itself with another bulldog power-dive that had me just hanging on, watching the line spool off the reel.

Well, it took another 10 minutes, but we eventually landed it, a 30-inch, nine-pounder. When most people fish for trout, they usually think in terms of catching a fish that will fit in a frying pan. With mackinaws, you think in terms of a trout that may not fit in your home freezer.

At Tahoe casinos, meanwhile, the gamblers keep putting their bets down on the tables, often watching their money disappear. With Dan Hannum, though, the chances are much better.

There is no such thing as a sure bet in fishing, weather or gambling, but at least when it comes to big mackinaw trout, Hannum has the ability to get the best odds available.

STEELHEAD
THE ULTIMATE POKER GAME

———————————— 🐟 ————————————

When big steelhead start jumping, it's like someone in a helicopter is dropping bowling balls into the water. From our vantage point from the cliff, we could see the fish jump, then hit the water and disappear with a splash and a big suction-like *voomph*, a sound that echoed off the granite walls of the river canyon. Only the big ones, the 15-pounders and up, make that sound.

"I bet there is a 25-pound steelhead in that hole," said Jim Csutoras, staring at the emerald-green flows of the Smith River. Betting is something Csutoras is good at, whether it is at a poker table or from a rock along a river while he casts for steelhead. He catches and releases more steelhead weighing 10 pounds or more than any angler in California—250 in an average year, and he does it by bank, not by boat.

The first time I really stared into this guy's eyes was when he was sitting across the table from me in a poker game. I had three jacks and was betting the hell out of them, and while Foonsky, Mr. Furnai and Rambob had dropped out, Jimmy not only matched my bet, but doubled it, adding to a huge pot. Then he took a nice long drink from his favorite bottled elixir, stared at me, with eyes as passionless as the gaze from a steelhead, waiting for my call. I looked at his up cards, which appeared as a possible straight, and matched his bet. It was as quiet as a sunrise on the Smith River as we all waited for him to reveal his hand. Finally he turned over his three down cards: All three cards were hearts, and going with two other cards in hearts face up, it made five, a heart flush, a winner.

The next day on the river, I noticed that Jim Csutoras had the same exact look as he approached a spot to cast to steelhead as he did when he made his bet at the poker table. By nature, he is a kind, warm soul with an equally warm family, a fellow who can get along with anybody. But when there are chips on the poker table or steelhead in a stream, something clicks inside him, and he raises the level of intensity, intuition, and mental sharpness several notches to the point where he enters a different orbit than the rest of the world. On this day, my own rocket boosters took me up there with him in the outer atmosphere, and we caught and released 13 steelhead ranging 12 to 18 pounds, the fightingest bank-caught fish in California. The irony was that the previous day, several guides had "guaranteed" we wouldn't catch anything because of poor river conditions and terrible catch rates.

You may understand the latter because 97 percent of California's anglers have never caught a steelhead, according to a Fish and Game survey. Of the three percent that have, perhaps just one percent have caught a 15-pounder. If you are an honorary member of the One Percent Club, you are probably both lucky and good, which is just what it takes to catch big steelhead and win at poker games. Just like Jim Csutoras.

If you are new to the game, the first thing to remember is that a steelhead is a trout, that is, a rainbow trout that lives most of its life in the ocean, getting big and strong, then returns to rivers during the winter to spawn. That is important because if you want to learn how to catch steelhead from the shoreline, you can use skills very similar to those necessary for fishing mountain trout streams during the summer. The difference between a summer trout stream in the mountains and a winter steelhead stream near the coast is the size: Everything is bigger. The water is bigger, the fish are bigger, and the tackle is bigger.

The type of water that holds steelhead is similar to that which holds trout, projected on a larger scale, of course. That became apparent from the edge of the cliff where Jimmy and I stood.

"Look!" he said, staring down at the water with binoculars. "You can see the dark outline of a steelhead at the lower end of that pool." Sure enough—and not just one, but several. During periods of low rainfall, rivers become so clear that some say steelhead can be seen but can't be caught. Not so. A key is using special techniques that Csutoras has developed, and reading the water.

"Steelhead use the river as a highway, then spawn in the tributaries," Csutoras explained. "They don't like to stop moving, but they will at certain areas in order to rest a bit, especially after swimming through some rough water. This is when you get your chance. I like to fish the holes, especially above whitewater. After a steelhead charges through that whitewater, it is bound to hole up for a while to rest before heading on upstream."

Early in the winter, when the seasonal rains are just starting and river levels are beginning to come up, steelhead will often wait for a storm (and higher stream levels) or higher tides before leaving the ocean. In small coastal streams, the steelhead will shoot through the mouth of the river during a high tide, then hole up in the lower river lagoon until stream flows are high enough upstream for them to venture onward. The recipe for steelhead is simple: Just add water. The ideal situation is enough rain to freshen up the river and attract the steelhead upstream, but not so much rain that the river is muddied up, or the stream is flowing too high and fast to fish.

If the stream is "greened up, freshened up," then you are in business. Steelhead will enter the river system and head upstream, stopping in the slicks just upstream of whitewater, in the holes just downstream of whitewater, occasionally along the edges of riffles, in holes on sharp bends in the river, aside large boulders, and in tailouts (especially on major rivers early in the season).

"I get up early and am on the water before first light," Csutoras said. "I never spend much more than 20 or 30 minutes at a spot. Instead I will hit a different spot each hour, and then when I'm on the spot, I'll fish the entire hole, the head of it, the middle of it, the tail of it. I'm always moving." Most steelhead streams in California are bordered by two-lane highways, with dirt pullouts alongside many of the best spots, which allow anglers to park, then hike down to the river.

That is exactly what Csutoras and I were doing. After parking at one of these pullouts, then scanning the river with binoculars from a cliff to spot several big steelhead in a hole located just below some whitewater, we started sneaking our way down to the spot. That was when I noticed that Csutoras was using the same exact tackle setup as I was.

We were both using 8 1/4-foot HMG Fenwick rods, Ambassadeur reels, and fresh Maxima line, light green in color. "Line can be absolutely critical with steelhead, especially if the river is clear," Csutoras said. "I only use light green Maxima, and I won't fish with somebody if they are not using it too." The reason is because more visible line can spook the wary steelhead. Thus the weight of the line is also a key. "In clear water, I will use as light as six-pound line," Csutoras said. "The heaviest I ever go is ten-pound line, and most of the time I use eight-pound line. But like the river, I am always changing, always gauging the river, then matching the line weight to the water clarity for that day."

For terminal rigging, use the three-way swivel concept. You tie on three feet of leader and your steelhead hook to one swivel (available pre-tied at tackle shops), and then four or five inches of leader with a dropper loop to another swivel. From the dropper loop, you clamp on a pencil sinker, or a "Slinky," which is a special sinker less apt to get snagged. Other options include putting a little styrofoam Glo Ball or plastic Corky on the line at the eye of the hook as an attractor, or using Puff Balls instead of bait. Some shoreliners will use lures, like the gold Little Cleo, Kastmaster, or artificial egg clusters, but this can get expensive, because snags are quite common as it is an absolute necessity for steelhead that you drift your offering near the stream bottom. Cleos can cost $3 a pop.

But with a three-way rig, if your sinker snags on a drift, you can just break it off, then quickly tie on another dropper loop, pinch on another piece of pencil lead, and you are ready to fish again—rather than having to re-tie the complete rig, or pay for another Little Cleo. Csutoras wears a fishing vest which is set up in advance with a few key tackle elements in separate pockets. He has a small spool of leader material (usually eight-pound Maxima), pencil lead, hooks, with a pair of clippers and pliers hanging from plastic ties, which are out and accessible. He also keeps a covered tub of roe for bait in another pocket. He can stand on a rock, and no matter what happens, he has all of his tackle completely self-contained in his vest, and when he snags up, breaks off, or needs to re-bait, he can retie, bait up, and be fishing in just a minute or two. He also always brings a huge net along, which sits along the shore ready, in case he needs to land the first documented 30-pound steelhead in California history.

"I do get a lot of fishing time in," Csutoras said. "Some people spend a lot of time tying rigs. I spend a lot of time fishing."

A viable option is hiring a guide who has a driftboat. This is especially beneficial if you are new to a river, new to the sport, or want the added excitement of a river trip. You get a fishing lesson, learn good spots on a river, and have a high chance of catching steelhead. Most guides are excellent companions as well. In addition, some rivers, such as the Eel and the Klamath, and parts of others, such as the lower Smith, are much easier to fish from a boat than from shoreline. By boat, you can rig the same when using bait. However, another good system is using Hot Shot or Wee Wart plugs, letting them flutter in the current behind the boat while the guide uses the oars to keep the boat near motionless in the river. Another system is to use a Hot 'N Tot plug, remove the hook, then add two feet of leader and a hook with a threaded nightcrawler for bait. Yet another option by boat is to use flies. The dark woolly worm, Brindle Bug and the Silver Hilton are the best patterns.

Most anglers, however, cannot afford to hire a guide every time they want to try fishing for steelhead. So inevitably they wind up on the bank, casting away, hoping for the best.

It turns out you can do more than hope. The initial approach to the chosen spot on a river is very important. You just plain cannot saunter up to the river bank and start casting. That is like throwing bricks in the river and then expecting the fish to bite. If the river is clear, particularly in canyons, Csutoras will stop 15 to 20 feet short of the shoreline, and then make his initial casts from there. "If the water is clear, any sight of casting motion, a shadow on the water, even the shadow of the rod on the water, anything strange at all that the fish can detect can tip your hand," he explained. "Once they're on to you, you don't have a chance. It's just like poker. If you know the other guy has a winning hand, you fold. That's what the fish do."

The first few casts should not be long casts across the river. You could be casting right over the heads of steelhead that are closer to the bank, and you are apt to scare them off. Instead, the first few casts should be along your side of the shore, then start reaching out farther with your casts, working your way across the river. Work the entire hole, not just the head of it, the tail of it, or the middle of it, and if you don't catch anything, get the hell out of there and get to another spot.

"After the cast, the bait must drift downstream, as if no line is attached, as if the drift of the roe is completely natural," Csutoras said. "The steelhead has to think this is for real. I remember that with every single cast. It is absolutely essential to get a good drift."

A big error many anglers make is "skidding" their baits. When the line is tight, instead of the bait drifting with the current, it is pulled across the current. You'll never get a bite with a skidded bait.

The bite of a steelhead is an exciting moment that you never forget. Like so many fish that are tremendous fighters, the bite is often quite light. The reason is because the fish are often resting, finning in place, head pointed upstream, when along comes this chunk of roe drifting downstream. Instead of a savage attack, they usually just move over a few feet in the stream to stop the passing bait. It takes time on the water to develop a "touch" to be able to discern the difference between a steelhead stopping the bait, and a sinker hitting a rock on the river bottom.

"You must be able to feel your sinker hitting the bottom," Csutoras said. "Then, after a while, you get the hang of getting a good drift out of each cast, feeling the sinker drifting down along the river bottom. After that, you suddenly become so tuned in that anything that feels weird at all, you know it's a fish, not a rock. The bite of a big steelhead usually feels more like a suction than a jolt, and when you're on top of your game, you will know it every time."

When the fish are very spooky, such as in clear, slow-moving water, sometimes the bites are so light that you will feel nothing at all. If you wait for a big yank, you might as well hire out as a statue. During these periods, Csutoras has taught me to watch the fishing line as it trails out across the river. When the bow in it tightens a bit—bang!—set the hook, because that is often the only discernable sign that a steelhead has stopped the downstream flow of the bait.

Like this one day when we reached the stream, stopping about 20 feet short of the shoreline along the sloping river canyon.

"We'll make our first casts from way up here," Csutoras said. "We don't want to scare 'em by getting too close." Just like a poker game, I thought, playing the first few hands close to the vest.

On my first cast and drift, I snagged up, then broke off. I quickly retrieved, tied on another dropper loop and then clamped a sinker on. I was just about to cast again when I saw the bow in Csutoras' line tighten just a bit, not more than six inches, and before I could shout to him, Csutoras saw it himself and set the hook. His rod bent down like a croquet hoop.

"A good one, a good one," he said. It flashed upstream, then jumped, landing with a tremendous splash—just like a bowling ball—then flashed across the stream and jumped again. A big steelhead is the fastest freshwater swimming fish in California, capable of covering 27 feet per second.

Then, Csutoras did something most anglers have never considered. No, he didn't cut the line. He knelt on a rock at streamside and pointed the butt of the fishing line at the steelhead, in the process putting a huge bend in the rod and tremendous pressure on the fish. For several minutes in this position, the fight remained a stalemate. The fish was unable to head downstream and escape into the rapids, but at the same time the fish was too powerful for Csutoras to gain any line. Giving steelhead "the butt," as it is referred, is the only way to keep a big one from saying "Adios, muchacho," then running downstream into whitewater to never-never land.

Suddenly, the steelhead ripped cross-stream right at Csutoras, the line went limp and Jimmy reeled like hell to catch up to the fish. Before he could, the steelhead jumped again, right in front of us, its shiny silver sides flashing in the sunlight, and then upon landing, shot away back to the other side of the river.

In the next ten minutes, the battle settled down to a give-and-take, with Csutoras kneeling and pointing the butt of the rod at the fish whenever it threatened to go downstream. Finally, after a 20-minute fight, the steelhead was persuaded to the shore, played out. It was huge, about three feet long and an honest 18 or 19 pounds, maybe even 20.

Csutoras gazed fondly at the fish, then unhooked it, grabbed it near the tail and worked the fish back and forth in the stream, forcing water through its mouth and gills to revive it. In a few minutes, the steelhead regained its strength, and with a flip of its tail was free, darting back into the depths of the river.

"A beauty, eh?" Csutoras said. "A real nice one."

Later that night, we were back at the poker table. And again at showdown time, seven-card stud, it was down to Csutoras and I staring at each other. Csutoras bet the limit, then stared at me. I noticed that unlike the previous evening, his bet was not followed by a long drink from his bottled elixir.

"Ah hah!" I thought to myself, a sure sign of nerves, a sign that he didn't have diddly squat. I immediately doubled his bet, then to show my own confidence, took an extra long drink of my own.

Csutoras saw this, then turned his cards over. "I fold," he said. "Your pot."

Heh, heh, heh. Little did he know, I didn't have diddly squat either, not even a pair, but I certainly convinced him otherwise. You see, Jimmy, poker is just like steelhead fishing. You have to watch for the smallest of signs.

STURGEON
THE KEITH FRASER SYSTEM

Sometimes the good old days aren't really so good.

When I remember how it was trying to catch a sturgeon in the good old days, I felt more like a prisoner of prayer than anything else. It was hour after hour waiting for a bite, and then when finally there would be a nibble, I never seemed to have a chance to set the hook.

"Oh, that's normal," I was told by an old curmudgeon at a boat ramp. "The average is about 40 hours per sturgeon."

Then, after a one-day lesson by a tall, bold gent named Keith Fraser, everything changed. I caught 100 and 150-pounders on back-to-back days, and went five years where I averaged nearly a sturgeon per hour, and never went a trip in that span where I got skunked.

The lesson started on a fall day on San Francisco Bay when the sky looked like a scene out of the Ten Commandments, with yellow and orange rays of sunlight refracting through clouds and across the water. The sun was just hitting Mt. Tamalpais to the west when there was a sudden downward pump on the rod tip. Then, just as quickly, there was nothing.

On my left, Keith Fraser, the master, pounced on the rod—but never jiggled it—and gently took hold and tilted it forward, using a unique rod board as an axis point.

"This looks like the start of a classic sturgeon bite," Fraser said. He stared at the rod tip as if his eyes were laser beams. A few quiet seconds passed. Suddenly, the rod tip pumped down again, just an inch, and instantly, Fraser reared back hard on the rod and set the hook home.

It was a sturgeon all right, an 80-pounder, and it jumped three times, ran off one time like it was headed for Hawaii, along with taking several shorter sprees. After 15 minutes, we had it alongside the boat, and it looked like it was played out.

"He's just playing possum," Fraser said. "A lot of anglers try to boat sturgeon the first time they get them alongside, but the fish are not ready and they'll get away right at the boat."

With the handle end of a net, Fraser gave the sturgeon a light nudge and it was like Fraser had shocked it with a cattle prod. In a few seconds, that sturgeon ran off 30 yards, jumped, then dove down to the bottom. It was another 10 minutes before the fish was alongside again.

"Now he's ready," Fraser said. The master leaned over the railing, and with a pair of pliers removed the hook. With a quick flip of the tail, the big sturgeon disappeared into the Bay's murky waters.

"I release just about everything," Fraser said. "My excitement comes in reading the bites right and setting the hook, and my satisfaction comes in releasing the fish."

A few years later, after having fished with Fraser many times, I asked him to start documenting his fishing trips. In 41 trips over the winter season, he hooked 86 sturgeon (keepers over 42 inches) and had only 10 missed sets. In one period he hooked 26 straight without a missed set. All but one of the fish were released, including two weighing over 200 pounds. I took part on three of those trips, in which we fished a total of 11 hours, and caught and released eight sturgeon.

On a trip that year with Fraser and John Beuttler of United Anglers of California, I had a potential world-record on my line for two hours, a 90-pound sturgeon on eight-pound test line. I finally had persuaded the fish within 30 feet of the boat, and with a swift outgoing tide running past, needed the help of my companions to back the boat down to the fish in order to land it; the tide was too strong to drag the fish the last 30 feet. But right then both Fraser and Beuttler hooked up and had their hands full with their own big sturgeons. After five minutes, my fish revived, went hurtling off on a 150-yard run, then finally jumped and landed on the line, snapping it, and was gone forever.

The key element in these hookups is a one-of-a-kind system Fraser has designed that parlays a fishing rod holder he calls a "Sturgeon Board" with a study of how tide patterns produce optimum three and four-hour periods.

The Sturgeon Board measures 58 inches long and 2 1/2 inches wide. At the top there is a 3/4-inch piece with a slot in the center where the rod is placed. There are also two vertical pieces three inches high on each side of the board located 16 inches from the bottom. Those vertical pieces keep the reel upright, and the pieces at the top of the board with the slot keep the rod in place.

The board, with the rod sitting in it, is rested at a 45-degree angle against the boat rail. The rod is left untouched until a fish bite is registered.

Fraser will cast out, reel in the slack, put the rod in place and stare at the rod tip. His focus is so intense that sometimes he looks like the Sphinx of Egypt. Should there come a bite, Fraser will carefully lift the butt of the rod, which tips the rod forward, using the slotted piece at the end of the Sturgeon Board as an axis point. If the rod tip is pulled down again—and often it can be less than an inch—he slams the hook home.

Mistakes are easily made, Fraser explained.

"The thing to remember is that even though sturgeon are huge, their bite is often very delicate. It is more of a soft pump than anything else. Also, the fish are very sensitive to anything unusual. If they feel any movement or agitation with the bait, it can spook them. If you jiggle the rod at all, they're gone."

That explains why sturgeon fishing had become such a dry slice of life for me before I switched to Fraser's system. By moving the rod around, even a few inches, I likely had been scaring the fish off.

"Whether anglers are holding their rod or not, what usually happens with most guys is that when they get a bite, they immediately pick the rod up, or get excited and move it around a bit," Fraser said. "Sometimes they will even stand up with it, getting ready to set the hook, waiting for another pumper. But sturgeon are so sensitive that just by moving the rod around like that, the fish get spooked off the bait. The sturgeon never comes back and the guy doesn't catch anything. It happens over and over."

A similar system is used by Delta guide Barry Canevaro (see text on striped bass), but instead of a Sturgeon Board, he uses what are called Balance Wedges for each rod. A Balance Wedge is a simple V-cut wedge, in which the rod sits, balancing like a suspended teeter-totter. When a fish bites, the rod tips forward. Canevaro then gently picks up the rod and points it toward the sturgeon, and stares hard at where the line enters the water. When the line moves a bit, sometimes just an inch or two as the fish tightens any slack, Canevaro sets the hook. That tightening line indicates that the fish has the bait in its mouth.

Using the Balance Wedge is also very effective when fishing in deep water or in San Francisco Bay when sturgeon are feeding on the roe of spawning herring. When a herring spawn occurs, you can gather the roe off of seaweed, pilings or rocks, then use it for bait. The roe is only effective for bait during a herring spawn, however. During non-spawn periods, it can be more effective to use whole herring for bait.

Quality tackle provides an additional edge. Use rods with sensitive (but not whippy) tips and enough backbone to handle a 100-pounder. The best market-produced rods are the seven-foot Fenwick 1870C, Sabre 870 and LCI graphite GBT704. Several reels are well-matched for these rods. The best is the Newell G344F. The Penn 4/0 is also quite good, although you can go smaller and get the job done.

Most anglers use 30-pound line. Some prefer 20-pound line to make casting easier; others like to go heavier, 40 and even 60-pound line, in case they hook one of those rare 300-pounders.

The terminal rigging is quite simple for sturgeon. You start by placing a "slider" over your fishing line. A slider is a hollow tube with a snap swivel connected to it, a cheap piece of tackle common at shops near where sturgeon are caught. With the line going through your slider, you tie on a strong snap swivel to the end of the fishing line. Clip on a pre-tied "sturgeon rig" to the snap swivel on your line, and then clip your sinker to the snap swivel on the slider.

Sturgeon rigs are plastic-coated wire line with a single 6/0 hook, or two 4/0 hooks opposed to each other. They are cheap and common to find. Use the single-hook rigs when using mud shrimp or ghost shrimp for bait, the two-hook rigs when using grass shrimp for bait.

Fraser has developed a few bonus tricks that are subtle but effective. To get hook penetration on the set, he tightens the drag 100 percent, so there is no line slippage at all. Once the fish is hooked, he immediately backs down on the drag for the fight.

In addition, another problem is that a variety of baitrobbers can knock the bait off the hook, particularly when using mud shrimp for bait. Fraser winds elastic thread around the mud shrimp a few times, which secures it more firmly to the hook.

Finally, Fraser is a student of tides and water flows. Both are critical to sturgeon. Tides are important because fast-moving tides, especially minus low outgoing tides, will kick up feed on the bottom, which can get the sturgeon on the prowl. Slow tides often can mean terrible fishing.

A "slow" tide is when there is little difference between a high tide and the following low tide. For instance, a high tide of 4.1 feet followed by a low tide of 3.6 feet has a differential of only 0.5 feet of moving water. That is very slow. In comparison, a high tide of 7.8 feet followed by a low tide of minus 0.2 feet has a differential of 8.0 feet of moving water, a fast tide.

During periods of high rainfall, when the push of outgoing freshwater is quite high, tides don't make much difference. But since heavy rain periods occur only rarely, sturgeon anglers must instead attune themselves to how tides affect the fishery.

The best fishing in the San Francisco Bay system is during outgoing tides just before (very good) and during (good) a cycle of minus low tides. More specifically, the best period is during the latter part of an outgoing tide, like on a Thursday afternoon, just before a weekend of minus low tides.

Since minus tides occur late in the day during winter, the sturgeon fishing is often best in the winter in late afternoon. To fine-tune it a step further, the best fishing is often during the two days just prior to when the minus low tides begin, from 3:30 p.m. to 5:30 p.m. Tide books identify these periods. They phase in and out in two-week cycles throughout the winter and spring.

Fraser is not one of these guys who is a slave to fishing, on the water for great numbers of hours in order to hook his fish.

"I often just fish for two or three hours," Fraser said. "Sometimes as much as four hours. Never more than that."

In fact, we have often just started fishing at 3:30 p.m., right when others are returning skunked from slaving away on the water all day, frustrated.

"Didn't get a bite," they'd say.

"Maybe next time," I'd answer, knowing the peak period for the day was about to arrive in the next two hours.

One time a friend of mine was angry at me for telling him that a certain day had a particularly positive outlook. I ran into him by accident at the dock at Loch Lomond Marina in San Rafael, right before a trip I had planned with Fraser.

"Nothing again," he said. "I can't understand what I'm doing wrong. Maybe next time I'll say my prayers."

Maybe next time, I thought, you will use a winning system.

An hour later, we were anchored between the Marin Islands and the Richmond Bridge. My rod tip dipped, I tipped the rod on the Sturgeon Board, the rod tip dipped again, and I rammed the hook home. Immediately a huge sturgeon jumped, over seven feet long.

I fought that fish for over an hour, and while doing so, Fraser and Jerry Goff, a third baseman for the Montreal Expos, caught and released other sturgeon weighing 70 and 90 pounds, respectively. It was nearly dark when the fish came alongside the boat, the lights of a traffic jam on the Richmond Bridge shining overhead. The sturgeon measured seven-foot-one, my largest by far.

There was a day when I would have prayed for a fish like this. No more. I just give thanks that I learned the Keith Fraser system.

STRIPED BASS
AND FRUSTRATION

Damn, stripers can be frustrating. I remember a story where a guy went berserk and started ramming his car into telephone poles, lamp posts and stop signs, before finally getting hauled into jail by the local gendarmes. The next morning, the judge stared down at the poor soul, who seemed to be suffering from some rare form of mental aberration, and asked simply, "What made you do it?"

"Striped bass," he answered. "Striped bass."

The judge, being an angler himself, quickly understood the man's problem, and immediately dismissed all charges and ordered him to go fishing with guide Barry Canevaro.

You may understand, too. You can chase striped bass across thousands of miles of waterways, try all matter of strategies, and after years of it, you end up being just what you were when you started: a prisoner of hope. What keeps people at it? Ah, it comes in those special periods when you find the fish and then start catching them as fast as if they were hungry bluegill.

Striped bass not only get big, but are a school fish. That combination means that when you hit it right, you have the chance to catch a lot of big fish fast. Once it happens to you, your perspective on the world changes, and it suddenly becomes a place where all greatness is possible. To recapture the feeling, you may even start chasing the fish on their migratory pathway, in the ocean, through the bays and Delta, maybe even to reservoirs, canals and the Colorado River lakes. Some anglers get almost possessed by the prospects, and in a worst-case scenario, start ramming telephone poles with their cars.

I have had a taste of the best and the worst of it. Imagine 13 striped bass to 25 pounds in three hours baitfishing in the Delta? Or 11 stripers to 28 pounds in two hours right under the Golden Gate Bridge? Or getting nearly a fish per cast for a 20-minute siege at O'Neill Forebay? Taking a 30-pounder right off Pacifica by beach surfcasting? Then there are the other times . . . not a nibble, not a strike, nothing at all for days. You might swear there isn't a striped bass left on the planet. When that happens to those who have a passion for this sport, it provides a mighty dry slice of life.

As for the cure, there are better answers than ramming your car into anything that is standing still. Take the advice of the masters of this sport: Barry Canevaro, Chuck Louie, Cliff Anfinson, and the Brothers Cuanang, Abe and Angelo.

■ Anchoring, Trolling And Plugging . . . Barry Canevaro

The first time I went fishing with Barry Canevaro, it was enough to practically clean the cholesterol right out of my veins.

This was in the Delta, where we cruised up a river slough, then anchored near a deep hole. We cast our baits out, and then he placed his rod in a strange, small balance wedge sitting on the back of his boat, the rod balancing perfectly with the wedge as an axis point, the line trailing out into the water. I looked at Barry like he had antlers growing out of his head.

"You're just going to leave your rod hanging like that?" I asked. "If you get a striper, it will pull your rod right in the water."

Barry just smiled. "Here, let me set yours up the same way."

"That's OK," I answered, "I prefer not to lose my gear."

A moment later, a memorable scenario unfolded: His rod suddenly tipped forward a few feet, and Barry picked it up gently, careful not to raise it, and pointed it toward the water.

"I'm getting bit," he said. "By using the wedge, even the lightest bites will pull the rod down, yet the fish won't feel a thing. With the wedge, you will see bites so light that if you were holding your rod or watching it, you wouldn't have a clue."

Just then, his line tightened a bit, and with his reel on free spool and thumb on the line, ever so slowly the line started to unroll from the reel. "He's starting to move with it." Two seconds later, the line started to spool off more quickly, and Barry flipped the brake on the reel, put his thumb on the line, and set the hook. It turned out to be a 15-pound striped bass, and seeing the way he caught it was like getting launched into the clouds and looking at the world with an entirely new perspective.

Canevaro specializes in anchoring and using bait, trolling, and more rarely, casting lures. He is the most successful striper fisherman in California, catching and releasing up to 1,300 striped bass over a single winter's season in the Delta. As a guide, he often takes two to four people along, and has stretches where he averages 10 bass per day for weeks, some days doing better. He's like my Johnson outboard. You turn him on and he runs.

The wedge system for balancing fishing rods is at the center of his success. It looks crazy. You will swear your rod will be pulled right in the water when you get a bite. Instead, it just tips forward like a teeter-totter with the wedge being the axis point. No matter how big the bass, the rod doesn't get pulled in the water. No matter how light the bite, you will never miss one.

The terminal rigging is straightforward. First, slip a slider on your line, those little tubes with the snap swivel attached, from which your sinker is attached. Tie a snap swivel to the end of the line, and from that, clasp on a three-foot striper leader with a 9/0 hook. That's it.

"For bait, I always use shad," Canevaro said. "What could be better? The Delta is loaded with shad." Bullheads, mudsuckers and ghost shrimp can also be good baits for striped bass. If you are unfamiliar with how to rig them on the hook, always ask for a demonstration at the bait shop. When using shad, for instance, Canevaro will fillet one side, poke the hook through three times—through the fillet, through the fish, and then back through the fillet—and then with the line, put a half hitch around the tail of the bait. It works. It not only works in the Delta, but also when stillfishing for striped bass in reservoirs or in the access points along the California Aqueduct.

The first time I used Canevaro's system of placing the rod in a balance wedge and using shad for bait, I caught 13 striped bass in three hours, keeping one for a photo and releasing the rest, including a 25-pounder. It was quite an introduction. On trips with Master Canevaro over a span of eight years, we have averaged about one striper per hour, although most of the fish are caught in two and three-hour periods when a school moves into the hole. Like I said, that is one way to reduce your cholesterol level. Those sieges are most common during the peak of tidal activity in the Delta, when the stripers are at their feeding peak.

In other waters, particularly reservoirs, lakes and canals, the best period is usually right at dawn, particularly during a period when the moon is dark. That early morning bite can be something else, but instead of baitfishing, it is usually better either trolling or plugging. Canevaro does both, and having spent years at it, has discovered how water temperatures affect the feeding behavior of the striped bass and how anglers should react to that.

"The first thing anybody should do is take a water temperature reading," he advises. "The magic number is 56. If it is 56 degrees or warmer, then it is excellent for trolling. If it is cooler than 56 degrees, then it is better for baitfishing. As the water gets colder, the trolling bite really tapers off."

The best trolling lure is the big Rebel minnow, both solid and jointed, but a number of other lures also work. They include plugs, jigs and spoons that resemble baitfish, such as the Bomber minnow, Rapala, Creek Chub Pikie and Big Mac; Worm-tail jig, Jet-Tail jig, Striper Razor, Hair Raiser and Bug-Eye; chrome Krocadile, Hopkins, Miki and Pet Spoon.

At times, a great strategy is to use a wire spreader while trolling, then use two lures simultaneously, usually a big plug on one line, a jig or chrome lure on the other. My two favorite combinations are a Rebel and a Worm-Tail jig, and also a Creek Chub Pikie and a Pet Spoon. Question: Guess which lure you will catch the majority of fish on, the big plug or the jig? Most people guess the plug, figuring the fish won't pass up the bigger meal. Actually, the opposite is more often true: The spoon or jig gets the fish. They must figure the darting "shad minnow" will soon escape, so they strike it first, then plan on returning for the larger, slow-moving baitfish.

Striper trolling can be productive in lakes and bays because the fish tend to be scattered, rather than tightly schooled as in the ocean. With trolling, you cover the maximum amount of water in the minimum amount of time. But when you find the fish while trolling, particularly in the vicinity of known underwater structure, it is often better to stop the boat and cast to the fish. This is called plugging.

Plugging allows the opportunity to use lighter gear, spinning rods and even fly rods. The one-ounce Striper Razor and Worm-Tail jig are very effective, because of that little twisty tail doing a little dance as it is retrieved. At lakes, casting deep-diving plugs such as the Big Mac also can take stripers, particularly at first light, and regardless of the reservoir, the best spots are often near the dam. As for fly patterns, the shad streamer tied by Ralph Kanz of Oakland is a beautiful and effective pattern for stripers, and won a national competition for the best-tied saltwater fly.

"Water clarity is important when tossing out a lure or a fly," Canevaro said. "If the water clarity isn't good, then I'd rather anchor and use bait."

When he does, Barry Canevaro really shines. The first time you see your rod teetering, balancing in one of those little V-wedges, you will swear you are about to lose your gear. Instead, you are about to gain the edge you may have always needed.

■ The Live-Bait Option ... Chuck Louie And Cliff Anfinson

Long-time skipper Cliff Anfinson and Captain Chuck Louie may be competitors these days out of San Francisco's Fisherman's Wharf, but they are bonded for life by spending so many days on the water together and having the same love for striped bass. For many years, Chuck Louie was the chief mate aboard Anfinson's boat, the *Bass-Tub*, and together they provided customers with unsurpassed enthusiasm and know-how. Eventually Chuck passed the Coast Guard test and then plunked his life's savings down, bought his own party boat and named it *Chucky's Pride*. They now each provide their own unique trips and strategies.

But both believe in one thing: Live bait. Be it anchovies, shiner perch, or mudsuckers, just make sure it is alive. Cliff Anfinson has spent more than 7,500 days on San Francisco Bay, and specializes in fishing its reefs during the summer months with daily trips leaving at 7 a.m. Chuck Louie, on the other hand, has designed what he calls "select fishing," where he matches a key part of a tidal period to a spot, providing the chance for sensational short binges.

Anfinson will neither anchor, troll or mooch, or turn his boat engine off. Instead he will allow his boat to drift with the tide over the prime reef areas. Meanwhile, the anglers aboard will dangle their live baits, usually anchovies, near the bay bottom.

"The rocks down there are home for the striped bass," Anfinson said. "When you bounce a sinker on his house, it's like knocking on his door. They like to come out and see who's there." Most of the reefs, he explains, are actually sloping ledges where baitfish get trapped and pinned during good tidal movement. That is why they are such good places to fish.

For terminal tackle, he uses the three-way swivel concept. From one of the swivels you just tie on your fishing line. From another, you tie off your sinker with about eight inches of leaders. From the remaining swivel, you tie on a short-shanked live-bait hook to three-foot leaders. Pre-tied rigs are available for $1. Anchovies should be hooked vertically through the nose, or in the upper gill collar. Shiner perch should be hooked horizontally through the nose. Mudsuckers should be hooked vertically through the upper lip.

As you drift over the reefs, you will learn to sense the sinker bouncing along the bottom, and develop a touch where you can walk the bait right up the side of an upsloping reef. It allows for the presentation of a bait in a life-like, natural manner. It takes some experience to tell the rocks from the bites, but after a few hours of it, you will suddenly realize the difference and start hooking striped bass and other fish. Some people get it right off. Having the right tackle helps plenty. You simply must be able to sense exactly what is going on down there during the drift. An excellent setup is the Fenwick 847 rod, Penn 2/0 Jigmaster reel, with fresh 20-pound line.

Cliff Anfinson has tremendous enthusiasm, and he is a daily example of how a zest for life can lead to perpetual happiness.

Chuck Louie also has a natural love of the sea and all its creatures, and it is the striped bass that is most compelling for him. In fact, he's the kind of guy who goes fishing on his days off, and at night, is apt to be in his workshop, designing and tying a new customized fishing rod. He is a craftsman, and in turn, approaches each day's fishing as a craft.

"Can you get here in an hour?" he asked on the phone one afternoon. "The stripers are going to be at the Tower tonight from 6 p.m. to 7:30 p.m." It was classic Chuck Louie. He goes when the fish go. The "Tower" is the South Tower of the Golden Gate Bridge in San Francisco Bay, where striped bass congregate during moderate outgoing tides, often during summer evenings in late June.

I remember the evening well. In 45 minutes, anglers on his boat caught 42 striped bass, landing nearly one per minute, one of the fastest bites I have ever taken part in. We were "using chromies" and "pumping the Tower." Oh yeah? Let me explain: "chromies" are three-ounce sinkers that are shaped like a cigar and are chrome plated. You tie one to your line, add 24 inches of leader and a 2/0 or 3/0 live bait hook, on which you hook an anchovy or shiner perch. It is called "pumping the Tower" because you let the bait down about 15 or 20 feet, then pump your rod up, then reel down to retrieve it.

"I love those bright and shiny cigar-shaped weights," Chuck said. "The fish can hit on the way down as well as on the way up, and when it happens at the Tower, it can be a red-hot bite, absolutely red-hot."

It can be a similar affair when fishing live bait in boats along the beach, where striped bass will corral schools of anchovies against the back of the surf line. The water is quite shallow, often just seven to ten feet deep, and you use very little weight. After tying on a No. 1 or 2/0 live-bait hook, add a half-ounce or one-ounce rubber-core sinker 15 inches above the hook. You use live anchovies for bait, hooking them through the gill cover, allowing them to roam near the bottom, and keeping your reel on free spool as they go.

All hell can break loose during a good beach bite, with diving birds, surf casters tossing lures out toward the boats, and five or ten people aboard hooked up simultaneously.

"The stripers can go on a feeding frenzy," Chuck said. "Sometimes we can take fish almost right off the surface."

When it happens, it makes for some of the best fishing in America. But when does it happen? Get on Chuck Louie's phone list and then be ready when he calls.

■ Beach, Bays And Canals . . . The Brothers Cuanang

Some children just seem ordained to become skilled anglers. That's how it was for Abe and Angelo Cuanang. As youngsters, they somehow convinced their father to drop them off every summer morning at a favorite fishing spot. Only after the elder Cuanang finished his work would he return to pick them up. In the process, the Brothers Cuanang spent years learning how to catch striped bass from shore, day-after-day, in all kinds of settings.

"When I first started fishing, all I had was a stick that had fishing line wound around it," said Abe, the older of the two. "I was five years old and I caught a bullhead. The thrill of catching that first fish on my very own was a special event I will always remember."

More recently, Abe and Angelo have traveled across the hemisphere in search of the world's most challenging fish. I remember one trip I took to the jungle waterways of Costa Rica, not far from the border of Nicaragua; I thought I was at a secret spot when I heard another skiff coming around the bend—I looked up and Abe and Angelo were waving at me. All these guys do is fish, and they have developed remarkable skills in all facets, yet still retain the enthusiasm of when they were just youngsters, catching bullheads.

But their specialty is striped bass from the surf, off the beach or off the rocks, and the lessons can also apply to the lakes and canals where stripers can be found.

"Nothing can match the sheer excitement of catching a big bass in the high surf, especially when the prospects of working over a school are imminent," said Abe.

I remember when I'd been tipped off about an evening surf bite, drove to the scene, and saw dozens of diving gulls and pelicans, with about a dozen anglers all fighting stripers at once. I grabbed my rod and started sprinting down the beach, just as several other anglers were doing so as well. It took me about five minutes to reach the spot, and all in one motion without stopping I cast out, then hooked up almost immediately. Another angler was right behind me, and attempted the same thing, but he was running so fast that when he cast out, the rod slipped out of his hands, and it went flying into the surf. Twenty minutes later, everybody on the scene had limited but this one poor guy, who was on his hands and knees in the water, still looking for his rod. He never did find it.

If you plan on fishing from shore for stripers, you can plan on similar unexpected encounters. It just comes with the territory. "Things just seem to happen," explained Angelo.

Most newcomers to the sport start by surf fishing from a beach, just as Abe and Angelo did as boys. What you discover quickly is that all the hoopla about "birds, bait and bass" doesn't seem to happen too often. So you end up casting away, with scarcely a sign of life and nary a bite, and wonder what it takes to get in on all the great beach fishing you've heard about.

"It takes a lot of time," says Abe. "Then, after a while, you will start recognizing signs of fish, and start cutting the odds down to your favor."

What you must recognize right off is the level of ocean surge, knowing the effects of tides, and keeping track of fish migrations. Once that is done and you start finding fish, you must have the technical ability to get a lure in front of them.

Ocean surge is critical, because when days of 20-knot winds cause a large inshore surge, the baitfish will move offshore and the striped bass will follow them right off. That makes it near hopeless for the surf angler. When the surge is down between late June and early September, the stripers are apt to corral anchovies against the surf line. But when? The answer, says Abe, "is usually when a tide turns over." By that, he means when a high tide tops out, or when a low tide bottoms. "The change gets them feeding. Generally, I like the incoming tide better."

Following the migrations and habits of striped bass is exciting in any water. In the Bay Area, they move out through the Golden Gate in late June, then head south along San Francisco, Pacifica and Half Moon Bay coasts in July and early August, and rarely make a showing at Muir Beach on the Marin coast as well. In September and October, some years they disappear temporarily, only to reappear for short binges near the mouth of the Salinas River in Monterey Bay. At most lakes, striped bass scatter about for most of the summer. But by fall, they school and chase threadfin shad as if they were in the ocean chasing anchovies.

When fishing from the beach, long casts are critical to reach the feeding bass. The longest casts are made with revolving spool reels, or the Australian Alvey reel, with low-diameter 20-pound line, and an 11-foot surf rod. From the beach, the best success is with metal lures and live anchovy baits that have been snagged. The best lures are the chrome Krocadile, Hopkins and Miki. You tie one on and let 'er rip.

When there are large amounts of anchovies in the area, a "snag rig" provides the opportunity to fish with live bait. A snag rig consists of tying a barrel swivel to the end of your line, then adding four feet of 50-pound test leader and tying on a snap swivel, clipping on a five-ounce sinker. Midway on the leader, tie a dropper loop and add a 4/0 treble hook. When birds are diving, cast the rig, snag an anchovy, then let it sit. "The stripers can't resist a wounded bait," says Abe.

Another exciting prospect is to abandon the beach areas and clamber out to the rocky points. In recent years, this is where the larger bass have been caught. Instead of heavy metal jigs, you use giant plugs, such as a 10-inch Pencil Popper, Striper Strike, Giant Pikie Minnow, and the largest Rebel Minnow. Because these plugs are lighter than the metal jigs, for casting ease you are better off using a spinning reel than a revolving spool reel. This is also true when fishing the access points on the California Aqueduct.

"Be imaginative," says Abe. "Don't stick to the same monotonous straight retrieve. Should a bass continue to follow, speed up, then slow down, or jerk the lure away from the bass, then allow it to rest briefly on the surface. Jig it, dance it, try anything that might induce a fish into striking."

When it comes to being imaginative, Abe and Angelo lead the league. One day, after hearing that big striped bass had been pinning anchovies into a rocky cove during high tides, they immediately started plotting a way to get in on it.

"We surveyed it, and it turned out there was no way to reach it by shore," Abe said. "Access was blocked off from the prime rock to stand on by water. You couldn't get there by boat either. Too rocky, too dangerous."

So what did they do? Only Abe or Angelo Cuanang would think of this: They bought a pair of wet suits and then actually swam out to the rock, keeping their rods airborne as they made their way through the water. Then later, as the high tide came in, so did the stripers, and the Cuanangs had a wild spree using surface lures.

"The fish were breaking right on the surface," Angelo said.

And out there on that rock were two men with rods, casting away with the same zeal they had as young boys catching bullheads.

With times being tough for the striped bass, a lot of people defer to other fish, saying it just "isn't like the good ol' days." But with the right approach, some skill and a zest for adventure, these are the good ol' days right now.

SALMON
A CANDID CAMERA REVEALS SECRETS

Comes a time for every angler when an experience seems to open a new door, allowing a glimpse of something rare and fantastic. Such a phenomenon hit me while salmon fishing one day, and it was like getting whacked in the head by a two-by-four. What I learned dramatically improved my ability to catch more and bigger salmon. Anybody can do the same.

It was a warm July morning on the Pacific Ocean, one of those summer days where the dawn light makes the clouds look like little red cotton balls. We were a bit tense over the day's plan. My angling compadre, Dick Pool, had invented a new way to suspend an underwater TV camera behind his boat so that it was focused on our trolled baits and spoons. On the boat deck, we could actually view the underwater picture on video screen, and any fish that might strike. It was like looking into a crystal ball and being able to tell the future.

But instead of viewing savage attacks, another scenario unfolded: Salmon of all sizes would race up to our baits, follow them for a while, then veer off into the briny blue without striking. It was a classic paradox—after three hours we had not caught a fish, but had captured many on camera following our baits.

"Judging by the bites we got, we would have thought that there were no fish down there," Pool said, "but the underwater TV camera disproved that."

Later in the morning, I was watching the trolled baits on the TV video when I noticed one of the baits was curiously tumbling like a pinwheel.

"Look," I said, "something's wrong with that one."

"We'll have to fix it," Pool responded.

Suddenly out of nowhere, a big salmon surged into the picture and ripped into that bait like a hungry lion pouncing on a zebra. Ten minutes later, a 15-pound king salmon was netted.

Something clicked in our minds. That event started several years of study involving thousands of hours of underwater filming by Pool. The first lesson, however, was obvious: "Bait action, that's a key right there," observed Pool. In the next year, he invented the Salmon Rotary Killer, which allows anglers to simply clip anchovies in the plastic bait holder (rather than a more complex rigging process), and also imparts a spinning, wounded look to the bait.

But for Pool, coming up with the Rotary Killer was like a young fawn learning how to walk. In the years since that first event, his underwater filming techniques have evolved to state-of-the-art quality, and so have the fishing secrets that we have learned because of it. The techniques are applicable to virtually any trolling situation, not just salmon.

We have had many fantastic trips together: salmon to 60 pounds . . . catching a dozen fish in a few hours when no other boat in the area even raised a net . . . never getting skunked in 10 years of salmon fishing together. The secrets revolve around four themes: bait action, fishing depth, color selection, and proper use of dodgers.

■ The "Wounded Look"

The reason that the darting action of a lure or the pinwheel motion imparted by a Rotary Killer is effective is not because it looks good. In fact, salmon in the ocean do not rely primarily on their sight and smell to feed. What is much more important is that they detect the vibrations of baitfish through what is called their lateral line sensors, which run the length of their bodies. It is like a built-in sonar, where the salmon can detect sound and vibrations through the water.

Salmon use their lateral lines more than anything else in order to find food. When water clarity is poor, or when you fish very deep, the importance of good bait action becomes critical.

"A perfect-looking bait or lure is almost useless under these conditions if it doesn't send the right vibrations to the fish," advises Pool.

That is why Rotary Killers can also work so well for yellowtail off Southern California, or why a smaller version can be effective for large trout in lakes where threadfin shad or other similar baits are legal. The scarcely detectable vibrations of baitfish are just

SECRETS OF THE MASTERS

what big fish are looking for. When a salmon sees the "wounded baitfish," the vibrations from the bait reinforce his attack instincts. Once you understand the salmon's sensory system—and make sure that your bait is always putting out the right message—you will have the chance to start catching more fish.

■ Fishing Depth

"How deep should I go?" This is always one of the first questions on many fishing trips, whether trolling in lakes or ocean, whether off Morro Bay, Half Moon Bay . . . or Alaska. The variables that determine depth are water temperature, water clarity and baitfish concentrations.

Salmon prefer water that is 52 to 54 degrees, and will tolerate water 48 to 59 degrees. If you don't have a temperature gauge, then you are missing out on a major clue—I never go on any fishing trip without a temperature gauge. Off the Southern California coast, where salmon roam during the spring, it can require trolling 100 to 300 feet deep in order to find the preferred cooler water. Off the Bay Area and Northern California coast, the water temperature can fluctuate so much during the season that fishing without a temperature reading is like walking blindfolded.

Water clarity also has an effect on how deep the fish are. That is because fish do not have eyelids, and thus the only way they can avoid bright light is to swim deeper.

The ideal condition for salmon is when water clarity is low. This will occur on a gray-sky day where the wind is causing a light chop on the water, and when plankton production is high. It is ideal because salmon are most apt to be shallow, rarely deeper than 40 feet down. The opposite condition is a blue-sky day with no wind and no plankton, and in turn, the salmon must go deep in order to avoid bright sunlight penetration.

Another factor for depth is baitfish concentrations. When salmon are feeding on juvenile rockfish at reef areas, which is common when no schools of anchovies are in the area, they are often 240 to 300 feet deep. When salmon are feeding on squid or shrimp, which is common in early spring, the best depth is usually 70 to 90 feet. When salmon are feeding on large schools of anchovies or herring, the salmon will often be just 25 to 40 feet deep. Remember this and get it right.

Put it all together: Water temperature, water clarity and bait-fish concentrations, and you will determine the proper trolling depth. Often you can fish shallow at daybreak, but as the sun gets high in the sky, causing great light penetration in the water, you will have to go deeper to reach the fish.

■ Color Selection

On some days, there seems no clue as to why some colors are effective, and others give you a one-way ticket to zilchville. But for the most part, there are some definite rules about color use.

As sunlight penetration in the water diminishes, so does the appearance of the color. In fact, as you go deeper, all colors eventually turn black, but do so at incredibly different rates.

For instance, bright red, the same hue used on police emergency lights and fire trucks, turns black faster than any other color underwater. That makes it effective only when used in shallow water, where light penetration is highest. If you fish deeper than 40 feet during typical ocean water clarity, red can lose its powers as an attractant. To the fish, it will actually appear black. The best time to use red for salmon is during the fall, when the salmon's spawning mode kicks into overdrive, and also when the fish will school outside the entrances to major rivers just 25 to 35 feet deep.

On the opposite end of the spectrum, blue is capable of reflecting the smallest glimmers of light. That is why blue is the most effective color when fishing deep, or in ocean water that is thick with plankton or otherwise provides low water clarity. Some anglers have told me that blue should never be used, since "blue is disguised by the water color and fish can't see it." According to a series of tests, the opposite is true. It shows up in deep water better than any color.

In the middle of the color spectrum is light green, or chartreuse. It shows up very well between 25 and 45 feet deep.

This is exactly how deep most salmon are during the summer months when the plankton is thick and salmon are corralling schools of anchovies. That is why the chartreuse Rotary Killer, or the clear with chartreuse fin, is the best-selling Rotary Killer. The best-selling Krocadile spoon is the four-inch model, chrome with a green reflective strip. When in doubt, go with chartreuse. Another trick is to use a "teaser leader", a six-foot salmon trolling leader which has a chartreuse hoochy placed midway on it for an attractor.

■ Dodgers And Flashers

"I always troll with at least one or two dodgers, but only rarely with a flasher," Pool said. "With the underwater TV camera, it has been proven to me why dodgers work so well." The best on the market for salmon is the No. 0 brass/silver model made by Luhr Jensen.

A dodger shakes back and forth in the water, emitting a signal that acts like a homing beeper for salmon's built-in radar. The salmon can "hear" the action of the dodger, and are then attracted to the area. "It's my opinion that a dodger simulates the back-and-forth action of the tail of an attacking salmon," Pool said. "Other salmon pick up the vibrations through the water and figure one of their buddies has found some food, so they race to the scene."

To prove it is the action of the dodger that attracts the salmon, and not the flash, Pool painted a dodger flat black so it was invisible to the fish. Yet it still attracted salmon by the vibrations that it produced. The underwater TV camera never lies.

"It is very important when using dodgers to use them exactly as detailed in the directions," Pool said. "If it says to use 24 inches of leader between the dodger and your bait, then use exactly 24 inches."

Flashers are longer than dodgers, measuring up to two feet, are tied far behind your weight, and are built to slowly turn and wobble in large loops as they are trolled. When light catches the sides, it reflects flashes similar to the shiny scales from a school of baitfish. We don't like them much, for two reasons. One is that they travel in large circles and often tangle with other lines. The other is that relying on flash for attraction rather than action is going against every lesson learned on the underwater TV camera.

The underwater filming has shown salmon rushing up to a dodger, only to veer off at the last minute. To counter this, a trick is to troll a dodger from the rod that is furthest forward on the boat, and then from the other rods fished from the stern, to troll a few baits without a dodger. "The dodger at the front will get the salmon's attention, and the other rods behind it will get the fish," said Pool.

If you have your own boat, you would be wise to get it set up with downriggers, which allow trolling at precise depths to 200 feet deep, with no strain on your rod. A downrigger has a separate spool filled with wire line, and a metal arm to withstand the heavy weight on the downrigger line. The fishing line is clipped to the downrigger line, which releases when a fish strikes. So not only can you fish precise depths, but you can use light fishing rods.

If you fish on a party boat, on the other hand, a variety of trolling techniques are used. The most common in the San Francisco Bay Area is a sinker release, in which a two or three-pound sinker is placed. When the salmon strikes, the sinker is released to the bottom, and you fight the fish, not the weight. In other areas, it is more common to use plastic trolling planers, such as the Deep Six or Pink Lady.

Regardless of what you choose, it is rod position on the party boat that becomes important. I always fish only one of three places: on the bow, so my bait is the first one a school of fish will see; right next to the window looking into the cabin, so I can see the fishfinder and always be aware of baitfish concentrations and their depth; on the stern, so I can let out more line and fish deep if necessary (from 10 a.m. on) without tangling any other lines on the boat.

One other phobia shared by salmon anglers is losing big fish. Some people make up for it by losing the small ones too. The reason for so many lost fish is one simple thing: Failure to keep the rod bent while fighting the fish. Keeping your rod bent during a fight guarantees a tight line; slack line allows salmon to throw the barbless hook.

For trollers using a cannonball sinker for weight, a popular rod and reel combination is the Fenwick 1870C, Penn 3/0 reel, filled with fresh 20-pound test line. But if you use a downrigger, a plastic diving-planer, or mooch, you can go much lighter. My favorite salmon rod is now the LCI 7 1/2-foot GBB764, setup with an Ambassadeur level-wind reel and 16-pound test line. This setup is ideal for trolling with a downrigger, or mooching.

It takes a bit of a detective, seaman and athlete to chase down California's big salmon. Dick Pool is all three, and I often think of a July trip out of Bodega Bay that proved it.

My brother Rambob was along, and an armada of boats were trolling just outside the harbor at a spot called the Whistle Buoy.

Nobody was catching anything. After two hours of testing using the methods detailed in this story, we finally found the salmon 60 feet deep. In a three-hour span, the three of us landed 12 salmon, including a 30-pounder, keeping just a few for the barbecue.

Mysteriously, other boats began following us around, the skippers watching with binoculars, including some captains on commercial boats. When Dick released a 10-pounder—and no other boat in the armada had even raised a net—the radio waves went wild.

Fishing trips don't always work that way, of course, but when they do, I flash back to that first day with the underwater TV camera. It has allowed a rare glimpse in a new and wonderful world of more and bigger salmon.

■ The Mooching Alternative

Ed Migale has one mission in life: to help people catch more fish. He has become so good at it that he quit his old job and now works 100 percent as a "professional fisherman."

Actually, Ed has accomplished this by building custom fishing rods, designing unique saltwater terminal tackle, and giving fishing lessons on his specialty, mooching for salmon.

Mooching is best from midsummer through fall, when the fish are no longer traveling great distances, but are holding in schools, feeding on hordes of anchovies. You turn your engine off and let the boat drift, keeping your rod in hand to sense every bite, set every hook.

Since salmon strike from the underside, their forward motion toward the boat can create some immediate slack in the line. As a result, you must react instantly by reeling the line taut, as in "reeling down to the fish." If you don't do it, you will rarely get the hook set. If the tip of your rod is too soft, this can also cause some missed sets.

Migale's favorite mooching setup is with the standard two-hook rig. If you are not familiar with how to hook your bait with a mooching rig, board a party boat and have the deckhand show you exactly how to do it. The bait should have a bend in it, so it bobs and weaves as the boat drifts in the current. "When the salmon are biting very lightly, then I will switch to a single hook rig," Migale says.

The rigging is very simple. From a snap swivel, attach a crescent or banana-shaped sinker, and from there, clip on your mooching leader. That's it. "The keel shape of the crescent weight causes them to ride upwards in the water," Migale explained. "That eliminates main-line tangles and helps facilitate a proper drift."

Another rig, popular in Monterey Bay, is to use a sinker slider (such as described in the section on sturgeon fishing), then attach a teardrop sinker to the clip on the slider. This works best when mooching in water deeper than 75 feet. In fact, off Santa Cruz, it is popular to mooch this way, with the anglers just propping their rod in a holder until the tip starts bouncing.

There are times when you can go even simpler. Just tie on a one-ounce Shim Jig, bait it with a one-inch anchovy fillet (including the tail), then let it flutter in the current as the boat drifts. When the salmon are on the bite, this is a favorite of mine. But when the salmon are not on the bite, you can get deluged with baitrobbers, particularly kingfish.

So what should you do? Troll or mooch? According to my logs of the Golden Gate Fleet, trolling produces higher numbers of fish, while mooching produces a larger average size. Take your pick.

■ A Word About Piers

The ultimate fishing experience from a pier is catching a big salmon, and there are two times in the San Francisco Bay Area when the prospects can be quite good. The first comes from mid-June through July, when schools of anchovies attract salmon to Pacifica Pier on the San Mateo County coast. The second is in September, as schools of salmon swim through the Bay and head upriver, when anglers at the pier at Fort Baker (north side of Golden Gate Bridge) have a chance at intercepting them.

Either time, the strategy is the same: Offer an anchovy rigged mooching-style under a large styrofoam float. It is almost like fishing in a lake for bluegills, but on a much grander scale. When that bobber starts to dance it might be a 20-pounder doing the tugging.

This setup also can be effective in the tidal lagoons of the Smith, Eel and Klamath rivers when the salmon first enter the lower river during the fall.

If you try to catch salmon from a pier, always remember to bring along a crab trap in order to hoist up the fish when it is played out. Otherwise it will be impossible to land it. By shore, bring a large net.

The one time I forgot a net was on the Smith River. My longtime pal Michael Furniss hooked a 15-pounder on his second cast of the day, and after a 15-minute fight, I tried to land it by hand. At the moment of truth, I slipped from a rock, instantly fell completely in the river, and then while underwater, struggled with the fish in my arms for a moment before it slipped away. It was gone forever.

Poor Mike never got over it, and to this day, he thinks he is afflicted with some rare form of jinx.

■ A River Adventure

Some people's stories are best told by the lines on their face, rather than the lines on a page. Such is the case for Al Vasconcellos, a salmon guide based on the Sacramento River at Balls Ferry Resort near Anderson.

In a two-month span here on the Sacramento River, he directed his customers to 300 salmon, including a 56-pounder. Al doesn't brag much, some days he doesn't say much, but you can tell that he's something special. You can see it in his face.

"I get my fish," Al said, and he doesn't speak with a forked tongue.

I have fished with Al many times and have had some great days with him. On a cold early-winter day with Al and my old friend, Dave Beronio, we caught six salmon between 15 and 35 pounds in just two hours. Another time, I caught 32 and 28-pounders on back-to-back casts. It doesn't come much better than that, anywhere.

Salmon start moving upriver during late summer and fall on California's major river systems, with the best fishing in September and October, and fair prospects in August and November. The major rivers are the Sacramento, Feather, American, Klamath, Trinity, and Smith. In big rain years, the San Joaquin system also can attract salmon.

You need a boat to do it right. Vasconcellos will position his boat at the head of a river hole, the boat headed upriver with the engine still running. The motor is given just enough gas so the boat remains almost motionless in the river, then Al will ease up a touch on the motor, allowing the boat to slowly drift downriver, just a foot at a time. That is why it is called "backtrolling."

With rod in hand, anglers will allow their bait, roe or a Flatfish lure (with a sardine fillet tied with thread to the underside), to trail off the bottom about 40 or 50 feet behind the boat. With roe, you keep the sinker along the bottom, "walking" it down the river holes. It takes a light touch to detect the bites, and a ramrod strike to set the hook.

It can be a long grind of a day waiting for a pick-up, but when it comes, it has the chance to be the biggest salmon of your life. The salmon in rivers are mostly spawners, bigger than 10 pounds, with a good number of 20-pounders and a sprinkling going bigger. The state record 88-pounder was caught by Lindy Lindberg on the Sacramento River, and 80-pounders have also been taken on the Smith.

Maybe the next nibble on your line will be one even bigger.

By shore, it is quite a bit more difficult to catch salmon. Salmon rest in the course of their upriver journey on the bottom of deep river holes, and getting a bait or lure to drift properly and deep enough through these holes is very difficult from shore. The exceptions are on the Trinity River and South Fork Smith River, where nature has placed many a shoreline rock adjacent to some of the best deep river holes, and also at the mouth of the Klamath River, where shoreliners can wade the prime lower river near the US 101 bridge.

Salmon provide one of the most multi-faceted fisheries in California. They are a bulldog on the hook, but provide gourmet eats when on the table. You can chase them across the ocean and up rivers, and in the process discover some of California's most beautiful natural areas.

SHARKS
PUTTING THE BITE ON THEM

Mankind always has been fascinated with sharks for one reason: Every once in a while, they eat somebody.

"They're really not such bad fellows," said Jim Siegle, "except that they have this biting problem now and then."

Siegle is a big, strong guy, a former pro football player and now a gun dealer, bred in a family of very rugged individuals. "I feel so small next to a big shark," he says. "I have dreams about them."

Jim Siegle started with a curious fascination about nature's perfect eating machines, and then developed a system that finally turns the tables and really puts the bite on them. It works for most of the 20 species of sharks common along California's coast and bays, and for the granddaddy, the man-eating Great White, he has developed the most unique strategy of all.

It was Siegle I first contacted when I started fishing for Great White sharks. We spent hours and hours talking strategy, developing rigs, and ultimately, many days on the water together on sheer, wild adventure. Later, I also fished for Great Whites with Abe and Angelo Cuanang (see striped bass), Ski Ratto, and Dick Pool (see salmon), and between them all, have had some of the scariest but exhilarating fishing trips imaginable.

Our intent is never to kill a Great White, but rather to have the excitement of fighting a fish that weighs over 1,000 pounds and is capable of eating you in a few gulps, then cutting the line. Because of the erosive qualities of saltwater and the juices in a shark's mouth, the hook dissolves quite quickly. Great Whites are a key part of the ocean environment, the only predator capable of keeping populations of sea lions under any semblance of control, and therefore are a key link in the balance of the marine food chain. In fact, we have seen Great Whites devour a six-foot sea lion in less than two minutes, leaving just a few scraps for the seagulls. There have been other episodes as well.

In one, a giant shark came up behind the boat and broached like a whale, then with its head out of the water, began barking like a dog, making woof sounds at us as it gulped air. I guess it wanted a bone.

On another, Angelo Cuanang hooked up with a Great White and had his boat towed off at five knots. "See ya."

Imagine this one: We were fishing quietly with no sign of sharks, at a spot where the bottom of the ocean was registering as 110 feet deep on the electronic depthfinder. Suddenly, the bottom registered as 70 feet deep, then 60 feet, then 50 feet, before falling off again to 110 feet—but the boat had not actually moved at all. "It's the Big Guy down there under the boat," said Abe Cuanang. "He's so big that the sonar thinks he's the bottom."

Another time, Ski Ratto was tying a knot when he felt like something was watching him. He looked up, and there, just a few feet behind the boat, was a Great White that was four feet across at the head, staring at him. Lunch served yet?

If you become fascinated with sharks, you should start by fishing for species that bite baits on hooks, and not the legs of surfers and scuba divers. Many species of such sharks are abundant, but most all of them are scavengers, roaming and feeding along the bottom. The most common big sharks that are bottom scavengers along the entire California coast and in bays are the seven-gill, six-gill, and thresher shark, along with the smaller leopard shark, gray smoothhound (sand shark), soupfin, and stickleback (dogfish). The biggest of those species that I have tangled with is a 170-pound seven-gill shark that was eight feet long and had a mouth that looked like a salad bowl full of razor blades.

"Always remember that the fish are always right on the bottom," Siegle said. "That means you have to get deep with them, right on the very bottom, and make them an offer they can't refuse."

He designed a terminal rigging that has become the standard for shark fishing: A one-pound sinker (less when depths and currents allow it), from which five feet of 25-pound plastic-coated wire leader extends to a size 14/0 hook. "This absolutely makes sure the bait is on the bottom," Siegle said.

And what for bait? Try to think like a fish, Siegle advises: If you were a shark, what would you want to eat? A Fish and Game director? No, no, no, you would want something that actually gets outside now and then, the most natural bait possible.

"The best bait is often another smaller shark," Siegle believes. "Large hunks of fish, squid, or combinations of them can also work." The baitfish called a midshipman can also attract Jaws Jr., as Barry Canevaro has proved.

Reno Montanelli demonstrated the effectiveness of Siegle's directive by using a whole stickleback (dogfish) shark to catch a 337-pound seven-gill shark that measured 10 feet long. Now get this: When the giant shark was landed, it had another three-foot stickleback lodged in its throat, yet was still trying to eat.

Even though these sharks aren't known to chase down and attack people, they will still bite just about anything in reach, particularly if they are brought aboard a boat. My dad, Bob Stienstra Sr., once caught a skinny little two-foot stickleback that tried to bite the toe of his right boot off, leaving permanent teeth marks in the leather.

"They just can't help it," Siegle said. "This biting fixation is just something they have to do."

As a result, you must always use extreme caution around all sharks, even the smaller ones, regardless of how docile they might appear or how small they are.

"Any shark larger than 4 1/2 feet should not be brought aboard any sportfishing boat," Siegle recommends. "They should be tied off to the boat and kept in the water." Of course, that lesson is not difficult to remember the first time you look down into the water and see an eight-footer coming up, mouth open, teeth exposed, and jaws snapping.

"For the bigger ones, you should always use a bang stick to dispatch them," Siegle said. "Always think safety. You don't want your hand or anything else to end up in their stomach."

A bang stick is actually a long pole on which a .410 shotgun shell is mounted on one end. When loaded and active, you plunge the end of the stick into the shark's head, whereupon the shell fires a direct hit.

Once under control, all sharks should be bled immediately in order to preserve the meat. This is accomplished by cutting a gash across the backbone of the fish near the tail or head. If this is not done, the blood will permeate the meat of the shark, making it smell something like a high school science project. When this happens, the meat must then be thrown away, which represents a terrible waste of life. Never kill a fish that you do not intend to eat, and shark meat is decent enough, provided the fish is bled immediately upon being caught.

When it comes to a Great White, however, don't even dream about bringing one home. They don't like that. It is extremely dangerous, even for specialists such as Frank Mundus on the East Coast, who has a big boat, specialized rig, and crew trained for Great Whites. In fact, Frank is the guy whom Hollywood patterned the possessed shark master after in the first *Jaws* movie.

A typical Great White off California is a 12-footer that weighs about 1,500 to 1,700 pounds, with 15 to 17-footers in the 2,500 to 3,000-pound range rare, but out there. But they come bigger. Great Whites measuring 19 feet and weighing more than 5,000 pounds have been chummed up and tagged by both John McCosker of Steinhart Aquarium and Peter Klimely of Scripps Institute on separate episodes.

The key to the expanding population of Great Whites is the Marine Mammal Protection Act of 1974. Since sea lions and elephant seals have been protected, they have provided a much larger food source for the Great Whites. In turn, the baby Great Whites started having much higher survival rates in the early 1980s. Now in the '90s, there are so many Great Whites that someone gets bit nearly every year, usually a surfer dressed up to look just like shark food.

But unlike surfers, we try to take a minimum of chances when shark hunting.

"First, we must have a calm ocean," Siegle said. "Imagine a rough ocean, losing your balance, and then falling in by accident? All Whitey would see would be your legs kicking back and forth as he came up the chum line. It gives me nightmares."

We also work out precise emergency teamwork maneuvers: Keeping a knife nearby at all times if cutting the line is necessary, having the boat ready to start and getting the hell out of there if the shark attacks and tries to ramrod us, and having a shotgun aboard with deer slugs at the ready.

That done, we start the trip by laying a chum line. All matter of fish carcasses, obtained from commercial fish buyers, are fed into a grinder, which leaves fish bits and chunks and a slick from fish oil in the water. If the carcasses are a few days old, the smell is so overwhelming that without a gas mask you may do some chumming yourself from a five-point stance.

You might think that sharks of all kinds would respond instantly to the chum line. That just hasn't happened. Only rarely, in the fall when blue sharks are more common, has there been even a tremor of visible response. Regardless, we keep at it, because we have learned that just because a Great White looks at the bait doesn't mean he will take it. They are actually quite difficult to entice, not the wild-abandoned biters you might think.

"The hope is that if a shark is in the area, the chum line may get him in the biting mood," Siegle said. "We could always dangle our feet in the water to do the same, of course, but for now have decided against that strategy."

For tackle, we use heavy, world-class rods, reels, and line. We have used the heaviest rod Sabre makes, rated at 130-pound test, with a 16/0 Penn reel loaded with 700 yards of 130-pound Andy line. It is so heavy you practically need a hoist to strap it on. To support it, you must have a full shoulder and back harness, to which the rod and reel are connected. We also use Penn International reels set up on heavy tuna rods, 80-pound class, which are a lot easier to handle.

The shoulder harness represents a touch of danger when shark fishing. If you hook the Big Guy, get a backlash, and then he takes off on a long run, you would be pulled right into the water because you are connected to the rod by the harness. That is why we always keep a knife at the ready.

"If you are outfitting your boat for a Great White shark expedition, I suggest using a fighting chair, as if you were fishing for marlin," Siegle says. "That way, you can be strapped into the chair, and Whitey won't be able to pull you into the water if you get a backlash or a reel malfunction and no line can go out."

The terminal rigging is an awesome sight. We use giant hooks, 18/0 if available, 16/0 at the minimum, connected by three feet of case-hardened chain, and then 12 feet of leader, four separate wound-strand wires, each testing at 1,000 pounds strength. Siegle designed this rigging, using no knots for connectors, but only wire clamps that can take 10,000 pounds of stress. If we use a live bait, Angelo Cuanang came up with the idea of using a large, red balloon as a bobber.

For bait, we use whatever is available for each trip. The best is a live lingcod, about a 15 or 20-pounder. Another very good bait is a ray in the 40 to 50-pound class. We have also used two or three stickleback (dogfish) sharks, or combinations of small sharks and rockfish.

One time we made a trip to a rural tallow works, where a fellow named Jake was fascinated with our adventure. He gave us several bags of dried blood to feed our chum line, and also a stillborn calf for bait. Alas, neither attracted any sharks at all, and the sight of it all caused everybody to get seasick. The best advice is to use only ground-up fish carcasses for chum, and large fish for baits.

You can spend a tremendous amount of time on the water and never even see a Great White. In the process, you can miss out on excellent nearby fishing. For that reason, my taxidermist has been working on making me a "sea lion lure." By starting with a mold for an elk mount, he is carving a sea lion shaped "lure," which will be sealed and painted black, then rigged with two large hooks. It will look like a giant Flatfish lure, wiggling back and forth, and I plan to troll it along when I troll for other fish.

If you think that sounds crazy, well, maybe it is. But you have to be a little deranged to fish for Great Whites.

Consider the tale of Hank the Tank out of Bodega Bay, who lost the biggest salmon of his life off Tomales Point when a Great White came up and bit it in half. The half of fish that remained weighed 25 pounds. Hank was enraged, and the next day returned to the same spot. He poured all matter of fish carcasses in the water, and after a hour, Whitey returned to the scene of the crime.

Hank responded by tossing out the half of salmon on a giant hook—which was connected by cable to a power winch he'd taken from his four-wheel drive. Well, sure enough, the shark took the bait, and Hank winched the shark right up to the back of the boat, and then started firing at it with a deer rifle. The shark responded by swimming away, actually reversing the direction of the power winch, then pulled the winch right off the floorboard of the boat and into the water.

Whitey wasn't done yet. He returned and bit the guy's propeller right off.

At last report, Hank had moved to the mountains, renamed his boat *The Mackinaw King*, and was fishing at Lake Tahoe.

ROCKFISH
BLIND MAN FRANK IS CALIFORNIA'S KING

The life of Frank Bodegraven was forever changed in the flash of a shocking moment on July 11, 1966. Frank was working as an elevator installer, and while working in a shaft, an elevator suddenly came hurtling down and struck him square in the back of the head, wedging his face into a metal boom. His nose was torn off and he was knocked unconscious, but he survived it.

"While I was in the ambulance, I remember coming to and going out again," Bodegraven said. "Four days later, I finally came out of it, regaining consciousness, and discovered I was blind." He also lost the hearing in his right ear.

Now turn the clock forward to the 1990s. It's a cold, foggy day on the ocean, and 25 miles out to sea there is a solitary figure on the bow of a big sportfishing vessel. The man ties his rig, baits his hook, then casts, all with the aplomb of a master, yet without ever seeing what he is doing. It's Blind Man Frank, California's deep sea king. Blind or not, his catches are amazing. He wins rockfish and lingcod jackpots so routinely on deep sea trips that some anglers feel like they are simply making a donation to the Frank Bodegraven Retirement Fund. His life-best catches include a 53-pound salmon, 35-pound lingcod, 19-pound goldeneye rockfish, and 12 albacore in one day.

"I still have the indentation of the elevator in my head, right where the edge of it hit me," Frank says. "I can't see nothing, but I've got one good ear left. When I cast, I listen real close to the plop of it landing in the water, so I can put my thumb down to stop the reel from getting a backlash."

Frank started fishing four years after the accident and has since developed a winning touch to go with a winning system. In the process, Frank has become an example for us all, both as an individual overcoming adversity, and as an angler who has mastered his craft.

"Because of his sensitivity, he has developed a fantastic touch with the rod and his line, and he is a highliner with large fish and getting the coveted jackpot," said Captain Bob Smith of the party boat *Cobra*. "He has the sensitivity that when he does get a big fish on, he is able to tune his reflexes to the fish. His capture rate of getting large fish off the bottom is phenomenal."

For years it has been standard on deep sea rockfish trips to use a pre-tied leader that has three shrimpflies, baiting them with a strip of squid, then adding a cannonball sinker or a 16-ounce Diamond Jig for weight, and letting it down to the bottom. No more. Not with Blind Man Frank.

"When I first went out there, I didn't know what to do," Frank said. "Then I started working at it, getting the hang of it. I'd go up on the bow and try casting a jig without a hook (for safety), trying to learn how to cast. Pretty soon, I started to get it right."

Frank ties on a Banana Bar, Diamond Jig, chrome Hex Bar, or maybe even a Tady jig. Sometimes he will put hooks on both ends of the chrome bar, or add a dropper a foot above the bar, then add a Hair Raiser or another small jig as a "cheater." He senses the wind direction, then lets fly with a cast, reaching as far out to sea with it as possible.

"If the wind is hitting me in the face, then I know to cast the opposite way," Frank explained. "You see, the boat is drifting sideways, getting pushed by the wind. So when I cast a Banana Bar the same direction as the drift, the boat will go toward the bar instead of away from it. That makes it a lot easier to get deep, and gives you more fishing time on the drift. Often a rockfish will take it on the way down. Most of the time it goes right down to the bottom, and then I work off of the bottom."

Blind Man Frank said that sometimes the bites are obvious, just good solid rips, but with big lingcod, sometimes they aren't so obvious.

"When I feel a slight difference in the weight of the bar, that is often all you feel with the real big lings," he said. "The second I feel that, I crank up five or ten turns real fast. That gets those big lings off the bottom so they won't get into the rocks. I work them up in easy stages."

It is an amazing sight to see Frank at work. On several occasions, he has even caught two big lingcod on a single chrome bar, made possible by rigging with hooks at both ends of the bar.

One of his favorite strategies is to use a cheater jig above the bar. "A lot of time you get the better size rockfish on the cheater hook," he said.

On deep sea trips, a variety of jigs can catch fish. The most popular jig over time has been the squid-baited shrimpfly, with the shrimpflies that are tied with yarn outperforming those in plastic. In recent years, however, many new jigs have entered the market that have become very successful. The most widely marketed is the split-tail Scampi, which ranges in size from six to 12 inches. Its fluttering tail action is a key, especially with school fish. A lesser-known alternative that some swear by is the Live-Action shrimp. Another option are a variety of Hair Raisers and hoochies, best in phosphorescent white, which simulate a deep water squid. A great combination is using a dark blue Banana Bar, with a phosphorescent Hair Raiser tied on a foot above it as a cheater.

"If I go two or three drops without a hookup, then something isn't working right," advises Blind Man Frank. "I always experiment. The best color can be unpredictable, because the amount of plankton in the water and water clarity changes from trip to trip. The fish are funny, they'll bite one day on one color, the next day they'll ignore it. You never know what color to use. It might be weird, but it seems to work out that way."

Watching Blind Man Frank at sea is a study of a person in close touch with himself. He asks for no help, tying his rigs himself, baiting his hooks, landing his fish, and even getting them off the hook and into the fish bag. His mind and body are one. He is the kind of guy who could be your hero, living proof of the value of courage, persistence and a zest for life.

■ The Light Tackle Option

The sea is often foggy and cold along the coast, but the changing future of using light tackle for rockfish to offer world-class sportfishing is growing clear and hot. The tide has turned. This new dimension adds newfound excitement to the 1990s.

The key is that skippers are designing trips where anglers can use freshwater tackle for saltwater fish; long, light, graphite rods, fitted with revolving spool reels, and 12 to 14-pound line. It looks like an outfit suited for steelhead or largemouth bass, but instead you fish the Pacific Ocean for a fantastic array of rockfish. It works at inshore reefs, around kelp beds, or at shallow offshore reefs near islands.

Captain Kurt Hochberg of the boat *C-Gull* is one of the pioneers of this conversion over to light tackle. "It is a fantastic opportunity for anglers," Hochberg said. "All of a sudden, members of black bass clubs can make an ocean trip and use their freshwater rods and reels, and catch rockfish that are bigger and stronger than the freshwater fish they are accustomed to."

The rigging is very simple. Tie on the jig of your choice. The most preferred setup is a three-ounce jig head, rigged with a split-tail Scampi, but many options are possible. The Gibbs Minnow, Point Wilson Dart, Hair Raisers, Worm-Tail jigs, and even black bass jigs such as a large Gits-It all work well.

On one such trip, I was using a 8 1/4-foot Fenwick HMG rod, Abu 5 level wind, and eight-pound line—that's right, on the ocean—and tied on a Point Wilson Dart. When the boat stopped, I flipped it about 60 feet and let it sink, the Dart fluttering and shimmering as it sank, just like a wounded anchovy. As it went down, you could feel the bites: Nibble, tap, rip, then wham, I hooked up, and tussled away with a three-pound rockfish, the graphite rod bending and bouncing.

It can be like this for hours, non-stop, for as long as you are on the fishing grounds. There are days when if you go more than a minute without a bite, then get ready, because your time is due. If you want bigger fish, you just put on a bigger jig and go deeper, or use the deep sea techniques detailed by Blind Man Frank Bodegraven. But it is the light-tackle element that is attracting new clientele to an old business.

This unique-styled trip is the future for the California coast, for rockfish and lingcod populations are experiencing huge increases in many coastal areas. The reason for that is very simple: No more gillnetting. As more areas are protected from gillnets along the California coast, one of the primary benefits will be increased numbers of rockfish and lingcod.

This is clear in areas that are already protected. It is as clear as the tug, tug, tug, you get before setting the hook. Sound good? It is. It will provide some of the best fishing in America in the backyards of multiple millions of California residents who live near the ocean.

HALIBUT
JAWS THEY ARE NOT

―――――― 🐟 ――――――

A confused angler walked into the pier's bait shop holding a fish he'd just caught, looked at the owner with a mystified look on his face, then asked innocently: "How can you tell the difference between a flounder and a halibut?"

The shop owner looked at the fellow with a curious glance, then said, "Put your finger in its mouth. If your finger gets bit off, it's a halibut."

Well, the fellow responded by sticking his finger in the mouth of the fish, whereupon the fish immediately bit it off. The guy pulled his hand away, and stared at the little red stub.

"Guess it's a halibut," said the shop owner.

Some resemblance of that story actually happened, according to bait shop owner Bill Dittman. The irony of it is that halibut are not nearly as ferocious in the water as they are out of it. After being landed, a big halibut can become dangerous, bouncing around the deck like a flying manhole cover, using its sharp teeth in its small mouth to take a chunk out of whatever is close. On a party boat, I once saw a 25-pound halibut flip then flop into a guy's shin, bruising it as if the guy had been hit with a billy club, then the fish flipped again and took a bite out of a wood deck railing. The skipper, Cliff Anfinson, tried to use his boat insurance to pay for the repairs to the railing, but the claims officer thought it was all just another fish tale. It wasn't. But you can't blame him. After all, halibut are not known as savage attackers.

Just the opposite. Even though they are equipped with a sharp set of chompers to slice up anchovies, they rarely slam into a bait, lure or jig with much ferocity. Rather they frustrate most anglers, nibbling, nibbling and nibbling, doing everything possible to keep from being hooked. This is the case regardless of how big they are. I have caught halibut so big in Alaska that I needed a forklift to get the fish from the boat to the cleaning table, but even those nibbled like wary dogs sneaking licks on their masters' dinner plates.

Once you hook a halibut, you will discover it a decent fighter, more bulldog than greyhound, with a few surprises on the way. At first, during the initial, critical transition of bite, hookup, then fight, confusion sets in as to whether you are indeed hooked up, because they never just take the bait and run with it. In fact, during the first 20 or 30 seconds, it can seem like you are just reeling in a heavy weight, then suddenly, reality finally connects in that tiny pea-sized fish brain. The halibut realizes it is hooked, and is likely to roar off right back down to the bottom where you first hooked it. The bigger the fish, the more powerful the runs, of course, and the latter half of the fight really can wear down an angler, with the fish hovering and circling in the water like a Darth Vader spacecraft.

Once landed, the fight is far from over. Halibut can appear to be within seconds of its last gill flap when finally brought aboard, but upon hitting the deck, go bonkers, flipping and flopping everywhere, high and wide. Some anglers will attempt to whack them in the head with a billy club, but this just seems to get them even more angry, and maybe even a bit snappy with those teeth, too. The answer is to give them a good whack in the back, not the head, and that can settle them down soon enough.

There are four primary techniques to catch halibut: live bait, jigging and trolling from a boat, or baitfishing from a pier. Each technique requires its own touch to develop success.

■ **Live Bait**

Using live anchovies for bait is a lot of fun, but it can be frustrating for halibut. It is fun because you get to sense all the nibbles before setting the hook; it is frustrating because you get to sense all the nibbles before setting the hook. After you develop a touch, soon the twain will meet. Otherwise, all you get are nibbles, not hookups.

The rigging depends on the depth. In shallow areas, all you need to do is tie on a 2/0 live-bait hook, and add on a one-half ounce or two-ounce rubber core sinker, depending on tidal surge. Anywhere 20 feet deep or deeper, or where more weight is needed to get the bait on the bottom, it is more effective to use a three-way swivel rig. Tie your line off one swivel, a one or two-inch dropper and your sinker off another swivel, and then on the remaining swivel, tie 24 inches of leader and your hook. With a three-way rig, the most common mistake is using too much line on the dropper where you sinker is tied. When fishing rocky areas with live bait, an eight-inch dropper is ideal, but when fishing sandy areas for halibut, a very short dropper is necessary to insure the bait is right on the bottom.

That is where the halibut are: right at the bottom. The boat is allowed to drift in the tide along these sandy spots while the anglers aboard allow the bait to dangle along the bottom. If the tide is too strong or water too muddy, the halibut will often move out or go off the bite. If the tide is too weak, concentrations of baitfish can be in short supply. It can be necessary to run the boat in gear at very slow speeds, as if you were motor mooching, in order to simulate a drift. According to my logbook, the best tidal period for halibut is the beginning of a moderate outgoing tide.

After rigging up, always select a lively anchovy for bait, picking one that is not scraped or missing any scales. Then hook the anchovy through the nose vertically, starting the hook through the lower jaw and running it through the nose. Drop it over the side, let it spool down to the bottom, then get ready. This is where the fun/frustration starts.

When a halibut first nibbles at the bait, your first inclination will be to set the hook. As Waylon Jennings likes to say: "Wrong!" Do that and you get only bites, not fish. Halibut, unlike virtually every other fish, eat anchovies from the tail first. When they start to munch, you have to give them time to get up to the hook, which is located at the nose of the bait. When getting a bite, some anglers believe the proper technique is to bow the rod down to the fish, some will put the reel on free spool and thumb off some line; some will do nothing but wait. When I haven't fished halibut for a while, my preference is to bow the rod down a bit, count to three, then set the hook. When I feel I'm really on the fish, I'll rely on touch alone, free-spooling the bait until there is just the right tension spooling off the reel before setting the hook.

By the way, I've tried adding a stinger hook on the tail of the anchovy as a trick to catch these tail-striking halibut, but it never seems to work. If the fish are consistently scraping the tails of baits and never getting hooked, I switch over to jigs.

■ Jigging

Jigs can work when bait does not because of the hook placement: It's right at the tail, where the halibut starts his bite, right where your chances are best of getting a hookup. But halibut are more apt to bite a bait than a jig, so live-bait drifting is always preferable. Regardless, this is a good alternative, especially in shallow water. An additional bonus is that you are apt to catch other species of fish while hoping for a halibut to get interested.

The best jigs for halibut are the Striper Razor, Worm-Tail jig, Hair Raiser and Shim jig. You should tip the jig with a fillet of anchovy, best prepared by cutting a fillet off one side of a bait, starting midway on the anchovy and including the tail in the fillet. The little anchovy fillet gives the jig some taste and smell. I then spray the jig with Bang!, which is a fish attractant.

I've caught my biggest halibut with this setup. Setting the hook is a lot easier than with live bait, because you don't have to wait, wait, wait for the halibut finally to eat its way up to the hook. The bite often starts as a very subtle nibble, just strong enough to alert you, then a moment later, transitions into a quick yank. Wham! Set the hook right then, and you will have your hands full with a big fish.

■ Trolling

Not many people troll for halibut, but it provides a preferred alternative in the spring and early summer, when the fish are scattered and just arriving to inshore areas and bays. The best catch rates for trollers is not from using the most sporting method: using wire line, a heavy cannonball sinker on the end, then a series of green hoochies baited with squid, with a hoochy placed every two feet. This system is used by commercial hook-and-line halibut anglers who fish out of small boats. It can provide tremendous results when other methods are just hit-and-miss.

For the sport angler, a trolling option is using lures such as the four-inch Rapala, or chrome spoons such as the 3 3/4-ounce Krocadile or Hopkins. It is necessary to add weight ahead of the lure in order to get it down to the bottom. This is best done with a three-way swivel, rigging it as when using live bait, except that instead of tying on a hook, you tie on the lure. Trolling speed is critical, and you should always let the lure "swim" alongside the boat to check for proper action before letting it down to the bottom.

The catch rate is poor for most sport halibut trollers, but the ratio of strikes-to-caught fish is high. That is because no special touch is required to set the hook, with the halibut often hooking itself when it hits a trolled lure.

■ Pier Fishing

Few fish provide more of a surprise or satisfaction than a big halibut for anglers who are fishing from a pier. Of the 60 piers detailed in this book, more than 20 provide such an opportunity. It is a long shot, to be sure, but long shots can come in.

The best way to rig up is to use the sliding sinker system. You start by placing a "slider" over your fishing line. A slider is a hollow tube with a snap swivel connected to it, a cheap, common piece of tackle at shops. With the line going through your slider, you tie on a strong snap swivel to the end of the fishing line. Tie on 24 inches of leader to the snap swivel, and then to the end of the leader, tie on a 2/0 live-bait hook. For bait, use a whole anchovy, live if available, and hook it through the lower jaw and nose. Cast it out and start waiting; from a pier, you must wait for the fish to come to you. But often enough, they do just that. In addition, you may catch many other desirable species of fish during the wait. Always have a crab net available, which is necessary to hoist a big, played-out fish up to the pier deck.

If you catch a large, flat-like fish, brown on one side, white on the other and are not sure exactly what it is, let me give you some advice: Do not stick your finger in its mouth!

YELLOWTAIL, BONITO, ALBACORE
SOUTHERN CALIFORNIA'S BEST

───────────── 🐟 ─────────────

"No matter how much you know," observed Pat McDonell, "the fish always seem to know more." But there have been many times when McDonell has taught yellowtail, bonito and albacore a thing or two himself.

He is in an extraordinary position to both give and take fishing lessons along the Southern California coast. McDonell is the editor of *Western Outdoor News,* and has had the chance to fish with more than 50 skippers, study the systems they use, and then glean the better techniques to further refine his own skills.

"I've seen all the bad ways to fish and a few good ways," he says with a laugh.

The first thing you notice about Pat McDonell on a fishing trip is that even though he has a tremendous breadth of experience, he is still willing to listen, willing to learn something new. That approach separates him from most anglers. Then, like many of the masters profiled in this book, you notice the natural enthusiasm he has for adventure. By profession, fishing is his business, taking notes, snapping photographs, and writing stories. He takes more trips in a year than many anglers do in their lifetimes. Regardless, he always seems to have a glow about him on the cruise out to sea, envisioning what may be possible in the coming day, and still seems to have sparks shooting off him during every hookup. Pat also fishes a lot with his father, Mac, which adds a lot to his enjoyment of the sport.

■ **Yellowtail**

Yellowtail are the kind of fish that can get inside your mind and realign your senses. All it takes is one wide-open surface bite and you will be afflicted; that is where you use no weight, a live squid for bait, and get near-instant hookups of big yellowtail that immediately burn 40, 50 even 60 yards of line before you have a chance to figure out what's happening.

One enchanted morning on the briny green, Pat McDonell found himself in the midst of one of these bites and landed 13 yellowtail in just a few hours, the biggest going 22 pounds, and from that day on, he always gets this strange, excited look in his eye whenever he hears of a yellowtail run. Yellowtail are among the fightingest fish in California, and also one of the tastiest. They can get big, 30 to 40 pounds—the "Homeguards"—and fishing them is demanding but also rewarding.

"Yellowtail are along the Southern California coast all summer long and into fall," McDonell said. "But getting them to bite is another thing."

Anglers use three methods for yellowtail: trolling, free-spooling live squid, and jigging. The ideal situation arrives in the fall, when squid become abundant. Skippers and deckhands often chum yellowtail right up to the surface. But when the situation is less than ideal, which is most common, other strategies need to be employed.

"Do you have chum?" McDonell asked rhetorically. "If not, it can be difficult to locate the yellowtail unless you see them breaking."

In that circumstance, it is best to troll a large Rapala, the one that is painted to look like a mackerel. Coronado Island, San Clemente Island, the Catalina Islands and La Jolla coast are good areas to work, but when you are not sure where specifically to start, trolling is the only way to cover a lot of water in a short amount of time. In the process, you should continually scan the sea surface, hoping to see the fish boiling. If you get a hookup, circle the area trolling, or stop and either try to chum the yellowtail up or cast jigs.

The big party boats rarely troll because the skippers either provide the chance to catch squid for bait, or will have spent the previous evening rounding up enough for the trip.

"A lot of success can revolve around getting the squid," McDonell said. "The squid can get the yellowtail into a frenzy. It's most abundant in late summer, early fall. Sometimes the skippers will go out the night before, and with bright lights, get the squid to float on top and scoop them right up, and have the bait ready when you get on board. Sometimes you have to catch it yourself." To catch live squid, you use small jigs, let them down near the bottom, then catch squid that are eight to ten inches long.

If you see yellowtail breaking the surface, you can be on the verge of some of California's most exciting fishing. Approach the school cautiously, being sure not to spook them, then stop short and cast to them. On the party boats, what occurs more often is anchoring near an undersea pinnacle, where the deckhands chum away with anchovies to attract the yellowtail toward the boat.

The standard rigging is to tie on a 2/0 to 4/0 hook, then double hook the tail of the squid: bring the hook through once, then bring it through again. That secures the bait. If the yellowtail are near the surface, no weight is necessary. If you need to get down 20 or 30 feet, a splitshot will do the trick. Much deeper? Add a rubber-core sinker.

"What often happens on a party boat is that you will be anchored up at an island, chumming anchovies, getting the yellowtail to come up the chum line," McDonell said. "With luck, maybe 40 yellowtail will start coming up, swimming up the chum line. You can't wait for the fish to get to the boat. If you want to get bit often, get a longer rod, with a reel that can really cast, and cast that squid as far back to them as you can, way up the chum line. Get that bait in front of them."

Line weight can be a critical factor at this point, both in the odds of getting bit as well as the odds of landing the fish. When the yellowtail are picky, and Lord knows they can be, Pat uses 30-pound line in order to minimize its visibility in the water. During a wide-open bite, when that is a moot point, he uses 40 or 60-pound line.

"When you have to use light line to get bit, yellowtail can really rock you," Pat said. "It's nothing for them to run 60, 70 yards and get into the rocks. A trick with light line is that if the fish gets into the rocks, just free spool them until they come out, then you can play them again. What can happen when you're fishing over a pinnacle is that the yellowtail get picky, and everybody on board has to drop down to 30-pound line. That's how a boat can get 100 pickups and catch only four fish.

"The idea behind the heavy line is to keep them out of the rocks. If the yellowtail are on a heavy bite, they're not that picky."

After a hookup, the ability to stop a yellowtail from a long run is critical not only in the rocks, but around the oil rigs stationed along the coast. The metal legs of the oil rigs are not only sharp, but protrude outward to create a more stable base. When the yellowtail hits, it can break you off every time on those legs. As a result, you must have a strong reel, 4/0 is a good size, that you can cinch the drag down and limit them to a 30 or 40-yard run.

"You're playing tug of war and after awhile you pray your reel can take it," Pat said.

While squid can inspire the yellowtail into a frenzy, it is always the exception. What is more common, especially in the early summer, is to chum lots of anchovies to attract the fish, then "throw iron," or cast metal jigs. Of course, it's not quite that simple.

On one trip with Pat, the yellowtail were busting on the surface just forward of the boat, then they suddenly dove to the bottom. Everybody but one angler kept casting and retrieving near the surface. That one angler let his jig go all the way to the bottom, and had a fish on right off. It was like a little light bulb went off in everybody's head. All of the four other anglers on the bow immediately let down, hit bottom, gave the reel a single turn and hooked up simultaneously.

"That taught me something obvious about using jigs," Pat said. "But it's something that is sometimes overlooked. Down you go, up you come, but you obviously must focus on the area where the fish are. Always count the number of cranks on the reel, then when you get bit, you return to the exact same depth."

To make this easier, he advises using high-speed reels with 6-to-1 retrieve ratios. While long rods are necessary for casting, short rods do fine for jigging straight up and down. The six-ounce Tady jig is a mainstay, with either a single or treble hook, but there are a variety of jigs that will work. The best colors are blue and white, mackerel, solid chrome, and what is called scrambled eggs (brown and yellow).

The bigger yellowtail, the 30 and 40-pounders, the big boys, the "Homeguards," are usually caught right near the bottom, often so deep that to land one requires so much work that it can feel like your arm is going to fall off.

On one trip, Pat and his dad, Mac, were fishing with jigs, with no chum and no squid available. Mac, more accustomed to using bait, decided to try something different and placed a whole mackerel on the hook of the jig, then sent it down to the bottom.

"Some of the diehard yellowtail anglers laughed at him, and I was a bit skeptical myself," Pat remembered. "But he got hit with a big yellowtail, and after a 40-minute fight, finally landed it. It just wouldn't come in. It turned out to weigh 38 pounds." Many longtime yellowtail anglers never catch one that big.

"It looked like that was either a real dumb fish or my dad was real smart," Pat said with a grin. "Then, sometimes just being lucky is also part of the equation."

■ Bonito

If you were to try to conduct a brain scan of a bonito, it would probably short circuit the machine. These fish are just plain nuts. They are vicious attackers, then when hooked, zigzag all over the place. Pound-for-pound, this little tuna may be the best fighting fish around. They most commonly range three to five pounds, with a few to seven or eight pounds in the mix, rarely over ten pounds.

They provide tremendous sport on all kinds of tackle, even flyfishing gear. Bonito are not picky eaters. Find them and you catch them.

"They usually are not too difficult to locate," said McDonell. "Sometimes you can see them crashing bait and boiling on the surface, and you cast to them. Sometimes they are right around kelp areas." If there is no sign of fish, troll a feather jig to locate them. When you get a strike, stop the boat and get ready for some fun.

Most people use live anchovies for bait, and bring along a large collection of hooks, No. 2, 4 and 6. You must match the size of the hook to the size of the bait, gill hooking the anchovy in its collar bone. Be certain the bait is fresh, and try not to squeeze it when you hook it. Keep your reel on free spool and thumb the line out, and be ready at all times for a strike. Boom! When it happens, let the fish run off for just a second, no more, no less, put the reel in gear, set the hook, and get ready to run around the boat chasing the fish. Like I said, these fish have short circuits in their brains.

"It's even more exciting when you see them crashing into bait," McDonell said. "You can charge up to them in a boat and then sight-cast to them." The best lures are twin-tailed plastics such as Scampi or Mojo jig, best with three or four-ounce leadheads.

Flyfishers can have tremendous excitement when the bonito are on the surface. Use a No. 6/7 or 8 weight rod with a saltwater fly reel that can take plenty of pressure. You cast bonito feathers, see the strike, then hang on for the ride. When schools of three and four-pound bonito are marauding anchovies, flyfishing for them is as fun as for any fish in California.

One note is that bonito become inedible if they are not bled immediately and are allowed to sit uncleaned for long periods. Many people release all the bonito they catch. But if you are going to keep them, then bleed each fish immediately and keep them on ice. Never waste the life of a fish. Either release them or eat them. There is no middle ground.

■ Albacore

What newcomers to albacore fishing discover is that you practically troll your little petunia off looking for fish. It is like a long fuse to a stick of dynamite. You troll, troll, troll, looking for the fish, an unpredictable, time consuming and sometimes frustrating affair. But when you connect, you can connect big time. A wide-open albacore bite is one of the biggest jackpots of ocean fishing.

The trips can range far offshore, with the schools of torpedo-shaped tuna following the warm currents in summer and fall along the California coast. In good years, they can be reached within five, 10 miles of coast. In bad years, they can be well over 100 miles offshore, a hell of a boat ride. Skippers often will study sea surface temperature reports, look for gradients where warm water meets cold, then fish the warm water side. Albacore sometimes migrate through underwater seamounts and canyons. Once the general area is determined, the boat will head to the spot, then start trolling.

Troll, troll, troll. They use standard feather tuna jigs, six to eight inches long, with four rods across the back of the boat. The anglers aboard alternate in sequence as to who is credited with what rod. "One of the little tricks I use is to try and get one of the outside rods, and then let a little bit of extra line out," McDonell said. "That is because the albacore come up at an angle. If your feather jig is on the outside, and out a little bit farther than the others, you can catch the first albacore that comes up to take a look."

When a troll rod gets a fish on, the boat immediately circles, then stops. The deckhands aboard will chum scoops of anchovies overboard. The hope is to attract the entire school of albacore to the surface, and turn the scene into a wide-open melee.

Meanwhile, the anglers aboard will grab their rods and either use live anchovies for bait, or cast jigs. It's a wild affair, with everybody rushing to the bait tank and to the railing simultaneously.

"Your bait is absolutely critical," McDonell said. "If it doesn't swim right, you don't have a chance. Pick out a green bait and handle it very carefully, hook it quickly through the collar, and start fishing. If you drop it, then kick it overboard, forget it. If any scales come off, it's worthless. You don't want a bait with a red nose, sore from banging away at the side of the bait tank. If you haven't been bit by an albacore after one minute, bring it up, snap it off, put on another. You just plain must have a quality live bait."

The exception is when the albacore get chummed right up to the surface. When that happens, casting metal jigs can result in instant hookups.

Usually a few bigeye tuna run amid the school of albacore. Bigeyes are the awesome line-burners of the California coast. Get one, and you will never forget it. McDonell has a trick to try and catch them.

"When the boat stops, everybody is crazy going after the albacore," he said. "What you can do is drop a jig or a heavily-waited Scampi down 50 to 60 yards, then reel up. That's how you can get in on the bigeye or large albacore, because they're underneath the school. The bait is on top, the school fish are under the bait, and then the big guys are on the bottom of the school. If you want the bigger fish, you have to go down to get them."

Because of the crazed state of anglers during such a spree, occasionally somebody gets hooked in the back of the head, back or arm by some self-obsessed angler trying to cast. It hurts plenty. No matter how wild it gets, there is a method to cast safely in a crowd: Always watch your jig as you cast, keeping your eyes on your hook so you are under control of it at all times. The mistake people make is that they gaze out in the direction of where they are casting, then while winding up, hook some poor guy alongside they don't see.

On one trip, I saw a guy get hooked in the side of the head. Now get this: He continued fishing, the lure hanging there, jangling whenever he moved. He claimed it didn't hurt, kept casting away, and then ended up catching several albacore, including a 25-pounder. Back at the dock, a doctor was waiting to remove it. After micro surgery was performed on the spot, the doctor was awarded with the 25-pounder for his deed. Strange? Anything is possible on these crazy trips.

CHAPTER FOURTEEN

THE SEA WOLF
POKE-POLING THE COAST

In the tiny coastal town of Pescadero, he was known simply as the Sea Wolf, a man who had mastered the art of catching fish from the rocks on the Pacific Coast.

Now most anglers wouldn't even consider standing precariously with a pole on the edge of a rock while the Pacific Ocean roars upon them. That's not fishing, the purists argue, it's an act of faith. It has been suggested that the few who play games with the ocean may be offspring from a unique species of man, a holdover from prehistoric times, such as the shark is in the world of fish.

The Sea Wolf just laughs at this notion, and remembers when he learned his tricks many years ago from his father. Of course, when one has fish in the bag, it is easy to laugh.

You see, there are several ways to try and catch fish from a rock in the ocean. The Sea Wolf way works.

Few attempt it. The generally accepted tactic is to fish as if you were surfcasting from a sandy bank. This quickly becomes a fatal mistake as you find that rocks can bite better than fish. You may have witnessed people out trying to catch fish from the rocky shoreline, solitary figures engaged in one of mankind's most primitive sports . . . the long, willowy rod and large spinning reel . . . the long casts . . . the waiting for the fish. The snags.

The Sea Wolf disdains such a rig on the rocks, and he's the one with the fish.

It was a clear, cold February morning many years ago when I was propped up on one of my favorite rocks just south of Pescadero, which is about 20 miles south of Half Moon Bay. I had my expensive surf gear in action. I was "rockfishing," but how little I truly knew. Like most people who go rockfishing, I had donated half of my tackle box to the ocean bottom because of snags, been soaked by a surprise wave when my back was turned, and had a seagull make off with some unattended bait. But I was happy. After all, I had somehow caught a fish, a fat 22-inch lingcod. Already, I was envisioning that evening's barbecue. Then I saw him.

He was half man, half reptile. He wore a wet suit bottom and walked knee deep in water among the rocks. In one hand was a bag, and in the other was a long, stout, bamboo pole. No fishing rod, no reel, no tackle box.

"A possible extraterrestrial life form," I chuckled to myself. But in a few minutes, it became clear that this was the legend of Pescadero I'd heard about, the Sea Wolf. He quickly spotted me, stopped whatever he was doing and approached. "Any luck?" he asked.

I proudly exhibited my lingcod.

"Better than most," he answered.

"How about you?" I countered.

The Sea Wolf hoisted his bag. My eyes about popped out of the sockets. It was half-filled with wonders of the rocks: cabezone, lingcod, sea trout, and a few eels.

My face plainly asked, "How?"

The Sea Wolf looked out to the sea for a long time, then looked me directly in the eye and spoke.

"My friend, just watch. Too few people today know how to fish my way. It's called poke-poling."

The man worked his way among the rocks. At the end of his pole was a two-inch piece of wire, and attached to that was a 2/0 hook and a touch of bait. It looked like abalone. With his pole, he searched and proved every crevice, every hole, working the bait in places right beneath the rock on which I had been sitting.

The Sea Wolf suddenly jolted, struggled with his pole for a moment, then lifted up a long, fat eel, caught practically right at my feet. I couldn't believe it.

"Long ago, everybody laughed at me because they thought I looked funny," he said. "Before that, they laughed at my father. But we catch the fish and the people who laugh don't catch any."

He went on to explain several of the key points of the art. You can maximize your success by fishing low tides, particularly minus tides. When the Pacific Ocean rolls back on low tides, it will unveil the shallow reef areas in the prime rocky sections along the Pacific Coast. This is the only time when you can walk far out on reefs and poke-pole in areas rarely fished by anybody—and never by anglers attempting to cast from shore. It also forces the fish into the remaining holes.

Anybody attempting to cast from shore to these spots snags up on the rocks, and quick. One time, this well-meaning gent hung up on five straight casts and then finally just sat down in frustration and watched the seagulls fly by. I remember this well because that fellow was me.

The best area for poke-poling, the Sea Wolf explained, is anywhere along the Pacific Coast where rocky areas and shallow reefs are abundant. If you can't locate a bamboo pole, an old CB antenna or worn-out surf rod can be a substitute. The best bait is abalone, but squid is also a preferred entreaty. The slimy meat from a mussel is also attractive, but is easily dislodged from the hook.

You have to conjure up the detective in you, exploring the rocks, poking the bait in the tidal crevices and, under the ledges. One time I probed my poke-pole through a hole in a rock that had a six-inch diameter. Almost immediately, I hooked a big lingcod that had entered from the other side, whose head was simply too big to get through that six-inch hole. I tussled away for several minutes before I finally figured out what had happened.

"You don't need no fancy rod to catch fish," said the Sea Wolf. "The fish don't know the difference. Just remember one thing: Doing good beats looking good."

The Sea Wolf picked up his bag and continued his day along the rocks, poking his pole as he went.

THE TEN COMMANDMENTS
GETTING KIDS HOOKED

The dad and his boy were going camping, and maybe they'd catch a fish, see some wild animals or explore some new country. Regardless, the possibilities are the stuff of dreams when people separated by so many years are linked by a common adventure. You could see the happiness in the dad's face, and the excitement in the kid's eyes. "That kid is going to grow up loving the outdoors," I remember thinking.

The future of fishing and camping depends on people like those two. The child who learns to love the outdoors in the 1990s will be the adult 20 years from now who will help protect it. A key problem is that 90 percent of today's youth live in urban areas, so they don't have the opportunity for a weekend adventure unless an adult takes them on one. A recent survey showed that if a kid hasn't camped and fished by age 14, he likely never will.

Children who don't camp or fish rarely develop a love for the outdoors or do much later to help protect it.

How do you get a boy or girl excited about the outdoors? How do you compete with a remote control and a television? How do you prove to a kid that success comes from persistence, spirit and logic, which the outdoors teaches, and not from pushing buttons?

The answer is in the Ten Camping/Fishing Commandments for Kids. They are lessons that will get youngsters excited about the outdoors, and will make sure adults help the process along, not kill it. Some are obvious, some are not, but all are important:

1. Trips with children should be to places where there is a guarantee of action without complicated techniques required. A good example is camping in a park where large numbers of wildlife can be viewed, such as squirrels, chipmunks, deer, and even bear. Other good choices are fishing at a small pond loaded with bluegill, or a hunting trip where a kid can shoot a .22 at pine cones all day. Boys and girls want action, not solitude.

2. Enthusiasm is contagious. If you are not excited about an adventure, you can't expect the child to be. Show a genuine zest for life in the outdoors, and point out everything as if it is the first time you have ever seen it.

3. Always, always, always be seated when talking to someone small. This allows the adult and child to be on the same level. That is why fishing in a small boat is perfect for adults and kids. Nothing is worse for youngsters than having a big person look down at them and give them orders. What fun is that?

4. Always show how to do something, whether it be gathering sticks for a campfire, cleaning a trout or tying a knot. Never tell. Always show. A button often clicks to "off" when a kid is lectured. Instead, they learn most behavior patterns and outdoor skills by watching adults—when the adults are not even aware they are being watched.

5. Let kids be kids. Let the adventure happen, rather than trying to force it within some preconceived plan. If they get sidetracked watching pollywogs, chasing butterflies, or sneaking up on chipmunks, let them be. A youngster can have more fun turning over rocks looking at different kinds of bugs than sitting in one spot, waiting for a fish to bite.

6. Expect young peoples' attention spans to be short. Instead of getting frustrated about it, use it to your advantage. How? By bringing along a bag of candy and snacks. When there is a lull in the camp activity, out comes the bag. Don't let them know what goodies await, so each one becomes a surprise.

7. Make absolutely certain the child's sleeping bag is clean, dry and warm. Nothing is worse than discomfort when trying to sleep, but a refreshing sleep makes for a positive attitude the next day. In addition, kids can become quite scared of animals at night. The parent should not wait for any signs of this, but always play the part of the outdoor guardian, the one who will "take care of everything."

8. Kids quickly relate to outdoor ethics. They will enjoy eating everything they kill, building a safe campfire, and picking up all their litter, and they will develop a sense of pride that goes with it. A good idea is to bring extra plastic garbage bags to pick up any trash you come across. Kids long remember when they do something right that somebody else has done wrong.

9. If you want youngsters hooked on the outdoors for life, take a close-up photograph of them holding up fish they have caught, blowing on the campfire, or completing other camp tasks. Young children can forget how much fun they had, but they never forget if they have a picture to remind them of it.

10. The least important word you can ever say to a kid is "I." Keep track of how often you are saying "Thank you" and "What do you think?" Not very often? Then you'll lose out. Finally, the most important words of all are: "I am proud of you."

OUTDOOR LORE

■ Predicting Weather

Jeff "Foonsky" Patty climbed out of his sleeping bag, glanced at the nearby meadow, and scowled hard.

"It doesn't look good," he said. "Doesn't look good at all."

I looked at my companion of 20 years of adventures, noted his discontent, and then I looked at the meadow and immediately understood why: "When the grass is dry at morning light, look for rain before the night."

"How bad you figure?" I asked him.

"We'll know soon enough, I reckon," Foonsky answered. "Short notice, soon to pass. Long notice, long it will last."

When you are out in the wild, spending your days fishing, and your nights camping, you learn to rely on yourself for weather predictions. It can make or break you. If a storm hits the unprepared, it will quash the trip and possibly endanger the participants. If you are ready for it, what could be a hardship ends up as an added adventure.

You can't rely on TV weather-casters either, people who don't even know that when all the cows on a hill are pointed north, it will rain that night for sure. God forbid if the cows are all sitting. But what can you expect from TV's talking heads?

Foonsky made a campfire, started boiling some water for coffee and soup, and we started to plan the day. But in the process, I noticed the smoke of the campfire: It was sluggish, drifting and hovering.

"You notice the smoke?" I asked, chewing on a piece of homemade jerky.

"Not good," Foonsky said, "not good." He knew that sluggish, hovering smoke indicates rain.

"You'd think we'd have been smart enough to know last night this was coming," Foonsky said. "Did you take a look at the moon or the clouds?"

"I didn't look at either," I answered. "Too busy eating the trout we caught." You see, if the moon is clear and white, the weather will be good the next day. But if there is a ring around the moon, you can count the number of stars inside the ring, and that is how many days until the next rain. As for clouds, the high, thin clouds called cirrus indicate a change in the weather.

We were quiet for a while, plotting strategy, but while we did so, some terrible things happened: A chipmunk scampered past with its tail high. A small flock of geese flew past very low. A little sparrow was perched on a tree limb quite close to the trunk.

"We're in for trouble," I told Foonsky.

"I know, I know," he responded. "I saw 'em, too. And come to think of it, no crickets were chirping last night either."

"Damn! That's right!"

These are all signs of an approaching storm. Foonsky pointed at the smoke of the campfire, and shook his head as if he had just been condemned. Sure enough, now the smoke was blowing towards the north, a sign of a south wind. "When the wind is from the south, the rain is in its mouth."

"We'd best stay hunkered down until it passes," Foonsky said.

I nodded. "Let's gather as much firewood now as we can, get our gear covered up, get a rain channel dug around the tent, then plan our meals."

"Then we'll get the poker game going."

As we accomplished these camp tasks, the sky clouded up, then darkened. Within an hour, we had gathered enough firewood to make a large pile, enough wood to keep a fire going no matter how hard it rained. The day's meals had been separated out from the food bag, so it wouldn't have to be retrieved during the storm. We buttoned two ponchos together, staked two of the corners with ropes to the ground, and tied the other two with ropes to different tree limbs to create a slanted roof/shelter. A channel was dug around the tent, so we wouldn't be camping in a pond if the rain was intense.

As the first raindrop fell with that magic sound on our poncho roof, Foonsky was just starting to shuffle the cards.

"Cut for deal," he said.

Just as I did so, it started to rain a bit harder. I pulled out another piece of jerky and started chewing on it. It was just another day in paradise . . .

Weather lore can be valuable for anglers. Small signs provided by nature and wildlife can be translated to provide a variety of weather information. Here is the list that I have compiled over the years:

When the grass is dry at morning light,
Look for rain before the night.

Short notice, soon to pass.
Long notice, long it will last.

Evening fog will not burn soon.
Morning fog will burn 'fore noon.

When the wind is from the east,
'Tis fit for neither man nor beast.

When the wind is from the south,
The rain is in its mouth.

When the wind is from the west,
Then it be the very best.

Red sky at night, sailor's delight.
Red sky in the morning, sailors take warning.

When all the cows are pointed north,
Within a day rain will come forth.

Onion skins very thin, mild winter coming in.
Onion skins very tough, winter's going to be very rough.

When your boots make the squeak of the snow,
Then it is certain that very cold temperatures will show.

If a goose flies high, fair weather ahead.
If a goose flies low, foul weather will come instead.

A thick coat on a woolly caterpillar means a big, early snow is coming.

Chipmunks will run with their tails up before a rain.
Bees always stay near their hives before a rainstorm.

When birds are perched on large limbs near tree trunks, an intense but short storm will arrive.

On the coast, if groups of seabirds are flying a mile inland, look for major winds.

If crickets are chirping very loud during the evening, the next day will be clear and warm.

If the smoke of a campfire at night rises in a thin spiral, good weather is assured for the next day.

If the smoke of a campfire at night is sluggish, drifting and hovering, it will rain the next day.

If there is a ring around the moon, count the number of stars inside the ring, and that is how many days until the next rain.

If the moon is clear and white, the weather will be good the next day.

The high, thin clouds called cirrus indicate a change in the weather.

The oval-shaped clouds called lenticular indicate high winds.

Two different levels of clouds moving in different directions indicate changing weather soon.

Huge, dark billowing clouds called cumulonimbus, suddenly forming on warm afternoons in the mountains, mean that a short but intense thunderstorm with lightning can be expected.

When squirrels are busy gathering food for extended periods, it means good weather is ahead in the short term, but a bad winter is ahead in the long term.

And God forbid if all the cows are sitting down . . .

■ **How Big Was That Fish?**

The question is inevitable. People just have to know, and not knowing can drive the curious crazy. "So," they ask with their best attempt at innocence, "just how big was that fish?"

The stock answer these days is: "It was a real nice one, a nice fish." With largemouth bass, anything in the 12, 13-inch range suddenly is "about a three-pounder." Trout that are nine or ten inches are suddenly "about a foot." For larger species, such as sharks, lingcod, striped bass, sturgeon or salmon, the answer is usually: "It was a real nice fish, but there wasn't a scale around to know for sure."

If the curious asks where, how, and with what the fish was caught, you can answer: "I caught a real nice fish in the water, right in the mouth on a hook."

If you have not caught anything at all, why it isn't your fault, because, "I just got here and have barely started." In Canada, it is popular to insist you are having a great day of it, "just fishing for the odd one."

But it is the question of size that confounds the imagination. Some people actually think there is just one big fish, and it is passed around for pictures. If you fish enough, however, sooner or later you will hook a big one. Sometimes they get away, and that is when legends are made.

You tell the tale, but eventually, the question pops out. "How big was that fish?" they ask.

Well, this is how big:

It was so big that when it jumped, a boat fell in the hole.

It was so big that when I took it out of the water, the lake level dropped three feet.

It was so big that it was a good thing we were wearing our life preservers, because when it splashed water on us with its tail, we nearly drowned.

It was so big that it attacked the boat, and we had to fight it off with the oars.

It was so big that I had to hire a forklift operator to get it to the cleaning table.

It was so big that I had to fold the fillets over several times to get them to fit in my freezer.

It was so big that after I tied it to the side of the boat, it swam the boat out to sea by flipping its tail and I had to jump ship to survive. Luckily, I was able to flag down a passing freighter, and I was rescued.

It was so big that I fought it all day long without gaining an inch, so I tied the line to the trailer-hitch on my four-wheel drive, figuring I'd pull it out like a boat. But the last I saw of my truck was the hood ornament disappearing in the water.

It was so big that I fought it all day long without gaining an inch. Finally, I tied the line off and swam down to see how big it was, and found it inside of a junked car. I tried to get it out, but every time I started reaching in, it rolled the windows up.

NORTHERN
CALIFORNIA

RATING SYSTEM

POOR——————————— FAIR ——————————GREAT

NORTHERN CALIFORNIA MAP SECTIONS

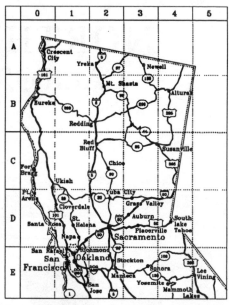

MAP AØ

NOR-CAL MAP. see page 120
adjoining maps
NORTH.........................no map
EAST (A1)..........see page 136
SOUTH (BØ)......see page 166
WEST............................no map

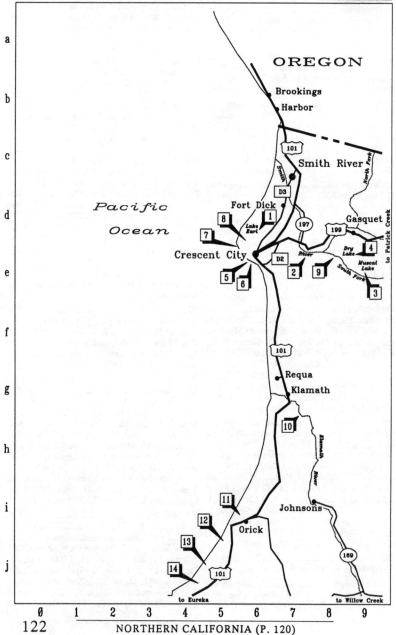

1.   LAKE EARL

Reference: near Crescent City; map AØ grid d6.

How to get there: From Crescent City, drive one-half mile north on US 101. Turn northwest on Northcrest-Lake Earl Drive. To get to the boat launch, go northwest on Lake View Road. For campsites, drive west on Morehead Road, or north on Lower Lake Road, or west on Kellogg Road.

Facilities: Six environmental walk-in campsites are provided. No piped water is available.

Cost: Campsite fee is $7 per night.

Who to contact: Write to Camp Lincoln at 4241 Kings Valley Road, Crescent City, CA 95531, or call (707) 464-9533.

About Lake Earl: Lake Earl is the largest lake by far in Del Norte County, but because tourists can't see it from Highway 101—and because it provides only mediocre fishing results—the lake gets very little attention. It is in a unique setting, though, set near sea level less than a mile from the Pacific Ocean. Its neighboring lake to the west, Lake Talawa, which is connected to Lake Earl by a short, narrow, curving piece of water, borders coastal sand dunes and after heavy rainfall sometimes runs into the ocean.

The lake is large and shallow, and no trout are stocked. There are no bass, bluegill, catfish or other typical lake sportsfish either. Instead, a few sea-run cutthroat enter adjoining Lake Talawa from the ocean in winter, then spend the rest of their lives roaming both Talawa and Lake Earl. Some approach good size, like 15 or 16 inches, but they are few and elusive. Flounder are also in the lake and tend to congregate in the narrow connector section between Talawa and Earl.

In any event, the fishing is usually poor, and unless you get into a batch of cutthroat or flounder, you might swear there are no fish at all.

---

2.   SMITH RIVER

Reference: East of Crescent City in Six Rivers National Forest; map AØ grid d7.

How to get there: At the junction of US 101 and US 199, drive east on US 199. Direct access is available.

Facilities: Several campgrounds are available, including Jedediah Smith Redwoods State Park and a few low-cost Forest Service camps. The camps are located along US 199 and provide streamside access. In addition, the Wagon Wheel Motel, near Gasquet, offers rooms, and a streamside cabin rental service is available by phoning Eileen Peterson at (707) 457-3267. For tackle and expert advice, Smith River Outfitters

---

and Hiouchi Market are the best sources.

Cost: Campsite fee ranges from $12 during the winter at Jedediah Smith Redwoods State Park to $17 at private campgrounds.

Who to contact: For fishing information or to hire a fishing guide with a driftboat, call Six Rivers Guide Service at (707) 458-3577, or Smith River Outfitters at (707) 487-0935. For camping information, write to Six Rivers National Forest Headquarters at 500 5th Street, Eureka, CA 95501, or phone (707) 442-1721; or Jedediah Smith Redwoods State Park at (707) 458-3310 or (707) 464-9533.

Special note: The Smith River is subject to emergency closures starting in October if flows are below the prescribed levels needed to protect migrating salmon and steelhead. The Department of Fish and Game has a recorded message that details the status of coastal streams. The number is (707) 442-4502.

About Smith River: The Smith River is the crown jewel of the nation's streams, a fountain of pure water, undammed and unbridled, running free through sapphire blue granite canyons. It needs no extra pushing. The river grows California's biggest salmon and steelhead, which arrive to the Smith every fall and winter, respectively, and beguile anglers as much as excite them. A decent fishery for sea-run cutthroat trout is also provided during summer months in the lower river.

When you see the Smith, the first thing you will say is, "Look how beautiful the water is." Even after heavy rains during winter, which can turn most rivers into brown muck, the Smith still often runs blue and clear. That is because of the river's hard granite base and the large volume of water drained from a huge mountain acreage. That combination gives the river a unique ability to cleanse itself.

Alas, there are some drawbacks. The fish are very difficult to catch, especially when compared to the nearby Chetco River to the north, which enters the sea at Brookings in southern Oregon. Some people might spend an hour talking about how beautiful the Smith River is, without mentioning even once that they haven't caught a fish in a week. It takes years to learn how to fish this river. But once that process is underway, it can feel like the magic secrets of nature are being revealed.

The best way to start that process is to hire a guide, get in his driftboat, and fish the lower river. Most driftboat trips average a fish or two per day, and in the process, you will get an excellent fishing lesson and have the excitement of tangling with a Smith River-bred salmon or steelhead. I also advise getting a lesson from shore from a guide who specializes in bank fishing, so you can make many return trips in future years, and fish by yourself.

One of the great rewards here is the size of the fish. In the fall and early winter, the ratio of salmon ranging 25 to 40 pounds to those smaller is better than any other river in the western U.S. In fact, salmon in the 50 and 60-pound class are caught each year, and rarely, 70 and 80-pounders are landed. Like I said, the river just grows big fish. The same is true with steelhead. A 10-pounder is the average fish, 15-pounders are common, and more 20-pounders are caught here than any river in California. The state record steelhead, 27 pounds four ounces, was taken from the Smith—and several over 30 pounds have been hooked and lost.

But they just don't come easy. I once went 2,000 casts without a bite on the Smith, then caught 15-pound steelhead on back-to-back casts. Another time, I went four days without a fish, then the next day caught 11 steelhead, all over 10 pounds — the best day I have ever had with steelhead anywhere in the world. It doesn't take luck, I know that. It takes persistence with spirit.

Although technique and strategy are detailed in the Secrets of the Masters portion at the beginning of this book, one key element required on the Smith is light line. If your reel has anything but Maxima Chameleon Green, six to 12-pound test, the strength of the line dependent on river clarity, many guides will immediately strip your line off and replace it. Because the water is so clear on the Smith, any line that is more visible will be avoided by the fish as if you were throwing large boulders into the river. If the river is low and clear, I use 6-pound test. I know it sounds crazy, but that is what it takes.

In addition, because the fish are big, you must have a big net with you. A lot of out-of-towners don't have nets big enough, and figure "I'll be okay with what I've got," then spend years howling at the moon over how they lost a 45-pound salmon with their little net.

When fishing for migratory fish, timing is always a critical factor. In October, salmon will start stacking up in river holes in the lower river, and only after a few rains will they venture far upriver. During the winter, steelhead use the river as a highway, that is, they head straight through and then spawn in the tributaries. Almost every year, there is a week-long period in January, and often again in March, where it doesn't rain. That is when the steelhead will slow their journey, and anglers have the opportunity for hookups at the prime holes.

You can make a lot of casts and spend a lot of days here before you are rewarded. But in the process, you will refine your craft, and the days spent learning will be along one of America's most beautiful rivers. There have been many days when that is reward enough.

---

3.   **MUSLATT LAKE**

Reference: Near Crescent City in Six Rivers National Forest; map AØ grid d8.
How to get there: From Crescent City, drive five miles north on US 101

to Highway 199. Turn east and drive five miles, through Hiouchi, to South Fork Road. Turn east on South Fork Road. Cross two bridges, then bear left after the second bridge. Continue 15 miles to Big Flat; the road changes to Forest Service Road 16 in Big Flat. Continue for five miles and turn right at the sign for Muslatt Lake.

Facilities: No facilities are provided. Big Flat Camp is available on South Fork Road near Hurdy Gurdy Creek, and the more developed Jedediah Smith State Park is available on Highway 199.

Cost: Lake access is free.

Who to contact: Write to Six Rivers National Forest at 500 5th Street, Eureka, CA 95501, or phone (707) 442-1721.

About Muslatt Lake: Little Muslatt Lake is set at the foot of Muslatt Mountain (3,468 feet), and has a small outlet stream that eventually winds all over the mountains and pours into the Smith River. The lake is stocked from the Fish and Game airplane each year with 3,000 fingerling-size rainbow trout.

If you arrive after a recent stock, all you will see and catch are trout in the four and five-inch class. But the bigger fellows are in there, usually deeper and more wary, having lived through a summer or two. The DFG airplane usually makes its stocks in early summer, so my advice is to stay clear of this one until early fall, when those little trout have had a chance to grow a few inches and make for a decent evening fish fry.

---

4. DRY LAKE

Reference: Near Crescent City in Six Rivers National Forest; map AØ grid d8.

How to get there: From Crescent City, drive five miles north on US 101 to Highway 199. Turn east and drive five miles, through Hiouchi, to South Fork Road. Turn east and cross two bridges, then bear left after the second bridge. Drive 13 miles to Big Flat Station and turn left on County Road 405 (Big Flat Road), then drive 6.5 miles north to Dry Lake.

Facilities: No facilities are provided. A primitive Forest Service camp (no piped water) is available where Hurdy Gurdy Creek enters the South Fork Smith River, and a developed state park campground, Jedediah Smith Redwoods, is available on Highway 199.

Cost: Lake access is free.

Who to contact: Write to Six Rivers National Forest at 500 5th Street, Eureka, CA 95501, or phone (707) 442-1721.

About Dry Lake: Dry Lake is a tiny, bowl-like lake set amid national forest that even the locals don't go to. No trout are stocked, and because of it, fish are scarce, limited to a light sprinkling of what we call dinkers.

But it is a pretty spot, set near the headwaters of Hurdy Gurdy Creek.

One side note: If you continue on the Forest Service road north up over Gordon Mountain (4,153 feet) and down the other side to Camp Six, about a 10-mile drive from the lake, you will reach the rainiest place in America's Lower 48. It rained 256 inches there in 1983, the highest amount ever recorded in the contiguous United States. Dry Lake? As the locals say, "Dry it ain't."

---

5. CRESCENT CITY DEEP SEA

Reference: At Crescent City Harbor; map AØ grid e6.

How to get there: From Crescent City, drive one mile south on US 101 and turn west on Anchor Way.

Facilities: A boat ramp, tackle shops, and restaurant are provided at the harbor. Party boat charters, lodging and campgrounds are available nearby. For weather information and sea conditions, a U.S. Coast Guard station is also available.

Cost: $35-$50 per person for a spot on party boats. Reservations and deposit required.

Who to contact: Phone The Chart Room at (707) 464-5993. For general information and a free travel packet, write to the Del Norte Chamber of Commerce at 1001 Front Street, Crescent City, CA 95531, or phone (707) 464-3174.

Party boat list: Lenbrooke and Stinger, phone (707) 464-7684; Top Cat and Pogie Cat, phone (707) 464-2420.

About Crescent City Deep Sea: Crescent City is where the redwoods meet the sea, and also where a lot of out-of-towners meet fish. Salmon fishing is best in July and August, and decent in June and September, while rockfish and lingcod are large and abundant year-round. In the fall, the rockfishing here is among the best anywhere on the Pacific Coast.

If you arrive from the south, your first sight of the harbor is a beautiful one from the lookout on Highway 101, especially at night. It is a natural half-moon shaped harbor that provides refuge from the terrible spring winds out of the northwest. Thus whether you own your own boat or plan to get aboard a charter, the most important part of your trip is calling ahead for wind and sea projections. In the winter, the storms can be nasty and frequent, yet ironically, between fronts the ocean is often its calmest of the year.

When the ocean is calm, that is when to jump. Most of the salmon trips during summer will take a 260-degree heading out of the harbor and often run into fish after an hour's run. In the fall, boats will head north and troll outside the mouth of the Smith River. Catch rates are not as high during this period, but the chance of a 40-pounder is the best anywhere in California.

If you want the closest thing to a guarantee for fish, take a deep sea trip to the St. George Reef, which is located just northwest of Point St. George. The reef near Star Rock, Whale Rock and Long Rock provide outstanding habitat for rockfish and lingcod, and they are abundant and big. Lingcod in the 20 and 30-pound class are common, and every fall, a few 40-pounders are caught.

If it sounds good, it's because it is. There are a few drawbacks, however. It rains a lot up here, and when it doesn't rain, it is often foggy. That means private boaters should venture out only in seaworthy boats that are equipped with competent navigation equipment. The exception is in late summer and fall, when the skies are clear and warm, the ocean usually calm, and the fish eager. If you make the trip then, you might just spot me at the boat launch.

---

6.   CRESCENT CITY HARBOR

Reference: In Crescent City; map AØ grid e6.

How to get there: South of Crescent City, drive north on US 101 and turn west at Citizen's Dock.

Facilities: Several privately-operated campgrounds are available in Crescent City. One of the more popular ones is Naco West Shoreline Campground, which has 242 sites for tents or motorhomes.

Cost: Access to the jetty is free.

Who to contact: For general information and a free travel packet, write to the Del Norte Chamber of Commerce at 1001 Front Street, Crescent City, CA 95531, or phone (707) 464-3174.

About Crescent City Harbor Jetty: Rock jetties along the coast are natural fish attractants, since the sprawling, underwater boulders provide marine habitat. Thus starts the marine food chain, from algae through lingcod. The latter is what you want, although you will discover the rocks can also grab your gear.

The best prospects are in the fall, when the lings move in from the depths of Davy Jones' Locker and congregate in holes amid the rocky shallows. Right there is the key: You might offer your bait in one of the holes along the jetty. Neglect this key point and you might swear there isn't a single fish in the entire ocean. Accomplish it, however, and you are on your way to some of the better shorefishing available.

For newcomers, the best strategy is to arrive during a very low tide. The reason is that when the ocean rolls back, much of the undersea world along the jetty is revealed. With your own eyes, you will see where the big rocks are, and at the same time, where the deeper holes are that hold fish. That is where to toss your bait. Get ready, because the bottom of a very low tide is one of the two key times when fish that live next to a jetty start feeding.

In addition, with those holes committed to memory, you can then return at the high tide and be the only one on the jetty who knows the prime spots. Timing is always important when ocean fishing because all species are tidal dependent, and are active feeders during certain key parts of the tide, but take a siesta the rest of the time. For inshore jetty fishing, always spotlight the three hours around the highest of that day's high tide. That is when the big lingcod decide to eat. Otherwise, they are often content to sit in their hole all day long, scarcely budging an inch.

7. CRESCENT CITY SHORELINE

Reference: In Crescent City; map AØ grid e6.

How to get there: On Highway 101 in Crescent City, head north on Northcrest Drive. Turn left on Washington Boulevard and continue to the shoreline. To the north is the sandy beach area, to the south is the rocky area.

Facilities: Several campgrounds are available in Crescent City. One of the more popular ones is Naco West Shoreline Campground, which has 242 sites for tents or motorhomes.

Cost: Shoreline access is free.

Who to contact: For general information and a free travel packet, write to the Del Norte Chamber of Commerce at 1001 Front Street, Crescent City, CA 95531, or phone (707) 464-3174.

About Crescent City shoreline: Few people fish the shoreline of the Crescent City area. The reason is all the rocks between Crescent City and Point George, which often bite better than the fish. But there are ways to go about it.

If you fish on high tides, all you are likely to catch are snags, because you will be casting in the blind. When surf fishing rocky areas, select only very low tides, when the shallow reef will be unveiled amid pockets of deeper water. Those deep holes are where you should cast. They are the only areas that will be holding rockfish, sea trout, cabezone and lingcod. All you have to do is take a look at the rocky shoreline just north of Crescent City and you will see why this approach applies so perfectly. Regardless, you can expect to lose some tackle. As shoreliners know, along the coast's rocky areas, losing tackle just comes with the territory.

You can avoid that here by fishing for perch instead along the beach area just north of Point George. The shoreline along Pelican Bay consists of a 10-mile long sand dune, and much of it is rarely traveled or fished. The perch fishing is only fair, best during the first two hours of an incoming tide just after a minus low tide. During such low tides, this is a prime spot for clams. So if you time it right, you can dig for clams while a minus low tide is bottoming out, then turn around and catch a few perch when the tide is running in.

8. DEAD LAKE

Reference: In Crescent City; map AØ grid e6.

How to get there: From US 101 in Crescent City, take Washington Boulevard west and continue almost to the airport. Turn north on Riverside Road and drive to the lake.

Facilities: Facilities are provided at the lake. However, all services and lodging are available two miles away in Crescent City.

Cost: Lake access is free.

Who to contact: The ranger can be reached by phoning (707) 464-9533.

About Dead Lake: This is one to file away in the back of your mind, then make sure you try it out when you are in the area. This little lake provides good bass fishing, is easy to reach, and is missed by virtually every angler that passes through the area.

Back in 1985, the lake was appropriately named, because it did indeed seem like a "dead" lake. No more. An experimental plant of largemouth bass took hold, and the lake has come alive. The fishing can be quite good, especially in spring evenings casting floating lures along the lake's shoreline. Though a small lake, it is not round, but long and narrow. That is ideal for bass, providing the type of shoreline habitat they desire.

9. SOUTH FORK SMITH RIVER

Reference: East of Crescent City in Six Rivers National Forest; map AØ grid e7.

How to get there: From Crescent City, drive four miles north on US 101 and turn east on US 199. Continue for six miles to the small town of Hiouchi, then continue on for one mile and turn right on South Fork Road. Continue south. Direct access is available.

Facilities: A primitive Forest Service campground, called Big Flat Camp, is available adjacent to where Hurdy Gurdy Creek enters the South Fork Smith. No piped water is available. The nearest facilities are available in Hiouchi.

Cost: The campsite fee at Big Flat Camp is $3-$6, depending on services available.

Who to contact: Write to Six Rivers National Forest Headquarters at 500 5th Street, Eureka, CA 95501, or phone (707) 442-1721.

Special note: The South Fork Smith is subject to emergency closures starting in October if flows are below the prescribed levels needed to protect migrating salmon and steelhead. The Department of Fish and Game has a recorded message that details the status of coastal streams. The number is (707) 442-4502.

About South Fork Smith: This stream seems placed on earth for the Lone Wolf types who hunt steelhead. Along South Fork Road you will find many small dirt turnouts, often with room for just one or two vehicles. That is where the Lone Wolf steelheader parks, scrambles down to the river, and then finds a streamside perch to make casts for the elusive Smith River steelhead.

If there is already a vehicle in the turnout, you must drive on to the next. It is considered steelhead sacrilege to crowd a Lone Wolf on his spot. But you probably know that well if you're way out here on the South Fork Smith. No matter. There are a dozen or so spots along the South Fork where a shoreliner can cast away in seclusion, hoping the next cast invites the attraction of a big steelhead. They don't come often or easy.

The ideal way to approach the river is to get up before dawn, already fully rigged so you don't have to tie any knots in darkness, then get on the river at first light. Hit a spot, drive on to the next one, then hit again. In a day, you should fish six to 10 spots. This is a problem on weekends, when more anglers are on the river, and the few spots available get taken.

If you have the idea that this isn't for everybody, well, you are right. It isn't. It is highly specialized, requiring that difficult skills be mastered, with long odds for the uninitiated. But it is Man vs. Nature, you against the river, no help provided, no crowd watching. For some anglers, that is exactly what they want.

---

10.   KLAMATH RIVER

Reference: Near Klamath in Six Rivers National Forest; map AØ grid g7.

How to get there: From Eureka, drive 60 miles north on US 101 to the town of Klamath. At the junction of US 101 and Highway 169, drive east on Highway 169. River access is available along the highway.

Facilities: Several motels, public campgrounds, private campgrounds, and motor home parks are available. Steelhead Lodge offers motor home spaces, a motel, restaurant and bar. Redwood Rest is a popular privately-owned motor home park.

Cost: River access is free.

Who to contact: For lodging information, phone Damm's Drifters at (707) 482-6635. For general information, write to Six Rivers National Forest Headquarters at 500 5th Street, Eureka, CA 95501, or phone (707) 442-1721.

About the Lower Klamath: Come Labor Day and the Lower Klamath

---

River looks like the salmon capital of the western world. Maybe it is.

The annual fall salmon run on the lower Klamath peaks in September, and the river is lined elbow-to-elbow with wading fishermen casting spinners or bait, sitting in oared drift boats or high-powered jet sleds. Every campground, public and private, will be full or close to it, and the same goes for lodges and hotels. From all the hoopla, you'd probably figure that everybody is catching huge salmon, right? Well, the reality is that the catch rates are only fair, especially for shoreliners, although a few know-hows have learned how to get an edge on the rest of the masses.

In the '90s, the better fishing has been upstream from the mouth, both at Terwer riffle and farther upstream at the mouth of Blue Creek. Other popular spots are at Glen, Waukell and Blake riffles. Most of the salmon are in the 10-pound class, a few range to 20 pounds. Only very rarely do they seem to come much larger on the Klamath.

The season begins with a run of "springers," that is, salmon that arrive in late May and June. These are quick-moving fish and intercepting them is a difficult experience, but it can be done. Then by mid-July, the fall-run salmon begin arriving, and most people fish in the tidal zone to try and catch them. The run peaks in the lower Klamath between mid-August and mid-September, and the fish then head upstream (for details, trace the Klamath River using this book's map grid system).

By September, what are called "half-pounders" begin arriving at the mouth and heading upstream. Half-pounders are actually juvenile steelhead that range from 12 to 15 inches. They often arrive in big schools and can provide some exciting fishing. My friend Ed Neal, the former outdoors editor of the *San Francisco Examiner*, once was casting from a point when a big school of half-pounders cruised through—and Ed caught and released 81 of them in an afternoon.

The key to the future success of this river is simply the number of fish that return to swim upstream and spawn. Because of high numbers of salmon caught by commercial anglers and in Indian gillnets, the populations have suffered. Meanwhile, sport anglers have been paying the freight, and had seasons and limits shortened, despite taking less than 10 percent of the overall catch. The hope is that a Klamath River Power Troika, a committee split between commercial, Indian and sport use, can agree on harvest quotas and equitable split in order to ensure the salmon return to this stream in large numbers.

The habitat is there. The Klamath River is capable of supporting runs of over 100,000 salmon every fall. With proper management techniques, those numbers could return again.

If so, all those people out on Labor Day Weekend will be doing more than just casting into the light fall breeze. They will have a realistic chance of catching a nice salmon, the king of the Klamath, and the greatness of this once-great river will be reclaimed again.

---

11. REDWOOD CREEK

Reference: Near Orick in Redwood National Park; map AØ grid i6.

How to get there: From Eureka, drive 42 miles north on US 101 to the town of Orick. Access to Redwood Creek is available off US 101 north of Orick.

Facilities: Tackle and supplies are available at Orick Store in Orick. Campgrounds are provided a few miles north in Prairie Creek Redwoods State Park.

Cost: Creek access is free.

Who to contact: Phone Prairie Creek Redwoods State Park at (707) 488-2171 or (707) 445-6547.

About Redwood Creek: Sometimes all you might want in this world is woods and water. That is what Redwood Creek provides, along with a chance for some fresh-run steelhead every winter.

Redwood Creek is one of the small coastal streams that attracts a modest steelhead run. Access is very easy, and fishing spots are similarly obvious. The best approach is to wear hip waders, then make casts in the slow-moving riffles upstream of the US 101 bridge.

Like all of the small coastal streams, timing is absolutely critical. If you arrive during a siege of drought, the river will be closed to fishing to protect the fish. If you arrive during a siege of rain, the stream will be too high and muddy to even make a cast. So you have to hit it just right, that being a few days after a fair rain. The infusion of freshwater attracts steelhead into the stream, and if water clarity is at least two to three feet, you can wade and cast with the hopes of hooking one of the sea-run migrants.

The catch rates on Redwood Creek are not high, and most of the success goes to know-how locals who are able to jump on the stream on a moment's notice that the steelhead are moving through. That being the case, your telephone and your car may be the most important pieces of fishing equipment you can have for this spot.

The area is quite beautiful, being located close to both Redwood National Park and Prairie Creek Redwoods State Park. Some of the biggest trees in the world are in this region, and when the filtered sunlight cascades down, it takes on the appearance of a cathedral. Spending some time here is one way an angler can get some religion.

---

12.   FRESHWATER LAGOON

Reference: North of Trinidad in Humboldt Lagoons State Park; map AØ grid j5.

How to get there: From Trinidad, drive 16 miles north on US 101.

Facilities: A large, flat area to the west of the highway is a popular spot to park motor homes. Sometimes they are lined up for a mile. Three campgrounds for tenters are located to the south at Stone Lagoon. Two tackle shops are located in Trinidad, Salty's and Bob's Boat Basin.

Cost: Access is free.

Who to contact: Phone the Eureka Department of Fish and Game at (707) 445-6499. A visitor information center is located just north of Freshwater Lagoon, north of Lookout Point on the west side of the highway.

About Freshwater Lagoon: The name gives it away: "Freshwater Lagoon." From that alone, all the vacationers cruising US 101 figure out that this is freshwater, not saltwater. Of the three lagoons in the immediate area, this is the only one on the east side of the highway. Right, another tipoff.

That is why visitor traffic pours into this spot, while Stone Lagoon and Big Lagoon to the south get a relative trickle. The shoreline fishing is good for rainbow trout; abundant stocks of trout from the Department of Fish and Game make sure of it. Some 30,000 rainbow trout are stocked each year, and these fish make for some nice stringers for shoreline baitdunkers. If you don't mind the company, Freshwater Lagoon often provides the best catch rates of any freshwater spot in the area. As mentioned, the area gets absolutely loaded with motor homes, all lined up on the west side of the highway. The owners of them make the short walk across US 101, set out a lawn chair, toss out their bait, and wait for the trout to start biting.

13.   STONE LAGOON

Reference: North of Trinidad in Humboldt Lagoons State Park; map AØ grid j5.

How to get there: From Trinidad, drive 14 miles north on US 101. The boat ramp is located directly off the highway.

Facilities: A boat dock and ramp are provided. Three campgrounds are available, including Ryan's Cove, located on the western shoreline across the lagoon. It's the best of the lot. Two good tackle shops are located in Trinidad, Salty's and Bob's Boat Basin.

Cost: $7.50 campsite fee per night; $5 fee for extra vehicles.

Who to contact: Phone the Eureka Department of Fish and Game at (707) 445-6499.

About Stone Lagoon: This is my favorite of the three freshwater lagoons set on a 10-mile piece of Del Norte County coast. You get a boat-in, shoreline campsite at Ryan's Camp, prime canoeing water, and decent trout fishing. It is also overlooked by many out-of towners. Like Big Lagoon to the south, most folks believe this lagoon is saltwater, not freshwater, and doesn't have any fish or campsites. Wrong again. It is stocked every two weeks with rainbow trout. The limit is two fish.

Even if the fish decide not to bite, the pleasure of the adventure is worth the energy to get here. After all, how many other campsites can you find where you can park your canoe near your campground, then go out for an evening paddle? In this part of California, the answer is none. This is it.

In the 1990s, the DFG started a new program to develop a sea-run cutthroat trout fishery. Some of these trout can get quite large. Because of this, special regulations are in effect; always check the DFG rule book before fishing here.

---

14.   BIG LAGOON

Reference: North of Trinidad in Humboldt Lagoons State Park; map AØ grid j5.

How to get there: From Trinidad, drive eight miles north on US 101 and turn west on Big Lagoon Road. The boat ramp is located on the east side of the lagoon off US 101.

Facilities: A boat ramp and bathrooms are provided. A campground is available at nearby Stone Lagoon. Two tackle shops are available in Trinidad, Salty's and Bob's Boat Basin. Campgrounds are available at Patrick's Point State Park in Trinidad, and also at Stone Lagoon to the immediate north.

Cost: Access is free.

Who to contact: Phone the Eureka Department of Fish and Game at (707) 445-6499.

About Big Lagoon: At first glance, a lot of out-of-towners cruising Highway 101 think that Big Lagoon is saltwater, not freshwater. That is because it is west of Highway 101, and is separated from the ocean by only a long, thin sand dune. But freshwater it is, and Big Lagoon provides trout fishing in this unusual coastal setting.

It is an ideal place to plunk in a canoe, paddle around and catch a few trout in the process. The lake is stocked every two weeks with rainbow trout from spring to mid-July, and the catch limit is two. Access is easy and campsites are available nearby, but regardless, it seems that only rarely is anybody paddling around on the lagoon. They just keep on driving by, day after day, on Highway 101. After all, they think it's saltwater.

MAP A1

9 LISTINGS
PAGES 136-145

NOR-CAL MAP. see page 120
adjoining maps
NORTH........................no map
EAST (A2)..........see page 146
SOUTH (B1).......see page 182
WEST (AØ) ....see page 122

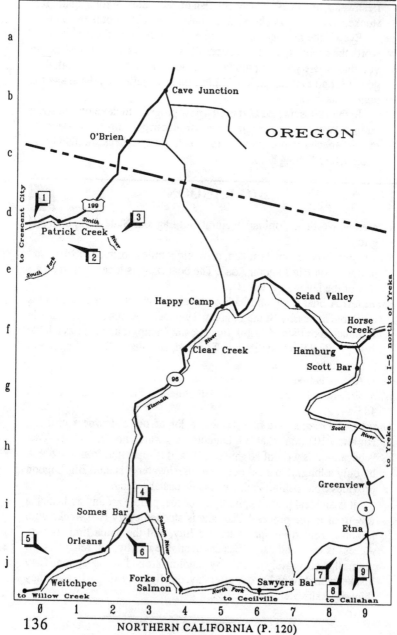

a

b

Cave Junction

O'Brien

OREGON

c

to Crescent City

1

199

3

Patrick Creek

Smith River

2

d

South Fork

e

Happy Camp

Seiad Valley

Horse Creek

f

River

Clear Creek

Hamburg

Scott Bar

96

g

Klamath

Scott River

to I-5 north of Yreka

h

to Yreka

Greenview

i

3

4

Somes Bar

Salmon River

Etna

Orleans

6

5

j

Weitchpec

Forks of Salmon

North Fork

to Cecilville

Sawyers Bar

7

9

8

to Callahan

to Willow Creek

Ø   1   2   3   4   5   6   7   8   9

SMITH RIVER

Reference: Northeast of Crescent City in Six Rivers National Forest; map A1 grid dØ.

How to get there: From Crescent City, drive five miles north on US 101 to US 199. Turn east and travel 14 miles to the small town of Gasquet. Continue northeast on US 199. Direct access is available off the highway.

Facilities: A campground is provided at Patrick Creek, about seven miles east of Gasquet. Supplies can be obtained in Gasquet at the Gasquet Store.

Cost: The campsite fee is $5 per night.

Who to contact: For fishing information, phone Six Rivers Guide Service at (707) 487-0935. For camping information, write to Six Rivers National Forest Headquarters at 500 5th Street, Eureka, CA 95501, or phone (707) 442-1721, or Jedediah Smith Redwoods State Park at (707) 458-3310 or (707) 464-9533.

Special note: The Smith River is subject to emergency closures starting October 1 if flows are below the prescribed levels needed to protect migrating salmon and steelhead. The Department of Fish and Game has a recorded message that details the status of coastal streams. The number is (707) 442-4502.

About Smith River: Just a small piece of the Smith River is in this map grid, but it is one of my favorites. It is the upper end of the Middle Fork Smith, set right along US 199, with both streamside camps and good fishing spots easily accessible.

The river is narrow, similar to a mountain trout stream, but instead of dink-size trout you are fishing for 20-pound steelhead. You must approach with complete stealth, lest you tip the fish off to your presence. One of the better tricks for this stretch of river is to make your casts a good 30 feet away from the river, so the steelhead cannot see your casting motion, or even the shadow of your fishing rod on the water. Light lines, such as six or eight-pound test Maxima, are mandatory in such clear water with such cautious fish.

They fight anything but cautiously. The steelhead run hell-bent for leather, and if they get downriver on you into fast water, it's "Goodbye Mabeline." You'll lose 'em for sure.

This section of the Smith is particularly pristine. Sometimes it can be pleasure enough just to watch the river go by. It is that pretty.

2. SIX RIVERS NATIONAL FOREST

Reference: East of Crescent City (a hike-in lake); map A1 grid d1.

How to get there: Several Forest Service access roads leading into the park can be found off US 199.

Facilities: Several campgrounds are provided, including Bluff Creek and Bluff Creek Group Camp, Aikens, and Pearch Creek.

Cost: Access is free.

Who to contact: Phone Six Rivers National Park at (707) 442-1721. For a detailed Forest Service map, send $2 to USDA-Forest Service, Office of Information, Pacific Southwest Region, 630 Sansome Street, San Francisco, CA 94111.

About Six Rivers National Forest: The miles and miles of Six Rivers Forest are among the lesser-traveled of the 20 million acres of national forest in California. It is an area of big trees and many streams, but relatively few lakes. Six Rivers National Forest has been cut extensively by loggers, but there remains untouched land in the Siskiyou Wilderness that makes for prime backpacking.

Only a few lakes provide viable fisheries. They are Buck Lake (which is just outside the Six Rivers Forest boundary) and Island Lake, which requires a gut-thumping, straight-up climb of a hike. Of the two, Buck Lake has the better fishing, particularly early in the season following Memorial Day weekend. Island Lake always seems to be loaded with the inevitable dinkers, which makes sense, since it is stocked with fingerling-size rainbow trout. If you don't get turned on by the fishing, the climb up to the top of Jedediah Mountain on the backside of the lake is not too difficult and provides wondrous views of the Siskiyou backbone.

Don't be too quick to bypass this area as a hike-in retreat, however. Devil's Punchbowl (Siskiyou Wilderness) and Bear Mountain (6,424 feet) are premium destinations. The ambitious can head into the adjoining Klamath Forest. The Kelsey Trail, which starts off a signed spur road off the South Fork Smith Road, goes all the way to the Marble Mountains and beyond to the east. The trout? Dinkers to be sure. But there are times when the size of trout becomes almost irrelevant. Almost.

3. SANGER LAKE

Reference: Near Gasquet in Six Rivers National Forest; map A1 grid d1.

How to get there: From Crescent City, drive five miles north on US 101 to US 199. Turn east and travel 14 miles to the small town of Gasquet. Continue 17.5 miles east on US 199. Turn east on Forest Service Road

18N02 and travel 13 miles, then bear left and travel a short distance to Sanger Lake.

Facilities: No facilities are available on-site. Camping is possible on a do-it-yourself basis.

Cost: Access is free.

Who to contact: Phone the Six Rivers National Forest at (707) 442-1721.

About Sanger Lake: Little Sanger Lake is an oblivious, little cold water pond that provides peace, quiet and a chance to catch little brook trout. It is set just below Sanger Peak (5,862 feet) to the north, and the long drive to get here via dirt roads is enough to keep most folks away, far away.

That makes it better for you, providing you don't mind the dink-size brookies. Fish and Game plants 6,000 of them per year, using their airplane to drop in the pint-size variety, with the theory that the fish will later grow to larger sizes. Well, that just doesn't seem to happen too often. That's OK. With the tranquility available here, any fish you can get are a bonus.

---

4. SALMON RIVER

Reference: Near Orleans in Klamath National Forest; map A1 grid i3.

How to get there: From the junction of Highways 169 and 96 at Weitchpec, drive approximately 15 miles north on Highway 96 to the town of Orleans. Continue seven miles northeast to the town of Somes Bar, then turn east on Salmon River Road. Access is available along Salmon River Road.

Facilities: Campgrounds are available nearby, off Highway 96 on the Klamath River. Camps are also available upstream on the Salmon. Supplies can be obtained in Orleans or Somes Bar.

Cost: River access is free.

Who to contact: For a free booklet, write to Shasta Cascade Wonderland Association at 1250 Parkview, Redding, CA 96001, or phone (916) 243-2643.

About Salmon River: The first time I fished the Salmon River, I witnessed one of the most amazing fishing episodes of my life.

I was with the late Ted Fay, a legendary fly fishermen who invented the dropper system of nymphing with two flies. We were sitting in my pickup truck, watching a black bear in the river trying to catch a steelhead. After a half hour, the bear gave up, and still hungry, probably went off to see if he could find a camper from the Bay Area, or maybe an outdoor writer.

Well, later that day, Ted and I had not caught anything either. And on our way driving out, I pulled over to the same spot where we had watched the bear make his fruitless attempt.

"If the bear knew a steelhead was in there, then we know there's a fish there, too," said Ted.

We approached the spot quietly, walking lightly. Then Ted Fay did the kind of thing that makes for legends. He caught the steelhead that the bear couldn't catch. His cast was delivered so lightly, the fly, a customized Silver Hilton, drifted from riffle to hole as if no line was attached. An instant later, it was a hook-up, and Fay, an older man at this point in his life, was taken to the limit to land the fish. After 15 minutes, he did.

For a young outdoors writer, it was a baptismal indoctrination to the Salmon River, the purest-running tributary to the Klamath. It is not a large river, but it is set at the bottom of a very deep canyon. Because little sunlight makes it to the river, the water runs much colder than the adjoining Klamath. The result is a special strain of steelhead that are bigger, stronger, and fresher than those on the Klamath. Alas, they are also much more difficult to catch.

A good suggestion is to get your fill of half-pounders on the Klamath to get your ya-yas out of your system. Then head over to the Salmon for something more serious, a sport that demands the best of a California steelheader. The water is small and clear, so fly fishing or light-tackle shorefishing is best suited.

And if you see a bear that can't catch a fish, well just remember: Ted Fay did it. Maybe you can, too.

---

5. FISH LAKE

Reference: Southwest of Orleans in Six Rivers National Forest; map A1 grid j1.

How to get there: From the town of Weitchpec at the junction of Highways 169 and 96, drive seven miles north on Highway 96. Near the Bluff Creek Ranger Station, turn west on Fish Lake Road and drive five miles to the lake.

Facilities: A campground is provided at the lake.

Cost: Campsite fee is $5 per night, mid-May through mid-October.

Who to contact: Phone the Six Rivers National Forest at (707) 442-1721.

About Fish Lake: In many ways, this lake provides the ideal summer camping/fishing destination. The key is that it is just enough out of the way to get missed by most everybody, yet it really isn't that difficult to reach.

When you get there, you discover that Fish Lake is quite pretty, set in the woods with a Forest Service road going right around it. You get a lakeside camp that is practically just a cast's distance from the water. Because this part of California has relatively few lakes, little Fish Lake receives generous stocks of rainbow trout from the Department of Fish and Game. The lake usually provides excellent fishing in June, when the weather is just starting to warm up, yet the water is still cold.

Fish Lake is well suited for anglers who like to fish from a pram, raft, or float tube. Since almost everybody sticks to the shoreline, they are limited to the spots where the vegetation is broken and the lake accessible. With a small raft or the like, you can explore the entire lake quite easily.

6.   KLAMATH RIVER

Reference: Near Orleans in Six Rivers National Forest; map A1 grid j2.
How to get there: From the junction of Highways 169 and 96 at Weitchpec, drive north on Highway 96 to the town of Orleans. Continue northeast on Highway 96, which runs parallel to the river. Direct access is available off turnouts along Highway 96, as well as short spur roads that lead to the river.
Facilities: Several Forest Service campgrounds are located along Highway 96. Supplies can be found in the towns of Klamath River, Weitchpec, Somes Bar, Happy Camp, Seiad Valley, Horse Creek, and Orleans.
Cost: Access is free.
Who to contact: For a free booklet, write to Shasta Cascade Wonderland Association at 1250 Parkview, Redding, CA 96001, or phone (916) 243-2643.
About the Klamath River: The dark silhouette of the steelhead could scarcely be discerned in the river far below, and my breath quickened as I stared at it, binoculars pressed tightly to my eyes.

"It'll only take a few minutes to get down there and make a cast," I thought, glancing across the canyon from my lookout along two-lane Highway 96.

This is one place where nature's artwork can seem perfect. The Klamath River tumbles around boulders, into gorges, then flattens into slicks, all framed by a high, tree-lined canyon rim and an azure blue sky.

As I started the hike down to the stream, an osprey suddenly appeared overhead. It slowed, hovered, then suddenly dive-bombed my intended fishing spot. Instantly, the bird emerged with a trout, and in a few seconds was gone.

Well, I may not have even gotten a chance to cast for that fish, but the abundance of wildlife and the easy access to prime fishing spots make the central Klamath River one of California's best fishing rivers. The steelhead start arriving in August and just keep on arriving all the way through April, although the peak period is from mid-September through early November. It is one of the longest steelhead runs in America, spanning some nine months, and it is ideal for shoreliners or guides with driftboats.

The best bite is in the fall, before the water has cooled below 46 degrees. The steelhead and the "half-pounders," or juvenile steelhead in the 12 to 15-inch class, are most active when the water temperature is 52 to 58 degrees, striking flies, Glo Bugs, and nightcrawlers. When the water temperature drops below 46 degrees, the steelhead stop hitting flies, and their grabs on nightcrawlers become a lot more subtle.

The beauty of the central Klamath is the many premium spots to fish along the shoreline. All you have to do is cruise Highway 96, then when you spot heads of riffles, tail-outs, and deep bends, stop and make a few casts. In a day of hitting and moving, you get to fish almost as many spots as those who use drift boats. There are many pull-outs along Highway 96, a winding two-laner, with short trails that are routed down to the river. My favorite spots are the mouth of the Shasta River (see map A2), the mouth of the Scott River, a five-mile stretch through Seiad Valley just upstream from the town of Happy Camp, and from T-Bar on downstream to Somes Bar.

Most of the steelhead on the Klamath are not huge, like those on the Smith River, but they do come in good numbers. Steelhead here are in the two to four-pound class. The average fish is about a 19-inch, three-pounder. Rarely they reach six pounds, and the largest I personally have seen on the Klamath was a 12-pounder. On a good day, you might catch a dozen half-pounders, with maybe a pair of two to three-pounders in the mix.

Even though the Klamath's clarity is typically poor, which helps hide anglers, the bite can really shut off during mid-day if there is bright sunlight and hot weather. That makes fishing shaded areas a key, as well as being on the water at both dawn and dusk.

One year I rafted the entire river, from its headwaters in Oregon all the way to the Pacific Ocean. It is a waterway vibrant with life, not only fish, but many species of birds and wildlife. They say Bigfoot also lives up here, with many sightings in the Bluff Creek area.

Is there really a Bigfoot? Well, animals I've seen 'em all, but Bigfoot? Just can't recall.

7.　TAYLOR LAKE

Reference: Southwest of Etna in in The Russian Wilderness; map A1 grid j8.

How to get there: Etna is located about a half-hour's drive west of Interstate 5 via Highway 3 from Yreka, or from the Gazelle turnoff located just north of Weed. From Etna, head west on Sawyers's Bar

Road and continue over Etna Summit, then just a mile down the other side. Make a left turn at the signed dirt road that says "Taylor Lake." A short walk is required to reach the lake, and it is wheelchair accessible.

Facilities: A primitive campground is provided, but no facilities are available.

Cost: Access is free.

Who to contact: Phone Klamath National Forest headquarters at (916) 842-6131. For a detailed map of the area, send $2 to Maps, Office of Information, U.S. National Forest, 630 Sansome Street, San Francisco, CA 94111.

About Taylor Lake: If you want the wilderness experience without the grunt of a serious overnight hike, you came to the right place. The fishing is good here, too, with rainbow trout and more rarely, brown trout, eager to take a fly or a Panther Martin spinner during the evening rise.

Because it is set just inside the wilderness boundary, many people who spot this lake on a map mistakenly believe it is very difficult to reach. It isn't. The walk is about 100 yards. None of the lakes in the Russian Wilderness are very large, but this is one of the biggest, shaped kind of like a kidney bean, with the outlet creek set along the access trail.

For many people making their first overnight trip into a wild area, this lake provides what may be an ideal setting: remote area, a short hike, and good trout fishing.

---

8.   MARBLE MOUNTAIN WILDERNESS

Reference: Northeast of Eureka near Klamath National Forest; map A1 grid j8.

How to get there: From the town of Etna on Highway 3, turn west on Sawyer's Bar Road. There are many trailheads in the area, detailed on a Forest Service map.

Facilities: No facilities are available in the wilderness area. Primitive campsites can be found at trailheads off Forest Service Roads that junction with Highway 96 to the north and Salmon River Road to the south.

Cost: Access is free.

Who to contact: Phone Klamath National Forest Headquarters at (916) 842-6131. For a map, send $2 to Maps, U.S. Forest Service, 630 Sansome Street, San Francisco, CA 94111.

About Marble Mountain Wilderness: Bay Area backpackers like Yosemite and Tahoe. L.A. backpackers like Kings Canyon and Mt. Whitney. Eureka and Redding backpackers like the Trinity Alps and Mount

Shasta. That leaves the Marble Mountains as one of the great, overlooked wilderness areas of the West. It is a large wilderness with more than a hundred lakes, several outstanding peaks, and, that's right, good fishing.

Because of the large number of lakes, it is possible to plan a week-long trip where you camp at a different trout-filled lake each evening. Of course, the deeper you get into the wilderness, the better the fishing is. That's always the law of the land.

Spirit Lake is such a lake. This is one of the prettiest lakes I have ever seen, always full, ringed by conifers, and loaded with brook trout and rainbow trout up to 10, 11 inches. In the evening, when the local osprey takes a dive, he never goes away empty-taloned.

There are many good lakes. Here is a selection of the lakes stocked each year from the air by the Department of Fish and Game: Bear Lake, Blueberry Lake, Buckthorn Lake, Burney Lake, Buzzard Lake, Calf Lake, Campbell Lake, Charimaine Lake, Chicaree Lake, Chimney Rock Lake, Chinquapin Lake, Clear Lake, Cliff Lake, all four of the Cuddihy Lakes, Deadman Lake, Deep Lake, the two Elk Lakes, Fisher Lake, Granite Lake, both Hancock Lakes, Hooligan Lake, Independence Lake, Kleaver Lake, Kidder Lake, Log Lake, Man Eaten Lake, Meteor Lake, Mill Creek Lake, Monument Lake, Onemile Lake, Pleasant Lake, Rainy Lake, Secret Lake, Shadow Lake, Sky High Lake, Snyder Lake, Spirit Lake, Steinacher Lake, Tickner Lake No. 3, Tom's Lake, Ukonom Lake, Wild Lake, Wolverine Lake, Wooley Lake, and the two Wright Lakes.

My personal preference is to hike in to the lakes for which there is no trail. The trout have never heard of hooks, and many of them have never even heard of people. At one such lake, my friend Michael Furniss tossed in a large boulder, making a tremendous splash. The trout actually swam toward it, rather than away from it, curious as to what all the commotion was about.

The Marbles are beautiful wilderness, and many sidetrips are possible. Take a daypack along so you can leave your backpack behind and scramble up Marble Mountain (6,880 feet), King's Castle (7,405 feet), Buckhorn Mountain (6,908 feet), or many of the shorter lookouts. If you like lush growth and big trees, the trail that runs along Wooley Creek provides it.

---

9.   RUSSIAN WILDERNESS

Reference: Northwest of Weaverville near Klamath National Forest; map A1 grid j9.

How to get there: There are several ways to access the Russian Wilderness. The best trailheads are off Forest Service roads that turn off Cecilville-

Callahan Road. That road can be reached from the west via Highway 96 at Somes Bar, and from the east at the town of Etna.

Facilities: No facilities are available.

Cost: Access is free.

Who to contact: Phone Klamath National Forest Headquarters at (916) 842-6131. For a map, send $2 to Maps, U.S. Forest Service, 630 Sansome Street, San Francisco, CA 94111.

About Russian Wilderness: Have you ever known a place that is so pristine, yet so small, that it just can't handle many visitors at a time? That is the way the Russian Wilderness is. If you go, please walk softly, take only pictures and leave only your footprints.

This is the smallest wilderness in the Forest Service system in California. It is only about two miles wide, six miles long, and it is best known as offering a prime stretch of the Pacific Crest Trail (PCT). The ambitious and skilled mountaineer can take off from the PCT and visit lakes that attract few visitors. But then again, the area can't stand many people. It's too small and too pristine for that.

Big Blue Lake is a good example. Getting in to it is a fairly rough task, but do-able cross-country style by those experienced at reading contour maps and the lay of the land. A campsite is available near the outlet of the lake, and the fishing during the evening rise is quite good. I saw a 20-incher slurping bugs on the surface, and after sneaking up and delivering a perfect cast, had a four-inch dinker grab the lure before the big guy had a chance for it.

There are several good lakes to fish in the area, though some, as mentioned, have no trails to reach them. The following are located in both the Russian Wilderness and surrounding Salmon-Scott Mountains and are stocked each year by air by the Department of Fish and Game: Both upper and lower Albert Lake, Big Blue Lake, Duck Lake, Hidden Lake, High Lake, Hogan Lake, Horseshoe Lake, Lipstick Lake, Mavis Lake, Paynes Lake, Poison Lake, Rock Lake, Ruffey Lake, both upper and lower Russian Lake, Syphon Lake and Waterdog Lake.

Many years ago, my friend Paul Wertz went in to the southern reaches of these wildlands. He brought a donkey with him that was strapped with 10-gallon milk cans—and in the milk cans were juvenile golden trout, sloshing around in the water. Well, Paul made it all the way to what is now known as Little Golden Russian Lake, and stocked the lake with those first baby golden trout. If you happen to make it to Little Golden as well, and maybe even catch the progeny trout, you may feel a special satisfaction in releasing the fish rather than eating it. After what Paul went through to get them there, they seem too valuable to be caught only once.

MAP A2

5 LISTINGS
PAGES 146-151

NOR-CAL MAP . see page 120
adjoining maps
NORTH.......................no map
EAST (A3)..........see page 152
SOUTH (B2).......see page 196
WEST (A1) ....see page 136

1. KLAMATH RIVER

Reference: Near Yreka in Klamath National Forest; map A2 grid f3.

How to get there: From Interstate 5 near Yreka, take the Yreka-Montague exit. Turn toward town and travel to the stop sign, then turn right on Hawkinsville Road (County Road 263). Drive six miles north (it is a narrow, twisty road), then turn west on Highway 96 to access the river. Good fishing spots include the mouth of Little Humbug Creek and the mouth of the Shasta River.

Facilities: A boat launch is located just south of Iron Gate Reservoir (see directions above). Several campgrounds can be found along the river; a good one is Trees of Heaven on Highway 96, about two miles west of Interstate 5.

Cost: River access is free.

Who to contact: Phone the Klamath National Forest Headquarters at (916) 842-6131.

About the Klamath River: The uppermost stretches of the Klamath River can provide some of its best winter steelhead prospects. From November through February, there are literally thousands and thousands of steelhead in the pockets from Iron Gate Dam on downstream to Trees under the Interstate-5 Bridge to Trees of Heaven Campground. Salmon arrive in October, and when a good school moves in, this stretch of water can become loaded with driftboats.

If there's a catch, it's that you need to fish from a boat to get it right. Shorefishing access is quite poor. That means hiring a guide for a trip down the river. But if you want to catch steelhead, this is the closest thing to a guarantee. The guide holds the oars, you hold your rod, letting a nightcrawler drift in the current downstream of the boat. In a morning, you might get 10 or 15 strikes. Even if you think you are hexed with a cataclysmic jinx, you are bound to luck into a few fish.

An option is to wade adjacent to where the Shasta River pours into the Klamath, which is located just a few miles west of Interstate 5 via Highway 96. It can be cold, especially in mid-December when the ice will freeze in your line guides, but this is when the fish arrive here. Because of the cold water temperatures in winter, there is no reason to be on the river early. In fact, during colder periods, the fish will often refuse to bite until the sun warms up the surface waters a degree or two.

Most of the steelhead run two to four pounds, about 18 to 22 inches. Rarely, larger ones are caught, but for the most part, it is the consistent action that is the attraction, not the size of the fish. About the only thing that can spoil it is a sudden increase in river flows from the outlet at Iron Gate Dam. If the flows suddenly increase, all matter of leaves, moss, and loose grass will be washed down the river, fouling hooks and spoiling the fishing.

For the most part, if you want steelhead, this piece of the Klamath River can solve your problem. You want fish—and here they are.

2. IRON GATE RESERVOIR & COPCO LAKE

Reference: Near Yreka near Klamath National Forest; map A2 grid f6.

How to get there: From Yreka, drive 12 miles north on Interstate 5 and take the Hornbrook exit. Drive ten miles east on Copco Road. You can reach one of several boat launches by following the road in.

Facilities: Four boat launches are provided at Iron Gate Reservoir, as well as a campground near Fall Creek. A boat launch and campground (located near the boat ramp) is also available at the adjoining Copco Lake. Tackle and supplies are available at Mitchell's Bait & Tackle at the south edge of the reservoir.

Cost: Access is free.

Who to contact: Phone the Shasta Cascade Wonderland Association at (916) 243-2643.

About Iron Gate Reservoir & Copco Lake: Yellow perch. If you want fish, loads of fish, you'll love 'em. If you want big fish, any fish just as long as it is big, you'll hate 'em. Since more people love catching lots of anything, as opposed to imitating statues, more people have learned to love these two adjoining lakes.

Copco Lake is the upper lake, Iron Gate is the lower lake. They both are loaded with yellow perch, the smallish fellow that can turn uninspired kids into enthusiastic, lifetime anglers. There are so many yellow perch up here that there is not even a limit on them. Catch all you want, keep all you catch. For a kid, what could be more perfect?

I'll tell you what: Eating them. Though these little fish may not get much bigger than five to seven inches, and they fight kind of like a tug-of-war between Goldie Hawn and Arnold Schwarzeneggar, they taste right up there with anything you can put on your plate. So let the kids catch them, and you can clean 'em and eat 'em.

Talk about easy: Use a little piece of red yarn on a hook, use a small piece of red worm on a hook, or even a little red lure. If you are using yarn or a piece of worm, just plunk it out in front of you. The best spot is the pier next to the boat ramp at Copco Lake, but if you can get out a little farther in a small raft or boat, it is hard to miss. If you use a lure, just jig it straight up and down. Test different depths, then when you get a strike, it's time to start filling your stringer. No kidding.

After a few hours of a good bite, you will wish you hadn't kept them all. It's common to catch 30 or 35 of the little buggers.

During the summer, there are times when people literally catch a hundred yellow perch. If you never experienced that kind of success, or are of the belief that you are vexed by some kind of jinx, you should make the trip at least once in your life.

3. JUANITA LAKE

Reference: Near Macdoel in Klamath National Forest; map A2 grid g8.
How to get there: From Interstate 5 near Weed, take the Weed-College of the Siskiyous exit. Drive north through town to the Highway 97 turnoff, then turn north and continue for approximately 40 miles to the town of Macdoel. Turn west on Meiss Lake-Sam's Neck Road and drive 8.5 miles to Butte Valley Road. Take Butte Valley Road south to the lake.
Facilities: A campground is provided. Supplies are available in Macdoel.
Cost: Campsite fee is $6-$8 per night.
Who to contact: Phone the Klamath National Forest Headquarters at (916) 842-6131.
About Juanita Lake: Juanita Lake is a perfect example of the kind of place that gets overlooked by so many Californians who hunger for exactly what it offers. It is small. It is out of the way, yet any car can reach it. It has lakeside camping, and decent trout fishing. But you don't know about it, do you? Don't feel bad. Not many folks do, or of the hundreds of lakes like it in the more remote areas of California.

The lake is stocked by Fish and Game with brook trout, and while the lake isn't exactly plugged with them, there are enough (2,000 a year) to provide fair prospects for the few folks who visit the lake. If you want Battlestar Galactica, this is not the place. If you want a quiet camp along a lake with a chance to catch some brook trout, well, the shoe just might fit.

4. CEDAR LAKE

Reference: Near Weed near Klamath National Forest; map A2 grid h5.
How to get there: From Interstate 5 near Weed, take the Weed-College of the Siskiyous exit. Drive north through town and take the Highway 97 turnoff. Drive nine miles north on Highway 97, then turn west on Highway A12. Drive 4.5 miles, then turn north on Harry Cash Road and travel 5.5 miles to Hart Road. Turn west and drive two miles to the lake.
Facilities: No facilities are available; tackle and supplies can be purchased in Weed.
Cost: Access is free.
Who to contact: Phone the Shasta Cascade Wonderland Association at (916) 243-2643.

About Cedar Lake: You never heard of Cedar Lake? No? That's OK. There are a lot of folks in the nearby town of Weed (named after a man, not a plant) who have no idea where it is either. But once you get in the area, access is easy, and you will find it a small, quiet spot with an outlet stream that pours into the Little Shasta River.

It is stocked by air each year by the Department of Fish and Game with 2,000 fingerling brook trout. Those are the dinkers of all dinkers. So get your focus in perspective. This is not the place where you are going to catch a world record. How about a foot-long brookie? Well, probably not one of them either. But if you can find contentment with five to eight-inchers, rarely one larger, as well as your own piece of turf at a lake that is virtually unknown, this trip can work out just fine.

---

5. LAKE SHASTINA

Reference: Near Weed near Klamath National Forest; map A2 grid j5.
How to get there: From Interstate 5 near Weed, take the Weed-College of the Siskiyous exit. Drive north through town and take the Highway 97 turnoff. Drive 2.5 miles northeast on Highway 97, then turn west on Ordway Road. Travel one mile and turn north on Edgewood-Big Springs Road. Watch for the signed turnoff and travel west to the lake. The boat ramp is located at the north end of the lake.
Facilities: A boat launch is provided, along with a few primitive campsites. Supplies can be obtained in Weed.
Cost: Access is free.
Who to contact: Phone the Shasta Cascade Wonderland Association at (916) 243-2643.
About Lake Shastina: Most people don't know this, but Lake Shastina is one of the best crappie lakes in California. What? A crappie lake in the mountains of Northern California? Is this possible? Yes, yes, and yes.

As spring makes its transition to summer, not only are the crappie abundant, but they are big. They often are caught in the 12 to 15-inch range, sometimes even larger. The first time you hook a big one you'll swear you have a bass on. But you don't. It's a crappie, and they are what make this place special.

The view is nice too. The lake is set on the northern slopes of Mount Shasta, the old giant volcano that rises like a diamond in a field of coal. Because of its proximity to the mountain, however, spring can be cold and windy, a time to stay off the lake. The key is to keep track of the weather up here. The first five-day binge of warm weather, and wham, it's time to hit Shastina for those crappie.

The lake is stocked with trout, and they can be caught with the traditional methods detailed in the Secrets of the Masters portion of this book. Most of the trout are in the 10, 11-inch class, and provide an alternative to the crappie.

This is one of the few lakes in California that has lakeside housing, with several small developments. It gets cold in the winter, quite windy in the spring, and that keeps the housing prices quite low compared to other vacation lakes. In addition, the lake level can be lowered in mid-summer, when it is sent via the Shasta River to the valley to the north to grow hay. It can get ugly. Some years, before the rains come, the lake has gotten so low that locals call it "River Shastina."

But they're just joking, hoping to scare people off. Like a lot of people with local knowledge, they're hoping nobody else finds out about the big crappie.

MAP A3

7 LISTINGS
PAGES 152-157

NOR-CAL MAP. see page 120
adjoining maps
NORTH.........................no map
EAST (A4)...........see page 158
SOUTH (B3).......see page 216
WEST (A2).........see page 146

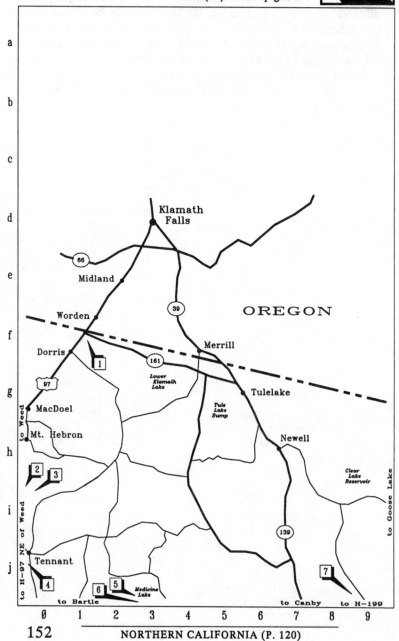

OREGON

Klamath Falls

Midland

Worden

Dorris

Merrill

Tulelake

MacDoel

Mt. Hebron

Newell

Tennant

to Weed

to H-97 NE of Weed

to Goose Lake

to Bartle

Medicine Lake

to Canby

to H-199

Lower Klamath Lake

Tule Lake Sump

Clear Lake Reservoir

1.   INDIAN TOM LAKE

Reference: Near Dorris; map A3 grid f1.

How to get there: From Interstate 5 near Weed, take Weed-College of the Siskiyous exit. Drive north through town to the Highway 97 turnoff, then turn north and continue for approximately 52 miles to the town of Dorris. Continue for 1.5 miles north on Highway 97, then turn east on Sheepy Creek Road and watch for the signed turnoff to the lake.

Facilities: No facilities are available. Supplies can be obtained in Dorris.

Cost: Access is free.

Who to contact: Phone the Shasta Cascade Wonderland Association at (916) 243-2643.

About Indian Tom Lake: The name "Indian Tom Lake" conjured up images for me of bark canoes, fall colors, and a quiet unknown spot similar to the little lakes in northern Minnesota. Wrong again.

This lake sits in flat, fairly stark country, has easy access, and is not the pristine setting the name suggests. But just the same, it offers a unique fishery like no other small lake in the state: a trophy trout fishery for Lahontan cutthroat trout. It comes with equally special fishing regulations. Always check the DFG rulebook before tossing in a line, because the regulations are often finetuned from year to year. The reason is because of two key elements at this lake: 1. The cutthroat trout; and 2. The lake's algae growth. This is one of the few waters in California that provides a decent chance to catch a good-size cutthroat troat. The DFG provides a boost by stocking 22,000 each spring.

However, the big problem most visitors have is that they arrive to the lake too late in the year for the better prospects. Come in midsummer, run into the algae growth, and your first response is, "What's the big deal about this place?" Well, the lake is not too deep, so it is vulnerable to weed growth in warm weather. But there is a window of opportunity between late spring and early summer when all the positive factors are aligned. The water is clear, but not too cold and not too warm, and the fish are hungry and vibrant. Come then.

2.   ORR LAKE

Reference: Near MacDoel in Klamath National Forest; map A3 grid i∅.

How to get there: From Interstate 5 near Weed, take Weed-College of the Siskiyous exit. Drive north through town to the Highway 97 turnoff, then turn north and travel approximately 40 miles to the town of MacDoel. Turn south on Old State Highway and travel 14 miles to the town of Bray, then turn north on a dirt road and drive two miles northwest to the lake.

Facilities: No facilities are available on-site.

Cost: Access is free.

Who to contact: Phone the Shasta Cascade Wonderland Association at (916) 243-2643.

About Orr Lake: Little Orr Lake is quite a place, both good and bad. You determine the rating. Want the bad news first? OK, this is it: The road in is in bad shape, the larger fish can be quite elusive, and in the hot summer months, visitors (especially those with kids) should be extremely careful about rattlesnakes. So have a vehicle that can take the bumps, bring along your angling smarts, and keep your eyes on the ground. That accomplished, you can be in for a treat.

The little lake is one of the few this size anymore that has both brown trout and bass in it. The trout fishing is best in the cool months, of course, and the bass in the warm months. The lake has a lot of little lily pads that provide ideal bass cover, and also a nice feeder creek, Butte Creek, which gives trout plenty of food. That makes for some big browns, but because the lake is small, those big fish are mighty wary. If you have a secret technique, this is the place for it to receive its litmus test. I suggest using a small jointed Rapala, which can attract strikes from both the bass as well as the browns. The bass are able to spawn naturally, but the DFG gives this lake a boost by planting 1,000 brown trout per year.

---

3. BUTTE CREEK

Reference: Near MacDoel in Klamath National Forest; map A3 grid i∅.

How to get there: From Interstate 5 near Weed, take Weed-College of the Siskiyous exit. Drive north through town to the Highway 97 turnoff, then turn north and travel approximately 40 miles to the town of MacDoel. Turn south on Old State Highway. Access is available along the road.

Facilities: No facilities are available. Supplies can be obtained in MacDoel.

Cost: Access is free.

Who to contact: Phone the Shasta Cascade Wonderland Association at (916) 243-2643.

About Butte Creek: When you first glance at Butte Creek, you immediately become aware that your work is cut out for you. The stream is just six to 10 feet wide, and while it flows freely, it is a slow-moving "chalk" stream. It is bordered by meadow, with a cut bank. Most of the trout hide in the shade of that cut bank. If you just saunter right up to the water and start casting, you'll swear there isn't a trout in existence.

That's because you're standing right on top of them, for one thing, and because you have scared them off for another. You have to sneak up on fish here, like a burglar sneaking through an unlocked window. It can help to stand some way back from the river to do your casting; if they see the shadow of your rod, detect any casting motion, or God forbid, see you, you're a goner for sure. The river is stocked with 2,000 rainbow trout each year, and if you hit it after a stock, it can be a confidence booster for the real test: fooling a native-born.

This is rattlesnake territory, so keep alert. Some years have been pretty bad, and you might consider packing a side arm. Also note that much of the river is bordered by private property and you don't want to offend your Modoc hosts, particularly if you are packing a gun.

---

4. ANTELOPE CREEK

Reference: Near Tennant in Klamath National Forest; map A3 grid jØ.
How to get there: From Interstate 5 near Weed, take Weed-College of the Siskiyous exit. Drive north through town to the Highway 97 turnoff, then turn north and travel approximately 40 miles to the town of MacDoel. Turn south on Old State Highway and travel 12 miles to Tennant Road. Turn left and travel south to the town of Tennant, then continue for one mile southwest on Tennant Road to access Antelope Creek.
Facilities: No facilities are available; supplies can be obtained in Tennant.
Cost: Access is free.
Who to contact: Phone the Shasta Cascade Wonderland Association at (916) 243-2643. For a map of the area, send $2 to Office of Information, 630 Sansome Street, San Francisco, CA 94111.
About Antelope Creek: Don't even think about fishing Antelope Creek unless you have a Forest Service map in hand. That way you can detail what is public and accessible, and what is private and not. Make the mistake and you can get nailed for trespassing. If you are from the Bay Area or L.A., they will particularly enjoy your plight.

This is a classic babbling brook, running over rocks and boulders and into pools and pocket water. It is stocked with just 1,000 trout per year, but always just on public-accessible areas. The native trout here have exceptional color, and while they are usually small, a few eight to 10-inchers can add a little spice to the day. Of course, so can a blast of rocksalt in the seat of your pants from Farmer John's shotgun, that is, if you have crossed onto private property. Remember that.

---

5. MEDICINE LAKE

Reference: Near McCloud in Modoc National Forest; map A3 grid j3.
How to get there: From Interstate 5 south of Mt. Shasta, take the McCloud-Reno exit and travel 12 miles on Highway 89 to McCloud.

Continue east for 17 miles to Bartle. From Bartle, drive 31 miles northeast on Powder Hill Road (Forest Service Road 46) to Medicine Lake Road. Take Medicine Lake Road to the lake.

Facilities: Three campgrounds are provided on the lake, and a good boat launch is available. Supplies are available in McCloud; limited supplies can be obtained at the Bartle Lodge.

Cost: Campsite fee is $5 per vehicle (trailers excluded).

Who to contact: Phone the Modoc National Forest District Office at (916) 667-2246.

About Medicine Lake: This is a place of mystery, a challenge and an answer. The mystery is that the lake was originally a caldera, that is, the mouth of a volcano. It draws a natural comparison to Crater Lake in Oregon, but it is not as deep and not as blue. Regardless, that gives it a sense of timeless history, which most lakes in California don't have. It is a beautiful lake with lakeside campsites and a paved road all the way in, with the snow cleared by June, sometimes earlier.

Undiscovered, however, Medicine Lake is not. The challenge is the fishing and the answer is that you can handle it. The trout fishing is good here, with the better results coming for trollers. In the summer, it is a typical morning and evening bite. In the spring and fall, when the bite is better day-long, beware of surprise storms which can pour snow on surprised visitors. Some folks are content to toss in their bait along the shore near the campgrounds, but the better results come by boat. To improve the boating experience, waterskiing is only permitted between 10 a.m. and 4 p.m. That means anglers who want quiet water for the prime times during morning and evening can get it. I really like this idea, a good solution to the unending waterskier/angler conflict, and suggest it be applied to other lakes in the state.

Medicine Lake receives more trout than any other lake in the region, getting almost 30,000 trout per year. They usually are all brook trout, although a few rainbow trout are rarely in the mix. At one time, arctic grayling were stocked in this lake, but little emphasis was ever focused on them. The stocking program ended, natural spawning did not take over, and now they are caught only rarely.

A few other notes: If you bring your dog, you'd better keep him tied up, because they are not allowed on the beach, and the rangers clamp down pretty hard here. On a brighter note, there are several exciting side trips in the area, including ice caves, an abandoned mountain top lookout, and also nearby Bullseye and Blanche lakes.

---

6. BULLSEYE LAKE

Reference: Near McCloud in Modoc National Forest; map A3 grid j3.
How to get there: From Interstate 5 south of Mt. Shasta, take the

McCloud-Reno exit and travel 12 miles on Highway 89 to McCloud. Continue east for 17 miles to Bartle. From Bartle, drive 31 miles northeast on Powder Hill Road (Forest Service Road 46) to Medicine Lake Road. Take Medicine Lake Road, past Medicine Lake, to Bullseye Lake.

Facilities: A primitive camp with no facilities is available. Supplies are available in McCloud; limited supplies can be obtained at the Bartle Lodge.

Cost: Access is free.

Who to contact: Phone the Modoc National Forest District Office at (916) 667-2246.

About Bullseye Lake: This tiny lake gets overlooked every year mainly because of its proximity to nearby Medicine Lake. But if you don't have a boat, this lake can provide better shoreline trout fishing than at the famed Medicine Lake. A surprise? You better believe it. The lake is shallow, but because snow keeps it locked up until late May or early June, the water stays plenty cold for the trout through July. The best results are for shoreliners using bait, or a bubble-and-fly combination. Don't expect large trout, especially with the number of brook trout in the lake. It is stocked each year with 2,000 rainbow trout and 1,000 brook trout. A nearby side trip are some ice caves, created by ancient volcanic action, which are fun to poke around in and explore.

7.　　　DUNCAN RESERVOIR

Reference: South of Tulelake in Modoc National Forest; map A3 grid j9.

How to get there: From the junction of Highways 139 and 299 at the small town of Canby, drive about seven miles north on Highway 139. Turn north on Loveness Road and drive 2.5 miles north, then turn right on a dirt road and continue two miles east to the reservoir.

Facilities: No facilities are available.

Cost: Access is free.

Who to contact: Phone the Modoc National Forest District Office at (916) 667-2246.

About Duncan Reservoir: Here's a little "sleeper" reservoir that few take notice of. And why not? It's out in the middle of nowhere, after all. I'll tell you why you should find it: Once you get the hang of the place, you can catch beautiful trout in the two to four-pound class. No foolin'. You will immediately notice that the trout here don't look like your average rainbow trout. That's because they aren't. They are a domesticated-strain of Eagle Lake trout, planted in fingerling size each May by the DFG air express. About 4,000 are stocked every year in this manner, survival rates are very high, and, well, if you get in on it, remember where you heard it.

MAP A4

11 LISTINGS
PAGES 158-165

NOR-CAL MAP. see page 120
adjoining maps
NORTH.........................no map
EAST ....no map
SOUTH (B4).......see page 232
WEST (A3).........see page 152

1.   JANES RESERVOIR

Reference: Near Davis Creek in Modoc National Forest; map A4 grid h2.

How to get there: From Alturas, drive north on US 395 to the town of Davis Creek. From the town of Davis Creek, drive 12 miles north on Westside Road, then turn west on South Main Road. Drive 14.5 miles west, then turn south on Crowder Flat Road and travel half a mile to Janes Reservoir.

Facilities: No facilities are available. Supplies are available in Alturas.

Cost: Access is free.

Who to contact: Phone the Modoc National Forest District Office at (916) 279-6116.

About Janes Reservoir: Ol' Janes gets very little fishing pressure because it's so far away. It even takes the Modoc locals a long time to reach it. So for a drive-to lake, the fish get a minimum of smart lessons from know-how anglers. That benefits the people who manage to make it out this far. Now listen to this: The lake is stocked with 2,000 brown trout and 6,000 Eagle Lake trout each year. These are not your average trout. Browns get big, and so do those Eagle Lake specials, and this lake has both. It is ironic, because many maps do not even put a name on this water. It's not the prettiest place in the world, set in the high plateau country, but if you have a canoe or car-top boat and are serious about fishing, it's an ideal spot to plunk in your boat and try to entice a few of these big trout.

2.   DIAMOND RESERVOIR

Reference: Near Davis Creek in Modoc National Forest; map A4 grid h2.

How to get there: From the town of Alturas, drive north on US 395 to the town of Davis Creek. From the town of Davis Creek, drive 12 miles north on Westside Road, then turn west on South Main Road. Drive 14.5 miles west, then turn north on Crowder Flat Road. Drive one mile north, past Crowder Flat Ranger Station, then turn west and travel one-half mile (stay to the right) to Baseball Reservoir (four-wheel drive vehicles are highly recommended). Bear left and travel one-half mile west to Diamond Reservoir.

Facilities: No facilities are available. Supplies are available in Alturas.

Cost: Access is free.

Who to contact: Phone the Modoc National Forest District Office at (916) 279-6116.

About Diamond Reservoir: This one is way out there in booger country. It's a lake that is hardly ever touched. The few people who know of it are the local cowboys, who occasionally run cattle in the general area. The annual stocks from the DFG are quite minimal, just 250 brown trout and 250 Eagle Lake trout, but since almost nobody ever fishes here, a few survive year after year and get quite big. You want obscure? You want cowboy country? You want a chance for a few nice trout? You want a long drive? This is the place. Guaranteed quiet, yes.

---

3.   CAVE LAKE

Reference: In Modoc National Forest; map A4 grid h8.

How to get there: From US 395 at New Pine Creek (on the Oregon/California border), drive six miles east on Forest Service Road 2.

Facilities: A campground is provided, as well as a boat ramp for small boats (all motors are prohibited on the lake). Supplies are available in New Pine Creek or Fort Bidwell.

Cost: Access is free.

Who to contact: Phone the Modoc National Forest District Office at (916) 279-6116.

About Cave Lake: A set of two lakes is found here, Cave Lake on one end and Lily Lake on the other. Together, they make a nice set, very quiet and little-traveled with decent fishing for trout in the foot-long class. Cave has very little vegetation around it, making Lily Lake the more attractive of the two. Cave Lake is worth tossing a line into, however. It is stocked with 1,000 trout per year, not big numbers to be sure, but decent relative to the number of anglers. Most of the fish are rainbow trout, but some brook trout are also available. Using a fly and bubble is by far the best technique at this lake. If you don't have a bobber handy, a piece of bark will float and do the same job just fine. A little "local knowledge" is that when there is a little ripple on the water from a light breeze, that is when the trout really seem to bite best—especially in the late spring and early summer.

---

4.   LILY LAKE

Reference: In Modoc National Forest; map A4 grid h8.

How to get there: From US 395 at New Pine Creek (on the Oregon/California border), drive 5.5 miles east on Forest Service Road 2.

Facilities: A campground is provided. Supplies are available in New Pine Creek or Fort Bidwell.

Cost: Access is free.

Who to contact: Phone the Modoc National Forest District Office at (916) 279-6116.

About Lily Lake: Little Lily is way out there in No Man's Land, but it is well worth the trip. It is one of the better destinations in Northern California that you can reach by car for camping, fishing and solitude. Because there are some conifers sprinkled around the lake, it is a lot prettier than neighboring Cave Lake. Alas, the fish are smaller than at Cave Lake. In fact, there are lots of the DFG dinker variety, the little five-inch rainbow trout. After a while, you'll catch an eight-incher, and you'll say, "Wow! A big one!" And you'll mean it. But those small ones make for a great trout fry around the evening campfire. For weary visitors who want their batteries recharged, this place is one of the best spots to do it.

---

5.   PINE CREEK

Reference: Near New Pine Creek in Modoc National Forest; map A4 grid h8.

How to get there: From New Pine Creek (on the Oregon/California border), drive one-half mile south on US 395 to Highgrade Road. Turn east. Access to the creek is available along Highgrade Road.

Facilities: No facilities are available. Supplies are available in New Pine Creek.

Cost: Access is free.

Who to contact: Phone the Modoc National Forest District Office at (916) 279-6116.

About Pine Creek: Imagine this scene: A little tumbling stream comes down a mountain side, and every once in a while you find a pool where the trout fin near motionless, waiting for a morsel to come floating by. Like it? Then Pine Creek may be your calling. If you like to hike, and then cast a line a little every now and then, this is a good spot for you. Very few anglers ever even consider trying it on for size. The trout tend to be little guys, but they are natives; the stream is not stocked. They can provide some fun with a fly rod. You do very little casting, but rather do what is called "nymph dipping." You use a weighted nymph and a seven and a half foot leader, then flip the nymph out so it drifts through pocket water. If the natural drift of the line is stopped, then strike, because that may be the only indication that a trout has stopped your fly. Because you are fishing pocket water only, this stream fishes better walking downstream than upstream.

---

6.   WILLOW CREEK

Reference: Near New Pine Creek in Modoc National Forest; map A4 grid i8.

How to get there: From New Pine Creek (on the Oregon/ California border), drive 5.5 miles south on US 395 to Fandango Pass Road. Turn east. Access to the creek is available along Fandango Pass Road and off short Forest Service Roads that junction with it.

Facilities: No facilities are available. Supplies can be obtained in New

Pine Creek or Davis Creek.

Cost: Access is free.

Who to contact: Phone the Modoc National Forest District Office at (916) 279-6116.

About Willow Creek: Let's admit the obvious: This is not much of a trout water. The stream is quite small, but it is worth mentioning because it does hold wild trout, and despite easy access it gets very little fishing pressure. The stream is in Modoc's high mountain plateau country, running through rolling hills en route to Goose Lake. I've never heard of a large trout in this stream, and it is never stocked, but it is quiet and pure. Sometimes that is enough.

---

7. LASSEN CREEK

Reference: Near New Pine Creek in Modoc National Forest; map A4 grid i8.

How to get there: From New Pine Creek (on the Oregon/California border), drive 7.5 miles south on US 395. Turn left on South Willow Ranch Road and drive 2.5 miles southeast, then turn east on Lassen Creek Road and travel south. Excellent access is available along Lassen Creek Road.

Facilities: No facilities are available. Supplies can be obtained in New Pine Creek or Davis Creek.

Cost: Access is free.

Who to contact: Phone the Modoc National Forest District Office at (916) 279-6116.

About Lassen Creek: Here is a surprise jewel in the north state, but only the local natives seem to know about it. Lassen Creek is a very small, narrow stream that supports a strain of wild red-banded rainbow trout that are as pretty as any anywhere. Small? Yes. This is one time it doesn't seem to matter. You should not kill any of these trout, but always release them. They are just too special.

In addition, a few local conservationists with Modoc National Forest have tried their best to restore the habitat here to improve trout populations. The best work has been with stream bank stabilization projects.

---

8. MILL CREEK

Reference: Near Fort Bidwell in Modoc National Forest; map A4 grid i9.

How to get there: From Alturas, drive north on US 395 to the town of Fort Bidwell. Then drive northwest on Bidwell Creek Road. Access is available all along Bidwell Creek Road.

Facilities: No facilities are available. Supplies can be obtained in Fort

Bidwell.

Cost: Access is free.

Who to contact: Phone the Modoc National Forest District Office at (916) 279-6116.

About Mill Creek: This stream is set apart from all the others in Modoc County because of the size of the trout here. Trout in the one to three-pound class are reality, not mirages, and if you tangle with a few here you will never forget it. Mill Creek tumbles out of the South Warner Wilderness. Access is good, with a trail along much of the stream, as well as the road which parallels it. Whenever fishing a trout stream, always refer to a national forest map to make sure you don't tromp on somebody's private property. That is doubly true in Modoc County, where trespassing without permission is considered sacrilege. The map will keep you out of trouble, and in the mean time, you can use sneak-fishing tactics in order to surprise the trout. The trout are surprisingly chunky, and also sometimes very dark, even almost black. They are a unique, native strain. The river eventually runs into Clear Lake, then drops over Mill Creek Falls and pours into the Jess Valley. There it enters the South Fork Pit River. Note that below Mill Creek Falls, most of the stream runs through private property. There is plenty of public access in other areas, however, to provide plenty of good trout water.

9.　　　　　　LAKE ANNIE

Reference: Near Fort Bidwell; map A4 grid i9.

How to get there: From Alturas, drive east on Highway 299 to Cedarville, then turn north on Surprise Valley Road and continue to the town of Fort Bidwell. In Fort Bidwell, turn north on Lake Annie Road and drive 2.5 miles.

Facilities: No facilities are available. Supplies can be obtained in Fort Bidwell.

Cost: Access is free.

Who to contact: Phone the Modoc National Forest District Office at (916) 279-6116.

About Lake Annie: Annie is the backyard fishing hole for the folks in the small town of Fort Bidwell, a unique community that time has passed by. It's an anachronism and a beautiful little spot, with a grocery store, a gas station, and hey, just west of town is a natural hot spring. The lake is set just to the west of Annie Mountain, from which it gets its name, and has good numbers of small rainbow trout. It is stocked by air—it's too far away for the DFG to drive to—and that means fingerling-size trout are plunked in each year, not the larger "catchables." It is set just east of the Warner Mountains, a lonely, quiet place.

The lake is surrounded by fairly sparse country, and one thing is for sure about it: Nobody gets here by accident.

---

10. BRILES RESERVOIR

Reference: Near Davis Creek in Modoc National Forest; map A4 grid j7.

How to get there: From Alturas, drive north on US 395 to the town of Davis Creek. Turn right on Westside Road (Forest Service Road 11) and drive 2.5 miles east. When the road forks, turn north (left) and travel four miles, then bear left again and travel a short distance to Briles Reservoir.

Facilities: No facilities are available. Supplies can be obtained in Davis Creek.

Cost: Access is free.

Who to contact: Phone the Modoc National Forest District Office at (916) 279-6116.

About Briles Reservoir: When you are cruising US 395, you can feel like you are out in the middle of nowhere. That's because you are. As a result, out-of-towners just start driving faster and faster and miss little spots like Briles Reservoir. It is set only a few miles east of the highway, tucked in a pocket of the foothills of the Warner Mountains in Modoc National Forest. It is stocked every May by the DFG airplane, which plants 4,000 fingerling-size rainbow trout. The best time to fish is in June and July, despite the high number of small fish you have to weed through to get a keeper. These months are best because this reservoir is used as a water supply to irrigate hay fields. By late summer, it can get fairly low.

---

11. FEE RESERVOIR

Reference: Near Fort Bidwell; map A4 grid j9.

How to get there: From Alturas, drive north on US 395 to Fort Bidwell. From Fort Bidwell, drive 7.5 miles east on Fee Reservoir Road, a good gravel road.

Facilities: No facilities are available. Supplies can be obtained in Fort Bidwell.

Cost: Access is free.

Who to contact: Phone the Modoc National Forest District Office at (916) 279-6116.

About Fee Reservoir: Fee Reservoir is one crazy place. It's barren around this lake, and it doesn't look like all that great a place to fish. After an hour or so, if you haven't caught anything, you might be apt just to forget the whole deal and head elsewhere. Most visitors do just that and it is a major error. There are some big trout in this lake, quality trout of the Eagle Lake strain that go two and a half to three pounds. Some are bigger. Yes, they can be hard to catch. But the persistent few who know how to present a nightcrawler are the ones who will fill their stringer with them. It takes a light touch, and it takes experience to know when to set the hook on the light bites. But that done, you are in business. Does the shoe fit?

The setting is typical of Modoc County's high desert country. You get a chance to see that special orange glow at dawn and dusk, and in early summer, the variety of blooming wildflowers makes a normally stark setting come alive in a multiplicity of colors.

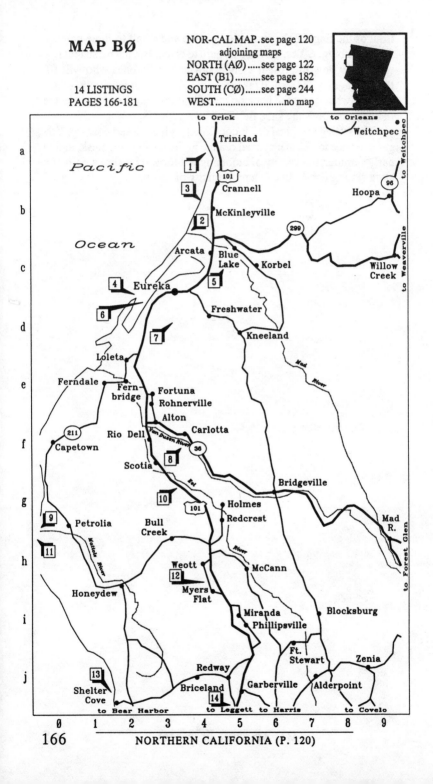

MAP BØ

14 LISTINGS
PAGES 166-181

NOR-CAL MAP.see page 120
adjoining maps
NORTH (AØ).....see page 122
EAST (B1)..........see page 182
SOUTH (CØ)......see page 244
WEST..........................no map

to Orick   to Orleans

Trinidad

Weitchpec

Pacific

1

101

3

Crannell

Hoopa

96

to Weitchpec

b

McKinleyville

299

Ocean

2

Blue
Lake

Korbel

to Weaverville

Arcata

c

Willow
Creek

4

Eureka

5

6

Freshwater

d

7

Kneeland

Mad River

Loleta

e

Ferndale

Fern-
bridge

Fortuna
Rohnerville

Alton

211

Rio Dell

Carlotta

Van Duzen River

f

Capetown

36

8

Scotia

Bridgeville

g

10

Holmes

Mad
R.

9

101

Redcrest

Petrolia

Bull
Creek

to Forest Glen

River

11

Mattole River

h

Weott

McCann

12

Myers
Flat

Honeydew

i

Miranda

Blocksburg

Phillipsville

Ft.
Stewart

Zenia

j

13

Redway

Garberville

Alderpoint

Shelter
Cove

Briceland

14

to Bear Harbor   to Leggett   to Harris   to Covelo

Ø   1   2   3   4   5   6   7   8   9

Reference: In Trinidad; map BØ grid a4.

How to get there: From Eureka, drive 22 miles north on US 101 and take the Trinidad exit. As you head west, the road becomes Main/Trinity/Edwards and goes all the way down to a parking lot adjacent to the Seascape Restaurant.

Facilities: Bob's Boat Basin provides a tackle shop, a restaurant, and a gift shop. Party boat charters are also available. A campground is available nearby at Patrick's Point State Park and good, low-cost lodging is available at several motels. No boat launch is available, but a boat hoist is provided at the pier.

Cost: Party boat fees are $45-$55 per person.

Who to contact: For general information and a free travel packet, phone the Trinidad Chamber of Commerce at (707) 677-0591 or (707) 677-3448. For fishing and party boat information, phone Bob's Boat Basin at (707) 677-3625. For fishing information and tackle, call Salty's at (707) 677-3874.

Party boat list: The *Shenandoah, Jumpin' Jack,* and Rod Woodson's 27-foot *Boston Whaler* are available out of Bob's Boat Basin.

About Trinidad Harbor: So many people miss out on Trinidad. But it only takes one good trip here and you will keep coming back for the rest of your life. It is a beautiful chunk of coast, a protected bay sprinkled with rock-tipped islands and prime fishing grounds just off the Trinidad Head. Just north is Patrick's Point State Park, one of the prettiest small parks in California—something of a rainforest jungle with Sitka spruce, heavy fern undergrowth, and trails that are like tunnels through vegetation.

Come July, every July, and the salmon move inshore here in a tremendous horde. Often these large schools of fish are within five miles of land, an easy trip for even small boats. You show up at dawn at the boat hoist, get dropped in the water, then make the quick cruise around Trinidad Head and to the fish. When the salmon move in, they are usually quite easy to find—you just join the flotilla of boats trolling for them. It can be very exciting, with fast hook-ups and a generous number of 15 and 20-pounders in the mix. At times, schools of silver salmon (identified by the white mouth) arrive and monopolize the fishery. These fish are more apt to jump than their big brothers, the king. As fall approaches, anglers tend to catch quality rather than quantity. That is, a few big king salmon, but sparse few silver salmon or school-sized kings. It takes more time, but the fall is when the sky is clear, the days are warm, and the ocean is its calmest of the year. That makes for very good rockfishing at the many inshore reefs, a bonus that most locals take for granted.

If there is a word of caution for summer visitors, it is to have honed your boat navigation skills. It is often quite foggy in the summer here, and the worst of it comes in July and August when the fishing is the best. Boaters unfamiliar with the area can find themselves cloaked in the stuff. That is why Loran navigation devices are so popular, along with professional charter boat services. The late winter and spring can be quite windy here, and you have to time it right to get on the water.

If you pick a good day, the crabbing provides a good option. The area is a natural for dungeness crab. You can set out a series of traps, spend the day rockfishing, then return to add a few big dungeness crabs to your bag. What a feast to be had for the wise!

2. MOUTH OF MAD RIVER

Reference: Near Arcata on the Pacific Ocean; map BØ grid b4.

How to get there: From US 101, drive north to the Janes Road exit. Turn west and drive one-half mile north on Janes Road, then turn left on Miller Lane and drive one mile west. Turn north on Mad River Road and drive to the river.

Facilities: A boat ramp is provided. Camping is available at Mad River RV Park in Arcata or at nearby Clam Beach County Park.

Cost: River access is free.

Who to contact: Phone the Arcata Chamber of Commerce at (800) 553-6569 (California only) or (707) 822-3619. For fishing information, phone Time Flies (a tackle shop) at (707) 822-8331.

About mouth of Mad River: When anglers assess the Mad River, they usually think of salmon and steelhead, both of which make runs upstream to the town of Blue Lake in the late fall and winter, respectively. But when you are fishing the mouth of the Mad, don't think salmon and steelhead. In fact, it is illegal to fish within a 200-yard radius of the mouth of the river from January 1 through July 31 in order to protect the sea-run migrants. It is summer and fall, especially in August and September, when the mouth of the Mad comes alive, and not with steelhead, but with perch.

It is one of the best shoreline fishing spots in the summer anywhere on the north coast. The adjacent surf zone near the mouth of the river is also loaded with perch. The perch are good size, clean and healthy, and taste great just battered up home-style and fried.

The tides and your selection of bait can make quite a difference in your prospects. The best hopes are after a minus tide has bottomed out, fishing during the first three hours of the incoming tide. As for bait, sand crabs are by far the preferred entreaty. The key here is to make sure their "mouths" are fully intact; perch seem to know the difference.

It you like the idea of tossing out your line from the beach and catching a nice batch of fish, this is the place.

3.   CLAM BEACH COUNTY PARK

Reference: Near McKinleyville; map BØ grid b4.

How to get there: From Eureka, drive north on US 101 to McKinleyville. Turn west at the sign for Clam Beach. Park at the north end.

Facilities: Clam Beach County Park provides a campground. Supplies are available in McKinleyville.

Cost: Campsite fee is $7 per night.

Who to contact: Phone Clam Beach County Park at (707) 445-7652.

About Clam Beach: This place didn't get its name by accident. During low tides in the winter, the ocean rolls back and unveils some of the North Coast's better clamming grounds, as well as a chance to follow it up by catching a few perch. It is a long, straight beach, and newcomers might feel it is so big that finding a good spot is like looking for a polar bear in the desert. Not so. You can find your polar bear.

The north end of the beach is where to start your search, by far the primary zone for clams, perch and prospects. For clams, you search the tidal flats for the telltale siphon hole. When spotted, you make a quick, knife-like incision into the sand with a narrow clammer's shovel. Do that and you'll be in business. At different times, I've seen people out here with garden shovels, looking like they are digging a garden. They see the bubbling hole, then start in. Before long, the beach starts looking like Craters of the Moon National Monument from the giant holes they have dug. Remember, these clams are crafty and quick. You have to be the same: A quick incision into the sand is what it takes.

The fishing gets far less attention, and for good reason. It's only fair, with perch arriving during the summer and fall. The fall is best, since the slope of the beach is flattest at that point, meaning there is less undertow, and less of a problem getting way out there after a low tide. Use sand crabs for bait, and bring a sand spike for your rod; it can get heavy while you wait for a bite. One sidenote: the campground here gets overlooked by a lot of out-of-towners cruising US 101. Why? Because it is a county park, not a state camp, and thus is not on the MISTIX reservation system. That's worth remembering.

4.   HUMBOLDT BAY

Reference: In Eureka; map BØ grid c2.

How to get there: From Eureka, drive south on US 101 to Field's Landing, or west on Road 255.

Facilities: Camping, lodging, food, bait and tackle are available in Eureka. Boat ramps are provided at the north end of Eureka and in the South Bay at Fields Landing.

Cost: Access is free.

Who to contact: For general information and a free travel packet, phone the Eureka Chamber of Commerce at (707) 442-3738. For fishing information, phone Bucksport Sporting Goods at (707) 442-1832.

About Humboldt Bay: Here is one of the vast bodies of water in Northern California that is constantly overlooked as a viable fishing spot. It is a long, narrow bay, with wetlands bordering the northern flats near Arcata.

The better fishing is in the vicinity of the mouth of the bay, which is quite narrow. That is where big seven-gill sharks hang out, and in the fall, salmon as well. Other good spots include near the PG&E plant and along the southern shoreline, best for perch.

The big surprise are the large sharks. Seven-gill sharks, also called cow sharks, often roam just north of King Salmon. They can reach seven feet and 200 pounds, rarely bigger, but very few people fish for them. These sharks have tremendous strength, and the power of their first run always surprises people who have never before tried to turn one. Wire line, 16/0 hooks, and enough weight to make sure your bait is right on the bottom are standard operating procedure. As scavengers, these sharks are right on the bottom, not the type that cruise around looking for the dangling legs of a surfer. Still, the big ones are dangerous if brought aboard alive. Unless released—and you should release anything you don't plan on eating—the sharks should be dispatched with a bang stick for safety reasons. Then, with the fish still in the water, cut the spinal column at the tail in order to bleed them out to protect the meat. Because of the sharks' unique circulatory system, their meat can be ruined if they are not bled out.

A less specialized sport is perch fishing. Red tail perch are particularly abundant in Humboldt Bay, especially in the winter. Year after year, the area adjacent to the old PG&E plant is quite productive for shorecasters using sand crabs for bait. Another productive area is that along the South Bay. If you are new to the area, Bucksport Sporting Goods can put you on the fish.

In the fall, owners of small boats who fear venturing out into the ocean get the unique opportunity to troll for salmon in the calm waters of Humboldt Bay. You just pretend you are in the ocean, trolling along, but instead of being in always potentially turbulent seas, you are in flat, calm water. Catch rates are not high during this "fall run," but when even the owners of small, aluminum boats have the chance to tie up with a salmon, it's worth it to fathom a chance.

Reference: Near Arcata; map BØ grid c5.

How to get there: From Eureka, drive nine miles north to Highway 299. Turn east on Highway 299 and drive six miles to the town of Blue Lake. From Blue Lake Boulevard, turn right on Greenwood Road. At the four-way stop, bear right; Greenwood Road turns into Hatchery Road. Take Hatchery Road to the Mad River Fish Hatchery. Most fishing is done between the hatchery and the bridge nearby.

Facilities: A picnic area and public restrooms are provided at the hatchery. RV camping is available at Mad River Rapid RV Park in Arcata.

Cost: River access is free.

Who to contact: Phone the Mad River Hatchery at (707) 822-0592. For fishing information, phone Time Flies (a tackle shop) at (707) 822-8331.

Special note: The Mad River is subject to emergency closures starting October 1 if flows are below the prescribed levels needed to protect migrating salmon and steelhead. The Department of Fish and Game has a recorded message that details the status of coastal streams. The number is (707) 442-4502.

About Mad River: This river is one of Northern California's biggest enigmas. Lord, it can tease you and please you with some of the best catch rates for salmon and steelhead. That's if you hit it right during the late fall or winter, respectively. But it can also frustrate you and humiliate you. That's if you hit it wrong during the common heavy rains in this part of the state. In heavy rain seasons, some people call the Mad River the "Mud River," since it has the capability of running brown for weeks on end. Arrive during such a period and you might as well try planting a crop of potatoes in the river as catching a fish. But hit it right . . . and dreams can be answered.

    The best fishing is downstream of the hatchery in the town of Blue Lake, where salmon and steelhead can stack up like cords of winter firewood. It can provide excellent shorefishing. The higher catch rates seem to be for salmon in the late fall, after the first rains of the season have raised the river high enough to attract the fish in from the sea, yet not enough rain has fallen to brown out the prospects. During such a period, shoreliners can catch several salmon in a weekend, and sometimes do even better. It is rarely mediocre here for salmon; either it's very good or very bad.

    As for the steelhead run, which is best from late December into February, anglers often do travel that middle ground. The key, of course, is the water conditions. A drive over the US 101 Bridge and a hard look at the river often provides all the clues you need. Is it green? Yes? Then get out your rod and get to it, because if the river has a little color to it, it is bound to have fish as well. As with all of the smaller coastal streams, timing is everything.

The most important piece of fishing equipment is your telephone. Those who track the week-to-week progress of the Mad River as it phases in and out of prime conditions will discover the Mad offers a chance at do-it-yourself quality; shorefishing for beautiful salmon and steelhead.

---

6. EUREKA COASTAL SALMON

Reference: In Eureka on Humboldt Bay; map BØ grid d2.

How to get there: From Eureka, drive 3.5 miles south on US 101 and take the King Salmon Avenue exit. Drive one-half mile west on King Salmon Avenue to the bay.

Facilities: A PG&E campground is provided. RV camping is available at Johnnie's Marina and RV Park. A boat ramp is available nearby. Supplies can be obtained in Eureka. Party boat charters are also available.

Cost: Party boat fees are in the vicinity of $50 per person.

Who to contact: Phone the Eureka Chamber of Commerce at (707) 442-3738. For fishing information, phone Bucksport Sporting Goods at (707) 442-1832.

Party boat list: Moku, King Salmon Charters, (707) 442-3474; *Celtic,* Celtic Charters, (707) 442-7580; *Kahuna,* Tom's Sportfishing, (707) 445-1630; *Sailfish,* Sailfish Charters, (707) 442-6682.

About Eureka Coastal Salmon: Eureka is one of the oldest towns in the state, established in 1850. In the many years since, logging and fishing have been the two primary industries, and when you talk fishing around these parts, you are talking salmon.

By July, the salmon can be practically jumping in the boat. Even in recent years when populations of Klamath River fish have shown declines, the salmon fishing has remained good along the nearshore Eureka coast. Most of the salmon are kings, usually ranging six to 10 pounds, and with a light sprinkling of bigger fellows in the 15 to 25-pound class. A few pods of silver salmon are often in the mix.

Early-season prospects are often hampered by windy weather and choppy seas, while late-season hopes bring with them the opportunity for the biggest fish of the year, although there are fewer of them. In between, this magic time of July and August is when anglers will come from near and far to chase the roaming coastal schools of wild fish.

The prime fishing zone is almost always between the mouth of the Eel River (just south of Humboldt Bay) and the mouth of the Mad River (just north of Humboldt Bay). From the Bay, the skippers will head straight "out front," or "out the jaws" and troll in the vicinity of this zone. Usually it is just offshore to just five or six miles out. In any case, it is within reach of private boats in the 18 to 24-foot class, as well as the larger charters.

In the fall, or after the quota of sport-caught salmon has been reached, many anglers switch over to deep sea fishing for rockfish. The average size of rockfish and lingcod is quite large, but the trip to the best fishing grounds is quite a long one to offshore Cape Mendocino. No matter. The sea is its calmest in the fall, and on many days, the trip can turn into a celebration of Poseidon's gifts.

7.   ELK RIVER

Reference: Near Eureka; map BØ grid d3.

How to get there: From US 101 at Eureka, drive south to the junction of US 101 and Elk River Road. Take that exit and head west toward the ocean.

Facilities: No facilities are provided, but all supplies are available in nearby Eureka.

Cost: River access is free.

Who to contact: Phone the Bureau of Land Management at (707) 462-3873, or Bucksport Sporting Goods in Eureka at (707) 442-1832.

About Elk River: Elk River is an obscure, meandering stream that provides an intimate opportunity for steelhead. Fishing is legal from the US 101 bridge on downstream, but virtually all the fish are caught in a 100-yard stretch of river below the railroad trestle bridge. Like so many of the small coastal streams that provide steelhead fishing, anglers are a prisoner of the calendar and the clock. You can visit here most days, including during the steelhead season in the winter, and there seems to be no fish in the river. That is because there aren't. They come in spurts, pushing into the river mouth during high water and high tides, then holing up for a while in the stretch of water below the railroad trestle to get acclimated to freshwater and water temperatures. That is when anglers have a chance to score here. So timing is absolutely critical.

8.   VAN DUZEN RIVER

Reference: Near Eureka; map BØ grid f3.

How to get there: From Eureka, drive 16 miles south on US 101. At the junction of US 101 and Highway 36, drive east on Highway 36. River access is available along the highway.

Facilities: Van Duzen County Park provides a campground east of Carlotta. Supplies are available there also.

Cost: Campsite fee is $7 per night.

Who to contact: Phone the Bureau of Land Management at (707) 462-3873, or phone Bucksport Sporting Goods at (707) 442-1832.

Special note: The Van Duzen River is subject to emergency closures starting October 1 if flows are below the prescribed levels needed to protect migrating salmon and steelhead. The Department of Fish and Game has a recorded message that details the status of coastal streams. The number is (707) 442-4502.

About Van Duzen River: A lot of out-of-towners miss out on the ol' Van Duzen, but not the locals. And even though they don't like to talk about it much—they don't want the word to leak out—this river can provide short periods of outstanding fishing. Of course, timing is everything.

If you know nothing of this stream, the key to remember is that it is actually a major tributary of the Eel River. That means that every fish that swims up the Van Duzen has first entered through the Eel. So if the Eel is getting its share of fish, the Van Duzen is likely getting them as well, even though it may not be publicized in any way. After all, folks can be tight-lipped around here.

The best of it starts in mid-October, when salmon enter the Eel, head upstream past Fernbridge, and bang, often stop right at the mouth of the Van Duzen. This provides a once-a-year chance to catch a big salmon from shore here. You won't be alone, either. Usually there are at least 10 rods at this spot, and they wouldn't be there if every one of them didn't think he was about to catch a big salmon. It can last for several weeks, with most of the salmon in the 10-pound class, a few to 15 pounds and bigger. As fall moves into winter, and Indian summer gives way to rains, the Van Duzen will have drastic changes in its water levels. That makes it a pesky water to track, but it is the rise in water levels that attracts the steelhead upstream. If the water is green enough and moving slowly enough to fish, it provides a good, lesser-fished option to nearby Eel, which gets hit quite hard by steelheaders. Before heading out here, I suggest you talk to Greg Rice at Bucksport Sporting Goods in Eureka, who not only fishes this river and has had some spectacular days on it, but is willing to share his timely secrets.

---

9. MATTOLE RIVER

Reference: Near Eureka; map BØ grid g1.

How to get there: On US 101, drive to the South Fork Road turnoff (just north of Weott) and head west on the sometimes winding road (it turns to gravel) to Honeydew, then continue west on Mattole Road to Petrolia. The road parallels the river, with the best public access closest to the mouth of the river. Fishing is permitted from the mouth of the river to the county road bridge at Petrolia.

Facilities: A.W. Way County Park provides a campground south of Petrolia.

Cost: Campsite fee is $7 per night.

Who to contact: To update river and fishing conditions, phone the Honeydew Store at (707) 629-3310. For camping or information about the adjacent lands, phone the Bureau of Land Management at (707) 462-3873.

Special note: The Mattole River is subject to emergency closures starting October 1 if flows are below the prescribed levels needed to protect migrating salmon and steelhead. The Department of Fish and Game has a recorded message that details the status of coastal streams. The number is (707) 442-4502.

About Mattole River: The Honeydew Valley is one of Northern California's little paradises that gets missed by most everybody. Nobody gets here by accident. It is out of the way, it can rain as much as anywhere in the Lower 48, and private land borders a lot of the river, preventing easy access to newcomers.

Ah, but then there is the Mattole River, which cuts a charmed path down the center of the valley. It is a beautiful stream that handles a lot of water—it can rain an inch an hour here during winter squalls—and that is the magic stuff that makes for big steelhead. They usually start entering the river in good numbers in late December, but the better fishing here is often much later in the season, often in early March. With the county campground near the mouth, this river can be an ideal winter camping/fishing destination, providing you have a rain-proof tent and bring plenty of dry clothes.

The steelhead on the Mattole are beautiful, bright fish, fresh from the ocean and full of fight. They aren't midgets either, but often range eight to 14 pounds, with a few bigger and smaller. One of my pals, Frank the Fishfinder, hits this river every year during early spring and has had some fantastic days, catching and releasing many steelhead.

Two problems confront anglers here, however. One is the rain. It downright pours. All the locals wear rubber boots throughout the winter as a matter of course. Because it can come fast and hard, the fishability of the river can often be questionable. So before heading out, a phone call to the Honeydew Store to get the latest river conditions is absolutely mandatory. Secondly, many of the prime spots for shoreliners are off limits because reaching them requires crossing over private land. What to do? Again, stop in at the Honeydew Store and talk to Bob Fuel, a hell of a guy who will keep you out of trouble by detailing the best public accessible spots.

Fishing is permitted from the mouth of the river to the county road bridge at Petrolia. For a river that handles such a large volume of water, the one disappointment is the relatively low numbers of salmon. They just aren't there. A local conservation effort is making a great push to enhance the Mattole's salmon populations, however, and it is just what is needed to complete the picture of this fine river.

---

10.   EEL RIVER

Reference: Near Eureka; map BØ grid g3.

How to get there: From Eureka, drive south on US 101. The river parallels the highway, and access is available off many spur roads, as well as through several small towns along the river such as Fortuna, Rio Dell, Shively and Holmes.

Facilities: Campgrounds are provided along the river. A good one is Stafford RV Park, near Scotia.

Cost: River access is free.

Who to contact: Phone Bucksport Sporting Goods in Eureka at (707) 442-1832; Brown's Sporting Goods in Garberville at (707) 923-2533; the Bureau of Land Management at (707) 462-3873.

Special note: The Eel River is subject to emergency closures starting October 1 if flows are below the prescribed levels needed to protect migrating salmon and steelhead. The Department of Fish and Game has a recorded message that details the status of coastal streams. The number is (707) 442-4502.

About Eel River: The Eel runs through some of the West's most easily accessible beautiful country. US 101 runs right alongside the river, bordered by redwoods, firs and other conifers. In some years, the scenery is even matched by the fishing, both for salmon and steelhead.

Tight restrictions on salmon catches in the Pacific Ocean have resulted in higher runs of fish on the Eel. In October, prior to heavy rains, the salmon will enter the Eel during high tides and start stacking up in the river between Fernbridge and Fortuna. As the rains come, the salmon will be sprung, heading upstream, which in the case of this river, is actually south. Since the highway follows along much of the main stem of the Eel, there are many access roads that provide an easy reach to good spots.

For salmon, always search out the deeper holes with slow-moving river current. They are perfect for salmon to rest in the course of their upriver journey. At times you can even see the salmon milling about near the stream bottom, providing you have a high enough vantage point. Now get this: The best bait for salmon on this river is a cocktail shrimp topped off with a small white marshmallow. Some guides swear by fresh roe, of course, but even they will try the sweet stuff now and then. The key here is to fish it on the drift, always keeping a close watch on your line. Many times the only indicator that you are getting a strike will be when the steady downstream bow in your line will straighten a bit. That is because a salmon has stopped the drift of your bait. If you wait for a tremendous strike, you are apt to turn into a statue.

Come winter, the rains and the steelhead arrive simultaneously. Because of the combination of past logging damage in watersheds, erosion, silt run-off, and heavy rains, the main Eel can muddy up more quickly than any river in California. If it keeps raining, it can stay muddy for weeks on end. When that happens, the only solution is to head upstream to the South Fork, where water clarity and fishable water is more reliable. During moderate rainy seasons, however, the main Eel will stay "greened up" and provide a tremendous steelhead fishery. In these conditions, many guides with driftboats will put in at the South Fork, then work their way downriver on the main Eel. The lesser the rains, the more apt the main Eel is to provide the best fishing. Eel River steelhead can get big. It is second only to the Smith River in the number of 20-pounders it produces, and the catch rates on the Eel are much, much higher than the Smith. The best opportunity is with a driftboat, either bumping roe or running Hot Shot or Wee Wart plugs downstream of the boat while the guide oars to keep you near motionless in the river. You usually start early and fish late, and in the process, hope to catch two or three bright-run steelies.

A few things to remember. In the summer, there is virtually no fishing at all. The river turns into a trickle, and the "little trout" you might see in the small pools are actually juvenile steelhead that should be left alone. The summer is also when so many out-of-staters clog up the highway around these parts. In the winter, however, it is a completely different scene. The tourists are few, the anglers are excited, and in every store and gas station, a sign could be posted that says: "Fishing is spoken here."

---

11.   MOUTH OF MATTOLE RIVER

Reference: Near Eureka on the Pacific Ocean; map BØ grid hØ.

How to get there: From Eureka, drive 13 miles south on US 101. Take the Ferndale exit and drive nine miles south on Mattole Road to Petrolia. Turn west on Lighthouse Road and travel five miles.

Facilities: A small campground is provided. Supplies can be obtained at Petrolia and in Honeydew.

Cost: River access is free.

Who to contact: Phone the Bureau of Land Management at (707) 462-3873.

About mouth of Mattole River: This stretch of land is known as the "Lost Coast," and it will take only one trip to figure out why. For such a pretty spot, you will be surprised at how few people are out here.

Compared to the rest of California's shore, some 1,200 miles of beachfront, it indeed feels lost.

The little county park campground near the mouth of the Mattole River provides a perfect layover out here in the boondocks. It also provides headquarters for your fishing trip, either for salmon or steelhead in fall and winter, respectively (see section on Mattole River), or for perch in the summer and early fall.

The mouth of the Mattole, like all the small coastal streams, is closed to fishing in the winter, spring and early summer in order to protect migrating steelhead.

But the area near the mouth attracts good numbers of perch, even when the mouth of the river is closed by the come-and-go sand bar. This is not complex fishing. You get your rod, your bait, and your bucket, cast out into the ocean, then wait for a perch to come around. Because this area gets so little fishing pressure, the wait is often not a long one. But, but, but . . . there is a catch. All saltwater species are tidal oriented. So are perch at the mouth of the Mattole. Mediocre tides, that is, tides with little variation between the high and the low, don't do much to whet the appetite of perch. So get a tide book, and select the lowest of the two low tides in a day, then time it so you are out fishing after it bottoms out and the incoming tide has started. Now you are in business.

In the meantime, you can explore this wonderful area. The Honeydew Valley to the east, Kings Mountain Range to the south, and the miles and miles of untouched ocean frontage all make for good fortune hunts.

---

12.   SOUTH FORK EEL RIVER

Reference: Near Garberville; map BØ grid h4.

How to get there: US 101 parallels much of the South Fork Eel, starting in Leggett to the south and running downstream (north) past Benbow, Garberville, Miranda, Myers Flat on to its confluence with the main stem of the Eel.

Facilities: Several campgrounds are provided along the river. The most famous is Richardson Grove State Park, located between Cooks Valley and Benbow. Tackle and supplies are available in Garberville at Brown's Sporting Goods.

Cost: River access is free.

Who to contact: For information, phone Brown's Sporting Goods at (707) 923-2533.

Special note: The South Fork Eel River is subject to emergency closures starting October 1 if flows are below the prescribed levels needed to protect migrating salmon and steelhead. The Department of Fish and

Game has a recorded message that details the status of coastal streams. The number is (707) 442-4502.

About South Fork Eel: Wanted: Big steelhead, a stream that can be fished effectively from shore, reliable reports on river conditions, and good choices for camping/lodging.

On the South Fork Eel, you get all that. The catch? The weather. It is always a chancy proposition here, with heavy rains turning the emerald-green flows of the South Fork Eel quickly to chocolate brown. When that happens, it can take several days of no rain before it clears enough to become fishable again—and by that time, it is bound to rain again. After all, that's why the trees are so tall up here. So what to do?

This is what: Get to know this river in its upstream (southerly) portions, which clear most quickly and also offer the better shorefishing areas. This is particularly true around Benbow, Cooks Valley, Piercy, and even as far upstream as Smithe Redwoods and sometimes even Leggett. There are many obvious areas at these places that are prime for shoreliners, with steelhead in the six to 15-pound class both the challenge and the reward. River conditions are critical here. The higher the clarity, the farther downriver (north) you will fish; either that, or you will be forced to switch over to lighter, less-visible line. Conversely, the lower the water clarity, the farther upstream (south) you must fish. It's that simple, and this is one place where you can get a reliable report on fishing conditions. Just call Darrin or Darrell Brown at Brown's in Garberville, and they will get you up to speed. I've been calling them for many years prior to my trips to the South Fork Eel.

Another bonus is the many choices for camping and lodging. Quality camps are available at Richardson Grove State Park, Standish-Hickey State Recreation Area, several privately-run parks, and overnight hotels in Garberville.

Virtually all of the shore-caught steelhead are taken on roe, fished with care and persistence in pockets at the tail ends of runs. A few guides specialize in the South Fork, and one who has quite high success, Jack Ellis of Santa Rosa, prefers putting in high upriver, near Leggett and also at Smithe Redwoods. Jack is quite a guy, and I credit him for being the first to discover the use of Wee Warts on the Eel.

One frustrating element about the South Fork Eel is that it can be difficult to make long-range plans that will stick. Because of the frequent rains, you need flexibility. If you expect the fish to fit into your hardened schedule, you stand the chance of getting the big zilch. But if you become flexible to the fish's schedule, well, then you are on your way to a hell of a trip on the South Fork Eel.

13.   SHELTER COVE

Reference: South of Eureka; map BØ grid j2.

How to get there: From Eureka, drive approximately 62 miles south on
US 101 to the town of Garberville. Take the Shelter Cove-Redwood
Road exit and drive 2.5 miles west on Redwood Road to Briceland-
Shelter Cove Road. Turn west and drive 24 miles, following the
truck/RV route signs. Turn south on Upper Pacific Drive and travel
one-half mile. A boat ramp is located near the campground.

Facilities: A campground is provided. A boat ramp, boat rentals, gas, and
supplies are also available.

Cost: Access is free.

Who to contact: Phone Shelter Cove Campground at (707) 986-7474.

About Shelter Cove: Nobody gets to Shelter Cove by accident; it is just
too far out of the way. For the people who keep returning here every
summer for the salmon fishing, that is just the way they like it. Shelter
Cove offers the ideal base camp for the traveling salmon angler with
an ocean-going skiff or cruiser on a trailer. The new boat launch is
outstanding, and the stocks of Klamath-run salmon also seem back on
the upswing.

This is one of the few places where anglers try not to keep too many
secrets. In fact, the opposite is true. Because there are no large party
boat operations chasing the fish every day, it is up to each skipper to
find the salmon. That can be aided a great deal by sharing information,
of course, so instead of having a case of lockjaw, visiting anglers love
rapping about strategies into the night. That is followed by the early
wake-up, then boom on the water and out to sea. Point Delgada
provides a natural shelter for the boat launch, reducing the surge from
offshore seaswells, making launching and loading easier.

For salmon, most all the fishing is done trolling, not mooching.
There are a preponderance of plastic planer-divers to get the bait down,
and not many cannonball sinkers on releases, such as off the Bay Area
coast. The salmon average in the five to eight-pound range, with a light
mix of bigger kings in the 10 to 15-pound class, rarely bigger. A few
schools of silver salmon also migrate through this area every summer,
usually in July.

Another bonus is good inshore rockfishing. Just get over any reef,
drop a jig down to the bottom and you will start catching fish. As long
as you are over rocks, you will be in business.

One note: If you are staying here a few days, always check with
the possession limit on salmon with the Department of Fish and Game.
In the 90s, part of the increased enforcement effort has been busting
vacationers who have coolers full of salmon from a week of limit
fishing.

14.   BENBOW LAKE

Reference: Near Garberville; map BØ grid j5.

How to get there: From Eureka, drive approximately 62 miles south on US 101 to the town of Garberville. Continue south on US 101 for two miles and take the Benbow State Recreation Area exit. The lake is located inside the park.

Facilities: A campground is provided. Tackle and supplies can be obtained in Garberville.

Cost: Fee for day use is $5 per vehicle. Campsite fee is $14; $5 for additional vehicles.

Who to contact: Phone the Benbow Lake State Recreation Area at (707) 923-3238. For fishing information or tackle, phone Brown's Sporting Goods in Garberville at (707) 923-2533.

About Benbow Lake: "Benbow Lake? Where's Benbow Lake? I can't find it anywhere on the map!" That's a typical response for visitors to this area. They can look all the want and only rarely will they find it on a map. That is because Benbow Lake is a seasonal lake, that is, it is actually the Eel River. Usually around Memorial Day Weekend, a temporary dam is placed across the river in Benbow, creating this little lake. It makes a popular spot for sunbathing and non-power boating.

No trout are stocked, lest they get mixed up with the runs of native steelhead. People actually go out and try to catch fish in the lake during the summer. But hey, let's be honest: This is one lousy spot. Why? Because those little "rainbow trout" that people catch now and then are not rainbow trout at all, but juvenile steelhead that are spending their summer in the river, trying to grow up big enough so they can head out to sea in the winter.

Because of this, fishing should not be permitted here in the summer, or at least certainly no take of any of these juvenile steelhead should be allowed. By killing any of these small "rainbow trout," anglers are undermining future runs of steelhead. All it takes is to catch one big sea-run steelhead during the winter and you'd never want to kill a baby again.

MAP B1

13 LISTINGS
PAGES 182-195

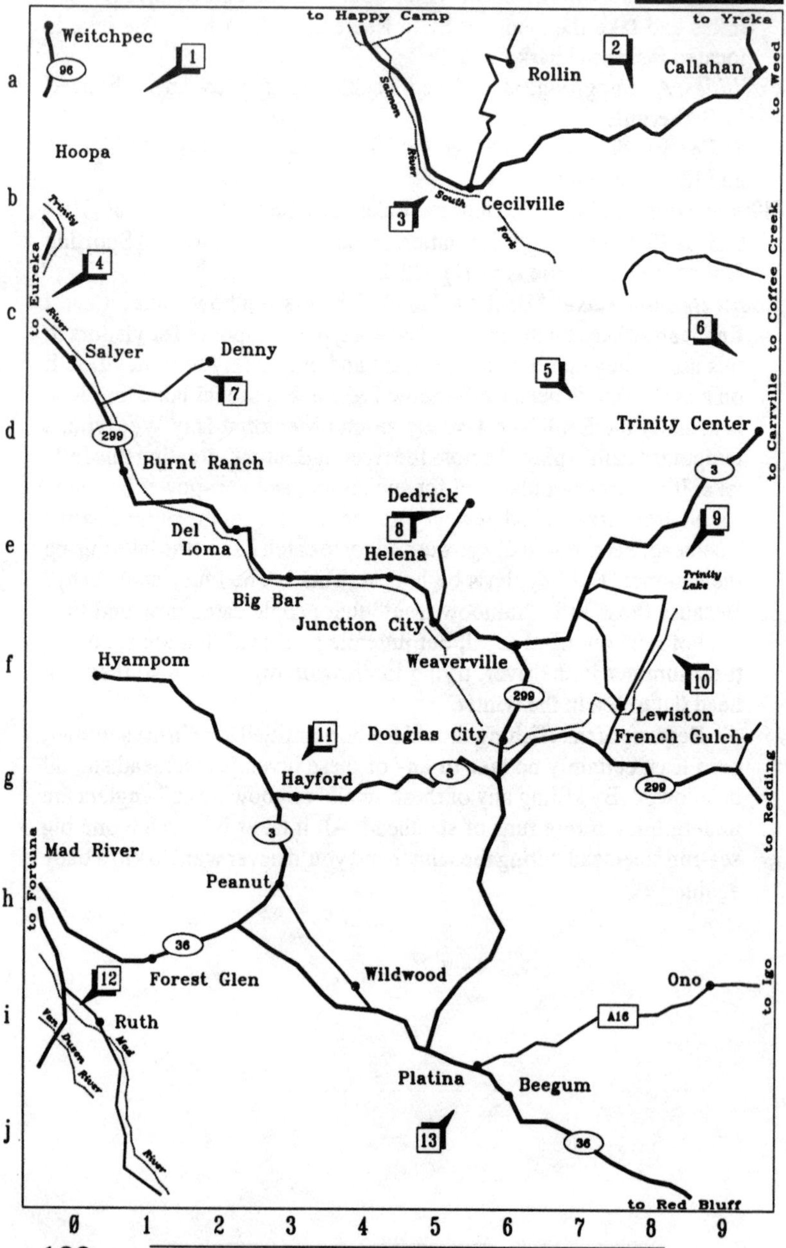

NOR-CAL MAP. see page 120
adjoining maps
NORTH (A1) ..... see page 136
EAST (B2) .... see page 196
SOUTH (C1) .... see page 256
WEST (BØ) .... see page 166

to Happy Camp
to Yreka

Weitchpec
96
1

Rollin
Callahan
2

to Weed

a

Hoopa

Trinity River

4

to Eureka

b

3
South Fork
Cecilville

to Coffee Creek

c

River
Salyer
Denny

6

5

7

Trinity Center

to Carrville

d

299
Burnt Ranch

3

Dedrick

e

Del Loma
8
Helena

9

Trinity Lake

Big Bar
Junction City

f

Hyampom

Weaverville

299

10

Lewiston
French Gulch

to Redding

g

11
Douglas City

Hayford

3

299

Mad River

3

h

Peanut

36

Wildwood

Ono

to Fortuna

12
Forest Glen

A16

i

Ruth

to Igo

Van Duzen River
Mad River

Platina
Beegum

j

13

36

to Red Bluff

Ø   1   2   3   4   5   6   7   8   9

1. SIX RIVERS NATIONAL FOREST

Reference: Northeast of Eureka; map B1 grid a1.

How to get there: Access is available off roads that junction with Highway 96 to the east.

Facilities: No facilities are available.

Cost: Access is free.

Who to contact: Write to Six Rivers National Forest at 500 5th Street, Eureka, CA 95501, or phone (707) 442-1721. For a detailed map showing hiking trails, send $2 to Office of Information, 630 Sansome Street, San Francisco, CA 94111.

About Six Rivers National Forest: This section of national forest is not loaded with lakes, but for that reason alone, it gets relatively low pressure from hike-in anglers.

The best prospect is Mill Creek Lake, located east of Hoopa and near North Trinity Mountain. It is stocked by airplane with 5,000 small rainbow trout each spring.

Six Rivers Forest is known for its myriad of small streams, all of which eventually feed into some of California's wildest rivers. A small creek seems to flow through the wedge at the bottom of almost every canyon. They provide the best qualities that makes this area popular for a handful of backpackers. But trout fishing? Pretty slim pickings.

For more information on this area, see Six Rivers National Forest listing on page 138.

2. RUSSIAN WILDERNESS

Reference: Near Klamath National Forest northwest of Weaverville; map B1 grid a7.

How to get there: From Interstate 5 at Yreka, take the Fort Jones-Highway 3 exit and drive approximately 45 miles west on Highway 3 to the town of Callahan. Turn right (south) on Cecilville-Callahan Road and continue driving southwest. On the northwest side of the road are Forest Service roads that lead to trailheads.

Facilities: No facilities are available.

Cost: Access is free.

Who to contact: Write to the Klamath National Forest Headquarters at 1215 Main Street, Yreka, CA 96097, or phone (916) 842-6131. For a detailed map showing hiking trails, send $2 to Office of Information, U.S. Forest Service, 630 Sansome Street, San Francisco, CA 94111.

About Russian Wilderness: It takes the skills of a mountaineer to reach many of the little lakes in the Russian Wilderness. Most of them are off-trail and access can be difficult, but the rewards are camps along small lakes with no one else around.

Because of that, you should also bring along the ethics of a mountaineer: Non-impact camping skills should be practiced to keep this small parcel of wildland as pristine as possible. The main access is via the Pacific Crest Trail, and from there, the freelance hiker heads off trail.

In this section of wilderness, several waters provide decent fishing for trout: Big Duck Lake, Little Duck Lake, Eaton Lake, High Lake, Bingham Lake, Jackson Lake, Russian Lake, Paynes Lake, South Russian Creek.

If you want a place where you just drive in, or where there is a nice, smooth trail to the lake or stream, well, head elsewhere. This here is booger country. For more information on this area, see Russian Wilderness listing on page 144.

---

3. SOUTH FORK SALMON RIVER

Reference: In Klamath National Forest; map B1 grid b4.

How to get there: From Interstate 5 at Yreka, take the Fort Jones-Highway 3 exit and drive approximately 45 miles west on Highway 3 to the town of Callahan. Turn right (south) on Cecilville-Callahan Road and continue southwest toward Cecilville. Excellent access is available off the road.

Facilities: Several campgrounds are provided on Cecilville-Callahan Road. A good one is Trail Creek campground.

Cost: River access is free.

Who to contact: Phone the Klamath National Forest Headquarters at (916) 842-6131.

About South Fork Salmon River: The South Fork Salmon can seem to have magic about it. The stream runs through the bottom of a deep canyon, the shade keeps the water and weather cold in fall and winter, and it is the most clear and pure of all the tributaries to the Klamath.

In turn, the steelhead that return here seem to be bigger, brighter and stronger than their Klamath counterparts. Difficult to catch? To be sure. But if you do tie into one, it will be one of the memorable moments in your life.

The reason is because the South Fork Salmon is a relatively small stream for steelhead. For the attuned angler, it creates a near religious experience. In the late fall-early winter, the river is fly-fishable, and it makes for a serious test of skill for know-hows. The rewards are steelhead to 6 pounds, sometimes a bit bigger, the kind that can bend a fly rod so it looks like a croquet hoop.

The best prospects on the South Fork are well downstream of Cecilville. River access is quite easy, with a gravel road running parallel to the stream. There are turnouts at the best fishing spots.

A few sidelights: Lots of bears are in the area, few people, and in the summer, the road gets some logging truck traffic. A few Forest Service camps provide a choice of base camps, and usually always have space, even on three-day weekends.

---

4. TRINITY RIVER

Reference: In Shasta-Trinity National Forest; map B1 grid cØ.

How to get there: To access the uppermost part of the river, drive north through the town of Lewiston on Trinity Dam Boulevard until you reach the bridge that crosses the river. Cross the bridge and turn left on Rush Creek Road. Direct access is available. To reach lower stretches of the river, drive west on Highway 299 to the town of Douglas City. Turn left (west) and follow Steiner Flat Road. Direct access is available off the road. Access is also available off several well-signed gravel roads and trails off Highway 299 west of Junction City. The stretch between Burnt Ranch and Hawkins Bar may be restricted; check current fishing regulations.

Facilities: Several campgrounds are available along Highway 299. Two good ones are Gray's Falls and Burnt Ranch. Supplies can be obtained in Lewiston.

Cost: River access is free.

Who to contact: Phone Brady's Sportshop in Weaverville at (916) 623-3121, Shasta-Trinity National Forest District Office at (916) 623-6106, Trinity River Lodge in Lewiston at (916) 778-3791, or guide Herb Burton at (916) 623-6757.

About Trinity River: Nature's artwork can seem perfect on the Trinity River. The stream runs clear and blue, tumbles around boulders and into deep holes, all framed by a high, tree-lined canyon. It makes a beautiful setting for shoreliners chasing steelhead.

The Trinity is the best steelhead river in California for shoreliners. Highway 299, a yellow-striped two-laner, runs right alongside with turnouts set perfectly above many of the prime fishing spots.

The best are just below the Lewiston Bridge, in the vicinity of Steel Bridge located midway between Lewiston and Douglas City, Steiner Flat (hike-in access) located below Douglas City, the mouth of Canyon Creek at Junction City, the confluence with the North Fork Trinity, and Hell Hole upstream of Big Bar. In addition, don't overlook Burnt Ranch Falls and Grey's Falls; although they are located far downstream, they can be two of the best spots in the entire river system, especially in the spring. By shore, you should approach the bank like a burglar sneaking through an unlocked window. Most fishing spots are identified as slicks, riffles with a defined edge, or pools above and below rapids. You should "quarter" your casts, which means casting at a 45-degree angle above the prime holding area, then "walking" the bait across the bottom downstream.

The Trinity provides some of the best flyfishing for steelhead in the state. That is because the river is not a wide stream, making it possible to reach the runs and pockets without difficult casts. The best patterns are the No. 10 Silver Hilton, Brindle Bug and pink Glo Bug.

A few years ago, I tested a fly tied by Dale Lackey that he called an "Assassin." It looked something like a black woolly worm that somebody had stepped on. Regardless of its appearance, it got destroyed by fish attacks on the Trinity.

One key element that really bodes well for the future is increased water releases from Trinity Dam, courtesy of the Bureau of Reclamation. They got spooked by the threat of a lawsuit from the Hoopa Indians, who were ready to prove in court that the Trinity had been devastated by low flows delivered by the Bureau. Well, more water in the 90s will equal more fish. It's that simple.

The steelhead start arriving in the fall and continue to arrive and move through the river all the way to spring, one of the longest runs anywhere. If you like to sleep in, this is the place to go. In winter, mid-day is the most productive period. The reason is that the river gets relatively small amounts of sunlight, and in combination with the cold temperatures, this makes the water frigid and the steelhead reluctant. When it warms up a degree or two while the sun is on it, the fish can really come to life.

It is times like these you never forget. After catching a steelhead here once, I remember just sitting on a rock and looking at my surroundings. The clouds were drifting through the trees, giving an ethereal feel to the area. I scanned the high mountain ridge, deep canyons and puffy cumulonimbus clouds sitting on the tree tops. It was the kind of scene you never forget.

---

5.   SALMON-TRINITY ALPS AREA

Reference: Northwest of Redding; map B1 grid c7.

How to get there: Trailheads leading into the primitive area can be found off Highway 3 to the west above Trinity Lake, and to the southwest of Callahan.

Facilities: No facilities are available.

Cost: Access is free.

Who to contact: Write to the Shasta-Trinity National Forest at 2400 Washington Avenue, Redding, CA 96001, or phone (916) 246-5222. For a map showing hiking trails, send $2 to Office of Information, U.S. Forest Service, 630 Sansome Street, San Francisco, CA 94111.

About Trinity Alps: Either from a mountain peak or from an airplane, the Trinity Alps look something like the high mountain backbone of Switzerland. For those who have hiked the southern Sierra, the Trinities look like they are 13,000 to 14,000 feet high, with conical peaks poking holes into the sky.

Not so, and that's the key to the trout fishing here. The elevation of most of the lakes and adjoining peaks range from 6,000 to 8,000 feet. Because of that, there is more than granite, ice and water, such as in the southern Sierra. There is more soil, more trees, more terrestrial activity. That adds up to more insect food and a longer growing season for the trout. The final result is some of the largest mountain-bred trout in California. Instead of the little seven-inchers you get in the high Sierra, the Trinity Alps offer trout topping out in the 14-inch class, rarely even to 17 or 18 inches. At Little South Fork Lake, which requires an excruciating off-trail grunt to reach, I had a trout run 40 feet on me—the only time in my life I've had a mountain trout do that.

I have visited most of the wilderness areas in California, and the backcountry lakes of the Trinity Alps offer the finest wilderness fishing—quality, quantity and scenic beauty—that I have experienced in the state.

The key? Pick a destination that is difficult to reach. The easier the access, the poorer the fishing. The reason is because camper/anglers tend to throw back the small ones, but keep the big ones. That results in a lake with a lot of small fish, and those little guys have already been taught a smart lesson by previous anglers.

The following hike-to lakes are the better spots in this part of the country (see adjoining map grid for more): Adams Lake, Holland Lake, Log Lake, Marshy Lakes, McDonald Lake, Snow Slide Pond, Bear Lakes, Tangle Blue Lake, Boulder Lakes, Long Gulch Lake, Stoddard Lake, Emerald Lake, Fox Creek Lake, Granite Lake, Little South Fork Lake, Grizzly Lake, Sapphire Lake, Papoose Lake, Smith Lake, Summit Lake, Canyon Creek Lakes.

They usually become accessible sometime in early summer, usually around mid-June, sometimes even earlier. The best fishing is usually in early July, when the water has had a chance to warm up a bit. That gets insects hatching, and in turn, gets the trout on the feed.

The Trinity Alps provide the opportunity for some tremendous day trips, hiking off to mountain tops or ridgelines for dramatic views. The most dramatic peak is Thompson, which juts out above the Sawtooth Ridge. The world is simple up here, a place where old glaciers have carved out a chunk of the world like no other.

6.   COFFEE CREEK

Reference: In Klamath National Forest; map B1 grid c9.

How to get there: From Trinity Center at the north end of Trinity Lake, drive nine miles north on Highway 3 to Coffee Creek Road. Turn west. Access is available along Coffee Creek Road.

Facilities: A campground is provided on Coffee Creek Road, about 21 miles west of the turnoff. No piped water is available, so bring your own. Supplies are available at Trinity Center.

Cost: Access is free.

Who to contact: Phone the Klamath National Forest Headquarters at (916) 842-6131.

About Coffee Creek: Coffee Creek should be renamed "Rock Creek." Why? Because there are mountains of rocks along parts of this river. Small rocks, big rocks, here a rock, there a rock, everywhere a rock. They are the result of past goldmining in the area, a symbol of an era long gone.

    The fish aren't long gone—they just aren't long. Most of the trout here are little buggers, true dinkers, and the number of areas with quality habitat for them is quite few.

    The best stretch of river is fairly close to where Coffee Creek enters the upper Trinity, but there are some "problems" with landowners here. Translation: They get mighty upset if you wander on their property while walking up the river. Farther upstream, where the river is bordered by National Forest, much of it is wide, shallow, and, of course, rocky.

7.   NEW RIVER

Reference: Near Salyer in Shasta-Trinity National Forest; map B1 grid d2.

How to get there: From US 101 at Eureka, drive five miles north to Highway 299 (a narrow, twisty two-laner). Turn right and travel about 50 miles east to County Road 402 (Denny Road), four miles east of the town of Salyer. If approaching from Interstate 5, take the Highway 299 west exit at Redding and drive approximately 90 miles west on Highway 299 to County Road 402 (Denny Road). Turn north and cross the river, then drive northeast on a winding road. Excellent roadside access is available.

Facilities: A campground is provided in Denny. Supplies are available in Salyer.

Cost: River access is free.

Who to contact: Phone the Shasta-Trinity National Forest District Office at (916) 623-6106. For a map of the area, send $2 to Office of Information, 630 Sansome Street, San Francisco, CA 94111.

About New River: The New River is an oft-forgotten tributary of the Trinity River. The reason it is oft-forgotten is because it feeds into the Trinity on the opposite side of the river from Highway 299. Yet it is here where a small, winding road traces the river up into the Salmon Mountains.

You can get access either off the road, or farther upstream where the road feeds into a trailhead that provides hike-in access to portions of the river that are rarely fished.

For a drive-to area so near a highway, it is quite remote. The trout are natives, with special regulations in effect; two-trout limit, 14-inch maximum.

---

8. CANYON CREEK

Reference: Near Junction City in Shasta-Trinity National Forest; map B1 grid e5.

How to get there: From Interstate 5 at Redding, take the Highway 299 west exit and travel approximately 55 miles west to Junction City. Turn north on Canyon Creek Road. Creek access is available off several roads and trails that junction with Canyon Creek Road.

Facilities: A campground, called Ripstein, is available on Canyon Creek Road. No piped water is provided, so bring your own. Supplies are available in Junction City.

Cost: Access is free.

Who to contact: Phone the Shasta-Trinity National Forest District Office at (916) 623-6106. For a map, send $2 to Office of Information, 630 Sansome Street, San Francisco, CA 94111.

About Canyon Creek: This is a pretty water, one that may not provide a chance at large trout, but that does offer scenic beauty and an opportunity for wild rainbow trout.

Sure they're little. Some rivers just seem to grow little fish. Fish and Game is attempting to increase the size of the fish by enforcing a 14-inch maximum size limit so that when a big one is caught, it will stay in the river rather than end up in a frying pan.

Canyon Creek is a tributary to the Trinity River, entering the Trinity near Junction City. The area has a lot of history, with a lot of gold mining having taken place on the stream's upper reaches.

Reference: Near Weaverville in Shasta-Trinity National Forest; map B1 grid e8.

How to get there: From Interstate 5 at Redding, take the Highway 299 west exit and drive approximately 45 miles to the town of Weaverville. Turn north on Highway 3 (Weaverville-Scott Mountain Road) and continue for 14 miles to the lake. The road will take you directly to a boat ramp; boat ramps are also available farther north off Highway 3 and off Trinity Dam Boulevard as well.

Facilities: Several campgrounds are provided around the lake. Two good ones are Pinewood Cove Campground and Tannery Gulch. Full-service marinas, boat ramps, boat rentals, picnic areas, groceries, bait and tackle are also available.

Cost: Campground fees range from free to $40 per night.

Who to contact: Phone the Shasta-Trinity National Forest District Office at (916) 623-2121. For lodging information, phone Shasta Cascade Wonderland Association at (916) 243-2643.

About Trinity Lake: If only Trinity Lake was a real lake, and not a reservoir, it would be a virtual mountain paradise for fishing, boating and camping. But it is a reservoir, subject to severe drawdowns as water is diverted and sent to the Sacramento River for farming. That means less water is around for Trinity Lake, as well as downstream on the Trinity River for steelhead and salmon. But there is enough water, even in dry years, to provide for one of the best smallmouth bass fisheries in the state, as well as good prospects for largemouth bass and rainbow trout. It is the smallmouth, however, that are the centerpiece.

The state record smallmouth was caught at Trinity, landed by Tim Brady of Weaverville. It weighed nine pounds, one ounce, and in fact, if you want to see the fish, it is mounted and on display at Brady's Sportshop, located on Main Street in Weaverville. It's worth a look. After that, your expedition to the lake will be undertaken with an entire new perspective of what is possible. Just don't wait until summer to take your trip, because the best fishing for smallmouth is when winter makes its transition to spring. Sure, it is cold. In fact, the breeze can really have a bite to it, especially in a fast boat, but that is when the smallmouth come out of hibernation. The fishing for them is best on the upper end of the lake, particularly around the dredger tailings, for anglers fanning the shoreline with casts using grubs or Gitsits.

As spring arrives in May, angler pressure here is still quite low, despite the fact that this is the best time to try for largemouth bass. The arms of the lake on the upper end are the best areas. Because Trinity Lake has almost zero structure, the bottom being practically barren and steeply sloped, the bass tend to be suspended and scattered off points and in the backs of coves. That means that covering a lot of water is critical. My best success here with largemouths has been with white spinnerbaits, casting ahead of the boat as we kept on the move. With 175 miles of shoreline to pick over, there are plenty of spots to sneak up on.

In June, the weather is often still quite cool here. Vacationers forget that this is the mountains, where summer doesn't arrive until July. But if you can pick a day when the wind is down, June is prime time for trout trolling. The better spots are Stuart's Fork and near the corners of the dam. No secrets about it; half of a nightcrawler trailed behind flashers is the way to get the most strikes.

As summer progresses, the weather can get quite hot, putting the fish down 25 to 40 feet. You either go down that deep in the thermocline to get them, or you get skunked. This is particularly frustrating for new arrivals who see all the fish pictures on the walls of tackle shops and resorts, then wonder why they never get a bite.

Trinity is a big lake with full-service marinas. You can rent houseboats, stay in cabins (Cedar Stock Resort), head out and set up a boat-in camp (a good one is located at Captain's Point on the west shore of the Trinity River arm), and have a variety of fish to try for. Even when the water level is down, there is still plenty of lake to explore and fish.

---

10. LEWISTON LAKE

Reference: Near Lewiston in Shasta-Trinity National Forest; map B1 grid f8.

How to get there: From Interstate 5 at Redding, take the Highway 299 west exit and drive approximately 30 miles west. Watch for Trinity Dam Boulevard on the right. Turn north and travel four miles to the town of Lewiston. From Lewiston, drive north on either County Road 105 (Buckeye Creek Road) or Trinity Dam Boulevard to reach the campgrounds and fishing access points. The boat ramp is located off Trinity Dam Boulevard.

Facilities: Several campgrounds are provided. The best is the Mary Smith camp. Lakeview Terrace Resort provides a nice headquarters for folks who don't want to rough it. A boat ramp is also provided. Supplies are available in Lewiston.

Cost: Campground fees range from free to $15 per night.

Who to contact: Phone the Shasta-Trinity National Forest District Office at (916) 623-2121.

About Lewiston Lake: When you first camp at Lewiston Lake, you might rub your eyes a bit to make sure you're on earth and not in heaven.

This is one of the prettiest lakes in California, always full to the brim and ringed by conifers, with the Trinity Alps providing a backdrop.

It provides quality camping (100 campsites), fishing, boating and hiking, yet is often overlooked in the shadow of its nearby big brother, Trinity Lake. Lewiston has 15 miles of shoreline, and best of all, a 10-mph speed limit that keeps the water quiet and calm, ideal for canoes and small aluminum boats.

Enjoy the beauty of the place, because the fishing can fluctuate wildly. One key is the Trinity Dam powerhouse at the head of Lewiston Lake. When the powerhouse is running, it pours feed right down the chute and into the head of the lake—and the trout fishing can be outstanding anywhere from Lakeview Terrace on upstream.

When the powerhouse is running, the best bet is to anchor in the current, then let a nightcrawler flutter near the bottom. When the powerhouse is not running, a better choice is to anchor near where the current flattens out into the lake, and use yellow Power Bait. The trout love the stuff here. Using more traditional trolling methods, such as a half of a nightcrawler trailed behind a set of flashers, you can usually pick up a trout or two, also. Flyfishing specialists should consider this lake, too. Some tules border the western shoreline near Lakeview Terrace, and it is here where anglers should wade out, then fish the evening rise. For those who don't flyfish, using a fly behind a bubble can also entice bites.

A bonus at this lake is that some rare, giant brown trout swim in the depths. Only rarely are they caught, but they are like mountain salmon, that is, measured in pounds, not inches.

---

11.   EWING GULCH RESERVOIR

Reference: Near Hayfork Trinity National Forest; map B1 grid g3.

How to get there: From Interstate 5 at Redding, take the Highway 299 west exit and travel approximately 40 miles west to the junction of Highways 299 and 3 at Douglas City. Turn south on Highway 3 and travel about 20 miles southwest to the town of Hayfork. Turn north on Brady Road and drive one mile, then turn east on Reservoir Road and follow the signs to the reservoir.

Facilities: Picnic tables and bathrooms are available for day use. No overnight camping is permitted; lodging and supplies are available in Hayfork.

Cost: Access is free.

Who to contact: Phone the Hayfork Ranger District Office at (916) 628-5227. For a map of the area, send $2 to Office of Information, 630 Sansome Street, San Francisco, CA 94111.

About Ewing Gulch Reservoir: Bet you never heard of this one. Right? Right.

This water is obscure even to many anglers who pride themselves on knowing the state and what it offers. The reason is because in the summer, the fishing is often rather poor, and nobody has a reason to even discuss the place.

It is a whole different ballgame come spring and fall, however. Around these parts, the winters come cold, the summers hot. That is zilch time. But when the seasonal transition arrives, so do the trout. Some 3,000 rainbow trout stocked in April and November, respectively, and the few anglers around do their best to keep it a secret.

The key is water temperature. That is why I always carry a thermometer (bought from an aquarium shop) with me. The lake is best when the water temperature is in the low to mid-50s. Check it out.

---

12.   RUTH LAKE

Reference: Near Mad River in Six Rivers National Forest; map B1 grid iØ.

How to get there: From Eureka, drive south on US 101 to Fortuna, then turn east on Highway 36 and continue on the long, winding two-laner to the town of Mad River. Turn on Mad River Road and drive six miles southeast to the lake.

Facilities: Two campgrounds are provided: Fir Cove Campground and Bailey Canyon. Boat-in camping is also available. A full-service marina, boat ramps, boat rentals, picnic areas, and a disposal station are also provided. Supplies are available in Mad River.

Cost: Campground fees range from $5-$20 per night.

Who to contact: Phone the Six Rivers National Forest at (707) 442-1721.

About Ruth Lake: Black bass on California's north coast? They are about as rare as Bigfoot in this part of the state, but Ruth Lake provides the exception. The lake provides a decent bass fishery, and trout as well.

For people who like driving fast, Ruth Lake is a difficult lake to reach. Winding Highway 36 demands patience, the route having been picked for horses and carriages, not fast cars. Once you get to Ruth Lake, you will discover that it is a long narrow lake set at 2,800 feet elevation in remote western Trinity County. Shoreline campgrounds are a big plus, especially when the lake is full of water.

Even though the lake is quite narrow, and both sides of the lake don't look all that different, the better fishing is on the west side of the lake. There are two reasons why. One is because the coastal winds come out of the west most of the year, and there is more protection from them on the west side of the lake. The other is that in late afternoon, the three major coves on the west side will get shade earlier than any other part of the lake. The lake is also stocked with trout, but only when the weather is cool. Fish and Game usually plants 10,000 rainbow trout in the spring, then another 5,000 in the fall. They provide an alternative when the bass don't bite.

The lake is open to all boating, and even though Ruth doesn't get a lot of traffic, even one water skier is too many for a basser trying to sneak up on a quiet cove. My suggestion is to cordone off half the lake, separating the skiers from anglers, just as is done at so many lakes in California.

---

13.   YOLLA-BOLLY WILDERNESS

Reference: West of Red Bluff in Shasta-Trinity National Forest; map B1 grid j5.

How to get there: From Interstate 5 at Red Bluff, take the Highway 36 west exit and drive west. Access to trailheads is available off several unimproved Forest Service roads that junction with Highway 36 near the town of Platina.

Facilities: No facilities are available.

Cost: Access is free.

Who to contact: Write to the Klamath National Forest Headquarters at 1215 Main Street, Yreka, CA 96097, or phone (916) 842-6131. For a detailed map showing hiking trails, send $2 to Office of Information, 630 Sansome Street, San Francisco, CA 94111.

About Yolla-Bolly Wilderness: Of the 43 wilderness areas in California, the Yolla-Bollies don't get rated high on the list, but they still have appeal for people in the know.

First, learn how to pronounce it. Yolla is pronounced "Yoe-La" and not "Yah-Lah." Bolly is pronounced "Bow-Lee" and not "Bah-Ley." OK, got it? If you do, and like primitive, rugged (and hot in the summer) country without many people around, this may be your place.

You see, there aren't any of the magnificent mountain peaks like you get in the Trinity, Marble, Russian or Sierra wilderness areas. There aren't a lot of lakes either, for that matter. The appeal is that this is where the headwaters of the Middle Eel River are found, along with other little feeder creeks at the bottoms of the steep ravines and canyon draws.

A relative handful of hike-to lakes provide decent fishing in the northern Yolla Bollies. They are Long Lake, Square Lake, Yolla-Bolly Lake, and Black Rock Lake. Each spring they are stocked by air by the Department of Fish and Game. It ain't love, but it ain't bad.

The appeal here, rather, is the primitive feel to the place. It can bring out gut-level feelings, and after a while the layers of civilization will start peeling off as if you are taking a good, long shower after getting caught in a dust storm.

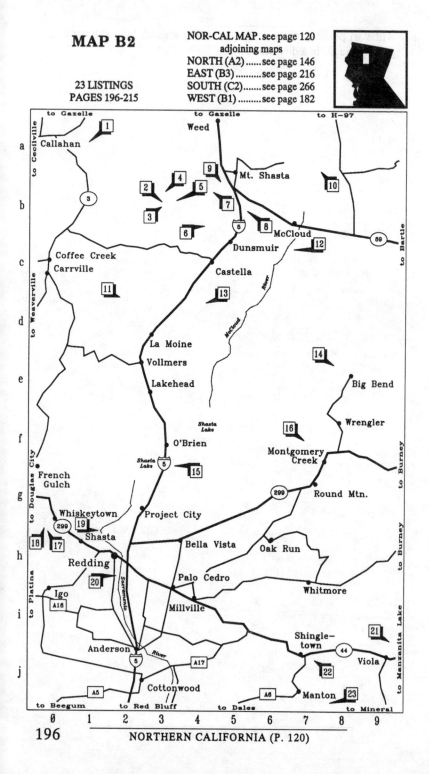

NOR-CAL MAP. see page 120
adjoining maps
NORTH (A2) ...... see page 146
EAST (B3) .... see page 216
SOUTH (C2) .... see page 266
WEST (B1) .... see page 182

to Gazelle
to Gazelle
to H-97

Callahan
Weed
to Cecilville

a

Mt. Shasta

b

Coffee Creek
Carrville
McCloud
Dunsmuir

c

Castella

River

d

La Moine
Vollmers
Lakehead

McCloud

Big Bend

e

Shasta
Lake
Wrengler

O'Brien
Montgomery
Creek

f

Shasta
Lake

to Burney

French
Gulch
Round Mtn.

g

Whiskeytown
Project City

Shasta
Bella Vista
Oak Run

Redding
Whitmore

h

Palo Cedro

to Burney

Igo
Millville

i

Shingle-
town
Viola

Anderson
River

to Manzanita Lake

j

Cottonwood
Manton

to Beegum
to Red Bluff
to Dales
to Mineral

to Platina
to Douglas City
to Weaverville

0 1 2 3 4 5 6 7 8 9

1.   KANGAROO LAKE

Reference: Near Callahan in Klamath National Forest; map B2 grid a1.

How to get there: From Interstate 5 at Yreka, take the Fort Jones-Highway 3 exit and drive about 45 miles southwest to the town of Callahan. Continue east for about two more miles on Highway 3 to Gazelle-Callahan Road. Turn left (north) and continue for about 15 miles. Look for the sign marking the Kangaroo Lake turnoff, then turn south on Rail Creek Road and continue to the lake. From Interstate 5 north of Weed, take the Gazelle exit, and once in Gazelle, turn west on Gazelle-Callahan Road, continue over the mountain, then turn south on Rail Creek Road and continue to the lake.

Facilities: A small campground is provided. Supplies are available in Callahan. The facilities are wheelchair accessible.

Cost: Campsite fee is $6-$8 per night.

Who to contact: Phone the Klamath National Forest Headquarters at (916) 842-6131.

About Kangaroo Lake: This little lake is nestled in the Scott Mountains, a perfect hideaway for campers/anglers who want to get away from it all. The road in is quite pretty, especially below Scott Mountain, where there are pristine, unpeopled valleys.

   The fishing is good, too. It is one of the few lakes in the region that is stocked with both yearlings and fingerlings from Fish and Game, each summer getting 12,000 trout in the foot-long class, and another 8,000 little guys to grow up for future years. A good spot is near the outlet, that is, where Rail Creek pours out toward the valley.

   Not many people know about Kangaroo Lake. But now you do.

---

2.   PICAYUNE LAKE

Reference: Near Mount Shasta; map B2 grid b3.

How to get there: From the town of Mount Shasta, drive 16.5 miles southwest on W.A. Barr Road (off Interstate 5), past Lake Siskiyou to South Fork Road and continue up the mountain, continuing past the Gumboot Lake turnoff (which is on the left). Continue up to the ridge, turn right (the lake will be below you to the left), and continue for another mile, then turn left and drive to the bar-type gate. Park and then hike the last half-mile to the lake.

Facilities: No facilities are available on-site. Camping is available nearby at Gumboot Lake. Supplies can be obtained in Mount Shasta.

Cost: Access is free.

Who to contact: Phone the Shasta-Trinity National Forest District Office at (916) 926-4511.

About Picayune Lake: This is one of the prettiest alpine lakes in the

Trinity-Divide Country, almost always full, lined by firs, pines and cedars, and bordered on the western side by a steep facing. It gets very little traffic because of the gate that blocks the last half-mile of the access road, the fact that most people just don't want to hike, and also because camping is prohibited. The fishing is only fair, however. Trout stocks are extremely rare, and even then, only by private interests and never by the state. That is because the lake is bordered by land owned by the Roseburg Lumber Company, not the U.S. Forest Service, and while public access is permitted, the gate is up to discourage it. Roseburg has built a nice cabin and dock at the lake, but they are strictly off limits to visitors.

---

3. GUMBOOT LAKE

Reference: Near Mount Shasta Shasta-Trinity National Forest; map B2 grid b3.

How to get there: From the town of Mount Shasta, drive 17 miles southwest on W.A. Barr Road (off Interstate 5), past Lake Siskiyou, and follow the signs to Gumboot Lake.

Facilities: A small campground is provided, but no piped water is available, so bring your own. No motorized boats are permitted on the lake.

Cost: Access is free.

Who to contact: Phone the Shasta-Trinity National Forest District Office at (916) 926-4511.

About Gumboot Lake: Little Gumboot has benefitted as much as any lake in the region from Fish and Game's decision to stock larger trout, albeit fewer of them. That is because Gumboot is so small, it doesn't need a lot of trout stocked to provide good fishing—and when you hook 12 and 13-inchers instead of those little Sierra Slim Jims it can get quite exciting.

A lot of folks from the local towns in the area have discovered this and Gumboot has been getting more fishing pressure recently than in past years. Most summer and fall weekends will find as many as a dozen rods on this little lake. The campsites are usually taken as well.

Why? Because for one, Gumboot is quite pretty, bordered by a meadow on the far side, then a steep face, and well-treed on the other. And for two, it provides good trout fishing, ideal from a float tube, canoe, pram or raft (no motors permitted or needed), or from shoreline for anglers using a fly and a bubble. A key here is water temperature. In the summer, when the water temperature is its warmest, you must fish the shaded areas of the lake. But in the fall, when the water temperature is cool, you must fish areas that are getting sun.

Many outstanding side trips are available here. My favorite is to scramble up the mountain behind the lake up to the ridgeline, hit the

Pacific Crest Trail, then turn left and claim the peak that is set just above the lake. It is a great lookout and quite an afternoon adventure as you are waiting for the evening bite to get started.

---

4. TOAD LAKE

Reference: Near Mount Shasta-Trinity National Forest; map B2 grid b3.

How to get there: From the town of Mount Shasta, drive 16.5 miles southwest on W.A. Barr Road (off Interstate 5), past Lake Siskiyou to South Fork Road and continue uphill (along the South Fork Sacramento River). Just past the concrete bridge, turn right (look for the sign) and continue for a short distance, then turn left on Morgan Meadow Road and continue for 10 miles to the parking area. A four-wheel drive vehicle is recommended. The lake is about a quarter-mile away from the parking area. A Forest Service map is also recommended.

Facilities: A small campground is provided, but no piped water is available. Supplies can be obtained in Mount Shasta.

Cost: Access is free.

Who to contact: Phone the Shasta-Trinity National Forest District Office at (916) 926-4511. For a map, send $2 to Office of Information, U.S. Forest Service, 630 Sansome Street, San Francisco, CA 94111.

About Toad Lake: Here is a classic spot that provides just about everything. Everything, that is, except good-size trout.

Because the road in is rough, particularly a terribly bumpy spot about a half-mile from the parking area, a lot of people stay clear of the lake. So that's a plus. It is a pretty lake, set in a rock bowl carved by glacial action, then filled each spring by snowmelt. Another plus.

It is excellent for swimming. Another plus. Hiking? A half-hour hike will take you above the rock bowl and on the Pacific Crest Trail, and another 15 minutes of walking will get you to Porcupine Lake, an absolute pristine setting. A mountain to climb? A three-mile grunt will get you to the top of Mount Eddy, 9,025 feet, the highest mountain in the local range.

Add it up and put it in your mental cash register: Right, quite a place. Ideal for camping, providing you don't mind carrying your gear in on the 10-minute walk to the lake.

If only the trout were bigger . . . if only . . . well, you can dream. It is stocked by air with fingerlings, both brook trout and brown trout, and some people swear that now and then somebody actually catches one that is more than six or seven inches long. However, I have not seen it with my own eyes.

---

5.   SHASTA-TRINITY NATIONAL FOREST

Reference: Near Mount Shasta; map B2 grid b3.

How to get there: Basic access roads are located off of Interstate 5, Highway 89, and Highway 299. There are several good fishing lakes off of roads that junction with W.A. Barr Road (west of Mount Shasta, off the Central Mount Shasta exit on Interstate 5). A Forest Service map is a necessity.

Facilities: Campgrounds are provided throughout the forest; a few primitive campsites are available at higher elevations.

Cost: Access is free.

Who to contact: Write to the Shasta-Trinity National Forest District Office at 2400 Washington Avenue, Redding, CA 96001, or phone (916) 926-4511. For a map, send $2 to Office of Information, U.S. Forest Service, 630 Sansome Street, San Francisco, CA 94111.

About Shasta-Trinity National Forest: This is God's country. It has to be because nobody else is clever enough to have invented it.

What you get are miles of wild land, good access via Forest Service roads, and dozens of lakes accessible from short hikes. Fish and Game keeps the lakes stocked with fingerlings, which have a decent opportunity to reach the pan-size range. It makes for ideal fishing/camping trips for people who don't feel like hiking to the end of the earth.

The country covers a large region, so the first step is to get a Forest Service map, cross-check lake names with the following list, and then start planning a trip.

These hike-in lakes provide the best fishing in this area: Deadfall Lakes, Bull Lake, Mumbo Lake, Grouse Lake, Cliff Lake, Gray Rock Lake, Echo Lake/Seven Lakes Basin, Twin Lakes, Crater Lakes, Bluff Lake, Devil's Lake, Highland Lake, Horseshoe Lake, Lost Lake, Masterson Meadow Lake, Slide Lake, Cabin Meadow Lake, Caldwell Lakes, Little Castle Lake, Dobkins Lake, Heart Lake, Helen Lake, Rock Fence Lake, Scott Lake, Terrace Lake, Timber Lake, West Park Lakes.

Lot of choices, right? Right. The best advice for newcomers is to pick the largest lakes possible, and then hit the smaller lakes in the area for side trip possibilities.

Because many of these lakes require just a half-hour to one-hour hike in, they do attract a lot of weekend attention from local residents. So if you are camping on a multi-day trip, it is a good idea to spend your time here during the week, or pick a destination that requires a little more effort to reach. You see, there is a magic, universal quotient: The harder it is to reach, the fewer the people that will go there. Ultimately, that translates to better fishing.

6. CASTLE LAKE

Reference: Near Mount Shasta-Trinity National Forest; map B2 grid b4.

How to get there: From the town of Mount Shasta, drive ten miles southwest on W.A. Barr Road (off Interstate 5), past Lake Siskiyou. Turn left on Castle Lake Road and continue to the lake.

Facilities: A small campground is provided, but there is no piped water. Supplies are available in Mount Shasta.

Cost: Access is free.

Who to contact: Phone the Shasta-Trinity National Forest District Office at (916) 926-4511.

About Castle Lake: Bring your camera. No, not to take pictures of all the big fish, because there are very few of those. But rather to take pictures from some of California's most scenic lookouts.

The view of Mount Shasta from the road in, just a half-mile below the lake, is absolutely spectacular. More magazine pictures of the magic mountain are taken here than from any other lookout. But . . . even a better photo opportunity is available if you hike in from Castle Lake to little Heart Lake, then take a photo of Shasta with the little lake in the foreground. You might get a photo award for that one; it's just beautiful!

The fishing at Castle Lake is usually just fair to middlin' for rainbow trout stocked by Fish and Game. Shoreliners can have a particularly difficult time. Even though the lake is small, the best success by far comes for anglers with some kind of craft, at least a raft or float tube, in order to cover some of the deeper areas. The reason is because shoreline areas are quite shallow in some parts of the lake, and those restricted to the shore won't reach the fish. If you do stick to the bank, then hike around to the far side, which offers the best shoreline prospects.

The few campsites are sprinkled on the east side of the lake, a do-it-yourself proposition. The lake is easy to reach, with a paved road all the way in. In the winter, it provides one of the few good ice-fishing opportunities in Northern California. But that is not what this lake is remembered for. The views, on the other hand, are unforgettable.

7. SOUTH FORK SACRAMENTO RIVER

Reference: Near Mount Shasta upstream of Lake Siskiyou; map B2 grid b4.

How to get there: From the town of Mount Shasta, drive southwest on W.A. Barr Road (off Interstate 5) past Lake Siskiyou. The river parallels W.A. Barr Road, and direct access is available in most places.

Facilities: Camping is available at Lake Siskiyou, Gumboot Lake, or in Mount Shasta. Supplies are available in Mount Shasta.

Cost: River access is free.

Who to contact: Phone the Shasta-Trinity National Forest District Office at (916) 926-4511.

About South Fork Sacramento River: This river isn't much more than a trickle most of the year, but enough water runs down to keep a small population of trout going. The prime riffle-fed deep pools that hold quality trout are practically non-existent, along with roadside turnouts. Instead you get pocket water, which requires short precise casts, and just a few places along the road with room to park. The best spot, however, is at the confluence of Wagon Creek, where Fish and Game makes rare stocks.

---

8. UPPER SACRAMENTO RIVER ❓

Reference: Near Mount Shasta upstream of Shasta Lake; map B2 grid b5.

How to get there: Direct access is available off Interstate 5 via nearly every exit between the towns of Lakehead and Mount Shasta.

Facilities: Several full-facility campgrounds and RV parks are available along the river and near adjacent towns. A few good ones are Sims Flat and Railroad Park (both near Dunsmuir), and Castle Crags State Park (near Castella). Supplies are available in Mount Shasta, Dunsmuir, Castella, Lakehead, and Redding.

Cost: River access is free.

Who to contact: Phone the Shasta-Trinity National Forest District Offices at (916) 926-4511 Mount Shasta area; or (916) 275-1587 Shasta Lake area; Ted Fay Fly Shop in Dunsmuir at (916) 235-2969.

About Upper Sacramento River: Here is America's mystery spot. What will happen to the Upper Sac in the future? Will it be flooded with hatchery trout? Will it turn into a wild, self-sustaining habitat with large, wild trout? Will it rival the streams of Yellowstone as a top quality, easily-accessed water?

Those questions are now posed since the worst inland toxic spill in California occurred here in the summer of 1991. A Southern Pacific train derailed just upstream of Dunsmuir and poured 13,500 gallons of an all-purpose plant killer into the river. Within a few days, every organism, from algae to insects to trout, had been murdered.

Regulations are apt to change year to year on this river in the 90s. Always check with the Redding Fish and Game office for an update by calling (916) 225-2300 prior to scheduling a trip. This is one stream to keep an eye on as the aquatic food chain is re-established and trout again start getting a foothold. The habitat available here is as good as any stream in California. How Fish and Game decides to fill that habitat in the 90s will be one of the most closely-watched management decisions in the state.

The Upper Sacramento is a beautiful piece of nature's artistry. Even if the fish take a while to get re-established, it is worth it just to sit on a rock and watch the water go by.

9. LAKE SISKIYOU

Reference: Near Mount Shasta in Shasta-Trinity National Forest; map B2 grid b5.

How to get there: From Interstate 5 at the town of Mount Shasta, take the Central Mount Shasta exit, then turn left at the stop sign, heading west over the freeway and drive one mile to another stop sign, which is W.A. Barr Road. Turn left and drive for a mile, then bear right on North Shore Road and continue to the far side of the lake, turning right at the sign marking Lake Siskiyou Marina and Campground.

Facilities: North shore access is limited to day use only; vault toilets are provided. Full facilities are provided at Lake Siskiyou Marina, including a campground, bathrooms, a marina, a boat ramp, small tackle shop and a grocery store. Boat rentals are available.

Cost: North shore access is free. Day-use fee at beach is $1; campsite fee is $10-$13 per night.

Who to contact: Phone (916) 926-2610.

About Lake Siskiyou: Indian legend has it that the great spirit poked a hole in the sky and shaped a tepee with the fallen pieces. Some of the fish in Lake Siskiyou seem big enough to have been created in similar fashion.

This lake sits at the veritable base of giant Shasta, 14,162 feet tall, creating one of the prettier settings for a man-made lake anywhere in America. This lake was created for the sole purpose of offering recreation, not for storing water for farmers, so while reservoirs in the foothills of California get drained, Siskiyou remains full. It is a jewel.

In the summer months, the lake gets a lot of traffic from motorhome campers, suntanners, and anglers as well. The standard fare is trolling for trout; after all, it is stocked with 20,000 trout by Fish and Game each year, but there are some surprises along the way.

The biggest surprise are the big brown trout. They range to 10 pounds and up in this lake—I hooked a monster brown here once, and could do nothing with it, until finally it wrapped the line around a stump and broke off. Another surprise are the largemouth bass, which provide a summer alternative. The best area is "the stumps," located on the north shore just upstream from the dam.

Many techniques have been developed specifically for this lake. One unusual method is using a lure called a Bingo Bug, available at the marina tackle shop, which can be slow-trolled at dawn during calm water and an insect hatch. It is a great fish catcher in those conditions. When the wind comes up, a quarter-ounce Z-Ray, gold with red spots, or a gold Little Cleo are both very good.

In the summer, using lead-core line and a Triple Teaser is quite effective, along with the traditional nightcrawler/flasher combination. Hey, in the summer, I've seen people swimming around in the middle of the lake next to their boat, using Power Bait 40 feet deep on an unattended rod, and outcatching the serious anglers.

---

10. TROUT CREEK

Reference: Near McCloud in Shasta-Trinity National Forest; map B2 grid b7.

How to get there: From Interstate 5 south of Mount Shasta, take the McCloud-Reno exit and travel 12 miles east on Highway 89 to McCloud. Continue east for two miles, then turn north on Pilgrim Creek Road and travel 20 miles. Turn left at the sign for Trout Creek and travel one mile.

Facilities: A small Forest Service campground is provided. No piped water is available, so bring your own. Supplies can be obtained in McCloud.

Cost: Access is free.

Who to contact: Phone the Shasta-Trinity National Forest District Office at (916) 964-2184.

About Trout Creek: You hear the name "Trout Creek" and that can be enough to get the blood pumping. Relax. Cool your jets. Sit down and take a few deep breaths.

This is a small stream with trout in the five to seven-inch class, the kind of place where the fishing is a bonus. The compelling thing is the setting, not the fishing. It's a quiet spot to camp, the water is pure, and so is the pine-scented air. After a while, you won't care that the biggest trout in the world aren't here. It won't seem to matter.

It is a beautiful place, easy to reach and easy to fish.

---

11. TAMARACK LAKE

Reference: Near Castella in Shasta-Trinity National Forest; map B2 grid c3.

How to get there: From the town of Castella on Interstate 5, drive 11 miles west on Road 25 (Castle Creek Road) to Twin Lakes Road. Turn south and travel three miles; when the road forks bear left and travel one mile to the lake.

Facilities: No facilities are available on-site. Primitive, do-it-yourself sites are available. Supplies can be obtained in Castella.

Cost: Access is free.

Who to contact: Phone the Shasta-Trinity National Forest District Office at (916) 926-4511.

About Tamarack Lake: Tamarack Lake is just good to look at. It is set deep in the Trinity-Divide country, a pretty alpine lake that provides a place of peace and beauty. Fishing? Well, it's not too shabby either.

There are actually three lakes in the immediate area. Tamarack is the biggest, and nearby to the west are Upper and Lower Twin Lakes. Tamarack also has the biggest fish. It is stocked with 3,000 foot-long rainbow trout each year, joined by 5,000 brook trout that are dropped from the DFG airplane. Upper and Lower Twin Lake, meanwhile, receive only fingerlings. Of those two, it is Upper Twin Lake that provides the better fishing.

It is a good base camp for people who like the idea of exploring. Of course, if you just want to look at it, that's OK too. It does just fine.

---

12. McCLOUD RIVER

Reference: Near McCloud in Shasta-Trinity National Forest; map B2 grid c7.

How to get there: From Interstate 5 south of Mount Shasta, take the McCloud-Reno exit and travel 12 miles east on Highway 89 to McCloud. To reach the lower portion of McCloud River, turn south on Squaw Valley Road. Drive 7.5 miles on the paved road, then turn south on an unpaved road near the southwestern shore of McCloud Reservoir and follow the signs to Ah-Di-Na Campground. To reach the upper portion of the river, drive five miles east on Highway 89 from McCloud. Turn right at the sign for Fowler's Camp. Access is available along a trail out of the camp.

Facilities: Lower McCloud River: The Forest Service camp Ah-Di-Na is available. Upper McCloud River: Camping is available at Fowler's Camp, Cattle Camp, and Algoma Camp. Supplies can be obtained in McCloud.

Cost: River access is free.

Who to contact: Phone thehone the Shasta-Trinity National Forest District Office at (916) 964-2184; Ted Fay Fly Shop at (916) 235-2969. To get a reservation to fish the section managed by the Nature Conservancy, phone headquarters at (415) 777-0487.

About McCloud River: This is about as close as you can get to standing in a time machine.

You can turn back the clock on the Lower McCloud, the section of river downstream of McCloud Dam which is managed by the Nature Conservancy. Access is restricted to no more than 10 rods at a time,

---

all trout hooked must be released, and anglers must use single barbless hooks on flies or lures. No wood cutting, hunting, or any impact activity is permitted. The idea is to keep the area in its natural state forever.

But the McCloud can be a difficult river to wade, fish, and have success. In addition, rattlesnakes, bears and mountain lions can cause some serious concern. And finally, the regulations are difficult to understand, with different rules for four parts of the river.

So let's get it straight: Upstream of Lake McCloud (the area accessed from Fowler's Camp), the limit is five fish with no special restrictions. Downstream of Lake McCloud from the Dam to the Nature Conservancy (near Ah-Di-Na Camp) the limit is two fish. On the 2.5 miles of river from the Nature Conservancy Cabin on downstream, all fish must be released. And finally, from the roped-off section on downstream for 2.5 miles, no fishing is permitted.

Confusing? Yes. But it is nothing compared to the confusion you will feel if the trout decide not to bite. The best results here are gained by highly skilled flyfishers using weighted nymphs, fishing pocket water. The trout rarely tattoo the fly. Most often they simply stop its flow in the current; know-hows watch their line, and any strange movement is often the only sign that they are getting a bite.

Chest waders with a belt are a must, along with a wading staff. The algae-covered rocks are extremely slippery and if you don't watch it, kerplunk, there you go, right in the drink. The upstream section, that is, near Fowler's Camp, is much easier to fish, and is stocked by Fish and Game. Like the Lower McCloud, it has spectacular beauty. A new trail from Fowler's Camp traces along the river upstream to Middle Falls, one of the prettiest waterfalls in Northern California. You can stop to fish on your way, zipping short casts to deep, clear pools.

Catch rates? There is no average to the average. Skunks are common, especially among newcomers. Those who keep returning for more punishment eventually figure out the river well enough to catch three or four trout per visit.

Occasionally, you hear of fantastic evening bites during a caddis hatch, or giant trout during the cold weather of early November. But more often when you run into folks here, they talk about the beauty. Pretty soon you figure it out: That's because they just got skunked.

---

13. HAZEL CREEK

Reference: Near Castella in Shasta-Trinity National Forest; map B2 grid d4.

How to get there: From the town of Castella, drive 5.5 miles south on Interstate 5 to the Sims Road exit. Turn left and travel east on Sims Road. Continue on Hazel Creek Road, past the turnoff for Sims Flat campground, to the creek.

Facilities: A campground is available at Sims Flat. Supplies can be obtained in Castella or Dunsmuir.

Cost: Creek access is free.

Who to contact: Phone the Shasta-Trinity National Forest District Office at (916) 926-4511.

About Hazel Creek: The future of this little trout stream is a mystery, as is that of its big brother, the Upper Sacramento. As a feeder stream to the Upper Sac, new rules are expected as the main river recovers from the toxic spill of the summer of '91.

Over the years, about 1,000 rainbow trout have been stocked each year at Hazel Creek, usually providing decent fishing in May, then poor in June, and zilch thereafter. As a feeder creek, it is dependent on each year's rains and snowpack, running highest in the spring, then very low by fall.

Before fishing here, a call to Fish and Game regional headquarters should be mandatory to learn the status and rules in effect. The number is (916) 225-2300.

---

14. IRON CANYON RESERVOIR

Reference: Near Big Bend in Shasta-Trinity National Forest; map B2 grid d7.

How to get there: From Burney, drive 14 miles west on Highway 299. Turn north on Big Bend Road and drive 17 miles to the town of Big Bend. Continue north for two miles, then turn left on Road 38N11 and drive three miles to the Iron Canyon Reservoir Spillway. Another turnoff farther west loops around the lake to Deadlun Camp.

Facilities: Two campgrounds are provided: Hawkins Landing and Deadlun. Neither has piped water, so bring your own. A boat ramp is also available; small boats are recommended. Supplies can be obtained in Big Bend or Burney.

Cost: Deadlun campground is free; the campsite fee at Hawkins Landing is $8-$9 per night.

Who to contact: Phone the Shasta-Trinity National Forest District Office at (916) 275-1587.

About Iron Canyon Reservoir: There are two Iron Canyon Reservoirs, the one that awaits you here in the spring, and the one that awaits in fall. One is good. One is bad. What kind of experience you have depends on which one you visit.

In the spring, the lake is full, the trout are hungry, and the campground always has plenty of room. In addition to rainbow trout, there is the chance for a big brown trout as well. I've caught some beautiful stringers of trout here, and they always seem to come in the spring.

In the fall, it's a different story. The lake is often low, exposing a long stump-ridden shore near Deadlun Camp. More people seem to be camping here, and the fish don't seem to bite as well. It's like a different lake. So you decide which Iron Canyon Reservoir to visit.

When the lake is full in the spring, it is a very pretty place, set in national forest, just above the elevation line where nature grows conifers instead of deciduous trees. Now and then, if you feel someone is watching, well, someone might just be. Look up; it is apt to be the lake's bald eagle on patrol.

15. SHASTA LAKE

Reference: Near Redding in Shasta-Trinity National Forest; map B2 grid f3.

How to get there: Fishing access is available all around the lake's shore, and can be reached by taking one of several exits off Interstate 5 north of Redding. A popular spot is Fisherman's Point at Shasta Dam. From Redding, drive four miles north on Interstate 5. Take the Shasta Dam Boulevard exit and drive to Lake Boulevard. Turn right and follow the signs to the dam.

Facilities: Several campgrounds are provided around the lake. Full-service marinas, boat ramps, boat rentals, houseboats, grocery stores, laundromats, gas, and recreation areas are available.

Cost: Campground fees range from $6-$17 per night for single camps; $40-$60 per night for group camps.

Who to contact: Phone Shasta Cascade Wonderland Association at (916) 243-2643; Shasta-Trinity National Forest District Office at (916) 275-1587; Digger Bay Marina, (916) 275-3072.

About Shasta Lake: Shasta Lake is one of the true outdoor recreational capitals of America, a massive reservoir with 365 miles of shoreline, 1,200 campsites, 21 boat launches, 12 marinas to rent houseboats, and 35 resorts. In addition, it is an easy lake to reach, a straight shot off Interstate 5.

A remarkable 22 species of fish live in the lake, but it is the bass, crappie and trout that provide the best results.

The best areas for bass are along big rockpiles, the backs of coves, submerged trees, and the downwind side of points. Most bassers fish long hours here and cover lots of water, their electric motors keeping them on the move, casting along the shoreline ahead of the boat.

The RattleTrap, Shad Rap, Zara Spook, and white spinnerbait are my favorite lures for Shasta. My favorite areas are the McCloud Arm and the Pit River arm, which are home to lots of fish. That includes big crappie, too.

On the Pit Arm, there are huge acreages of water loaded with submerged trees. It is here where the huge crappie hang out. The way to catch them is to use a live minnow for bait, roaming right into the lair of a big school of crappie, or to use a white crappie jig, then lower it down 20 feet and jig it straight up and down. The crappie can range to 14 or 15 inches, fight hard, and can really provide some fun.

If you like to be able to eat and drink to your heart's content while fishing—like if you rent a houseboat for a week—then trolling for the trout is likely to be higher on your list. The best fishing for trout is in early winter and late winter, often at the corners of Shasta Dam or the entrance of the Squaw Creek arm of the lake. It might be cold out, but the trout come during this time, averaging 14 to 18 inches, occasionally bigger, and rarely to six pounds and up.

If you see a photograph of one of these big trout, then arrive in the summer, you may discover the sport an exercise in futility. In summer, the surface temperature can reach 80 degrees and the trout respond by going very deep, way down to the thermocline, some 80 feet down. They can be impossible to catch without a downrigger to get you deep enough.

One thing about Shasta that is easy to get used to is the number of people on it. In summer, there are hundreds and hundreds of house-boats, and also lots of water skiers. This is one place where there is plenty of room for everybody. If you want quiet, just head into one of the quiet coves and you will get it.

---

16.   PIT RIVER

Reference: Northeast of Redding in Shasta-Trinity National Forest; map B2 grid f7.

How to get there: From Interstate 5 at Redding, take the Highway 299 east exit and drive about 30 miles east. Turn left on Fender's Ferry Road and travel four miles. Access is available on the left side of the river, below the dam. The river can also be accessed off several roads that junction with Big Bend Road, about 35 miles east of Redding.

Facilities: A few campgrounds are available off Highway 299. Supplies are available in Redding.

Cost: River access is free.

Who to contact: Phone the Shasta-Trinity National Forest District Office at (916) 275-1587; Vaughn's Sporting Goods, Burney, (916) 335-2381.

About Pit River: This place isn't for everybody. To reach the best sections of river, it takes a hike down a canyon, skillful and aggressive wading, precise casts during the evening rise, then a hike in darkness back out of the canyon. Get the picture? If you are still with me, maybe you should try it on for size.

The Pit is one of several quality trout streams in this area, but this is the toughest to get in and out of. PG&E has a series of powerhouses on the river, with each stretch of river unique. For the most part, the stream is brushy, so you have to get out in it and wade. Shoreliners don't have a prayer. Other stretches are at the bottom of canyons, and being in top physical condition is a must.

The best stretches of river are below Powerhouse No. 3, Powerhouse No. 5 (difficult access), and near the town of Bend (easiest access). The latter is best for a first trip here, casting to pools and pockets in this boulder-laden stream. If you want, a natural hot spring just downstream of town is available, and you can work out all your sore casting muscles.

---

17.   CLEAR CREEK

Reference: West of Redding; map B2 grid gØ.

How to get there: From Interstate 5 at Redding, take the Highway 299 west exit and drive 17 miles west, past Whiskeytown Lake, to Trinity Mountain Road. Turn right and travel north. Access is available off short roads that junction with Trinity Mountain Road, which parallels the creek.

Facilities: A small primitive campground is provided north of French Gulch. No piped water is available. Supplies can be obtained in Redding.

Cost: Access is free.

Who to contact: Phone the Shasta-Trinity National Forest District Office at (916) 623-2121.

About Clear Creek: "Psssst: Want to hear a secret? Just don't tell anybody about it."

That is how people talk about Clear Creek. You see, everybody in this area goes to nearby Whiskeytown Lake. They don't know Clear Creek exists, or the little campground here either. But it does. And not only that, but the stream has a fair population of trout, with many in the 10 to 12-inch class.

The stream has fishable sections both upstream and downstream of Whiskeytown Reservoir. The stretch downstream has the most fish, getting stocked with 4,000 trout per year from the DFG. The upstream section, in comparison, receives 1,000 trout per year.

If you visit nearby Whiskeytown Lake during the peak early summer season, little Clear Creek might just provide the alternative you are looking for.

Reference: Near Redding in Shasta-Trinity National Forest; map B2 grid gØ.

How to get there: From Interstate 5 at Redding, take the Highway 299 west exit and drive ten miles west. Turn left on Kennedy Memorial Drive, or continue west on Highway 299. The highway runs right over the Whiskey Creek arm of the lake.

Facilities: Three campgrounds are available: Brandy Creek, Oak Bottom, and Dry Creek Group Camp. No tents are permitted at Brandy Creek. A full-service marina, boat ramps, boat rentals, groceries, wood, and a sanitary disposal station are available.

Cost: Campsite fees range from free to $7 per night for single camps; $30-$50 per night for group camps.

Who to contact: Phone the Whiskeytown National Recreation Area at (916) 241-6584; Shasta Cascade Wonderland Association at (916) 243-2643; Whiskeytown Store at (916) 246-3444.

About Whiskeytown Reservoir: You may not believe this: Make sure you bring a can of corn if you visit Whiskeytown Lake. What? Corn? That's right, because that is exactly what the kokanee salmon like here.

Whiskeytown is incredibly easy to reach, is big enough (36 miles of shoreline) to spend a lot of time exploring, and has decent camping accommodations. If there is any problem, it is the wind during the spring, which is why it is the favorite lake in the area for windsurfers and sailboaters.

They will probably wonder why you have a can of corn. The reason is because you will use it for bait. Start with a set of flashers, add on a Luhr Jensen Wedding Spinner, then put a piece of corn on the hook for bait. The kokanee love it. And you, in turn, will love the kokanee, among the best tasting fish you can catch in freshwater.

Alas, if the kokanee aren't biting, just skewer on a nightcrawler instead of the kernel of corn and you're in business for trout. After all, it is stocked with 65,000 rainbow trout every year. The best areas are in the vicinity of the Highway 299 Bridge, and near the powerhouse. In fact, if the powerhouse is running, start your trip there and end it there. It is the best spot on the lake.

One bonus is that there is plenty of shoreline for anglers without boats. When the lake is full, the Whiskey Creek arm offers several hundred yards of accessible bank on each side.

19. KESWICK RESERVOIR

Reference: Near Redding Shasta-Trinity National Forest; map B2 grid h1.

How to get there: From Interstate 5 at Redding, take the Highway 299 west exit. Drive four miles west, then turn north on Iron Mountain Road and travel four miles to the reservoir. Follow the signs to the boat ramp.

Facilities: A boat ramp and a day-use picnic area are provided. Camping is available nearby at Whiskeytown Reservoir.

Cost: Access is free.

Who to contact: Phone the Whiskeytown National Recreation Area at (916) 241-6584.

About Keswick Reservoir: Well, you can't win 'em all. This is just a lousy place to fish. It is a narrow, deep and small lake, where you practically need a Jaws of Life to get the fish to open their mouths.

Yeah, there are some big ones in here, huge, I'm told, but I've never caught one of them, or even seen one. But I have been told that it takes deep-water trolling techniques, downriggers preferred, to get down to them.

As the rumors go, this lake is home to some monster-sized rainbow trout and brown trout, but scarce numbers of them.

Perhaps the answer is this: There is just one big trout here, and it is passed around for photographs.

---

20. LOWER SACRAMENTO RIVER

Reference: Near Redding; map B2 grid h2.

How to get there: From Redding, drive south on Interstate 5. Access is available via the Riverside, Balls Ferry, and Jellys Ferry exits off the freeway. Access is also available in the city of Redding, at Caldwell Park and near the Redding Civic Auditorium.

Facilities: Several full-facility campgrounds and RV parks are available along the river and near adjacent towns. A few good ones are Marina Motor Home Park, Sacramento River Motor Home Park, and Reading Island.

Cost: River access is free.

Who to contact: Phone Shasta Cascade Wonderland Association at (916) 243-2643.

About Lower Sacramento River: My first trip here was a special one. I fished with guide Al Vasconcellos and a north state legend, John Reginato. At first they were skeptical of me, the talking beard, but soon I hooked a 28-pound salmon and landed it after a fantastic fight that included several jumps. John got a photo of it jumping in mid-air with my profile and bent rod in the foreground, a picture that has run in more than 50 publications. Then 20 minutes later, I got another big one. This one went 32 pounds. I was an instant believer.

Right off I learned about the big salmon in the Sacramento River. They average 10 to 20 pounds, and bigger ones are common. The state record was caught here, 88 pounds, by Lindy Lindberg. But what I didn't learn that day I have learned in the many years since: The fishing for salmon is rarely fast-paced.

You tend to grind out the fish, working the river for hours, hoping to get a bite every hour or so. The salmon fishing starts to perk up around mid-August, peaks from mid-September to mid-October, then starts to wane through November. In the process, there will be hundreds of boats on the river every day, back-trolling over the deep river holes where salmon rest during their upstream journey.

Rig with a large silver Flatfish or Kwikfish, with a three-inch fillet of sardine tied on the underside of the lure. Place a three-way swivel four feet above the lure, and from the swivel hang your sinker, its weight dependent on the depth of the hole and river current. Four to eight ounces usually does the job. If you don't have a boat, then get a guide. Shasta Cascade has a complete list. One of the few bank-fishable spots for salmon is at the mouth of Old Battle Creek from the east side of the river.

Don't fish for salmon upstream of the Deschutes Bridge in Redding; it's illegal. But this stretch of water is good for rainbow trout on black woolly worm flies. My biggest trout in this section of river was a 21-incher. It can be fished by shore or by drift boat, but newcomers are best off making the trip with a guide to learn the water.

Another option are shad, which arrive in June and remain in force to early July. They provide a sport that is just the opposite of salmon fishing: Fast-paced, not huge, but a chance at a light-tackle or flyfishing sport. The best spot is the Tehama Riffle, located downstream of Tehama Bridge. Here you can wade out, cast Shad Darts, Teeney Rounders, or T-Killers and catch 10 shad or so in the two to four-pound class in an evening.

The Sacramento River is the lifeblood of Northern California, running some 400 river miles from its source at the base of Mount Shasta on south to San Francisco Bay. It has been damaged by water exports to points south, but as long as water keeps rumbling downstream, the fish will keep coming back.

21.   McCUMBER RESERVOIR

Reference: East of Redding; map B2 grid i9.

How to get there: From Redding, drive east on Highway 44 towards Viola, then turn north on Lake McCumber Road and drive two miles to the reservoir. Follow the signs to the boat ramp.

Facilities: A small campground is provided. A car-top boat launch is also available; no gas motors are permitted, but electric motors are OK.

Cost: Campsite fee is $8-$9 per night.

Who to contact: Phone the PG&E District Office at (916) 527-0354.

About McCumber Reservoir: Here's a little lake, easy to reach out of Redding, that gets missed by a lot of folks. They just keep on driving right on by. Whoa there. If you put your foot to the brake you'll find little McCumber Reservoir, part of PG&E's hydro system and stocked with foot-long trout by the Department of Fish and Game. It receives 8,000 per year.

　　McCumber was created when a dam was placed across the North Fork of Battle Creek. Remember that. In the warm summer months, most of the fish often hold near the original creek channel, which tends to be on the eastern side of the lake rather than right down the middle.

---

22.   GRACE LAKE

Reference: Near Shingletown in Shasta-Trinity National Forest; map B2 grid j7.

How to get there: From Redding, take Highway 44 east to Shingleton. From Shingletown, drive 2.5 miles south on Grace Resort Road to the lake.

Facilities: No facilities are available on-site. Campgrounds and RV parks are available near Shingletown.

Cost: Lake access is free.

Who to contact: Phone the Bureau of Land Management at (916) 246-5325.

About Grace Lake: Never heard of this one? Maybe you should listen up. Despite its tiny size, Grace Lake is stocked each spring with 14,000 rainbow trout, most in the 10, 11-inch range. That's a lot of fish for a small lake that doesn't get much fishing pressure. If you hit it, then hit it early in the season. By mid-June, the sun starts branding everything in sight around these parts. The water temperature gets cranked up and the trout get cranked down. But if you find yourself cruising in this vicinity in April or May, and have a hankering for a trout, roll on by for some good shoreline baitdunking.

Reference: East of Red Bluff in Lassen National Forest; map B2 grid J7.

How to get there: From Red Bluff on Interstate 5, drive about 13 miles northeast on Highway 36 to the town of Dales. Turn north on Road A6 (Manton Road) and drive about 22 miles. The road will fork; bear right at Forwards Mill Road and continue around Digger Butte. Direct access to Digger Creek is available here.

Facilities: No facilities are available on-site. Campgrounds are available southeast, on Highway 36. Supplies can be obtained in Red Bluff.

Cost: Access is free.

Who to contact: Phone the Lassen National Forest District Office at (916) 258-2141. For a map, send $2 to Office of Information, U.S. Forest Service, 630 Sansome Street, San Francisco, CA 94111.

About Digger Creek: This little unknown stream provides sneak-fishing opportunities. It is difficult to reach, and not easy to fish, but the rewards go well beyond the fishing.

The surrounding country is rugged and beautiful, the air clean with the scent of pines. The stream is pure, its headwaters located just to the east in Lassen National Park. Anglers who like rock-hopping along a stream in solitude will find that little Digger Creek provides such an opportunity.

Digger Creek receives small stocks of trout to a foot long, and if you are fishing but not catching, then keep on the move until you find a pocket of them—but don't take it for granted. This is a small stream and it must be approached quietly.

MAP B3

20 LISTINGS
PAGES 216-231

NOR-CAL MAP. see page 120
adjoining maps
NORTH (A3) ...... see page 152
EAST (B4) .... see page 232
SOUTH (C3)....... see page 278
WEST (B2) .... see page 196

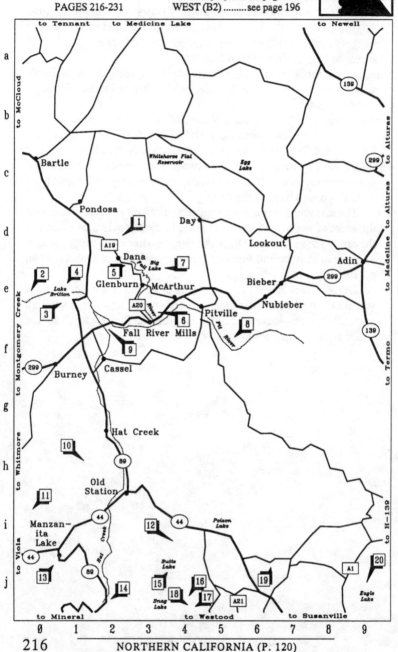

1. BEAR CREEK

Reference: Near McArthur Shasta-Trinity National Forest; map B3 grid d2.

How to get there: From McArthur on Highway 299, drive 11.5 miles northwest on Highway A19 (MacArthur Road). Turn left on Forest Service Road 24 (Ted Elder Road) and travel north. Access to the creek is available off roads that junction with Road 24.

Facilities: No facilities are available. Campgrounds and supplies are available near McArthur and at Lake Britton.

Cost: Creek access is free.

Who to contact: Phone the Bureau of Land Management at (916) 257-5381.

About Bear Creek: Like so many small streams and lakes, Bear Creek gets overshadowed by its famous nearby companions, Hat Creek and Fall River.

But Bear Creek provides a decent fishery from hatchery-reared trout, with some 4,000 stocked per year by Fish and Game. And these are not the dinkers, but the trout that range to a foot. They are quite a surprise to anglers accustomed to the smaller fish that usually come with smaller streams.

If you get skunked on the more famous waters, keep Bear Creek in mind—along with one of those large, black frying pans.

2. ROCK CREEK

Reference: Near Lake Britton; map B3 grid eØ.

How to get there: From Lake Britton on Highway 89, drive west on Forest Service Road 11. The road parallels Rock Creek, and direct access is available.

Facilities: A small, free primitive campground is located just below the intersection of the road and the creek. No piped water is available there. More campgrounds and supplies are available at Lake Britton.

Cost: Creek access is free.

Who to contact: Phone the Shasta-Trinity National Forest District Office at (916) 337–6502.

About Rock Creek: So, you have fished for bass at Lake Britton for a few days, maybe camped at the developed sites at nearby Burney Falls State Park, and would like something different. Like maybe a primitive camp along a small stream stocked with trout? This is the place. It is so close to Lake Britton, and also the state park, yet only rarely will you ever hear local folks talk about it. In fact, it is hikers who discover the good fishing by accident, since the Pacific Crest Trail is routed right across the creek. The best stretch of water is right below Lake

Britton on downstream a bit, where 2,000 rainbow trout are stocked at different times of the late spring and early summer. It provides a nice option.

---

3.   BURNEY CREEK

Reference: Near Burney; map B3 grid e1.

How to get there: One access point is the area around McArthur-Burney Falls: From the junction of Highways 299 and 89, drive seven miles north on Highway 89 to McArthur-Burney Falls Memorial State Park. Fishing access is available above and below the falls. Access is also available off side roads west of Burney: From Burney, drive west on Tamarack Road (across from the entrance to the Sierra Pacific mill) and drive one-quarter mile. Turn onto a cinder road that parallels the creek. Access is available directly off the Forest Service roads that junction with it.

Facilities: Camping is available nearby at Cassel Forebay on Hat Creek or at McArthur-Burney Falls Memorial State Park at Lake Britton.

Cost: A $5 parking fee is charged at McArthur-Burney Falls Memorial State Park. Other creek access is free.

Who to contact: Phone Vaughn's Sporting Goods in Burney at (916) 335-2381; or Bob's Sporting Goods in Burney at (916) 335-4949.

About Burney Creek: This stream provides a pretty setting, the river gurgling over rocks polished by centuries of rolling river water. Access is good, and often so is the trout fishing.

But get this: The most popular area to fish provides the worst results—and the least popular area provides the best results. Crazy? That's how it is here.

That is because so many campers stay at McArthur-Burney Falls State Park, then fish the section of Burney Creek which runs over the awesome waterfall, into the deep pool below, and on through the park. That stretch of river gets hammered every day of the season by campers at the park, giving the trout smart lessons in the process.

The stretch of water west of Burney is a completely different story. It is well stocked, uncrowded, and the catching is often as good as the fishing. If you need any help on access or fishing tips, stop in at Vaughn's Sportshop in Burney for assistance.

For the record, Lower Burney Creek gets 12,000 trout, Middle Burney Creek gets 2,500, and Upper Burney gets 7,000, rainbow trout all. It adds up to an opportunity you may have previously missed.

4.   LAKE BRITTON

Reference: Near Fall River Mills in Shasta-Trinity National Forest; map
B3 grid e1.

How to get there: At the junction of Highways 89 and 299 north of Burney,
drive north on Highway 89 for ten miles. Turn left on Old Highway
Road and drive one mile to the lake, or follow the signs to campground
entrances off Highway 89.

Facilities: Several campgrounds are provided. A good one is PG&E's
Northshore. Boat ramps, boat rentals, groceries, bait, and tackle are
available.

Cost: Campsite fees range from $8-$10 per night. Day use parking fee is
$5.

Who to contact: Phone the PG&E District Office at (916) 527-0354;
Vaughn's Tackle in Burney at (916) 335-2381.

About Lake Britton: You want an ideal camping/fishing/boating vacation? Lake Britton may be the place. Campgrounds are available on
the north shore of the lake, as well as at nearby MacArthur-Burney
Falls State Park. Boat ramps provide easy access, and a large variety
of species makes the fishing a special attraction.

Unlike many of the lakes in this region, Lake Britton has bass,
bluegill and crappie as well as trout. So all you have to do is tailor your
style according to the season and water temperature and you'll be in
business. For the most part, it is the bass and bluegill that provide the
best action, not the trout and crappie.

Also unlike so many lakes, this reservoir is not hidden. Highway
89 runs right across it, and many people learn of it simply by driving
over it while coming or going from Burney Falls State Park. The latter
makes an excellent side trip, with the waterfall a virtual fountain of
fresh water.

---

5.   FALL RIVER

Reference: Near McArthur; map B3 grid e3.

How to get there: Access to the premium upper stretch of the river is
limited to guests of Rick's Lodge, with the rest of the stream bordered
by private property. Public access is available, however, at the Cal
Trout Access at Island Bridge, off McArthur Road (but with room for
just a few cars). The lower part of the river can be reached via Glenburn
Road, just west of Fall River Mills, off Highway 299.

Facilities: Boats can also be launched at the PG&E dredge access where
Glenburn and McArthur Roads meet. Camping is available at Cassel
Forebay or Lake Britton.

Cost: River access is free.

Who to contact: Phone the PG&E District Office at (916) 527-0354; California Trout, Inc. at (415) 392-8887; Rick's Lodge at (916) 336-5300.

About Fall River: Snow-covered Mount Lassen sits above this trout paradise, watching as it has done since its last violent eruption 70 years ago. If you lose a few big trout, you might just blow your top too.

Come the warm days of June on through summer and fall, Fall River is the site of the most amazing insect hatch in California. There can be so many pools on the calm stream surface from hatching insects and rising trout that it can look like it is raining. It is a unique, world-class water: Water so clear that you can spot a dime on the bottom 30 feet deep and unconsciously reach in, thinking you can pick it up. The trout are wild and many are big, 16 to 20–inchers with a sprinkling in the five-pound class.

That is enough right there to inspire people from all over America to cast a line, but it takes more than inspiration here. It takes flyfishing skill, a knowledge of stream access, and a sense of ethics.

Fall River does not roll over rocks and boulders. It is a spring-fed stream, deep and slow-moving, slow enough to fish from a float tube. It is so clear that long leaders (12 feet is the average) and delicate casts are mandatory. This is a flyfishing-only stream, and all trout are released. It adds up to an exclusive, quality water.

Access can also be exclusive. The best bet is staying at Rick's Lodge, where you can get access to the prime upper stretch of river. Rooms cost $50 per night, $75 for a double, and boats with electric motors are available for $30 for the half-day, $40 for a full day. Fishing classes, flies, and a bar and restaurant also come with the territory. A sidelight worth even a quick stop is the amazing collection of trophy buck mounts owner Rick Piscatello has put together, located in the bar.

The favored patterns for flies are the paraduns, either in olive, tan or yellow, with a No. 16 the best starting size. You should also have Zug Bugs, a black Leech, and a Hare's Ear nymph in your fly box.

The Fall River experience is not for everybody. If somebody showed up with a frying pan, well, he might not make it out alive. But for those who appreciate a pristine, spring-fed stream that demands the best out of flyfishers, this is it.

---

6.   BAUM & CRYSTAL LAKES

Reference: Near Burney; map B3 grid e3.

How to get there: At the junction of Highways 89 and 299, drive two miles northeast on Highway 299 to Cassel Road. Turn right and drive two miles south, then turn left on Hat Creek-Powerhouse Road and continue to Baum Lake and the adjoining Crystal Lake.

Facilities: Camping is available nearby at Hat Creek or Lake Britton. Only non-motorized boats are permitted on Baum and Crystal Lakes. Supplies are available in Burney.

Cost: Lake access is free.

Who to contact: Phone the PG&E District Office at (916) 527-0354; Vaughn's Sporting Goods, Burney, (916) 335-2381.

About Baum Lake: This is big fish country, where brown trout and rainbow trout grow to surprising sizes. The biggest I've seen was a 24-pound brown trout. No foolin'.

Baum can be fished by boat or bank, but no motors are allowed on the lake. Most anglers dunk nightcrawlers, a few cast flies behind a bubble. They catch trout in the foot-long class, for the most part, until suddenly and unexpectedly, something giant is hooked. Many big fish are lost, with the angler stunned as to what actually occurred.

Fish and Game takes good care of Baum Lake, stocking it with 28,000 rainbow trout and 8,000 browns each year. Its those browns that grow to such large sizes and that also can be so elusive. Side trips in the immediate area include touring the Crystal Hatchery, which is located adjacent to the lake, or taking a jaunt on the Pacific Crest Trail, which is also nearby.

7.　　　　　　　BIG LAKE　　　

Reference: Near McArthur; map B3 grid e3.

How to get there: From the town of McArthur on Highway 299, turn left on Rat Ranch Road. Travel about 3.5 miles north, then turn right across a canal to the boat ramp.

Facilities: A boat launch is provided. A boat-access only campground is available across the lake at Ahjumawa Lava Springs State Park. Other campgrounds are available nearby at Baum Lake or Lake Britton. Supplies are available in Fall River Mills or MacArthur.

Cost: Access is free.

Who to contact: Phone Vaughn's Sporting Goods at (916) 335-2381.

About Big Lake: "There's no fish in Big Lake," I've heard people say. "After all, Fish and Game doesn't put any in."

Wrong and right. Wrong about the no fish, right about the no stocks. You see, Big Lake supports a low population of large trout, especially brown trout. Not many people try for them, but those who have figured them out aren't doing no yelpin'.

Big Lake is quite shallow, the fishing is generally only fair, and most people discover the place while visiting the adjacent Ahjumawa Lava Springs State Park. But know-hows who cast large bass-type

---

lures, such as Rapalas, Rebels, and Shad Raps from a boat, and who fan the shoreline with casts, can discover a whole new possibility, the big brown trout. They don't come easy, but an 18-incher is average, and they range much bigger.

If you have any good luck charms, you might bring them with you.

---

8. PIT RIVER

Reference: Near Fall River Mills; map B3 grid f5.

How to get there: West of Lake Britton: At the intersection of Big Bend Road and Hagen Flat Road in the town of Big Bend (accessible via Big Bend Road, off Highway 299 east of Burney), drive east on Hagen Flat Road. Access is available directly off Hagen Flat Road, near Powerhouses No. 3 and 5 and at several spots in between. Access is also available below the Lake Britton Dam. East of Lake Britton: At the junction of Highways 299 and 89, drive about seven miles north on Highway 299 to Powerhouse No. 1.

Facilities: Campgrounds are available at Lake Britton or McArthur–Burney Falls State Park. A few small, primitive Forest Service campgrounds are also available along the river, but they offer no piped water. Supplies can be obtained in Fall River Mills or McArthur.

Cost: River access is free.

Who to contact: Phone the Bureau of Land Management at (916) 257–5381.

About Pit River: Everybody says the Pit River is brushy, difficult to wade, and difficult to reach. They are right. It also provides good trouting to people who figure out how to beat it.

The best fishing is below Powerhouse No. 3, Powerhouse No. 4, and in the Bend area. The best areas require a fairly rugged hike in, aggressive wading with chest waders, belt and pole, and casting in pools and pocket water without getting hung up on the brush along the shoreline. For more information on the Pit River, see page 209.

---

9. HAT CREEK

Reference: Near Burney in Lassen National Forest; map B3 grid g2.

How to get there: Lower Hat Creek: From Burney, drive 7.5 miles northeast on Highway 299. Access is directly off Highway 299 where the road crosses the stream. The stretch between Powerhouse No. 2 and Lake Britton is a designated wild trout stream, and only flies and single, barbless hooks may be used. The area from Cassel Forebay to the Powerhouse No. 2 inlet may be fished with no special restrictions.

How to get there: Upper Hat Creek: From the junction of Highways 44 and 89, drive north on Highway 89-44 to Big Pine Camp. Access to the creek begins here. Continue north to the town of Old Station, then turn left and follow Highway 89 to Bridge Campground. From Bridge Campground to Cassel Forebay, Hat Creek runs through private property, and is not accessible to the public.

Facilities: Several campgrounds are located on Upper Hat Creek along Highway 89. A popular one is Big Pine Campground. Supplies are available in Burney and Old Station.

Cost: River access is free.

Who to contact: Phone the Lassen National Forest District Office at (916) 336-5521.

About Hat Creek: What kind of trip do you want? Do you want to camp along the stream, have a chance at catching trout up to 12 inches, then eating them for dinner? If so, Upper Hat Creek is the spot. Or do you want to fish a classic chalk stream, bringing a conservation-oriented fishing rod for wild trout, releasing what you catch? If so, Lower Hat Creek is the spot.

Upper Hat provides easy access off Highway 89, streamside campgrounds, and stretches of river that are stocked bi-weekly through the summer. Some 75,000 rainbow trout and 7,000 brook trout are stocked in Upper Hat, along with another 15,000 rainbow trout in Middle Hat. That adds up to a lot fish for happy campers in this neighborhood. Anything goes here, with Power Bait garnished with a salmon egg the preferred entreaty, and a five-fish limit.

Such is not the case at Lower Hat. No trout have been stocked for some 20 years in the section from Powerhouse No. 2 to Lake Britton. It is a flyfishing stream where anglers use floating lines, 2X and 3X tippets, and fly patterns as small as No. 20, though No. 16s often do well during the evening rise. The best patterns for Hat Creek are the Yellow Stone, Humpy, caddis, and duns.

Because all fish are released, some big trout roam these waters, most averaging 10 to 16 inches. The 18 to 22-inchers seem much more rare in the 1990s than in the past, but some monsters are still caught. The biggest I have heard of on Lower Hat is a 17-pound brown trout caught about 10 years ago.

The skills needed for Upper Hat Creek are the kind appropriate for any mountain stream stocked with trout. The skills required for Lower Hat, on the other hand, demand the absolute best out of flyfishers. Many say if you can master Lower Hat, you can fish anywhere in the world and be successful.

---

10. THOUSAND LAKE WILDERNESS AREA

Reference: East of Redding; map B3 grid h1.

How to get there: Basic access roads that lead to trailheads are available

---

off Highway 89 to the west. A Forest Service map is mandatory.

Facilities: No facilities are available in the wilderness area. Several campgrounds are available off Highway 89 between Hat Creek Work Center and Old Station.

Cost: Access is free.

Who to contact: Write to Lassen National Forest at 707 Nevada Street, Susanville, CA 96130, or phone (916) 257-2151. For a map, send $2 to Office of Information, U.S. Forest Service, 630 Sansome Street, San Francisco, CA 94111.

About Thousand Lake Wilderness: Get yourself a map of this area, start gazing and imagine the possibilities. It is hard to go wrong.

A good first trip is to start from the Cypress trailhead and hike in to Eiler Lake, a good trout lake set at 6,000 feet elevation. This is an easy in-and-outer, a one-day hike.

If you are more ambitious, a good option is to hit nearby Box Lake, then Barrett Lake as well, turning it into a five-mile loop hike. You want to stay longer? The following lakes are stocked with trout by airplane: Lake Eiler, Box Lake, Hufford Lake, Barrett Lake, Durbin Lake, Everett Lake, and Magee Lake. It is not a large wilderness, with most of the lakes set in the northeast sector, south of Freaner Peak in the Thousand Lakes Valley. If you want to expand your trip with some mountain climbing, a series of peaks with great views are accessible to the southwest out of Everett and Magee Lakes.

---

11. NORTH BATTLE CREEK RESERVOIR

Reference: Near Viola; map B3 grid iØ.

How to get there: From Redding, drive east on Highway 44 to Viola, then continue for 3.5 more miles. Turn north on Road 32N17 and drive five miles, then turn left on Road 32N31 and drive four miles. Turn right on Road 32N18 and drive one-half mile to the reservoir.

Facilities: A campground is provided, as well as a car-top boat launch. Electric motors are permitted on the reservoir, but no gas engines.

Cost: Campsite fee is $8 per night.

Who to contact: Phone the PG&E District Office at (916) 527-0354; Shasta Cascade Wonderland Association at (916) 243-2643.

About North Battle Creek Reservoir: A lot of folks miss this lake. They're too busy and excited en route to Lassen Park while heading east on Highway 44. But if they slowed down, they might just see the turnoff for North Battle Creek Reservoir, and in turn, discover a much lesser-used spot than the nearby national park.

The fishing is often better here than at lakes in Lassen Park as well. Each year, North Battle Creek Reservoir is stocked with 3,000 brown trout and 2,000 Eagle Lake trout, species which grow a lot bigger than the dink-size variety in most of the lakes at Lassen.

If the campgrounds are crowded at Lassen, what the heck, just roll on over to North Battle Creek Reservoir. You will probably end up catching more fish, anyway.

12.   BUTTE CREEK

Reference: Near Old Station Lassen National Forest; map B3 grid i4.

How to get there: From Interstate 5 south of Mount Shasta, take the McCloud–Reno exit and drive approximately 75 miles east to the turnoff for Highway 44. Turn east and drive 11 miles. Turn south on Road 18, which parallels the creek.

Facilities: A small, primitive campground is provided, but no piped water is available.

Cost: Access is free.

Who to contact: Phone the Lassen National Forest District Office at (916) 257-2151.

About Butte Creek: Thousands and thousands of vacationers drive right by Butte Creek on their way to Lassen National Park without even knowing it exists. But it does.

The stretch of river just outside the park boundary is the top spot, albeit for modest success. It is planted with about 1,000 trout each year, and while those modest numbers limit success, there is a short period of opportunity during the early summer.

If this stream grabs your fancy, you need to keep track of the annual winter road closure on Highway 89 in Lassen Park. When the snow melts enough for them to plow the road, boom, that is when Butte Creek is often planted. It usually is in mid to late May, sometimes early June.

By mid summer to fall, however, the flow on this stream turns into a little trickle. Just keep on driving.

13.   MANZANITA LAKE

Reference: In Lassen Volcanic National Park; map B3 grid j1.

How to get there: From Redding, drive east on Highway 44. Manzanita Lake is located just beyond the Visitor Center on Highway 44 at the western boundary of the park.

Facilities: A campground is provided. Groceries and propane gas are available nearby. A boat ramp is available; only non-motorized boats are permitted on the lake.

Cost: Campsite fee is $7 per night.

Who to contact: Phone the Lassen Volcanic National Park at (916) 595-4444.

About Manzanita Lake: The old volcano is the centerpiece of Lassen Park, of course, and climbing it is one of the best two-hour hikes in California. But on a good day, Manzanita Lake can provide the kind of fishing that could make you care less about hiking. Manzanita Lake is an idyllic setting and in many ways an ideal destination. The campground adjacent to the lake is Lassen's largest with 179 sites, so you will most always find a spot, and is also the easiest to reach, being located so near a major entrance to the park. The lake is small but quite beautiful and the conversion to a natural trout fishery has been a success. Rules mandate lure or fly only with a single, barbless hook, and a two-fish limit, none longer than 10 inches. By having a maximum size limit instead of a minimum size limit, it means the big trout that anglers prize, the 15 to 20-inchers, remain in the lake instead of ending up in a frying pan.

No power boats are permitted on the lake, making it perfect for a canoe, raft or pram. The best technique here is to offer the trout what they feed on: insects. Fly patterns that work the best are the No. 14 Callibatis, No. 16 Haystack, No. 14 or No. 16 Hare's Ear Nymph, or if a larger hatch is coming off, a No. 6, 8 or 10 leech in brown or olive. Flyfishers come ready with both sinking and floating lines, switching as is necessary. Most of the feeding is done sub-surface, however.

No fishing at all is permitted at Emerald or Helen lakes at Lassen Park. Considering what is provided at Manzanita, all is forgiven for that umbrage.

---

14.   SUMMIT LAKE

Reference: Near Manzanita Lake in Lassen Volcanic National Park; map B3 grid j2.

How to get there: From Redding, drive east on Highway 44 to Lassen Volcanic National Park. Enter at the western entrance. From Manzanita Lake, drive 12 miles south on Lassen Park Road.

Facilities: A campground is provided. Groceries and propane gas are available nearby. Only non-motorized boats are permitted on the lake.

Cost: Campsite fee is $5–$7 per night.

Who to contact: Phone the Lassen Volcanic National Park at (916) 595-4444.

About Summit Lake: This lake is a perfect example of a place where a put-and-take fishery is ideal, rather than a wild trout fishery. It has two campgrounds near the lake and shoreline access is excellent, making it perfect for a family fishing expedition. In addition, because of a lack of natural spawning habitat, the lake would be devoid of trout without any stocks.

So what happens? Almost no fish get stocked here, that's what happens. It's Dinkerville, U.S.A., that is, a 5,000-fish load of four-inch rainbow trout is plunked in every spring, and that's it for the year. Because of the large numbers of vacationing kids that fish here, a lot of those dinkers are caught and kept, so the lake has virtually no large fish.

It's a pretty camping spot, and I've seen lots of deer here, particularly on the southeastern end. I have yet to see a trout over six inches, however.

15. BUTTE LAKE

Reference: Near Burney in Lassen Volcanic National Park; map B3 grid j3.

How to get there: From Interstate 5 at Redding, take the Highway 299 east exit and drive to the town of Burney. Continue for five more miles and turn south on Highway 89. Travel 24 miles to the town of Old Station. Turn east on Highway 44 and drive 10.5 miles. Turn south on Road 18 and drive seven miles to the lake.

Facilities: A campground is provided. A boat ramp is available; only non-motorized boats are permitted on the lake.

Cost: Campsite fee is $7 per night.

Who to contact: Phone the Lassen Volcanic National Park at (916) 595-4444.

About Butte Lake: Some vacationers say the fishing at Butte Lake is the best they've had in a national park. Others wonder what the big fuss is all about.

The reason is because this lake receives generous stocks of trout in the 10 to 13-inch class. They come several times during the summer, totaling some 14,500 trout in all. If you happen to be camping here during a week when there is a fresh stock, well, you are in business.

Because access to the lake is via an obscure park entrance, it is often missed by visitors to the park. It borders the Fantastic Lava Beds to the southwest, with hikes available to Snag Lake to the south or Prospect Peak to the west.

16. CARIBOU WILDERNESS

Reference: In Lassen National Forest; map B3 grid j4.

How to get there: Access roads that lead to trailheads are located off Highway 44 to the west. A good scenic trailhead begins at Silver Lake, off Highway A21. A Forest Service map is mandatory.

Facilities: No facilities are available in the wilderness area. Campgrounds are available at Silver Lake. Supplies can be obtained in Westwood.

Cost: Access is free.

Who to contact: Write to Lassen National Forest at 707 Nevada Street, Susanville, CA 96130, or phone (916) 257-2151. For a map, send $2 to Office of Information, U.S. Forest Service, 630 Sansome Street, San Francisco, CA 94111.

About Caribou Wilderness: Elevations range from 5,000 to 7,000 feet in the Caribou Wilderness, offering hiking that isn't too rough and a chance to visit many alpine lakes with pan-size trout.

The highlights are exploring natural volcanic activity, several good one-day loop hikes to lakes, or the chance at a multi-day expedition into adjoining Lassen National Park. Some of the better fishing is at Black Lake and Turnaround Lake, both providing fairly easy access for hikers. On a longer trip, you could tie in Snag Lake or Juniper Lake, along with many others. The following hike-to lakes are stocked with trout by airplane: Beauty Lake, Betty Lake, Black Lake, Cypress Lake, Eleanor Lake, Emerald Lake, Evelyn Lake, Gem Lake, Hidden Lakes, Jewel Lake, Posey Lake, Rim Lake, Triangle Lake, Turnaround Lake. Other unique points of interest are the Black Cinder Rock, Red Cinder Cone and Caribou Peaks. Once you set up a base camp in the vicinity of these geologic wonders, you can take a lunch in a daypack and make a great side trip or two. Sound good? Is good.

---

17. SILVER LAKE

Reference: Near Westwood in Lassen National Forest; map B3 grid j4.

How to get there: From Susanville, drive west on Highway 36 to the town of Westwood (located east of Lake Almanor). Turn north on County Road A21 and drive 12.5 miles. Turn left on Silver Lake Road and continue to the lake.

Facilities: Two campgrounds are provided: Silver Bowl and Rocky Knoll. An unimproved boat ramp is available; only car-top boats are permitted. Supplies are available in Westwood.

Cost: Campsite fee is $6 per night.

Who to contact: Phone the Lassen National Forest at (916) 257-2151.

About Silver Lake: There are dozens of lakes in the adjacent Caribou Wilderness, but it is Silver Lake, accessible without hiking, that often provides the best fishing of the bunch.

While Silver Lake is the largest of the little alpine lakes in the region, it is completely dwarfed by Lake Almanor, Mountain Meadows Reservoir, and Butt Lake to the south. For that reason, it gets missed by many vacationers.

The lake has three species of trout: brook trout, Eagle Lake trout, and brown trout. They comprise a decent fishery that provides a variety of the smaller, easier-to-catch brookies and a few of the larger, more elusive brownies. About 12,000 trout are stocked each year.

Silver Lake makes a good first-night camp for an expedition into the adjoining Caribou Wilderness, with routes available both to Emerald Lake to the northwest, and Betty, Trail and Shotoverin Lakes nearby to the southeast.

If you don't like the company at Silver Lake, nearby Caribou Lake provides a option.

---

18. CARIBOU LAKE

Reference: Near Westwood in Lassen National Forest; map B3 grid j4.

How to get there: From Susanville, drive west on Highway 36 to the town of Westwood (located east of Lake Almanor). Turn north on County Road A21 and drive 12.5 miles, then turn left on Silver Lake Road and continue, past Silver Lake, to Caribou Lake.

Facilities: Campgrounds are available nearby at Silver Lake. Only non-motorized boats are permitted at Caribou Lake.

Cost: Access is free.

Who to contact: Phone the Lassen National Forest at (916) 257-2151.

About Caribou Lake: Everyone should fly an airplane over this area at least once to appreciate it. There are literally dozens of lakes in the area, most of them being pristine, little spots where you can hear the flowers bloom.

Caribou is one you can reach by car, and being set on the edge of the wilderness, provides a jump-off point to several other small lakes, including Jewel, Eleanor, Black, Turnaround, Twin and Triangle Lakes, which you hit in that order heading into the interior of the wilderness.

Caribou Lake is stocked each year with 2,000 rainbow trout, 6,000 Eagle Lake trout, and 1,000-plus brown trout. All of those fish are good size, most being in the foot-long class. Those with "local knowledge" realize this, and fish this lake year after year.

---

19. CRATER LAKE

Reference: Near Susanville in Lassen National Forest; map B3 grid j7.

How to get there: From Susanville, drive six miles west on Highway 299 to the Highway 44 turnoff. Turn northwest and travel 22 miles to the Bogard Work Center, then turn north on a Forest Service road and follow the signs for seven miles to the lake.

Facilities: A campground is provided. Well water is available. Only non-motorized boats are permitted on the lake. Supplies are available in Susanville.

Cost: Campsite fee is $6 per night.

Who to contact: Phone the Lassen National Forest at (916) 257-2151.

About Crater Lake: Little Crater Lake sits just below the top of Crater Lake Mountain, an obscure spot in Lassen National Forest. It provides an intimate setting for trout fishing. Most of the fish are brook trout, including some dinkers, with a sprinkling of larger Eagle Lake trout in the mix.

It receives a variety of stocks, including 5,000 trout in the 8 to 11-inch class, and another 8,000 fingerling brookies dropped in from the DFG airplane.

A good side trip here is taking the Forest Service road up to the top of Crater Lake Mountain, which has a loop near the summit.

---

20.   EAGLE LAKE

Reference: Near Susanville in Lassen National Forest; map B3 grid j9.

How to get there: From Susanville, drive three miles west on Highway 36. Turn north on County Road A1 and drive 15.5 miles, then northeast on County Road 201 to the lake. Follow the signs to the boat ramps.

Facilities: Several campgrounds are provided. Two good ones are Aspen Grove and Merrill. A full-service marina, boat rentals, boat ramps, a grocery store, and a sanitary disposal station are available.

Cost: Campsite fees range from $7-$9 per night for single camps; $55-$65 per night for group camps. Day use is free.

Who to contact: Phone the Lassen National Forest at (916) 257-2151; Spalding Tract at (916) 825-2191.

About Eagle Lake: You want big trout? You say you even dream about big trout? You'd do anything for big trout? Anything?

Well, you don't have to do anything. You just have to make a trip to Eagle Lake in the fall, then have some persistence, and you will indeed get your big trout.

The trout here are measured in pounds, not inches, and for those who are more accustomed to catching six-inch brook trout, well, an Eagle Lake trout would eat those for breakfast. Trout in the four and five-pound class is more like it, with a 20-incher about the average.

And get this: You don't need a boat. What you do need is some anti-freeze because it gets so cold up here that it can make your blood freeze. When the cold weather arrives, the big trout abandon their deep water haunts of summer and move in to the shallows just outside the tules at the north end of the lake. Know-how anglers will cast out a nightcrawler, inflated like a little balloon so it will float off the lake bottom, and wait for a big trout to cruise by. Sooner or later, one will.

Trolling is also good during the fall, especially with Needlefish lures. Eagle's Nest and northward provide the better spots. If you arrive in summer, it is a far different story. The shorefishing is poor, with the bigger fish often out of casting range. I've taken catch-rate surveys, talking to angler after angler who have nothing to show for several days effort.

Meanwhile, boaters must employ special deepwater techniques, trolling 30 to 40 feet down, or flyfishing with sink-tip lines. It is absolutely critical to be on the water very early, at dawn or before, when the lake is calm. Why? Because the wind can howl at Eagle Lake in the spring and summer, and the quick results are waves and white caps that can making boating unpleasant at the least, very dangerous at the worst.

The lake opens on Memorial Day Weekend every year and it is accompanied by a lot of hoopla, then usually followed by poor fishing in windy, often foul weather. I just wait. I know that come the cold weather of fall, instead of me having to search out the fish, I can wait at the north end of the lake and they will come to me.

MAP B4

NOR-CAL MAP . see page 120
adjoining maps
NORTH (A4) ...... see page 158
EAST .... no map
SOUTH (C4) .... see page 304
WEST (B3) .... see page 216

17 LISTINGS
PAGES 232-243

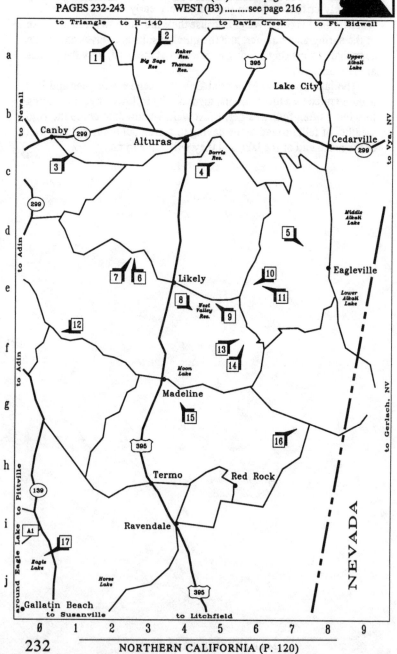

232   NORTHERN CALIFORNIA (P. 120)

1.   RESERVOIR C

Reference: Near Alturas in Modoc National Forest; map B4 grid a2.

How to get there: From Alturas, drive one mile west on Highway 299. Turn right on County Road 73 (Crowder Flat Road), and travel 9.5 miles north, then turn left on Triangle Ranch Road and drive seven miles to the reservoir.

Facilities: A small campground is provided, but there is no piped water, so bring your own. Toilets and picnic tables are also provided.

Cost: Access is free.

Who to contact: Phone the Modoc National Forest District Office at (916) 233-4611.

About Reservoir C: It is a hell of an exploration just to adventure to the "alphabet lakes," located in the remote Devil's Garden area of Modoc County. Reservoir C and Reservoir F are the best of the lot, but the success can go up and down like a yo-yo depending on water levels in the lakes. For the most part, the fishing is decent in late spring and early summer, then goes the way of the do-do bird.

Reservoir C gets a favorable listing because of the small camp that makes it acceptable for overnighters, and the hopeful prospects that come in early summer. Year-to-year results are very weather dependent. If the water level is up, then so is the fishing. It is stocked with both brown trout and Eagle Lake trout, 1,000 apiece, in late spring.

A sidelight to this area are the number of primitive roads that are routed through Modoc National Forest, perfect for four-wheel drive cowboys.

2.   BIG SAGE RESERVOIR

Reference: Near Alturas in Modoc National Forest; map B4 grid a3.

How to get there: From Alturas, drive four miles west on Highway 299. Turn north on Crowder Flat Road and drive six miles, then turn right on the dirt access road (Big Sage Road) and continue to the reservoir. The boat ramp is located nearby.

Facilities: A campground is provided, but no piped water is available, so bring your own. A boat ramp is also available.

Cost: Access is free.

Who to contact: Phone the Modoc National Forest District Office at (916) 233-4611.

About Big Sage Reservoir: Don't get scared off by the dirt road that provides access to this lake. It's smooth enough to trailer a boat over. That done, you will find a good ramp awaiting as well as some good waters for largemouth bass.

It is one of the few bass waters in the entire area, with a few islands providing shoreline habitat, in addition to several good coves along the southwest shoreline. Catfishing is also available here.

This is classic desert plateau country, with the land bordering the lake to the north particularly sparse. It is a good size lake, covering some 5,000 acres, and set at 4,400 feet elevation. It is one of the area's most popular lakes, and for Modoc County, that means you might actually see another person.

---

3. BALLARD RESERVOIR

Reference: Near Canby; map B4 grid c1.

How to get there: From Alturas, drive 17 miles west on Highway 299 to the town of Canby. Turn left on County Road 54 in Canby and travel 1.5 miles south until the road forks, then bear left and continue, following the signs to Ballard Reservoir.

Facilities: A few primitive campsites are available, but there is no piped water, so bring your own. Supplies are available in Canby.

Cost: Access is free.

Who to contact: Phone the Modoc National Forest District Office at (916) 233-4611.

About Ballard Reservoir: Fish this lake in May and June, and any later than that, well, in hot weather years you might as well fish in a bucket. It's not because the lake is small, it's because it was built by ranchers and they take what they think they deserve . . . and sometimes what they don't deserve as well. So the result is that dropping water levels and hot weather can cause an algae problem later in the fishing season at this lake. No problem: Get there early. Do that and you will find good fishing for Eagle Lake rainbow trout. Some 5,000 are stocked every spring. The lake is shaped kind of like a cucumber, with a dirt road along the southwest side providing access. With no ramp, anglers with car-top boats and canoes have a big advantage here.

---

4. DORRIS RESERVOIR

Reference: Near Alturas; map B4 grid c5.

How to get there: From the south end of Alturas, drive about three miles east on Parker Creek Road until the road forks. Bear right and travel a short distance to the boat ramp, or bear left and continue to the north end of the reservoir.

Facilities: An unimproved boat ramp is provided. Camping is available several miles east of the reservoir, near Cedar Pass. Supplies can be obtained in Alturas.

Cost: Access is free.

Who to contact: Phone the Modoc National Wildlife Refuge at (916)

233-3572.

About Dorris Reservoir: Locals can get a case of lock-jaw when asked about this lake. There are some big, big trout in this lake, as well as bass and catfish, and I'm not speaking with forked tongue. The reservoir is a decent-sized one, located a short drive out of Alturas on the Modoc National Wildlife Refuge. It is something of a wildlife paradise, so always bring your camera along. There is a diversity of birds and wildlife, especially large numbers of geese in the fall and winter, as well as coyotes, deer, quail, rabbits and even antelope. They make touring the adjacent refuge a must for first-time visitors. The ol' "Modockers" put a lot of faith in a good ol' nightcrawler, and you might do the same at this lake. They toss it out with a splitshot for weight, perhaps inflating the nightcrawler so it floats a bit off the lake bottom, then see what they get. In the early summer, when the trout, bass and catfish are all coming on, the gettin' is good. A boat provides a definite advantage here, almost a necessity.

---

5.   SOUTH WARNER WILDERNESS

Reference: Near Likely in Modoc National Forest; map B4 grid d7.

How to get there: From Alturas, drive 18.5 miles south on US 395 to the town of Likely. Turn left on Jess Valley Road and drive nine miles west, until the road forks. Bear left and continue north; access roads that lead to trailheads are located off Jess Valley Road. Access is also available off Highway 81 on County Road 40, just south of Eagleville. A trailhead is located at Emerson Camp.

Facilities: No developed campgrounds are located within the wilderness area, but Mill Creek Falls, Soup Springs, and Patterson campgrounds are located at the outskirts. Supplies are available in Likely or Eagleville.

Cost: Access is free.

Who to contact: Write to the Modoc National Forest at 441 N. Main Street, Alturas, CA 96101, or phone (916) 233-4611. For a map, send $2 to Office of Information, U.S. Forest Service, 630 Sansome Street, San Francisco, CA 94111.

About South Warner Wilderness: The Warner Mountains are a lonely area overlooked by many hikers, but it has a genuine mystique highlighted by a remote and extensive trail system. The west side of the Warners are something like the Sierra, with pine trees, meadows and streams. The east side, however, is high desert, sagebrush, and juniper, all quite dry and rugged.

   The best destinations for anglers are the following: North Emerson Lake, Clear Lake, Patterson Lake, Cottonwood Lake are the best lakes. Cottonwood Creek, Parker Creek, Pine Creek, East Creek are the best

---

streams.

One of the best backpacking trips available here is the 23-mile Summit Trail Loop, which traverses both sides of the ridgeline. That allows visitors to see the stark contrasts between the east and west slopes.

If you go, treat this area softly. After a while, you may even notice that you are talking in soft tones, not loud ones. The Warners can do that to you.

---

6.   BAYLEY RESERVOIR

Reference: South of Alturas; map B4 grid e3.

How to get there: From the south end of Alturas, drive about two miles south on Centerville Road to Westside Road. Turn left and drive 6.5 miles south. Turn right on Bayley Reservoir Road and travel ten miles southwest to the reservoir.

Facilities: No facilities are available on-site. Supplies can be obtained in Alturas.

Cost: Access is free.

Who to contact: Phone the Bureau of Land Management at (916) 257-5381.

About Bayley Reservoir: This lake is way out in the middle of nowhere. What makes it a great place? Just that it is far away from anything. In fact, the first time I stopped in nearby Likely, which consists of a gas station/store and a cemetery, I asked this old fella at the gas pump why they named the town Likely of all things.

"Because you are Likely not to get there," he answered. That's the way they are in Modoc. This is cow country, and if you want a lake to yourself, here you go. The trees are small, there is plenty of chaparral, but more trout than people. In fact, it is stocked each year with 8,000 foot-long Eagle Lake trout, along with 15,000 fingerlings. That is more than any other water in Modoc County.

Both Graven Reservoir to the north and Delta Lake to the south are very close in proximity to this lake, but don't get fooled. Graven gets only 1,000 trout per year, and Delta gets zero.

---

7.   GRAVEN RESERVOIR

Reference: South of Alturas; map B4 grid e3.

How to get there: From the south end of Alturas, drive about two miles south on Centerville Road to Westside Road. Turn left and drive 6.5 miles south. Turn right on Bayley Reservoir Road and travel six miles south, then turn right on Graven Reservoir Road and continue for 4.5 miles.

Facilities: No facilities are available on-site. Supplies can be obtained in Alturas.

Cost: Access is free.

Who to contact: Phone the Bureau of Land Management at (916) 257-5381.

About Graven Reservoir: If you are heading to nearby Bayley Reservoir, Graven Reservoir to the northwest provides an alternative. Not much of one, however, with trout stocks quite few and reportedly no spawning of resident trout taking place.

So why even try? Because even obscure spots like this can have little sprees. Do this: At the gas station in the nearby little town of Likely on US 395, ask the guy, "Anybody catching anything over at Graven?" Then watch his face very carefully. The inflection in his eyes will be his answer, rarely his words. If the body language is "yes," then yes, do take a crack at it.

---

8.   WEST VALLEY RESERVOIR

Reference: Near Likely; map B4 grid e4.

How to get there: From Alturas, drive 18.5 miles south on US 395 to the town of Likely. Turn east on Jess Valley Road and drive two miles. To reach the boat ramp, turn right at the sign for West Valley Reservoir and drive four miles south. The north end of the lake can be accessed via a short road off Jess Valley Road.

Facilities: A few unimproved campsites are provided, with water and toilets available. A boat ramp is also available. Supplies can be obtained in Likely.

Cost: Access is free.

Who to contact: Phone the Bureau of Land Management at (916) 233-4666.

About West Valley Reservoir: First the warning: Hazardous high winds can arrive here in the spring, and there have been several accidents. Some say there are ghosts that will hover over fishing boats.

But if you pick a calm day, this is one of the better choices in the entire region. West Valley Reservoir provides good access, a quality boat ramp, and usually gets filled during the winter with runoff from the South Fork Pit River.

You don't even need a boat here. Both shoreliners and boaters alike take the same approach: Pick a spot, then hunker down while waiting for a nibble on their bait. Bait? That's right. Very few people use lures here, only a sprinkling try trolling.

In the hot summer months, this is a good lake to swim in. And in the cold (and I mean c-o-l-d) winter, this lake is good for icefishing.

Up here on the Modoc plateau, it's often around zero degrees for several weeks starting in mid-December.

9. SOUTH FORK PIT RIVER

Reference: Near Likely in Modoc National Forest; map B4 grid e5.

How to get there: From Alturas, drive 18.5 miles south on US 395 to the town of Likely. Turn left on Jess Valley Road and drive east. Direct access is available along the road.

Facilities: Campgrounds are available at Mill Creek Falls and farther north in the town of Alturas. Supplies are available in Likely.

Cost: River access is free.

Who to contact: Phone the Modoc National Forest District Office at (916) 279-6116.

About South Fork Pit River: The South Fork Pit, which is fed by Mill Creek, is one of the little surprises in this remote part of California. It surprises because the stream runs right along the road and the adventurous angler will discover some good trout water.

When you turn off at Likely and first see the river, it may be murky but don't dishearten. It is murky because you are looking at water that has been released from West Valley Reservoir. Keep on, keep on.

Soon you will reach the South Fork Pit, which runs clear. It is a small stream, but home to eastern brooks and rainbow trout. It is a fishing delight to flyfishers who like a small water challenge.

10. MILL CREEK

Reference: Near Likely in Modoc National Forest; map B4 grid e6.

How to get there: From Alturas, drive 18.5 miles south on US 395 to the town of Likely. Turn left on Jess Valley Road and drive east until the road forks. Bear left and follow the road to Mill Creek Falls. Access is available off Forest Service Roads near Mill Creek Falls campground, and also along trails that lead into the South Warner Wilderness.

Facilities: A campground is available at Mill Creek Falls. Supplies are available in Likely.

Cost: Access to the creek is free.

Who to contact: Phone the Modoc National Forest District Office at (916) 279-6116.

About Mill Creek: Mill Creek comes right out of the South Warner Wilderness, those lonely mountains of the northeast. The best strategy here is to go in from Soup Springs Camp, and then hike into the South Warner Wilderness boundary. You will come off a hillside and into a valley floor, and at the bottom of that valley you will find Mill Creek.

It is best fished while walking upstream, and that is because it is a very touchy water. It requires finesse and sneak-fishing techniques. Tie up your rigs behind a tree, don't let 'em see your shadow, and stay low when you cast.

Your reward will be a unique strain of wild trout that are short, dark and chunky, appearing as if they have been somehow compressed. The trip is a lot of fun, a little work, and you won't see fish that look like this anywhere else.

11. CLEAR LAKE

Reference: Near Likely in Modoc National Forest; map B4 grid e6.

How to get there: From Alturas, drive 18.5 miles south on US 395 to the town of Likely. Turn east on Jess Valley Road and drive nine miles, until the road forks. Bear right and drive 2.5 miles, then turn right and travel two miles to Mill Creek Falls; the lake is a short hike away.

Facilities: No camping is permitted at the lake, but a campground is available at Mill Creek Falls. Supplies can be obtained in Likely.

Cost: Lake access is free.

Who to contact: Phone the Modoc National Forest District Office at (916) 279-6116.

About Clear Lake: Here is one of the prettiest spots in Modoc County. Clear Lake is a small, high mountain lake, but unlike so many small, high mountain lakes, some of the fish here are big. That goes especially for the brown trout here, though there are some rainbow trout too. Knowing that can add some sizzle to the adventure. The fishing is best in the evenings.

It's a paved road all the way in from Likely, then a short (half-mile) but beautiful hike in from the Forest Service camp near Mill Creek Falls.

Don't expect to catch a lot of fish here. There just plain aren't that many. (Nearby Blue Lake to the south is a better bet). But there are some big ones, and the surrounding beauty of the Warner Mountains and Mill Creek Falls makes it a good overnighter.

12. ASH CREEK

Reference: Near Adin in Modoc National Forest; map B4 grid f1.

How to get there: From Alturas, drive about 37 miles west on Highway 299 to the town of Adin. Turn east on Ash Valley Road and drive 7.5 miles southeast until the road forks. Bear left and travel along the paved road, which parallels the creek. Direct access is available.

Facilities: Ash Creek Campground is located off Ash Ash Valley Road. Supplies are available in Adin.

Cost: Access is free.

Who to contact: Phone the Modoc National Forest District Office at (916) 299-3215.

About Ash Creek: Know your water: Ash Creek is visible from Highway 299 north of Adin, with the lower stretch of it bordered by private land. So head instead east of Highway 299 to Ash Creek Campground, a cozy spot, and start your adventure there. There you will find pocket water with small trout. The pools are small and the shoreline is brushy, so the best strategy is to wade right down the middle of the creek, kneeling down while you cast, making short, precise casts to these small pockets.

---

13.   PARSNIP CREEK

Reference: Near Likely in Modoc National Forest; map B4 grid f5.

How to get there: From Alturas, drive 18.5 miles south on US 395 to the town of Likely. Turn left on Jess Valley Road and drive eight miles east until the road forks, then bear right and travel 5.5 miles south on Blue Lake Road. Turn right on a dirt road; direct access is available.

Facilities: Camping is available at Blue Lake and Patterson Campground. Supplies can be obtained in Likely.

Cost: Access to the creek is free.

Who to contact: Phone the Modoc National Forest District Office at (916) 299–3215.

About Parsnip Creek: This little creek enters and exits Blue Lake. The best stretch of water is below the lake not above, as it drops down through forest country.

At first glance, you may be unimpressed with the water. It is quite small, and you can walk a mile and find just a few spots to flick your line. But every once in a while you will find a deep pool where the fish are just sitting there, suspended in the current, gorging themselves as they pick up morsels floating by. Most of the trout are small, however.

The upper end of the stream above Blue Lake is high plateau country. If you are camping at Blue Lake and want to try something different, it is "worth a try" to hike upstream, rod in hand, using extreme stealth to sneak up on every spot.

---

14.   BLUE LAKE

Reference: Near Likely in Modoc National Forest; map B4 grid f6.

How to get there: From Alturas, drive 18.5 miles south on US 395 to the town of Likely. Turn east on Jess Valley Road and drive nine miles, until the road forks. Bear right and travel seven miles on Blue Lake

Road, then turn right at the signed turnoff and continue to the boat ramp at the lake.

Facilities: A campground and a picnic area are provided. An unimproved boat ramp is available. Supplies can be obtained in Likely.

Cost: Campsite fee is $5 per night; day use is free.

Who to contact: Phone the Modoc National Forest District Office at (916) 299-3215.

About Blue Lake: Some big brown trout roam this lake, like in the 10 to 12-pound class, and they provide something of a treasure hunt amid the good numbers of rainbow trout in the foot-long class.

For a lake located near a wilderness area (South Warner), access is quite good, with a paved road all the way to the northeast side of the lake. The campground is set in a pretty area, a good boat ramp is nearby, and anglers will discover consistent results trolling from late spring well into summer.

It is a pretty lake, shaped like an egg and rimmed by trees. It borders on pristine, one of the prettiest you can reach on a paved road—with a bonus of big fish.

---

15.   MENDIBOURE RESERVOIR

Reference: Near Madeline; map B4 grid g4.

How to get there: From Alturas, drive 31.5 miles south on US 395 to the town of Madeline. Turn south on Mendiboure Road and drive three miles, then turn east (left) on a dirt road and travel four miles to the reservoir.

Facilities: No facilities are available on-site.

Cost: Access is free.

Who to contact: Phone the Bureau of Land Management at (916) 257-5381.

About Mendiboure Reservoir: This lake is named after one of the local ranchers. Get the idea? Right, it was built to provide water to local ranchlands, and that means Mendiboure Reservoir is subject to fluctuations, depending on how much water it gets in the winter, and how much is taken out by the ranchers in summer.

It is stocked with Eagle Lake trout, about 3,000 in the foot-long class every spring, so fish it in May and June. Virtually only the locals know about this spot.

---

16.   DODGE RESERVOIR

Reference: Near Ravendale; map B4 grid h7.

How to get there: From Alturas, drive approximately 52 miles south on US 395 to the town of Ravendale. Turn east on Garate Road and drive four miles, then turn left on Mail Marr Road and drive ten miles north and west to Stage Road. Turn left and drive two miles north, then turn right on Tuledad Road and continue. Take the signed turnoff on the left for the reservoir.

Facilities: A campground is provided. No piped water is available, so bring your own. No boat ramp is available, and only non-motorized boats are permitted on the reservoir.

Cost: Access is free.

Who to contact: Phone the Bureau of Land Management at (916) 257-5381.

About Dodge Reservoir: Dodge is one of the larger reservoirs in this remote area of the Modoc Plateau and because of it, Fish and Game has taken a completely different approach with it. Instead of stocking a few thousand "catchables," some 25,000 fingerlings are planted every May. The hope is that the lake is big enough and provides enough feed for a high percentage of them to grow to adult sizes.

Alas, if you hit it wrong, that is, just after the big stock in May, it will seem like the Dodge Dinker Refuge. But because of its size, this lake provides more stable fishing conditions than so many of the reservoirs that are used for water storage. That means better fishing during the summer than the other lakes.

---

17.   EAGLE LAKE

Reference: Near Susanville in Lassen National Forest; map B4 grid jØ.

How to get there: From Susanville, drive three miles west on Highway 36. Turn north on County Road A1 and drive 15.5 miles, then northeast on County Road 201 to the lake. Or, drive north from Susanville on Highway 139 and take Merrillville Road, Eagle Lake Road, or Stone Road west to the lake. Follow the signs to the boat ramps and campgrounds. Boat ramps are located at the north and south ends of the lake.

Facilities: Several campgrounds are provided. Two good ones are Aspen Grove and Merrill. A full-service marina, boat rentals, boat ramps, a grocery store, and a sanitary disposal station are available.

Cost: Campsite fees range from $7-$9 per night for single camps; $55-$65 per night for group camps. Day use is free.

Who to contact: Phone the Lassen National Forest at (916) 257-2151; Spalding Tract at (916) 825-2191.

About Eagle Lake: You want big trout? You say you even dream about big trout? You'd do anything for a big trout? Anything?

Well, you don't have to do anything. You just have to make a trip to Eagle Lake in the fall, then have some persistence, and you will indeed get your big trout.

The trout here are measured in pounds, not inches, and for those who are more accustomed to catching six-inch brook trout, well, an Eagle Lake trout would eat those for breakfast. Trout in the four, and five-pound class is more like it, with a 20-incher about the average.

And get this: You don't need a boat. What you do need is some anti-freeze because it gets so cold up here than it can make your blood freeze. When the cold weather arrives, the big trout abandon their deep water haunts of summer and move in to the shallows just outside the tules at the north end of the lake. Know-how anglers will cast out a nightcrawler, inflated like a little balloon so it will float off the lake bottom, and wait for a big trout to cruise by. Sooner or later, they will.

Trolling is also good during the fall, especially with Needlefish lures. Eagle's Nest on northward are the better spots. If you arrive in summer, it is a far different story. The shorefishing is poor, with the bigger fish often out of casting range. I've taken catch-rate surveys and talking to angler after angler who have nothing to show for several days effort.

Meanwhile, boaters must employ special deepwater techniques, trolling 30 to 40 feet down, or flyfishing with sink-tip lines. It is absolutely critical to be on the water very early, at dawn or before, when the lake is calm. Why? Because the wind can howl at Eagle Lake in the spring and summer, and the quick results are waves and white caps that can making boating unpleasant at the least, very dangerous at the worst.

The lake opens on Memorial Day Weekend every year and it is accompanied by a lot of hoopla, then usually followed by poor fishing in windy, often foul weather. I just wait. I know that come the cold weather of fall, instead of me having to search out the fish, I can wait at the north end of the lake and they will come to me.

MAP CØ

NOR-CAL MAP. see page 120
adjoining maps
NORTH (BØ) ..... see page 166
EAST (C1) .... see page 256
SOUTH (DØ)...... see page 312
WEST .... no map

15 LISTINGS
PAGES 244-255

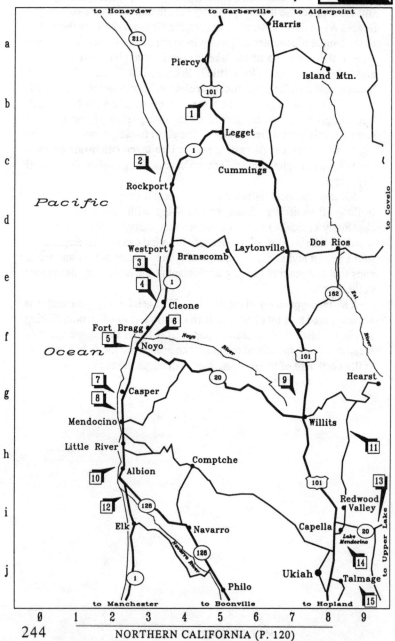

Pacific

Ocean

to Honeydew   to Garberville   to Alderpoint

Harris

211

Piercy

Island Mtn.

101

1

Legget

1

Cummings

2

Rockport

Westport

Branscomb

Laytonville

Dos Rios

3

4

1

162

Eel River

Cleone

6

Fort Bragg

5

Noyo

Noyo River

101

7

8

Casper

20

9

Hearst

Mendocino

Willits

Little River

11

Comptche

101

13

10

Albion

Redwood Valley

12

128

20

Elk

Navarro

Capella

Lake Mendocino

to Upper Lake

128

Navarro River

14

1

Ukiah

Talmage

Philo

15

to Manchester   to Boonville   to Hopland

to Covelo

Ø   1   2   3   4   5   6   7   8   9

NORTHERN CALIFORNIA (P. 120)

1. SOUTH FORK EEL RIVER

Reference: North of Leggett; map CØ grid b5.

How to get there: From Willits, drive approximately 44 miles north on US 101 to Leggett. Continue north on US 101. Access is excellent near the Smithe Redwoods State Reserve at Bridges Creek and Dora Creek, and near Standish Hickey Recreation Area, off the South Leggett exit. Access is also available off the Highway 271 exit (four-wheel drive is advisable here).

Facilities: Several campgrounds are available along the river on US 101, including Rock Creek, Standish-Hickey, and Redwood River Retreat. Supplies can be obtained in Leggett or Piercy.

Cost: River access is free.

Who to contact: Phone the Standish-Hickey Recreation Area at (707) 946-2311; Brown's Sporting Goods in Garberville at (707) 923-2533.

Special note: The South Fork Eel can be closed on October 1 if flows are below prescribed levels needed to protect migrating salmon and steelhead. The status of the stream is available by phoning a recorded message at (707) 442-4502.

About South Fork Eel: Steelhead anglers know well how muddy the Eel River can get. After a good rain in the winter, it can get so muddy, they say, that "you can plant a crop of potatoes." As for the fishing, it is zilched until the river starts to green up, and that can take a week to 10 days.

So what to do? Sit on your keyster praying for some sun? No way, not with the South Fork Eel available. You see, the heavy rains and corresponding high stream flows allow the steelhead to swim upriver, way upriver, and the section of the South Fork Eel just downstream of Leggett can provide greened-up, fishable water just a few days after a gullywasher.

Guide Jack Ellis has made a living for years by specializing on the Eel, focusing on this stretch of the South Fork when the rest of the Eel system is a brown out. There are several good spots between Leggett and Piercy. The best are at the deep bend in the river just south of Piercy, accessible by Highway 271, another deep bend just west (walking distance) of Standish-Hickey State Park, and just west of US 101 at Leggett. At the latter, a small road off adjacent Highway 1 provides a route down to the stream.

There are some other advantages to this section of river. One is the number of campgrounds in the area, providing options for a base camp. The other is its southern proximity, making it the closest major steelhead stream to the San Francisco Bay Area, a viable weekend trip with a Friday p.m. departure.

One note: This is a winter-only fishery. In the summer, the river is barely a trickle in this section and has no trout. Come the rains of winter, however, and if you hear something good about the South Fork Eel, you should raise your eyebrows and consider this stretch of river.

2. ROCKPORT SHORELINE

Reference: North of Fort Bragg; map CØ grid c3.
How to get there: From Fort Bragg, drive 20 miles north on Highway 1 to the town of Rockport. Turn west and travel to the coast.
Facilities: Campgrounds are located south of Rockport, off of Highway 1. Supplies are available nearby.
Cost: Access is free.
Who to contact: For general information, phone the Fort Bragg-Mendocino Coast Chamber of Commerce at (707) 964-3153. For fishing information, phone the Noyo Fishing Center in Fort Bragg at (707) 964-7609.
About Rockport shoreline: A good, hidden coastal spot can be discovered here. It is located in a small bay between Sea Lion Rock to the north and Cape Vizcaino to the south. This is where Cottaneva Creek pours into the ocean, creating a natural food basin for a number of marine species.

Perch are at the top of the list. Use sand crabs or chunks of anchovy for bait. Use a standard two-hook surf rig, small pyramid sinker and cast them out as far as you can near the river mouth. The perch can make for a great evening fish fry.

3. TEN MILE RIVER

Reference: North of Mackerricher State Park; map CØ grid e3.
How to get there: From Fort Bragg, drive three miles north on Highway 1 to MacKerricher State Park. Ten Mile River is located at the north end of the park, and is accessible by driving east on Camp 1 Ten Mile Road or south on Camp 2 Ten Mile Road.
Facilities: Camping is available at MacKerricher State Park. Supplies can be obtained in Fort Bragg.
Cost: Access is free.
Who to contact: Phone MacKerricher State Park at (707) 937-5804.
About Ten Mile River: Little Ten Mile River starts in the mountains just north of Bucha Ridge and tumbles some 20 miles in its short journey to the Pacific Ocean. It in the winter, when fierce coastal squalls pound into the ridge, water rushes down the canyon, forming this stream.

That water attracts a small run of steelhead upriver, a run which has suffered in numbers in recent years. Fishing them is difficult, limited to a small section of river near the mouth. The steelhead will enter the river after fresh rains and a high tide, then hole up in the lagoon for a while as they acclimate themselves to the cold, freshwater flows.

Few steelhead are caught on this river, but for people who are in the right place at the right time, it provides an intimate setting to deal with a powerful fish.

---

4.   CLEONE LAKE

Reference: Near Fort Bragg in Mackerricher State Park; map CØ grid e3.
How to get there: From Fort Bragg, drive three miles north on Highway 1 to MacKerricher State Park. The lake is located in the park.
Facilities: A campground is provided at MacKerricher State Park. Supplies are available in Fort Bragg. Non-motorized boats are permitted on the lake.
Cost: Campsite fees are $14 per night.
Who to contact: Phone MacKerricher State Park at (707) 937-5804.
About Cleone Lake: Little Cleone Lake is one of the few lakes in the state that is actually located west of Highway 1, nestled in a little pocket between the highway and Laguna Point. The lake and surrounding MacKerricher Park make an ideal weekend vacation.

It is stocked with rainbow trout, decent-sized ones at that, usually 11, 12-inchers that can provide a tussle. Shoreline baitdunkers do quite well after a stock, using the inevitable yellow Power Bait on one hook, half a nightcrawler on the other. The lake is stocked about every 10 days from spring to early summer.

Those trout join a resident population of largemouth bass, bluegill and brown bullhead. All three are warm-water fish that are most active in the summer and fall, but can be difficult to catch in any abundance. One reason is they get non-stop smart lessons every day of the summer.

Once the tourist season starts, a lot of people plan to camp at MacKerricher because of its idyllic location on the Mendocino coast. Many of them are not even aware of Cleone Lake. That changes quickly once they arrive, and if they have a fishing rod along, out it comes. What to do? Beat them to the punch by arriving in the spring, when the lake is full, the people are few, and the trout are biting.

---

5.   FORT BRAGG DEEP SEA

Reference: At Fort Bragg; map CØ grid f3.
How to get there: From Fort Bragg, drive south through town to North Harbor Drive (right before the Noyo Bridge). Turn left and travel west to Noyo Harbor.
Facilities: Several campgrounds and RV parks are available nearby,

including Dolphin Isle Marina, Woodside, and Pomo. A full-service marina, a boat ramp, bathrooms, groceries, bait, tackle, and party boat charters are available.

Cost: Party boat fees are $45-$55 per person.

Who to contact: For general information, phone the Fort Bragg Chamber of Commerce at (707) 964-3153. For fishing information, phone the Noyo Fishing Center at (707) 964-7609.

Party boat list: Noyo Fishing Center: *Misty II, Tally Ho II;* phone (707) 964-7604. Sportsman's Dock: *Trek II, Patty-C, Cavalier;* phone (707) 964-4550. Lady Irma: *Lady Irma II;* phone (707) 964-3854.

About Fort Bragg Deep Sea: Come summer and the Fort Bragg coast can provide some of the best salmon fishing anywhere in the world. The reason is because two runs of salmon can arrive here at the same time, with Klamath River salmon ranging this far south, and Sacramento River salmon ranging this far north. It usually happens between mid-June and mid-July. In addition, bottom fishing for rockfish and lingcod is outstanding as long as the sea is calm.

In the first part of July, a large number of salmon are caught straight out of Noyo Harbor. Anglers start trolling as soon as they reach open water. Another good spot for both salmon and rockfish is Cleone Reef, which is about three miles north of Fort Bragg in just 60 feet of water. And yet another close-to-port area is just two miles south of town, just offshore of a house that sits along the coast.

During September and October, the ocean is often its calmest of the year, and though the salmon have departed, the deep sea fishing is outstanding in its place. Some huge lingcod and a variety of rockfish will move into the local fishing grounds and provide limit bags that weigh 100 pounds.

Fort Bragg is the classic fisherman's town, out of the way but worth the trip. Because it is on Highway 1, tourists from all over America will visit here while cruising the coast highway. One time when I was waiting to be seated at a restaurant, a tourist tapped me on the arm, then asked: "What's the name of that big lake out there?" No kidding.

---

6. NOYO RIVER

Reference: Near Fort Bragg; map CØ grid f3.

How to get there: From Fort Bragg, drive south to North Harbor Drive (right before the Noyo Bridge). Turn west and travel to the harbor. Fishing is open from the mouth to below the Silverado Area Boy Scout Camp.

Facilities: Two boat ramps are provided on the south side of the river. Campgrounds, lodging, groceries, bait, and tackle are available nearby at Fort Bragg.

Cost: Access is free.

Who to contact: For general information, phone the Fort Bragg-Mendocino Coast Chamber of Commerce at (707) 964-3153. For fishing information, phone the Noyo Fishing Center at (707) 964-7609.

About Noyo River: Local know-hows catch 95 percent of the fish on this river, and it isn't because they have developed a special brand of expertise. It is rather because of their ability to jump when it is time to jump, that is, fish when the fish are in the river. The Noyo is a good-size coastal stream, running all the way from the mountains west of Willits on westward to Fort Bragg, pouring right out through the harbor.

What happens is that long periods of doldrums are interspersed by short, intense runs of fish as they leave the ocean and head upstream. When that happens, you flat have to be on the river. It can last for just a day or two, then they're gone upstream, and the wait starts again for another group of fish. Because of this, the most important piece of fishing equipment you can have is your telephone and a good local contact.

---

7.   CASPAR HEADLANDS STATE BEACH

Reference: Near Mendocino; map CØ grid g2.

How to get there: From Mendocino, drive three miles north on Highway 1. Take the Point Cabrillo exit and travel west to the beach. Fishing access is available on the shore and nearby at Caspar Creek.

Facilities: A full-facility campground is available across the street from the beach at Caspar Beach RV Park. Supplies are available in Mendocino.

Cost: Access is free; permit required.

Who to contact: For a use permit, contact Mendocino Recreation and Parks at (707) 937-5804. For lodging information, phone the Fort Bragg-Mendocino Coast Chamber of Commerce at (707) 964-3153.

About Caspar State Beach: This beach is protected in a bay, access is easy, and the gentle outflow of Caspar Creek here gets the marine food chain in gear, with perch on the top of it.

The irony is that the best fishing is when there are the least number of visitors. From Memorial Day through Labor Day, the perch fishing is only fair here, and in the spring, it can be quite poor. Yet that is when the tourists show up.

From September through early winter, however, the beach has its most gentle slope, run-off from fall rains raises the level of Caspar Creek and it begins flowing to sea, and the perch start biting. It is also excellent for swimming this time of year. Anybody around? Nobody but you.

---

8. MENDOCINO COAST

Reference: Near Mendocino; map CØ grid g2.

How to get there: From Mendocino, drive one-half mile south on US 101 to Mendocino Bay and the mouth of Big River. Direct access is available.

Facilities: A boat ramp is provided. Camping, groceries, gas, bait, tackle, and canoe rentals are available nearby.

Cost: Access is free.

Who to contact: Phone the Fort Bragg-Mendocino Coast Chamber of Commerce at (707) 964-3153.

About Mendocino coast: Mendocino Bay is pretty, the kind of place where Steinbeck would fit right in, one of the classic spots on the Pacific Coast. The little shops in town are loaded with little treasures, but the real treasure hunt comes to fishermen who venture on the inshore coastal waters.

The boat ramp provides easy access, and once on the water, you can be fishing in a matter of minutes. Good rockfishing is provided at many nearby reef areas, including just northwest of Goat Island around the northern point, and along the reefs southward to Stillwell Point.

Though the Big River flows to sea through Mendocino Bay, it attracts no salmon. Yet thousands and thousands of salmon swim past this area every summer. That presents what is called an "interception fishery," since the salmon that are here today are on the move, and will likely be gone tomorrow. That makes timing critical, and as at Fort Bragg, mid-July seems the best time to plan such a trip.

Boaters should not venture far out of Mendocino Bay without quality navigation equipment. It is very common for a giant fog bank to sit just off the coast, then suddenly move in and blanket everything. If you are offshore in a boat in clear weather, and then suddenly are cloaked, you will need that navigation equipment to safely return to harbor.

The fall is the prettiest time here, especially the calm evenings when the lights of Mendocino reflect off the bay. See it once and you will never forget it.

9. LAKE EMILY

Reference: Near Willits; map CØ grid g8.

How to get there: From the town of Willits on US 101, drive north on Sherwood Road to the Brooktrails Development. Turn left on Lupine Road and travel to the lake.

Facilities: No facilities are available on-site. Lodging and supplies are available in Willits.

Cost: Access free.

Who to contact: Willits Chamber of Commerce at (707) 459-7910; Department of Fish and Game at (707) 944-5500.

About Lake Emily: The locals are going to want to string me up to the yardarm for putting this one in the book, but hey, an author has a sworn duty.

It's not that Lake Emily is a spectacular setting. It isn't. It's not that the fish are giant. They aren't. What is it then? It's that Lake Emily is like a private, backyard fishing hole for the folks around Willits and they keep quiet about it.

Alas, access is so easy, just a short jaunt from US 101, that out-of-towners are bound to discover it anyway. Plus, the lake responds quickly after stocks, and it's hard to keep quiet when you see kids pedaling off with nice stringers of trout. So what you get at Lake Emily is an easy-to-reach, put-and-take fishery that can provide some good catch rates for rainbow trout. It's baitdunker time, so bring your chair and your bucket, and after a stock, wander on over and take a gander.

---

10.   ALBION COAST

Reference: Near Mendocino; map CØ grid h2.

How to get there: From Mendocino, drive 5.5 miles south on Highway 1 to the town of Albion. At the north side of the bridge, turn right and travel west to the harbor. A boat ramp is available at Schooner's Landing, located one mile north of the Albion Bridge.

Facilities: Camping, a boat ramp, canoe rentals, gas, groceries, bait and tackle are available nearby.

Cost: There is a fee to launch boats.

Who to contact: Phone Schooner's Landing at (707) 937-5707.

About Albion coast: It's a short cruise to the fishing grounds, either just around Albion Head to the north or make a left turn and head around Salmon Point to the south. There you will find good rockfishing, occasional salmon moving through the area in mid-summer, and big lingcod in September and October.

The area in the vicinity of Schooner's Landing is well protected, making for a good launch site for trailered boats. They have camp-grounds on grassy sites, and full hookups for motor homes, so this can make a good headquarters for a multi-day fishing trip.

A lot of people with trailered boats bypass this area because they usually do not even know a ramp is available. Well, it is. If you are touring the coast, it can add the missing piece to your vacation puzzle.

---

11.   VAN ARSDALE RESERVOIR

Reference: Near Ukiah; map CØ grid h9.

How to get there: From Ukiah, drive 4.5 miles north on US 101 to the junction with Highway 20. Turn east on Highway 20 and drive five miles east. Turn north on County Road 240 (Potter Valley-Lake Pillsbury Road) and travel to the reservoir.

Facilities: No facilities are available on-site. A PG&E campground is available nearby at Trout Creek. Supplies can be obtained in Ukiah.

Cost: Access is free.

Who to contact: Phone PG&E at (415) 973-8250.

About Van Arsdale Reservoir: This lake is proof that not all hidden lakes provide wondrous adventures. In fact, this lake doesn't serve much of a purpose except for screwing up the runs of steelhead in the Eel River that run head-on into Van Arsdale Dam.

   The lake is never stocked, no campgrounds are available in the immediate vicinity, no boat launch is provided, and the fishing is lousy. Other than that, it's a great place.

12.   NAVARRO RIVER

Reference: Near Mendocino; map CØ grid i2.

How to get there: From Mendocino, drive ten miles south on Highway 1. Turn left on Highway 128 and drive east. The highway parallels the lower river. Fishing is permitted from the river mouth to Greenwood Road Bridge. The upper river can be accessed through Hendy Woods State Park, located off Highway 128. A path at the south end of the bridge provides excellent access.

Facilities: A campground is available at Paul Dimmick State Park. Supplies can be obtained in Mendocino.

Cost: Access is free.

Who to contact: Phone the Fort Bragg-Mendocino Coast Chamber of Commerce at (707) 964-3153.

About Navarro River: Highway 128 follows this river all the way to the ocean, providing a good look at conditions and easy access. The best bet is to park at Paul Dimmick State Park and then hike upstream one to two miles. This is the best stretch of water for steelhead and a light sprinkling of silver salmon.

   The river brings with it a few surprises. It is quite wide near the mouth, and it is also quite clear and slow-flowing. During peak periods in the steelhead run in the winter, you can actually see the fish while hiking on the adjacent trail. You will get a mix of wonderment over the fish and frustration over the inability to hook many of them.

COLD CREEK

Reference: Near Ukiah; map CØ grid i9.

How to get there: From the junction of US 101 and Highway 20 north of Ukiah, drive five miles east on Highway 20. The mouth of Cold Creek is located at the junction on Highway 20 and East Side Road. Direct access is available off of Highway 20 driving southeast.

Facilities: Campgrounds and supplies are available at Lake Mendocino and Blue Lakes.

Cost: Access is free.

Who to contact: Phone the Bureau of Land Management at (707) 462-3873; Ukiah Sporting Goods at (707) 462-6036; Department of Fish and Game, (707) 944-5500.

About Cold Creek: Never heard of Cold Creek, eh? Well, some maps list it as the East Fork Russian River, but by any name, it provides the best summer trout fishing in a stream anywhere in this region. The locals call it Cold Creek, so referring to it as such shows a hint of inner knowledge.

The best section by far is the stretch of water just upstream from Lake Mendocino. This is where the DFG stocks rainbow trout, and not dinkers, but decent 11, 12-inch fish. In an area virtually devoid of trout streams—winter steelhead and summer rainbow trout just don't mix—Cold Creek provides an unique alternative. Access is easy and nearby Lake Mendocino provides campgrounds. Instead of searching for the hard-to-catch bass at Mendocino, you can just keep quiet, get your trout at Cold Creek, and return for the evening for a fish fry.

---

14. **LAKE MENDOCINO**

Reference: Near Ukiah; map CØ grid i9.

How to get there: From Ukiah, drive 4.5 miles north on US 101 to the junction with Highway 20. Turn east on Highway 20 and travel four miles to the lake entrance road. Turn right and continue to the lake.

Facilities: Several campgrounds are provided around the lake. A marina, boat ramps, picnic areas, and bait are available. Other supplies can be obtained in Ukiah.

Cost: Campsite fees range from $5-$8 for single camps; $70 for group camps.

Who to contact: Phone the U.S. Corps of Engineers, Lake Mendocino at (707) 462-7581; Ukiah Sporting Goods, (707) 462-6036.

About Lake Mendocino: If you like to swim, be careful about wading at Lake Mendocino. This is the home of the man-biting catfish. One summer, several swimmers were actually bit quite severely on their legs, leaving large red welts. You see, Fish and Game placed several "catfish condominiums" in the lake, that is, little homes for the catfish to hole up in, and when a wader stepped too close . . . wham! They got nailed.

This does not mean to use a human leg for bait, however. More traditional entreaties are in order, with summer evenings the prime time, when those catfish come out of their condos and go on the prowl for something to eat.

If you like fishing mornings instead, get up early before the waterskiers come to and cast small Rapalas in the coves. As long as the water is quiet and shaded, sunfish, bluegill, and bass will hang in these coves. But when the waterskiers start plowing up the water, and the sun heats up the surface temperatures, forget it, it's over.

There is another option, however, a real longshot for the gold ring. Believe it or not, there are some giant striped bass in this lake. The Department of Fish and Game provides a boost to the striped bass fishery each year by planting 4,500 yearling stripers. But they are very hard to catch, tend to hang quite deep, but feast by eating the other fish in the lake. It is illegal to use a live sportsfish for bait, but there is a way. Get on the water at first light at Coyote Dam, and cast large, deep-diving plugs, or troll a diving Rebel down the main river channel. A long shot? Definitely, but sometimes longshots come in.

After all, who ever heard of a man-biting cat.

---

15.   MILL CREEK PONDS

Reference: East of Ukiah near Cow Mountain Recreation Area; map CØ grid j9.

How to get there: From US 101 at Ukiah, take the Talmage turnoff. Turn right on East Side Road and drive one-quarter mile, then turn at the sign for Cow Mountain Recreation Area and travel a short distance to the ponds.

Facilities: Campgrounds are available nearby. Supplies can be obtained in Ukiah.

Cost: Access is free.

Who to contact: Phone the Bureau of Land Management, Cow Mountain Recreation Area at (707) 462-3873; Ukiah Sporting Goods at (707) 462-6036.

About Mill Creek Ponds: The trout at Mill Creek Ponds provide the finishing touch to a good idea that works.

Nearby is the Cow Mountain Recreation Area, a primitive area set in the Mayacmas Mountains, with hiking trails, some four-wheel drive roads, and a campground. The one thing that is missing is good trout fishing, but that is where Mill Creek Ponds come in. Fish and Game stocks the ponds with foot-long rainbow trout as long as water is high enough and cold enough to allow it. That means fall through early summer, generally about every two weeks. These fish want bait, not lures, and the ponds are small enough to make shoreline fishing ideal.

MAP C1

11 LISTINGS
PAGES 256-265

NOR-CAL MAP . see page 120
adjoining maps
NORTH (B1) ...... see page 182
EAST (C2) .... see page 266
SOUTH (D1) .... see page 322
WEST (CØ) .... see page 244

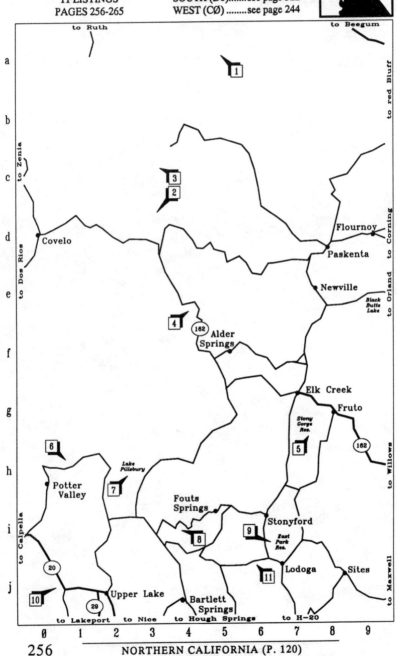

to Ruth

to Beegum

a

1

to red Bluff

b

to Zenia

c

3

2

to Dos Rios

d

Covelo

Flournoy

to Corning

Paskenta

e

Newville

to Orland

Black
Butte
Lake

4

162

Alder
Springs

f

Elk Creek

g

Fruto

Stony
Gorge
Res.

6

h

Lake
Pillsbury

5

162

Potter
Valley

7

to Willows

Fouts
Springs

Stonyford

i

8

9

East
Park
Res.

to Calpella

20

Lodoga

Sites

j

11

10

Upper Lake

29

Bartlett
Springs

to Maxwell

to Lakeport

to Nice

to Hough Springs

to H-20

Ø   1   2   3   4   5   6   7   8   9

1. YOLLA-BOLLY MIDDLE EEL WILDERNESS

Reference: West of Red Bluff in Mendocino National Forest; map C1 grid a5.

How to get there: From Red Bluff on Interstate 5, drive about four miles west on County Road A7, then turn left on Red Bank Road and drive 14.5 miles south. Bear right at Colyear Springs Road (County Road 356) and travel about 20 miles west. Park at Brown's Camp and hike into the wilderness area.

Facilities: No facilities are provided. No piped water is available, so bring your own.

Cost: Access is free.

Who to contact: Write to the Mendocino National Forest at 420 Laurel Street, Willows, CA 95988, or phone (916) 934-3316. For a map, send $2 to Office of Information, U.S. Forest Service, 630 Sansome Street, San Francisco, CA 94111. See Zone B1 for more information.

About Yolla-Bolly Wilderness: The Yolla-Bolly Wilderness is known for providing little-traveled routes to an intricate series of small streams, many of which provide the first flowing trickles into the Eel River. Lakes? Not too many. That's not the appeal here.

As a result, the fishing is often poor. Many of the little creeks scarcely even flow in late summer. However, hikers will discover the area is sprinkled with cold springs. In this sector of the Yolla Bollies, they will also discover just a few lakes that provide any fishing prospects.

Those lakes are Long Lake, Square Lake and Yolla-Bolly Lake; that's it. For other options, see the description of the Yolla Bolly Wilderness is neighboring Zone B1.

If you want great fishing, there are may other wilderness areas that rate higher. But if you want a wilderness hiking trip where you see few people and the climbs aren't killers, now you're talking. That is what the Yolly-Bolly Wilderness can offer.

---

2. HOWARD LAKE

Reference: Near Covelo in Mendocino National Forest; map C1 grid c3.

How to get there: From the junction of US 101 and Highway 162 at Longvale, drive northeast on Highway 162 to Covelo. Continue for thirteen miles east on Highway 162 to the Eel River Bridge. Turn left at the bridge and travel about 11 miles northeast on Forest Service Road M1 to Howard Lake.

Facilities: A campground, called Little Doe, is available just north of the lake. No piped water is provided, so bring your own. Supplies are

---

available in Covelo.

Cost: Access is free.

Who to contact: Phone the Mendocino National Forest District Office at (707) 983-6118. For a map, send $2 to Office of Information, U.S. Forest Service, 630 Sansome Street, San Francisco, CA 94111.

About Howard Lake: Little Howard Lake is tucked deep in the interior of Mendocino National Forest between Espee Ridge to the south and Little Doe Ridge to the north. For a drive-to lake, it is surprisingly remote and provides good fishing and primitive camping.

Howard Lake can be fished well from the shoreline, but is ideal for a small car-top boat such as a canoe, pram or raft. Whatever your preference, just plunk it in, paddle around, and fish all the area out of reach from shore. The trout are often good-size. It may seem hard to believe, but Fish and Game actually sends a tanker truck way out here, instead of stocking it by air. The result is trout in the foot-long class, instead of the midgets that take the one-way airplane rides.

Hammerhorn Lake, which is even smaller than Howard Lake, is located six miles north and provides an option. There are also some four-wheel drive roads that can provide a side trip opportunity.

---

3.   HAMMERHORN LAKE

Reference: Near Covelo in Mendocino National Forest; map C1 grid c3.

How to get there: From the junction of US 101 and Highway 162 at Longvale, drive northeast on Highway 162 to Covelo and continue for thirteen miles east on Highway 162 to the Eel River Bridge. Turn left at the bridge and travel about 17 miles northeast on Forest Service Road M1 to Hammerhorn Lake.

Facilities: A campground is provided at Hammerhorn Lake. Supplies are available in Covelo.

Cost: Access is free.

Who to contact: Phone the Mendocino National Forest District Office at (707) 983-6118. For a map, send $2 to Office of Information, U.S. Forest Service, 630 Sansome Street, San Francisco, CA 94111.

About Hammerhorn Lake: This is a veritable dot of a lake, just five acres, obscure and hidden, but it gets stocked with good-size fish and can provide good fishing, camping and adventuring for the few people who know of it. A population of golden shiners can drive you nuts robbing your bait in late summer, but most anglers can do just fine in early summer. No boat needed.

The lake is set near the border of the Yolla Bolla Wilderness, and some hikers will spend the night at Hammerhorn Lake before heading off the next day for the Mendocino wildlands, with the trailhead located nearby to the northeast. The irony is that they are apt to get better fishing at little Hammerhorn than anywhere in the adjacent wilderness.

If you want to explore the area further, a four-wheel drive can negotiate the primitive roads. The Hammerhorn Mountain lookout provides a great vista point. Either that, or bring a backpack and head northeast into the Yolla Bollies.

---

4. PLASKETT LAKES

Reference: Northwest of Willows in Mendocino National Forest; map C1 grid e4.

How to get there: From Willows on Interstate 5, turn west on Highway 162 and drive toward the town of Elk Creek. Just after you cross the Stony Creek Bridge, turn north on Road 306 and drive four miles. Turn left on Alder Springs Road and travel 31 miles, then turn left over the final piece of rough road to reach the lakes. Trailers over 16 feet are not advised.

Facilities: Two campgrounds are provided. Motorized boats are not permitted on the lake. Supplies are available in Elk Creek.

Cost: Campsite fee is $4 per night for single camps; $15 for group camp.

Who to contact: Phone the Mendocino National Forest District Office at (916) 934-3316.

About Plaskett Lakes: Plaskett Lakes are a pair of connected dot-size mountain lakes that form the headwaters of little Plaskett Creek. They are difficult to reach, set out in the middle of nowhere, but provide fishing for rainbow trout in the foot-long class. That is always a surprise for newcomers.

Of the two lakes, the better prospects by far are at the western-most one. The lake is not only bigger, but just plain seems to have more fish in it.

For a side trip option, there are some good hiking trails in the area to the south. One route heads along Plaskett Creek and then to the south up to Chimney Rock (which can also be reached from the south via Bushy Mountain Road).

---

5. STONY GORGE RESERVOIR

Reference: Near Elk Creek; map C1 grid g7.

How to get there: From the town of Willows on Interstate 5, drive west on Highway 162 for about 15 miles, then turn left at the signed entrance and travel one mile to the reservoir.

Facilities: Three free campgrounds are provided, but there is no piped water, so bring your own. A boat ramp is also available. Supplies can be obtained in Elk Creek.

Cost: Access is free.

Who to contact: Phone the Bureau of Reclamation at (916) 934-7066.

About Stony Gorge Reservoir: Stony Gorge is a long narrow lake set in a canyon, a classic foothill reservoir that gets hot weather and experiences summer water drawdowns, but also provides a decent warmwater fishery.

This lake could be something special if only they wouldn't tamper so much with the water levels—"they" being the Bureau of Reclamation, of course. The water is diverted out of Stony Creek and then delivered to farmers, many of whom then flood their fields with it. Because of their prehistoric irrigation techniques, you can actually see the water evaporating right off the fields and uncovered canals in the summer.

If you hit this lake in the early summer before it gets drained too much, you will find catfish, bluegill, crappie, and some largemouth bass. It is not a great bass lake, like Indian Valley Reservoir to the south, but it does provide good boating and a virtual smorgasbord of fishing opportunity.

---

6.   TROUT CREEK

Reference: Near Ukiah; map C1 grid h1.

How to get there: From Ukiah, drive north to the junction of US 101 and Highway 20. Turn east on Highway 20 and drive five miles. Turn northwest on County Road 240 (Potter Valley-Lake Pillsbury Road) and travel to Eel River Road. Turn right and continue 4.5 miles east to the Eel River Bridge. Drive two miles to Trout Creek.

Facilities: A PG&E campground is provided. Supplies are available in Potter Valley or Ukiah.

Cost: Campsite fee is $8 per night.

Who to contact: Phone PG&E at (415) 973-5552.

About Trout Creek: Trout Creek is a short feeder stream to the upper Eel River, a small but classic babbling brook that has enough pocket water to keep some small wild trout going. Don't expect anything big, and don't expect to catch a lot. But if you want a near-pristine stream, a nearby camp, and some pan-size trout, you found the place.

There are very few trout streams in this region, and most people don't have a clue about this one. Then when they hear about it and make a visit, they often are disappointed at the scaled-down size of the water and the fish. Don't be. It is quiet, peaceful and pure out here. Sometimes that is reward enough.

Reference: Near Ukiah in Mendocino National Forest; map C1 grid h2.

How to get there: From Ukiah, drive 4.5 miles north to the junction of US 101 and Highway 20. Turn east on Highway 20 and drive five miles. Turn northwest on County Road 240 (Potter Valley-Lake Pillsbury Road) and travel 26 miles to the lake.

Facilities: Several campgrounds are provided. Lodging, a marina, boat ramps, boat rentals, groceries, gas, bait, and tackle are also available.

Cost: Campsite fees range from free to $5 per night.

Who to contact: Phone the Mendocino National Forest District Office at (707) 275-2361.

About Lake Pillsbury: It seems that Lake Pillsbury is growing in popularity every year, bit by bit. At one time not so long ago, it was a mountain lake that had good weather, plenty of water, few people and lots of trout. Well, with all those attractions, it isn't surprising that more vacationers than ever before are heading here.

Covering some 2,000 acres, Pillsbury is by far the largest lake in Mendocino National Forest. It has lakeside camping and good boat ramps. Although the price "ain't great," groceries and gas are also available. Hey, there's even a county airport just north of the lake, with the runway just a long cast from lake's edge.

But it remains just hard enough to reach — via the little two-laners once you turn off US 101, or from Upper Lake — that it is unlikely to get inundated with people. That seems especially true with Clear Lake so much easier to reach to the south.

Pillsbury is well stocked with trout in the spring and the fall, and provides good trolling results. That continues into summer, when eventual hot weather drives the trout deep. At the same time that hot weather gets the resident populations of bass, bluegill and green sunfish active in the top 10 feet of water. It also makes the lake a good one for swimming, right off the Pogie Point Campground.

The better fishing is up the lake arms. Leave the main lake body to the water skiers, and instead explore up the Eel River arm, Horseshoe Gulch, or south of Rocky Point up the Rice Fork. Between vacation time from Memorial Day to Labor Day, you will never have this lake to yourself. But if you are interested in a visit, you can't blame other folks for having the same idea.

8. LETTS LAKE

Reference: West of Maxwell in Mendocino National Forest; map C1 grid i4.

How to get there: From Interstate 5 at Maxwell, turn west on Maxwell-Sites Road and drive to Sites, bear right on Peterson Road for one-half mile, then turn left on Sites-Lodaga Road and continue to Lodaga. Turn right on Lodaga-Stonyford Road and loop around East Park Reservoir to reach Stonyford. From Stonyford, drive eight miles west on Road M10 (Fouts Springs Road). Bear left at Forest Service Road 18N01 and travel six miles. Continue three miles southeast on Forest Service Road 17N02 to the lake. You can't miss it.

Facilities: Several campgrounds are provided. An unimproved boat ramp is available, but no motorized boats are permitted on the lake. Supplies can be obtained in Stonyford.

Cost: Campsite fees are $3-$5 per night.

Who to contact: Phone the Mendocino National Forest District Office at (916) 963-3128. For a map, send $2 to Office of Information, U.S. Forest Service, 630 Sansome Street, San Francisco, CA 94111.

About Letts Lake: OK, c'mon now, admit it: You've never seen directions like the ones provided here for Letts Lake, right? If you think they are confusing, imagine how difficult it would be to find without this book. Result? Advantage, you.

What you find when you eventually get here is a small lake set at 4,500 feet within the edge of Mendocino National Forest, with a few campgrounds on the north shore of the lake. Do not get it confused with the smaller Lily Pond to the immediate east, which has no fish (yet people are out there trying anyway). At Letts, however, there are trout to 12 inches, providing a good camping/fishing destination for folks who like to end the day with a trout fry. The lake is just big enough so that a small boat is a real help. Since no motors are allowed, and the access road is quite circuitous, car-top row boats, canoes or rafts are well suited.

You can add a dimension to your trip by taking a hike to one of several natural springs in the area: Fir Rock Springs, Summit Springs, Cold Springs, Freezeout Springs, Board Camp Springs, Young's Corral Springs, or Sylar Springs. The trails are detailed on a Forest Service map.

9.   EAST PARK RESERVOIR

Reference: Near Stonyford in Mendocino National Forest; map C1 grid i7.

How to get there: From Interstate 5 at Maxwell, turn west on Maxwell-Sites Road and drive to Sites, bear right on Peterson Road for one-half mile, then turn left on Sites-Lodaga Road and continue to Lodaga. Turn right on Lodaga-Stonyford Road and loop around East Park Reservoir to reach Stonyford. From Stonyford turn east on East Park Road and drive to the reservoir.

Facilities: A picnic area and an unimproved boat ramp are provided. Camping is available at Letts Lake in Mendocino National Forest. Supplies can be obtained in Stonyford or Lodaga.

Cost: Access is free.

Who to contact: Phone the Mendocino National Forest District Office at (916) 963-3128.

About East Park Reservoir: Damn, it can get hot here. In mid-summer, temperatures in the 90s and 100s are common, the lake levels drop a bit almost daily, and East Park Reservoir turns into a bathtub, complete with the ring.

So the smart angler gets here before the searing heat of summer, before the drawdowns, and before you need to wear ice under your hat to stay cool. Spring arrives early in the Central Valley foothills, and that can get the bass on a good bite here. What you should look for is the year's first three or four-day binge of weather in the 80s. That is when the bass will come out of their winter slumber and go on the attack.

The bass fishing remains quite good until the heat gets oppressive, then it is limited to sprees during early morning and late evening when the sun is off the lake. Anglers should respond by switching gears, fishing instead for bluegill, crappie or catfish.

East Park is shaped like a horseshoe, and when it is full, there is much more habitat for bass than the average reservoir. Many little fingers and coves on the southeast arm of the lake provide ideal haunts for bass. This is where to start your search, sticking and moving, casting along the shoreline during the first warm weather of spring.

10.   BLUE LAKES

Reference: Near Upper Lake; map C1 grid j0.

How to get there: From US 101 at Ukiah, drive 4.5 miles north to Highway 20. Turn east and continue for 12 miles to Blue Lakes. Lake access is available off Highway 20 or Blue Lakes Road.

Facilities: Several resorts and campgrounds are available, featuring camping, lodging, restaurants, boat ramps, boat rentals, groceries, bait, tackle and gas.

Cost: Campground fees are $14-$18 per night.

Who to contact: Phone the Le Trianon Resort at (707) 275-2262, or Pine Acres Blue Lake Resort at (707) 275-2811.

About Blue Lakes: Blue Lakes provides one of the few places in California where you can rent a lakeside cabin, go trout fishing, yet not have to endure a long, grinding drive to get there.

These Blue Lakes are in Lake County and are not to be confused with several other Blue Lakes elsewhere in the state. These Blue Lakes are stocked in the spring and fall with trout on a bi-weekly basis, and at times can provide the most consistent catch rates in the county. Those times, however, are always in the cooler months, not summer, and it can be frustrating for people who show up in July and say, "Where are all the trout I've heard about?"

The answer is that they have either already been caught, or are deep in the lake's thermocline, where the cool, oxygenated water is. When that happens, it is better to switch than fight. That means fishing instead for bluegill (during the day), largemouth bass (mornings/evenings), or catfish (night).

Blue Lakes are long and narrow, created from the flows of Cold Creek, which eventually flows into the East Fork Russian River and into Lake Mendocino. The lower lake is shaped like a peanut and is the larger of the two lakes.

Many people overlook Blue Lakes because of their close proximity to giant Clear Lake, located just 10 miles away to the southeast. In fact, visitors to Clear Lake often do not even know Blue Lakes exist. And if it is spring or fall and the bass aren't biting at Clear Lake, the trout at Blue Lakes can provide the ultimate insurance policy.

---

11.   LITTLE STONY CREEK

Reference: West of Maxwell; map C1 grid j6.

How to get there: From Interstate 5 at Maxwell, turn west on Maxwell-Sites Road and drive to Sites, bear right on Peterson Road for one-half mile, then turn left on Sites-Lodaga Road and continue to Lodaga. Turn right on Lodaga-Stonyford Road and start looping around East Park Reservoir, then turn left on Goat Mountain Road. Direct access is available from the road.

Facilities: Several campgrounds are provided along the creek. A good one is Digger Pine Flat on Goat Mountain Road.

Cost: Access to the creek is free.

Who to contact: Phone the Mendocino National Forest District Office at

(916) 963-3128.

About Little Stony Creek: This stream is appropriately named. It is little, and it is stony, and the little trout amid the stones fit right in.

It runs from Mendocino National Forest downstream into East Park Reservoir in the Colusa foothills, picking up help from Trout Creek and Sullivan Creek on the way. Because of the good access from adjacent Goat Mountain road, it is easy to fish much of this stream in an evening. You spot the hole, park and make the quick trip to the river, cast 10 times, then return to your vehicle and head further down the road.

The trout are small in here, have no illusions about that, but just the same, there are few other places in the Central Valley where you can head off Interstate 5 and be fishing in a trout stream within 20 miles of driving.

MAP C2

12 LISTINGS
PAGES 266-277

NOR-CAL MAP . see page 120
adjoining maps
NORTH (B2) ...... see page 196
EAST (C3) .... see page 278
SOUTH (D2)....... see page 340
WEST (C1) .... see page 256

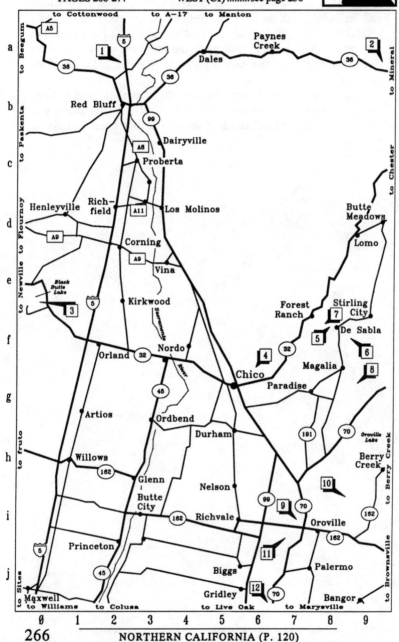

1. SACRAMENTO RIVER

Reference: From Red Bluff to Colusa; map C2 grid a3.

How to get there: Access is available off roads that junction with Interstate 5 near Red Bluff, Corning, and Orland. The river is also paralled by Highway 45 southeast of Orland, and direct access is available.

Facilities: Several campgrounds and RV parks are available along the river. A few good ones are Bend RV Park and Fishing Resort (near Red Bluff), Hidden Harbor RV Park (near Los Molinos), and Woodson Bridge State Recreation Area (near Corning). Lodging, boat ramps, boat rentals, and supplies are also available.

Cost: River access is free.

Who to contact: Phone Shasta Cascade Wonderland Association at (916) 243-2643.

About Sacramento River: The old river is a fountain of emerald-green, the lifeblood of Northern California, a living, pulsing vein in the heart of the state. Wow, what a writer, eh?

To put it to you a little more directly, this section of the river, from Red Bluff downstream to Colusa, is the prettiest part of California's Central Valley. I have canoed all of it, fished most of it, and it remains a place of beauty, power and big fish. For the folks who live on the river, they don't need a calendar. All they need to do is keep track of the migrations of fish, which tell time better than a watch. The river has resident trout and migrations of shad, salmon, striped bass, and sturgeon, some of which reach state-record sizes.

To fish it well, for the most part you must have a boat, and skill in operating it, or hire a guide who can do the job for you. The reason is because the banks of the Sacramento River for most of this section are quite deep, and wading is impossible in many areas. There are exceptions, however, and we will get to that.

In late May and June, the Sacramento River comes to life with the arrival of migrating shad. They will move through the entire section of river, from Colusa on upstream to the Red Bluff Diversion Dam. Shad provide the exception; they can be caught by anglers wading at two key areas: the Tehama Riffle and the Colusa area.

The Tehama Riffle is an outstanding spot. To reach it, take the Tehama/Los Molinos exit off Interstate 5, then drive east. At Tehama, turn right on County Road A8 and drive a few blocks, then cross the Sacramento River. Turn left on a dirt road and park immediately under the Tehama Bridge. The best stretch is just downstream of the bridge.

If you have a boat, you can launch at Woodson Bridge State Park, Mill Creek Park at Los Molinos or at the Red Bluff Diversion Dam. The best fishing is in the evening, when one can catch up to 20 shad in the two to five-pound class, using Shad Darts, T-Killers or Teeney

Rounders, quartering your casts and getting the lure deep.

The shad run continues into July, when the big females arrive, then starts to wane. By August, however, enough salmon begin moving through to change your entire perspective. These are all big spawners, mostly 10 to 20-pounders, and they can jump, strip line, and really raise hell. The salmon run peaks in September, continues through October, then peters out in November.

It's a long grind of a day fishing for these big salmon, though. You start early and end late, patiently back-trolling with roe, Flatfish, or Kwikfish lures, in the river's deeper holes. You need persistence with spirit, and it is worth it. The holes in the five miles of river downstream of the Red Bluff Diversion Dam are the top spots. It was here that Lindy Lindberg caught the state record 88-pounder, a fish so big that he had to strap it to the side of his boat a la "Old Man and The Sea." For details on the techniques required for both salmon and shad fishing on the river, see the Secrets of the Masters section at the front of this book.

Come winter and early spring, the sturgeon and striped bass start moving into this area. The better holes are in the stretch of water near Colusa, and some huge sturgeon are in the mix. Many of them beat the six-foot size limit now in effect. These are strong fish, and they can really put you through a war. Meanwhile, more stripers now spawn in the Sacramento River than in the San Joaquin Delta. Trolling Rebels is the way to catch them, though it can require many hours per hookup. They don't come easy, but they come big. Since the larger individuals are spawning females, I urge anglers to release them with the trade of guaranteed improved future fishing.

2.　　　　BATTLE CREEK

Reference: Near Red Bluff in Lassen National Forest; map C2 grid a9.

How to get there: From Red Bluff on Interstate 5, drive about 40 miles east on Highway 36. Direct access is available.

Facilities: A campground is provided just west of the town of Mineral. Supplies are available in Mineral.

Cost: Access is free.

Who to contact: Phone the Lassen National Forest District Office at (916) 258-2141.

About Battle Creek: Here is the best of trout streams in Lassen National Forest. You get rainbow trout up to a foot long, easy access off Highway 36, and a pretty setting on the edge of Lassen National Park. A lot of anglers drive right on by in both directions, not realizing there are fish in Battle Creek. But there are. Fish and Game makes sure of it by stocking catchables bi-weekly through much of the summer. Get rainbows and some brookies.

Adjacent Paynes Creek, set lower on Highway 36, provides a nearby alternative, though the fish tend to be smaller and the seasonal window of opportunity a bit shorter.

---

3.   BLACK BUTTE LAKE

Reference: Near Orland; map C2 grid eØ.
How to get there: From Interstate 5 at Orland, take the Black Butte Lake exit. Drive ten miles west on Newville Road to the lake.
Facilities: Two campgrounds are provided: Orland Buttes and Buckhorn.
     A full-service marina, a boat ramp, boat rentals, a sanitary disposal station, groceries, bait, tackle, and propane gas are available nearby.
Cost: Access to the lake is free.
Who to contact: Phone the U.S. Corps of Engineers, Black Butte Lake at
     (916) 865-4781.
About Black Butte Lake: Hit this lake wrong and you get a vacation from hell. Hit it right, and you wonder why more people aren't taking advantage of "paradise." The reality here is that there is rarely an in-between.

Connect here in late March, April and May and you will find a pretty lake amid fresh-green foothills, some 40 miles of shoreline, lakeside camps, and some of the best crappie fishing in Northern California.

But arrive in late July or August and you will find the lake level low, the hillsides brown and mostly barren, the camps like sweat pits, and fish with a terminal case of lockjaw. Thus there should be no doubt as to when you should plan your visit. Access is easy to Black Butte, being just a short jog off Interstate 5, making it a prime attraction to owners of trailered boats. In the spring, not only do the crappie go on the bite, but that is also the best time of year for a good fishery for largemouth bass.

The lake is shaped like a giant 7, and when the water level is up, the better area for fishing is on the north side just west of the dam and east of Buckhorn Store, where there are a series of protected coves and an island. Avoid open water at this reservoir and instead focus on the little coves and protected backwater areas. That is where you will find the fish.

Yeah, this place can be hell in the summer, when 100-degree temperatures are common. In the spring, however, it provides a far different scenario.

4.   BIG CHICO CREEK

Reference: Near Chico; map C2 grid f6.

How to get there: From Interstate 5 at Red Bluff, take the Chico exit. Or, farther south on Interstate 5, take the Chico exit at Orland. Continue to the town of Chico, then drive north on Chico Canyon Road, which borders the stream. Another option is to drive east on Highway 32 out of Chico, then turn north on Fourteen Mile House Road, which connects to Chico Canyon Road in the better fishing area.

Facilities: No facilities are provided. Lodging and Supplies are available in Chico.

Cost: Access is free.

Who to contact: Phone the Shasta-Cascade Wonderland Association at (916) 243-2643.

About Big Chico Creek: Big Chico Creek is just out of sight of Highway 32. Guess what? That is why everybody driving the highway rips right on by. No trout are stocked here, and the resident population of wild trout are not exactly worth bragging about . . . but the area has easy access and quiet spots. Sometimes just watching the river run by is reward enough.

---

5.   DE SABLA FOREBAY

Reference: Near Paradise; map C2 grid f8.

How to get there: From Interstate 5 at Orland, take the Highway 32-Chico exit. Drive about 18 miles east to Chico, then get on Highway 99 south and turn east on Skyway Road and drive ten miles, toward Paradise. Continue through the town and drive ten more miles north to De Sabla Forebay.

Facilities: No camping is permitted, but a recreational group picnic area is provided on the east side. No boating is permitted.

Cost: Fee for using the group picnic area is $50 per day; reservations are required.

Who to contact: Phone PG&E at (800) 552-4743.

About De Sabla Forebay: Ever wanted to fish somebody's personal fishing reserve? If so, De Sabla Forebay provides that opportunity.

This little lake is a private resort for a handful of PG&E hoity-toity types, but public access is permitted on the south and east side of the lake, with access off Skyway Boulevard. It's shoreline baitdunking time, with no boats allowed.

It is stocked with rainbow trout, and if you can get the vacation schedule of the PG&E hotshots who fish here, you will always know the best times to fish. Even though it is quite small, the water level always seems to be full, another PG&E virtue.

Note: The group picnic area is booked nearly every summer weekend, and if you plan on reserving it, do so far in advance.

---

6. PARADISE LAKE

Reference: Near Paradise; map C2 grid f8.

How to get there: From Interstate 5 at Orland, take the Highway 32-Chico exit. Drive about 18 miles east to Chico, then get on Highway 99 south and turn east on Skyway Road and drive ten miles, toward Paradise. Once in Paradise, turn north on Coutolenc Road and drive five miles.

Facilities: A day-use only picnic area is provided. No motorized boats are permitted on the lake. A campground is available north of Paradise Lake at Philbrook Reservoir. Supplies are available in Paradise.

Cost: Day-use fee is $1.

Who to contact: Phone Paradise Lake at (916) 873-1040.

About Paradise Lake: Anglers with any kind of imagination can conjure up all kinds of fantastic notions about a lake that is named Paradise. But keep your lid on before you overheat, because while it's nice, it's not quite t-h-a-t nice.

The best thing about Paradise Lake is that it provides a more intimate setting to fish for trout in the spring and bass in the summer than Lake Oroville to the south. Because no motors are allowed on the lake, you don't have to worry about getting plowed under by waterskiers, such as at Oroville. Instead you get quiet water, ideal for small paddle-powered boats.

In early summer, this can be a perfect place to bring a canoe, with the stern man paddling, the bow man casting along the shore for bass. Occasionally you might even pick up a large brown trout while casting for bass. They're in here, too.

Paradise Lake is stocked every spring with rainbow trout and brook trout, and in addition to largemouth bass, also has a resident population of catfish. The species are season-dependent, with the area getting huge swings in temperature from season to season. That is because it is set at 3,000 feet, getting both the heat of valley in summer, the cold of Lassen Forest in winter.

---

7. BUTTE CREEK

Reference: Near Paradise in Lassen National Forest; map C2 grid f8.

How to get there: From Interstate 5 at Orland, take the Highway 32-Chico exit. Drive about 18 miles east to Chico, then get on Highway 99 south and turn east on Skyway Road and drive ten miles, toward Paradise. Once in Paradise, drive five more miles north on Skyway Road, then

---

turn north on Doe Mill Road. Access is available at the bridge nearby, and also farther north along the road.

Facilities: No facilities are available on-site. A campground is available north of Butte Creek at Philbrook Reservoir. Supplies can be obtained in Paradise.

Cost: Access is free.

Who to contact: Phone the Bureau of Land Management at (916) 246-5325. For a map, send $2 to Office of Information, U.S. Forest Service, 630 Sansome Street, San Francisco, CA 94111.

About Butte Creek: For the angler who has grown tired of the reservoirs in the area, especially on a hot day when a cold stream sounds even better than a cold beer, Butte Creek provides the answer.

It is stocked with 8,500 trout starting in early summer, and these aren't the little Slim Jims, but range to a foot. It is just enough out of the way to get missed by virtually all out-of-towners. The drive to the stream can provide some fun, exploring the vicinity of Doe Mill Ridge and the surrounding Lassen National Forest.

---

8.   CONCOW RESERVOIR

Reference: Near Paradise; map C2 grid g8.

How to get there: From Interstate 5 at Red Bluff, take the Highway 99-Chico exit. Drive approximately 55 miles south on Highway 99 to Highway 149, then turn east and drive four miles to Highway 70. Turn north and travel twelve miles to Concow Road on the left. Turn north and continue for three miles to the reservoir. From the town of Paradise, drive south on Pentz Road to Highway 70, then north to Concow Road and proceed as above.

Facilities: No facilities are available on-site. Campgrounds are available nearby at Lake Oroville. Supplies can be obtained in Oroville.

Cost: Access is free.

Who to contact: Phone Paradise Lake at (916) 873-1040.

About Concow Lake: The key with Concow Lake is in what the lake doesn't have, rather than what it does. It does not have a campground, and in fact, it has no facilities at all. There are virtually no fish stocks of any kind. Boating access is poor too, with no ramp. Fishing? That's not so great either. These are some resident rainbow trout, a few big brown trout that hide out and are difficult, and scarce little else. The easiest area to fish is the southern end of the lake, where a road drops down to the lake. Other than that it's a great place, heh, heh, heh.

THERMALITO FOREBAY

Reference: Near Oroville in Oroville Lake State Recreation Area; map C2 grid i7.

How to get there: The forebay is divided into two areas: North Forebay and South Forebay. To reach the North Forebay from Oroville, drive about two miles north on Highway 70. Turn west on Garden Drive and travel one mile to the picnic area. To reach the South Forebay, drive three miles west on Grand Avenue to the parking area.

Facilities: A day-use picnic area and a boat ramp are provided at the North Forebay. No motorized boats are permitted. Motors are permitted on the South Forebay, and a boat ramp is provided there as well. Camping is available nearby at Lake Oroville. Supplies can be obtained in Oroville.

Cost: A parking fee of $6 is charged.

Who to contact: Phone the Lake Oroville State Recreation Area at (916) 538-2200; Feather River Bait, Thermolito, (916) 534-0605.

About Thermolito Forebay: With so many boaters, campers and anglers heading to nearby Lake Oroville, Thermolito Forebay is becoming a surprisingly viable option to those who prefer a quiet water with no motorized boats.

It may seem small compared to the giant Lake Oroville, but the Forebay is no pint-sized lake, and provides some good fishing as well. The best of it is for trout in the spring, then bass in the early summer. Shoreline prospects are decent, especially for anglers who keep on the move, exploring new spots, rather than sitting like a statue all day.

The quality of camping is also seasonal dependent. At less than 1,000-feet elevation, this area gets blowtorch heat day after day once midsummer arrives. You might as well camp in the caldera of a volcano.

---

10.   LAKE OROVILLE

Reference: Near Oroville; map C2 grid i9.

How to get there: From Oroville on Highway 70, drive east on Highway 162 or north on Highway 70 to the lake.

Facilities: Several campgrounds are provided, including Bidwell Canyon and Loafer Creek. Boat-in camping is also available. A full-service marina, boat ramps, boat rentals, groceries, gas, bait, and tackle can be obtained nearby.

Cost: Fee for day use is $6. Campsite fees are $12-$22 for single camps; $18.75-$37.50 for group camps. The boat launch fee is $3.

Who to contact: Phone the Lake Oroville State Recreation Area at (916)

538-2200; Feather River Bait, Thermolito, (916) 534-0605.

About Lake Oroville: Lake Oroville is a huge, manmade reservoir with extensive lake arms and a large central body of water, covering more than 15,000 acres. Fish? It's got 'em, a huge variety, including rainbow trout, brown trout, largemouth bass, catfish, bluegill, crappie, and even a modest salmon population.

So at first glance, Oroville seems to have it all: campgrounds, enough water for all kinds of boating, and a fish for every angler. But at second glance, the vision becomes more of a mirage.

Water? So much is drained every year that it can look like the Grand Canyon of Oroville, with acres and acres of exposed lake bottom. Campgrounds? They're too far from the water, and the state has broken its promise to provide more of them. The weather? At 900 feet elevation in foothill country, very hot temperatures are typical in the summer, and anybody who isn't prepared for it will shrivel like a prune. The fishing? Well, it only rarely lives up to expectations.

The bass fishing should be as good as at Shasta Lake, another big reservoir, but it isn't. Because of the lake drawdowns, much of the bass spawn in the shallows is left high and dry every spring, so this lake never seems to get the big spawns that later make for quality fishing. In addition, much of the lake bottom is barren and steep, and little structure equals few bass.

Some big trout are in this lake, and they provide good trolling during the seasonal transitions from winter to spring, and again from fall to winter. The best of it is well up the lake arms, particularly for big browns trolling a jointed Rapala during the cool fall months, or for small rainbow trout using the traditional flasher/nightcrawler combination. But for most of the year, because the surface waters get so warm, the trout are very deep, like 60 to 80 feet down, sometimes even deeper, and nobody likes to fish that deep in a lake.

That is why Fish and Game tried planting salmon, but they went deep too, and unlike the success with salmon at Lake Almanor and Don Pedro Reservoir, not many folks have been able to catch them here.

Another problem are the water skiers. Because the surface water becomes so warm in summer, owners of high-powered boats find it is like skiing in a huge hot tub. In turn, they like to go up the narrow lake arms, instead of sticking to the large central body of water, and can plow up what should be calm and quiet fishing territory.

There is hope for all of this. The Lake Oroville Fishery Enhancement Committee (LOFEC) is demanding improved management of fishery habitat, water levels and recreation sites. Already, some black bass habitat projects have been completed, although what is needed is a large scale, state-funded program. If LOFEC keeps the noise up, though, they can't help but improve this lake.

---

11. THERMALITO AFTERBAY

Reference: Near Oroville; map C2 grid j6.

How to get there: From Oroville, drive west on Highway 162 (Oroville Dam Boulevard). Right before the bridge on the Afterbay, turn left on a dirt road and travel a short distance to the launching area.

Facilities: No paved boat launch is provided, but all boats are permitted. Campgrounds are located nearby at Lake Oroville. Supplies are available in Oroville.

Cost: Access is free.

Who to contact: Phone the Lake Oroville State Recreation Area at (916) 538-2200; Feather River Bait, Thermolito, (916) 534-0605.

About Thermalito Afterbay: After a day at Lake Oroville, owners of canoes, row boats and rafts might be ready to throw their boats over Feather Falls. But Thermalito Afterbay provides a much saner option, with some good bass fishing as a bonus.

Owners of small boats who poke and probe will get good bass fishing in spring and early summer, during the early morning and late evening. When the water temperature is 65 to 70 degrees, the southeastern part of the lake can provide quite a surface bass bite.

The problem for small boats at neighboring Oroville is that they can just about get plowed under by a speeding ski boat rounding a point on one of the upper lake arms. That just doesn't seem to happen here. The key is the non-paved ramp. Most of the owners of the power boats just don't like the idea of it, but for an owner of a car-top boat, it will do just fine.

In addition, the Afterbay doesn't look like a lake is supposed to look. It is squarish to the southwest, then shallow to the east. The latter provides good habitat for waterfowl in the winter.

---

12. FEATHER RIVER

Reference: Near Oroville; map C2 grid j6.

How to get there: Access is available south of Oroville, off Highway 70. The area north of the Table Mountain Bicycle Bridge is closed to all fishing. Areas south of the bridge are open seasonally; check current DFG regulations.

Facilities: Campgrounds, lodging, and supplies are available in the Oroville area.

Cost: River access is free.

Who to contact: Phone the Oroville Wildlife Area at (916) 538-2236;

Feather River Bait at (916) 534-0605.

About Feather River: You either have a boat or you don't. Your approach to this river varies dramatically according to that.

It doesn't mean you are out of luck if you don't have a boat; you just have to play ball by the fish's rules, not your own. For salmon, which arrive in both the fall and the spring, it means heading to the Thermolito Afterbay Outlet Hole. That is where the salmon often congregate, though a lot of them seem to be jumpers, not biters, and it can drive you nuts. The persistent few wait them out with anchovies for bait.

For shad, which move into the river in good numbers in May, Shanghai Bend is one of the best spots in the state. It is located downriver from the mouth of the Yuba River, a prime, wadable piece of water that can provide some tremendous fishing. In the first and second weeks of May, anglers can sometimes catch 20 to 25 shad in an evening. The best years are those when stream flows are up, not down. There can be long periods, of course, when the catches are sparse, but if you ever get in on one of these runs, you never forget it.

The odds are better, however, if you have a boat. The shad arrive at Feather's confluence with the Sacramento River at Verona, where boaters will anchor and be able to cast right where the two rivers blend together. This is one of the top shad spots anywhere.

If you have a boat, it is also much easier to chase the migrating salmon and striped bass. Both the mouth of the Feather, and upstream at Shanghai Bend and the Thermolito Afterbay Outlet Hole are prime spots. So are a number of river holes in between those spots, which can be located with a depthfinder. They are best fished by positioning the boat just upstream of the hole, keeping the boat pointed upriver, and either anchoring or keeping the engine running enough to maintain river position. Then the angler drops his bait or lure downstream into the hole, right along the river bottom where the big fish are. Before the Oroville Dam was built, the Feather River was one of the top salmon and shad streams in America. Although downscaled a bit from the good 'ol days, there are still periods when it reclaims that former excellence.

MAP C3

35 LISTINGS
PAGES 278-303

NOR-CAL MAP . see page 120
adjoining maps
NORTH (B3) ...... see page 216
EAST (C4) .... see page 304
SOUTH (D3) .... see page 348
WEST (C2) .... see page 266

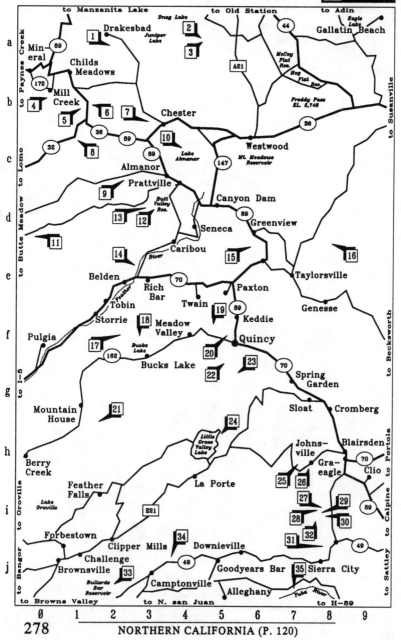

NORTHERN CALIFORNIA (P. 120)

1. WILLOW LAKE

Reference: Near Chester in Lassen National Forest; map C3 grid a2.

How to get there: From Susanville, drive approximately 26 miles west on Highway 36 to the town of Chester. Turn north on Warner Valley Road and drive about five miles north. When the road forks, bear left for one mile, then bear right and continue on a dirt road to Willow Lake.

Facilities: A primitive campground is provided, but no piped water is available. Supplies can be obtained in Chester.

Cost: Access is free.

Who to contact: Phone the Lassen National Forest District Office at (916) 258-2141.

About Willow Lake: The little egg-shaped lake always comes as a surprise. It is well off the ol' beaten path, but is located so near some of California's top vacation destinations that it gets missed by out-of-towners every time.

Willow Lake is set in national forest just west of Kelly Mountain, only three miles from the southeastern border of Lassen National Park at Drakesbad, and only 10 miles northwest of giant Lake Almanor. It provides an intimate, quiet setting for the camper/angler, and is stocked in early summer with 1,000 brown trout and 1,000 Eagle Lake trout, primarily 10 and 11-inchers. Shoreline fishing is easy and often good. After setting up camp, just walk around the lake, stopping to cast a few times as you go. A fly-and-bubble, Panther Martin, or 1/8-ounce Kastmaster or Z-Ray can usually do the job. If nobody has fished the lake recently, approach the shallows of the lake at the Willow Creek inlet and outlets. Unless they get scared off, trout often hold here.

Drakesbad at Lassen Park provides a great side trip for hikers, with destinations such as Devil's Kitchen and several alpine lakes within an hour's walk.

2. ECHO LAKE

Reference: Near Chester in Lassen National Forest; map C3 grid a5.

How to get there: From Susanville, drive approximately 18 miles west on Highway 36 to Chester Dump Road (about eight miles east of the town of Chester). Turn left on Chester Dump Road and drive west a short distance on a connector road, then continue north for 9.5 miles to Echo Lake.

Facilities: A primitive campground is provided, but no piped water is available. Supplies can be obtained in Chester.

Cost: Access is free.

Who to contact: Phone the Lassen National Forest District Office at (916) 258-2141. A map is available for $2 from Office of Information, U.S.

Forest Service, 630 Sansome Street, San Francisco, CA 94111.

About Echo Lake: Obscure? Hard to reach? Primitive camping? Good fishing? Not many people around?

That is exactly what most people want on a vacation, and that is exactly what Echo Lake provides. Its one drawback is its small size, a problem only on extended trips. But in the short run, it is to your advantage, with 2,000 rainbow trout and 2,000 brook trout stocked each year in late spring. That is double the number of trout stocked in Willow Lake to the west, which provides a similarly styled destination.

The lake is set less than a mile from the Caribou Wilderness to the northwest. With a national forest map in hand to help you route your trip, it can be easy to make a quick trip into the nearby wilderness and hit a lake loop. Hidden Lakes, Long Lake, Posey Lake and Beauty Lake are all on the same loop trail.

---

3. STAR LAKE

Reference: Near Chester in Lassen National Forest; map C3 grid a5.

How to get there: From Susanville, drive approximately 18 miles west on Highway 36 to Chester Dump Road (about eight miles east of the town of Chester). Turn left on Chester Dump Road and drive west a short distance on a connector road, then continue north for about nine miles to the trailhead. It's a short hike to the lake.

Facilities: No facilities are available on-site. A primitive campground is available at nearby Echo Lake, but there is no piped water.

Cost: Access is free.

Who to contact: Phone the Lassen National Forest District Office at (916) 258-2141.

About Star Lake: Of three small trout lakes in this area north of Almanor, Star Lake provides the best chance of seeing the fewest people. Unfortunately, it also provides the best chance of catching the smallest fish.

This little mountain lake has those DFG dinkers in it, you know, the little five-inch brook trout. If you catch an eight-incher, you may need to call the hospital to get resuscitated. The lake is not exactly loaded with these little brookies either. It gets only 500 per year.

But it is quiet and pretty, and if you have some mountain goat in you, climbing the adjacent Star Butte to the east provides a good boot-thumping side trip.

---

4. MILL CREEK

Reference: Near Mineral in Lassen National Forest; map C3 grid b0.

How to get there: From Interstate 5 at Red Bluff, take the Highway 36 exit and drive about 45 miles northeast to the town of Mineral. Turn south on County Road 172 and drive five miles to the town of Mill Creek. Turn right at a signed Forest Service road and continue for three miles to a parking area and trailhead. A hiking trail follows Mill Creek for several miles.

Facilities: Campgrounds are available off the road that leads to the trailhead. Supplies are available in Mineral.

Cost: Access is free.

Who to contact: Phone the Lassen National Forest District Office at (916) 258-2141. For a map, send $2 to U.S. Forest Service, 630 Sansome Street, San Francisco, CA 94111.

About Mill Creek: Don't try fishing Mill Creek without a Forest Service map. A lot of the land bordering this trout stream is privately owned, and the ranchers are apt to give you a load of buck salt in your rear end if you get caught trespassing.

So pay close attention to the advised directions. This stretch of stream is where the trout stocks are usually made, some 2,000 per summer, and also where public access is best. Besides, too much salt isn't good for you.

---

5. GURNSEY CREEK

Reference: East of Mineral in Lassen National Forest; map C3 grid b1.

How to get there: From Interstate 5 at Red Bluff, take the Highway 36 exit and drive about 45 miles northeast to the town of Mineral. Continue east on Highway 36 for about 15 miles; direct access is available off the highway near Fire Mountain.

Facilities: A campground is provided on Highway 36. Supplies are available in Mineral.

Cost: Access is free.

Who to contact: Phone the Lassen National Forest District Office at (916) 258-2141.

About Gurnsey Creek: This is a very small stream that provides a viable fishery in early summer before stream flows turn into a trickle. Highway 36 crosses Gurnsey Creek twice, just before and then after the "town" of Fire Mountain. This is your access point.

The fishing here is dependent on stocks and streamflows. It gets only 1,000 trout per year and the flows are usually best around mid-May. It's not anything great, to be sure, but it does provide a road-side hit if you're cruising through the area on Highway 36.

---

6. WILSON LAKE

Reference: Near Mineral in Lassen National Forest; map C3 grid b1.

How to get there: From Interstate 5 at Red Bluff, take the Highway 36 exit and drive about 45 miles northeast to the town of Mineral. Continue east for 8.5 miles, just past Childs Meadows. Turn left on Wilson Lake Road and travel 2.5 miles north to the lake.

Facilities: No facilities are available on-site. A primitive campground, called Willow Springs, is located a short distance east of Wilson Lake, but no piped water is provided. Supplies are available in Mineral.

Cost: Access is free.

Who to contact: Phone the Lassen National Forest District Office at (916) 258-2141.

About Wilson Lake: If you want a pretty spot to visit, but wouldn't want to live there, Wilson Lake is worth consideration.

You see, the trout fishing just doesn't seem to be up to snuff at ol' Wilson Lake. It's pretty enough, a round lake bordered by meadows on one side and a few little islands dotting it, but it is shallow on the northeast side. At least the salamanders like it.

If you don't catch anything, consider the short hike southeast of the lake to the Ice Cave, created by ancient glacial action, or the more rigorous adventure to the top of Ice Cave Mountain.

---

7. LITTLE NORTH FORK FEATHER RIVER

Reference: Northwest of Lake Almanor in Lassen National Forest; map C3 grid b3.

How to get there: From Susanville, drive approximately 26 miles west on Highway 36 to the town of Chester. Turn north on Warner Valley Road and continue northwest. Access is available directly off Warner Valley Road and off several Forest Service roads and trails that junction with it.

Facilities: Several campgrounds are available near the river. Supplies can be obtained in Chester.

Cost: Access is free.

Who to contact: Phone the Lassen National Forest District Office at (916) 258-2141. For a map, send $2 to Office of Information, U.S. Forest Service, 630 Sansome Street, San Francisco, CA 94111.

About Little North Fork Feather River: The best spots are hard to reach—you have to be willing to hike—but the Little North Fork can provide some very good fishing, depending on where you fish it.

The central access points, just off Forest Service roads in Warner Valley, are the same places where Fish and Game stocks trout. These are not the real little guys, but for the most part are rainbow trout sized in the nine to 11-inch class, some 17,000 per year. That can provide some fun, in an intimate, small water setting.

But if you hike onward, brush bashing and rock-hopping your way to the difficult-to-reach pools, you will find water with some brown trout of surprising size. The theory is that these browns are from Lake Almanor. They are difficult to catch, and there are not a lot of them, so tread lightly, and if you are lucky enough to hook one, maybe it's time to let 'em go and leave some seed for the future.

---

8. DEER CREEK

Reference: Near Mineral in Lassen National Forest; map C3 grid cØ.
How to get there: From Interstate 5 at Red Bluff, take the Highway 36 exit and drive about 45 miles northeast to the town of Mineral. Continue for about 12 miles southeast on Highway 36. Turn right on Highway 32 and travel south. Direct access is available off Highway 32.
Facilities: Campgrounds are provided on the creek on Highway 32. Supplies are available in Mineral.
Cost: Access is free.
Who to contact: Phone the Lassen National Forest District Office at (916) 258-2141.
About Deer Creek: Try to envision the ideal trout stream: A trail goes along the stream, providing access; the stream is pure and clear, winding its way over rocks and into pools; there seem to be trout in the foot-long class in all of the good-looking spots, even though you can't always catch them.

Want more? A small, yellow-striped two-lane highway runs right alongside much of it, allowing anglers to hit several different stretches of river the same day.

You have probably figured out by now that Deer Creek provides all of this. It is consistently one of the better stream producers from the trout opener on the last Saturday in April on through June. In that span, it is stocked with 54,000 rainbow trout and 6,000 brook trout.

The trail along much of the stream on this premium upper stretch really makes the river. You get a good look at the better spots, then get the feeling that you are sneaking up on the fish, and ultimately have a realistic opportunity of coming up with a nice stringer.

---

9. BUTT CREEK

Reference: Near Lake Almanor in Lassen National Forest; map C3 grid c3.
How to get there: From the town of Chester, drive three miles west on Highway 36. Turn south on Highway 89 and travel four miles south

---

to Humbug Road. Turn right (south) and drive three-quarters of a mile, then bear right at Humboldt Road and travel west. Creek access is available directly off Humboldt Road and off trails that junction with it.

Facilities: Campgrounds are available nearby at Lake Almanor. Supplies are available in Chester.

Cost: Access is free.

Who to contact: Phone the Lassen National Forest District Office at (916) 258-2141.

About Butt Creek: Butt Creek is an very short stream system set upstream of Butt Lake. When the flows are suitable in late spring, usually mid-May, the DFG will stock it lightly a few times. In the past, only the locals have fished it. Even then, many local folks have no idea there are any trout in here.

That is because there usually aren't. This stream does not grow trout on its own, so it is the prisoner of the tanker truck. If you hit it in May after a stock, it can seem pretty good. Any other time, however, you might as well fish in a bucket.

---

10.   LAKE ALMANOR

Reference: East of Red Bluff in Lassen National Forest; map C3 grid c4.

How to get there: From Susanville, drive approximately 28 miles west on Highway 36, past the town of Chester, to Highway 89. If approaching from Interstate 5, take the Highway 36 exit at Red Bluff and travel about 75 miles east to the Highway 89 turnoff. Turn south on Highway 89 and proceed to the lake. Another option is to drive five miles east of Chester on Highway 36 and turn south on Road A13 (Lake Almanor Road).

Facilities: Campgrounds are provided on the northern and southwestern shorelines of the lake. Lodging, boat ramps, a boat dock, groceries, gas, bait, and tackle are available.

Cost: Campsite fees area $7-$15 per night.

Who to contact: For fishing information, boat rentals, cabins, camping or guides, call Lassen View Resort at (916) 596-3437. For a free travel packet, write the Plumas County Chamber of Commerce, Box 11018, Quincy, CA 95971 or phone at (916) 283-2045. For Forest Service campgrounds, phone the Lassen National Forest District Office at (916) 258-2141.

About Lake Almanor: Lake Almanor is Northern California's answer to Lake Tahoe, a jewel ringed by conifers, the opportunity for a lakeside vacation home or rental cabin, and a great chance of catching a big fish.

It is one of the best lakes in the state for large rainbow trout, brown

trout, and lake-raised salmon. It also has smallmouth bass, which come
to life at mid-summer, right when the cold-water species go into a short
lull.

The keys at Almanor are the natural springs, the huge population
of minnows, and large stocks of trout and salmon. The natural springs
keep the lake cold, in circulation, and in combination with sunlight
penetration, help start the aquatic food chain. The numbers of minnows
are thus abundant, providing large amounts of feed for the growing
sportsfish. Finally, Fish and Game stocks more than 200,000 fish each
year, including almost 60,000 salmon, 100,000 Eagle Lake trout and
23,000 browns. Those are all species that can get big, and with the
abundant food supply at Almanor, they do.

If there is a drawback at Almanor, it's the weather. In the spring,
when the salmon fishing is so good, it is often very cold and windy.
In fact, a key is to be out before daybreak, because the wind often
comes up by 10 a.m. and forces everybody off the lake. In the fall, it
is also quite cold, with mornings absolutely frigid. And in the winter,
Almanor gets a lot of snow, often 10 feet, and the place is just about
abandoned. That leaves a narrow window of good weather in July and
August, and that is when the fishing is the worst.

The best period is in October, when the big brown trout and Eagle
Lake trout are on the prowl. It is common to catch browns and Eagle
Lakers in the three to five-pound class during a two to three-week
period in October when it isn't raining. Another peak period arrives
from April through early June, when the salmon can provide fantastic
fishing. They average in the five-pound, 20-inch class, and can rip line
like no other fish in any California lake.

A big problem is that most people want to visit Almanor in July
and August, when the weather is guaranteed, even though the fishing
is not. The smallmouth provide the bridge during this period for anglers
using crickets for bait. With a splitshot for weight, you cast along the
shoreline drop-offs, let the cricket sink to about 30 feet deep, then
twitch it and reel in a few feet—right then is when you will often get
a bite.

The salmon fishing, however, is much more exciting. The Big
Springs area, located on the east side of the lake just north of the
Hamilton Branch, is the most consistent area on the lake. It is only a
five-minute boat ride from Lassen View Resort, which provides the
best fishing information (especially on location) of any place on the
lake. Another good spring that attracts big fish is adjacent to the
"A-Frame," another famous spot on the lake. You anchor in the
vicinity of these springs, then use either a small chunk of anchovy or
an entire nightcrawler, letting the bait descend to the lake bottom.
When the bait gets picked up, the technique I prefer is to point the rod

at the water, and then when the slack in the line is pulled a few inches, wham, I slam the hook home. The first day I tried this, I caught five salmon that weighed a cumulative 25 pounds and every one had long runs of 35, 40 yards.

Another technique is to jig straight up and down. Crappie jigs and Gitsits both work well. While anchored, you simply drop the jig to the lake bottom, jerk it up in two foot pulls with your rod, then let the jig settle back down. This can get very monotonous, but can often entice bites when bait will not, particularly after the main bite is over at 9:30 a.m.

This is a big lake, some 13 miles long and covering 28,000 acres. That alone can be frustrating to newcomers who don't know where the heck to start their expedition. The answer is always to call Lassen View Resort at (916) 596-3437 to get the lowdown. Otherwise, it can take a few days of zilches before you figure out where to fish. With such large fish in the prospects, it's not worth the wait.

Although Almanor is a reservoir built by PG&E, it looks more like a natural lake since it is kept so full most of the year. The inside word is that lake levels are kept high during the summer because a number of PG&E executives have cabins on the exclusive Almanor Peninsula, and they don't like looking at bare shoreline. That might explain why the lake levels always seem so low at Mountain Meadows Reservoir to the east, which feeds into Almanor, and Butt Lake to the south, which gets its water from Almanor.

Regardless, Lake Almanor is big and beautiful, with sapphire blue waters and snow-capped Mount Lassen off to the northwest. Everybody should try it on for size at least once. You might find it fits pretty good.

---

11. PHILBROOK RESERVOIR

Reference: Near Paradise in Lassen National Forest; map C3 grid dØ.

How to get there: From Interstate 5 at Orland, take the Highway 32-Chico exit. Drive about 18 miles east to Chico, then get on Highway 99 south and turn east on Skyway Road and drive ten miles, toward Paradise. Once in Paradise, continue for 27 miles north on Skyway Road. Bear right at Humbug Summit Road and travel two miles, then turn right on Philbrook Road and drive four miles.

Facilities: A campground is provided. A car-top boat launch is also available.

Cost: Campsite fee is $9 per night.

Who to contact: Phone the Lassen National Forest District Office at (916) 258-2141.

About Philbrook Reservoir: The first time I visited Philbrook, I figured they got the name wrong. Even though Paradise Lake is located so close to the southwest, it looked like this lake should have been named Paradise, and not the original.

It is just hard enough to reach to keep most folks away. It is larger than expected, and when I rolled up, insects were hatching and trout were rising, leaving little pools all over the surface. The road is too rough to bring a trailered boat in, but it looked ideal for the canoe sitting on top of my Ford 4x4. Shortly thereafter, I realized why this lake was not named Paradise: It's Dinkerville, U.S.A. That's right, it is loaded with little rainbow trout, and stocked each year with more little rainbow trout, and it can take a hell of an effort to catch anything else. If you get here at midsummer, it is even worse, with the weather very hot, and the fishing poor.

---

12. BUTT LAKE

Reference: Near Chester; map C3 grid d3.

How to get there: From Susanville, drive approximately 26 miles west on Highway 36 to the town of Chester. Continue three miles west on Highway 36, then turn left on Highway 89 and drive 6.5 miles south. Turn southwest on Butt Valley Road and travel three miles to the reservoir.

Facilities: Two campgrounds are provided on the eastern shoreline. A boat ramp is available. Supplies can be obtained in Chester.

Cost: Campsite fee is $9 per night.

Who to contact: Phone Sportsmen's Den in Quincy at (916) 283-2733; Phone PG&E at (916) 527-0354.

About Butt Lake: Most people show up to Butt Lake, take a look and say, "What's all the fuss about?"

After all, the lake is often quite low, with lots of stumps on the bare lake bed, the campground is some distance from the water, and it can be intolerable if you get some self-obsessed moron with a boombox or a generator for a neighbor. Then you discover the trout can be difficult to catch, and you are bound to say, "I should have gone to Almanor."

The answer is that if the powerhouse is running, you should not have gone to Almanor. The powerhouse, you see, is located on the northern end of this long, narrow reservoir, and when it is running, remarkable numbers of little minnows come down the tunnel from Almanor and get funneled by the PG&E turbines right into the narrow channel at the head of Butt Lake. In turn, every big trout in Butt Lake will congregate in the small area—and you can catch the trout of your life.

Rainbow trout ranging 10 to 15 pounds have been caught here when the powerhouse is running. One month, something like 20 10-pounders were documented coming from this channel, most taken on Countdown Rapalas. The biggest I've heard of was a 17-pound rainbow trout caught by a woman who casted out a Phoebe, of all things.

So Butt Lake can be a disaster, or it can be a fishing heaven. It rarely is somewhere in between.

---

13.   YELLOW CREEK

Reference: Near Lake Almanor in Lassen National Forest; map C3 grid d3.

How to get there: From Susanville, drive approximately 26 miles west on Highway 36 to the town of Chester. Continue two miles south on Highway 36. Turn south on Highway 89 and travel about four miles to the signed turnoff for Humbug-Humboldt Road. Turn right and drive about one-half mile. At the fork, bear left and continue to Longville. Cross Butt Creek and continue straight through the middle fork of the road. Continue to Humbug Valley. Direct access is available.

Facilities: A PG&E campground is provided. Supplies are available in Chester.

Cost: Campsite fee is $8 per night.

Who to contact: Phone PG&E at (916) 527-0354.

About Yellow Creek: This is the classic spring creek, that is, a meandering, slow-flowing stream that rolls gently through a valley. It is not the kind of stream that rushes over rocks into pools.

It is similar to Hat Creek near Burney, except Yellow Creek doesn't have nearly the numbers of people. It is very challenging and difficult—regulations mandate flyfishing only—use dry flies and matching hatches. The evening rise is a classic scene here for skilled flyfishers. That is another way of saying that the trout can be damn hard to catch.

But a secret is that the stream's biggest fish rarely rise to a hatching caddis. Instead, they lay under the cut bank, that is, the underwater indentation that is unique to spring creeks, and wait for morsels to drift by.

A good campground is available here, as well as a fence that keeps the cows out of the creek. You can thank the fine organization California Trout for that.

You should always check fishing regulations before heading out on any water, but it is critical here, with different rules for different parts of the river.

The middle of the valley is considered something of a temple, however. Catch-and-release flyfishing is the religion practiced.

14. NORTH FORK FEATHER RIVER

Reference: South of Belden Forebay in Plumas National Forest; map C3 grid e3.

How to get there: From Oroville, drive northeast on Highway 70. Just after passing Little Haven, turn left (north) on Prattville-Butt Reservoir Road. The North Fork Feather borders this small road all the way to Belden Forebay.

Facilities: Three campgrounds are set right along the river, with access off Prattville-Butt Reservoir Road. Others are provided off Highway 70. A good one is Gansner Bar. Supplies are available along Highway 70.

Cost: River access is free.

Who to contact: Phone the Plumas National Forest Headquarters at (916) 283-2050.

About North Fork Feather River: The North Fork Feather River has been a top trout producer ever since the Fish and Game purposely poisoned it in 1982. The idea was to clear out the squawfish, which were eating baby trout, then restock the river and let nature take over again.

But the local outrage was vehement. In response to that, the DFG has since stocked the river quite heavily, especially from the opening of trout season on the last Saturday of April through early summer.

It has made visiting campers quite happy, and as for the stream, it has come back quite strong. All aquatic life is vibrant and productive, and since the stream was pretty to begin with, this has become a favorite area for those who have followed its recent progress.

The natural place to start fishing is at the campgrounds. But that is where everybody, and I mean everybody, fishes.

Instead, drive up to Belden Forebay and work over the stretch of water in the first 150 yards below the dam. This can be an excellent spot. From there, continue on downstream, making hits along the way, and eventually you will return to the campgrounds. By then, you will likely have your fish. Watch. All the hard-pressed campers ask you, "Where did you catch those?"

You can just smile and say: "In the water, on a hook, right in the mouth."

15. ROUND VALLEY RESERVOIR

Reference: Near Greenville in Plumas National Forest; map C3 grid e6.

How to get there: From Susanville, drive approximately 28 miles west on Highway 36, past the town of Chester, to Highway 89. If approaching from Interstate 5, take the Highway 36 exit at Red Bluff and travel about 75 miles east to the Highway 89 turnoff. Turn south on Highway 89 and drive about 25 miles to the town of Greenville. Turn south on Greenville Road and drive three miles to the lake.

Facilities: A private campground is available. A picnic area is provided for day use. A boat ramp is also available. Supplies can be obtained in Greenville.

Cost: Access is free.

Who to contact: Phone Sportsman's Den in Quincy at (916) 283-2733; the Plumas National Forest District Office at (916) 284-7126.

About Round Valley Reservoir: Even the best bassers sometimes go years without fishing Round Valley. They forget, just like so many people, that a good bass lake can be located in the mountains.

Round Valley is one of the few high-altitude bass lakes in California. It has ideal bass habitat, with a lot of stumps, and in the summer, lily pads and some weed cover. That is why the bass get big here. Before the introduction of the Florida strain of largemouth bass, Round Valley had the state record with a 14-pounder.

Bluegill and catfish also are available in this lake, but it is the bass that make it special. The lake becomes productive in early May, and by midsummer, provides a lot of topwater action.

---

16. TAYLOR LAKE

Reference: Near Taylorsville in Plumas National Forest; map C3 grid e8.

How to get there: From Quincy, drive about 18 miles north on Highway 89 to the turnoff for Highway 22. Turn right and drive five miles east to Taylorsville. Turn north on County Road 214 and drive about two miles. Turn right onto Forest Service Road 27N10 and drive about ten miles east (stay to the left). Turn left onto Forest Service Road 27N57 and travel one mile to the lake.

Facilities: A few primitive Forest Service campsites are available, but there is no piped water, so bring your own. Supplies are available in Taylorsville.

Cost: Access is free.

Who to contact: Phone the Plumas National Forest District Office at (916) 284-7126. A map is available for $2 from Office of Information, U.S. Forest Service, 630 Sansome Street, San Francisco, CA 94111.

About Taylor Lake: This is a quality brook trout water. The water is clear, the fish are shy, but the careful approach in the evening with light line and a 1/16-ounce black Panther Martin spinner can make for a nice stringer of brookies for the evening fish fry.

It's a good lake to fish from a float tube or raft, a small, obscure mountain lake that gets little attention from most anglers and campers.

Some good drive-to side trips in the area are to the lookout point west of Taylor Lake near Kettle Rock, and also north to the remote area between Rattlesnake and Eisenheimer Peak.

---

17. SILVER LAKE

Reference: Near Quincy in Plumas National Forest; map C3 grid f3.

How to get there: From Quincy on Highway 89, drive seven miles west on Bucks Lake Road to Spanish Ranch. Turn north on Silver Lake Road and travel seven miles.

Facilities: A campground is provided, but there is no piped water available. Supplies are available in Quincy.

Cost: Access is free.

Who to contact: Phone the Plumas National Forest District Office at (916) 283-0555.

About Silver Lake: If you want a pan-size fish fry, Silver Lake can provide it. This lake has lot of brook trout that seem sized perfectly for the frying pan, though about one trout out of five here seems to be a rainbow trout.

The surrounding area is quite attractive. The Pacific Crest Trail is routed just above (west of) the lake, and little Gold Lake is located just south of Silver Lake. Silver also has quite a few brookies. They need to be thinned out so a few have the chance to get a bit bigger.

---

18. BUCKS LAKE

Reference: Near Quincy in Plumas National Forest; map C3 grid f3.

How to get there: From Highway 70 at Quincy, turn west on Bucks Lake Road and drive 16.5 miles to the lake.

Facilities: Several campgrounds are provided on or near the lake. A full-service marina, boat ramps, boat rentals, groceries, bait and tackle are available.

Cost: Campsite fees range from free to $9 per night.

Who to contact: Phone Sportsman's Den in Quincy at (916) 283-2733; the Plumas National Forest District Office at (916) 283-0555.

About Bucks Lake: You want fish? You get fish. Instead of searching all over creation to find them, at Bucks Lake they can come to you.

Bucks Lake is one of the most consistent trout producers in the western U.S. It is a good lake for the family, with good, clean camps available, and it is also good for know-hows who want to try for something special. The lake record is a 16-pound brown trout, but there are also some big mackinaw trout (the biggest weighed 11 pounds, 16 ounces) and rafts of rainbow trout and a sprinkling of kokanee salmon.

The best fishing here is for the rainbow trout, and the best spot is by Rocky Point, near where Bucks Creek enters the lake. The old river

---

channel near where Mill Creek pours in is also quite good, and has a sprinkling of the big mackinaws here. Bucks Lake is set at 5,150 feet, and that means it gets snow, lots of it. As soon as the ice melts and the access road is plowed clear, the fishing is often the best of the year. That usually happens in May, but is dependent on the amount of late snow. The stocks early in the season are large and consistent.

When I was a kid, I latched onto a friend's family who made a trip to Bucks Lake, and I limited on trout on back-to-back days. The next morning, just before leaving for home, I decided to brag about it in the little store there, and found a game warden with willing ears.

After listening patiently to the 12-year-old, who was a misguided missile who needed a straitjacket to stand still, the warden informed me that I had been fishing in a closed area—because it was where all the fish were planted—and that I must go to jail.

I started crying, figuring it was the end of my life.

Then the warden put his arm around me and said: "Well, son, maybe I don't have to take you to jail after all. But from now on, make sure you check the fishing regulations every time before you start fishing."

It is a promise I've never broken.

---

19. SNAKE LAKE

Reference: Near Quincy in Plumas National Forest; map C3 grid f5.

How to get there: From Quincy on Highway 89, drive five miles west on Bucks Lake Road. Turn north and drive five miles.

Facilities: A campground is provided. No piped water is available, so bring your own. A car-top boat launch is available. No motors are permitted on the lake. Supplies can be obtained in Quincy.

Cost: Access is free.

Who to contact: Phone the Plumas National Forest District Office at 283-0555.

About Snake Lake: The hard freeze of December 1990 really did a number on this lake. Snake Lake nearly froze all the way to the bottom, killing about 70 percent of the fish here.

You see, Snake Lake is quite shallow, in fact, so shallow that the summer sun heats up the lake so much that it provides habitat for warm-water fisheries despite its mountain setting. Snake Lake has bass, catfish and bluegill, which are certainly a surprise for newcomers who think the Plumas Forest lakes grow only trout, not bass. Until 1995, as the lake recovers from the freeze, expect smaller, fewer fish.

20.   SPANISH CREEK

Reference: Near Quincy in Plumas National Forest; map C3 grid f5.

How to get there: From Quincy, drive west on Bucks Lake Road or north on Quincy Junction and Oakland Camp Roads. Excellent access is available.

Facilities: Campgrounds and lodging are available nearby. Supplies are available in Quincy.

Cost: Access is free.

Who to contact: For camping information, phone the Plumas National Forest District Office at (916) 283-0555. For fishing information, phone the Sportsmen's Den in Quincy at (916) 283-2733.

About Spanish Creek: On the opening day of trout season in California, some one million people try to go fishing, according to the Department of Fish and Game. Spanish Creek is an ideal bet for such a situation. The name "Spanish Creek" by itself doesn't mean anything to most anglers, but it should.

Access is good, there is a multitude of hatches, and a good mix of rainbow trout, brown trout, as well as a light sprinkling of quality browns. In addition, there has been a habitat enhancement program on Greenhorn Creek, a tributary to Spanish Creek, which is restoring the river back to the quality of the good old days.

---

21.   MIDDLE FORK FEATHER

Reference: Northeast of Oroville in Plumas National Forest; map C3 grid g2.

How to get there: From Oroville: At the junction of Highways 70 and 162, drive 26 miles north on Highway 162 (Oroville-Quincy Highway). At the town of Brush Creek, turn south on Bald Rock Road and drive one-half mile to Forest Service Road 22N62 (Milsap Bar Road). Turn left and continue northeast. The road is steep and rough. Access is available directly off the road. From Blairsden: Drive north on Highway 70/89. Access is available off the highway between the towns of Blairsden and Sloat, and off trails that junction with it.

Facilities: Campgrounds are available along the river. Supplies can be obtained in Oroville and Blairsden.

Cost: River access is free.

Who to contact: Phone the Plumas National Forest Headquarters at (916) 283-2050. For a map, send $2 to Office of Information, U.S. Forest Service, 630 Sansome Street, San Francisco, CA 94111.

About Middle Fork Feather River: The Middle Fork Feather is one of the top 10 trout streams in California. That is, providing you know

---

which part to fish. The stretch of river above Quincy is decent, but nothing unique. It is stocked by Fish and Game, provides easy access, and if you want a quick evening hit, it can answer the request. But the stretch of river down below the confluence of Nelson Creek is a different chunk of territory. This is hike-in wilderness, the river is unbridled, and so are the trout. This is for those with pioneering spirit, which is another way of saying it takes one hell of a hike to get in and out of this canyon. A Forest Service map, a lookout for any rattlesnakes, and some brush bashing can all be mandatory on your way down to the river. Once there, you will find an untouched stream and wild trout that have never seen a Purina Trout Chow pellet in their lives.

Six-piece backpack rods are ideal, the kind that can be converted instantly to a spinning rod or fly rod, such as the Daiwa pack rod. During most of the day, when hatches are few and the trout are feeding sub-surface, you can use the rod as a spinning rod and cast small lures into the heads of pools. At dawn or dusk, when trout are rising to hatching insects, you can convert the rod to a fly rod and cast dry flies.

Obviously, this is not for everybody, but that is just one more thing that makes it special.

---

22.   SOUTH FORK ROCK CREEK

Reference: Near Quincy in Plumas National Forest; map C3 grid g5.
How to get there: From Quincy, drive 3.5 miles west on Bucks Lake Road. Turn south on Forest Service Road 24N28 and travel about seven miles. Direct access is available.
Facilities: A free, primitive campground is provided on the creek. No piped water is available. Supplies can be obtained in Quincy.
Cost: Access is free.
Who to contact: Phone the Plumas National Forest District Office at (916) 283-0555.
About South Fork Rock Creek: I can't imagine anybody going here on purpose to catch a fish. Maybe to watch the water go by and have some solitude, but not to catch a fish.

All the trout are very small natives, and the fishery is flow-dependent, so if there isn't a big snowpack, forget it. Hey, if you like a pure, quiet spot, fine. If you want fish, not fine.

---

23.   PLUMAS NATIONAL FOREST

Reference: South of Lake Almanor; map C3 grid g5.
How to get there: Access is available off roads that junction with Highway 70.
Facilities: Several campgrounds are provided on and near Highway 70.

Supplies are available in neighboring towns.

Cost: Access is free.

Who to contact: Write to Plumas National Forest Headquarters at P.O. Box 1500, Quincy, CA 95971, or phone (916) 283-2050. For a map, send $2 to Office of Information, U.S. Forest Service, 630 Sansome Street, San Francisco, CA 94111.

About Plumas National Forest: Many of the lakes in Plumas Forest have been detailed in other sections of this zone. But three that have not been mentioned are Smith Lake (located just north of Snake Lake) and Big Bear Lake and Long Lake in the Gold Lakes Basin.

They all have fish in them, but it is Long Lake that is the premier attraction of the three. It is particularly beautiful, a very clean, very deep lake, that only requires a half-mile hike to reach it. The evening trout fishing can be good here. Long Lake, as well as the little Big Bear Lakes to the immediate south, add an extra hike-in dimension to the Gold Lakes Basin as a premier destination.

---

24. LITTLE GRASS VALLEY RESERVOIR

Reference: Near La Porte in Plumas National Forest; map C3 grid h5.

How to get there: From East Quincy on Highway 89-70, drive one mile east, then turn south on Quincy-La Porte Road and drive approximately 30 miles on a narrow, twisty road until you reach Little Grass Valley Road. Turn north and travel three miles to the reservoir.

Facilities: Several campgrounds are provided. Two good ones are Wyandotte and Running Deer. A boat ramp is available.

Cost: Campsite fees are $8-$10 per night.

Who to contact: Phone the Plumas National Forest District Office at (916) 283-0555.

About Little Grass Valley Reservoir: This is your standard trolling/hardware lake. That means get a boat, rig with flashers trailing a nightcrawler, and troll slow for rainbow trout in the foot-long class.

It is set at 5,000 feet in Plumas National Forest, provides popular lakeside camping, and decent catch rates. By summer, when the fish go down to the thermocline, a number of boaters will use lead-core lines to get 35 to 40 feet deep. Stocks are quite good, with some 35,000 foot-long trout planted each year.

Add it up: Lakeside camps, boat ramps, good trout stocks, a mountain lake with a decent amount of water. Now put it in your cash register: Don't plan on being alone out here. This lake gets plenty of visitors.

---

25. EUREKA LAKE

Reference: Near Graeagle in Plumas-Eureka State Park; map C3 grid h7.

How to get there: From Quincy on Highway 89, drive approximately 25 miles southeast on Highway 89 to the town of Graeagle. Turn west on County Road A14 (Johnsonville-Graeagle Road) and drive five miles west. Turn right and drive one mile, then turn left at the sign for Eureka Lake and travel about one mile.

Facilities: Two campgrounds are provided in Plumas-Eureka State Park. No motorized boats are permitted on the lake. Supplies are available in Graeagle.

Cost: A day-use fee of $5 per vehicle is charged at the park.

Who to contact: Phone Plumas-Eureka State Park at (916) 836-2380.

About Eureka Lake: The smartest thing rangers ever did was close the access road here from Fridays through Sundays. That means that nobody gets here by accident on the crowded weekends. It isn't a difficult walk to reach Eureka Lake, but any time you have to walk, the fishing always seems to improve a clear notch for it. It's a beautiful little lake that provides its best trout fishing during the first part of the season, usually in June. If you are camping at the park, it is well worth the hike. There are primarily rainbow trout, but a few browns are occasionally in the mix.

26. JAMISON CREEK

Reference: Near Graeagle in Plumas-Eureka State Park; map C3 grid h7.

How to get there: From Quincy on Highway 89, drive approximately 25 miles southeast on Highway 89 to the town of Graeagle. Turn west on County Road A14 (Graeagle-Johnsville Road). Creek access is available off the road near the campgrounds.

Facilities: Two campgrounds are provided. Reservations are required. Supplies are available in Graeagle.

Cost: Campsite fee is $12-$14 per night.

Who to contact: Phone Plumas-Eureka State Park at (916) 836-2380.

About Jamison Creek: Most streams are not good family spots. Extensive hiking, special fishing techniques, and lack of elbow room makes most stream fishing better for folks who don't mind splitting up. Jamison Creek is the exception, however. It is stocked with nice trout year-after-year, and the nearby campground and squirrels can keep the kids busy. In addition, access is quite easy, and no extensive hiking is required.

27.   GOLD LAKE

Reference: Near Sierraville in Plumas National Forest; map C3 grid i8.

How to get there: From Interstate 80 at Truckee, drive about 30 miles north on Highway 89 to Sierraville. Turn left (west) on Highway 49 and drive about 20 miles to the Bassetts Store. Turn right (north) on Gold Lake Road and drive about six miles, following the signs to the lake.

Facilities: Lodging and campgrounds are available nearby. A boat ramp is provided. Limited supplies are available at nearby resorts; other supplies can be obtained in Graeagle or Bassetts.

Cost: Access is free.

Who to contact: Phone Plumas National Forest District Office at (916) 836-2575. For a map, send $2 to Office of Information, U.S. Forest Service, 630 Sansome Street, San Francisco, CA 94111.

About Gold Lake: All anglers hate wind, right? It's the one thing that can kill the fishing, right? Nobody catches anything when it's windy, right?

When it comes to Gold Lake, the answers are wrong, wrong and wrong. Because the water is extremely clear, when it is calm, the trout are easily spooked and the lake presents a tremendous challenge. But ah, when it is windy . . . the trout get a lot braver. The big brown trout, rainbow trout and mackinaw trout will emerge from the depths and cruise the shallows, feeding primarily on minnows and juvenile trout.

That is when you can catch the trout of your life. A 10-pound brown trout and 14-pound mackinaw trout have been documented in recent years out of this lake, and there will be more in this class. Why? Because of the minnows, the favorite forage. The lake is loaded with them.

Gold Lake is set at 6,400 feet in Plumas Forest and is bigger than most newcomers expect. Since it is a natural lake, it is always full of water, a beautiful sight. Never curse the wind here. You need it. Otherwise Gold Lake is a very challenging lake.

But if you hit one of those windless stretches where finding a fish at Gold Lake is like finding Bigfoot, there are many hike-to options in the surrounding Gold Lakes Basin. Good destinations include Summit Lake, Bear Lake, Round Lake, Long Lake, Silver Lake, and Squaw Lake. Of those, Squaw Lake provides the steadiest fishing, although they are all little brook trout.

28.   HAVEN LAKE

Reference: Near Sierraville in Plumas National Forest; map C3 grid i8.

How to get there: From Interstate 80 at Truckee, drive about 30 miles north on Highway 89 to Sierraville. Turn left (west) on Highway 49 and drive about 20 miles to the Bassetts Store. Turn right (north) on Gold Lake Road and drive about five miles.

Facilities: A few primitive campsites are available, but there is no piped water. Other campgrounds and lodging are available nearby. Supplies are available in Sierra City or Bassetts.

Cost: Access is free.

Who to contact: Phone the Plumas National Forest District Office at (916) 836-2575.

About Haven Lake: You don't see quality at Haven Lake, such as is possible at nearby Gold Lake to the north. But you do see quantity, which is something unreliable at Gold.

This small lake is very pretty, always full of water, and is stocked each year with 2,200 fingerling-sized brook trout. These are the king of dinkers. Shoreliners have to wade through quite a few little brookies before getting one with much to it.

You can improve the experience by fishing from a float tube with a fly rod, using damsel and small nymphs, strip retrieve. You will be in the center of this beautiful place and the size of the brook trout will hardly seem to matter.

---

29. SNAG LAKE

Reference: Near Sierraville in Plumas National Forest; map C3 grid i8.

How to get there: From Interstate 80 at Truckee, drive about 30 miles north on Highway 89 to Sierraville. Turn left (west) on Highway 49 and drive about 20 miles to the Bassetts Store. Turn right (north) on Gold Lake Road and drive about five miles.

Facilities: A primitive campground is available nearby, but there is no piped water. No boat ramps are provided; only hand-launching is permitted. Supplies are available in Sierra City or Bassetts.

Cost: Access is free.

Who to contact: Phone the Tahoe National Forest Headquarters at (916) 265-4531.

About Snag Lake: There are better lakes in this area, and then there are worse. So as far as the competition goes, it rates in the so-so range. But when you consider what a beautiful area this section of Plumas National Forest is, on a larger scale you could do a lot worse.

It is stocked with 4,000 trout per year, split evenly between rainbow trout and brook trout, most in the seven to nine-inch class. The larger resident fish that have avoided getting caught for a year or two are very smart, and you might see them cruising the lake, but darn if they'll bite something with a hook in it.

Snag Lake is a neat little spot and it doesn't get much fishing pressure. That is the best thing it has going for it.

30. SALMON LAKE

Reference: Near Sierraville in Tahoe National Forest; map C3 grid i8.

How to get there: From Interstate 80 at Truckee, drive about 30 miles north on Highway 89 to Sierraville. Turn left (west) on Highway 49 and drive about 20 miles to the Bassetts Store. Turn right (north) on Gold Lake Road and drive about three miles north, then turn left at the sign for Salmon Lake and drive one mile to the lake.

Facilities: Lodging is available at Salmon Lake Lodge. Campgrounds are available nearby. No boat ramp is provided, but boats can be launched at the shore. Supplies are available in Sierra City and Bassetts.

Cost: Access is free.

Who to contact: Phone the Tahoe National Forest Headquarters at (916) 265-4531, or phone Salmon Lake Lodge at (415) 771-0150.

About Salmon Lake: Salmon Lake is a nice spot for a family to make an overnight outing and catch some trout while they're at it. It's baitdunker time, with most of the trout here caught from shoreline by folks using nightcrawlers, Power Bait, or crickets under a float. The lake is stocked with 6,000 trout averaging 10, 11 inches.

If you are more ambititious and don't mind a steep hike, then the reward can be quite spectacular in the surrounding area. Lower Salmon Lake, Horse Lake and Deer Lake are all nearby, with Deer Lake absolutely pristine and beautiful. It has crystal-clear water and Golden trout. It is also accessible via a trail out of Packer Lake.

31. SARDINE LAKES

Reference: Near Sierraville in Tahoe National Forest; map C3 grid i8.

How to get there: From Interstate 80 at Truckee, drive about 30 miles north on Highway 89 to Sierraville. Turn left (west) on Highway 49 and drive about 20 miles to the Bassetts Store. Turn right (north) on Gold Lake Road and drive one mile north. Turn left at Sardine Lake Road and drive one mile to the lakes.

Facilities: Lodging, boat rentals, and limited supplies are available at Sardine Lake Lodge. A campground is provided at Lower Sardine Lake. Supplies can be obtained in Sierra City or Bassetts.

Cost: Lake access is free.

Who to contact: Phone Sardine Lake Resort at (916) 862-1196; Tahoe National Forest Headquarters at (916) 265-4531.

About Sardine Lakes: Sometimes there is just no substitute for spectacular natural beauty. That is why there is no substitute for Sardine Lakes in a visit to the Plumas area.

The Sardine Lakes are among the prettiest drive-to lakes in California, set in a rock bowl with the Sierra Buttes nearby, always full with water from the drops of melting snow. Right there, that is plenty to attract a visit. The lakes need no extra pushing, but they get it.

Lower Sardine Lake is stocked with 25,000 trout per year, all at least 10 or 11 inches, and with holdover fish, provide a consistent summer fishery. The lodge, boat rentals, and a chance to get a fishing report make this a unique setting. Most of the fishing is trolling or shoreline baitfishing, using standard techniques.

Upper Sardine Lake can't really compare with the lower lake as a fishery. It is stocked with only 3,000 fingerling-sized rainbow trout each year. The catches bear this out, with fish tending to be small and more difficult to catch. After hearing about the Sardine Lakes, some anglers mistakenly fish the Upper Lake, then wonder what all the fuss is about.

---

32.   PACKER LAKE

Reference: Near Sierraville in Tahoe National Forest; map C3 grid i8.

How to get there: From Interstate 80 at Truckee, drive about 30 miles north on Highway 89 to Sierraville. Turn left (west) on Highway 49 and drive about 20 miles to the Bassetts Store. Turn right (north) on Gold Lake Road and drive one mile, then turn left on Packer Lake Road and drive two miles.

Facilities: A small primitive camping area and a picnic area are provided. No piped water is available. More campgrounds and lodging are available at nearby lakes. Supplies can be obtained in Sierra City or Bassetts.

Cost: Access is free.

Who to contact: Phone the Tahoe National Forest Headquarters at (916) 265-4351.

About Packer Lake: It seems that Packer Lake gets fished by just as many people as Lower Sardine Lake, yet Packer is stocked with 6,500 trout. That is only 25 percent of the number going in Lower Sardine, and yes, the fishing seems to be about 25 percent as good.

The reason this happens is because during the summer, folks show up to Lower Sardine and figure there are too many people, so they drive onward to Packer. Enough visitors do this so Packer gets hit pretty hard, way too hard considering the number of trout that are stocked.

Regardless, it is a very pretty spot.

33. BULLARDS BAR RESERVOIR

Reference: Near Camptonville in Tahoe National Forest; map C3 grid j2.

How to get there: From Marysville on Highway 99, drive about 12 miles northeast on Highway 20 to Marysville Road. Turn north and continue for approximately 30 miles on the narrow, winding road to Bullards Bar Reservoir. The road will take you directly to a boat ramp at the south end of the lake.

Facilities: Several boat-in campgrounds are provided, but they offer no piped water and require reservations. Campgrounds are also available near and on the shoreline. A marina and boat ramps are available. Supplies can be obtained in Marysville, Camptonville, and Dobbins.

Cost: Campsite fees range from free to $7.50 per night.

Who to contact: Phone the Emerald Cove Resort and Marina or the Yuba County Water Agency at (916) 692-2166 or (916) 741-6278.

About Bullards Bar Reservoir: Bullards Bar Reservoir is like a silver dollar in a field of pennies compared to the other reservoirs in the Central Valley foothills.

So many of the 155 major reservoirs in California are just shameless water storage facilities, drawn down at the whims of the water brokers regardless of the effects on recreation and fisheries. The folks who control the plumbing at Bullards Bar somehow manage to keep this lake near full through July, even in low water years when other reservoirs are turned into dust bowls. So right off, you get good lakeside camping, boating and general beauty that goes with a lot of water. The lake is set at 2,300 feet elevation, and with 55 miles of shoreline covers a lot of territory.

The fishing is quite a bonus, with excellent trolling for both rainbow trout and kokanee salmon. One of the best techniques is to start with a set of Cousin' Carl Half-Fast Flashers, then hook on a No. 0 Luhr Jensen Wedding Spinner, which comes with a pre-tied leader. Then add a small piece of nightcrawler on the hook, and slow troll until you find fish.

The main feeder stream to this reservoir is the North Fork Yuba River. That's a good place to start fishing, and if the lake is full, boat-in camps are available at Frenchy Point (east side) and Madrone Cove (west side, well upstream).

---

34. TAHOE NATIONAL FOREST

Reference: East of Oroville; map C3 grid j3.

How to get there: Access is available directly off Highway 49 and off roads that junction with it.

Facilities: Several campgrounds are provided on or near Highway 49. Supplies are available along the highway.

Cost: Access is free.

Who to contact: Write to Tahoe National Forest Headquarters at Highway 49, Nevada City, CA 95959, or phone (916) 265-4531. For a map, send $2 to Office of Information, U.S. Forest Service, 630 Sansome Street, San Francisco, CA 94111.

About Tahoe National Forest: This chunk of national forest is known for four-wheel drive roads, small hike-to lakes, and alas, small trout.

The best lakes in this sector are the following: Horse Lake, Deer Lake, Lower Salmon Lake, Tamarack Lakes, Hawley Lake and the Spencer Lakes.

A Forest Service map is available which details the back roads, trails and hidden lakes. It is the large number of roads that makes this perfect for four-wheel drive cowboys.

It can snow a lot in this country, and it usually does not become accessible to hikers until early June, later if there is a particularly large snowpack.

---

35.   NORTH YUBA RIVER

Reference: Near Sierra City in Tahoe National Forest; map C3 grid j7.

How to get there: From Sierra City, drive east or west on Highway 49. Direct access is available.

Facilities: Numerous campgrounds are available off Highway 49. Two good ones are Union Flat and Chapman Creek. Supplies are available in Bassetts, Sierra City, Downieville, and Camptonville.

Cost: River access is free.

Who to contact: Phone the Tahoe National Forest Headquarters at (916) 265-4531.

About North Fork Yuba River: If you have ever driven along Highway 49 in this region, you inevitably saw the North Yuba and said to yourself, "That's pretty. I wonder if there are any trout in it?"

Enough vacationers stop to find out for themselves that this stretch of the North Yuba gets a lot of activity. But Fish and Game figures it that way, and stocks some 27,000 trout per year so folks who are asking that initial question can be answered with a yes.

One problem on this river, however, is the number of goldmining operations in progress. These guys don't own the river, but they act like they do. If you start fishing near a claim, you can have problems. Some of these guys are completely self-obsessed and paranoid that someone is going to get their gold, and they can get mighty testy.

Tell 'em to go suck on a rock. They don't own the river, and you don't want their piddly little amounts of gold anyway.

MAP C4

7 LISTINGS
PAGES 304-311

NOR-CAL MAP . see page 120
adjoining maps
NORTH (B4) ...... see page 232
EAST .... no map
SOUTH (D4) .... see page 382
WEST (C3) .... see page 278

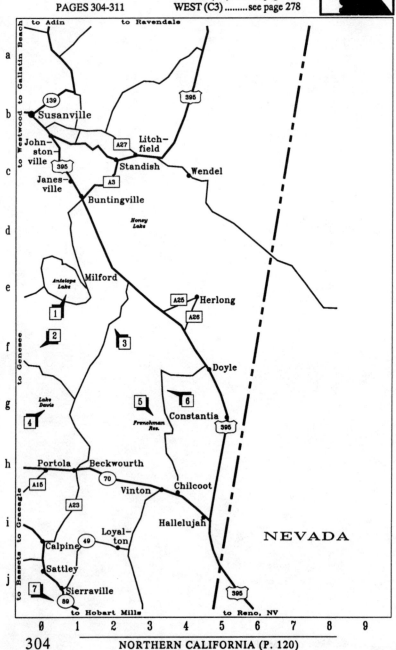

to Adin   to Ravendale

to Gallatin Beach
to Westwood

139 Susanville

Johnstonville

A27 Litchfield

395

Janesville **395**

A3 Standish • Wendel

Buntingville

Honey Lake

Antelope Lake Milford

□1

to Genesee

□2   □3

A25 • Herlong
A26

• Doyle

Lake Davis   □5   □6

□4   *Frenchman Res.* Constantia **395**

Portola Beckwourth

to Graeagle **A15** **70**
Vinton • Chilcoot

A23

Hallelujah

to Bassets Calpine **49** Loyalton   **NEVADA**

Sattley

□7 Sierraville
89
to Hobart Mills   to Reno, NV

0   1   2   3   4   5   6   7   8   9

304   NORTHERN CALIFORNIA (P. 120)

1. ANTELOPE LAKE

Reference: Near Taylorsville in Plumas National Forest; map C4 grid e1.

How to get there: From Quincy, drive about 18 miles north on Highway 89 to the turnoff for Highway 22. Turn right and drive five miles east to Taylorsville. From Taylorsville, drive 24 miles northeast on Beckworth and Indian Creek Roads to the lake.

Facilities: Campgrounds are provided at the lake. A boat ramp and small store are available. Supplies can be obtained nearby in Taylorsville.

Cost: Lake access is free.

Who to contact: Phone Plumas National Forest Headquarters at (916) 283-2050.

About Antelope Lake: Wanted: Mountain lake circled by conifers with secluded campsites and good fishing.

Some people might want to put an advertisement in the newspaper to find such a place, but it isn't necessary with Antelope Lake available in northern Plumas County. Antelope Lake is set at 5,000 feet, ringed by forest, with campgrounds located at each end of the lake, and also a boat ramp a few miles from each camp. Indian Creek provides an option, located just below the Antelope Valley Dam.

Antelope Lake is just about perfect for a fishing/camping vacation. It is secluded, about 100 miles by our estimate from Oroville, yet accessible for trailered boats. It isn't a huge lake, but big enough, with 15 miles of shoreline and little islands, coves and peninsulas to give it an intimate feel. And then there is the fishing.

It is good, particularly in the early summer. Fish and Game stocks it with 30,000 rainbow trout and 5,000 Eagle Lake trout, all in the 11, 12-inch class, which join a few large resident brown trout. Most folks either use standard trolling techniques, that is, a nightcrawler trailing a set of flashers, or will anchor up along a shoreline point or cove and baitfish.

The lucky part is that reaching it requires quite a drive for most visitors. If it was any closer, it would be loaded with vacationers every day of the summer.

2. INDIAN CREEK

Reference: South of Antelope Lake in Plumas National Forest; map C4 grid fØ.

How to get there: From Quincy, drive about 18 miles north on Highway 89 to the turnoff for Highway 22. Turn right and drive five miles east to Taylorsville. From Taylorsville, drive north on Beckwourth and Indian Creek Roads. They parallel the creek, and direct access is available.

Facilities: Campgrounds are available at Taylorsville or Antelope Lake. Supplies can be obtained in Taylorsville.

Cost: Access is free.

Who to contact: Phone the Plumas National Forest Headquarters at (916) 283-2050.

About Indian Creek: If Antelope Lake is crowded, Indian Creek provides a good alternative for the skilled stream angler.

Indian Creek pours from the Antelope Valley Dam, then tumbles well downstream into Genesee Valley, and down past Taylorsville. Two-lane roads border much of this section, and you will find small pull-outs along the road and little trails that are routed down to the better spots on the river. No trail? Likely not a great spot.

One of the best stretches of water is the two miles below the dam. This is where the bigger fish seem to be, including some nice brown trout. In addition, the area where Cold Stream Creek enters Indian Creek holds some small rainbow trout. Note: The Cold Stream Creek that is a small tributary to Indian Creek in Plumas County should not be confused with the Cold Stream Creek (see page 310) in Sierra County, located south of Sierraville near Highway 89.

---

3. WILLOW CREEK

Reference: Near Milford in Plumas National Forest; map C4 grid f2.

How to get there: From Susanville, drive south on Highway 36 to US 395, then continue south to the town of Milford. Turn south on Milford Grade Road and travel three miles. Bear right (toward Beckwourth), and continue for six more miles to the pavement. Access is available past the bridge that crosses the creek.

Facilities: A campground is available on Milford Grade Road, and another on Willow Creek. Neither one offers piped water, so bring your own. Supplies can be obtained in Milford.

Cost: Access is free.

Who to contact: Phone the Plumas National Forest District Office at (916) 253-2223. For a map, send $2 to Office of Information, 630 Sansome Street, San Francisco, CA 94111.

About Willow Creek: Bet you didn't know about this one, right? But if you want a quiet, small stream with good access, you will want to know about this one.

Willow Creek is an obscure little stream in the Diamond Mountains southwest of Honey Lake (little water, no fish). There are a number of four-wheel drive roads in the area, and to the south, a prime deer area in the Dixie Mountain State Game Refuge. The trout are on the small side, but they are wild fish, no planters, and the area is quiet and gets little traffic.

Considering the good access from the bridge on, it makes for a rare combination that is little-known.

---

4. DAVIS LAKE

Reference: Near Portola in Plumas National Forest; map C4 grid gØ.

How to get there: From Portola on Highway 70, drive two miles east on Highway 70. Turn north on Grizzly Road and drive six miles. Turn north on Lake Davis Road and continue to the lake.

Facilities: Campgrounds are available at the lake. Boat ramps are provided. Supplies are available near the campgrounds and in Portola.

Cost: Lake access is free.

Who to contact: Phone Sportsmen's Den, Quincy, (916) 283-2733; Plumas National Forest Headquarters at (916) 283-2050.

About Davis Lake: An experiment in the mid 1980s has added a facet to this mountain lake, making it quite unique in the area.

Davis Lake has always been a good trout lake, as well as a beautiful spot to camp, boat and hike. Then bass were added, and while there may be some feasting on juvenile trout, the bass provide a safety valve during the warm summer months when trout become more difficult to catch, particularly late July and August.

Davis Lake is located in the southern reaches of Plumas National Forest, just 50 miles from Reno, a bonus if you want to end your trip with a little gambling binge. It's a good-size lake, with 30 miles of shoreline, and set high in the northern Sierra at 5,775 feet, so it gets a lot of snow in the winter, and despite its size, can freeze over.

The ice-out in late spring is often a peak time to fish for the trout, which span all sizes, from dinkers to 24-inch trophies. This lake is ideal for flyfishing from a float tube, particularly on the northwest end of the lake near the outlets of Freeman Creek (best) and Grizzly Creek (second best). In fact, the whole northwestern end of the lake seems to hold more of the larger, resident trout, and the southern end more of the smaller planters.

There are a lot of the latter. The lake is stocked each year with 30,000 rainbow trout and 50,000 Eagle Lake trout in the 10 to 12-inch range, along with 300,000 Eagle Lake trout fingerlings.

All boating is permitted here and trolling is quite popular. But if you arrive early in the year, you should beware of afternoon spring winds, which can howl pretty good out of the north. So dress warm, get out early and enjoy the quiet time. As summer comes on, the evening trout rise can be a pretty good one. But once the midsummer sun starts heating up the lake, the bass fishing provides a good substitute. The best of it is on the northeastern shoreline, though it can get weedy in the shallows. If you have never bass fished in a mountain

---

lake, it can really be a unique feeling to be plugging the shoreline with casts, using Shad Raps, Rattletraps, and or Countdown Rapalas, and then not only catch bass—but a big brown trout. That can happen here, and does.

It makes for a multi-dimensional experience.

---

5. FRENCHMAN LAKE

Reference: Near Portola in Plumas National Forest; map C4 grid g3.

How to get there: From the junction of US 395 and Highway 70 (Hallelujah Junction), drive west on Highway 70 to the town of Chilcoot. Turn north on Frenchman Lake Road and travel about ten miles to the lake.

Facilities: Several campgrounds are provided. A good one is Spring Creek. A boat ramp is also provided. Groceries are available near the campgrounds.

Cost: Access is free.

Who to contact: Phone Plumas National Forest Headquarters at (916) 283-2050.

About Frenchman Lake: Frenchman Lake sat in relative obscurity for years until one day in 1987 when a fisherman caught a long, greenish fish with a mouth full of teeth that looked like the spikes on the bottom of a track shoe. By 1990, the lake was famous across America for it. You see, the fish was a pike, which makes a living by eating other fish, and its illegal introduction and possible spread threatened the survival of other sportsfish in the state.

As a result, the lake was poisoned out in the summer of '91, completely cleaned out of all fish including the pike, and now the lake is being re-established as a viable put-and-take trout fishery.

While some people were opposed to the poisoning, the pike presented too great a danger to other fisheries to be allowed to exist. In addition, it is the past policy of the Department of Fish and Game to stock any water that has been chemically treated with bonus plants of a variety of trout.

For Frenchman Lake, it means two things: First, unknown thousands of trout in the foot-long class will be stocked for several years, along with the likely addition of some huge brood-fish in the five-pound class. Second, the regular stocks of smaller trout will continue, and that represents some 150,000 rainbow fingerlings and 70,000 Eagle Lake fingerlings.

This is a good lake to fish from shore, particularly from the inlet on the west side of the lake, directly accessible from the road. This same area is good from a float tube or small raft on either side of the road because it is well protected from any winds.

By boat, most slow-troll with nightcrawlers until getting a strike, then re-work the area. The mistake a lot of folks make is rushing off from the boat ramp area. It is my experience that this is one of the better spots to fish, along with the narrows and upstream near the creek inlet.

Because of water demands, the lake level often drops substantially in late summer and fall. During this time of the year, it is advisable to phone the Forest Service before planning a trip with a boat—to make sure the water level isn't below the ramp.

The lake is in fairly high country, 5,500 feet, and it gets cold and windy in the spring and fall. A good side trip is just to the northwest to the Dixie Mountain State Game Refuge, or to another favorite, Reno, which is only 35 miles away. Stream anglers should consider Little Last Chance Creek, just below the dam.

6. LITTLE LAST CHANCE CREEK

Reference: Near Milford in Plumas National Forest; map C4 grid g4.

How to get there: From the junction of US 395 and Highway 70 (Hallelujah Junction), drive five miles west to the town of Chilcoot. Turn north on Frenchman Lake Road. Direct access is available off the road.

Facilities: A campground, called Chilcoot, is provided on Frenchman Lake Road.

Cost: Access is free.

Who to contact: Phone the Tahoe National Forest District Office at (916) 253-2223.

About Little Last Chance Creek: Over the years, I have caught some beautiful trout in this stream, with the best section the first 200 yards below the outlet at Frenchman Lake Dam.

But when Frenchman Lake was poisoned in the summer of '91, the chemical killer got into the stream and apparently wiped the stream out, too. So in the 1990s, Fish and Game will have to stock this stream with trout or results will be zilch. Usually, no trout are planted in this stream.

Too bad, because Little Last Chance Creek was a real quality trout fishery with some big native fish. I once released a 16-incher while a local baitdunker was standing by and he practically gagged to death. Just couldn't believe it.

"Why fish if you're going to throw 'em back?" he said. "Because I'd like to catch 'em again next year," I answered. He just shook his head.

It's a beautiful stream, full of riffles, bends and pools, and easy access off of Highway 284, a little two-laner. Even though it is only a 45-minute drive to Reno, it provides a clean, remote setting.

One other note: Following the poisoning of every lake or stream in the past 20 years, the DFG stocks the heck out of it in order to get the local public opinion back on their side. That will likely apply here in the '90s.

---

7. COLD STREAM CREEK

Reference: North of Truckee in Tahoe National Forest; map C4 grid j1.

How to get there: From Interstate 80 at Truckee, drive north on Highway 89; access is available directly off the road north of the Bear Valley Road turnoff. Continue to Old Truckee Road (about one mile south of Sierraville). Turn north; the road parallels the stream, and direct access is available.

Facilities: A campground is available on Highway 89. Supplies are available in Truckee or Sierraville.

Cost: Access is free.

Who to contact: Phone the Tahoe National Forest District Office at (916) 994-3401.

About Cold Stream Creek: If you want to learn how to fish a small trout stream, and have a very good chance of catching rainbow trout in the nine to 11-inch class, then Cold Stream Creek provides a destination.

This little stream provides mountain-style fishing, but with easy access and planted trout. The easy access is off Old Truckee Road, which runs right along the river, and the planters are rainbow trout, of which some 1,620 are stocked each summer. The area is quite pretty, and there are often lots of deer in the vicinity, especially during evenings. If you are driving Highway 89 or 49 to get here, be sure to slow down, because deer can jump out of the woods and cross the road at any time.

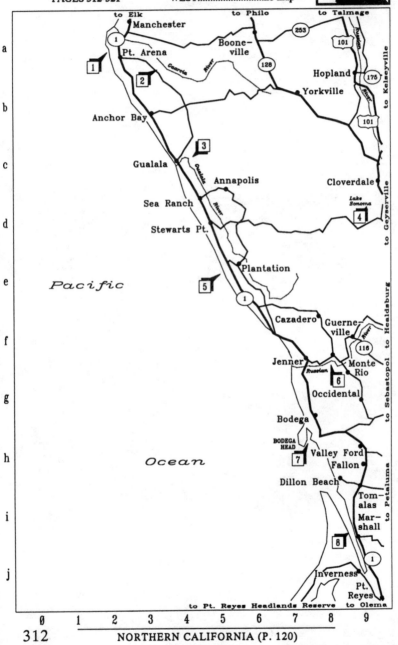

MAP DØ

8 LISTINGS
PAGES 312-321

NOR-CAL MAP. see page 120
adjoining maps
NORTH (CØ) ..... see page 244
EAST (D1).......... see page 322
SOUTH (EØ) ...... see page 410
WEST...........................no map

to Elk
Manchester
to Philo
to Talmage

Pt. Arena
253
101
a
Boone-
ville
128
Hopland
175
b
Yorkville
Anchor Bay
101
3
c
Gualala
Annapolis
Cloverdale
Sea Ranch
Lake
Sonoma
d
Stewarts Pt.
4
Plantation
Pacific
e
5
1
Cazadero
Guerne-
ville
f
Jenner
Monte
Rio
116
6
Occidental
g
Bodega
BODEGA
HEAD
h
7
Valley Ford
Ocean
Fallon
Dillon Beach
Tom-
alas
i
Mar-
shall
8
1
j
Inverness
Pt.
Reyes
to Pt. Reyes Headlands Reserve
to Olema

to Kelseyville
to Geyserville
to Healdsburg
to Sebastopol
to Petaluma

Gualala River
Russian River
Navarro River

1. POINT ARENA COVE

Reference: South of Mendocino; map DØ grid a2.

How to get there: From Mendocino, drive about 30 miles south on Highway 1 to the town of Point Arena. Turn west on Port Road and travel to the coast.

Facilities: Campgrounds are available at Manchester State Beach (north of Point Arena) and near Gualala. One charter boat, called *Second Semester,* is available. Diving equipment can be rented at Gualala Hardware in Gualala.

Cost: Party boat rates are $50 per person, three person minimum.

Who to contact: For party boat reservations, phone Second Semester Charters at (707) 882-2440. For fishing information, phone Gualala Sport & Tackle at (707) 884-4247.

About Point Arena: This chunk of Mendocino Coast is wild and rocky, and fishing here provides a rare chance to test waters that are relatively untouched.

The Second Semester Charter business, although sometimes an on-and-off proposition, fills a needed niche for visitors to the area. Because there are no boat ramps in the immediate area, fishermen with trailered boats are out of luck here. Regardless, this is a pristine coastal area that offers a unique opportunity for inshore fishing.

The inshore reefs, in particular, are loaded with rockfish and lingcod, especially in late summer and fall. No long boat ride is required. You can use light ocean tackle, three-ounce leadheads with split-tail Scampis and start getting the magic tug, tug, tug almost immediately. A huge variety of rockfish hang out here, some 200 species in all, including hordes of blues and yellows during the fall months. Lingcod are also big and abundant, but prefer a large jig such as the dark blue Banana Bar or chrome Diamond Jig.

The salmon fishing is less predictable, but can offer periods of high quality fishing during the summer months. Because there are no streams that salmon return to in the immediate vicinity, fishermen must intercept salmon that are migrating through the area. That can be an unpredictable, up-and-down affair, with excellent fishing for week-long periods, then nothing. It is usually the best in mid-July.

For shoreliners, the best area is the southern end of Point Arena Cove, casting in the vicinity of the mouth of Point Arena Creek. Perch fishing is good here, sometimes outstanding in late fall. The combination of a calm sea and a little bit of freshwater flow from the creek to sea makes a perfect combination for perch in this rarely-fished area.

2. GARCIA RIVER

Reference: Near Point Arena; map DØ grid a3.

How to get there: From Point Arena, drive five miles east on Eureka Hill Road. The upper fishing limit is at the bridge located there. The river can be accessed by foot downstream of the bridge. Or, drive west from Point Arena on Miner Hole Road to a parking area that offers nearby access.

Facilities: Camping is available at Manchester State Beach. Supplies can be obtained in Point Arena.

Cost: Access is free.

Who to contact: Phone guide Craig Bell at Greenwater Guide Service at (707) 882-2150.

About Garcia River: What is California's fastest clearing coastal river after a big storm? The answer is right here, the Garcia River, a short steelhead stream that runs out to sea just north of the town of Point Arena. The prime spot is the tidewater at the Miner Hole, and the prime time is high tide and the first two hours of the outgoing tide in January and February. You can often see the steelhead rolling, which can really get your juices running. The Miner Hole is located a short walk from the parking area on Miner Hole Road. When the fish are in, you'll see the other cars parked here.

Waders are a must here, working downstream, casting as you go. The preferred technique is to cast a Little Cleo or an F7 Flatfish, with the best colors gold, orange and silver. The critical factor with the Garcia River is timing, of course. You either hit it when the steelhead are in or you get skunked, and the latter is a common result for out-of-towners. Always phone first before planning a trip.

The Garcia has about 10 miles of fishable water, but the best bet is sticking exclusively to the tidewater. This is where fresh-run steelhead hole up for awhile, acclimating themselves to the freshwater. They are strong and bright. Hook a big one and you'll never forget it.

---

3. GUALALA RIVER

Reference: South of Point Arena; map DØ grid c4.

How to get there: To reach the upper fishing limit of the river, drive south on Highway 1 from Point Arena for 20 miles to Annapolis Road. Turn left (east) and travel to the twin bridges. To access the lower river, turn on Road 501, then Road 502 from the town of Gualala. Direct access is available.

Facilities: Campgrounds are available near Gualala. Supplies can be obtained in Gualala.

Cost: Access is free.

Who to contact: For fishing information, phone Gualala Sport & Tackle at (707) 884-4247; guide Craig Bell at Greenwater Guide Service at (707) 882-2150.

About Gualala River: Among most California steelhead streams, the Gualala River is a lance of light in a field of darkness. The steelhead runs are improving, not declining, thanks primarily to protecting habitat and a local project that has resulted in releasing 30,000 steelhead smolts per year from rod-and-reel caught spawners. Some beautiful, big steelhead in the 15-pound class can be caught on the Gualala, but alas, the word is out: When the fishing is on, you can expect a very crowded setting. The worst-case scenario is "the gauntlet," that is, when a line of anglers are all working shoulder-to-shoulder in the same prime piece of water. It may sound crazy, but it happens here fairly often without many feathers getting ruffled.

The key? Get on the water early, being the first to fish several holes. The steelhead can spook here, and will once the river gets crowded. So get there first.

Want some secrets? Here's a few, provided by guide Craig Bell. During an evening high tide, fishing the stretch of river just below the Highway 1 Bridge at Mill Bend can be outstanding, casting in the direction of rolling steelhead with Little Cleos or peach-colored Puff Balls. During the morning, a better bet is to start upstream at Switchvale, cross upstream and fish the North Fork Hole. From here on down, there are about 10 good spots for steelhead. My best luck on the Gualala has been early in the winter, when the steelhead will enter the river and hole up in the tidewater for awhile. The Miner Hole, located near the Sonoma County Park parking lot, often can hold many dozens of steelhead. It provides an opportunity for flyfishers, with Comets and sinking lines mandatory. The key is getting deep with your offering and getting as natural a drift as possible in the slow moving water here.

If you don't mind the company and the competition, the Gualala provides a rare opportunity to catch a large steelhead on a small stream. If you arrive when steelhead are moving through, you will discover some big, strong fish as well. Certainly, that represents two big "ifs," but few things worth remembering come easy.

---

4. LAKE SONOMA

Reference: North of Santa Rosa; map DØ grid d9.

How to get there: From Santa Rosa, drive 12 miles north on US 101 to the town of Healdsburg. Take the Dry Creek Road exit and turn left. Travel 11 miles to the lake.

Facilities: Primitive, developed, and group campsites are provided at the lake. A full-service marina, boat ramps, and boat rentals are available. Supplies can be obtained in Healdsburg.

Cost: Day-use fee is $4 per vehicle. Primitive boat-in campsites are free; developed sites are $6 per night. Group sites require reservations.

Who to contact: For general information and reservations, phone the U.S. Corps of Engineers, Lake Sonoma at (707) 433-9483. For fishing information, phone the Lake Sonoma Marina at (707) 433-2200. For a map, write Corps of Engineers, Lake Sonoma, 3333 Skaggs Springs Road, Geyserville, CA 95441.

About Lake Sonoma: Lake Sonoma is one of the few times when the government did something right. With Warm Springs Dam came the creation of this lake, an ideal spot for camping, fishing and waterskiing in specific areas, with the bonus of an adjacent 8,000-acre wildlife area with 40 miles of hiking trails. Just don't expect to catch any trout here. None are planted because of the fear of the genetic-cloned hatchery fish getting mixed up with wild strains of steelhead downstream on the Russian River. Instead, this lake provides a good fishery for largemouth bass and sunfish, with excellent habitat well upstream on each of the lake arms. It is a big lake set in rich foothill country with thousands of hidden coves. From the dam, the lake extends nine miles north on the Dry Creek Arm and four miles west on Warm Springs Creek. Each of the lake arms has several fingers and miles of quiet and secluded shore. The public boat launch is located near the junction of the lake arms. In addition, boat rentals are available from the marina.

The waterskier/fisherman conflict has been solved by providing a large area in the main lake body for water skiers and jet skis. Yet some two miles of the Warm Springs Creek arm and five miles on the Dry Creek arm are off limits to skiing, and it is here where the bass fishing is best. The preferred technique is to use live minnows for bait, available from the Dry Creek Store, which is located on the approach road just south of the lake.

On the lake arms, there are lots of "stickups," or submerged trees. It is here where you should cast your lures or let your minnows roam. Bass and sunfish are abundant, and while there are few large fish, the numbers of the smaller fellows often make up for it.

---

5.   SALT POINT STATE PARK

Reference: North of Fort Ross; map DØ grid e5.

How to get there: From the town of Jenner, drive 20 miles north on Highway 1 to the park entrance.

Facilities: A campground and picnic areas are provided at the park. Reservations are required for camping on weekends. Diving equipment can be rented at Gualala Hardware in Gualala.

Cost: Day use fee is $5 per vehicle.

Who to contact: Phone the park at (707) 847-3221.

About Salt Point State Park: Hard to reach? It is. Obscure? It is not. Salt Point State Park is the preferred destination for abalone divers from all over the Bay Area and Northern California. That is because of the abundance of abalone in both Gerstle Cove and the adjoining shallow reef area. It takes skill in snorkeling, diving and swimming, as well as quickness with a pry bar, but that done, you are probably more apt to get your abalone here than at any public beach in California. It is safe too, with virtually no sharks in the area, unlike farther south at the Farallones and Pigeon Point areas.

The key with abalone is to surprise them. Once they know you are there, they can clamp down so hard that it is almost impossible to dislodge them, particularly if they are in a crevice, or a deep area, where holding your breath becomes something of an act of faith. The key to the future of abalone diving here is allowing the juveniles to grow to mature size in order to get at least one or more spawns out of them before they are taken. That is why size limits are so critical for abalone. It is also why the Department of Fish and Game is cracking down on size and take limits at Salt Point. During the first few weekends of the season, the DFG has even set up roadblocks on the access highways and made many arrests. Do yourself a favor and help out the abalone resource in the process: adhere to the legal limits. And remember that the first word in sportsman is "sport."

---

6.   RUSSIAN RIVER

Reference: Northwest of Santa Rosa; map DØ grid f8.

How to get there: At the junction of Highways 1 and 116 near Jenner, drive east on Highway 116. Direct access is available.

Facilities: Several campgrounds are available on and near the river. A good one is Casini Ranch Family Campground. A boat ramp and boat rentals are available there as well. Another boat ramp is located near Monte Rio, off Church Street.

Cost: Access is free.

Who to contact: For fishing information, phone Steve Jackson at King's Sport & Tackle in Guerneville at (707) 869-2156. Sonoma Coast State Park at the mouth of the river can be reached at (707) 875-3483 or (707) 865-2391.

About Russian River: Sometimes just watching the mouth of the Russian River can be an illuminating experience. In late fall, the mouth of the

Russian is like a revolving door, with a sand bar opening and closing according to the strength of river flows. After heavy rains, it busts a hole through the sand bar, opens the mouth, and the river again flows to sea. At the same time, that allows anadromous fish such as salmon, steelhead, and in the spring, shad, to enter the river, depending on the time of the year.

Those should be all the clues you need for fishing here. During the summer, when the mouth is closed, the fishing is quite poor. But from winter through spring, when the mouth is open, it can be decent. Not great, but decent.

The runs of fish on the Russian vary quite a bit from year to year. With increased production of salmon and steelhead upstream from the Dry Creek Hatchery, there is some optimism for the future. But without corresponding increased river flows, courtesy of releases from Lake Sonoma and Lake Mendocino, those runs can be undermined.

The sea lions also seem to be a problem, although historically large runs of steelhead and large numbers of sea lions co-populated the river. One day in January, I saw something like 75 sea lions lined up practically shoulder-to-shoulder at the mouth of the river, trying to pick off steelhead as they swam through. The balance seemed out of whack.

The key here is water, and when early-winter rains provide it, the salmon have a chance to enter the river in September and October, followed by steelhead around Thanksgiving. The bigger steelhead usually show up around mid-January. The fish can be elusive, but there are also good sprees every year that always provide a lot of excitement and disbelief to those who have never experienced it.

Where to fish? The best spots for salmon are in the lower river, from the mouth on up at Markham Pool, Duncan Pool, Brown Pool, below the Monte Rio riffle, and Northwood. The best spots for steelhead are between the mouth of Dry Creek and Duncan Mills, though access for shorefishing is only fair. Though I have not personally done this, Steve Jackson, the owner of King's Tackle, suggests launching a small pram or drift boat to get the best access in this stretch of river. Good launch areas include Wohler Bridge, Mirabel Park, Midway Beach, Vacation Beach, Monte Rio Beach, and Cassini's Campground.

In spring and summer, fishing activity tapers off on the Russian River. In May, the remainder of a once-great shad run moves through the Russian, with the best spots below the Healdsburg dam on to Duncan Mills. I caught my first shad on the Russian River in 1966 upstream near Cloverdale, a run of fish that is extinct because of the dam at Healdsburg. In the summer, the county places several temporary dams in the river, turning it from a river into a series of greenish sloughs. Some small catfish and smallmouth bass hang out in the Alexander Valley area, but are rarely fished. The river gets a lot of canoe traffic in the summer, and to be honest, a lot of fishermen show up in the hopes of seeing topless women paddling away down the river. No kidding. It happens.

7.   BODEGA BAY SALMON & DEEP SEA

Reference: North of San Francisco; map DØ grid h8.

How to get there: From Highway 101 at Petaluma, turn west on Bodega Avenue (signed turnoff), drive through Petaluma and continue west for about eight miles, then turn north (right) on Valley Ford Road and continue for about 10 miles. Take the Valley Ford/Highway 1 cutoff west to Bodega Bay.

Facilities: Campgrounds are available nearby. A good boat ramp is available on the west side of Bodega Bay on West Shore Road. A full-service marina is also available. Supplies can be obtained in the town of Bodega Bay. Party boat charters are also available.

Cost: Party boat rates range from $38-$44 per person.

Who to contact: For general information and a free travel packet, phone the Bodega Bay Chamber of Commerce at (707) 875-3422. For fishing information, phone Bodega Bay Sportfishing at (707) 875-3344.

Party Boat List: New Sea Angler and *Jaws,* both at (707) 875-3495; *Mary Jane* and *Sea Dog III,* both at (707) 875-3344; *Challenger* at (707) 875-2474.

About Bodega Bay Salmon and Deep Sea: One time while returning from a salmon trip here, I actually saw a deer swimming straight out of the harbor, heading out to sea. The Coast Guard sent a boat out and rescued it. That is as strange as it gets here, despite the area's legendary status as the place where the Alfred Hitchcock thriller "The Birds" was filmed.

Instead of attacking birds, what you are more likely to see are attacking fish. Though you may not have to beat them off the boat with oars, there are large rockfish and big salmon, and a fun trip is made more enjoyable by beautiful surroundings.

Though it is in relatively close proximity to the Bay Area, Bodega Bay retains a rural feel to it. The drive here is a nice one, along a two-laner that is routed through rolling hills and country-styled dairy farms. What draws people here is the sea, a goldmine of fish and good times. The most abundant fish are the rockfish, with trips to Cordell Bank, Point Reyes, and north off of Fort Ross the specialty. Limits are virtually a daily affair, and so are very heavy bags of rockfish. Cordell Bank is one of the most consistent producers in California, about a 2 and a half hour trip to reach, and deep at 300 to 340 feet, but the rewards are large goldeneyes, reds, and bocaccios that often average 6 to 10 pounds. A 15-fish limit can weigh 90 and 100 pounds, more if you catch some bonus lingcod.

If you don't like to fish so deep, Captain Rick Powers of the *New Sea Angler* offers light-tackle "anything goes" trips to the shallows of Fort Ross every fall. It is one of the most fun rockfish trips available in California. While rockfish provide consistent day-in, day-out results, it is the salmon that provide the sizzle. I have fished here many times when a horde of salmon were located just west of Bodega Head at the Whistle Buoy, a short cruise from the excellent boat ramp. Other good spots for salmon are south just off Tomales Point, and north just outside the mouth of Salmon Creek. Typically the salmon are in the five and six-pound class early in the season. That is also when it is windiest here, and believe me, the north wind can really howl over the top of Bodega Head. Come summertime, however, and the wind lays down and the salmon get bigger. There are periods when there seem to be more 20-pound salmon than any other area of the coast. This normally sedate area can turn into a madhouse on July weekends when the salmon are running. By late August, however, only a sprinkling of fish remain in the area, and catch rates for salmon are only fair.

Several adventures on land are also available. In winter, minus low tides come in cycles every two weeks, uncovering miles of tidal flats in Bodega Bay, especially on the western side. Though it is gooey, this is prime clamming area. On high tides, perch, flounder, and rarely in the summer, halibut can be caught by shorefishing. This area is fast becoming a favorite fishing port and weekend vacation site. After a trip here, you will likely understand why.

---

8.   TOMALES BAY

Reference: North of San Francisco; map DØ grid i8.

How to get there: From US 101 in San Rafael, take the Sir Francis Drake Boulevard exit and drive west to Olema. Turn right and continue on Sir Francis Drake Boulevard (note that it jogs left just before reaching Point Reyes Station). Continue and then turn right on Pierce Point Road, and look for the Tomales Bay State Park entrance on the right side.

Facilities: A small campground is provided for bicyclists at Tomales Bay State Park. Camping is also available nearby at Bodega Bay.

Cost: Day-use fee at Tomales Bay State Park is $5 per vehicle.

Who to contact: Phone Tomales Bay State Park at (415) 669-1140.

About Tomales Bay: The inventive few with small boats can explore the quiet waters of Tomales Bay in the summer and discover huge halibut on the northwestern side of the Bay. Schools of perch also can be found, though there can be a lot of searching before much finding. For non-boaters, clamming is quite good in season during minus tides at Tomales Bay State Park. It is one of the more unique places in California, a long narrow bay that is cut by the San Andreas Fault, one of the world's most feared earthquake epicenters. Because Point Reyes shields the Bay from north winds, it is good place to paddle kayaks or motor around in small boats (a hoist is available in Inverness; look for the sign on the east side of the road).

Tomales Bay is largely undeveloped, bordered by the Point Reyes National Seashore to the west, and Highway 1 and very small towns to the east. It provides a quiet, wind-protected area. A few warnings, however. Every year, dozens of clammers get nailed at Tomales Bay State Park for not having a state fishing license in possession. It is required for clamming, and the rangers will check. Another note: It is unwise to try to "shoot the jaws" and head through the mouth of Tomales Bay and out into the ocean in a small boat. It is very shallow near the buoy here, and the water can be choppy and dangerous. In addition, this is a breeding area for Great White sharks. In fact, a Great White actually bit the propeller off a boat once in this area. That is warning enough.

MAP D1

18 LISTINGS
PAGES 322-339

NOR-CAL MAP . see page 120
adjoining maps
NORTH (C1) ...... see page 256
EAST (D2) .... see page 340
SOUTH (E1) .... see page 414
WEST (DØ) .... see page 312

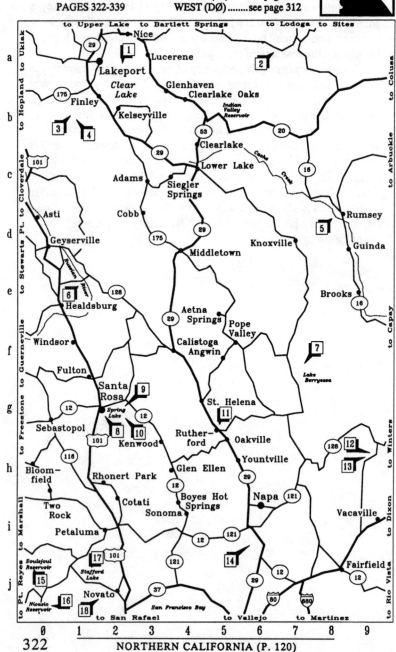

to Upper Lake   to Bartlett Springs   to Lodoga   to Sites

Nice

㉙

▢ 1   Lucerene

▢ 2

a

Lakeport

Clear Lake

Glenhaven
Clearlake Oaks

to Ukiah   to Hopland

⑰⑤   Finley

Kelseyville

Indian Valley Reservoir

b

▢ 3   ▢ 4

㊼

⑳

to Cloverdale

⑩①   Clearlake

㉙

Lower Lake   *Cache Creek*

⑯

c

Adams   Siegler Springs

Asti   Cobb

to Stewarts Pt.

Geyserville

㉙   ⑰⑤

Knoxville   Guinda

▢ 5

Rumsey

to Arbuckle   to Colusa

d

Middletown

Russian River

⑫⑧   Brooks

e

▢ 6   Healdsburg

㉙   Aetna Springs   Pope Valley

⑯

to Capay

Windsor

Calistoga
Angwin   ▢ 7

Lake Berryessa

f

Fulton

to Freestone   to Guerneville

Santa Rosa   ▢ 9

Spring Lake   St. Helena

⑫   ▢ 11

Sebastopol   ⑫

g

①⑩①   ▢ 8   ▢ 10   Rutherford   Oakville

⑫⑧   ▢ 12

Kenwood

Yountville   ⑬

to Winters

⑪⑥

Bloom-field   Rhonert Park   Glen Ellen   ㉙

h

to Marshall   to Pt. Reyes

Two Rock   ⑫

Cotati   Boyes Hot Springs   Napa   ⑫①

Sonoma   Vacaville

to Dixon

i

Petaluma   ⑫   ⑫①

▢ 14   ⑫

Fairfield

⑫

j

▢ 17   ①⑩①

Stafford Lake

▢ 15   *Soulajoul Reservoir*   ⑫①

㉙

⑧⓪   ⑥⑧⓪

to Rio Vista

Nicasio Reservoir   ▢ 16   Novato

㊲   *San Francisco Bay*

▢ 18

to San Rafael   to Vallejo   to Martinez

Ø   1   2   3   4   5   6   7   8   9

Reference: North of San Francisco; map D1 grid a2.

How to get there from the Bay Area: Take Highway 80 north over the Carquinez Bridge, then turn north on Highway 29, continue through Vallejo and Napa (jogging left just after Napa College), and continue on Highway 29 through the Napa Valley, past Middletown to the town of Lower Lake.

How to get there from Sacramento/Interstate 5: Take Interstate 5 north to Williams, then turn west on Highway 20 and continue the town of Clearlake.

How to get there from the North Coast: Take US 101 to Calpella (17 miles south of Willits), then turn south on Highway 20 and continue to the town of Nice.

Free boat ramps: Public boat ramps are available at Clearlake, at Rosebud County Park; in Kelseyville, at Lakeside County Park; in Lakeport, at First Street, Third Street, Fifth Street, Clear Lake Avenue, and at the junction of Lakeshore Boulevard and Crystal Lake Way; in Lucerne, at Lucerne Harbor County Park; in Nice, at H.V. Keeling County Park, Nice Community County Park, and at Hudson Avenue.

Facilities: Camping is available at Clear Lake State Park (near Kelseyville), as well as at several private campgrounds and resorts around the lake. Full-service marinas, boat ramps, boat rentals, bait, tackle, and supplies are also available.

Cost: Lake access is free.

Who to contact: For general information and a free travel packet, phone the Lakeport Chamber of Commerce at (707) 263-5092, or the Lake County Visitor Information Center at (707) 263-9544 or toll-free (California only) (800) 525-3743. For fishing information, phone Konocti Harbor Inn at (707) 279-4291, ext. 280, or Ferndale Marina (on the west side of the lake) at (707) 279-4866; Lakeport Tackle in Lakeport at (707) 263-8862; Shaw's Shady Acres in Lower Lake at (707) 994-2236; Rod & Gun in Upper Lake at 275-2045; Tally's Family Resort in Nice at (707) 274-1177.

About Clear Lake: Maybe Clear Lake should be renamed. Maybe call it "Fish Lake" or "Green Lake," because it is full of fish and it is shaded the color emerald green. But clear it is not, with high nutrient and algae levels clouding water levels, and you can thank nature for creating such a wonderful problem.

    You see, these high amounts of nutrient, phytoplankton and algae and huge numbers of minnows support a high carrying capacity at Clear Lake. In simpler terms, it means a lot of aquatic food equals a lot of fish, including some giant bass, catfish and crappie, along with scads of bluegill. In the 1970s, people said the lake had "wall-to-wall" crappie. In the 1980s, people said the lake had "wall-to-wall" catfish. Now in the '90s, the same folks are saying it has "wall-to-wall" bass. In any case, you get the idea.

The lake is quite pretty, covering more than 40,000 surface acres amid the foothills of Lake County. It is the largest natural freshwater lake within California borders, and often seems full right to the brim, with Highway 20 running aside the eastern shore. It can accommodate huge numbers of visitors without feeling crowded, with dozens of resorts and private campgrounds sprinkled along the 100 miles of shoreline. Reservations are advised in the summer, of course.

Outstanding fish habitat makes for outstanding fishing. Pro bassers named it the number one bass fishing lake in America, and it also produces more big crappie and more sheer numbers of catfish than any lake in California.

What makes it so attractive for bass fishing is that there is ample habitat, there are plenty of bass in the five to 10-pound class, and the bass seem to be in shallow water almost year-round. Much of the southwest shore, in the vicinity of the state and county parks, has one cove after another lined with tules, ideal haunts for bass, crappie and bluegill. In the central part of the lake, the shoreline of a small island and peninsula also hold a lot of bass. At the north end of the lake, there are a series of old pilings and docks where the bass often hug.

Unlike the great bass lakes of Southern California, bait is rarely used. Instead, anglers use crankbaits such as the Rattletrap, Shad Rap, Fat Rap and Rapala, large spinnerbaits in white or black, and many plastics such as the motor-oil colored plastic worm, Salt-and-Pepper grubs, and Gitsits. Casts must be precise, tossing the lure within inches of the desired mark, either next to a piling, tule berm, or rockpile. Keep doing that and it becomes difficult not to catch fish.

And you are apt to catch more than bass. That is because Clear Lake has a population of huge black crappie, running to 15, 16 inches. They often are caught by accident on bass plugs. If you catch one, then switch over to a crappie jig in white, yellow or white-with-a-spinner, or let a live minnow roam down there. Crappie stay tightly schooled, and the angler must present the lure or bait right in front of them. The most difficult part is finding the school, not getting bites.

As a 10-year-old misguided missile, I had my one of my first personal successes at Clear Lake, catching dozens of crappie on a warm summer night. You still can. Private resorts will hang bright lights from their dock, which attract gnats, and in turn, attract minnows. Ultimately, the crappie show up to eat the minnows, and you just toss out a small white jig and start catching fish.

If you have a boat, you can get a kid hooked on fishing by taking a similar approach for bluegill. Just use a red worm under a bobber, toss it out the near the tules, and watch that bobber start to dance. For a young kid who thinks no fish exist at all, it is quite a thrill. The coves near the state park are excellent for this sport.

For anglers who prefer to relax, the catfishing provides the answer. The deep holes near Jago Bay, Rattlesnake Island, and just outside the entrance to Cache Creek at the south end of the lake and Rodman Slough at the north end are excellent spots. For a primer on specialized catfish techniques, see the story in the front of this book on the late George Powers, the "Mr. Catfish" of America.

If all this sounds too good to be true, you are right, it is. A few problems provide a few thorns. One is the traffic, which is horrendous on summer weekends on the little two-laners that provide access to the lake. Another is the wind in the early spring, when the north wind can put the fish off the bite for days on end. And lastly, by late summer, algae blooms can turn the surface waters into a soupy mess. Waterskiers can get coated with the stuff.

But that green mess is the stuff of life for Clear Lake. Without it, the lake would likely just provide average feed and fish populations. Maybe they should just change the name of the lake.

---

2. INDIAN VALLEY RESERVOIR

Reference: Near Clear Lake; map D1 grid a6.

How to get there from the west: From the north end of Clear Lake at the town of Nice, drive one mile south on Highway 20, then turn left on Bartlett Springs Road. The road is quite twisty, but is routed to the north end of the lake, where a boat launch is located.

How to get there from the east: From Interstate 5 at Williams, turn west on Highway 20 and drive about eight miles. Turn right on Lees-ville/Walnut Road, and drive to Leesville (very twisty at Windy Point). Continue a half-mile past Leesville, and jog left on Bear Valley Road, drive two miles, then turn right on Brim/Bartlett Springs Road to the north end of the lake, where a boat launch is located.

Facilities: Campgrounds, a boat ramp, bait, tackle, and supplies are available at the Indian Valley Store.

Cost: Day-use fee is $2 per vehicle (two people per vehicle; $1 for each additional person). Campsite fees are $5 per vehicle (same vehicle restrictions as day-use).

Who to contact: Phone the Indian Valley Store at (916) 662-0607 for camping reservations and fishing information.

About Indian Valley Reservoir: Imagine a lake so ugly that it is beautiful. That is the way it is at Indian Valley Reservoir.

Ugly? To some people, it is the Roseanne Barr of lakes. The water level is often very low, turning the lake into a long narrow strip with

---

miles of exposed shore. For most of the year, the surrounding hills are brown and barren. The road in from either side is a twisted nightmare.

But after awhile, Indian Valley Reservoir becomes like an ugly dog that you love more than anything in the world. Because inside beats a heart that will never betray you.

Indian Valley Reservoir is one of the best bass lakes in America, with days of fantastic catches every spring. You need a boat, but that done, two anglers might catch 40 or 50 bass during a warm, windless day from mid-March through early June. It happens. In fact, it happens a lot.

One key is the large amount of "stick-ups," or submerged trees, in the lake that provide perfect habitat for bass and crappie. Winter inflows from Cache Creek and Wolf Creek provide fresh, cool oxygenated water and an influx of feed, and then the hot weather that follows gets the bass, crappie and redear sunfish active and feeding.

In the late winter and spring, a real surprise here is the quality trout fishing. It is usually best near the creek inlets and along the dam. Although most of the spring trout are planted rainbows, a sprinkling of larger trout occasionally are caught. When the hot weather arrives for keeps, the trout say adios and head for the depths. No problem. This is primarily a bass lake anyway.

When full, the lake covers about 4,000 acres and has 41 miles of shoreline. But it never seems to be full. Remember, this is an ugly lake. But it is also beautiful. A 10-mph speed limit, clear water, and hot days makes for a quiet setting and good swimming in the summer.

If you have a small boat, want to catch bass, then Indian Valley Reservoir is the spot. Just don't expect Racquel Welch to float by on a piece of driftwood and ask to come aboard.

---

3.   HIGHLAND SPRINGS RESERVOIR

Reference: West of Clear Lake; map D1 grid b1.

How to get there: From Highway 101 at Hopland, drive east on Highway 175 to Kelseyville. Turn west and drive four miles northwest on Highway 29. Turn left on Highland Springs Road and travel four miles south.

Facilities: Picnic areas and boat ramps are provided. No gasoline motors are permitted on the lake.

Cost: Access is free.

Who to contact: Phone Lake County Flood Control at (707) 263-2343.

About Highland Springs Reservoir: People can drive to giant Clear Lake for a lifetime and never learn about Highland Springs Reservoir and adjacent Adobe Creek Reservoir. Yet they are so nearby, only about 10 miles west of Clear Lake, and between them provide needed options.

Highland Springs Reservoir is located in the foothills just southwest of Big Valley, about a mile west of Adobe Creek Reservoir. It covers about 150 acres, created from a dam on Highland Creek, a tributary of Adobe Creek.

Since no motors are allowed on the lake, Highland Springs offers a perfect alternative for anglers with small, hand-powered boats, such as canoes, rafts, or prams. That guarantees quiet water, even on three-day weekends when nearby Clear Lake just about gets plowed under from the hot jet boats.

With the quiet water comes a variety of warmwater fish, including largemouth bass, sunfish, bluegill, catfish and bullhead. The best fishing is during the first warm snaps during spring, often in April and early May, especially for the bass and bluegill. As summer heats up this reservoir, the fishing is better for catfish. A bonus is that if your luck is not good at Highland Springs, you can just make the quick trip over to Adobe Creek Reservoir.

---

4.   ADOBE CREEK RESERVOIR

Reference: West of Clear Lake; map D1 grid b1.

How to get there: From US 101 at Hopland, drive east on Highway 175 to Kelseyville. Turn west and drive one mile northwest on Highway 29. Turn left on Bell Hill Road and travel about four miles, then turn south on Adobe Creek Road and continue to the reservoir.

Facilities: No facilities are available on-site. No motors are permitted on the lake.

Cost: Access is free.

Who to contact: Phone Lake County Flood Control at (707) 263-2343.

About Adobe Creek Reservoir: This reservoir is the little brother of adjacent Highland Springs Reservoir, located about a mile to the west. Adobe Creek Reservoir covers 60 acres, and is a quiet spot in the foothills of the Mayacmas Mountains. Because Mount Konocti to the east helps separate these two lakes from giant Clear Lake, they are often overlooked.

Adobe Creek Reservoir provides a fair fishery for bass, bluegill, and sunfish, but has a more squarish shape, fewer coves, and as a result, less fish habitat than adjacent Highlands Creek Reservoir. Of the two lakes here, this one comes in second. But . . . whenever you can find a lake where no motors are allowed, there is always the chance for a quality fishing experience. This lake is good for float tubers casting poppers or small floating Rapalas along the shore during the spring bite. Just don't expect large fish.

---

5. CACHE CREEK

Reference: Southeast of Clear Lake; map D1 grid d8.

How to get there: From Interstate 5 at Williams, take the Highway 20 exit. Turn west and continue for approximately 20 miles to the turnoff for Highway 16. Turn south on Highway 16; direct access is available from the town of Rumsey to four miles upstream, at the confluence of Bear Creek. South of Rumsey the creek runs on private property; be aware of the boundaries.

Facilities: Cache Creek Canyon Regional Park offers a campground about 10 miles north of Rumsey. Supplies are available in the Clear Lake area.

Cost: Access is free.

Who to contact: Phone Cache Creek Canyon Regional Park at (916) 666-8115.

About Cache Creek: Cache Creek is better known as the closest white-water rafting opportunity to the San Francisco Bay Area. What is lesser-known is that some huge catfish and a light sprinkling of smallmouth bass roam the slower flows of the river.

You don't believe it? Then stop in at the little tackle shop in the town of Guinda. Seeing is believing: A 30-pound catfish caught in Cache Creek, then mounted, is on display.

Much of the upper reaches of Cache Creek (just below Clear lake) are inaccessible, though a two-mile stretch of bass water can be fished on the little road that runs out of Anderson Flat. It is rarely hit. The more accessible area is right along Highway 16, the little two-laner that connects tiny towns such as Guinda and Rumsey and then heads north to the raft put-in spot near the confluence of Bear Creek.

6. RUSSIAN RIVER

Reference: North of Santa Rosa; map D1 grid e1.

How to get tthere: Many access points are available. From the Bay Area, drive north on US 101 to Healdsburg. Take Westside Road and head west (the road then bends south), for walk-in access. Or continue on US 101 just past Cloverdale, where there is access to the river under the old US 101 Bridge. Another option is driving farther north, where there are several pullouts on the road and access points between Cloverdale and Hopland. An excellent map of the river is available at local tackle shops.

Facilities: Fishing supplies can be obtained at Dry Creek General Store, (west of Healdsburg), or King's Sport & Tackle in Guerneville, or Mike's Tackle in Santa Rosa.

328

Cost: Access is free.

Who to contact: Phone King's Sport & Tackle in Guerneville at (707) 869-2156, or Mike's Tackle in Santa Rosa at (707) 544-9456.

About Russian River: The future of this section of river is closely tied to the success or failure of the Warm Springs Hatchery set below Lake Sonoma.

If it works, and runs of steelhead return to historic levels, then the stretch of river from Healdsburg on down will provide the closest quality steelhead opportunity for Bay Area anglers. If it doesn't work, they might as well dynamite the two dams that are depriving this river of water, which is about all anadromous fish really need.

When the steelhead return to the Russian River in the winter months, they now often stop at the mouth of Dry Creek, then make the turn north there for the trip up to the hatchery. From Thanksgiving on, as long as stream conditions are fishable, you can always plan to see at least a few bank anglers casting here. It is located just a mile downstream from Healdsburg. Dry Creek, a key spawning tributary, is closed to all fishing, of course. Upstream of Healdsburg, the river takes on a different scope. Because of the concrete fish block at Healdsburg, steelhead are few in the winter, shad are now extinct in the spring, and what is left are primarily small trout in pocket water during the early summer.

I used to fish the Squaw Rock area between Cloverdale and Hopland and had some success, but in recent years, the results have been poor to fair at best. Access is not difficult on the Russian River in this area, but catching anything decent certainly is. A better prospect is fishing the East Fork Russian River (Cold Creek) just above Lake Mendocino, which is stocked with trout by Fish and Game.

For more information about the lower river, turn to zone DØ. For more information about the upper river above Lake Mendocino, turn to zone C1.

---

7.   LAKE BERRYESSA

Reference: North of Vallejo; map D1 grid f7.

How to get there: From Vallejo, drive north on Interstate 80 to the Suisun Valley Road exit. Take Suisun Valley Road to Highway 121, then turn north and travel five miles. Turn left (north) on Highway 128 and drive five miles, then turn right (north) onto Berryessa-Knoxville Road and travel north.

Facilities: Several campgrounds are available around the lake. A full-service marina, boat ramps, boat rentals, lodging, gas, bait, tackle, and groceries are also available.

Cost: Lake access is free.

Who to contact: Lakeside accommodations are offered at Putah Creek Resort, (707) 966-2116; Steele Park Marina, (707) 966-2330. Tent and RV camping is available at Rancho Monticello, (707) 966-2116; Berryessa Marina, (707) 966-2161; Spanish Flat Resort, (707) 966-2338; South Shore, (707) 966-2172; Putah Creek and Steele Park. Houseboat rentals are available from Markley Cove Marina, (707) 966-2134. For general information, phone the U.S. Bureau of Reclamation at (707) 966-2111.

About Lake Berryessa: A trophy-trout fishery, scads of small bass, and 750 campsites at seven resort areas make Lake Berryessa the Bay Area's most popular vacationland. It is a big lake, covering some 21,000 acres with 165 miles of shoreline, complete with secret coves, islands, and an expanse of untouched shore (eastern side) where people are off limits.

If it sounds good, it's because it is. However, that causes the one problem this lake has—too many people on weekends. It is particularly frustrating if you cross paths with self-obsessed water skiers, ripping up and down the lake during the summer with little regard for anything but themselves. The campgrounds can get loaded, too, so this is hardly a pristine experience.

But what you do get is quality fishing. If you can visit during the week, avoiding the party-goers, you will get a chance at quiet water and good fishing. On a Thursday morning, for instance, Berryessa seems like it is on a different planet compared to a Saturday afternoon.

Like many large reservoirs, your approach to fishing is dependent on water temperature. If you want numbers, try during the spring, when the bass move in along shoreline cove areas in the lake arms. The prime areas are the three major lake arms at the south end of the lake, as well as the Putah Creek Arm at the north end of the lake. Avoid the main lake body.

It is common to catch 10 or 15 bass in a day, casting a variety of lures along these protected shoreline coves. During the evening, surface lures such as the Rebel Pop-R can provide some exciting fishing. Most of the bass are small, many in the 10 to 12-inch class, but there are enough bigger to keep it interesting. There are nowhere near the numbers of large bass in Berryessa as are in Clear Lake to the north, however.

No problem. Because Clear Lake doesn't have trout, much less a trophy-trout fishery. Berryessa does, and it provides excellent trolling opportunity from spring through summer. Depth is the key, and once the hot weather arrives, it is like the trout are locked in jail the way they stay in the thermocline about 40 feet deep. You either get down that deep or get skunked. Guide Claude Davis out of Markley Cove Marina has mastered the art of using two trolling lines on a single downrigger, then using red **Rainbow Runner** spoons to catch trout in the 12 to 18-inch class. You can also use lead-core trolling line or a planer-diver to get deep easy.

If you don't like trolling deep, then wait until the lake "turns over," that is, when the stratified temperature zones do a flip-flop, bringing cool water and the trout to the surface. It usually happens around the third week of October. When it does, the lake surface will have thousands of tiny pools from rising trout, a spectacular scene, best on Hope Creek, Putah Creek, the Markley Cove arm, and around the island. The lake record rainbow trout, 38 inches and 14 pounds, was taken during such a period. That is when using live minnows for bait is so effective. You let your boat drift, letting a live minnow roam about, either with or without a bobber. It's like a potluck affair, where you bring minnow for dinner and plenty of your guests might decide to try it.

It was during the fall when I paddled my canoe well up the Putah Creek arm, which is off limits to power boats. Everything was quiet and pretty as I casted along the steep, granite drop-off on the west side. Suddenly, I felt like somebody was watching me. Somebody was. On the east shore, a deer and two fawns had come out at dusk to drink at lake's edge. They had not heard the canoe until it was very close to them, and for 10 seconds, we just stared at each other at point blank range.

It was a special moment, the kind that many who live in metropolitan areas should experience more often.

---

8. RALPHINE LAKE

Reference: In Santa Rosa at Howarth Park; map D1 grid g2 .

How to get there: From US 101 in Santa Rosa, drive east on Highway 12 until it becomes Hoen Avenue. Continue for about three miles to Summerfield Road. Turn left and travel to Howarth Park.

Facilities: Picnic facilities are provided in the park. A boat ramp and boat rentals are available. No motors are permitted on the lake. A campground is available nearby at Spring Lake. Fishing supplies are available at Mike's Tackle.

Cost: Access is free.

Who to contact: Phone Howarth Park at (707) 539-1499, or Mike's Tackle at (707) 544-9456. For lodging information, phone the Santa Rosa Chamber of Commerce at (707) 545-1414.

About Ralphine Lake: This is one of two backyard fishing holes in Santa Rosa, the other being Spring Lake, and some inside knowledge is that both lakes are always stocked on the same day with the same amount of trout.

Ralphine is the smaller of the two, one-third the size at 26 acres. It is fished primarily by baitdunkers, both from shore and small rowboats. You can go far here with a jar of Power Bait, tub of nightcrawlers, and two size six hooks.

It is stocked solely by the Department of Fish and Game, and that means no large bonus trout; anything over 12 inches is an accident. But the stocks are consistent, 2,000 trout plunked in twice a month when the lake temperatures are cool enough to allow it, usually October through March. In the summer, some small bass and bluegill provide an opportunity for kids.

---

9. SPRING LAKE

Reference: In Santa Rosa in Spring Lake County Park; map D1 grid g2.

How to get there: From US 101 in Santa Rosa, drive east on Highway 12 until it becomes Hoen Avenue. Turn left on New Angle Avenue and drive to the end of the road.

Facilities: A campground is provided at the lake. A boat ramp (no motors permitted), boat rentals, and bait are available. Fishing supplies can be obtained at Mike's Tackle.

Cost: Day-use fee is $2 per vehicle; campsite fee is $11 per night.

Who to contact: Phone Spring Lake County Park at (707) 539-8082, or Mike's Tackle at (707) 544-9456. For lodging information, phone the Santa Rosa Chamber of Commerce at (707) 545-1414.

About Spring Lake A precious handful of lakes in the San Francisco Bay Area have campgrounds, and this is one of them. The others are Lake Del Valle, Lake Chabot, Uvas Reservoir, Coyote Lake, and Pinto Lake.

Since Spring Lake is stocked with trout twice a month from fall through spring, it provides the chance for a fishing/camping trip right in Santa Rosa, of all places. Crazy? It may sound so until you see the lake, which is fairly good size (75 acres), and surrounded by parkland.

It provides a very similar fishery to nearby Ralphine Lake, with trout in the cool months, some small bass and bluegill in the summer.

---

10. LAKE ILSANJO

Reference: In Santa Rosa in Annadel State Park; map D1 grid g2.

How to get there: From US 101 in Santa Rosa, drive east on Highway 12. Bear right at Montgomery Drive, then turn right on Channel Drive and continue to the park. To reach the lake requires a 2.5-mile hike.

Facilities: A campground is available nearby at Spring Lake County Park. Supplies can be obtained in Santa Rosa.

Cost: Day-use fee is $5 per vehicle.

Who to contact: Phone Annadel State Park at (707) 539-3911.

About Lake Ilsanjo: "You've got to walk there" can seem like the most frightening sentence ever spoken to a angler. It certainly is enough to scare most folks away from Lake Ilsanjo.

Ilsanjo is the centerpiece at Annadel State Park, which has 5,000 acres of rolling hills, meadows, and oak woodlands, with a few seasonal creeks. The lake is a classic bass pond, which many anglers never get a chance to fish. Well, here is your chance. Alas, you must walk, a five-mile roundtrip. It takes a little more than an hour in both directions, and always bring a full canteen to make the trip a little easier.

That done, it is a perfect lake to take a light spinning rod and small bass lures for the spring bite. A great lure for this lake is a one-inch Countdown Rapala, black over gold. A key is not to be too quick to walk up to the shoreline and cast as far as possible, because most of the bass are right along the shore. So instead creep up and cast along the bank, moving deeper with each cast.

While most of the bass are small, they are fun to catch and there are a few big fellows in here. The lake record is an eight-pounder.

---

11. LAKE HENNESSEY

Reference: North of Napa in Lake Hennessey City Recreation Area; map D1 grid g5.

How to get there: From Napa, drive east on Trancas Street to Silverado Trail. Turn north and travel about 15 miles, then take the Highway 128 east turnoff and continue for three miles to the park entrance.

Facilities: A boat launch is provided (no engines over ten horsepower are permitted on the lake). Supplies are available in Napa.

Cost: There is an annual access fee of $2. A boat launching fee is also charged.

Who to contact: Phone the Department of Parks and Recreation, Public Works & Water, at (707) 257-9520; Department of Fish and Game, Napa, (707) 944-5500.

About Lake Hennessey: The City of Napa owns this lake, and they do a good job of keeping quiet about it. Most people elsewhere in the Bay Area have never heard of it.

Then when they do, and curiosity compels them to take a look, they are often stunned at its size: 20,000 acres, 12 miles long, four miles wide. What? Impossible? It is, and it is not. Fishing? Well, at least you can fish. There are some other lakes in this area that are off limits to the public. Fish and Game provides some assistance by stocking 10 to 11-inch rainbow trout in the fall, winter and spring, and some resident bass, bluegill and sunfish provide poor to fair hopes in the summer. A little inside knowledge always helps, however. The impoundment east of Highway 128 is where the trout are stocked. The main reservoir rarely gets trout plants, unless the impoundment is very low on water.

12.   LAKE SOLANO

Reference: Near Lake Berryessa in Lake Solano County Park; map D1 grid h9.

How to get there: From the town of Winters on Interstate 505, turn west on Highway 128. Drive about five miles and turn left (south) on Pleasant Valley Road. Continue to the park.

Facilities: A campground, a boat ramp, and boat rentals are available at the park. Supplies can be obtained nearby.

Cost: Campsite fee is $10-$12 per night.

Who to contact: Phone Lake Solano County Park at (916) 795-2990.

About Lake Solano: Sometimes a lake is not a lake at all. That is the case with Lake Solano. The lake is actually Putah Creek with a small dam on it.

It provides a quiet alternative to nearby Lake Berryessa. That is because no motor boats are allowed on the water here, making it a good bet for folks with canoes, rowboats or other small people-powered crafts.

Lake Solano is stocked once a week with rainbow trout, and also supports a resident population of sunfish and small catfish. The campgrounds are popular on summer weekends, but they fill during the week on only rare occasions. When nearby Berryessa just has too many people and too many fast boats, Lake Solano provides a much quieter option.

13.   PUTAH CREEK

Reference: Downstream of Lake Berryessa; map D1 grid h9.

How to get there: From the town of Winters on Interstate 505, turn west on Highway 128. Drive about five miles. Putah Creek runs along the road, with the best fishing in the two miles just below the dam at Lake Solano.

Facilities: The nearest campground and facilities are at Lake Solano County Park, located just upstream of Putah Creek.

Cost: Access is free.

Who to contact: Department of Fish and Game at (707) 944-5500.

About Putah Creek: Putah Creek may be a prisoner of the DFG tanker truck, but it is a model prisoner.

The fishable section is actually quite short, set just below the little dam at Lake Solano, all just downstream from Lake Berryessa. When

Putah Creek is stocked, the results are good. When it isn't, then they aren't. It is that simple.

Some Bay Area flyfishers use Putah Creek to hone their craft before heading off for more serious stuff in the mountains. Sometimes they even catch a trout, providing they are fishing after a stock.

What to do? This is one water where you have to follow the weekly DFG stocks, which are listed weekly in *Western Outdoor News*.

---

14.   NAPA RIVER

Reference: Near Napa; map D1 grid i6.

How to get there: To reach the boat ramps, drive southwest on Highway 121-Highway 12 from Napa. Turn left on Cuttings Wharf Road and travel to the end of the road.

Facilities: A public boat ramp is provided at Moore's Resort. A private fishing area is available in the immediate vicinity at Sea Ranch. Bait and tackle are available nearby. Lodging is available in Napa.

Cost: Access is free.

Who to contact: For general information, phone the Napa Chamber of Commerce at (707) 226-7455. For fishing information, phone Napa Valley Marina at (707) 252-8011, or Moore's Landing at (707) 226-7026.

About Napa River: "If only" . . . those magic words seem appropriate whenever I look at the Napa River.

If only the steelhead returned here during the winter like they used to. If only the striped bass once again arrived in hordes in the spring. If only the water looked like a real river instead of a green slough. If only. But reality replaces daydreams when it comes to casting a line, and that reality is that the Napa River has degenerated from a once-great fishery to hardly being able to qualify for a mention in this book.

What seems left are what I call "Napa River Trout," that is, six and seven-inch striped bass that can be caught, then released, on trout gear during the summer. A few gallant steelhead still manage to return during the winter, but they are better left alone to complete their spawning mission.

The one viable area to fish the Napa River is the lower section, where an excellent pier is available that provides a chance for sturgeon and large striped bass. For information, see Zone EØ.

---

15.   SOULEJULE LAKE

Reference: Near Novato; map D1 grid jØ.

How to get there: From US 101 at Novato, take the San Marin exit and continue west to Novato Boulevard. Turn right and drive nine miles.

Turn right on Petaluma-Point Reyes Road and travel one-quarter mile, then turn left on Wilson Hill Road. Drive three miles northwest, then turn on Marshall-Petaluma Road and continue for five miles to the signed turnoff on the left. Park at the base of the dam and hike a short distance to the lake.

Facilities: No facilities are available on-site. Lodging and supplies are available in Novato or Petaluma.

Cost: Access is free.

Who to contact: Phone Western Boat in San Rafael, (415) 454-4177; North Marin Water District at (415) 897-4133.

About Soulejule Lake: Start here by trying not to butcher the name of this lake. It is pronounced Soo-La-Hooley and not Sole-Ley-Jewl. It may not sound right to you, but after you start catching the bass here, pronouncing it will come easier.

This is a little-known, hike-in lake in northern Marin. You can drive to the base of the dam, then make the short hike to the lake's edge. The quiet and crafty will discover many small largemouth bass, a few elusive big fellas, and the best crappie fishery in Marin County.

Timing is a key, with the first warm weather of the year the prime time for the crappie. Tie on a crappie jig, either white, chartreuse or yellow, then make a cast, walk on, make a cast. If you hit crappie, then stick to that spot; they're a school fish. The evening bass fishing can also be decent on small crankbaits, though most of the fish are small.

Now, one more time: How do you pronounce Soulejule?

---

16.   NICASIO LAKE

Reference: Near Novato; map D1 grid jØ.

How to get there: From US 101 at Novato, drive seven miles west on Sir Francis Drake Boulevard. Turn right on Nicasio Valley Road and travel five miles to the lake.

Facilities: No facilities are available on-site. Lodging and supplies are available in Novato.

Cost: Access is free.

Who to contact: Phone the North Marin Water District at (415) 897-4133.

About Nicasio Lake: Nicasio Lake is set in open hills without even a picnic table around. On spring evenings during the week, it can seem abandoned. Therefore, is it even worth a look?

You bet your butt. Nicasio is one of the surprises of the hidden lakes in Marin, with lots of small bass making it a good destination for a parent/child team who want action. You can add to the action by using surface lures, so you get to see all the strikes. The way to do it here is to cast small Jitterbugs, let 'em sit, then give 'em a twitch, and get lots of strikes from bass in the eight to 12-inch class. It happens like this as the first warm weather arrives and spring gives way to summer.

After that, the picture changes. You need to cast Green Weenies or mid-level swimming lures in shad patterns. As long as you don't expect big fish, you won't have any big disappointments.

Nicasio is by far the biggest lake in Marin County, covering some 825 acres, more than three times as large as the second largest lake, Alpine Lake (225 acres).

---

17. STAFFORD LAKE

Reference: Near Novato; map D1 grid j1.

How to get there: From US 101 at Novato, take the San Marin exit and continue west to Novato Boulevard. Turn right and drive about five miles to the lake.

Facilities: A picnic area is provided on the west side of the lake. Lodging and supplies are available in Novato.

Cost: There is a $1 parking fee; walk-in access is free.

Who to contact: Phone Western Boat in San Rafael at (415) 454-4177; North Marin Water District at (415) 897-4133.

About Stafford Lake: Imagine sitting along this lake, fishing and enjoying the scenery, with your rod propped up on a stick. Then whoosh! Gone! The rod gets ripped into the lake and disappears forever.

That is exactly what was happening at Stafford Lake. Rumors started circulating about some giant fish that was stealing rods, "The Monster of Stafford Lake." Now and then, someone would hook it, lose all their line, and the legend would grow. Nobody could handle it.

Then the water district decided to drain the lake in order to work on the dam, and what happens? As the water got low, a five-foot sturgeon was spotted—The Monster. In its honor, the sturgeon was rescued, transported to its rightful home in San Pablo Bay and released. All was well again.

All is well at Stafford Lake, too. When it was drained, volunteers completed a major habitat improvement project for bass and bluegill. Now it is full of water and fish, and it has become one of the better little lakes for bass fishing in the Bay Area. At 245 acres, it is big enough to provide a quality fishery during the '90s.

The one regret is that no boats or even float tubes are allowed on the water. That addition could make a decent and improving bass water a great one.

---

18. NOVATO CREEK

Reference: In Novato; map D1 grid j2.

How to get there: From US 101 at Novato, take the San Marin exit and drive west on San Marin Drive, past the high school. Continue west on San Marin Drive-Sutro Avenue to Novato Boulevard. Turn left on Novato Boulevard and travel a short distance to Mi-Wok Park, or continue on San Marin Drive-Sutro Avenue and cross a bridge to O'Hare Park (an undeveloped area).

Facilities: Mi-Wok Park offers picnic facilities. There are no facilities at O'Hare Park. A KOA campground is available in Petaluma. Lodging and supplies are available in Novato.

Cost: Access is free.

Who to contact: Phone the Department of Fish and Game at (707) 944-5500; Novato Chamber of Commerce at (415) 897-1164.

About Novato Creek: You don't have to drive 250 miles to fish a trout stream. Not with Novato Creek available.

It is one of three streams in the Bay Area that is stocked with trout during the summer months. The others are Alameda Creek in Niles Canyon east of Fremont and Coyote Creek downstream of Anderson Dam just south of San Jose.

Novato Creek often provides the best success, however. That is because the two key access points, Mi-Wok Park and Sutro Avenue picnic area (O'Hare Park), are the same places that are stocked by the Department of Fish and Game. Stocks are made twice each month during the summer with trout averaging 10, 11 inches. It isn't the wilderness, true. But for a suburban fishing opportunity, it is the next best thing.

MAP D2

6 LISTINGS
PAGES 340-347

NOR-CAL MAP . see page 120
adjoining maps
NORTH (C2) ...... see page 266
EAST (D3) .... see page 348
SOUTH (E2) .... see page 466
WEST (D1) .... see page 322

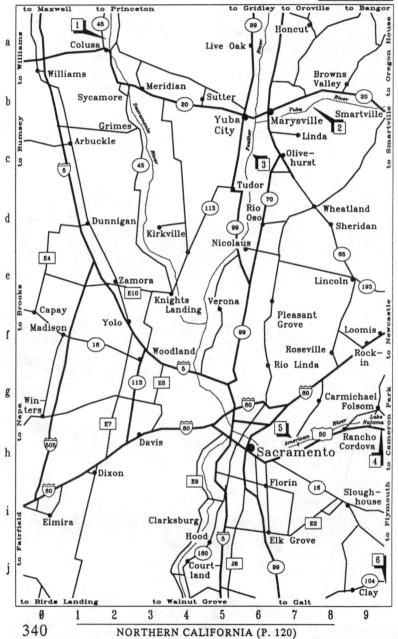

Reference: From Colusa to Sacramento; map D2 grid a2.

How to get there: Access is available off roads that junction with Interstate 5. Boat ramps are placed at the following locations: Colusa-Sacramento River State Recreation Area in Colusa; Ward's Boat Landing on Butte Slough Road, south of Colusa; Joe's Landing, on Garden Highway in Verona; Elkhorn Boat Launch, northwest of Sacramento on Bayou Way; Alamar Marina, on Garden Highway in Sacramento; Discovery Park in Sacramento, at the confluence of the Sacramento and American Rivers; Sacramento Harbor, in south Sacramento at Miller Park; Clarksburg Flat on South River Road, south of Sacramento.

Facilities: Campgrounds, lodging, boat rentals and supplies are available in the Sacramento area.

Cost: River access is free.

Who to contact: For general information, phone the Sacramento Chamber of Commerce at (916) 443-3771. For fishing information, phone any of the following tackle shops: Fran & Eddy's Sports Den, (916) 363-6885; Knight's Landing Sport Center, (916) 735-6355; Sherwood Harbor Marina, (916) 371-3471; Freeport Marina, (916) 665-1555.

About Sacramento River: From Colusa to Sacramento, this river represents the best and worst of the Central Valley.

The best includes prospects for big salmon, striped bass and sturgeon, and many shad too, during their respective migrations upriver. The worst is what the Army Corps of Engineers has done to much of the area here.

When I canoed the entire Sacramento River, this particular section left the strongest memories. Many long sections of river have been converted to canal by the Army Corps, the river banks now being rip-rapped levees, complete with beveled edges and 90-degree turns. These parts of the river are tree-less, virtually bird-less, and the fish simply use it as a highway, migrating straight upriver without pausing to stop. They have little reason to.

But in the Colusa and Sacramento areas, it is a different world. Near Colusa, the river is quite beautiful as it winds its way southward. The banks are lined with trees, with deep holes, gravel bars and good fishing in season. Near Sacramento, while the river is leveed off, there are also some good holes where fish will hold up on their upriver journey. In between? There are precious few spots, the best being in the vicinity of Grimes and Knight's Landing.

The Colusa area of the river is most attractive. It is here in the spring where striped bass are now spawning in large numbers. Some 75 percent of the striper spawning originally took place in the San

Joaquin Delta, but the giant state and federal water pumps at Clifton Court have virtually destroyed the stripers in the south Delta, and they are instead heading up to Colusa on the Sacramento River to do their thing.

If you have a boat, graph, and good supply of lures, you can do your thing too. Except for shad, the river cannot be fished effectively from shore, and the graph helps locate the key holes and bottom drop-offs where the fish hold. It is these spots where you troll the large Rebel minnows for striped bass (March and April); T-55 or M-2 Flatfish for salmon (mid-August through mid-October); anchor and use mud shrimp or ghost shrimp for sturgeon (December through March); or cast Darts, T-Killers or Teeney Rounders along the edges of runs and riffles for shad (May and June).

In the Sacramento area, there are many natural areas that will hold the fish in the course of their respective migrations. The most famous are the Minnow Hole, located just south of Sacramento; mouth of the American River at Discovery Park; mouth of the Feather River at Verona. There is no secret about this, and you can expect plenty of company on the water when the fish are moving through.

Other good spots: Highway 880 Bridge; Government Dock, north of Discovery Park; Miller Park in south Sacramento; Brickyards, south of Minnow Hole; Garcia Flat, just north of Freeport; Freeport Flat in Freeport; Clarksburg Flat in Clarksburg.

A newcomer to the area may seem puzzled as to where to begin. There is no puzzle. Either the fish are moving through or they are not. When they are, then get on the river, pick one of the suggested spots—and get in line with the rest of the boats.

---

2. YUBA RIVER

Reference: East of Marysville from Browns Valley to Marysville; map D2 grid b7.

How to get there: At the junction of Interstate 5 and Highway 20 just north of Williams, drive about 30 miles east on Highway 20 to Yuba City. Access is available at the Simpson Park Bridge in Marysville and at the E Street Bridge on Highway 20.

Facilities: A campground called Live Oak is available north of Yuba City. Lodging and supplies are available in Yuba City.

Cost: River access is free.

Who to contact: Phone Johnson Tackle in Yuba City at (916) 674-1912.

About Yuba River: Like so many rivers in the Central Valley, the Yuba is a prisoner of the water releases from reservoirs located upstream. In the case of the Yuba River, the fact that Bullards Bar Reservoir is always so full translates into the Yuba often being quite low.

This section of the Yuba has the ability to attract steelhead in the winter and shad in the spring. But the key with anadromous fish is freshwater. That is what attracts them. When the flows are low, there is little else that can compel them onward. But in the years where the river is flowing sufficiently, the Yuba provides know-how anglers with a unique opportunity. The shad arrive in May, the steelhead in January and February, and though access is limited, some fine catches are made anyway. One friend of mine, guide Jack Ellis, prefers the Yuba because there are relatively few other rods on the river. When everything is right, it can be an exceptional water. But there are few times when everything is right.

---

3.   FEATHER RIVER

Reference: From Marysville to Sacramento; map D2 grid c6.

How to get there: There are two excellent fishing spots on the Feather River: Shanghai Bend and the mouth of the Feather River.

To reach Shanghai Bend: At the junction of Interstate 5 and Highway 20 just north of Williams, drive about 30 miles east on Highway 20 to Yuba City. Turn south on Highway 99 and travel two miles to Lincoln Road. Turn left and travel to the end of the road, then turn right on Garden Highway and travel two miles to Shanghai Bend road. Turn left and continue via a dirt road to the parking area.

To reach the mouth of the Feather River: At the junction of Interstate 5 and Highway 99 north of Sacramento, drive eight miles north on Highway 99 to Sankey Road. Turn left and travel two miles west to the Verona Marina.

Facilities: A campground, called Live Oak, is available north of Yuba City. More campgrounds and lodging are available in the Sacramento area. Boat ramps are available near Yuba City and at Verona Marina. Fishing supplies are available in Yuba City.

Cost: River access is free.

Who to contact: Phone Johnson's Tackle in Yuba City at (916) 674-1912, or Feather River Bait, at (916) 534-0605.

About Feather River: You want fish, lots of fish? Show up at Shanghai Bend during the second week of May and you get fish.

The Feather River is turning into the number one shad river in the Central Valley. Why? With low flows most years on the American River to the south, a lot of shad seem to be bypassing the American and heading farther up the Sacramento River, then turning right at the Feather.

You hear the tales . . . 35, 40, 50 shad in an evening, sometimes even more. It actually happens here in May, when the shad arrive en masse and head upstream. If you are in a boat at the mouth of the

---

Feather River at Verona, or wading at Shanghai Bend, and the shad army moves through, greatness is possible. But what is more likely is catching five to 10, enjoying the first warm days of the year, maybe getting a sunburn. This happens every year, with the best fishing somewhere in a 10-day span starting in early May. Johnson's Tackle provides the most reliable information on the timing of strength of the run.

The rest of the year is a different story. The river gets doses of striped bass (fall and spring), salmon (fall), and steelhead (winter), but they are sprinkled in holes from Marysville on upstream to the Thermolito Bay Outlet Hole.

A boat is a virtual necessity to do it right here. Two good spots north of Yuba City are the Car Body Hole and Long Hole, and two good spots south of Yuba City are the Boyd's Pump (there's a boat ramp near here) and Star Bend. Johnson's Tackle can provide specific directions.

---

4. LAKE NATOMA

Reference: East of Sacramento at Nimbus Dam; map D2 grid g9.

How to get there: From Sacramento, drive east on Madison Avenue or Greenback Lane as far as you can go. Turn right and continue to Negro Bar. Or, drive east on Highway 50 and take Hazel Avenue to the boat ramp at the west end of the lake.

Facilities: A campground is available at Negro Bar. Ramps for launching small boats are located at the east and west ends of the lake at Negro Bar and Nimbus Flat.

Cost: Day-use fee is $6 per vehicle.

Who to contact: Phone Folsom Lake State Recreation Area at (916) 988-0205, or Fran & Eddy's Sports Den in Rancho Cordova at (916) 363-6885.

About Lake Natoma: Every major reservoir has a small lake below it called an afterbay, and Lake Natoma is such for big Folsom Lake to the east.

Natoma is a narrow lake covering 500 acres, and since it gets water from the bottom of Folsom Dam, Natoma tends to be colder than its big brother Folsom. That is why this is a decent trout lake, both from stocked rainbow trout from the Department of Fish and Game, and from a few large resident fish that hang near the upper end and gobble up the passing morsels in the flows from Folsom Dam. The biggest trout I have heard of out of Natoma weighed 12 pounds.

Waterskiing is prohibited and a five-mph speed limit is enforced, so you won't have to compete with jet skis and speed boats. Instead you get quiet trolling water, and with 13 miles of shoreline, many good spots to baitfish from the bank. There are a few bass and sunfish in Natoma, but nearby Folsom is a much better lake for bass fishing.

---

5.   AMERICAN RIVER

Reference: From Fair Oaks to Sacramento; map D2 grid h7.

How to get there: Easy access is available off the roads in Rancho Cordova and Fair Oaks that cut off from Highway 50. A free map is available from Fran & Eddy's Sports Den. By boat, the best, and most easily accessible spot is at the confluence of the Sacramento and American Rivers in Discovery Park in Sacramento. Excellent shorefishing access is also available at the following locations in Sacramento: Nimbus Basin, Ancil Hoffman Park, Goethe Park, the Sunrise Avenue access areas, the Watt Avenue Bridge area, Paradise Beach, the area behind Cal Expo, Dredger Hole.

Facilities: Boat ramps are provided at Discovery Park and near Watt Avenue. Campgrounds, lodging, and supplies are available in the Sacramento area.

Cost: River access is free.

Who to contact: For general information, phone the Sacramento Chamber of Commerce at (916) 443-3771. For fishing information, phone Fran & Eddy's Sports Den at (916) 363-6885.

About American River: Don't like the action? Just stick around. Another run of fish always seem to be on the way on the American River.

Steelhead arrive from December through mid-March, shad from late April through early June, striped bass in July and August, and salmon from September through November. By December, the cycle starts anew. No fish? What, me worry?

This section of the American flows from the outlet at Nimbus Basin on downstream past Fair Oaks and Rancho Cordova before entering the Sacramento River at Discovery Park. In that span, there are several excellent access points, by boat or bank (though chest waders are a necessity at several spots).

One of my favorite spots in May is Goethe Park, where I walk downstream a bit, then wade in and start casting for shad.

There's a footbridge overhead, and from the view there, kids can often see the shad and tell me where to cast. Cheating? Maybe, but I release all the fish anyway. Another favorite spot is Sunrise Avenue, where a lot more shad are caught than at Goethe Park, but this area is usually loaded with anglers.

The shad need decent water flows to be attracted upstream, and if they are provided, the American is one of the best shad rivers anywhere. The same is true for the other anadromous species that migrate here: salmon, steelhead, and striped bass. The converse is also true, however.

If the flows are very low, as can be the case, the river turns into a skunkhole. Little water equals few fish.

In the best years, the late summer striped bass fishing is best in the section of river just upstream from its confluence with the Sacramento River. You need a boat to have much of a chance. Salmon and steelhead, on the other hand, are sprinkled throughout the river all the way to Nimbus Basin during fall and winter, and can be caught from shore as well as by boat. Though a driftboat/guide service specializing in the American is not available anymore, if the fishing were to return to prominence, you can bet that the availability of guided trips would also return.

The last peak steelhead fishing was in the early 1980s, when it seemed everyone was catching a 10-pounder. It got so good that a local tackle shop started a steelhead derby, and week-after-week, huge steelhead in the 15 to 20-pound class were winning it. Nobody had ever seen so many huge steelhead on the American.

But at the state fish hatchery, biologists noticed some fish had disappeared. Then, late one night, game wardens hid in darkness as they watched more than a dozen poachers sneak into the hatchery and steal brood-stock steelhead—future winners of the American River Steelhead Derby.

Well, this time there were no winners. The midnight bandits were all arrested, fined and sent to jail. And ever since, folks have noticed that there haven't been very many large steelhead caught in the American River anymore.

---

6. RANCHO SECO LAKE

Reference: Southeast of Sacramento in Rancho Seco Recreation Area; map D2 grid j9.

How to get there: From Sacramento, drive about 12 miles south on Highway 99. Take the Highway 104 exit and drive 12 miles east on Highway 104 (Twin Cities Road). Turn right at the signed entrance for Rancho Seco Recreation Area and continue to the lake.

Facilities: A picnic area is provided. A boat ramp is available. No motorized boats or live bait are permitted on the lake. Camping, lodging, and supplies are available in Sacramento.

Cost: Entrance fee is $3 per day.

Who to contact: Phone Rancho Seco Recreation Area at (209) 748-2318.

About Rancho Seco Lake: Here's a spot that is ideal for a family picnic, with dad or mom getting away after dinner for some evening fishing. The lake is part of 400-acre Rancho Seco Recreation Area, with a boat ramp (no motors permitted), picnic area, and several docks for shorefishing.

The lake covers 160 acres and provides a variety of prospects, all weather dependent. In the spring and fall, the bass fishing can be good here, best in April, May and October. The lake record is a 12-pounder. In late winter and spring, with the water cold, some 4,000 trout are stocked. They are sought after primarily by shoreline baitdunkers. In the summer, it really heats up here and most of the fishing is by kids trying for sunfish, or persistent oldtimers waiting for a catfish. The park provides day-use only, closing each day at sunset. With no motors on the lake, you get quiet water, fair fishing, and good access and picnic sites. Take the family.

MAP D3

45 LISTINGS
PAGES 348-381

NOR-CAL MAP. see page 120
adjoining maps
NORTH (C3) ...... see page 278
EAST (D4) .... see page 382
SOUTH (E3) .... see page 478
WEST (D2) .... see page 340

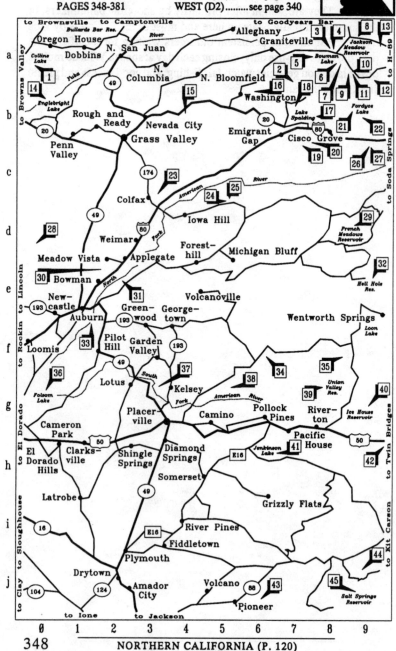

to Brownsville   to Camptonville   to Goodyears Bar
Bullards Bar Res.
Oregon House   Alleghany
River   Graniteville
Dobbins   N. San Juan   Jackson Meadow Reservoir
Collins Lake
1   Bowman Lake
N. Columbia   **5**   **10**
N. Bloomfield   **2**   **6**
14   N.   **16**   **18**   **7**   **9**   **11**   **12**
Englebright Lake   Washington   **17**
Rough and Ready   Lake Spalding   **21**   **22**
20   Nevada City   **20**
Penn Valley   Grass Valley   Emigrant Gap   Cisco Grove
174   **23**   **19**   **20**   **26**   **27**
Colfax   River
American   **24**   **25**
49   Iowa Hill   **29**
28   Weimar   French Meadows Reservoir
Meadow Vista   Forest-hill   Michigan Bluff
30   Bowman   North   **32**
New-castle   **31**   Volcanoville   Hell Hole Res.
193   Greenwood   George-town   Wentworth Springs
Auburn   **193**   Loon Lake
Loomis   Pilot   Garden   **193**
33   Hill   Valley
36   **49**   **37**   **35**
Lotus   Kelsey   **38**   **34**   Union Valley Res.   **40**
Folsom Lake   South   **39**   River-ton
Fork   American   River   Pollock   Ice House Reservoir
Placer-ville   Camino   Pines   Riverton
Cameron Park   **50**   Pacific   **50**
El Dorado   Clarks-   Shingle   Diamond   **41**   House
Hills   ville   Springs   Springs   Jenkinson   **42**
Somerset   Lake   E16
Latrobe   **49**   Grizzly Flats
16   River Pines   **44**
E16   Fiddletown
Plymouth
Drytown   **45**
104   **124**   Amador   Volcano   **88**   **43**   Salt Springs Reservoir
City   Pioneer
to Ione   to Jackson

0   1   2   3   4   5   6   7   8   9

348   NORTHERN CALIFORNIA (P. 120)

1. COLLINS LAKE

Reference: North of Marysville in Collins Lake Recreation Area; map D3
    grid aØ.

How to get there: From Marysville at the intersection of Highways 70
    and 20, take Highway 20 east and drive 12 miles. Turn north on
    Marysville Road and travel ten miles to the lake entrance on the right.

Facilities: Campgrounds, a full-service marina, a boat ramp, boat rentals,
    and supplies are available at the lake.

Cost: Day-use fee is $4 per vehicle, four person maximum; $1 fee for each
    additional person. Fee for entering with a boat is $9. Campsite fees are
    $10-$15 per night.

Who to contact: Phone the park at (916) 692-1600.

About Collins Lake: Every reservoir goes through a unique evolution,
    and Collins Lake seems to be peaking in productivity in the 90s.

It is one of the few lakes where both bass and trout can thrive. Trout
fishing is excellent in the spring, when the cool, pure flows of Dry
Creek and Willow Glen Creek fill the lake. Then in early summer,
when the surface temperatures warm significantly, the largemouth bass
come to life.

Collins Lake is set at 1,200 feet elevation in the foothill country of
Yuba County, a pretty spot, ideal for the camper/boater/angler. My
preference is for April and early May, and then again from mid-September
through October, when the lake is quiet, the surface temperatures cool, and the fishing is best. In between, during the hot summer
months, the trout are deep (but good fishing using deepwater trolling
techniques), the bass are a dawn/dusk affair, and you can run into
waterskier traffic.

Regardless, this lake gets a good rating. It has about 12 miles of
shoreline, and in a weekend, you can explore most of it while trolling
for trout. That is how most of the trout are caught here, using standard
techniques. The key is always depth, with the trout shallow in the cool
months, then going deeper and deeper month after month into summer.
By late July, it is common to fish 40, 45 feet deep for trout.

But the reward are rainbow trout that average in the foot-long class,
a few similar-sized brown trout mixed in, and then every once in a
while, a huge brown that will make you think you've hooked Moby
Trout. It is scheduled to be stocked each year with about 25,000
rainbow trout and 1,500 brown trout, and occasionally receives bonus
plants as well.

This is a good fishing lake. If you are one of the poor anglers who
believes they are afflicted with a terrible jinx, show up here during late
April or early May and get the cure.

Reference: Northwest of Lake Tahoe; map D3 grid a7.

How to get there: Access is available off roads and trails that junction with Interstate 80 to the north and south.

Facilities: Several campgrounds are available off Interstate 80 and near adjacent towns. Supplies are available in Nevada City and off Interstate 80.

Cost: Access is free.

Who to contact: Write to Tahoe National Forest at Highway 49, Nevada City, CA 95959, or phone (916) 265-4531. For a map, send $2 to Office of Information, U.S. Forest Service, 630 Sansome Street, San Francisco, CA 94111.

About Tahoe National Forest: This chunk of national forest is marked by beautiful lakes in rock bowls, granite peaks, and a mixed conifer forest where the trees seem sprinkled from heaven.

There is a special look to the area, and it becomes apparent immediately. It isn't so heavily wooded as the national forests of Northern California. It isn't so sparse as the high southern Sierra near Mount Whitney. Instead it is a perfect granite backdrop. In addition, you can be witness to some fantastic thunderstorms of just an hour's duration on some summer afternoons, when the thunder rolls will rattle down the canyon and lightning bolts harpoon ridgetops.

Nearby Desolation Wilderness (see zone D4), located southwest of Lake Tahoe, gets so many people that quotas on trailheads always seem filled. There seems to be a camper at every lake, no matter how difficult it is to reach. The adjacent national forest to the west provides a good option, with similar-styled country and lesser-known destinations.

The following hike-to lakes are stocked by air and provide the best fishing in the area, though most of the trout are on the small side: Lake of The Woods, Upper and Lower Lindsey Lakes, Feeley Lake, Island Lake, Long Lake, Round Lake, Milk Lake, Sanford Lake, Downey Lake, Lower Beyers Lake, Blue Lake, Warren Lake, Devil's Oven Lake, Upper and Lower Lola Montez Lakes, Upper and Lower Loch Leven Lakes, Fisher Lake, Hysink Lake and Huntley Mill Lake.

While this area does not provide the isolation of some of the lesser-traveled wildlands of the state, it does have great natural beauty in its spectacular mountain scenery. It also provides quiet camps along jeweled lakes, where the rising trout leave little pools each evening.

3.   WEAVER LAKE

Reference: North of Emigrant Gap in Tahoe National Forest; map D3 grid a8.

How to get there: From Sacramento, drive east on Highway 80 to Emigrant Gap. Take the offramp, then head north on the short connector road to Highway 20. Drive west one-half mile on Highway 20, then turn right on Bowman Road and travel 12 miles north. Turn right (east) on Meadow Lake Road and drive one mile, then turn north on McMurray Lake Road and travel two miles to Weaver Lake. Trailered boats are not advised.

Facilities: No facilities are available on-site. A free primitive campground is available at Bowman Lake. No piped water is provided.

Cost: Access is free.

Who to contact: Phone the Tahoe National Forest Headquarters at (916) 265-4531. For fishing information, phone the camera department at the SPD Grocery Store in Nevada City, (916) 265-4596.

About Weaver Lake: For the mom and dad who want to get away from it all, but whose family is not ready for the wilderness experience, Weaver Lake provides a rare drive-to alternative.

It is one of dozens of lakes within a 10-mile radius tucked away in the granite slopes of Sierra Nevada country. On the way in, you will pass several lakes, including both little McMurray Lake and large Bowman Lake within a mile to the south.

Weaver has a good mix of trout, primarily rainbow trout, some browns, and a even a few elusive mackinaws. The lake is on the DFG's route for regular stocking, the first plants starting when the access road is cleared of snow in late spring, then continuing into mid-summer. About 10,000 "catchables" are stocked during this period, along with 4,000 fingerlings.

This is the place for a car-top boat and a family camping experience.

4.   MCMURRAY LAKE

Reference: North of Emigrant Gap in Tahoe National Forest; map D3 grid a8.

How to get there: From Sacramento, drive east on Highway 80 to Emigrant Gap. Take the offramp, then head north on the short connector road to Highway 20. Drive west one-half mile on Highway 20, then turn right on Bowman Road and travel 12 miles north. Turn right (east) on Meadow Lake Road and drive one mile, then turn north on McMurray Lake Road and travel one mile to the lake. Trailered boats are not advised.

Facilities: No facilities are available on-site. Free primitive campgrounds are available at Bowman Lake and Weaver Lake.

Cost: Access is free.

Who to contact: Phone the Tahoe National Forest Headquarters at (916) 265-4531. For fishing information, phone the camera department at the SPD Grocery Store in Nevada City, (916) 265-4596.

About McMurray Lake: Little McMurray Lake is often lost in the shadow of its nearby big brothers: Weaver Lake, a half-mile to the north, and Bowman Lake, a half-mile to the south. This little lake doesn't have a campground either.

But it does have trout. And folks who don't connect at Weaver or Bowman should saunter on over to McMurray and make a few casts. The lake is stocked with 2,200 rainbow trout in the 10, 11-inch class, and while that is certainly not a great amount of fish, it is plenty for little McMurray. If you hit it after a plant, it will be plenty for you, too.

The lake is ideal to fish from a float tube, which provides the mobility to fish much of the lake in an evening.

---

5. **BOWMAN LAKE**

Reference: North of Emigrant Gap in Tahoe National Forest; map D3 grid a8.

How to get there: From Sacramento, drive east on Highway 80 to Emigrant Gap. Take the offramp, then head north on the short connector road to Highway 20. Drive west one-half mile on Highway 20, then turn right on Bowman Road and travel 12 miles north. Turn right (east) on Meadow Lake Road and drive one mile. The lake will be on your right.

Facilities: A free primitive campground is provided at the lake.

Cost: Access is free.

Who to contact: Phone the Tahoe National Forest Headquarters at (916) 265-4531. For fishing information, phone the camera department at the SPD Grocery Store in Nevada City, (916) 265-4596.

About Bowman Lake: Many get their first glimpse of Bowman Lake from the access road, fully intending to drive onward to Weaver Lake nearby to the north or Jackson Meadow Reservoir six miles to the northeast. But Bowman is so pretty, a sapphire jewel set in granite at 5,568 feet, that it is difficult to pass by without making camp.

Then you might discover Bowman's secret: The brown trout. It is the best lake in the immediate region for them. These brownies strike hard, fight hard, and after you take them out of the frying pan, go down easy.

It helps tremendously here to have a boat, but alas, there is no boat ramp. That means using a car-topper, or a canoe, raft, pram, anything—

just get on the water for increased access and mobility. In early summer, the better fishing is on the upper end of the lake, near where Canyon Creek and Jackson Creek feed the lake. This is also a good area in the fall, when some big browns prowl around this area. But once the flows of those feeder creeks are reduced to a trickle, the fish seem to scatter about the lake, and your search is best rewarded by trolling about 30 yards off the shoreline, covering most of the lake. That way you cover the maximum amount of water in the minimum amount of time.

Bowman is stocked each summer with 4,000 rainbow trout and 10,000 brown trout, the latter having an excellent year-to-year carry-over.

---

6.   SAWMILL LAKE

Reference: North of Emigrant Gap in Tahoe National Forest; map D3 grid a8.

How to get there: From Sacramento, drive east on Highway 80 to Emigrant Gap. Take the offramp, then head north on the short connector road to Highway 20. Drive west one-half mile on Highway 20, then turn right on Bowman Road and travel 16 miles (past Bowman Lake) to Jackson Creek Campground. Turn right (south) on a Forest Service road and travel about two miles to Sawmill Lake.

Facilities: No facilities are available on-site. Camping is available at Jackson Creek.

Cost: Access is free.

Who to contact: Phone the Tahoe National Forest Headquarters at (916) 265-4531. For fishing information, phone the camera department at the SPD Grocery Store in Nevada City, (916) 265-4596. For a map, send $2 to Office of Information, U.S. Forest Service, 630 Sansome Street, San Francisco, CA 94111.

About Sawmill Lake: No campground. No large trout. Several nearby lakes provide both. Why then, would you come here? Because it is beautiful, and sometimes that is enough.

Sawmill Lake is home for the inevitable DFG dinker, those puny five-inchers that go into a swoon when hooked. They do make a pretty sight rising atop the still waters during a windless dusk. But if you want to camp and fish, then move it on down the line.

---

7.   FAUCHERIE LAKE

Reference: North of Emigrant Gap in Tahoe National Forest; map D3 grid a8.

How to get there: From Sacramento, drive east on Highway 80 to Emigrant

---

Gap. Take the offramp, then head north on the short connector road to Highway 20. Drive west one-half mile on Highway 20, then turn right on Bowman Road. Drive 16 miles (past Bowman Lake) to Jackson Creek Campground, then turn right (south) on a Forest Service road and travel about two miles past Sawmill Lake and on four more miles to Faucherie Lake.

Facilities: A small, primitive campground is provided at the lake. There is no piped water.

Cost: Access is free.

Who to contact: Phone the Tahoe National Forest Headquarters at (916) 265-4531. For fishing information, phone the camera department at the SPD Grocery Store in Nevada City, (916) 265-4596. For a map, send $2 to Office of Information, U.S. Forest Service, 630 Sansome Street, San Francisco, CA 94111.

About Faucherie Lake: It can seem hard to believe that you can drive to Faucherie Lake. But here it is, a classic alpine lake in the Sierra Nevada, created with the clear, pure water from melting snow filling a glacial-carved granite bowl.

This is the kind of place I have backpacked many miles to reach. It is quiet and pristine, with fair fishing for rainbow trout. Those are courtesy stocks of 10 to 12-inchers from Fish and Game, about 1,300 planted per year.

Imagine arriving to Faucherie Lake on a summer afternoon, plopping in a canoe, then a paddling around, enjoying the natural beauty. While you're at it, you have a lure trailing behind the boat, the fishing rod propped against your shoulder while you paddle. There's a decent chance of a trout or two coming along for the ride, and of you completing a perfect day with an evening trout fry over a campfire.

---

8.   JACKSON MEADOW RESERVOIR

Reference: Northwest of Truckee in Tahoe National Forest; map D3 grid a9.

How to get there: From Sacramento, drive east on Highway 80 to Truckee. Turn north on Highway 89 and drive 17.5 miles. Turn west on Forest Service Road 7 and travel 16 miles west to the reservoir.

Facilities: Several campgrounds, including a boat-in campground, are provided. Boat ramps and picnic areas are also provided. Supplies are available in Truckee or Sierraville.

Cost: Campsite fees range from free to $8 per night for single camps; $25-$50 for group camps.

Who to contact: For general information, phone the Tahoe National Forest District Office at (916) 587-3558, or the Truckee Chamber of Commerce at (916) 587-2757. For fishing information, phone Tahoe

Truckee Sports at (916) 587-1154, Mountain Hardware at (916) 587-4844, or Tourist Liquor & Sporting Goods at (916) 587-3081. For a map, send $2 to Office of Information, U.S. Forest Service, 630 Sansome Street, San Francisco, CA 94111.

About Jackson Meadow Reservoir: Campers use Jackson Meadow Reservoir as headquarters for multi-day trips into this multi-faceted mountain country. The lake is set at 6,200 feet, a pretty area with forest, meadows and the trademark granite look of the Sierra Nevada. There are also many lakes in the vicinity that provide options, and the trailhead for the Pacific Crest Trail is located just east of the lake along the lake's access road.

The lake itself is quite beautiful because its levels are often kept higher than other mountain reservoirs. Lakeside camping, a decent boat ramp and fair fishing add up to a pleasant trip for most visitors.

The lake is stocked with some 5,600 rainbow trout, 1,700 brown trout, all "catchables" and no dinks. They are planted in early summer after ice-out has cleared the lake and snowplows have cleared the access road. Standard trolling techniques and shoreline baitdunking are popular and usually do OK, best early in the summer.

This isn't the wilderness, this isn't A-1 fishing, but it is a pretty mountain lake to camp and boat, and maybe catch a trout now and then.

---

9. CATFISH LAKE

Reference: North of Emigrant Gap in Tahoe National Forest; map D3 grid a9.

How to get there: From Sacramento, drive east on Highway 80 to Emigrant Gap. Take the offramp, then head north on the short connector road to Highway 20. Drive west one-half mile on Highway 20, then turn right on Bowman Road. Drive 19 miles (past Bowman Lake), then turn right on Meadow Lake Road and drive one mile to Catfish Lake.

Facilities: No facilities are available on-site. Campgrounds are available nearby at Jackson Meadow Reservoir. Supplies are available in Truckee.

Cost: Access is free.

Who to contact: Phone the Tahoe National Forest Headquarters at (916) 265-4531.

About Catfish Lake: Who knows how this lake got its name? There isn't a catfish in sight. Not much else either.

This little dot of a mountain lake is a nice picnic site, a pretty spot just to look at and enjoy yourself. But fishing? It's not exactly Excitement City. There are some tiny brook trout here, most in the four and five-inch class, and scarce little else.

French Lake and Meadow Lake farther down the road heading south are much better prospects.

---

10. JACKSON LAKE

Reference: North of Emigrant Gap in Tahoe National Forest; map D3 grid a9.

How to get there: From Sacramento, drive east on Highway 80 to Emigrant Gap. Take the offramp, then head north on the short connector road to Highway 20. Drive west one-half mile on Highway 20, then turn right on Bowman Road. Drive 18 miles (past Bowman Lake), then turn right on Jackson Lake Road and drive one mile to Jackson Lake.

Facilities: No facilities are available on-site. Campgrounds are available nearby at Jackson Meadow Reservoir. Supplies are available in Truckee.

Cost: Access is free.

Who to contact: Phone the Tahoe National Forest Headquarters at (916) 265-4531.

About Jackson Lake: Jackson Lake, like its neighbor Catfish Lake, just doesn't cut the mustard. The few trout in the lake are midget-sized brook trout, and with so many other waters to pick from in the area, this is not the place to wind up at. There is not a campground here, either.

But if you just want a spot to sit and enjoy the scenery, Jackson does provide a classic mountain view. It is set below a high back wall, in a granite cirque, like a mountain temple.

---

11. FRENCH LAKE

Reference: North of Emigrant Gap in Tahoe National Forest; map D3 grid a9.

How to get there: From Sacramento, drive east on Highway 80 to Emigrant Gap. Take the offramp, then head north on the short connector road to Highway 20. Drive west one-half mile on Highway 20, then turn right on Bowman Road. Drive 19 miles (past Bowman Lake), then turn right on Meadow Lake Road and drive four miles. Turn right on French Lake Road and drive two miles to French Lake.

Facilities: No facilities are available on-site.

Cost: Access is free.

Who to contact: Phone the Tahoe National Forest Headquarters at (916) 265-4531. For a map, send $2 to Office of Information, 630 Sansome Street, San Francisco, CA 94111.

About French Lake: For a remote mountain lake, French Lake has surprising size and grandeur. It covers close to 350 acres and has a maximum depth of 150 feet, surrounded by rugged country in the 6,000-foot elevation range.

But alas, the fishing is largely hit-and-miss, with a lot of misses and the hits being mostly small trout. Catch anything larger than 10 inches and you might as well head to Reno, because luck is with you. Because of the difficulty in reaching it and the poor to fair fishing as a reward, French Lake gets little attention by visitors to Tahoe National Forest. If you want a remote spot that is reachable by car, where you can tromp around a bit and have a near-wilderness experience, French Lake is a good destination. Just make sure you bring something to eat for dinner.

---

12. MEADOW LAKE

Reference: Northwest of Truckee in Tahoe National Forest; map D3 grid a9.

How to get there: From Sacramento, drive east on Highway 80 to Emigrant Gap. Take the offramp, then head north on the short connector road to Highway 20. Drive west one-half mile on Highway 20, then turn right on Bowman Road. Drive 19 miles (past Bowman Lake), then turn right on Meadow Lake Road and drive about six miles to Meadow Lake.

Facilities: No facilities are available on-site.

Cost: Access is free.

Who to contact: For general information, phone the Tahoe National Forest District Office at (916) 587-3558, or the Truckee Chamber of Commerce at (916) 587-2757. For fishing information, phone Tahoe Truckee Sports at (916) 587-1154, Mountain Hardware at (916) 587-4844, or Tourist Liquor & Sporting Goods at (916) 587-3081. For a map, send $2 to Office of Information, U.S. Forest Service, 630 Sansome Street, San Francisco, CA 94111.

About Meadow Lake: Of the five lakes in the immediate vicinity—Catfish Lake, Jackson Lake, French Lake, Tollhouse Lake and Meadow Lake—it is Meadow Lake that provides the best fishing. It isn't like the reincarnation of Star Wars, but compared to the others, it is the best.

You pass by those five lakes, as well as several others, on the route in from Emigrant Gap. The lake is good-sized for a mountain lake, nearly as large as French Lake, set below Hartley Butte to the south. A good side trip for hikers is to explore to the south, where a trail is routed to the Meadow Lakes Mine, an old gold mine.

The lake is stocked each year with 1,200 rainbow trout in the 10 to 11-inch class, sometimes reaching a foot. The best fishing is in early summer, well after ice-out, when the wildflowers are blooming in the surrounding meadow. Most folks do just fine by taking a tour around the lake, stopping to cast every 50 feet or so, using a small Panther Martin spinner, 1/16-ounce, black body with yellow spots.

Webber Lake to the north provides an option, accessible by driving about 10 miles north on Meadow Lake Road.

---

13.   WEBBER LAKE

Reference: Northwest of Truckee in Tahoe National Forest; map D3 grid a9.

How to get there: From Truckee, drive 17.5 miles north on Highway 89. Turn east on Forest Service Road 7 (Henness Pass Road) and travel 7.5 miles to the signed turnoff for Webber Lake. Turn left (south) and drive one mile to the lake.

Facilities: A campground is provided at the lake. Supplies can be obtained in Truckee.

Cost: Access is free.

Who to contact: For general information, phone the Tahoe National Forest District Office at (916) 587-3558, or the Truckee Chamber of Commerce at (916) 587-2757. For fishing information, phone Tahoe Truckee Sports at (916) 587-1154, Mountain Hardware at (916) 587-4844, or Tourist Liquor & Sporting Goods at (916) 587-3081. For a map, send $2 to Office of Information, 630 Sansome Street, San Francisco, CA 94111.

About Webber Lake: Webber Lake is one of the better choices in the area for a family camping expedition. Once the snow has cleared, it is reached easily enough by car, has a camp set near the lake, and the chance of crowning the day with a fish fry is decent enough. There are a variety of trout species in the lake: brook trout, brown trout and rainbow trout. The brookies are the most amenable to jumping into the skillet, averaging about eight inches and keeping the kids happy. The browns come bigger, with a sprinkling of large fish among the pan-sized. Your chances for them are best right at dusk, when they often cruise near the outlet into the Little Truckee River on the east side of the lake, hunting down those little brookies.

The lake is stocked with 1,520 eastern brook trout catchables and 2,100 brown trout catchables each year. At 6,000 feet, the lake receives a lot of snow in winter, and visitors should always be prepared for snow even in early June, and short-lived afternoon thunderstorms later in the summer.

---

14.   ENGLEBRIGHT LAKE

Reference: Northeast of Marysville; map D3 grid bØ.

How to get there: From Marysville, drive 20 miles east on Highway 20 to Mooney Flat Road, (just past Smartville). Drive three miles north to the lake.

Facilities: A campground is provided, in addition to several boat-in campsites. Boat ramps, boat rentals, groceries and bait are available also.

Cost: Access is free.

Who to contact: Phone the U.S. Corps of Engineers, Englebright Lake, at (916) 639-2342, or Skipper's Cove at the lake, (916) 639-2272.

About Englebright Lake: Remember this place. Englebright always seems to have plenty of water, waterskiing is prohibited on its upper end, and in the spring, it seems like Englebright has a trout war with Collins Lake to the north to see who can provide the best fishing.

Englebright Lake has an unusual appearance. The reservoir looks something like a water snake winding its way in the Yuba River Canyon, with 24 miles of shoreline in the Yuba County foothills, about 500 feet elevation.

The weather gets hot here in the summer, and waterskiers really like this place because the nearby shoreline provides a greater illusion of speed than on a wide-open lake. So anglers are better off visiting in the spring, when the water is cool, the skiers few, and the trout are near the surface. That is also when the fish planting starts in weekly increments, 25,000 rainbow trout planted in all, sized from 10 to 12 inches, rarely bigger.

If you visit during the peak summer months, you can escape the waterskiers by heading upstream. Waterskiing is not permitted upstream of a line of demarcation called Upper Boston, and the trolling is often quite good near where the South Fork Yuba enters, especially in the fall.

---

15. SCOTTS FLAT RESERVOIR

Reference: East of Nevada City in Scotts Flat Recreation Area; map D3 grid b4.

How to get there: From Nevada City, drive five miles east on Highway 20. Turn south on Scotts Flat Road and drive four miles south.

Facilities: A large campground, boat ramp, and picnic area are provided on the north side of the lake. Boat rentals, groceries, bait, and tackle are also available.

Cost: Day-use fee is $4 per vehicle. Campsite fee is $12 per night; reservations are strongly recommended in the summer.

Who to contact: Phone Scotts Flat Recreation Area at (916) 265-5302.

About Scotts Flat Reservoir: When Scotts Flat Lake is full to the brim, it is one of the prettier lakes in the Sierra Nevada foothills. The lake is shaped like a teardrop, with 7.5 miles of shoreline circled by forest at

---

3,100 feet elevation. With the campground near the lake's edge, decent trout stocks and a nearby boat launch, it makes for an ideal family camping destination.

The trout stocks usually start in April and continue well into summer, with 21,000 rainbow trout "catchables" planted, including some 5,000 that go in the foot-long class. Most of the fish are caught by boaters using standard techniques, slow-trolling with flashers trailed by a nightcrawler, using a zigzag course about 30 yards adjacent to the shore. But some shoreline baitdunkers also catch some fish from the camp on the north side of the lake, which is only a quarter-mile from where the fish are planted.

If you want to avoid the developed area (store/boat ramp/large campground) on the north side, a campground is also available on the more primitive southern shore.

---

16.   SOUTH FORK YUBA RIVER

Reference: East of Nevada City in Tahoe National Forest; map D3 grid b6.

How to get there: Direct access is available from Interstate 80 near Donner Summit, via the Eagle Lakes or Big Bend/Rainbow Road exits. Another option is also available from Nevada City: Drive 12 miles east on Highway 20, turn north on Washington Road and travel about eight miles, then turn right (east) on Maybert Road. Access is available near the campgrounds and picnic areas.

Facilities: Campgrounds are available off Washington Road and near Interstate 80. Supplies can be obtained in Nevada City or off Interstate 80.

Cost: River access is free.

Who to contact: Phone the Tahoe National Forest Headquarters at (916) 265-4531.

About South Fork Yuba River: The South Fork Yuba provides good trout fishing in a beautiful blue stream that flows over smooth boulders that have been polished by centuries of river water.

The best bet is the area just off Interstate 80 in the Donner Summit area. My preference is the stretch of water downstream from the Eagle Lakes area. I have always caught fish here, and after getting hold of the DFG's stocking schedule, I discovered why: About 10,000 trout are stocked here every year. They join a population of small natives.

If you fish the area near Interstate 80, carry along a Forest Service map, which details the public and private areas. That will keep you off private property. The area gets enough traffic that any trespasser is viewed as intolerable.

I first fished the South Fork Yuba 20 years ago and remain

fascinated with its beauty. It is bordered by stark granite country, and its flows are such a deep blue that it looks like a picture on a postcard.

17. LAKE SPAULDING

Reference: Near Emigrant Gap in Tahoe National Forest; map D3 grid b7.

How to get there: From Sacramento, drive east on Highway 80 to Emigrant Gap. Take the offramp, then head north on the short connector road to Highway 20. Drive east on Highway 20 for two miles, then turn left on Lake Spaulding Road and travel one-half mile to the lake.

Facilities: PG&E provides a campground and a boat ramp. Supplies are available in Nevada City.

Cost: Campsite fee is $9 per night.

Who to contact: Phone PG&E at (800) 552-4743. For fishing information, phone the camera department at the SPD Grocery Store in Nevada City at (916) 265-4596.

About Lake Spaulding: Here are the requirements: Spectacular beauty. Easy to reach. Good boat ramp. Campground. Decent fishing. Good side trip options.

Lake Spaulding is one of the few lakes that can provide all of those things. About the only thing it doesn't provide is warm enough water to enjoy swimming—I froze my buns off after taking a dare to take a dunk.

It is set at 5,000 feet in the Sierra Nevada, classic granite country, with huge boulders and a sprinkling of conifers around a gray, slab-like shoreline. The entire area looks like it has been cut and chiseled. The drive here is nearly a straight shot up Interstate 80, the boat ramp is fine for small aluminum boats, and if there is a problem, it is to expect plenty of company at the campground.

The trout fishing is good, with morning and evening bites. The fish are scattered about, however, since this lake is just a big rock canyon filled with water and has almost no natural holding areas. That mandates trolling and gives boaters a huge advantage over shoreliners. In addition, there are a few giant brown trout in this lake, but they are caught only rarely.

It is stocked each year with 18,040 rainbow trout ranging 10 to 12 inches, more than the many other lakes set in the mountain country to the immediate north. They can make for excellent side trips, lakes like Bowman, Weaver, Faucherie. Visitors should take a half-day and make a tour of it.

18.   FULLER LAKE

Reference: East of Nevada City in Tahoe National Forest; map D3 grid b7.

How to get there: From Sacramento, drive east on Highway 80 to Emigrant Gap. Take the offramp, then head north on the short connector road to Highway 20, drive west a half mile on Highway 20, then turn right on Bowman Road. Drive four miles and to Fuller Lake on the right.

Facilities: A free primitive campground is provided. No piped water is available. A small unimproved boat ramp is also available. Supplies can be obtained in Nevada City.

Cost: Access is free.

Who to contact: Phone the Tahoe National Forest Headquarters at (916) 265-4531. For fishing information, phone the camera department at the SPD Grocery Store in Nevada City, (916) 265-4596. For a map, send $2 to Office of Information, U.S. Forest Service, 630 Sansome Street, San Francisco, CA 94111.

About Fuller Lake: It can be tough to drive by Fuller Lake. This is the first lake you come to while driving north on Bowman Road, with dozens of other lakes set farther back in the mountains here. But stopping can be a good idea.

Fuller Lake is not only much easier to reach than the other more remote lakes in this region, but provides much better fishing. Remember that it is not only easier to reach for campers, but also easier to reach for the Department of Fish and Game, and they plant the heck out of it. They stock almost 20,000 trout per year, mostly rainbow trout but including brown trout as well. It is also one of the few lakes in the entire backcountry region that provides any semblance of a boat ramp.

The lake is set at 5,600 feet and the road in is usually free of snow by mid-May. Late snowstorms are common in this area, however, so always phone the Forest Service first in order to get road conditions.

---

19.   LAKE VALLEY RESERVOIR

Reference: Near Yuba Gap in Tahoe National Forest; map D3 grid b7.

How to get there: From Interstate 80, take the Yuba Gap exit, heading south. Turn right on Lake Valley Road for one mile until the road forks. Bear right and continue for 1.5 miles.

Facilities: PG&E provides a campground. A picnic area is nearby. A boat ramp is available. Supplies can be obtained off Interstate 80.

Cost: Campsite fee is $9 per night.

Who to contact: Phone PG&E at (800) 552-4743. For fishing information, phone the camera department at the SPD Grocery Store in Nevada

City at (916) 265-4596.

About Lake Valley Reservoir: Lake Valley Reservoir is gorgeous when full, its shoreline sprinkled with conifers and boulders. It provides a similar setting to nearby Lake Spaulding, which is located just north of Interstate 80, although the fishing is not quite as good and the lake is not quite as large. No waterskiing is permitted at Lake Valley Reservoir.

It is set at 5,786 feet, has a surface acreage of 300 acres, and a decent campground with nearby boat ramp. It is stocked each year with 4,000 rainbow trout, and after an initial period where they congregate around the boat ramp, they scatter about the lake. There is little in the form of underwater structure to hold them to a specific area.

That is why trollers, not shoreline baitdunkers, have the best luck. You need a boat to best cover this elliptical-shaped lake. In the spring, it can get quite windy, and you can turn off your engine and let the wind push you, which is often a perfect speed to present a nightcrawler trailing behind flashers.

---

20.   KELLY LAKE

Reference: East of Nevada City in Tahoe National Forest; map D3 grid b7.

How to get there: From Interstate 80, take the Yuba Gap exit, heading south. Turn right on Lake Valley Road for one mile; the road forks. Bear to the left and continue for 1.5 miles to the lake.

Facilities: A picnic area is provided. A campground is available nearby at Lake Valley Reservoir. No motorized boats are permitted on the lake.

Cost: Access is free.

Who to contact: Phone PG&E at (800) 552-4743. For fishing information, phone the camera department at the SPD Grocery Store in Nevada City at (916) 265-4596.

About Kelly Lake: Kelly Lake is the little brother to nearby Lake Valley Reservoir. It has a similar look, being set at 5,900 feet, surrounded by granite boulders and conifers, but is just 15 percent the size of Lake Valley.

It gets planted with far fewer trout as well, only 1,250 rainbow trout per year. Of the two lakes, it is better to fish from the shore at Kelly, where one can get access to much of it by hiking. It is also a good lake for small car-top boats, and ideal for a canoe.

---

21.   FORDYCE LAKE

Reference: East of Nevada City in Tahoe National Forest; map D3 grid b9.

How to get there: From Interstate 80, take the Cisco Grove exit and head to the north side of the highway. Immediately turn left on the frontage road, then right on Rattlesnake Road. Travel three miles north. When the road forks, bear left (this road is recommended for four-wheel drive vehicles only) and travel three miles to the lake.

Facilities: No facilities are available on-site. A primitive campground is available nearby at Lake Sterling. Supplies can be obtained off Interstate 80.

Cost: Access is free.

Who to contact: Phone the Tahoe National Forest Headquarters at (916) 265-4531. For a map, send $2 to Office of Information, U.S. Forest Service, 630 Sansome Street, San Francisco, CA 94111.

About Fordyce Lake: Dams in Sierra gorges can create strangely shaped lakes, and Fordyce is one of them. This is a long, curving lake, with a very deep southern end near the dam, several coves, and six feeder streams.

It is ideal for four-wheel drive cowboys with car-top boats, who can make their way to the west side of the very narrow part of the lake, then hand-launch their craft. It takes some muscle and spirit, but if you get the job done, the fishing can be decent for rainbow trout and brown trout. It is stocked with 5,000 rainbow trout and 3,000 fingerling brown trout, the latter having high survival rates.

In fact, there are some downright huge browns in the lake. A 15-incher is a small one. It takes persistence with spirit to hook up with one, best on trolled Rapalas near the inlets, especially in the fall and spring.

There are some good hiking trails in the area, which are detailed on a Forest Service map. If your car can't handle the access road, you can camp at nearby Lake Sterling to the south and make the short hike to Fordyce on a well-marked trail.

---

22.   LAKE STERLING

Reference: East of Nevada City in Tahoe National Forest; map D3 grid b9.

How to get there: From Interstate 80, take the Cisco Grove exit. Turn left at the frontage road, then right on Rattlesnake Road. Drive 6.5 miles to the lake. (The road is rough and steep; trailers are not recommended.)

Facilities: A small primitive campground is provided. An unimproved boat ramp is available. No piped water is available.

Cost: Access is free.

Who to contact: Phone the Tahoe National Forest Headquarters at (916) 265-4531.

About Lake Sterling: Lake Sterling is a small lake perched in a granite pocket at 7,000 feet, a very pretty lake with sparse results for anglers. Before you make this your destination, though, call ahead first and ask the key question: "How high's the water?" Because throughout its history, Lake Sterling has been subject to severe fluctuations.

The trout are few, primarily rainbows, and most visitors are not serious anglers but rather campers who like the beauty of the area, and who then take off hiking. A good trail routes north to Fordyce Lake.

---

23. ROLLINS LAKE

Reference: Southeast of Grass Valley; map D3 grid c3.

How to get there: From Interstate 80, take the Colfax exit. Turn left and head northwest (the road will become Highway 174), and drive to the lake. At the lake off of Highway 174, take one of two access roads: Orchard Springs, Greenhorn, or You Bet Road to reach campgrounds and launch ramps.

Facilities: Campgrounds, boat ramps, and picnic areas are provided. Supplies are available in Grass Valley or Colfax.

Cost: Day-use fee is $4 per vehicle; campsite fees are $9-$14 per night.

Who to contact: For camping and fishing information, phone the Tahoe National Forest Headquarters at (916) 265-4531, or Rollins Lake Resort at (916) 272-6100.

About Rollins Lake: OK, OK, you want decent-sized trout? The search ends at Rollins Lake, where 14,000 trout are stocked each spring, including about 7,000 in the foot-long class. Add in the trout holdovers from previous years, and you have the opportunity to come up with a nice limit. When the weather makes the switch to summer, then anglers make the switch to bass.

Rollins Lake is set at 2,100 feet elevation, a short drive north of Colfax, right where foothill country becomes forest. In late winter, the snow line is about here as well. The result is a lake that crosses the spectrum as both a trout lake and a bass lake. It can get quite hot here in summer and that makes the lake popular for swimming and waterskiing.

Boat ramps are available near all four campgrounds, with the most remote being on the Peninsula (reached via Highway 174 and You Bet Road). The lake extends far up two lake arms, covering 900 acres with 26 miles of shoreline. The best trout fishing is in the spring in the lower end of the lake near the dam, while the best bass fishing is in the coves midway up the lake arms.

---

24. SUGAR PINE RESERVOIR

Reference: Northeast of Auburn in Tahoe National Forest; map D3 grid c5.

How to get there: From Auburn on Interstate 80, take the Foresthill Road exit at the north end of town and drive 20 miles northeast on Foresthill Road to the town of Foresthill. Continue east on Foresthill Road (it becomes Baker Ranch-Soda Springs Road) for eight miles, then turn north on Sugar Pine Road. Drive five miles, and then turn left on Iowa Hill Road and drive to the lake (turn right at the first short access road to reach the boat launch).

Facilities: Campgrounds, picnic areas, and a boat ramp are provided. Supplies are available in Foresthill.

Cost: Campsite fees are $6-$8 per night for single camps; $40 per night for group camps.

Who to contact: Phone the Tahoe National Forest District Office at (916) 367-2224.

About Sugar Pine Reservoir: Just two lakes are available within an area of 150 square miles surrounding Sugar Pine Reservoir and Big Reservoir, and here they are, set within a mile of each other. Don't make the mistake of thinking they resemble each other. They don't.

Sugar Pine has the fish, Big Reservoir (also called Morning Star Lake by some folks) has the better-known campground. Rarely do the twain meet. Given the choice, head to Sugar Pine, a relatively new reservoir with new facilities and better fishing. Why? Because it is stocked with 12,000 rainbow trout each year, while nearby Big Reservoir gets none. The plants usually start in late April and continue into early summer. That makes sense, with the lake set at 3,500 feet elevation.

---

25. BIG RESERVOIR

Reference: Northeast of Auburn in Tahoe National Forest; map D3 grid c5.

How to get there: From Auburn on Interstate 80, take the Foresthill Road exit at the north end of town and drive 20 miles northeast on Foresthill Road to the town of Foresthill. Continue east on Foresthill Road (it becomes Baker Ranch-Soda Springs Road) for eight miles, then turn north on Sugar Pine Road and drive about seven miles. Turn right on the signed access road and drive one mile to the lake.

Facilities: A campground and picnic areas are provided. No motorized boats are permitted on the reservoir. Supplies are available in Foresthill.

Cost: Campsite fee is $8 per night.

Who to contact: Phone the Tahoe National Forest District Office at (916) 367-2224, or DeAnza Placer Gold Mining Company at (916) 367-2129.

About Big Reservoir: This lake is quite pretty, a 70-acre pocket of freshwater surrounded by forest. It is also quiet, with no gas-powered boats permitted. A picnic area is available at lake's edge.

Sound about perfect? Well, it needs more fish to be perfect. Trout? Doesn't seem to be many, and the Department of Fish and Game does not have any stocks scheduled. Bass? A few, providing a rare opportunity to bass fish at a mountain lake (elevation: 4,000 feet). Small, paddle-powered boats are ideal for this lake. If you are spending a weekend up here, you might consider Big Reservoir for one day, then nearby Sugar Pine Reservoir the next day.

---

26.   KIDD LAKE

Reference: West of Truckee in Tahoe National Forest; map D3 grid c9.

How to get there: From Truckee, drive 12 miles west on Interstate 80. Take the Norden exit. Turn south on Soda Springs Road and travel one mile to Pahatsi Road. Turn west and drive one mile. When the road forks, bear south and drive one mile south, then one-half mile west.

Facilities: PG&E provides both single and group campsites. Group sites require reservations. An unimproved boat ramp is available. Supplies are available in Truckee.

Cost: Campsite fee is $15 per night.

Who to contact: Phone the Tahoe National Forest District Office at (916) 587-3558. For fishing information, phone Tahoe Truckee Sports at (916) 587-1154, Mountain Hardware at (916) 587-4844, or Tourist Liquor & Sporting Goods at (916) 587-3081.

About Kidd Lake: Kidd Lake is the first of three lakes bunched in a series along the access road, and one of seven in a six-mile radius. A campground and primitive boat ramp make it one of the better choices.

Question: But what can you catch? Answer: Alas, the DFG dinker. Those little four-inch brook trout are stocked here, about 3,000 per year. No matter how much you pray, or how many times you cast, it is extremely rare to catch anything else. The lake is set in the northern Sierra's high country, 6,500 feet, and gets loaded with snow every winter. In late spring and early summer, always call ahead for conditions on the access road.

---

27.   CASCADE LAKES

Reference: West of Truckee in Tahoe National Forest; map D3 grid c9.

How to get there: From Truckee, drive 12 miles west on Interstate 80. Take the Norden exit. Turn south on Soda Springs Road and travel one miles to Pahatsi Road. Turn west and drive one mile. When the road forks, bear south and drive one mile south, then three miles west, past Kidd Lake, to Cascade Lakes.

Facilities: No facilities are available on-site. A campground is available nearby at Kidd Lake. Supplies can be obtained in Truckee.

Cost: Access is free.

Who to contact: Phone the Tahoe National Forest District Office at (916) 587-3558. For fishing information, phone Tahoe Truckee Sports at (916) 587-1154, Mountain Hardware at (916) 587-4844, or Tourist Liquor & Sporting Goods at (916) 587-3081.

About Cascade Lakes: Somewhere in the Department of Fish and Game is somebody who thinks that people actually like catching four and five-inch trout. There must be. Because like neighboring Kidd Lake, that is all you seem to catch at Cascade Lakes.

A check of the stocking schedule explains why: Once the ice melts here, it's "time to plant some dinkers." That's right, some 3,000 dinker rainbow trout are planted in Lower Cascade Lake, and 2,000 dinker brook trout are planted in Upper Cascade Lake. Let me tell you, those dinker brookies are the dinkers of all dinkers.

Otherwise, it is a pretty lake that can be used as a jump-off point for a backpack trip. A trailhead is located at the northwest side of the lake that is routed south into Tahoe National Forest, up into the drainage to the headwaters of the North Fork American River.

28.   CAMP FAR WEST RESERVOIR

Reference: East of Marysville; map D3 grid dØ.

How to get there: From Sacramento on Interstate 80, drive east to Roseville and take Highway 65. Turn north and drive on Highway 65 to the town of Sheridan. Turn northeast on Camp Far West Road and drive six miles to the reservoir. A road circles around the west side of the lake, providing access to camps and boat launches at both the north and south entrances to the lake.

Facilities: Campgrounds, a full-service marina, boat ramps, and picnic areas are provided. Boat rentals, bait, tackle, and groceries are also available.

Cost: Day-use fee is $3.50 per vehicle, $7 if entering with a boat (four person maximum, $1 for each additional person). Campsite fees are

$8.50 per night, $12 if camping with a boat.

Who to contact: For camping and fishing information, phone Camp Far West at (916) 645-8069.

About Camp Far West Reservoir: You see this lake and you instantly say: "Bass." You should, with 29 miles of shoreline, cove after cove, and perfect weather for bass. This lake has turned into one of the better bets in the Central Valley.

It is set at 320 feet elevation in the foothill country, which means an early spring followed by a hot summer. Give this lake four straight days of warm weather in the spring and in return, this lake will give you bass on the bite.

There are many obvious, good spots on each section of the lake: the Bear River arm, Rock Creek arm, and a rock-studded area just north of the dam. Most bassers prefer the Rock Creek arm, where there are several deep coves that you can approach quietly, then stick a cast right on top of a big largemouth. The main lake body, both in front of the two launch ramps and the dam area, should be avoided. There is a lot less bass habitat here, and this is where most of the waterskiing activity takes place as well. No problem. Many other places provide what you will be looking for. The reservoir receives a bonus plant of 3,000 yearling striped bass each year.

---

29. FRENCH MEADOWS RESERVOIR

Reference: Northeast of Auburn in Tahoe National Forest; map D3 grid d9.

How to get there: From Auburn on Interstate 80, take the Foresthill Road exit at the north end of town and drive 20 miles northeast on Foresthill Road. Just before the town of Foresthill, turn right on Mosquito Ridge Road and travel 36 miles east to the French Meadows Reservoir Dam. Cross the dam, then turn east and drive along the lake.

Facilities: Several campgrounds, two boat ramps, and two lakeside picnic areas are provided. Supplies are available in Foresthill.

Cost: Campsite fees range from free to $8 per night for single camps; $25-$50 per night for group camps.

Who to contact: Phone the Tahoe National Forest District Office at (916) 367-2224.

About French Meadows Reservoir: It's a long, winding drive to reach this lake, and if you get stuck behind a motorhome that refuses to pull over, you may feel like adding an army tank-style gun turret to the front of your rig. What's the big rush? The trout, that's what. They're waiting for you.

French Meadows Reservoir, set at 5,300 feet on a dammed-up section of the Middle Fork American River, has turned into one of the top trout lakes in the Sierra Nevada. It is stocked each year with more than 30,000 rainbow trout in the foot-long class, joining a population of resident brown trout and holdovers from stocks of rainbow trout in previous years.

It is a big lake, covering nearly 2,000 acres when full in the spring, but the water bully boys who control the dam have a way of turning it into a little lake by fall. That's right, they drain this sucker down until acres and acres of lake bottom are exposed and all kinds of stumps and boulders start poking through the surface. It creates a multitude of navigational hazards. But when you see all these stumps and boulders, you realize why the trout like it here: Lots of habitat. The big browns especially like to hang out around the submerged logs, similar to how a bass acts in a warmwater lake.

30.　　　　HALSEY FOREBAY

Reference: North of Auburn; map D3 grid e2.
How to get there: From Auburn, drive two miles north on Interstate 80 and take the Dry Creek Road exit. Turn right on Christian Valley Road and travel one mile, then turn north on Bancroft Road and drive a short distance.
Facilities: A picnic area is provided by PG&E. A campground, lodging, and supplies are available in Auburn.
Cost: Access is free.
Who to contact: For general information, phone the Auburn Chamber of Commerce at (916) 885-5616. For fishing information, phone Bill's Bait & Tackle in Auburn at (916) 885-9200.
About Halsey Forebay: This is a small lake fed by the Bear River Canal, known only by locals who track the latest trout stocks. Get 'em it does, some 6,000 rainbow trout as spring turns into summer.

It is set at 1,800 feet in the foothill country north of Auburn. Rock Creek Lake, Lake Arthur, Lake Theodore, and Siphon Lake are all similar small lakes located within five miles of Halsey Forebay, but Halsey is the only one stocked with trout, getting good-sized ones at that from Fish and Game.

31.　　　　CLEMENTINE LAKE

Reference: Northeast of Auburn on the American River; map D3 grid e2.
How to get there: At the north end of Auburn on Interstate 80, take the Foresthill Road exit and drive five miles east. Turn north on Clementine Road and drive four miles to the boat ramp.
Facilities: A boat ramp is provided. A small, primitive boat-in campground is available on the west shore of the lake. Supplies can be

obtained in Auburn.

Cost: Access is free.

Who to contact: For general information, phone the Auburn Chamber of Commerce at (916) 885-5616. For fishing information, phone Bill's Bait & Tackle in Auburn at (916) 885-9200.

About Clementine Lake: Sometimes you just plain must have a boat. When you visit Clementine Lake, you will discover that this is one of those times.

    The shoreline is very brushy, and trying to walk along the bank of this reservoir is damn near impossible. Ah, but the boater, on the other hand, has it made. From the water, facing the shore, the boater can zip casts along that brush—right where the bass often hang out.

    The lake is long and narrow, a dammed-up gorge on the North Fork American River. As you get well upstream, you will discover the water temperature is cooler; this is where the lake's modest population of trout will congregate. Get your boat as far upstream as possible, anchor, then toss out a nightcrawler, letting it flutter a bit in the current.

---

32.   HELL HOLE RESERVOIR

Reference: In Eldorado National Forest Northeast of Auburn; map D3 grid e9.

How to get there: From Auburn on Interstate 80, take the Foresthill Exit at the north end of town. Drive 20 miles northeast on Foresthill Road to the town of Foresthill. Turn east on Mosquito Ridge Road (the route to French Meadows Reservoir) and drive 36 miles to French Meadows Dam. Cross the dam and turn south on Forest Service Road 48, then travel 13 miles to the reservoir.

Facilities: A Forest Service campground (Big Meadows) is available about a two-mile drive west of the reservoir. Another primitive camp is available at the south end of the reservoir; access is available only by foot or boat. Supplies can be obtained in Foresthill.

Cost: Lake access is free.

Who to contact: Phone the Eldorado National Forest District Ranger at (916)333-4312.

About Hell Hole Reservoir: The first time I saw this lake was from an airplane, which provided a spectacular view of one of the most awesome drive-to destinations in California. The lake is set at the bottom of a massive granite gorge, with water the color of sapphire blue, and from an airplane, it has the look of a mountain temple.

    Close up, Hell Hole Reservoir is just as sacred. The lake elevation is only 4,700 feet, but the surrounding walls and mountain country rise steep and high above the water. The water is crystal pure, fed by the most remote stretches of the pristine Rubicon River.

For newcomers, fishing always comes second. Just gazing at the water and surrounding country is plenty.

Soon, though, you will want to get on the water and explore further. Small trailered boats as well as car-top boats are well suited. The long, winding access road is too far, too twisty, and too slow for pulling anything but a light, aluminum boat. But once on the water, the surprises keep on coming.

The primary trout in this lake are brown trout and mackinaw trout. Not brook trout, not rainbow trout, but brownies and lakers. Fish and Game plans to keep it that way, too, by stocking 9,000 brown trout and 9,000 mackinaws (fingerlings) each year. This provides a new dimension for most anglers who visit mountain lakes.

Browns and mackinaws can get giant, and they do just that at Hell Hole. There are fish in the 10-pound class here, and while they might be your goal, there are enough brownies in the foot-long class to keep things interesting while you pursue the big fellows.

Don't try to get here quick. It's impossible; the access road is too long and twisty. Don't make it a fast hit, either. Big brown trout and lake trout play by their own rules and timing, not yours. Besides, the place is too beautiful not to spend some slow days getting a real sense of the spirit of it.

Also, because the fishing is for brown trout and mackinaws, and the water is often very clear, this reservoir can require special deep-water techniques during the day and in the evening a very quiet, careful approach. Shoreline fishing is not usually productive.

---

33.   NORTH FORK AMERICAN

Reference: Near Auburn; map D3 grid f1.

How to get there: From Auburn, drive east on Highway 49. Access is available where the bridge crosses the river. Limited access is also available off roads that junction with Interstate 80 near Colfax. Access to the North Fork of the North Fork American is available farther north, off Interstate 80 via the Emigrant Gap exit.

Facilities: A boat ramp is located off Highway 49 north of Folsom Lake, on Rattlesnake Bar Road. Campgrounds are available in Auburn and off Interstate 80 at the above locations. Supplies can be obtained in Auburn, Colfax, and in the Emigrant Gap area.

Cost: River access is free.

Who to contact: Phone Bill's Bait & Tackle in Auburn at (916) 885-9200 or Performance Marine in Colfax at (916) 346-8555.

About North Fork American River: Access is extremely limited on this section of river. The one decent access point is at the Highway 49 Bridge, just below the confluence of the North and Middle Forks.

What you find here is a good spot for smallmouth bass, either flyfishing with dark woolly worms, or plugging with crankbaits. Don't expect large fish—there aren't many. But there are enough in the nine to 12-inch class that a smallmouth fan can feed his addiction.

34. STUMPY MEADOWS RESERVOIR

Reference: Northeast of Placerville in Eldorado National Forest; map D3 grid f6.

How to get there: From Placerville on US 50, drive 12 miles north on Highway 193 to Georgetown. Turn right (east) on Georgetown-Wentworth Road and travel 20 miles to the lake. The boat ramp is located just south of the dam.

Facilities: Campgrounds, picnic areas, and a boat ramp are provided. Supplies are available in Placerville or Georgetown.

Cost: Campsite fees are $7-$12 for single camps; $25 for group camps.

Who to contact: Phone the Eldorado National Forest District Office at (916) 333-4312, or Russell's Sportsman's Corner in Placerville at (916) 621-2483.

About Stumpy Meadows Reservoir: Don't let the name Stumpy Meadows fool you into thinking this is a stodgy old place full of algae. It is just the opposite. The water is cold and clear, it is surrounded by national forest, and it is an ideal place to camp, fish and boat. A bonus is that a five-mph speed limit for boaters keeps the lake quiet, perfect for fishing.

Stumpy Meadows covers 320 acres and is set at 4,400 feet in Eldorado National Forest, up in the snow country. The access road gets shut down every winter by snow, but when it is plowed (usually in April), the fishing is often excellent right off. It is stocked each year with nearly 30,000 rainbow trout, the plants coming nearly every week once the access road is cleared. That makes it a popular lake for angler/campers, and most of the trout are caught using standard trolling techniques, adjusting for depth according to time of year. A bonus is that in the early spring and late fall, some big brown trout will move up into the head of the lake near where Pilot Creek enters the lake.

35. GERLE CREEK RESERVOIR

Reference: West of Lake Tahoe in Eldorado National Forest; map D3 grid f8.

How to get there: From Placerville, drive about 20 miles east on US 50 to the town of Riverton. Turn north on Ice House Road and drive about 25 miles (passing Union Valley Reservoir), continuing straight at Loon Lake Road (on the right), and driving three miles to the Gerle Creek turnoff on the left.

Facilities: A campground is provided. No motors are permitted on the lake. Supplies are available in Placerville.

Cost: Campsite fee is $7 per night.

Who to contact: Phone the Eldorado National Forest District Office at (916) 644-2349.

About Gerle Creek Reservoir: This is a small, pretty, but limited spot at 5,300 feet in Eldorado National Forest.

Small? No boat ramp is available, making it perfect for those with car-top boats that are easily hand-launched, such as canoes. Pretty? Definitely, set in the Gerle Creek canyon, which feeds into the South Fork Rubicon. Limited? That too is affirmative.

This little lake rarely gets stocked with trout, and unless there are bonus fish available, it can go the entire year without a plant. That leaves it up to the native fish to do their thing, and with no catch-and-release regulations in force, makes for a small resident population.

The campground is quite nice, the scenery excellent. It's decent for a layover, but nearby Loon Lake, Union Valley Reservoir and Ice House Reservoir all provide much better fishing.

---

36. FOLSOM LAKE

Reference: Northeast of Sacramento in Folsom Lake State Recreation Area; map D3 grid gØ.

How to get there: From Sacramento, drive northeast on Interstate 80. Take the Douglas Boulevard exit and travel nine miles east on Douglas Boulevard to Granite Bay at the lake.

Facilities: Campgrounds, a full-service marina, boat ramps, boat rentals, bait and tackle are available at the lake.

Cost: Day-use fee is $6 per vehicle, $5 for a boat. Campsite fees range from $12-$14 per night.

Who to contact: Phone the Folsom Lake State Recreation Area at (916) 988-0205, or Fran & Eddy's Sports Den in Rancho Cordova at (916) 363-6885.

About Folsom Lake: This is Sacramento's backyard playland, where thousands and thousands of people visit to fish, waterski, camp, or just lay around in the sun.

Because of the lake's shallow lake arms, the water levels can fluctuate as dramatically from winter to spring as any lake in California. I've seen this lake look almost empty before any rains start in December, then seem to fill to the brim virtually overnight. When it is full, it covers some 12,000 acres with 75 miles of shoreline.

Its character changes from month-to-month almost as fast as the water level. In late winter and spring, this is an excellent trout fishing lake. The water is cool and fresh, and rainbow trout are stocked weekly as long as it remains that way, totaling 61,000 trout in the 10 to 12-inch class. Year after year, it seems that the Dike 8 area, located between the dam and Folsom Marina, produces more trout than any other area for trollers. In early May, hot weather starts hammering away at the Central Valley. Suddenly, out come hundreds of mermaids to get a suntan. Just as fast, the lake converts more to a bass lake than a trout lake. If you want trout, you'd best get on the water at daybreak and get it done by 9 a.m. After that, the waterskiers take over, and the sun sends the trout down to the abyss.

The largemouth bass, on the other hand, respond quickly to the warming water. There are miles of decent bass water up both lake arms, the North Fork American and the South Fork American, and it is here where a skilled basser can do very well. Skill? Required. Over the course of a few months, these bass will see damn near every lure ever invented. You have to make the offering in a way that fools them into thinking the thing is actually alive.

One reason Folsom Lake has such a productive bass fishery is because it is stocked by 35,000 fingerling-sized large mouth bass each year.

You can plan on seeing a lot of young drunken sailors out at Folsom, and if you stick around long enough, you'll see just about every stunt imaginable that comes with hot sun, cold suds, and lots of people.

---

37.   SOUTH FORK AMERICAN

Reference: Near Placerville in Eldorado National Forest; map D3 grid g3.
How to get there: Excellent access to the upper South Fork American is available off US 50 east of Placerville; there are several turnouts where you can park and hike down to the river. The best area is near Riverton. Two good spots are also available on the lower South Fork American. From Placerville, drive north on Highway 193 to Chili Bar. Direct access is available there, and trails are available for hiking downstream. Another option is near Coloma. From Placerville, drive north on Highway 49/193 then northwest on Highway 49, which crosses the river just north of town.
Facilities: Campgrounds are available off US 50. Supplies are available in Placerville.
Cost: River access is free.
Who to contact: Phone Eldorado National Forest District Office at (916) 644-2349, or Russell's Sportsman's Corner in Placerville at (916) 621-2483.
About South Fork American: There is one excellent spot on the upper South Fork American River near US 50, and two good stretches on

the lower South Fork just north of Placerville. Take your pick.

The stretch of water near Riverton along Highway 50 is the top piece of river in the entire canyon. Why? There are just plain more trout here than any place else on the river. My spy tells me the DFG plants nearly 20,000 rainbow trout at Riverton. It is also very pretty here. Anyone who makes the trip up Highway 50 to Tahoe should keep a rod rigged and ready, then park at a turnout and make a few casts to reclaim some sanity.

The lower stretch of the American, from Chili Bar on downstream to Placerville, is very popular for rafters in various stages of dress. The trout are smaller here and also more wary, and sneak-fishing techniques must be employed. On weekends, there can be so many rafts that it can disrupt the fishing in this area.

The answer is to head farther upstream in the Coloma area, where 7,000 trout are stocked, adding to a fair base of native fish.

---

38.   FINNON LAKE

Reference: North of Placerville; map D3 grid g5.
How to get there: From Placerville, drive eight miles north on Highway 193. Turn right (east) on Rock Creek Road and travel eight miles.
Facilities: A campground and picnic areas are provided. No gasoline motors are permitted on the lake. Supplies are available in Placerville.
Cost: Day-use fee is $2 per vehicle. Campsite fee is $5 per night.
Who to contact: Phone Finnon Lake at (916) 622-9314, or Russell's Sportsman's Corner in Placerville at (916) 621-2483.
About Finnon Lake: Most folks just keep on driving when they see the Rock Creek Road turnoff that leads to little Finnon Lake. And why not? Finnon is set at 2,200 feet and has a light mix of bass, red ear sunfish, bluegill and perch. It's a county recreation lake, set up for small boats that are hand-launched and paddle powered, with a small campground and a few hiking trails. This is the kind of lake where you could put a red worm under a bobber, then watch it dance a little. If you are more ambitious, well, keep on driving.

---

39.   UNION VALLEY RESERVOIR

Reference: West of Lake Tahoe in Eldorado National Forest; map D3 grid g8.
How to get there: From Placerville, drive about 20 miles east on US 50 to the town of Riverton. Turn north on Ice House Road and drive about 20 miles (past the turnoff to Ice House Lake). When you reach the lake, three roads provide access, with boat ramps available at the first left turn and the third left turn, and campgrounds at all three turns.

Facilities: Campgrounds and picnic areas are provided. Boat ramps are available. Supplies can be obtained in Placerville.

Cost: Campsite fees range from $7-$12 per night for single camps; $25 for group camps.

Who to contact: Phone the Eldorado National Forest District Office at (916) 644-2349, or Russell's Sportsman's Corner in Placerville at (916) 621-2483.

About Union Valley Reservoir: The Crystal Basin Recreation Area is one of the most popular backcountry regions for campers from the Sacramento area. Union Valley Reservoir, a big lake covering nearly 3,000 acres, is one of the centerpieces.

The area gets its name from the prominent granite Sierra ridge, which looks like crystal when it is covered with frozen snow. The lake is set at 4,900 feet, with nearby Ice House Reservoir to the south and Loon Lake farther to the north.

Union Valley is stocked with 18,000 rainbow trout per year, providing both shoreline prospects for campers, and good evening trolling results. The lake is shaped kind of like a horseshoe, with several feeder streams located up each of the lake arms. The better fishing is typically in these two areas.

---

40. ICE HOUSE RESERVOIR

Reference: West of Lake Tahoe in Eldorado National Forest; map D3 grid g9.

How to get there: From Placerville, drive about 20 miles east on US 50 to the town of Riverton. Turn north on Ice House Road and drive 10 miles, then turn right on the Ice House Reservoir access road and drive two miles east to the boat ramp.

Facilities: Two campgrounds and a boat ramp are provided. Supplies are available in Placerville.

Cost: Campsite fee is $7 per night.

Who to contact: Phone the Eldorado National Forest District Office at (916) 644-2349, or Russell's Sportsman's Corner in Placerville at (916) 621-2483.

About Ice House Reservoir: Of the three major lakes in the beautiful Crystal Lakes Basin, Ice House is the first one you reach. The others are Union Valley Reservoir, and then father north, Loon Lake.

It is Ice House which attracts most of the anglers during the summer, while Union Valley gets many more campers. Ice House is stocked every summer with more than 30,000 trout, and not just a bunch of dinkers, but rainbow trout in the 11, 12-inch class. They join a decent resident population that includes brown trout, and adds up to very good trout fishery.

A lot of limits are taken here, most by trollers. The fish tend not to congregate at any key area at Ice House Reservoir, so trolling allows the best way to search out the lake, picking up a fish every now and then.

Ice House was created by a dam on South Fork Silver Creek at 5,500 feet elevation, covering about 650 acres when full. The deepest spot I could find was 130 feet, which explains why the lake seems to have a good holdover population through the ice-cold winters.

---

41. JENKINSON LAKE

Reference: East of Placerville in Sly Park Recreation Area; map D3 grid h6.

How to get there: From Placerville, drive 11 miles east on US 50 to the town of Pollock Pines. Take the Sly Park Road exit and travel five miles south on Sly Park Road.

Facilities: A campground and picnic areas are provided. A boat ramp is available. Supplies are can be obtained in Placerville.

Cost: Day-use fee is $3.50 per vehicle, $6 for motorized boats. There is no fee for kayaks or canoes.

Who to contact: Phone Sly Park Recreation Area at (916) 644-2545, or Russell's Sportsman's Corner in Placerville at (916) 621-2483.

About Jenkinson Lake: Jenkinson Lake is hardly a secret, but that is about the only thing wrong with it. In fact, in many ways Jenkinson Lake is the ideal destination.

The trout fishing is excellent in the spring, the bass fishing comes on strong in the summer, the upper end of the lake has a five-mph speed limit, which keeps all the waterskiers out of your hair, and a series of five lakeside camps are set along the north shore on the upper end of the lake.

Sound good? It is. And that means you can expect plenty of company. This is a popular, easy-to-reach lake with a paved, three-lane boat ramp. But once on the water, heading well up the main lake arm out of the way of the waterskiers, you will hardly notice the others.

Jenkinson Lake is set at 3,500 feet elevation in the lower reaches of Eldorado National Forest, with a climate that is perfect for fishing.

It gets cold with snow in the winter, and in the spring and early summer, cool water temperatures make it ideal for trout. In response, a lot of them are stocked, some 35,000 per year, including many in the foot-long class. Just plain forget trying to fish the main lake body. Instead head straight up the lake, trolling from the narrows on upstream, exploring both of the lake's arms.

Then when the hot weather arrives, get out your bass gear. A surprisingly good largemouth bass population has been established in this lake. As with the trout, the better fishing is well up the lake arms. The irony is that you can be peppering shoreline haunts with casts, hoping a big bass gets riled up enough to strike, and instead a big brown trout can nail your lure. It happens.

42. SILVER FORK AMERICAN RIVER

Reference: In Eldorado National Forest east of Placerville; map D3 grid h9.

How to get there: From Placerville, drive 29 miles east on US 50 to Kyburz Resort. Turn south on Silver Fork Road; the road parallels the river, and direct access is available.

Facilities: A campground, called China Flat, is located on Silver Fork Road. Supplies are available in Placerville.

Cost: Campsite fee is $7 per night.

Who to contact: Phone Eldorado National Forest District Office at (916) 644-2349, or Russell's Sportsman's Corner in Placerville at (916) 621-2483.

About Silver Fork American River: Kyburz isn't a big town. In fact, it's a veritable dot. But it's a key place on US 50 and the adjacent American River. There are two reasons. One is that the snow line often starts right at Kyburz, and in the early season, that can make the difference between easy or terrible access. The second reason is because on the South Fork American along US 50, fish populations are very low upstream of Kyburz. The wise few ignore this stretch of the American River, and instead turn off at Kyburz and fish the Silver Fork.

That is because Silver Fork American is stocked with 13,500 rainbow trout in the 10, 11-inch class, some bigger, and join a light sprinkling of natives. Together, they provide much better fishing than anything you can get upstream of Kyburz along US 50.

43. TIGER CREEK AFTERBAY

Reference: Northeast of Jackson; map D3 grid j6.

How to get there: From the junction of Highways 49 and 88 at the town of Jackson, drive 18 miles east on Highway 88. Turn right on Tiger Creek Powerhouse Road (at Buckhorn Lodge) and travel one mile. Bear south at the junction and drive one mile to the reservoir.

Facilities: A PG&E picnic area is provided. Supplies are available in Jackson.

Cost: Access is free.

Who to contact: Phone the Eldorado National Forest District Office at (209) 295-4251.

About Tiger Creek Afterbay: Little Tiger Creek Afterbay is one of the more overlooked spots along the Highway 88 corridor. At 2,400 feet elevation, most people probably figure that the weather is too hot and the lake too small to provide much of anything.

Wrong again. In the spring, it's not hot at all here. It is stocked with nearly 6,000 rainbow trout in the cool spring months, providing good prospects for those who time it right. Most of the trout range in the 10, 11-inch class.

That can make it an ideal lake for someone with a car-top boat who wants a spot devoid of big power boats.

---

44. BEAR RIVER RESERVOIR

Reference: Southwest of Lake Tahoe in Eldorado National Forest; map D3 grid j9.

How to get there: From Stockton on Highway 99, turn east on Highway 88 and continue for 75 miles, through the foothill country and into the mountains. Turn right on Bear River Road and drive two miles, then turn left and drive a half-mile to the Bear River Resort, campgrounds, and boat launch.

Facilities: Campgrounds are provided. Boat ramps, boat rentals, bait, tackle, and groceries are available nearby.

Cost: Campsite fees range from $7-$18.50 per night.

Who to contact: Phone the Eldorado National Forest District Office at (209) 295-4251.

About Bear River Reservoir: As you venture into the mountains on Highway 88, this is the first of three quality mountain lakes you will come to. The others are Silver Lake and Caples Lake.

One advantage at Bear River Reservoir is its lower elevation, 5,900 feet. That means the ice melts off sooner here than at its brothers farther up the line, Silver and Caples, and correspondingly, the spring stocks and fishing get going earlier, too.

Another edge is that Bear River Reservoir gets a double-barreled dose of trout, coming both from the Department of Fish and Game as well as the private resort that adds bonus trophy fish. The DFG stocks 43,000 rainbow trout in the 10 to 12-inch class, and get this, a plant of 1,700 fingerling-sized mackinaw trout. The resort adds thousands of trout on top of that, all on top of a small number of large resident brown trout.

You get the idea: There's a lot of fish here. Almost every week someone catches a trout in the five to 10-pound class, and the resort at the lake does a good job of providing detailed fish reports.

The lake is decent size, 725 acres, and deep too. During the summer, most trollers use lead-core trolling line to get to the desired depth, and catch the majority of fish. Shoreliners do only fair at the campgrounds on each side of the boat ramp on the western shore.

A side trip possibility is hiking up to Upper Bear River Reservoir, which involves about a two-mile hike and 100-foot climb. Piece of cake, right? That lake just seems to have dinkers, four and five-inch rainbow trout.

---

45.   SALT SPRINGS RESERVOIR

Reference: East of Jackson in Eldorado National Forest; map D3 grid j9.

How to get there: From the junction of Highways 49 and 88 at the town of Jackson, drive 22 miles east on Highway 88. Turn south at Inspiration Lodge and drive five miles on Ellis Road. When the road forks, bear south and cross the bridge that goes across Bear River. Continue three miles to the dam. The boat launch is located at the north end of the base of the dam.

Facilities: A PG&E picnic area is provided at the reservoir. Three free, primitive campgrounds are available nearby on the Mokelumne River. No piped water is available. No motorized boats are permitted on the reservoir. Supplies are available in Pioneer.

Cost: Access is free.

Who to contact: Phone the Eldorado National Forest District Office at (209) 295-4251. For a map, send $2 to U.S. Forest Service, 630 Sansome Street, San Francisco, CA 94111.

About Salt Springs Reservoir: This lake has just about everything, a place everyone should visit at least once in their life. It's a long, narrow lake set in the Mokelumne River Gorge, a dramatic canyon with spectacular surroundings for boaters. It's a good spot for hikers, too. A trail that is routed into the Mokelumne Wilderness starts just north of the dam. Want more? Got more. A series of small, primitive campgrounds are set west of the lake, below the dam along the Mokelumne River, all very pretty spots.

The lake is set at 4,000 feet elevation and covers 950 acres, and even though it has a fairly obscure location, its beauty attracts returning vacationers year after year.

But what of the fishing? Well, like I said, it has just about everything. It does not seem to have a lot of fish, nor any stocks planned to provide them. Skilled anglers that boat upstream to the lake's Mokelumne River inlet can find trout congregating there in the early summer. Below the dam, the Mokelumne River itself seems to provide higher catch rates.

MAP D4

33 LISTINGS
PAGES 382-409

NOR-CAL MAP.see page 120
adjoining maps
NORTH (C4) ......see page 304
EAST ....no map
SOUTH (E4).......see page 492
WEST (D3).........see page 348

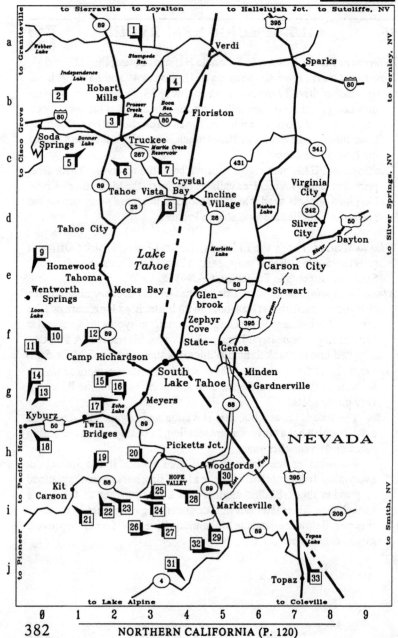

1.   STAMPEDE RESERVOIR

Reference: North of Truckee in Tahoe National Forest; map D4 grid a3.

How to get there: From Truckee, drive seven miles east on Interstate 80 and take the Boca-Hirschdale exit. Continue north (past Boca Reservoir) for eight miles on Stampede Meadows Road to the reservoir. The launch ramp and campgrounds are located on the south side of the lake.

Facilities: Several campgrounds are provided. A boat ramp is available. Supplies can be obtained in Truckee.

Cost: Campsite fees are $7-$9 per night for single camps; $25-$50 for group camps.

Who to contact: Phone the Tahoe National Forest District Office at (916) 587-3558, or California Land Management at (916) 582-0120. For fishing information, phone Tahoe Truckee Sports at (916) 587-1154, Mountain Hardware at (916) 587-4844, or Tourist Liquor & Sporting Goods at (916) 587-3081.

About Stampede Reservoir: Stampede Reservoir offers the classic Sierra Nevada experience, and for an easy-to-reach, drive-to lake, that is hard to beat.

The lake is a big one at 3,400 acres, the largest in the area besides Lake Tahoe. It is set at 6,000 feet in the Sierra granite country, usually becoming accessible by late May. It has just about everything: an extended launch ramp, a half dozen campgrounds, and good fishing.

There's just one problem. Note the "extended" launch ramp. Why would a ramp need to be extended? Right, because the water gets quite low here in late summer and fall, when the water is poured out the dam via the Little Truckee River and Boca Reservoir to keep the fish going in the Truckee River along Interstate 80.

So locals always focus on the early season, picking days when the wind is down, then getting good results catching foot-long rainbow trout along the southern shoreline and near the inlet of the Little Truckee River. A bonus is an honest chance at a monster brown trout or mackinaw trout. The best way to entice 'em is to be on the water at dawn or dusk, then troll a Rapala directly across from the boat launch along the northern shoreline.

This big lake provides a good option from Tahoe, and the DFG knows it. That is why they stock it with 38,000 rainbow trout and a bonus of 8,700 fingerling-sized mackinaw trout.

Stampede also has an excellent fishery for kokanee salmon—what may be the finest tasting of fresh water fish. The best prospects are in the fall starting the last week of August and running through early October. Kokanee approaching the state record of four pounds have been taken here.

2. INDEPENDENCE LAKE

Reference: North of Truckee in Tahoe National Forest; map D4 grid b1.

How to get there: From Truckee, drive 17.5 miles north on Highway 89 to Forest Service Road 7 (Jackson Meadow Road). Turn west and travel 1.5 miles to Independence Lake Road. Turn south and drive 6.5 miles to the lake.

Facilities: An undeveloped campground is provided at the lake. No piped water or sewage facilities are available. A primitive boat ramp is available. Supplies can be obtained in Truckee.

Cost: Anyone entering the lake area must register at the caretaker's house. Day-use fee is $3 per vehicle; additional $3 for a boat. Walk-in access is free after registering. Campsite fee is $5 per night.

Who to contact: For camping information, phone Lands of the Sierra in Reno at (702) 323-0807. For fishing information, phone Tahoe Truckee Sports at (916) 587-1154, Mountain Hardware at (916) 587-4844, or Tourist Liquor & Sporting Goods at (916) 587-3081.

About Independence Lake: When you turn left off Highway 89 and start heading west into the interior of Tahoe National Forest, this is the first of three lakes you come to, set at 5,600 feet elevation. The others are Webber Lake (another seven miles) and Jackson Meadow Reservoir (another 14 miles). For information on those lakes, see zone D3.

It's a good thing there are options, because sometimes things just don't pop at Independence. The lake is primarily set up for water storage, not recreation. For a longer trip, Jackson Meadow offers a lot more of just about everything.

But Independence does offer something that Jackson Meadow does not: Lahontan cutthroat trout. In fact, it is the only species of trout stocked at this lake, getting 6,500 fingerlings per year. The little ones aren't worth worrying about, of course, and the few larger ones don't fight a heck of a lot.

The fishing is best in the fall, after the cold weather puts a snap in the air, and before any heavy snows have arrived. That is when the larger cutthroats start cruising along the shoreline, providing fair prospects for both shoreliners and trollers.

3. PROSSER RESERVOIR

Reference: North of Truckee in Tahoe National Forest; map D4 grid b2.

How to get there: From Truckee, drive about one-half mile north on Highway 89 to the Prosser Reservoir turnoff on the right. Turn east and travel about four miles on Prosser Dam Road to the dam. Or, continue north on Highway 89 for three miles, then turn east at the signed turnoff and travel to the north shore of the reservoir.

Facilities: Campgrounds are provided around the lake. Boat ramps are available. Supplies can be obtained in Truckee.

Cost: Campsite fees range from free to $8 per night for single camps; $35 for group camps.

Who to contact: Phone the Tahoe National Forest District Office at (916) 586-3558. For fishing information, phone Tahoe Truckee Sports at (916) 587-1154, Mountain Hardware at (916) 587-4844, or Tourist Liquor & Sporting Goods at (916) 587-3081.

About Prosser Reservoir: Feel kind of hungry? Hey, stop looking at my arm like that. Yeah, this is the lake where the survivors of the Donner Party did their thing in the winter of 1846-47, munching away on arms and legs because the cattle they had along was "too tough chewing."

A lot of people think Donner Lake was the site of that winter party. Wrong. It was here, with their picnic set up on the southwest arm of the lake at what is now called the "Donner Picnic Site." Hey, got a leg in that picnic basket? Now wait a minute, Herschel, I meant a chicken leg.

Well, if you hit Prosser Reservoir wrong and planned to eat trout for dinner, you'd best plan on dinner in Truckee. There are times here where you will swear there isn't a trout left in the world that is over five inches. That is because Fish and Game stocks 100,000 rainbow trout dinkers here; that's right, those little swooners. Eventually, these fish are supposed to grow bigger. Oh yeah? When?

Ah, but hit it right and you will expect to be crowned the World's Great Fisherman at any second. That is because the DFG also plants 20,100 rainbow trout in the foot-long class, joining the holdovers of plants from past years, and providing a decent shoreline fishery.

It's a pretty spot, set at 5,800 feet elevation, and a 10-mph speed limit keeps the fast boats off. Prosser Campground is the best camp, perched on a wooded lake overlook. It's the last camp you come to as you drive in on the access road from west to east.

Whatever you do, don't plan to eat trout for dinner. That will guarantee you will not catch any, and then what will you eat?

Say, what's in that picnic basket?

---

4. BOCA RESERVOIR

Reference: Northeast of Truckee in Tahoe National Forest; map D4 grid b3.

How to get there: From Truckee, drive seven miles east on Interstate 80. Take the Boca-Hirschdale exit and drive two miles to Boca Reservoir. The boat ramp is located in southwest end of the lake.

Facilities: Two free primitive campgrounds are provided. A boat ramp is available. Supplies can be obtained in Truckee.

Cost: Access is free.

Who to contact: Phone the Tahoe National Forest District Office at (916) 586-3558. For fishing information, phone Tahoe Truckee Sports at (916) 587-1154, Mountain Hardware at (916) 587-4844, or Tourist Liquor & Sporting Goods at (916) 587-3081.

About Boca Reservoir: A few giant brown trout join a sampling of stocked rainbows to make Boca a decent lake for campers who want a chance to catch a trout or two. Access to the lake is very easy, just a quick hop off Interstate 80, yet a lot of folks miss it because the dam faces the highway—unlike nearby Donner Lake, which is set right aside the highway.

It is stocked with 12,210 rainbow trout per year, and in some years, also receives a bonus stock of rainbow trout in the five to eight-pound class. The best prospects are on the west side of the lake, where there are a series of coves from the dam all the way up to the north side where the Little Truckee River enters the lake.

Like so many lakes in this region, Boca is also very pretty, set at 5,700 feet, covering 1,000 acres. Once on the water, it can seem hard to believe that Interstate 80 is only two miles away. No foolin'.

---

5. DONNER LAKE

Reference: West of Truckee in Donner Memorial State Park; map D4 grid c1.

How to get there: From Truckee, drive two miles west on Donner Pass Road to the lake.

Facilities: A campground and a boat ramp are provided. Supplies are available in Truckee.

Cost: Day-use fee is $5 per vehicle; campsite fees are $12-$14 per night.

Who to contact: Phone the park at (916) 587-3841. For fishing information, phone Tahoe Truckee Sports at (916) 587-1154, Mountain Hardware at (916) 587-4844, or Tourist Liquor & Sporting Goods at (916) 587-3081.

About Donner Lake: Even though Donner Lake has become a common stop for millions of vacationers cruising past on Interstate 80, the first glimpse is always a stirring one. Its remarkable beauty evokes a heartfelt response. Was it good for you, too? Hey, this is the genuine article.

It is a big, oblong-shaped lake, three miles long and three-quarters of a mile wide, gem-like blue, set near the Sierra crest at 5,900 feet. It is easy to reach and a good choice for family camping. The area is well developed, with cabins and maintained access roads. Those exact reasons, however, are often cited as to why some people never stay at

Donner. They want more seclusion. A public boat ramp is available at the west end of the lake at Donner Village Resort, and it is near here where the trout fishing is often good. Because the lake is so big, it is best fished by boat, but shoreliners do have a chance tossing Kastmasters. If you do go by boat, take fair warning that afternoon winds can run you off the lake during the spring, and afternoon thunderstorms can cause a similar result in late summer.

Donner Lake is stocked with 81,310 rainbow trout, along with 8,820 fingerling-size mackinaw trout. Because of the lake's extreme depth, 800 feet in spots, the mackinaws seem to disappear for much of the year, then reappear in decent sizes. The lake gets fished hard by trollers, and the primary fare are the planted trout.

But there is just enough chance to catch a real beauty—a rainbow, brown or mackinaw trout in the 10-pound class—that a wise few know that the next nibble may be the trout they have been waiting for all their lives.

---

6. TRUCKEE RIVER

Reference: Near Truckee in Tahoe National Forest; map D4 grid c2.

How to get there: From Truckee, drive south on Highway 89. The road parallels the river for 14 miles to Tahoe City, and excellent roadside access is available. To reach the section of river east of Truckee, drive east on Highway 267 and turn right on Glenshire Drive. Glenshire Drive parallels the river for several miles, with direct access available. Access is also available off Interstate 80 east of Truckee.

Facilities: Several campgrounds are available on Highway 89 and in the Truckee area. Lodging, bait, tackle, and groceries can be obtained in Truckee.

Cost: River access is free.

Who to contact: For general information, phone the Tahoe National Forest District Office at (916) 586-3558. For fishing information, phone Tahoe Truckee Sports at (916) 587-1154, Mountain Hardware at (916) 587-4844, or Tourist Liquor & Sporting Goods at (916) 587-3081.

About Truckee River: Of the great trout streams in California, the Truckee stands apart as one of the few that provides both easy access and quality trout fishing. It has a mix of both wild trout and planters, providing good fishing for flyfishers and family baitdunkers alike.

The Highway 89 section, where the highway runs aside the river from Truckee to Tahoe City, is stocked with 50,340 rainbow trout every summer. That's a hell of a lot of fish for a small stream, but if you have ever seen the traffic on 89, then you understand very quickly why. The river gets quite a bit of people pressure. In fact, so many rafts go down it on weekends that many of the better holes can get spooked.

Regardless, if you are in the area and making the drive here, always keep your rod ready, and if you see a spot that looks good (there are lots of them), pull off the road, hoof it down to the stream and make a few casts. It is always worth it. Farther downstream, east of Truckee along Glenshire Drive, there are fewer fish but far fewer anglers. Access is still quite easy, though, and the trout hold in pockets and pools in this stretch. This area is quite good during the evening for flyfishers who take a careful approach and can make short, gentle casts.

The Truckee has become a famous river because so many people have driven right beside it. Only the people who have fished it, however, know its best qualities.

---

7. MARTIS CREEK LAKE

Reference: Near Truckee; map D4 grid c3.

How to get there: From Truckee, drive 2.5 miles southeast on Highway 267 to the signed entrance to the lake. Turn left and travel two miles.

Facilities: A free developed campground is provided at the lake. No motorized boats are permitted on the lake, and fishing is limited to catch-and-release with single, barbless hooks and artificials. No bait is permitted.

Cost: Access is free.

Who to contact: Phone the U.S. Corps of Engineers, Martis Creek Lake at (916) 639-2342; California Trout, Inc., at (415) 392-8887.

About Martis Creek Lake: What began as an experiment is now an established victory for flyfishers, with Martis Lake, 5,700 feet elevation, one of the few lakes in America set aside exclusively for wild trout. But if you want wild trout, you must also demand catch-and-release fishing. It just comes with the territory. Otherwise a water can be fished out because there is no tanker truck showing up every other week to replenish what has been taken. So catch-and-release fishing is the law at Martis, and it is working.

The first thing that happens when no fish are killed in a water is that the average size becomes much larger than most anglers are accustomed to. That is because in most situations, given no restrictions, most anglers like to throw back the little ones, but always keep the big ones. That is a worst-case scenario for any river or stream, because soon all you get are lots of little fish. At Martis, all fish are returned, so not only do the little ones have a chance to get big, but the big ones have a chance to get even bigger.

The result at Martis are Lahontan cutthroat trout that range to 25 inches, and a sprinkling of equally-huge brown trout. But they are difficult to catch, and with special regulations in place, this is not the place to come for the family camper. Whatever you do, don't show up with one of those big, black frying pans. No motors are allowed on the lake. Instead, most flyfishers arrive with float tubes or prams, using sinking lines, leech or woolly worm patterns, and a strip retrieve. You rarely hear stories about large numbers of trout caught at Martis Lake. Instead you hear about the size of the trout, and the challenge of the adventure.

---

8.   LAKE TAHOE

Reference: East of Sacramento in Lake Tahoe Basin; map D4 grid d3.

How to get there: From Sacramento, drive east on Interstate 50 to get to the south shore. An alternate route is to take Interstate 80 to Truckee, then head south on Highway 267 to Tahoe City (west shore) or Highway 89 to Kings Beach (north shore).

Boat ramps: Boat ramps are located at the following locations: (South Lake Tahoe) El Dorado Boat Ramp, at the junction of US 50 and Lakeview Avenue; Ski Run Marina, South Lake Tahoe; Timber Cove Marina, South Lake Tahoe; Meeks Bay Resort, Meeks Bay; Obexers Boat & Motor Sales, Homewood (North Lake Tahoe); Kings Beach Boat Launching Facility, Kings Beach; Alpine Marina, Tahoe Vista; Tahoe Vista Yacht Harbor, Tahoe Vista; Sierra Boat Company, Carnelian Bay; Lake Forest Public Ramp, two miles north of Tahoe City off Highway 28; Sunnyside Resort, Tahoe City; Tahoe Boat Company, Tahoe City.

Facilities: Campgrounds, lodging, marinas, boat ramps, boat rentals, groceries, bait, and tackle are available at several locations around the lake.

Cost: Lake access is free.

Fishing guide: Guide Dan Hannum can be reached through Tahoe Bait & Tackle at (916) 541-8801.

Who to contact: Phone the Lake Tahoe Basin Management Unit at (916) 573-2600, or the North Lake Chamber of Commerce at (916) 581-6900, or the South Lake Chamber of Commerce at (916) 541-5255. For fishing information, phone (North Lake Tahoe) Swigards Hardware, (916) 583-3738; Homewood Hardware, (916) 525-6367. (South Lake Tahoe) Rich's Fishing Charters, (916) 541-5550; Tahoe Bait & Tackle, (916) 541-8801; Woody's Sportfishing, (916) 544-3086.

About Lake Tahoe: So many places don't evoke any feeling, but Lake Tahoe is one of the few places that does. Along with Crater Lake in Oregon, and Yosemite Valley, Lake Tahoe is one of the rare natural wonders that makes you feel something special just by looking at it. Of course, it is huge, but it also has unmatched pureness. Huge? It is 22 miles long, 12 miles wide, and 1,645 feet deep at its deepest point.

It is filled with 39 trillion gallons of water, enough to cover California to a depth of 13.8 feet, and enough so that it would take 300 years of severe drought for it to drain significantly. Pure? It is 99.9 percent pure, similar to the purity of distilled water. It is so clear that on a calm day, you can see a dinner plate 75 feet below the surface.

It is that pureness, however, that prevents Tahoe from becoming a world-class fishery. It undermines the lake's ability to support large amounts of aquatic life. Regardless, it is still a quality fishery. The mackinaw trout are the lake's trophy fishery, the rainbow trout provide the most predictable results, and the kokanee salmon offer wild sprees in most years in late summer.

What I learned first about Tahoe is that the fish hold in relatively small pockets, and that 95 percent of the water has no fish at all. Newcomers arriving green are unlikely to catch anything at all. But once you start to figure this lake out, great things become possible (see the section on mackinaw trout in Secrets of the Masters in the front of this book).

It is the mackinaw that can provide the best battle. They average five pounds, but commonly go eight, and rarely much bigger, with 10 to 25-pounders. Some say that 50 and 60-pounders swim in the depths of the lake, but nobody has ever landed one that big from this lake; the record is 38 pounds.

When mackinaws get over 10 pounds, they are usually called "lakers," as in lake trout. Well, most of the lakers are taken in a few key spots: the northwest section of the lake along the steep underwater ledge, 160 to 220 feet deep; in the southern part of the lake in the vicinity of Emerald Bay; and near underwater nobs and domes, such as the one that rises to 160 feet below the surface about a mile offshore of casino row at South Shore. The water is so clear that light penetration causes the mackinaws to live quite deep, commonly 150 feet down, much deeper during periods of full moons at night and bright sun by day. That is why anglers are on the water at first light at Tahoe, prefer overcast days (252 days a year are sunny at Tahoe, on the average), always troll deep for the lakers, and usually have their fishing done by 9 or 10 a.m.

It's a different deal, however, for the rainbow trout and kokanee salmon; it's not nearly so specialized.

The rainbow trout trolling is decent sport at Tahoe. It is aided by the stocking of 40,000 trout, a fairly sparse number considering the huge amount of water available. But wait: These fish avoid areas with sandy bottoms at Tahoe, and instead congregate where rocky subterrain provides for more aquatic life and better feeding. Such spots are found along the northwestern shore near Kings Beach, and also along the southeastern shore, just inside the Nevada line. The bonus is that every once in awhile, somebody catches a monster brown trout by accident in these areas while trolling for trout. The browns like to eat the small trout, you see.

The kokanee bite can be a wild affair when it happens, a one-after-another proposition. When does it happen? Like a longshot romance, sometimes it never happens. When it does, it is usually in late summer or early fall, and by September, there are enough kokanee either caught or not caught to know whether the year is a winner or loser.

Always remember that Tahoe is a special place. You may never see water so clear anywhere else, and thus, it requires a special approach. You must be up early or late. In between? After you've had your fill of the casinos, maybe you can sit on the ridge above Emerald Bay, or take the chairlift to the top of Heavenly Valley, and just look at the lake. It is one of the great feelings of the world.

9.　　　　　　RUBICON RIVER

Reference: East of Lake Tahoe; map D4 grid e1.

How to get there: Note: The road that parallels the Rubicon River is suitable only for four-wheel drive vehicles. From the town of Homewood on Highway 89 (on the west shore of Lake Tahoe), drive three miles south on Highway 89 to McKinney Rubicon Springs Road. Turn right and travel east along the river on a rough, primitive road. The road ends after about ten miles at the trailhead to the Desolation Wilderness.

Facilities: No facilities are available. Camping, lodging, and supplies are available in the Lake Tahoe area.

Cost: Access is free.

Who to contact: Phone the Lake Tahoe Basin Management Unit at (916) 573-2600.

About Rubicon River: A lot of anglers talk about the Rubicon River in hushed, secretive tones. Once you see it, you will understand why.

The Rubicon is one of the prettiest streams in California. It is bound to stay that way as long as access remains limited to people with four-wheel drive vehicles and those willing to hike quite a bit and then sneak-fish the better spots. It is tough to reach and takes talent to fish, but the reward is a crystal pure stream with pretty, stream-bred trout.

I also think the water in the Rubicon is the best-tasting anywhere in this hemisphere. It makes the water at the drinking fountains at the rest stops along Interstate 5 in the San Joaquin Valley taste like toxic waste. Of course, always use a water filteration device.

The Rubicon is wild and free, requiring anglers to quietly sneak up on pools where miniature waterfalls or riffles are poured into. Then short, precise, yet soft casts are required and a natural drift with your offering to make it appear as if no line is attached. The trout will accept nothing less. After all, these wild fish have never seen a Purina Trout Chow pellet. It is a great mountain trout stream. Nothing extra is needed.

---

10. LOON LAKE

Reference: South of Lake Tahoe in Eldorado National Forest; map D4 grid fØ.

How to get there: From Sacramento, drive east on US 50 to the town of Riverton. Turn north on Ice House-Loon Lake Road and drive 32 miles to the Ice House Lake turnoff. Turn right and drive one mile to the lake.

Facilities: One drive-to campground is provided. Another primitive campground can be accessed by boat or trail. A boat ramp is available.

Cost: The primitive campsites are free; developed campsites are $7 per night.

Who to contact: Phone the Eldorado National Forest District Office at (916) 644-2349; Russell's Sportsman's Corner in Placerville at (916) 621-2483; Ice House Resort at (916) 293-3321.

About Loon Lake: Loon Lake is a good destination for a weekend camping trip, (especially if you have a small boat), or a jumpoff point for a week-long backpacking trip.

The lake is set near the Sierra crest at 6,400 feet elevation, a good-size lake with 600 acres and a depth of 130 feet at its deepest point. It is bordered by Eldorado National Forest, with a trail available that is routed out to Winifred Lake, Spider Lake, and Buck Island Lake, all set to the east. If you don't like roughing it, Ice House Resort is available on the access road in, about three miles from the lake.

You want trout? This lake has 'em. It is stocked with 34,250 rainbow trout each year, and with a late opening due to heavy snow, it tends to get stocked just about every week once accessible. It's a good thing, because this is a popular lake and can get quite a bit of fishing pressure once the weather turns good for keeps in the summer. A sprinkling of kokanee salmon are also in the lake, but are less predictable.

No boating restrictions are in effect, and in the early summer, afternoon winds can drive anglers off the lake. They are cheered, however, by sailboarders. Union Valley Reservoir to the north provides a viable option.

ELDORADO NATIONAL FOREST

Reference: Southwest of in Lake Tahoe; map D4 grid fØ.

How to get there: Access to roads and trailheads is available off US 50 and Highway 88 to the north and south.

Facilities: Campgrounds and supplies are available off US 50 and Highway 88.

Cost: Access is free.

Who to contact: Write to Eldorado National Forest at 100 Forni Road, Placerville, CA 95667, or phone (916) 622-5061. For a map, send $2 to Office of Information, U.S. Forest Service, 630 Sansome Street, San Francisco, CA 94111.

About Eldorado National Forest: With so many hikers heading into the Desolation Wilderness, the adjacent Eldorado Forest provides a viable option that a lot of backpackers miss out on.

This national forest has many of the qualities of the wilderness, but gets a lot less hiker traffic. The hikes into the better fishing lakes are often not as long as is required when entering Desolation.

Start by getting a map, then scan for the following lakes, which are stocked by airplane by the Department of Fish and Game: Richardson Lake, McKinstry Lake, Winifred Lake, Spider Lake, Emigrant Lake and Cody Lake.

Many of these lakes provide good day hikes from trailheads at drive-to lakes listed in this zone.

---

12.   DESOLATION WILDERNESS

Reference: In Eldorado National Forest; map D4 grid f1.

How to get there: Trailheads can be reached at the following locations: out of Loon Lake, off Highway 89 west of Lake Tahoe, out of Fallen Leaf Lake, out of Echo Lakes, and off US 50.

Facilities: No facilities are available.

Cost: Access is free.

Who to contact: Write to Eldorado National Forest at 100 Forni Road, Placerville, CA 95667, or phone (916) 622-5061. For a map, contact the Office of Information, U.S. Forest Service, 630 Sansome Street, San Francisco, CA 94111.

About Desolation Wilderness: If it is possible to love something to death, hikers are trying their best at Desolation Wilderness.

The attraction is natural, love at first sight. The wilderness is one of the most stunning with lookouts of Lake Tahoe, more than 120 pristine lakes, and a diverse trail system that ranges from 6,330 feet to 9,900 feet elevation. The Pacific Crest Trail is routed through here, and hikers that have completed the PCT—from the Mexico border to Canada—say the stretch that runs through Desolation is one of the prettiest.

But once the snow melts off enough to provide access to backpackers, it seems that there is a camper at every lake. Because of the area's popularity, entry is on a strict permit system which allows no more than 700 overnight visitors at any one time. Getting a permit in advance is a necessity.

That done, you can spend many hours gazing over a map of the wilderness and dream of visiting a different lake every night. Many of them provide decent fishing, though the trout are universally small.

The following hike-to lakes are stocked by air by the Department of Fish and Game: Rockbound Lake, Rubicon Reservoir, Hidden Lake, Shadow Lake, Stony Ridge Lake, Eagle Lake, Middle Velma Lake, Forni Lake, Highland Lake, Horseshoe Lake, Lower Q Lake, Middle Q Lake, Lake Number 3, Granite Lake, Lake Number 5, Lawrence Lake, Lost Lake, Doris Lakes, Maud Lake, Gertrude Lake, Tyler Lake, Gilmore Lake, Kalmia Lake, Snow Lake, Tallac Lake, Floating Island Lake, Grass Lake, Cathedral Lake, Triangle Lake, Lake LeConte, Cagwin Lake, Ralston Lake, Lake of The Woods, Ropi Lake, Pyramid Lake, Toem Lake, Avalanche Lake, Clyde Lake, Twin Lakes, Hemlock Lake, Sylvia Lake, Grouse Lake and Cup Lake.

The trailhead out of Echo Lake provides access to some of the best lookouts and prettiest lakes in Desolation Valley, located just below the Crystal Range. It is also one of the busiest areas of the wilderness, however. Arranging a trip here in September, when the nights are cold and most of the vacation traffic has passed by, can provide a setting similar to what John Muir found so compelling a hundred years ago.

13.　　　　　WRIGHTS LAKE

Reference: Southwest of Lake Tahoe in Eldorado National Forest; map D4 grid gØ.

How to get there: From South Lake Tahoe, drive 15 miles west on US 50 to Wrights Lake Road. Turn north and travel eight miles to the lake.

Facilities: A campground is provided. Supplies can be obtained in South Lake Tahoe.

Cost: Campsite fee is $8 per night.

Who to contact: Phone the Eldorado National Forest District Office at (916) 644-2349.

About Wrights Lake: Wrights Lake is an ideal jump-off point for a backpacker, day-hiker, or an angler with a car-top boat.

It is a classic alpine lake, fairly small at just 65 acres, set high in the Sierra Nevada at 7,000 feet elevation. Anglers with hand-launched boats can poke around this lake, trolling for rainbow trout and brown trout. Both are stocked and year-to-year holdover rates are decent, providing the chance for the large but elusive brownies.

The beauty of this little lake is the number of options available. You can drive less than a mile to little Dark Lake, and from there, hike farther north to the Beauty Lakes or Pearl Lake. For multi-day trips, another consideration is routing a backpack trip to the east in the Crystal Range and the Desolation Wilderness (permit required).

---

14.   DARK LAKE

Reference: Southwest of Lake Tahoe in Eldorado National Forest; map D4 grid gØ.

How to get there: From South Lake Tahoe, drive 15 miles west on US 50 to Wrights Lake Road. Turn north and travel eight miles. Bear left at the Wrights Lake campground and travel one mile, and take the short cutoff road on the left to Dark Lake.

Facilities: No facilities are available on-site. A campground is available nearby at Wrights Lake.

Cost: Access is free.

Who to contact: Phone the Eldorado National Forest District Office at (916) 644-2349.

About Dark Lake: Most people first check out Dark Lake as just a curiosity. This is the little lake that is set just a mile to the west of Wrights Lake, a more popular destination point. As long as they are visiting Wrights, they figure, they might as well make the quick trip over to Dark and see what's happening.

What they will find is a little lake in the high Sierra, about a quarter of the size of Wrights Lake, with decent numbers of both rainbow trout and brown trout. Most range 10 to 12 inches, with decent prospects for shoreliners.

At the north end of Dark Lake you will find a trailhead for a path that is routed north to the Beauty Lakes, and then Pearl Lake. All three of them are small alpine lakes, smaller that Dark Lake.

---

15.   FALLEN LEAF LAKE

Reference: Near South Lake Tahoe in Lake Tahoe Basin; map D4 grid g2.

How to get there: From South Lake Tahoe, drive two miles north on Highway 89 to Fallen Leaf Road. Turn south and travel two miles to the lake. The boat ramp is located at the south end of the lake.

Facilities: A campground and a boat ramp are provided. Supplies are available nearby.

Cost: Campsite fees are $10-$12 per night.

Who to contact: Phone the Lake Tahoe Basin Management Unit at (916) 573-2600.

About Fallen Leaf Lake: Millions of people drive within a mile of this large, beautiful lake and don't even know it's there. It is located just one mile from Highway 89 along Lake Tahoe, and only three miles from the town of South Lake Tahoe.

Fallen Leaf Lake is almost as deep a blue as nearby Lake Tahoe. It is set at 6,300 feet elevation. It's a big lake, three miles long, three-quarters of a mile wide, and is also quite deep, 430 feet at its deepest point. Because the lake is circled by forest, some of it is on private property, and you need a boat here to do it right.

Most anglers will slow-troll near the shoreline for rainbow trout, or toss bait out from spots near the campground at the north end of the lake. Fishing success is only fair. There are many days when the lake is better for looking at than fishing.

---

16. ECHO LAKE

Reference: South of Lake Tahoe in Lake Tahoe Basin; map D4 grid g2.

How to get there: From South Lake Tahoe, drive 15 miles west on US 50 to the signed Echo Lake turnoff. Turn east and travel 1.5 miles to the boat ramp at Echo Chalet.

Facilities: Lodging, picnic areas, a marina, a boat ramp, groceries, bait and tackle are available at Echo Chalet. Campgrounds are available nearby at Lake Tahoe.

Cost: There is a fee for boat launching. Other access is free.

Who to contact: Phone Echo Chalet at (916) 659-7207.

About Echo Lake: Afternoon sunlight and a light breeze will cover the surface of Echo Lake with slivers of silver. By evening the lake, now calm, takes on a completely different appearance, deep and beautiful, almost foreboding. It's like watching the changing expressions of a person you care for.

Echo Lake is carved out of granite near the Sierra ridge, set at 7,500 feet elevation, the gateway to the southern portion of the Desolation Wilderness. The lake is big and blue, covering 300 acres with depths ranging to 200 feet. It was once actually two lakes, but a small dam on Lower Echo Lake raised the water level, and now there is a narrow connecting link to Upper Echo Lake.

It is Lower Echo that gets most of the traffic, both from waterskiers and anglers. A variety of stocks are made: 11,500 rainbow trout in the foot-long class, 9,000 rainbow trout fingerlings, and 10,000 Lahontan cutthroat trout fingerlings. They join a fair population of kokanee salmon and brown trout, though the latter can be difficult to locate.

On the main lake, there can be tons of waterskiers during the hot summer months. On Upper Echo Lake, waterskiing is not permitted, so you get guaranteed quiet water. But you can also have a quiet rod; the fishing just is not as good up here.

On the north side of the lake, the Pacific Crest Trail is routed up to Upper Lake, and then beyond into the Desolation Wilderness. If you hike into the wilderness, a permit is required from the Forest Service, and because of the area's popularity, trailhead quotas are enforced. Many outstanding destinations are possible along the PCT, including Tamarack Lake and many other nearby lakes, but you can expect plenty of company.

---

17. ANGORA LAKES

Reference: South of Lake Tahoe in Lake Tahoe Basin; map D4 grid g2.
How to get there: From South Lake Tahoe, drive two miles north on Highway 89 to Fallen Leaf Road. Turn south and travel three miles. When the road forks, bear left for one-quarter mile, then bear right on a dirt road and continue for about six miles. Park at the lot provided and hike about one-half mile to Angora Lakes.
Facilities: Piped water and restrooms are provided. A campground is available nearby at Fallen Leaf Lake. Supplies are available in South Lake Tahoe.
Cost: Access is free.
Who to contact: Phone the Lake Tahoe Basin Management Unit at (916) 573-2600.
About Angora Lakes: For many visitors to Lake Tahoe, a day trip to the Angora Lakes provides the perfect side trip.

It is just a short drive from South Tahoe, followed by a short walk, but that alone keeps most people from making the trip. There are two small lakes, set in a bowl below Echo and Angora peaks, each stocked by air with fingerling-sized cutthroat trout. Fishing is fair, with the lower lake a shade better first thing in the morning.

First thing in the morning? That's right, because what these lakes are popular for are swimming, not fishing. There are a lot of big boulders to jump off.

Hey, this isn't the wilderness, anyway. Sometimes a nice little old lady even shows up with a cart and sells ice cream bars and the best lemonade ever made.

---

18. SOUTH FORK AMERICAN

Reference: East of Placerville in Eldorado National Forest; map D4 grid hØ.

How to get there: From Placerville, drive east on US 50. From South Lake Tahoe, drive west on US 50. Direct access is available off the road betweeen Pollock Pines and Echo Summit.

Facilities: Several campgrounds are available off US 50. Supplies can be obtained in towns on US 50.

Cost: River access is free.

Who to contact: Phone the Eldorado National Forest District Office at (916) 644-2324.

About South Fork American River: This river looks fishy, and access is easy. But after a while on the stream, reality sets in: Catch rates are very poor.

For most folks, this is one of the bigger disappointments in an otherwise very pretty and much-traveled area. The South Fork American runs through granite chutes, over boulders and around bends, then drops into nice pools. It is admired by millions of drivers every year as they cruise US 50 to and from Tahoe.

Some even stop to cast a line a few times. After all, access is so easy from pullouts along US 50. The only time it's a problem is when the traffic is heavy, when waiting for a gap in the traffic to pull back onto the highway can take a while.

Then you get down to the river and make a few casts, and voila!—you don't catch anything. This happens time and time again. The stream just doesn't seem to produce very often.

A better bet is farther downstream (see zone D3) near Kyburz on the Silver Fork American. Now that's a stretch of water where there are trout to be caught.

---

19. KIRKWOOD LAKE

Reference: South of Lake Tahoe in Eldorado National Forest; map D4 grid h1.

How to get there: From the junction of Highways 88 and 49 at the town of Jackson, drive approximately 60 miles east on Highway 88 to the Kirkwood Lake entrance.

Facilities: A campground and picnic areas are provided. No motorized boats are permitted on the lake.

Cost: Campsite fee is $7 per night.

Who to contact: Phone the Eldorado National Forest District Office at (209) 295-4251; Kirkwood Resort at (209) 258-6000.

About Kirkwood Lake: The Carson Pass area has become a great alternative to nearby but crowded Tahoe to the north (it's an hour's drive to the casinos). At the center of it is Kirkwood Ski Resort, which now offers year-round accommodations, and a deluxe base of operations for a fishing or hiking trip.

Nearby is little Kirkwood Lake, set in a beautiful Sierra setting at 7,600 feet. It's a good lake to get kids started on, with good shoreline access, quiet water, some little rainbow trout and not much else. That's right, it's Dinkerville, U.S.A. For larger trout there are many nearby options, all worth fishing.

---

20.   WEST FORK CARSON RIVER

Reference: Near Markleeville in Toiyabe National Forest; map D4 grid h3.

How to get there: At the intersection of Highways 88 and 89 at the small town of Woodfords, drive east on Highway 88/89. Good roadside access is available in Hope Valley. Several camps are also available in this area. It can also be reached from the west out of Stockton, by making the long, circuitous drive east up Highway 88.

Facilities: Campgrounds are available off Highway 88 near Woodfords and also in Hope Valley. Cabins are available at Sorensen's Resort in Hope Valley.

Cost: River access is free.

Who to contact: Phone the Toiyabe National Forest District Office at (916) 694-2911; Monty Wolf's Trading Post at (916) 694-2201; Sorensen's Resort at (916) 694-2203.

About West Fork Carson River: Imagine a camp where you can set up your tent just a cast's distance from a beautiful trout stream. Or stay in a log cabin located a five-minute walk from several good trout holes. A mountain stream where there's a good chance of catching a three-pound cutthroat trout. Most of the fish, however, are rainbow trout in the nine to 11-inch class.

The impossible dream. Not on the West Fork Carson River. It provides all those elements.

The best section of the West Carson runs through Hope Valley. This is where most of the 21,500 trout planted in the West Carson are plunked in every summer, along with 500 big cutthroats. It is also where a series of small Forest Service campgrounds are set along the stream, and where genuine log cabin rentals are available at Sorensen's Resort. An option is to fish the West Carson where Highways 88 and 89 intersect. But a ton of people hit this spot every day, and though quite a few trout are planted here, I always avoid it.

One surprise can be the early season weather in this area. On one

---

trout opener on the West Carson, I got hit by quite a snow storm the night before. It turns out that snow is common in late April and early May, and that the fishing doesn't really get started here until late May and early June.

It is a fairly small stream, but larger than a babbling brook, with the better spots often below the bridges that cross over it. This is often where you find the trout-filled pools, where a well-presented 1/16-ounce Panther Martin is difficult for them to resist.

---

21. SILVER LAKE

Reference: In Eldorado National Forest; map D4 grid i1.
How to get there: From the junction of Highways 88 and 49 at the town of Jackson, drive 52 miles east on Highway 88 to Silver Lake. The boat ramp is located at the northwest corner of the lake, just off Highway 88.
Facilities: Two campgrounds, picnic areas, a boat ramp, boat rentals, and supplies are available at the lake.
Cost: Campsite fee is $7 per night.
Who to contact: Phone the Eldorado National Forest District Office at (209) 295-4251.
About Silver Lake: The Highway 88 corridor provides access to several excellent lakes, including three right in a row from west to east: Lower Bear River, Silver and Caples. Of the three, it is Silver Lake that is most often overlooked.

Why? Because both Lower Bear River Reservoir and Caples Lake have developed resorts nearby that promote the fishing. Silver Lake does not, yet it provides quality trout trolling and a chance at a big brown or mackinaw trout.

It is set at 7,200 feet elevation in a classic granite cirque, just below the Sierra ridgeline. It provides a solid opportunity for trouting by boat or shoreline, with 37,000 rainbow trout stocked each year, and a bonus of 1,760 fingerling-size mackinaw trout. The top spots are the northwest corner near the boat ramp, especially at dawn and dusk, and also in the narrows along Treasure Island on toward the inlet stream, the headwaters of the Silver Fork of the American River.

---

22. CAPLES LAKE

Reference: South of Lake Tahoe; map D4 grid i2.
How to get there: From the junction of Highways 49 and 88 at the town of Jackson, drive 63 miles east on Highway 88 to Caples Lake on the right side of the road.
Facilities: A campground is available across the road. A boat ramp, boat

rentals, groceries, and bait are available nearby.

Cost: Campsite fee is $7 per night.

Who to contact: Phone the Eldorado National Forest District Office at (209) 295-4251; Kirkwood Resort at (209) 258-6000.

About Caples Lake: Just pray the wind doesn't blow. In early summer, when fishing is best at Caples, that cold wind can just about turn you into petrified wood.

Caples is one of the best mountain lakes for fishing in the Sierra, as long as the wind doesn't blow. The trout are abundant, include a variety of species, and can come big. Once the ice has melted, wait two weeks, and the next four weeks that follow are often the best of the year.

This is a high mountain lake, 7,950 feet elevation, with dramatic surroundings and easy access off Highway 88. The lake covers 600 acres, restricts boats to 10 mph, and there are good hiking possibilities in the adjacent national forest. The best is a trail that starts just off the highway near the dam at the westernmost portion of the lake, and is routed into the Mokelumne Wilderness.

The lake gets a lot of anglers at midsummer, but not nearly so many in early summer and fall. The stocks are quite large: 41,000 rainbow trout, 1,100 brook trout, and 2,800 brown trout, all in the 10 to 12-inch range. The DFG also plants 4,000 mackinaw trout fingerlings. The best fishing is gained by trolling the northern shoreline near the surface during early summer.

Just pray the wind is down.

---

23. WOODS LAKE

Reference: In Eldorado National Forest; map D4 grid i2.

How to get there: From the junction of Highways 88 and 49 at the town of Jackson, drive 70 miles east on Highway 88 to the signed turnoff for Woods Lake. Turn south and drive two miles on Woods Lake Road to the lake.

Facilities: A campground and picnic area are provided. No motorized boats are permitted on the lake. Supplies are available nearby.

Cost: Campsite fee is $7 per night.

Who to contact: Phone the Eldorado National Forest District Office at (209) 295-4251.

About Woods Lake: Woods Lake is only two miles from Highway 88, yet it provides the feeling that you are visiting some far-off distant land.

This is the high Sierra, 8,200 feet elevation, and the small lake comes with a campground and area to launch car-top boats. The lake always seems to be full, making it very pretty against the granite Sierra backdrop.

It is stocked with 960 rainbow catchables and 240 brook catchables, which provide fair hopes for shoreliners. The best area to fish is a radius of 50 yards near the outlet of Woods Creek, which pours downstream into Caples Lake.

---

24. FROG LAKE

Reference: South of Lake Tahoe in Eldorado National Forest; map D4 grid i3.

How to get there: From the junction of US 50 and Highway 89 at the town of Meyers (two miles south of South Lake Tahoe), drive 20 miles southeast on Highway 89 to Highway 88. Turn right and drive 15 miles southwest on Highway 88 to the turnoff for Frog Lake. Turn left and continue to the lake.

Facilities: No facilities are available on-site. A campground is available nearby at Woods Lake.

Cost: Access is free.

Who to contact: Phone Eldorado National Forest at (209) 295-4251.

About Frog Lake: It's a good thing Frog Lake is a great place to look at. Because it sure isn't much for fishing.

Frog Lake is a veritable dot of a lake set just below Carson Pass, amid stark granite country that gives the entire area a pristine sense. That's lucky, because otherwise, all you will find in the way of fish are rainbow trout that are about five inches long.

What to do? Hike on, that's what. The trail out of Frog Lake heads south to Winnemucca Lake, a lake that is easy to hike to and provides decent prospects, though the fish are not a heck of a lot bigger. Winnemucca is an ideal choice to get newcomers hooked on backpacking. On your way in, you might stop and look at Frog Lake. It is, at least, good to look at.

---

25. RED LAKE

Reference: South of Lake Tahoe in Toiyabe National Forest; map D4 grid i3.

How to get there: From the junction of US 50 and Highway 89 at the town of Meyers (two miles south of South Lake Tahoe), drive 20 miles southeast on Highway 89 to Highway 88. Turn right and drive 12 miles southwest on Highway 88 to the turnoff for Red Lake. Turn left and continue for one mile to the lake.

Facilities: No facilities are available on-site. A campground is available nearby at Woods Lake.

Cost: Access is free.

Who to contact: Phone Toiyabe National Forest at (702) 882-2766.

About Red Lake: Red Lake is the brook trout capital of Toiyabe National Forest. That's kind of like being the best second baseman in Austria, but what the heck, an award is an award.

Here a brook trout, there a brook trout, every once in a while a brook trout. And not just dinkers, though you can be guaranteed that there are plenty of those. A fair mix of seven to nine-inchers help flesh out the frying pan.

Red Lake is a high mountain lake, set at 8,200 feet just southeast of Carson Pass. It is a fair-sized lake, about four times the size of nearby Woods Lake, shaped like a lima bean, and stocked with 10,560 "catchable" brook trout and 15,345 brook dinkers.

The problem with this lake is the people who own land adjacent to the lake. Sometimes they act like they own the water. They don't. Regardless, shoreline fishing is not encouraged. Instead, bring a car-top boat and do your thing. No motors permitted.

---

26. BLUE LAKES (Upper and Lower)

Reference: South of Lake Tahoe in Toiyabe National Forest; map D4 grid i3.

How to get there: From the junction of US 50 and Highway 89 at the town of Meyers (two miles south of South Lake Tahoe), drive 20 miles southeast on Highway 89 to Highway 88. Turn right (west) and travel about six miles southwest to Blue Lakes Road (just before Red Lake). Turn left and drive about six miles to Upper Blue Lake.

Facilities: Several PG&E campgrounds are available in the vicinity. A boat ramp is available.

Cost: Campsite fee is $10 per night.

Who to contact: Phone PG&E at (415) 973-5552 or (415) 973-8250; Toiyabe National Forest at (702) 882-2766.

About Blue Lakes: This is the high country, 8,200 feet, where the water is cold and the fishing can be hot. The Blue Lakes, both upper and lower, are two of the most consistent producers of rainbow trout in the region.

Upper Blue Lake is the first of the two lakes, which are linked by Middle Blue Creek. Of the two, Upper Blue seems to be better for shoreline fishing, particularly near the boat ramp on toward the west for about 200 yards. Lower Blue is decent from shore, but can be deadly trolling from a boat. It's best at the north end of the lake, just off the drop-off there.

Both lakes are well stocked each year. Upper Blue gets 22,000 rainbow trout per year, plus a bonus of 20,000 cutthroat fingerlings. Lower Blue Lake receives 25,000 rainbow trout. The first time I fished the Blue Lakes was on a trip to nearby Hope Valley, where the mission was to fish the Carson River, then head over to the Rubicon. But the Carson was a zilch that day, and a freak snowfall blocked access to the Rubicon. So it was off to Blue Lakes, which had just become ice free and had a clear access road. They turned out to be the best insurance policy for a fishing trip that you could ask for.

Now when I visit this area, I go to Blue Lakes first, and keep the Carson and Rubicon in mind as side trips.

---

27. LOST LAKES

Reference: South of Lake Tahoe in Toiyabe National Forest; map D4 grid i3.

How to get there: From the junction of US 50 and Highway 89 at the town of Meyers (two miles south of South Lake Tahoe), drive 20 miles southeast on Highway 89 to Highway 88. Turn right (west) and travel about six miles southwest to Blue Lakes Road (just before Red Lake). Turn left and drive about five miles, and then turn left (east) on the primitive access road one mile to Lost Lakes.

Facilities: No facilities are available on-site. Campgrounds are available nearby at Blue Lakes.

Cost: Access is free.

Who to contact:

About Lost Lakes: If it's the middle of summer or a three-day weekend and you run into too much traffic at nearby Blue Lakes, then the two little Lost Lakes provide a quiet alternative.

Alas, they do not provide quality fishing. Each of the two lakes are stocked with brook trout fingerlings, the fish for which the term "dinker" was first invented. Regardless, the lakes are small, intimate and set in high granite country, a nice spot for a picnic. Mountaineers might consider scrambling to the peak to the southwest of the lakes, which is aptly named "The Nipple." Another option is connecting with the Pacific Crest Trail, which is routed right along Blue Lakes Road at the turnoff for Lost Lakes.

---

28. BURNSIDE LAKE

Reference: Southeast of Lake Tahoe; map D4 grid i4.

How to get there: From the junction of US 50 and Highway 89 at the town of Meyers (two miles south of South Lake Tahoe), drive 20 miles southeast on Highway 89 to Highway 88. Cross the highway and continue straight on Burnside Lake Road (a dirt road) for eight miles to Burnside Lake.

Facilities: No facilities are available on-site. Cabins are available at Sorensen's Resort.

Cost: Lake access is free.

Who to contact: Phone Toiyabe National Forest at (702) 882-2766.

About Burnside Lake: The first time I fished little Burnside Lake, I didn't bring my canoe along.

Instead I walked along the shoreline near the outlet, casting a variety of small lures. By 11 a.m., I had caught one little five-inch rainbow trout. My buddies Ed the Owl and Buster Brown had each caught just one also. By noon, we were all in South Tahoe, sitting at a blackjack table. I had much better luck there.

The irony was that there were these two women in a small rowboat on the middle of the lake, just rowing along, with their lines trailing behind the boat, trolling. They caught a rainbow trout about every 10 minutes, and while they too caught a few small ones, they ended up filling their stringer with two limits and returning to shore right when we were leaving.

The lesson: Bring your boat and your nightcrawlers, and troll.

---

29.   EAST FORK CARSON RIVER

Reference: Near Markleeville in Toiyabe National Forest; map D4 grid i5.

How to get there: From the small town of Markleeville on Highway 89 (southeast of Lake Tahoe), drive south on Highways 89 and 4 for six miles. Direct access along the highway is available in this area. Access is also available off Wolf Creek Road (paved for one mile, then a rough, unimproved road), six miles south of Markleeville off Highway 4. Park off the road and hike down the trails to the river. It is also accessible from the west out of Stockton, heading east into the mountains on Highway 4, a long, circuitous drive.

Facilities: A campground is available near Markleeville. Supplies are available in Markleeville.

Cost: River access is free.

Who to contact: Phone the Toiyabe National Forest District Office at (916) 694-2911, or Monty Wolf's Trading Post at (916) 694-2201.

About East Fork Carson River: The East Fork Carson provides a more stark, remote setting than the West Fork, and gets much less fishing traffic—but just as many trout are stocked.

It not only gets 23,000 rainbow trout in the nine to 11-inch class, but also gets 825 of the big cutthroats that range three pounds and up. The stream is just enough out of the way that many anglers don't get over to try it out, despite very easy access right along the road.

The section along Wolf Road is my favorite, just upstream from Highway 4. There is a lot of pocket water and several pools here, and the water is clear, cold and pure. On summer weekends, there can be kayakers going through at mid-day, but they cause few problems, since the better fishing here is during the evening hatch. Wear mosquito repellent.

Another good section is just downstream from where Monitor Creek enters the East Fork. That is located at the junction of Highway 89 and Highway 4. There just always seems to be good numbers of fish in this area.

---

30.   INDIAN CREEK RESERVOIR

near Markleeville

Reference: In Indian Creek Reservoir Recreation Area; map D4 grid i5.

How to get there: At the intersection of Highways 88 and 89 at the small town of Woodfords, drive three miles south on Highway 89 to Airport Boulevard. Turn left and travel eight miles to the reservoir. The campgrounds and launch ramp are on the west side of the lake.

Facilities: Campgrounds, picnic areas, and a boat ramp are provided. Supplies are available nearby.

Cost: Campsite fees are $4-$6 per night.

Who to contact: Phone the Bureau of Land Management at (702) 882-1631.

About Indian Creek Reservoir: In the space of just a few miles, the terrain completely changes in this country. When you cross from the western Sierra over the ridge to the eastern Sierra, the land becomes sparsely forested, with far fewer of the classic granite features. That is why Indian Creek Reservoir gets missed by so many. It's on the eastern side, at 5,600 feet elevation, and most vacationers are off yonder. But access is quite easy (there's even a small county airport within a mile of the lake), and the trout trolling is fair. Not great. Fair.

A side trip is taking the one-mile hike to little Summit Lake, located just west of Indian Creek Reservoir. The trailhead is located just southwest of the campground area.

---

31.   KINNEY RESERVOIR

Reference: South of Markleeville in Toiyabe National Forest; map D4 grid j4.

How to get there: From the junction of Highways 88 and 89 at the small town of Woodfords, drive south on Highway 89 to Highway 4. Turn south and drive about ten miles to Kinney Reservoir on the right. If approaching from Interstate 5 to the west, take Highway 4 east from Stockton, a long, circuitous drive.

Facilities: No facilities are available on-site. A campground is available nearby on Silver Creek. Supplies can be obtained in Markleeville.

Cost: Access is free.

Who to contact: Phone the Toiyabe National Forest District Office at (916) 694-2911.

About Kinney Reservoir: The Kinney lakes, three in all, are perched high in granite country, just east of Ebbetts Pass along the Pacific Crest Trail.

Each of the three lakes has its own niche for anglers. The biggest of the three, Kinney Reservoir, is set right along Highway 4 and provides shoreline fishing prospects for rainbow trout in the nine to 11-inch class, and an equal mix of small brook trout. The lake is small enough and often calm enough to fish from a raft or float tube.

The other lakes are called Upper and Lower Kinney lakes, and can be reached with short hikes. The first you will come to is Lower Kinney, the prettiest of the three lakes and nearly as big as Kinney Reservoir. It has only small brook trout, however. Upper Kinney is set just a short jaunt upstream, feeding into Lower Kinney through a creek. After close inspection, the feeling is that Upper Kinney has no nuthin'.

One of the lesser-traveled sections of the Pacific Crest Trail runs just west of Upper Kinney, a good spot to start a backpack hike. Head north over Reynolds Peak, around Raymond Peak and you will be routed into a basin with eight small lakes.

---

32. SILVER CREEK

Reference: Near Markleeville in Toiyabe National Forest; map D4 grid j5.

How to get there: From the small town of Markleeville on Highway 89 (southeast of Lake Tahoe), drive south on Highways 89 and 4 for six miles, to the confluence of the Carson River and Silver Creek. Continue southwest on Highway 4; direct access is available. It is also accessible from the west out of Stockton, heading east on Highway 4, a long, circuitous drive.

Facilities: A campground is provided on Silver Creek. Supplies are available in Markleeville.

Cost: Creek access is free.

Who to contact: Phone the Toiyabe National Forest District Office at (916) 694-2911, or Monty Wolf's Trading Post in Markleeville at (916) 694-2201.

About Silver Creek: Here is a small, pristine stream that is out of the way yet easy to reach. It is set along Highway 88 east of Ebbetts Pass, running pure over small boulders for about six miles until it pours into the East Fork Carson River.

Most of the stream is bordered by large granite slabs, on which you walk along from spot to spot. The little two-lane highway crosses the river several times, and it is just downstream from these spots where the largest numbers of trout hold in pools.

The stream is stocked with 3,850 rainbow catchables, and 50 big bonus cutthroats, decent amounts for such a short stretch of river.

---

33. TOPAZ LAKE

Reference: On California/Nevada border in Toiyabe National Forest; map D4 grid j7.

How to get there: Drive north on US 395 to the California/Nevada border and Topaz Lake on the right.

Facilities: An RV park is located off US 395. There's a boat ramp here. Tent camping is available at Douglas County Park on the northeast side of the lake.

Cost: Lake access is free.

Who to contact: Phone Topaz Lake Trailer Park at (916) 495-2357.

About Topaz Lake: The wind can howl at Topaz but so can your fishing reel when the big trout go on the bite.

The lake doesn't have the greatest scenic quality, but it does have the trout, big ones, often averaging 14 to 18 inches, with a sprinkling going bigger and smaller. Topaz is set at 5,000 feet in the eastern Sierra, surrounded by the high desert country, with the Nevada border running right through the lake. Some people say the place is cute, as in "cute like an iguana," and when the wind kicks up, it can get downright ugly. If you fish out of a small aluminum boat, always remember: Safety first.

That done, come prepared for extensive trolling, a realistic chance for trophy-size trout, and please, please, please remember to bring a net big enough to land a big fish. They're in here, and every week someone gets a five to eight-pounder up to their boat and then loses it because the net is too small.

There are lots of trout in the foot-long class too, since the lake is stocked by both Nevada and California. On one trip at Topaz, Ed "The Dunk" Dunckel looked at his fishfinder and just about croaked (see trout trolling in Secrets of the Masters in the front of this book).

"There are so many black spots that it looks like an attack of gnats," he said.

They weren't gnats, of course, but trout, some 40,000 of them from a recent plant near the Topaz Marina ramp. Ironically, none of the fish would bite. After some intense effort, they were left for better prospects, and by day's end, The Dunk had one of the most beautiful stringers of trout I've ever seen.

MAP EØ

2 LISTINGS
PAGES 410-413

NOR-CAL MAP . see page 120
adjoining maps
NORTH (DØ) ..... see page 312
EAST (E1) .... see page 414
SOUTH .... no map
WEST .... no map

to Inverness   to Tomales
Olema

PT. REYES
LIGHT STATION

PT. REYES
NATIONAL
SEASHORE

to San Francisco

a

1

Pacific

b

Ocean

2

Noonday
Rock

North
Farallon

Farallon
Islands

c

Island of
St. James

d

FARALLON
NATIONAL
WILDLIFE
REFUGE

Middle
Farallon

Mauitop
Island

Southeast
Farallon

e

f

g

h

i

j

Ø   1   2   3   4   5   6   7   8   9

410   NORTHERN CALIFORNIA (P. 120)

1.　　　CORDELL BANK

Reference: Off the San Francisco coast; map EØ grid a3.

How to get there: Cordell Bank is located approximately ten miles north of the Farallon Islands and can be reached by charter boats out of Bodega Bay.

Facilities: Bait and tackle rentals are available on the party boat.

Cost: Party boat fees range from $38-$44 per person.

Party boats: New Sea Angler, (707) 875-3495; Bodega Bay Sportsfishing, (707) 875-3344; *Cobra,* Richmond, (510) 283-6773.

About Cordell Bank: The sacks of fish caught at Cordell Bank are so heavy that few anglers can carry them to their car. It is common when a 15-fish rockfish limit, with maybe a bonus lingcod or two, weighs 100 pounds, with a chance of it approaching 125 pounds or even more.

This is the attraction for Cordell Bank, a deep underwater reef that has the largest rockfish of any area along the great Bay Area coast. It's a long trip out of Bodega Bay, a two and a half hour pull, longer going back, and out of reach of all Bay Area boats except for the 96-foot, three-engine Cobra out of Richmond. Cordell is also very deep, with the best area 320 to 340 feet deep, which demands fairly heavy gear. Only that keeps it from being rated a "10."

But the results are big red rockfish that average five to 10 pounds, bocaccios, golden eyes and cow cod to 15 pounds, and a light sprinkling of lingcod that range from 10 to 50 pounds. Cordell Bank was just about cleaned out in the early 1970s by Soviet netters, but since America kicked them out in 1978, this area has flourished.

On one trip, I saw a guy having tremendous difficulty reeling up his rig. When he finally did so, he called the deckhand for the gaff. From a distance, the deckhand looked down the rail and spotted about a five-pound rockfish on the guy's line, and became irritated about having to gaff such a fish. Usually, they are just lifted aboard.

But a closer look revealed one of the most bizarre scenarios I have ever seen on a party boat: The guy had connected five shrimpfly rigs, three shrimpflies on each rig, totalling 15 jigs in all—and had caught a five to seven-pound rockfish on each jig. The boat had drifted over a school of fish, and in the span of about 20 seconds, the guy had hooked his 15-fish rockfish limit on one drop. It weighed 65 pounds. No wonder he had such difficulty bringing it up.

2.　　　FARALLON ISLANDS

Reference: Off the San Francisco coast; map EØ grid c6.

How to get there: The Farallon Islands are located 27 miles west of the Golden Gate and can be reached by charter boat.

Facilities: Bait and tackle rentals are available on each boat.

Cost: Party boat fees range from $40-$50 per person.

San Francisco boats: Chucky's Pride (during the fall months only), (415) 564-5515.

Emeryville boats: C-Gull, (510) 654-6040; *New Donna D,* (510) 222-4158; *Jubilee,* (510) 654-6040.

Richmond boats: Cobra, Richmond Marina, (510) 283-6773.

Half Moon Bay boats: Outlaw, Huck Finn Sportsfishing, (415) 726-7133; *Captain John,* Captain John's Sportsfishing, (415) 726-2913.

About Farallon Islands: The resurgence of life at the Farallon Islands has returned a world-class fishery to California anglers.

The rebirth is due to one thing: the banning of gillnets within three miles of the Farallones, turning the area into a virtual fish and wildlife sanctuary. By 1987, gillnets had depleted greatly the common murre, the friendly little seabird that breeds at the Farallones, as well as basic stocks of dozens of species of rockfish, lingcod and cabezone. The only difference between today and 1987 is that the nets are gone—and the remarkable diversity of marine life has returned in huge numbers. The first species to rebound was the school fish, especially the yellow and blue rockfish. I have seen quiet fall mornings where the fish were swirling on the surface and would take a large silver streamer delivered by a fly rod, or a Hair Raiser cast from a spinning rod. Then the juvenile lingcod returned, with fantastic numbers of lings in the five-pound class, which holds much promise for future years. Finally, the coppers, china rockfish, vermillions, and to a lesser extent, cabezone, reds and bocaccios also started coming back in historical numbers.

The murres seem to be returning as well. It was their protection that required the banning of the nets. The little seabirds were being drowned when caught in the nets while diving and chasing anchovies and shrimp. That violated the federal Migratory Bird Act, and after the patient had just about died, the federal doctor finally prescribed the right medication. Rejuvenating the fishery is a fortunate side effect, and there are a variety of trips now available out of several harbors that sample the great fishing out here. The trips leave early, usually by 5:30 a.m., and traveling at 12 knots, usually reach the Farallones by 8:45 a.m. I have reached the Farallones in 56 minutes from the Golden Gate, however, in a fast skiff on a flat, calm sea.

Much of the area is now loaded with rockfish, but the vicinity of the South Farallon Island seems most abundant.

Skippers turn their engines off and drift, the boats floating across the top of tremendous schools of yellows and blues 50 to 100 feet deep, and large numbers of lingcod on the bottom, 120 to 200 feet deep. This allows the opportunity for light tackle fishing for the shallow school fish, or the traditional bottom-style for lings and the wide variety of rockfish that live on the bottom. For techniques, see "Rockfish—Blindman Frank," in Secrets of the Masters.

The Farallon Islands are actually the emerging tops of an underwater mountain range that provides perfect habitat for the aquatic food chain. To the north is "The Pimple," and beyond that, the North Farallon Islands. All three areas provide rich marine regions where rockfish thrive. The South Island is the largest, has a few structures on it, and is used as a research lab by the Scripps Institute. The Pimple is just a single rock, and the North Islands are a collection of sharp-tipped rocks that look similar to the mountain peaks in the jagged southern Sierra near Mount Whitney.

In the winter and spring, huge schools of krill can actually tint the surface water red, and in the process attract large schools of salmon. During the first week of the salmon season, the vicinity of the North Farallones is particularly attractive if the weather is calm enough to make the long trip. All through spring, balls of shrimp, squid and the number of juvenile rockfish will attract salmon to the area. As for rockfish, they tend to be deep during this time of the year, often 200 to 300 feet down.

As summer arrives, the salmon move inshore with the arrival of large schools of anchovies. In addition, rockfish start moving to more shallow and easier-to-fish areas, with the mid-water schoolfish becoming abundant by mid-June. By fall, salmon move out and rockfish take over, available shallow and deep, with a bonus of large numbers of lingcod. Of the latter, most are in the five to 10-pound class, with about 10 percent in the 15 to 20-pound range, a few more even larger.

It all adds up to one of the best fisheries in California, diverse and vibrant with marine life. To get it, all they did was kick out the gillnets.

MAP E1

81 LISTINGS
PAGES 414-465

NOR-CAL MAP . see page 120
adjoining maps
NORTH (D1) ...... see page 322
EAST (E2) .... see page 466
SOUTH (F1) .... see page 542
WEST (EØ)......... see page 410

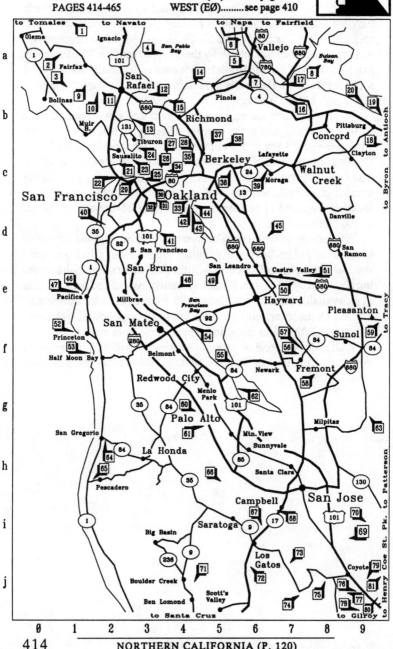

1. NICASIO LAKE

Reference: Near Nicasio; map E1 grid a1.

How to get there: From US 101 in Marin, take Sir Francis Drake Boulevard and head west for about seven miles. Turn right on Nicasio Valley Road. Continue for five miles to the lake.

Facilities: No facilities are available. Boat and water contact are not permitted. Open from sunrise to sunset.

Cost: Access is free.

Who to contact: Contact the Marin Water District at (415) 924-4600, North Marin Water District at (415) 897-4133, or call Western Boat in San Rafael at (415) 454-4177.

About Nicasio Lake: Nicasio is the biggest lake in the North Bay Area, covering 825 acres, and it has been one of the angling surprises among the Bay Area's 43 lakes that provide public fishing.

In the spring, it provides good bass and crappie fishing during the evening. Shoreliners can cast surface plugs such as a small Jitterbug, then with a hesitating retrieve, entice strikes from smallmouth bass in the eight to 13-inch class. They aren't big, but it is surface action and it's fun. Some big bass are also in the lake, but they are wised up.

No trout are stocked. There are also no picnic tables at the lake, and since the area isn't wooded, set in rolling hills, hiking is only fair.

2. KENT LAKE

Reference: Near Lagunitas; map E1 grid a1.

How to get there: From US 101, take Sir Francis Drake Boulevard and travel west for about 10 miles. Go through the Town of Lagunitas and park on Sir Francis Drake Boulevard just before reaching Samuel P. Taylor Park. A small sign is on the gate on the left side of the road (a ranch road that is the trail to the lake, about a one-mile hike).

Facilities: No facilities are available. Boat and water contact are not permitted. The lake is open from sunrise to sunset. The only way to get to this lake is to hike in.

Cost: Access is free.

Who to contact: Phone the Marin Water District at (415) 924-4600, North Marin Water District at (415) 897-4133, or call Western Boat in San Rafael at (415) 454-4177.

About Kent Lake: The only way to get here is to hike, and when you first see the lake, its size will surprise you. It covers 460 acres, set in a canyon on Lagunitas Creek. The fishing is not easy, with stocks quite rare—and when they are made, they are small fingerlings that are supposed to grow to catchable sizes. It doesn't seem to work out that way.

Specialists can still catch trout and bass, however. The best way is to bring a minnow trap to the lake, catch your own minnows, then use the live bait. The best area is to the left of the dam, along the back side.

Parking access is lousy, and once you've found a spot, it's about a half-hour walk to the lake.

---

3.   ALPINE LAKE

Reference: Near Fairfax; map E1 grid a1.

How to get there: From US 101, take the Sir Francis Boulevard exit and head west to Fairfax. In Fairfax, turn left on Pacheco and travel less than a block to Broadway. Turn right and drive past the Fairfax Theatre. Turn left on Bolinas Road and continue for five miles; the road borders the lake.

Facilities: No facilities are available. Boats and water contact are not permitted. The lake is open from sunrise to sunset.

Cost: Access is free.

Who to contact: Phone the Marin Water District at (415) 924-4600, North Marin Water District at (415) 897-4133, or call Western Boat in San Rafael at (415) 454-4177.

About Alpine Lake: Alpine is one of the prettiest lakes in the Bay Area, a good-sized reservoir (224 acres) by Bay Area standards, set in a tree-bordered canyon on the slopes of Mt. Tamalpais. Most newcomers find it much larger and prettier than they expect. A bonus is that trailheads for excellent hikes are available at the dam.

This lake has very few rainbow trout; there are a small number of large ones, and a similar light number of largemouth bass. It is not stocked and the resident fish seem to have gone to Smart School. The best bet is walking (no boats or water contact permitted) around the back side of the lake, casting plugs such as a deep-running Wee Wart, Rapala or Shad Rap.

---

4.   SAN PABLO BAY

Reference: From Richmond Bridge to Carquinez Bridge; map E1 grid A4.

Boat ramps: Launch ramps for private boats are available at Loch Lomond Marina, San Rafael, (415) 456-0321; Benicia Marina, Benicia, (707) 745-2628; Crockett Marina, Crockett, (510) 787-1049; Glen Cove Marina, Vallejo, (707) 552-3236; Rodeo Marina, Rodeo, (510) 799-4436.

Piers: Several piers and shoreline jettys are available (for more information on Bay Area piers, see page 431 or individual pier listings).

Who to contact: Loch Lomond Live Bait, San Rafael, (415) 456-0321; M&M Market & Bait, Vallejo, (707) 642-3524; Point Pinole Regional Park, (510) 237-6896.

Party boats: *Superfish,* San Rafael, (415) 898-6989; *Bass-Tub* (from October through March), San Rafael, (415) 456-9055; *New Keesa,* Pt. San Pablo, (510) 787-1720.

About San Pablo Bay: Keith Fraser was walking down the dock at Loch Lomond Marina one day, when suddenly a 5-foot sturgeon jumped out of the water and landed right on the dock. Fraser then wrestled with the fish, pinned it, and after having proclaimed it caught, poured it back into the water.

Usually sturgeon are a good deal more difficult to come by, but if you could create a perfect place to position yourself to intercept migrations of sturgeon, as well as striped bass, San Pablo Bay would be the place. It also provides the opportunity for perch and shark fishing in late fall.

San Pablo Bay, set between the freshwater of the Delta and the saltwater of San Francisco Bay, is in the center of the migration path for thousands of fish coming and going every year. Sturgeon and striped bass provide the best fishing. During years of heavy rainfall, the magic area where saltwater mixes with freshwater shifts down into western San Pablo Bay. Some 90 percent of the marine food production in the Bay-Delta takes place in this saltwater-freshwater mixing zone, and with enough rain, it will position itself in an area I named the Sturgeon Triangle. The Triangle is bordered by the "Pumphouse" (it looks like an outhouse on stilts, three miles east of Hamilton Field), China Camp to the southwest, and Buoy 5 to the southeast. The pumphouse and China Camp attract sturgeon during outgoing tides, and Buoy 5 is a good spot on incoming tides.

There are several other excellent spots. They include the Richmond Bridge area, both above and below the bridge on outgoing tides, particularly in the fall, and just off the Point Pinole Pier, especially in March. In the east side of the Bay, just south of the Mare Island Rock Wall is a good spot, along with offshore Rodeo, on the edge of the channel, but usually only after periods of significant rain runoff.

During years of high rainfall, large numbers of sturgeon will abandon the ocean and enter the Bay-Delta system to spawn. Sturgeon live primarily in the ocean, capable of lifespans to 70 and 80 years, and only spawn once every seven or eight years. They often wait for ideal conditions before heading upstream, which explains the apparent dramatic fluctuations in population levels from year to year. They need a reason to leave the ocean, and it is high streamflows moving through the Bay system that provide it.

Striped bass, though down in overall population numbers, are more predictable in their annual cycles. They arrive in the spring months to San Pablo Bay, and again (often in better numbers) in the fall from September through early November. If the water isn't too muddy from storm runoff, they provide a good trolling opportunity. The best period is during the top of high tides, and the first two hours of a moderate outgoing tide. The best spots are along the Marin shoreline from San Quentin Prison on northward, including along the Marin Islands, the Brickyard, Pumphouse, and on the southeast side of San Pablo Bay at Point Pinole and the Rodeo flats.

Water clarity is a key for striper trolling. If it's muddy, you might as well search for a polar bear in the desert. If it's clear, and you time it right, you have decent prospects for 4 to 8-pound fish using white, one-ounce Worm-Tail jigs.

An option is in the early summer when the larger striped bass move down from the Delta. The reefs adjacent to the Brothers Islands (on the east side) and Sisters Islands (on the west side) provide a habitat where the striped bass can pin baitfish against the rocks. Anglers allowing their boats to drift, dangling live shiner perch, mudsuckers or bullheads near the bottom, can get some beautiful fish. These spots are real tackle grabbers, however, so come forewarned and prepared.

Shoreline fishing also can be quite good. McNear's Pier in San Rafael and Point Pinole Pier provide a rare opportunity for sturgeon in the winter, striped bass in the spring. During the spring, the Loch Lomond Jetty is a fair spot for big bat rays, with some reaching 60 pounds.

There are periods when the fishing in San Pablo Bay is among the best anywhere in America. One March day after very heavy rains, there were 14 sturgeon in the 100-pound class caught in a two-hour span at the Richmond Bridge.

Then there was the day a sturgeon actually jumped on the dock. If you spend enough time on the water, you see the moments like these that make San Pablo Bay a special place.

---

5. CARQUINEZ STRAIT

Reference: From Carquinez Bridge to Mothball Fleet; map E1 grid a6.

Boat ramps: Glen Cove Marina, Vallejo, (707) 552-3236; Martinez Marina, Martinez, (510) 372-3585; Benicia Public Ramp, (707)746-4200.

Piers: Several piers are available (for more information on Bay Area piers, see page 431 or individual pier listings).

Who to contact: Tackle Shop, Benicia, (707) 745-4921; Martinez Bait, (510) 229-3150; M&M Market & Bait, Vallejo, (707) 642-3524. Party boats: *New Keesa,* Pt. San Pablo, (510) 787-1720; *Nobilis,* Martinez, (510) 757-2946; *Morning Star* and *South Pacific,* Crockett, (707) 745-1431.

About Carquinez Strait: Joey Pallotta hooked a sturgeon one day here off Benicia, and when it rolled near the surface, it looked as big as a whale. It turned out, it was. The fish weighed 468 pounds and measured 9 feet, 6 inches, a world record.

Now get this. Bigger fish have been seen in this area. Some divers laying cable on the bottom say they came across a sturgeon that they paced off at something like 12 feet long. Another time, a big ship's propeller cut a big sturgeon in two, and according to the story, both pieces added up to 11 feet.

So you'd think this is the spot everyone would fish for sturgeon, right? Well, it doesn't work that way.

The reason is because the best area is in the deep water, 70 to 90 feet deep off Benicia. Because of strong tides here, and in the spring, heavy freshwater outflows, it requires heavy sinkers just to get the bait near the bottom where the sturgeon are prowling around. It also requires a huge amount of anchor line to get your boat to stay put, especially in the spring when freshwater outflows double the strength of an outgoing tide. So this remains a sport for specialists.

An option is striped bass, which provide short periods of excellent fishing. They migrate through Carquinez Strait in the spring and can provide some excellent evening trolling. The key? Water clarity. It tends to clear at the top of the tide here. In recent years, the Department of Fish and Game has taken to planting juvenile salmon in Benicia, and when it happens, the striped bass go into a feeding frenzy. A number of anglers catch quick limits of stripers here, casting Rebels, Pencil Poppers, Hair Raisers, or using threadfin shad for bait.

A number of complaints have been forwarded to the DFG over the situation. Those hatchery-raised salmon have become the most expensive fish chum in the world, and by inducing the stripers into a frenzy, can undermine two of the most valued Bay fisheries simultaneously.

---

6.   **VALLEJO PIER**

Reference: Near Vallejo; map E1 grid a6.

How to get there: From Highway 80 in Vallejo, take the Highway 37 exit and head west (or head east from Highway 101 in Marin). Take the turn-off for Wilson Avenue at the east end of the Napa River Bridge.

Facilities: Restrooms, benches, fish cleaning sinks, lights, and bait shop are available.

Cost: Access is free.

Who to contact: Phone the Greater Vallejo Recreation District at (707) 648-4600.

About Vallejo Pier: This is one of the more popular piers in the Bay Area for the opportunity to catch sturgeon and striped bass. Set on the Napa River, near its confluence with San Pablo Bay. The largest fish ever caught from a Bay Area pier was landed here (for more information on Bay Area piers, see page 431).

---

7. CROCKETT PIER

Reference: In Crockett; map E1 grid a6.

How to get there: From Highway 80 in Crockett, take the Crockett exit to Pomona Street. Turn left on Port Street and left at the end of Port on Dowrelio Road.

Facilities: A snack bar with bait sales and restrooms is available.

Cost: Access is free.

Who to contact: Phone the Crockett Marine Service at (510) 787-1049.

About Crockett Pier: Old Crockett Pier extends out near the bridge on the west end of Carquinez Bridge, right in the path of migrating striped bass (for more information on Bay Area piers, see page 431).

---

8. SUISUN BAY

Reference: From Mothball Fleet to Pittsburg; map E1 grid a8.

Boat ramps: Pierce Harbor, north of Benicia, (707) 745-3222; Pittsburg Marina, Pittsburg, (510) 439-3440; Harris Harbor, West Pittsburg, (510) 458-1606; Martinez Marina, Martinez, (510) 372-3585.

Piers: Several piers are available (for more information on Bay Area piers, see page 431 or individual pier listings).

Who to contact: Martinez Bait, (510) 229-3150; Harris Harbor at Pittsburg, (510) 458-4904; M&M Market & Bait, Vallejo, (707) 642-3524.

Party boats: Nobilis, Martinez, (510) 757-2946; Morning Star and South Pacific, Crockett, (707) 745-1431.

About Suisun Bay: The rod tip dipped, then straightened. Fish on? Fish off? With the reel on free spool, I thumbed the line, waiting like a safe-cracker for any detectable sign.

Suddenly, again I felt pressure, and under my thumb, I felt the line start to peel off the fishing reel.

"One, two, three," I counted out loud, while some 15 feet of line was stripped, then locked the spool, and set the hook home. Fish on! A nice striped bass.

This is how anglers fish the fall and winter runs of striped bass in Suisun Bay and adjacent Honker Bay: You should be in a boat, anchored, and using bullheads for bait. It is exciting, because you keep your reel on free spool and must have the nerve to wait to set the hook until you are sure the striped bass has the hook in its mouth.

While you are anchored and waiting for a big striped bass to come by, a giant sturgeon might just wander by and gobble your bait by accident. Some of the biggest sturgeon ever caught have been taken this way by complete accident. It provides an additional opportunity.

The best spot to anchor and "bullhead for stripers" is just east of the Mothball Fleet, in the shallows of Hunters Bay, along the Firing Line, located across from Pittsburg, and in holes and ledges in Montezuma Slough. When the stripers are in during the fall and winter, this is some of the most productive fishing in the Bay-Delta system.

Sturgeon, on the other hand, provide a more steady fishery, but can require long hours on the water in this area. The best spots are at the Glomar Explorer (located between the Martinez/Benicia Bridge and the Mothball Fleet), the third row of ships at the Mothball Fleet, just off the sandbar at the Mothball Fleet, just east of the Mothball Fleet, and in the center of the channel adjacent to the Pittsburg PG&E plant.

The rule of thumb is to locate where the mixing zone is for Delta freshwater and Bay saltwater, then anchor in the best spot in that area. This mixing zone is where most of the aquatic food is produced for the Bay system and is a natural holding area for sturgeon. Depending on rainfall and reservoir releases, this mixing zone can shift through the year, and adds some detective work to your quest.

A bonus for anchor fishing here, as compared to San Pablo and San Francisco Bays, is that there are far fewer bait robbers in Suisun Bay. That not only keeps the bait bill down, but lets you know that when you are getting a bite, it is not likely to be from a pesky crab or bullhead—but from a big striped bass or sturgeon.

---

9.   BON TEMPE LAKE

Reference: Near Fairfax; map E1 grid b1.

How to get there: From US 101, take the Sir Francis Boulevard exit and head west to Fairfax. In Fairfax, turn left on Pacheco and travel less than a block to Broadway. Turn right and drive past the Fairfax Theatre. Turn left on Bolinas Road and drive 1.5 miles, then turn left at Sky Oaks Road and continue to the lake.

Facilities: A parking area is available. Boats and water contact are not permitted. The lake is open from sunrise to sunset.

Cost: Day-use fee is $3 per vehicle.

Who to contact: Phone the Marin Water District at (415) 924-4600, North Marin Water District at (415) 897-4133, or call Western Boat in San Rafael at (415) 454-4177.

About Bon Tempe Lake: Pretty Bon Tempe Lake has the highest trout catch rate of any lake in Marin County. When stocks were suspended at nearby Lagunitas Lake, they were doubled at Bon Tempe from November through April. That has resulted in a lot of smiling faces for anglers, with many five-fish limits of trout in the 9 to 11-inch class. There is no secret how: shoreline baitdunking.

This is the most popular of the eight Marin lakes. It seems to get more sun than the others, picnic areas are available, and a network of outstanding hiking trails start near the lake. The lake covers 140 acres, and is set on the slopes of Mt. Tamalpais, quite near Lagunitas Lake and Alpine Lake.

---

10. LAGUNITAS LAKE

Reference: Near Fairfax; map E1 grid b2.
How to get there: From US 101, take the Sir Francis Boulevard exit and head west to Fairfax. In Fairfax, turn left on Pacheco and travel less than a block to Broadway. Turn right and drive past the Fairfax Theatre. Turn left on Bolinas Road and drive 1.5 miles, then turn left at Sky Oaks Road and continue to Lagunitas Lake (located directly above Bon Tempe Lake).
Facilities: A parking area is available. Boat and water contact are not permitted. The lake is open from sunrise to sunset.
Cost: Day-use fee is $3 per vehicle.
Who to contact: Phone the Marin Water District at (415) 924-4600, North Marin Water District at (415) 897-4133, or call Western Boat in San Rafael at (415) 454 454-4177.
About Lagunitas Lake: This little lake, covering just 22 acres, has gained national attention as a testing ground for providing a natural, wild trout fishery in an urban area. The idea is to have very few stocks, primarily catch-and-release fishing, and allow the trout to spawn on the lake's feeder streams.

The best technique is using flies behind a Cast-A-Bubble or a Kastmaster (with the hook removed). Success fluctuates tremendously according to season, with the bite very slow in summer and winter. Regulations can be adjusted here to react to changing spawning success, so always, always, always check the rules before heading out.

---

11. PHOENIX LAKE

Reference: Near Ross; map E1 grid b2.
How to get there: From US 101 in Marin, take Sir Francis Drake Boulevard heading west. Turn left on Lagunitas Road and continue for a few miles

into Natalie Coffin Green Park. You can't see the lake from your car. After parking, hike a quarter of a mile on the signed road.

Facilities: No facilities are available. Boat and water contact are not permitted. Open from sunrise to sunset.

Cost: Access is free.

Who to contact: Phone the Marin Water District at (415) 924-4600, North Marin Water District at (415) 897-4133, or call Western Boat in San Rafael at (415) 454-4177.

About Phoenix Lake: Phoenix Lake is a prisoner of the DFG tanker truck. When the stocks come, fishing is quite good for three or four days, then slacks off until the next stock. Water conditions determine the plants, but they usually take place twice per month from mid-November through mid-April.

The best bet is shoreline baitfishing from the southern side of the lake. An option during the spring is flyfishing where the little creeks enter the lake. The parking area for Phoenix Lake is terrible; you have to wedge your way in someplace along the side of a small road.

Two bonuses, however, are a network of hiking trails starting at the lake, and the lake itself is quite pretty, tucked in a pocket on the slopes of Mt. Tamalpais.

---

12.   MCNEAR'S PIER

Reference: In San Rafael at McNear's Beach; map E1 grid b3.

How to get there: From Highway 101 in San Rafael, take the Central San Rafael exit and go east on 2nd Street. 2nd Street becomes San Pedro Road. Follow this road for about 4 miles to Cantera Way. Turn right and continue to the park.

Facilities: Restrooms, parking, drinking water, fish cleaning stations, a swimming pool, tennis courts, a beach and a concession stand are available.

Cost: Entrance fee is $5 per vehicle on weekends, $3 on weekdays.

Who to contact: Phone Marin County Parks at (415) 499-6387.

About McNear's Pier: This provides the top opportunity to catch a sturgeon of any pier in the Bay Area (for more information on Bay Area piers, see page 431).

---

13.   PARADISE PIER

Reference: In Tiburon in Paradise Beach County Park; map E1 grid b3.

How to get there: From San Francisco, travel north on US 101. Take the Tiburon exit and proceed on Paradise Drive to the pier.

Facilities: Benches, tap water and fish sinks are provided. Restrooms and picnic tables are available nearby.

Cost: Entrance fee is $5 on weekends, $3 on weekdays.

Who to contact: Phone Marin County Parks at (415) 493-6387.

About Paradise Pier: This pier is part of an 11-acre county park, well-landscaped. During winter, there is a chance for a sturgeon here; during summer, prospects for striped bass (for more information on Bay Area piers, see page 431).

---

14. POINT PINOLE

Reference: Near Pinole; map E1 grid b4.

How to get there: From Highway 80 in Richmond, take the Hilltop exit. Proceed west on Hilltop to the intersection with San Pablo Avenue. Turn right onto San Pablo Avenue and proceed north to the intersection with Atlas Road. Turn left onto Atlas. Take the park shuttle bus or enjoy the hike out to the pier. The shuttle operates daily from 7:30 a.m. to 6 p.m. in the summer, and 7:30 a.m. to 5 p.m. in the winter. From the parking lot, the hike out to the pier is about 1.5 miles.

Facilities: Restrooms, drinking fountains, benches with windscreens and shaded picnic sites are provided. Bicycle trails and a beach path also are available.

Cost: Fee is $2.50 per vehicle, $1 for dogs. The shuttle costs 50 cents for people 12 years and older, 25 cents for kids 6-11 years. The shuttle is free for seniors 62 years and older, kids under 6 years old, and the handicapped.

Who to contact: Phone the East Bay Regional Park District at (510) 531-9300, ext.2208.

About Point Pinole: Part of a regional park that offers long, undisturbed shoreline and a chance for striped bass, sturgeon, and more often, kingfish (for more information on Bay Area piers, see page 431).

---

15. RED ROCK PIER

Reference: In Richmond; map E1 grid b4.

How to get there: From Highway 17, take the Point Molate exit near the Richmond-San Rafael Bridge toll plaza. North of the freeway are three forks in the road. Take the left fork to the marina.

Facilities: No facilities are available.

Cost: A small admission fee is sometimes charged.

Who to contact: Contact the East Bay Regional Park District at (510) 531-9300, ext.2208.

About Red Rock Pier: Located within the Red Rock Marina, this area can be decent for perch in early winter (for more information on Bay Area piers, see page 431).

16.   MARTINEZ PIER

Reference: In Martinez; map E1 grid b7.

How to get there: From Highway 80 in Martinez, take the Highway 4 exit and follow to the Alhambra Avenue off-ramp. Travel through Martinez to the end of Ferry Street. Follow signs to the parking area and pier of Martinez Regional Shoreline Park.

Facilities: Benches, fish cleaning sinks, restrooms (at marina headquarters), and a bait shop are available.

Cost: Access is free.

Who to contact: Phone the Martinez Park and Recreation Department at (510) 372-3510, or phone the marina at (510) 372-3593.

About Martinez Pier: You get a fine view of the bay and marina activities, and a fair chance for passing fish in season, including striped bass in the spring and fall, sturgeon in the winter, and get this, steelhead in late fall (for more information on Bay Area piers, see page 431).

17.   BENICIA PIERS

Reference: In Benicia; map E1 grid b7.

How to get there: To get to the 9th Street Park and pier, take Interstate 680 coming from Concord to Interstate 780 and take the West Military exit. Stay to the right as you exit and you will be on West K Street. Follow West K Street to 9th Street and turn right. Continue down 9th Street to the park. To get to Benicia Marina and pier, take Interstate 680 coming from Concord to Interstate 780 and take the East 5th Street off-ramp. Turn left on 5th Street and follow down to the end. Off to the right is the marina.

Facilities: The 9th Street Park has restrooms, a picnic area and a launching facility. The Benicia Marina has restrooms, a general store, benches, and parking.

Who to contact: Phone the Benicia Park and Recreation Department at (707) 746-4285.

About Benicia Piers: Striped bass are hard to catch in the fall months. There are lots of bullheads, though; the best bet is catching bullheads, then using them for bait for striped bass (for more information on Bay Area piers, see page 431).

18.   CONTRA LOMA RESERVOIR

Reference: Near Antioch; map E1 grid b9.

How to get there: In Antioch, take Contra Loma Boulevard south to the park entrance.

Facilities: A boat launch, a fishing pier, picnic areas, canoe rentals, and a snack bar are available. Boats with electric motors are permitted on the reservoir (limit 17 feet), but no gasoline motors. The facilities are wheelchair accessible.

Cost: Parking fee is $4 per vehicle. A fishing permit is required; fee is $2 per person, per day.

Who to contact: Phone (510) 757-0404.

About Contra Loma Reservoir: Striped bass, and more recently, stocked rainbow trout, have always provided a reason to pray at Contra Loma.

The striped bass are in this lake because they get sucked in. Contra Loma, 81 acres, gets its water via the fish-stealing California Aqueduct. Most of the striped bass in Contra Loma seem to be on the small side, but there is hope for those on the southern shoreline.

With the 90s, however, came a new trout planting program that has been successful. Both the park district and Department of Fish and Game made modest trout stocks. Relatively few anglers are taking advantage of it, even though the fishing has been good during spring. In the summer, with the trout on the wane, fishing success is poor to fair. In addition to the striped bass, some small catfish are available.

---

19. ANTIOCH PIER

Reference: In Antioch; map E1 grid b9.

How to get there: From Interstate 80 near Pinole, take Highway 4 eastbound to Antioch Bridge. Take the Wilbur Avenue off-ramp just before the toll plaza. Follow the frontage road to the pier, which is just to the right of the bridge.

Facilities: Restrooms, parking and picnic tables are available. No swimming is permitted.

Cost: Access is free.

Who to contact: Phone the East Bay Regional Park District at (510) 531-9300, ext.2208.

About Antioch: This is one of the better prospects for striped bass, and it has a good view of the waterway (for more information on Bay Area piers, see page 431).

---

20. PITTSBURG PIER

Reference: In Pittsburg; map E1 grid b9.

How to get there: From Interstate 680 in Martinez, take the Highway 4 exit eastbound. From Highway 4, take the Railroad Avenue exit and turn left on Railroad Avenue. Follow to the end and then turn left on 3rd Street. From 3rd Street travel to Marina Boulevard and turn right. Follow Marina Boulevard to its end and you will come to the harbor.

To get to another pier, follow the same directions except turn left on Marina Boulevard and keep to the right until you come to Bayside. Turn right and follow to the road's end. You will see signs indicating the access road to the pier.

Facilities: The newer pier has restrooms, parking, picnic tables and drinking water.

Cost: Access is free.

Who to contact: Phone the Pittsburg Department of Parks and Recreation at (510) 439-3440, or phone the Harbormaster's Office at (510) 439-4958.

About Pittsburg Pier: Fish are attracted to this spot from the warm water coming from the nearby PG&E outfall. It can be one of the best pier spots in the Bay Area for striped bass (fall), sturgeon (winter through spring), and even steelhead (late fall). For more information on Bay Area piers, see page 431.

---

21. EAST FORT BAKER

Reference: West of Sausalito; map E1 grid c2.

How to get there: Located on the Marin County side of the Golden Gate Bridge. From Highway 101, take the Alexander Avenue exit, turn left on Danes Drive, then right on Bunker Road.

Facilities: Restrooms are provided.

Cost: Access is free.

Who to contact: Phone the Golden Gate National Recreation Area at (415) 556-0560.

About East Fort baker: This is a beautiful spot just inside the entrance to the Bay near the Golden Gate Bridge. For more information, see Bay Area Piers on page 431.

---

22. FORT POINT

Reference: In San Francisco; map E1 grid c2.

How to get there: In San Francisco from Lincoln Boulevard, turn off on Long Avenue and proceed to Marine Drive. Turn left and continue to Fort Point.

Facilities: Restrooms are available near the entrance to the fort.

Cost: Access is free.

Who to contact: Golden Gate National Recreation Area at (415) 556-1693.

About Fort Point: Fort Point was a pre-civil war fortification that once guarded the entrance to the Bay, located just under the Golden Gate Bridge on the San Francisco Bay. Now it is an attractive spot which offers fishing along the sea wall. During late June evenings, there is a chance for striped bass.

---

23. SAUSALITO JETTY

Reference: In Sausalito; map E1 grid c2.

How to get there: From San Francisco, travel north on US 101. Take the Alexander Avenue exit into Sausalito. Turn right on Second Street, then right on Richardson Street.

Facilities: No facilities are available.

Cost: Access is free.

Who to contact: Phone the Sausalito Parks and Recreation Department at (415) 289-4125.

About Sausalito Jetty: It is a seawall, not a pier, where herring often spawn at high tides during the winter, providing a unique opportunity for some light-tackle excitement.

---

24. ELEPHANT ROCK

Reference: In Tiburon; map E1 grid c3.

How to get there: From San Francisco, travel north on US 101 and cross the bridge. Take the Tiburon exit and turn west on Highway 131 to the intersection of Paradise Drive and Mar West Street.

Facilities: No facilities are available.

Cost: Access is free.

Who to contact: Phone the Tiburon Parks and Recreation Department at (415) 435-4355.

About Elephant Rock: An excellent view of the Belvedere Peninsula and Angel Island is provided here. In winter, herring spawn in this area. For more information, see Bay Area piers, page 431.

---

25. FORT MASON

Reference: In San Francisco; map E1 grid c4.

How to get there: The entrance for parking access is on the Fort Mason waterfront, located at the intersection of Marina Boulevard and Buchanan Street. From the Golden Gate Bridge, proceed east on Doyle Drive to Marina Boulevard. From San Francisco Civic Center, follow US 101 by way of Van Ness Avenue and Lombard Street to Fillmore Street. Turn right on Fillmore and then right on Marina Boulevard.

Facilities: Restrooms are located near the entrance to the dock parking area on the Marina Green. Picnic areas are located up the hill behind the dock area. A brochure describing park facilities and points of interest is available at the headquarters of the GGNRA in Building Number 308 near the main entrance.

Cost: Access is free.

Who to contact: Phone the Golden Gate National Recreation Area at (415) 556-0560.

About Fort Mason: Just west of Aquatic Park in San Francisco, Fort Mason offers picnic facilities in a semblance of a wooded setting. The pier is nearby (for more information on Bay Area piers, see page 431).

---

26. GOLDEN GATE SALMON

Reference: Along Bay Area Coast; map E1 grid c4.

Launch ramps: Launch ramps for private boats are available at Berkeley Marina, (510) 849-2727; Caruso's in Sausalito, (415) 332-1015; Loch Lomond Marina in San Rafael, (415) 456-0321; Richmond Marina, (510) 236-1013; Oyster Point Marina, South San Francisco, (510) 952-0808.

Party boats: Party boats leave at 6 a.m. daily from San Francisco, Sausalito, Emeryville, and Berkeley. Skippers ask that fishermen arrive at 5:30 a.m. for orientation. Bait is provided, and tackle and rod rentals are available on each boat.

Cost: Party boat fees range from $40-$50 per day.

San Francisco boats: Argo, (415) 321-3344; *Butchie B,* (415) 457-8388; *Carrie,* (415) 756-6178 or (415) 944-FISH; *Chucky's Pride,* (415) 564-5515; *Edibob,* (415) 564-2706; *Ketchikan,* (415) 981-6269; *Lindy Su,* (415) 664-6014; *Lovely Martha,* (415) 621-1691; *Miss Farallones,* (415) 352-5708; *New Easy Rider,* (415) 285-2000; *New Florie S,* (415) 878-4644 or (415) 991-4366; *New Holiday IV,* (415) 673-9815 or 924-5575; *Pik Nik,* (415) 939-5306; *Quite A Lady,* (415) 821-3838; *Viking,* (415) 566-2916 or (415) 334-9096; *Wacky Jacky,* (415) 586-9800.

Sausalito boats: Flying Fish, (415) 898-6610; *Ginnie C II,* (415) 454-3191; *Lenora II,* (415) 676-3509; *Louellen,* (415) 668-9607; *Mister Bill,* (415) 892-9153; *New Merrimac,* (415) 388-5351; *New Rayanne,* (415) 924-6851; *Pacific Queen,* (415) 479-1322; *Salty Lady,* (415) 348-2107; *Stardust,* (415) 924-1367; *Endigo,* (415) 332-4903.

San Rafael boats: Superfish, (415) 898-6989.

Berkeley boats: Dandy, (510) 233-5838; *El Dorado,* (510) 222-4054; *El Dorado II,* (510) 223-7878; *Happy Hooker,* (510) 222-5388; *New Captain Pete,* (510) 581-4000; *New Donna D,* (510) 222-4158.

Emeryville boats: Jubilee, (510) 881-7622; *New Fisherman III,* (510) 837-5113; *Rapid Transit,* (510) 685-0466; *Sea Master,* (510) 654-6040.

About Golden Gate Salmon: The richest marine region on the Pacific Coast from Mexico to Alaska is along the San Francisco shore, and it is salmon that are king of the coast.

The key is that an underwater shelf extends about 25 miles out to sea before dropping off to never-never land. The relatively shallow area is perfect for ocean upwelling in the spring, which brings cold, mineral-rich waters to the surface. Sunlight then penetrates that mineral-rich water and results in large births of tiny aquatic organisms. In turn, that plankton-rich water attracts shrimp, squid, anchovies and herring. The final result is that hordes of feeding salmon will search for the baitfish, roaming the Bay Area coast year-round, feeding and moving. It is the only coastal area on the Pacific Coast where salmon can be found year-round.

The season starts in March and runs through October, and in the process, fishermen get some widely varied and quality fishing. In the spring, the primary feed is shrimp and squid, which are in tight balls often near the Farallon Islands, along with a sprinkling of juvenile rockfish and small schools of anchovies off Pedro Point near southern Pacifica, the Deep Reef southwest of Half Moon Bay, and Duxbury Reef offshore Marin. The best fishing is usually around the shrimp balls, offshore near the Farallon Islands in water 55 to 90 feet deep.

The best results in the early season are by trolling, not mooching, often well offshore. The big charter boats will fan out like the turning spokes of a bicycle wheel in their search for the fish, and when one skipper finds the fish, he will often alert the rest of the fleet. If you are on the water in a private boat, you can listen in by tuning your marine radio to Channel 67, and more rarely, Channel 59.

By mid-June to early July, however, large migrations of anchovies arrive to inshore waters off Half Moon Bay, Pacifica and Marin. This causes the salmon to swarm together in large schools, then move inshore to corral the newly-arrived baitfish. This often results in the best fishing of the year, with calm seas and packs of salmon on the bite in nearby range.

Drift-mooching becomes popular by this time; the boat engine is turned off and the boat is allowed to drift with the current. Trolling tends to result in higher catch rates, and mooching results in larger fish, since anglers can use lighter tackle and sense every bite, and can be a lot more fun. For special techniques on trolling and mooching, see the Secrets of the Masters section at the front of the book.

By fall, many of the salmon will school in the vicinity of the Channel Buoys, located 10 miles west of the Golden Gate, getting ready for their journey through the Bay and upriver to their spawning grounds. Catch rates are often lower during this period, but the largest salmon of the year are also caught, with a sprinkling of 25 to 40-pound fish in the area from mid-August through early October.

If you are new to the game, learning how is as easy as tumbling out of bed in time for the boat departure. You should bring a lunch, drinks, warm clothing, and if vulnerable to Neptune, seasick pills. Before heading out, the skippers will provide brief instructions on the techniques planned for the day. If at any time you need help, a professional deckhand is available to provide it.

The salmon fishery is still one of the best fisheries in the state, despite dramatic fluctuations in populations because of perpetually troubled water conditions in the spawning areas of Northern California and the San Joaquin Delta.

I haven't missed an opening day since 1980, and have closed out the season several years as well. One year, on the last day of the season aboard the boat *Wacky Jacky,* I took my buddy Dave "Hank" Zimmer out on his first salmon trip. About midway through the day, I hooked a salmon I figured for a 10-pounder, then passed the rod to ol' Hank.

"Here ya go, Hank," I said. "Enjoy it."

Well, 40 minutes later, he finally brought a 32-pounder alongside. It was one of the greatest fights with a salmon I have ever seen, the fish streaking off on long runs the first three times it saw the boat. Afterwards, Hank just sat down kind of stunned, and looked at the giant fish.

Then he calmly said: "Hey, this is fun."

---

27.   BAY AREA PIERS

Reference: Throughout Bay Area waters; map E1 grid c4.

About Bay Area Piers: Waiting is the one thing most people find so despicable in city life, whether it be at a traffic light or a gas station. But it is the very heart of pier fishing, an activity which provides a medicine savored by thousands.

More than 30 piers in the Bay Area provide spots in which to take the proper dosage. These crusty old structures that withstand ill treatment by tides, wind and fishermen alike are available to those who want a simple day in the sun with a chance to catch fish. Here, you will find people who pay little heed to the pace at which they are catching fish, but who are content to be out of life's fragile fast lane and on something as solid and time-tested as a pier.

A wide variety of fish can be caught off the piers in the Bay Area. The most common are shark, bullhead, kingfish, perch, flounder and jacksmelt. Rarely, large gamefish can be caught. This includes salmon at Pacifica Pier, and sturgeon at San Mateo Pier, Dumbarton Pier, McNear's Pier, Point Pinole Pier, Vallejo Pier and Martinez Pier. In the 1990s, kingfish have been the most abundant of all pier-caught fish.

The Bay record for largest fish ever caught from a pier is a 194-pound sturgeon caught in 1980 by George Gane of Vallejo at

---

Vallejo Pier, located near the mouth of the Napa River. However, in late May of the same year, an angler hooked something giant at 11 a.m., never lost or gained more than 25 yards over a 12-hour span, then had the line break at 10 p.m. Some say it may have been the 400-pound sturgeon that Joey Pallotta later caught off Benicia to set a world record.

For the most part, anglers are content with the simple. All that is required is your favorite saltwater rod and reel combination, along with a bucket containing a knife, a few hooks, leaders, sinkers and bait. Most people use pile worms, grass shrimp, anchovies or squid for bait. They pick a high tide and give it a few hours.

In most cases, fishermen just toss out their bait and enjoy themselves as they wait for the fish. While they're at it, the anglers may nibble at a loaf of French bread and savor a few relaxing hours.

---

28. BERKELEY PIER

Reference: In Berkeley; map E1 grid c4.

How to get there: From Interstate 80 in Berkeley, take the University Avenue exit and follow the signs to the Berkeley Marina. The pier is at the foot of University Avenue, just past the bait shop and marina.

Facilities: Restrooms, fish cleaning racks, overhead lighting, and benches are provided.

Cost: Access is free.

Who to contact: Phone Berkeley Marina Sports Center at (510) 849-2727.

About Berkeley Pier: Berkeley Pier is one of the most popular in the Bay Area, extending some 3,000 feet out into Bay waters. Perch fishing can be very good along the pilings in winter months, with a chance for halibut in the early summer (for more information on Bay Area piers, see page 431).

---

29. MUNI PIER

Reference: In San Francisco; map E1 grid c4.

How to get there: In San Francisco, drive west to the foot of Van Ness Avenue.

Facilities: Restrooms, a snack shop and a drinking fountain are located near the pier. Benches, bleachers and green lawn are available for picnicking.

Cost: Access is free.

Who to contact: Phone the Golden Gate National Recreation Area at (415) 556-0560; Muni Bait at (415) 673-9815.

About Muni Pier: This pier sits just west of the Aquatic Park and offers views of the Bay and wharf activity, and prospects for jacksmelt, shiner perch and flounder (for more information on Bay Area piers, see page 431).

30.　　　　PIER SEVEN

Reference: In San Francisco; map E1 grid c4.

How to get there: The pier is located at the end of Broadway in San Francisco.

Facilities: No facilities are available.

Cost: Access is free.

Who to contact: Phone the Port of San Francisco at (415) 274-0400.

About Pier Seven: The principal use of this pier is as a parking lot, but benches and a fishing area exist at the far end (for more information on Bay Area piers, see page 431).

31.　　　　AGUA VISTA PIER

Reference: In San Francisco; map E1 grid c4.

How to get there: In San Francisco, travel north on Third Street to the intersection with China Basin Street.

Facilities: A thousand square feet of pier is available, with picnic tables provided. Restrooms, a public phone, a bait shop, and a restaurant are at the adjoining Mission Rock Resort.

Cost: Access is free.

Who to contact: Phone the Port of San Francisco at (415) 274-0400.

About Agua Vista: Jacksmelt in the spring and shiner perch in the summer are the most common catches from this spot (for more information on Bay Area piers, see page 431).

32.　　WARM WATER COVE PIER

Reference: In San Francisco; map E1 grid c4.

How to get there: From Third Street, drive east on 23rd Street, turn right on Illinois Street and proceed a short block to 24th Street.

Facilities: A small T-shaped pier, benches and a chemical toilet are provided.

Cost: Access is free.

Who to contact: Phone the Port of San Francisco at (415) 274-0400.

About Warm Water Cove: It doesn't look like much, being located in an industrial area adjacent to a power plant outfall. The warm water from the outfall attract a wide variety of fish throughout the year and makes it popular with local anglers (for more information on Bay Area piers, see page 431).

33.   FRUITVALE BRIDGE

Reference: In Oakland; map E1 grid c4.

How to get there: In Oakland, take Highway 17 to the High Street exit. From High Street turn onto Alameda Avenue and travel west to the intersection with Fruitvale Avenue. The pier is on the southeast shore of the Oakland Estuary next to the Fruitvale Bridge.

Facilities: Benches are available.

Cost: Access is free.

Who to contact: Phone the Oakland Parks and Recreation Department at (510) 273-3866.

Trip note: Two piers are located at each end of the Fruitvale Bridge. The Oakland side is open 24 hours a day, while the Alameda side closes nightly at 9 o'clock. Striped bass roam through this area in summer months (for more information on Bay Area piers, see page 431).

---

34.   GOLDEN GATE STRIPED BASS

Reference: In San Francisco Bay and coast; map E1 grid c4.

Launch ramps: Launch ramps for private boats are available at Berkeley Marina, (510) 849-2727; Caruso's in Sausalito, (415) 332-1015; Loch Lomond Marina in San Rafael, (415) 456-0321; Richmond Marina, (510) 236-1013; Oyster Point Marina, South San Francisco, (510) 952-0808.

Piers: There are many piers available (for more information on Bay Area piers, see page 431).

Party boats: Party boats leave at 7 a.m. daily from San Francisco, Emeryville, Berkeley, San Rafael, Pt. San Pablo and Crockett. Skippers ask that fishermen arrive at 6:30 a.m. for orientation. Bait is provided, and tackle and rod rentals are available on each boat.

Cost: Party boat fees range from $40-$50 per day.

San Francisco boats: *Bass-Tub,* (415) 456-9055; *Chucky's Pride,* (415) 564-5515.

Berkeley boats: *Happy Hooker,* (510) 223-5388.

Emeryville boats: *Huck Finn,* (510) 654-6040; *New Donna D,* (510) 222-4158; *New Mary S,* (510) 654-6040.

Point San Pablo boats: *New Keesa,* (510) 787-1720.

About Golden Gate Striped Bass: The trip starts with a boat ride among national treasures like Alcatraz, the Golden Gate Bridge and views of the Bay Area skylines. It ends with a treasure chest of striped bass, halibut and rockfish. In between, you get top fishing excitement by dangling a live anchovy or shiner perch for bait, having the chance to catch a variety of fish while getting a great view. It is called potluck fishing, starting in June when the striped bass begin arriving to San Francisco Bay after having spent the winter upstream in the Delta. First come the scout fish, the five to 10-pound striped bass, but by the third week of June, the best Bay fishing of the year starts up. That is when halibut also arrive to the Bay, and when rockfish can be found at the reefs just west of the Golden Gate Bridge.

During weekday evenings in late June and mid-July during moderate outgoing tides, anchovies will become trapped along the South Tower of the Golden Gate Bridge, and big schools of striped bass will move in right along the pillar and attack the baitfish. Meanwhile, earlier in the day during incoming tides, the stripers will congregate along the rocky reefs west of Alcatraz: the rockpile, Harding Rock, Shag Rock and Arch Rock.

It provides some of the fastest fishing of the year.

Greatness is possible. On one trip, I caught and released 13 striped bass ranging from eight to 22 pounds in two hours. Captain Chuck Louie, owner of *Chucky's Pride*, often has a fantastic limit streak in late June and early July.

All saltwater species are tidal-dependent, and that is especially true for halibut and striped bass. During slow-moving tides, halibut provide the best fishing, and during stronger tides, the striped bass come to the front. Since tide cycles will phase in and out from fast to slow, skippers have quality stripers or halibut to shoot for most of the days of summer. The only tides to be wary of are minus low tides, which muddy the water and put a damper on all fishing in the Bay. Dredge dumping, a serious problem in the late 1980s, caused a similar problem, but has since been greatly reduced.

Those minus low tides cause swift outgoing water, which seems to push a big school of stripers out the Golden Gate and along the inshore coasts by early July. That is when surf fishing becomes good at Thornton Beach and Pacifica, and when the Happy Hooker, Huck Finn and other boats that specialize in beach fishing have tremendous results along Pacifica.

August is the one slow period in the Bay, because most of the fish have migrated to the Pacific Ocean. They start returning in September, however, and the period from mid-September to mid-October provides another good spree for striped bass. During this time, they usually show up at the reef off Yellow Bluff, located upstream of the Golden Gate Bridge on the Marin shore, during outgoing tides.

The striped bass fishery has been hammered by water pumping in their spawning grounds in the San Joaquin Delta, where giant pumps take some 80 million gallons of water per second and send it to points south. After a spawn, the eggs of a striped bass must remain suspended in the water for 48 hours before hatching, and the strong pull of the pumps sucks the spawn and baby stripers right down the hole. That is why the species has suffered such declines since the California Aqueduct pumps began running full blast in 1968.

What remains is a troubled population that provides windows of opportunity for wise anglers. The fish have bulldog strength and provide a mercurial sensation at the rod for the angler who has hooked one.

An option for Bay fishing is sharks, with leopard sharks in the 40 to 45-inch class most common. The best spots are near the Bay Bridge, west of Angel Island, and just north of Belvedere Point on the east side.

It is the striped bass that provide an indicator for the health of San Francisco Bay. I have prayed many times that we will never look at the Bay and say, "The striped bass used to live here." Getting the Delta pumps turned off during the spring striper spawn could do much to solve that.

---

35. EMERYVILLE PIER

Reference: In Emeryville; map E1 grid c4.

How to get there: Take the Powell Street exit from Highway 80 to Emeryville. Travel west on Powell Street to its end in the Emeryville Marina. The pier is at the foot of Powell Street.

Facilities: Seats, lighting, water taps and fish cleaning racks are provided on the pier. Also in the marina are restrooms, a picnic area, a fish market with bait and tackle sales, and a choice of restaurants.

Cost: Access is free.

Who to contact: Phone the City of Emeryville at (510) 596-4300; Emeryville Marina at (510) 596-4340; Emeryville Sportsfishing at (510) 654-6040.

Abot Emeryville Pier: This pier should not be confused with the Emeryville Boardwalk, from which fishing is not permitted. It extends about 350 feet and is located just Bayward of Scoma's Restaurant along the frontage road. Fish high tides only (for more information on Bay Area piers, see page 431).

---

36. LAKE TEMESCAL

Reference: In the Oakland Hills; map E1 grid c5.

How to get there: From Highway 24 in Oakland, take the Broadway exit. Follow the signs to Highway 13. Look for the parking entrance on the right, just before the Highway 13 on-ramp.

Facilities: No boats are permitted on the lake. Picnic areas and a snack bar are available. Most facilities are wheelchair accessible.

Cost: Parking fee is $2.50 per vehicle when the kiosk is attended; free when it's not.

Who to contact: Phone (510) 531-9300, ext.2208

About Lake Temescal: Don't show up at Lake Temescal and plan on having a BBQ. This whole place was BBQd in the terrible fire of the fall of 91. The surrounding hills were torched and the lake decimated by ash, some polluted run-off, and serious oxygen depletion that led to a fish kill. How soon will this lake recover? It will probably be at least well into 1992 and maybe 1993 before the trout planting program resumes here.

Temescal covers 15 acres, and because of its small size, it always has responded instantly to trout plants. When the trout plants do resume, expect the commorants to respond quickly, too. One of the ironies at Temescal has been that after a plant, it becomes a fish-catching contest between the birds and the anglers. The trout are caught, and quick. Even when Temescal has its full scale fishing programs, it is still a dud in the warm summer months. An attempt to improve it by stocking small catfish will be likely in the rest of the 1990's.

---

37.   SAN PABLO RESERVOIR

Reference: Near Orinda; map E1 grid c5.

How to get there: From Orinda, drive northwest on San Pablo Dam Road to the park entrance.

Facilities: A boat ramp, boat rentals, groceries, bait, and tackle are available.

Cost: Parking fee is $4 per vehicle. A fishing permit is required; the fee is $2 per person, per day. The money is used to purchase bonus trout stocks from an independent source.

Who to contact: Phone (510) 223-1661.

About San Pablo Reservoir: Daybreak at San Pablo Reservoir is one of the most pastoral scenes in the Bay Area, with blues, greens and placid water, and boats leaving fresh, white trails. Anglers are scattered about the lake, many landing rainbow trout. San Pablo is the Bay Area's No. 1 lake, providing a unique combination of beauty, good boating and good fishing.

It receives more trout stocks than any lake in California, some 7,000 to 10,000 per week in season. The trout average a foot, with a genuine dose of three to five-pounders and a few every year in the 10-pound class. Shorefishing is good right in front of the Tackle Shop, and there are often excellent results along the far shore just inside leeward points. A bonus is good bass fishing, but usually only right at first light and last light. The Waterfowl Area at the south end of the lake holds some nice bass. The key for trout at San Pablo is depth. The magic level is

---

25 to 30 feet deep, either baitfishing or trolling. If you use bait, use two hooks with yellow Power Bait and a half a nightcrawler, or use one hook loaded with mushy salmon eggs. Trollers do best with flashers trailed by a Needlefish lure or half a nightcrawler.

It is a large, beautiful lake, 854 acres, with a good boat ramp. If there is a problem, it is its popularity on three-day weekends, when the catch rates always drop significantly. Most of the time, however, San Pablo offers one of the most consistent fisheries in the state.

---

38. LAKE ANZA

Reference: In Berkeley in Tilden Regional Park; map E1 grid c5.

How to get there: From Orinda, take Highway 24 to Fish Ranch Road. Turn right on Grizzly Peak Boulevard and continue to South Park Drive. Turn right and travel one mile, then turn left on Wildcat Canyon Road. Turn right on Central Park Drive, then right again on Lake Anza entrance road, just before the merry-go-round.

Facilities: Picnic areas and bathrooms are provided. The facilities are wheelchair accessible.

Cost: Access is free.

Who to contact: Phone Tilden Regional Park at (510) 531-9300.

About Lake Anza: This lake doesn't do much to get the heart pumping. It is just 11 acres, and the main attraction is the surrounding parkland, not the fishing. There are a few bluegill here, some small bass, but it is generally poor and does not pan out too much.

---

39. LAFAYETTE RESERVOIR

Reference: Near Walnut Creek; map E1 grid c6.

How to get there: From Walnut Creek, drive east on Highway 24. Take the Acalanes exit and travel south to the reservoir.

Facilities: Picnic areas, restrooms, hiking and bicycle trails are provided. No motors are permitted on the lake. Canoe and rowboat rentals are available.

Cost: Access is free.

Who to contact: Phone (510) 284-9669.

About Lafayette Reservoir: Because of its nearby proximity to San Pablo Reservoir, Lafayette Reservoir often is overlooked by anglers. It shouldn't be. For its size, 53 acres, it provides surprising results for the anglers who fish from winter through early summer. It has regular trout stocks, and some large but elusive bass. When fishing from a boat or the shoreline, most all of the trout caught here are taken by baitfishing. The East Cove is the most consistent producer.

If you limit on trout, before going home you might test the shoreline and docks for bass. Some big ones are in here, like 10-pounders, but they are rarely ever hooked and few people try for them.

---

40.   LAKE MERCED

Reference: In San Francisco; map E1 grid d2.

How to get there: From Interstate 280, take John Daly Boulevard west, turn right at Skyline Boulevard and continue to the lake.

Facilities: Row boats, canoes and boats with electric motors are available for rental. Rod and reel rentals are also available. Boat ramps are available for both lakes.

Cost: A Lake Merced fishing permit is required for anglers aged 16 and over. The fee is $2.50 for the North Lake and $1 for the South Lake. An annual fee for the South Lake is available for $8, with a $4 discount for anglers 62 or over. Permits are available at the Merced Bait Shop.

Who to contact: Contact the Merced Bait Shop at (415) 753-1101.

About Lake Merced: If you try sitting in a boat along the tule-lined shore, San Francisco's 700,000 residents will seem like they are in a different world. That is because they are. This is a place of peace. It also is a place with a fantastic bonus of a chance of catching a 10-pound rainbow trout.

There are actually three lakes here in all: Lake Merced North (105 acres), Lake Merced South (203 acres), and the Merced Impoundment (17 acres). Unlike most of the Bay Area lakes, trout fishing remains good in the summer. That is because daily morning and evening fog keeps the water temperatures cool, allowing continued stocks.

The North Lake has the highest catch rates and biggest fish. The average is about 1.5 to 2.25 trout per rod, with about one trout out of four 15 inches or larger. Because of the lake's high population of freshwater shrimp, always use bait, not lures. The cove offshore the 18th hole of the adjacent golf course, as well as the northwest corner, are the best spots. An option is bass fishing on the far side of the little bridge.

The South Lake, on the other hand, is more of a recreation lake for rowers and sailboats, but it can provide very good fishing for trout in the 10 or 11-inch class. The best spots are along the tules on the east shoreline, just inside the points, and also near the dam. Some large catfish and bass live along the tules, but few people have figured out how to catch them.

The Impoundment is smaller than many expect. In low rain years, it is reduced to a puddle and no trout are stocked. When water conditions are high and cool, this lake gets stocked about once every six weeks by the Department of Fish and Game. That sets off quick limit fishing for shoreliners casting small lures that lasts for about three days.

Lake Merced has a long, colorful history. In 1893, 90,000 muskies were planted in the lake, but never heard from again. Now, some 100 years later, about 225,000 trout are planted a year, making it one of the most successful urban fishery programs in America.

---

41. CANDLESTICK POINT

Reference: In San Francisco; map E1 grid d3.

How to get there: Southbound from San Francisco, take the Third Street exit off US 101 and follow the signs to the vicinity of Candlestick Park. Candlestick Point is located off Hunters' Point Expressway and Jamestown Avenue. Northbound from San Mateo, take the Candlestick Park exit off US 101 and continue to the point.

Facilities: Benches and tables for cutting bait and dressing fish are provided on the pier. Restrooms and picnic facilities shielded by windbreaks are available nearby.

Cost: Access is free.

Who to contact: Phone Candlestick Point State Recreation Area at (415) 557-4069.

About Candlestick Point: As baseball fans can tell you, it can get windy out here, and the adjacent neighborhood at Hunter's Point can be dangerous to non-locals (for more information on Bay Area piers, see page 431).

---

42. ESTUARY PARK PIER

Reference: In Oakland; map E1 grid d4.

How to get there: From Highway 17 in Oakland, take the Jackson Street exit and travel south on Jackson. Turn left on Embarcadero and continue four blocks to the park.

Facilities: Restrooms, benches, a drinking fountain and tables are provided. A bait shop and a choice of restaurants are available eight blocks away at Jack London Square.

Cost: Access is free.

Who to contact: Phone the Oakland Parks and Recreation Department at (510) 273-3866.

About Estuary Park: This pier is one in a series of piers in the Oakland-Alameda Estuary. It offers fine views of estuary activities, including ship repair work, and a chance for perch in winter months, with an outside shot at striped bass in the summer (for more information on Bay Area piers, see page 431).

43. MIDDLE HARBOR PARK

Reference: In Oakland; map E1 grid d4.

How to get there: Take Highway 17 to Oakland. If traveling south, take the Cypress Street exit and follow it west to the intersection with Seventh Street. Turn left and continue south to the intersection with Adeline Street. Turn right onto Adeline and continue west. Adeline turns into Middle Harbor Road. Continue on Middle Harbor Road to the intersection with Ferro Street, near the Middle Harbor Terminal. Turn left onto Ferro Street and follow it around the terminal on the Oakland Estuary. If traveling north, take the Oak Street exit, turn right onto Oak Street and travel one block east. Turn left onto Seventh Street and travel north to the intersection of Adeline Street. Proceed on Adeline as above.

Facilities: Benches, tables and a drinking fountain are provided. A water tap is available at the pier.

Cost: Access is free.

Who to contact: Phone the Port of Oakland at (510) 272-1100.

About Middle Harbor Park: The pier is adjacent to a landscaped strip with picnic tables, set in Oakland's Middle Harbor (for more information on Bay Area piers, see page 431).

44. PORT VIEW PARK

Reference: In Oakland; map E1 grid d4.

How to get there: Take Highway 17 to Oakland. If traveling south, take the Cypress Street exit and follow it south to Seventh Street. Turn right onto Seventh and follow it to its end at the Seventh Street Marin Terminal. The park and circular pier are just south of the terminal near the Oakland Estuary entrance. If traveling north, take the Cypress/Eighth Streets exit. Turn left from Eighth Street onto Cypress and travel one block west. Turn right onto Seventh Street and proceed as above.

Facilities: Benches and lighting are provided on the pier. Restrooms, a drinking fountain and an observation tower are available at the park area.

Cost: Access is free.

Who to contact: Contact the Port of Oakland at (510) 272-1100.

About Port View Park: Good prospects for striped bass, especially at night in the early summer. This area gets heavy use during this period (for more information on Bay Area piers, see page 431).

45.   **LAKE CHABOT**

Reference: Near Castro Valley; map E1 grid d6.

How to get there: The key is to get to Interstate 580, then travel to San Leandro and turn east on Fairmont Drive, which goes over a ridge and merges with Lake Chabot Road. Follow Lake Chabot Road into the park.

Facilities: Restrooms, parking, boat rentals, horseback riding rentals, camping spots, bicycle trails, picnic areas and drinking water are available. No private boats are allowed. A small marina office has bait and tackle for sale.

Cost: Day-use fee is $3 per vehicle. Fishing pass fee is $2. Camping ranges from $10-$16. Boats range from $7 per hour to $20 for five hours. Horses range from $12-$15 per hour.

Who to contact: Phone the East Bay Regional Park District at (415) 531-9300, ext. 2200, or phone the Lake Chabot Marina at (415) 881-1833.

About Lake Chabot: Here's a lake that just plain "looks fishy." And it is, with abundant trout stocks in the winter and spring, catfish in the summer, and a resident population of the biggest largemouth bass in the Bay Area. There are also schools of crappie and bluegill in several coves. The best spots are Coot Landing, Honker Bay and Bass Cove; avoid the open lake body.

Too bad they don't allow private boats to launch here, because otherwise this lake would offer a program nearly as strong as that at San Pablo Reservoir. But rentals are available, and shorefishing for trout is often quite good anyway.

The lake covers 315 acres and is the centerpiece for a 5,000-acre regional park that includes 31 miles of hiking trails, horseback riding rentals, and a campground.

---

46.   **PACIFICA**

Reference: From Devil's Slide to Mussel Rock; map E1 grid e1.

Boat ramps: There is no boat ramp available in Pacifica. Some hardy souls hand launch small boats through the surf at the southern end of Linda Mar Bay. The nearest boat ramp is at Pillar Point Harbor at Princeton in Half Moon Bay.

Piers: Pacifica Pier is located off Sharp Park Road, with access off Highway 1.

Who to contact: Coastside No. 2, (415) 355-9901; Pacifica Pier, (415) 355-0690.

Party boats: *Happy Hooker,* Berkeley, (415) 223-5388; *Huck Finn,* Emeryville, (510) 654-6040; *New Donna D,* Emeryville, (510) 222-4158.

About Pacifica: During a magical five-week period from the last week of June, through July, into the first week of August, the inshore coast off Pacifica can provide some of the best fishing in America.

The rocky coast here is made up of a series of small bays where striped bass can corral schools of anchovies and pin them against the back of the surf line. In addition, salmon often move in as well, rounding up the anchovies just a mile offshore. Want more? Got more: Halibut also are common off the sandy flats, especially in the Devil's Slide area.

If there is a problem, there can sometimes just be too many fish—kingfish, or white croaker. They can be so abundant that they can disrupt attempts to catch salmon while drift-mooching.

The key here every year is wind and the resulting ocean surge it causes. If the wind is up and the waves are high, it disrupts the ocean bottom and the anchovies will move offshore. When that happens, the inshore striper and salmon fishing goes belly up. But when the wind is down and there is no ocean surge, the anchovies will move right in, and with them, large marauding schools of striped bass and salmon.

That is when the live-bait boats will show up from Berkeley and Emeryville and chum the stripers into a frenzy. The anglers aboard will use live anchovies for bait and catch one striper after another until limits have been reached. These big boats back into the surf line near Mussel Rock or in Linda Mar Bay, and some owners of small boats will get in the general area and either use live bait (available at J&P Bait at Fisherman's Wharf) or cast Hair Raisers. Small boats should stay clear of the surf zone, an area where it is very easy to capsize and drown. Meanwhile, surf casters on the beach will send casts out to the fish, using chrome Hopkins, Krocadile or Miki jigs. There are also runs of striped bass independent of those started by the chumming, usually in late June at Center Hole (north of Mussel Rock), then in July off the Manor Apartments (north end of town) and Rockaway Beach. In August, the better fishing is from the rocks at Mori Point using large Pencil Poppers. Tides are always important, with the best fishing at the high tide.

Salmon fishing also can be outstanding, but some years it just doesn't happen here. According to my logbook, salmon often show up just off Pedro Point in mid-March, then disappear until July, when they return about a mile offshore the Pacifica Pier. When this happens, there can be so many boats on the water that it looks like a virtual flotilla.

Since most of the fishing here is in the magical period from July through early August, the question is what do you do the rest of the year? Maybe crab a little at Pacifica Pier in the winter, hope for a perch at Linda Mar Bay in the spring, and try rockfishing off Pedro Point in the fall—and dream of the magical time during the summer.

47.   PACIFICA PIER

Reference: In Pacifica; map E1 grid e2.

How to get there: From San Francisco, travel south on Highway 1 to Pacifica. Take the Paloma Avenue exit. At the west end of Paloma, turn left on Beach Boulevard.

Facilities: Drinking fountains, restrooms, benches, lighting, and fish cleaning facilities are provided. A snack shop with bait and tackle sales is also available.

Cost: Access is free.

Who to contact: Call Pacifica Parks, Beaches and Recreation at (415) 738-7380, or phone the bait shop at the pier (415) 355-0690.

About Pacifica Pier: Provides a rare chance in summer months to catch salmon, using anchovy under pier bobber. Good spot for crabbing in winter (for more information on Bay Area piers, see page 431. For more on Pacifica, see page 442).

48.   SOUTH SAN FRANCISCO BAY

Reference: From the Bay Bridge to Alviso; map E1 grid e1.

Boat ramps: Launch ramps for private boats are available at Oyster Point Marina, (415) 952-0808; Coyote Point County Park, (415) 573-2592; Alviso Boat Dock, (408) 262-3885; Alameda Estuary (510) 422-4100; San Leandro Marina, (510) 577-3472; Port of Redwood City, (415) 365-1613.

Piers: Several piers and shoreline jettys are available, including at Oyster Point, Coyote Point, San Mateo Pier, Dumbarton Piers (from both East Palo Alto and Newark), Palo Alto Baylands, and Alameda estuary (for more information on Bay Area piers, see page 431 or individual pier listings).

Who to contact: Sun Valley Bait, San Mateo, (415) 343-4690 (daily fish report recording) or (415) 343-6837; Jailhouse Bait, South San Francisco, (415) 952-4240; Lew's Bait, Alameda, (510) 534-1131; Central Bait, Alameda, (510) 522-6731; Dumbarton Pier, Fish and Wildlife Service, (510) 792-0222; Alviso Boat Dock, (408) 262-3885.

About South San Francisco Bay: What an expanse of water that is ignored! The South Bay is huge and unique, but the tremendous declines in many fish species have caused it to be largely bypassed by anglers—as well as the government bureaucrats that could start a plan for its restoration.

The South Bay is actually not a bay at all, but an estuary that experiences huge changes in water temperature and salinity levels throughout the year. Rain and the resulting storm runoff into the South Bay is one key. It can provide just the right freshwater/saltwater mix during the spring, which then results in huge bumper crops of grass shrimp. That is the favorite food of most fish in the South Bay, especially perch and sturgeon.

When the South Bay does get heavy amounts of rain, the first thing to look for are upturns in the number of perch and sturgeon. Perch are common during good moving tides along rocky areas (such as the cement blocks breakwater at Coyote Point), pilings (such as the Dumbarton and San Mateo Bridges, and also at the pilings adjacent to the San Francisco and Oakland airports), and in sloughs where there is a good tidal flush (such as Burlingame's Showboat Slough and the Alameda estuary). What for bait? Live grass shrimp, of course.

The same bait is good for sturgeon, although bullheads and small sharks can be pests. After decent rains, the areas in the main channel just south of the San Mateo Bridge, and also in the vicinity of the Dumbarton Train Bridge, are often excellent spots. After very heavy rains, big sturgeon can be discovered farther south along the PG&E Towers. Another option is waiting for herring spawns in late December and January, then anchoring off of Candlestick or Alameda, and using herring eggs (during a spawn) or whole herring for bait. Some of the best sturgeon scores in the past 10 years have come in these areas aboard the party boat *Chucky's Pride* out of San Francisco.

What is so disappointing about the South Bay is the lack of striped bass. Once you could toss out a cut chunk of sardine from the shore and catch 20-pounders. In fact, I caught my first striped bass at age 6 in an obscure South Bay slough near Palo Alto. That slough has been unfit for any fish for more than 10 years, and to catch a striper anywhere in the South Bay now requires highly specialized skills and precise timing.

Sometimes school-sized striped bass will arrive in mid-March and early April in the vicinity of Coyote Point, where they can be taken by trolling white, one-ounce Hair Raisers during high tides. Sometimes not. They also can show near the flats off Candlestick and at the nearby Brisbane Tubes, and also off the Alameda Rock Wall in June during high and incoming tides, and even more rarely, again in September. The higher the rainfall during the previous winter, the more apt these bites are to occur.

The same formula is true for excellent runs of jacksmelt in the spring, primarily from mid-February through early April. After decent winter rains, the best fishing is on the western side of the South Bay in the vicinity of Burlingame's Fisherman's Park, using a chunk of pileworm under a big float. Timing is important, of course. Be there at the top of the tide, then focus during the first two hours of the outgoing tide, when the tide will take your float out to deeper areas.

It will take more than heavy rains to bring the South Bay back to decent standards. A big problem is the pollution from metals, particularly mercury, from the computer companies and Kodak lab along the south Peninsula. Local governments demonstrated a willingness to provide upgraded sewage treatment plants in Palo Alto and San Jose, but stopping the heavy metal pollution is a much more serious priority for all aquatic species in the South Bay.

---

49.   SAN LEANDRO PIER

Reference: In San Leandro; map E1 grid e5.
How to get there: Take Highway 17 to the Marina Boulevard exit in San Leandro. Travel west on Marina to the intersection with Neptune Drive. Turn left onto San Leandro and Marina. The pier is on South Dike Road in the marina.
Facilities: Restrooms, drinking water and picnic tables are provided.
Cost: Access is free.
Who to contact: Phone the San Leandro Recreation Department at (510) 577-3462, or the Harbormaster's Office at (510) 357-7447.
About San Leandro Pier: This is the southernmost pier available in the East Bay (for more information on Bay Area piers, see page 431).

---

50.   DON CASTRO RESERVOIR

Reference: In Hayward Hills; map E1 grid e7.
How to get there: From Interstate 580 eastbound in Castro Valley, take the Center Street exit and head south to Kelly Street. Turn left on Kelly Street. Follow Kelly to Woodroe Avenue and turn left. Continue to the entrance.
Facilities: Parking, restrooms, a fishing lake, a swimming lagoon, a hiking trail around the lake, picnic areas, several fishing piers and a food concession are available. There are no boating facilities and no boating allowed.
Cost: Entrance fee is $2 during the summer, $1 for dogs. Fishing permit fee is $2 per day.
Who to contact: Phone the East Bay Regional Park District at (415) 531-9300, extension 2200.
About Don Castro Reservoir: Little Don Castro, just 23 acres, is the focal point of a small regional park in the Hayward hills that doesn't get

much attention. And why should it? No boats allowed, very few trout, and a few dinker-sized catfish don't add up to a heck of a lot. Well, there is one time when it does deserve a look. That is in the spring and early summer when small bass and bluegill can provide some shoreline fun. Dunk a worm under a bobber and see what happens.

---

51.   CULL CANYON RESERVOIR

Reference: In Castro Valley; map E1 grid e7.

How to get there: From Interstate 580 eastbound in Castro Valley, take the Center Street exit. Turn north on Center Street to Heyer Street and turn right. Follow Heyer to Cull Canyon Road and turn left. Continue to park entrance.

Facilities: Restrooms, parking, drinking water, trails for hiking, picnic areas, a fishing lake, a swimming lagoon, and a food concession stand are available. There are no boating facilities and no boating allowed.

Cost: Fishing permit fee is $2 per day. Swimming fee is $2 per day. Swimming fee for children under 16 and seniors over 62 is $1.

Who to contact: Phone the East Bay Regional Park District at (415) 531-9300, extension 2200.

About Cull Canyon Reservoir: Cull Canyon covers just 18 acres, and with the East Bay heat hammering away at this lake all summer, supports small populations of warm water fish, including catfish, bass and sunfish.

   The results won't exactly make you cancel the trip you had planned for Alaska. The best hopes are during the summer for small catfish, which are stocked once or twice per month.

   Otherwise, fishing is quite poor, and visitors are apt to say "forget it" and hike around the surrounding parkland instead .

---

52.   PILLAR POINT PIER

Reference: In Princeton; map E1 grid f1.

How to get there: Travel on Highway 1 to Princeton. Turn west at the lighted intersection at Capistrano Road.

Facilities: Restrooms, a drinking fountain, a restaurant, a snack bar, and a bait store where tackle may be purchased are available. The pier is open 24 hours, daily.

Cost: Access is free.

Who to contact: Phone the San Mateo County Harbor District, Pillar Point Harbormaster at (415) 726-5727.

About Pillar Point Pier: Once quite good, now quite bad. The outer jetty provides much better prospects for variety of rockfish, sea trout, some perch (for more information on Bay Area piers, see page 431).

---

53. **HALF MOON BAY**

Reference: From Martin's Beach to Devil's Slide; map E1 grid f1.

Boat ramps: A boat ramp is available at Pillar Point Harbor at Princeton in Half Moon Bay. Lines are common.

Piers: The Pillar Point Harbor Pier offers very limited success (for more information on Bay Area piers, see page 431).

Who to contact: Capt. John's Sportsfishing, (415) 726-2913; Huck Finn Sportsfishing, (415) 726-7133; Hilltop Market & Tackle, (415) 726-4950.

Party boats: The Red Baron, Queen of Hearts, Huck Finn and *Outlaw* are available out of Huck Finn Sportsfishing, (415) 726-7133; *The Capt. John* and *Morning Star* are available out of Captain John's Sportsfishing, (415) 726-2913.

About Half Moon Bay: One of the great success stories of the California coast is here at Half Moon Bay.

It was just about a lost cause in the mid-1980s. Gill-netters were wiping out the inshore fisheries, commercial fishermen were shooting sea lions, the old launch ramp had lines extending out to the highway, the marina was old and dilapidated, the party boats were slow and needed painting, and there wasn't enough parking. Other than that, it was a great place.

But one by one, all of those elements were fixed. Gillnetting was banned in water shallower than 240 feet, commercial fishermen stopped shooting anything that moved, a new launch ramp was completed, a new breakwater was added inside the harbor and new boat slips added, new skippers brought in fast and quality-maintained boats, and a new parking lot was added.

Suddenly, it is a quality act. So is the fishing. The most consistent is the rockfishing at the Deep Reef, 12 miles southwest of the harbor, and offshore Pescadero and Pigeon Point to the south, and Devil's Slide and Pedro Point to the north. The rockfish are coming back in decent numbers after the gillnet devastation of the '80s, and should respond with increased sizes as well in the '90s.

The salmon are less predictable. Because no salmon stream is located near Half Moon Bay, it is an interception fishery, where boaters try to intercept passing fish. There are usually two periods of great success, however. The first is in late June and early July, when salmon often are located at the Southeast Reef (marked by three buoys, adjacent to the Miramar Restaurant) and Martin's Beach to the south. After a lull, another large batch of small salmon, 20 to 24-inchers, show up in early August off the far buoy northwest of Pillar Point. At other times, from March through September, there are usually at least a sprinkling of salmon in the area.

For the owner of a small boat, it can be ideal when the fish are schooling. During the week, you can launch at 5:30 p.m., cruise out to the fishing grounds, limit out between 6 p.m. and 8 p.m., and be back at the ramp by nightfall.

There are other options in this area as well. Perch fishing along the beach just south of the Princeton jetty is excellent during the first two hours of an incoming tide, just after a good low tide has bottomed out. They use a unique system with plastic grubs here, which are available at Hilltop Grocery & Tackle on Highway 92.

The Princeton jetty offers an opportunity for shoreliners, with lots of snags but a decent number of fish. It is best just after low water, fishing the incoming tide with bait. Other possibilities are beach runs of striped bass during the summer. Although now rare, they still occur, usually during the second week of June, then on and off in July. Venice Beach is the most common spot.

Harbormasters at ports along the California coast that are considering revamping their harbors should take a look at Half Moon Bay. They did it right.

---

54.   SAN MATEO PIER

Reference: In San Mateo; map E1 grid f4.
How to get there: From the US 101 Bayshore Freeway just outside Foster City, take the Hillsdale exit and drive east by way of Hillsdale Boulevard and then Beach Park Boulevard to the pier.
Facilities: No facilities are available.
Cost: Access is free.
Who to contact: Phone the San Mateo County Parks and Recreation Department at (415) 363-4021; Sun Valley Bait, San Mateo, (415) 343-6837.
About San Mateo Pier: The old San Mateo Pier was converted into this fishing pier, which extends adjacent to the San Mateo Bridge nearly to the main channel of the South Bay. Prospects for sharks, rays, and in the winter, sturgeon (for more information on Bay Area piers, see page 431).

---

55.   DUMBARTON PIER

Reference: In Newark; map E1 grid f5.
How to get there: From Redwood City, take Highway 84 east and cross the Dumbarton Bridge. Just past the tollbooth turn right onto Thornton Avenue and travel south for about one-quarter mile to Marshlands Road. Turn right again and drive into the San Francisco Bay National

---

Wildlife Refuge. Drive past the visitor center and follow signs for about three miles to the pier.

Facilities: Running water for drinking and cleaning fish is provided. Restrooms and windbreaks are also available.

Cost: Access is free.

Who to contact: Phone the U.S. Fish and Wildlife Service at (415) 792-0222.

About Dumbarton Pier: This is an example of the government doing something right, with the pier extending to the channel of the South Bay from the Newark shoreline. During periods of heavy rain, many sturgeon congregate in this area. During summer, there are a lot of small sharks. There are plaques along the pier that show the different species of fish available (for more information on Bay Area piers, see page 431).

---

56. SHINN POND

Reference: In Fremont; map E1 grid f7.

How to get there: From Interstate 680 in Fremont, take the Mission Boulevard exit and drive northwest for about three miles to Niles Canyon Road. Turn left and drive to Niles Boulevard. Turn right and continue to H Street. Turn left and drive to Niles Community Park. You can walk to the pond from the park.

Facilities: Restrooms and drinking water are available at the pond. Parking is available at the park.

Cost: Access is free.

Who to contact: Phone the East Bay Regional Park District at (510) 531-9300, ext. 2208.

About Shinn Pond: Once an old gravel pit, it was filled with water, then stocked once with bass and bluegill. The pond covers 23 acres and does not provide much of anything.

In the summer, the Department of Fish and Game makes a special stock of 300 yearling striped bass. Small catfish rarely are stocked. Some folks sit there with their lines in the water, and after a few hours, you wonder if they are real or statues.

---

57. ALAMEDA CREEK

Reference: Near Fremont in Niles Canyon; map E1 grid f7.

How to get there: From San Francisco, take the Bay Bridge, then Highway 17 south to Decoto Road in Fremont. Turn left and travel east, toward the hills, and turn right on Niles Boulevard. Continue for several miles to Niles Canyon Road. If approaching from Highway 680, take the Sunol exit and head west on Highway 84.

Facilities: No facilities are available on-site. However, tackle and fishing information are available nearby in Fremont.

Cost: Access is free.

Who to contact: Phone the Fisherman Bait and Tackle shop at (510) 794-3474. For general information, call the East Bay Regional Parks District at (510) 531-9300, ext.2208.

About Alameda Creek: Alameda Creek is the emerald-green stream that flows along Highway 84 in Niles Canyon, and thousands and thousands of people drive along it every day without a clue as to the fishing that is possible.

That's right, this is one of three streams in the Bay Area that is stocked with trout in the nine to 11-inch class on a bi-weekly basis during the summer. The others are Novato Creek (see Zone E1) and Coyote Creek. They offer a rare opportunity to stream fish without having to drive to the mountains.

The best place to fish is about a mile upstream of Fremont's Mission Boulevard. You will see a small concrete coffer dam, over which the river flows. Try from there on upstream a few miles. Most of the success is on bait.

---

58.   LAKE ELIZABETH

Reference: In Fremont; map E1 grid f8.

How to get there: From Highway 17 in Fremont, turn northeast on Stevenson Boulevard and proceed to the park.

Facilities: A boat ramp, boat rentals, restrooms.

Cost: Access free.

Who to contact: Phone (510) 791-4356.

About Lake Elizabeth: During the hot summer in the East Bay flats, Lake Elizabeth and the surrounding parkland provide a relatively cool spot. It is located in Fremont's Central Park, covering 63 acres.

The fishing is also quite cool, no matter what the temperature is. A few small bass, bluegill and catfish provide some longshot hopes. At one time, trout were stocked here in the winter months by Fish and Game, but all plants have long been suspended.

---

59.   SHADOW CLIFFS LAKE

Reference: In Pleasanton; map E1 grid f9.

How to get there: From Interstate 680, take the Pleasanton exit. Turn northeast on Sunol Boulevard and continue to the lake.

Facilities: A boat launch, boat rentals, picnic areas, and a snack bar are available. Boats with electric motors are permitted on the lake (limit

---

17 feet), but no gasoline engines. Some facilities are wheelchair accessible.

Cost: Parking fee is $3.50. A fishing permit is required; fee is $2 per person, per day.

Who to contact: Phone (510) 846-3000.

About Shadow Cliffs Lake: Shadow Cliffs is a good idea that works. It was a good-size (143 acres) water hole for a former rock quarry that has been converted to a lake for fishing and boating.

Its squarish shape and steep banks give it an odd, submerged appearance, but you'll get used to it. Stocks of trout are supplied by both the Regional Park District as well as the DFG, and together it offers a viable fishery in the cool months. Included in the mix are trout in the five-pound class. The better fishing is always in the panhandle area, or in the vicinity of the third dock. Don't ask why, it just works out that way.

The weather gets very hot over here in the summer, and instead of planting trout, the Regional Park District stocks small catfish. Nobody ever seems to catch any, though.

---

60.   BORONDA LAKE

Reference: Near Palo Alto in Foothills Park; map E1 grid g5.

Special note: Access is presently limited to Palo Alto residents and guests of Palo Alto residents only, but the park may be opened to non-residents in the 1990s.

How to get there: From Palo Alto, drive west on Page Mill Road. The exit to Foothills Park is 2.7 miles beyond Interstate 280 off of Page Mill Road.

Facilities: A parking area, drinking water, picnic tables, and restrooms are available at this park, which is for Palo Alto residents only. A small boat dock is also provided; however, only non-motorized boats are allowed. There is no swimming or wading allowed.

Cost: Entrance fee is $2 per vehicle, $1 for walk-ins.

Who to contact: Phone Foothills Park at (415) 329-2423.

About Boronda Lake: Here is a perfect example of how government can screw up a good idea. This lake is set in a deep canyon, and after being dammed, could have provided a fantastic habitat for bass, bluegill, sunfish and catfish.

Instead, the bureaucrats decided to fill in the canyon with dirt and cap it, making the lake very shallow. That allows sunlight to penetrate to the bottom, which causes high water temperatures, intense weed and algae growth, and has ruined the chance of the lake providing a decent fishery.

What you get are a few dinker-size bass and a few sunfish. You also get a lot of weeds. This is a perfect case where fishery habitat decisions should be taken out of the hands of the pseudo-intellectual Palo Alto bureaucrats and handed over to fishery biologists who could still make the lake a good thing. As it is: Hopeless.

---

61. ARASTRADERO LAKE

Reference: Near Palo Alto in the Peninsula Foothills; map E1 grid g5.
How to get there: The park is located in the foothills above Palo Alto. From Interstate 280, take the Page Mill Road exit and head west. Turn right on Arastradero Road. A signed parking lot is available on the right side of the road. A 20-minute hike is required.
Facilities: There are a few marked hiking trails.
Cost: Access is free.
Who to contact: Phone headquarters at Foothills Park at (415) 329-2423.
About Arastradero Lake: A 20-minute hike through pretty foothill country will get you to this classic bass pond. There are good hiking trails in the area, with lots of squirrels, chipmunks and hawks. It's part of a 600-acre preserve.

The pond is small and circled by tules, with only a few openings along the shoreline where fishermen can find enough space to make a cast. You'll see the snarled line on adjacent branches. There are some big bass in here, but they are hard to catch.

One royal pain in the rear end is the idiotic rule the Palo Alto Recreation Department has come up with that keeps all rafts or float tubes off the pond. This is a perfect setting for a float tube, which would allow flyfishing with poppers, sending casts along the tule-lined shore. But no, that is forbidden. The fools.

---

62. PALO ALTO BAYLANDS

Reference: In Palo Alto; map E1 grid g6.
How to get there: Take Highway 101 to Palo Alto, then take the Embarcadero East exit. Head toward the Bay, past the Palo Alto Airport, Yacht Harbor and park near the Interpretive Center. Walk out on the "catwalk," which extends over the water.
Facilities: No facilities are available.
Cost: Access is free.
Who to contact: Phone the Baylands Interpretive Center at (415) 329-2261.
About Palo Alto Baylands: Fishing is limited to high tides; you'll find only mud flats during low tides. Use squid for sharks and rays. I spent many days fishing here as a young boy.

---

63.   SANDY WOOL LAKE

Reference: Near Milpitas in Ed Levin County Park; map E1 grid g9.

How to get there: From San Jose, take Interstate 680 north to Milpitas. Take the Calaveras Road East exit and follow to the park.

Facilities: Restrooms, parking, a golf course, horseback riding, and picnic areas are available.

Cost: Day-use fee is $3 per vehicle.

Who to contact: Phone the Santa Clara County Parks and Recreation at (408) 358-3741, or phone the park at (408) 262-6980.

About Sandy Wool Lake: This is a small lake, just 14 acres, but it is surrounded by parkland with 16 miles of hiking trails. They also allow non-powered boats on the lake, making it a nice spot to paddle a raft, canoe or rowboat around.

Yeah, but what about the fishing? Well, it spans from fair to downright terrible. The best hopes are in the winter, when it is stocked with trout twice per month by the Department of Fish and Game. That provides the one decent chance to catch fish here. In the summer, when the water heats up, you might as well dunk a line in a bucket.

64.   SAN GREGORIO CREEK

Reference: South of Half Moon Bay; map E1 grid h2.

How to get there: From Half Moon Bay, drive south on Highway 1 for about ten miles. Creek access is just to the east of San Gregorio Beach. You can park on the east side of the highway.

Facilities: No facilities are available. Fishing is permitted from the bridge east.

Cost: Access is free.

Who to contact: Phone Peterson's and Alford's General Store in San Gregorio at (415) 726-0565; Hilltop Grocery & Tackle in Half Moon Bay at (415) 726-4950.

About San Gregorio Creek: A meager steelhead run still returns to little San Gregorio Creek, but they are hard-pressed to make it upstream, and anglers have an even more difficult task trying to intercept them.

The runs can vary in size from year to year, but what does not vary are the conditions that attract them. It always starts with good heavy rains in December and early January, then during high tides from around January 10 to mid-February, pods of steelhead will come shooting out of the river, head under the Highway 1 Bridge and move eastward toward their spawning grounds. Fishing is permitted only on Wednesdays and weekends, so timing becomes very difficult. Most of the steelhead are caught in the 150 yards upstream of the Highway

1 Bridge by anglers using nightcrawlers or roe for bait. Occasionally, small trout are caught as well.

If nothing is doing, Pescadero Creek to the nearby south provides an alternative and has larger runs of fish.

---

65. PESCADERO CREEK

Reference: South of Half Moon Bay; map E1 grid h2.
How to get there: From Half Moon Bay, drive south on Highway 1 for about 13 miles. Creek access is to the east of Pescadero State Beach. You can park on the east side of the highway.
Facilities: No facilities are available. Fishing is permitted from the bridge eastward.
Cost: Access is free.
Who to contact: Phone the Pescadero Store at (415) 879-0541; Hilltop Tackle in Half Moon Bay at (415) 726-4950.
About Pescadero Creek: Most of the steelhead caught here are tricked just upstream of the Highway 1 Bridge in the lagoon. It happens right at sunrise and at dusk, when a high tide and good river flows out to sea allow pods of steelhead to enter the stream.

Those circumstances are rarely aligned, and since fishing is permitted only on Wednesdays and weekends, timing becomes the most difficult aspect of the trip. But it can happen. This stream still attracts steelhead in the 15-pound class, though four to eight-pounders are the average, along with a fair numbers of juvenile steelhead that people around here call rainbow trout.

The steelhead are difficult to catch, usually taken by anglers wading in the lagoon, and by baitfishing with roe or nightcrawlers in the near-still flows. It can take remarkable persistence, staring at your line where it enters the water for any movement, a sign that a fish is moving off with the bait. Once hooked, the steelhead are outstanding fighters, both jumping and streaking off on runs. Although catching them has become a rare event, they remain the fightingest fish in the Bay Area.

If you decide to wait for a tremendous strike, then call the Pescadero Store. I hear they are looking for a Cigar Store Indian.

---

66. STEVENS CREEK RESERVOIR

Reference: Near Cupertino; map E1 grid h5.
How to get there: Take Interstate 280 in San Jose to the Foothill Boulevard exit and follow south. Foothill Boulevard becomes Stevens Canyon Road. Stay on it and follow it to the reservoir. The approximate mileage from the original exit to the reservoir is four miles.

Facilities: This reservoir is located in a county park, so there are full facilities, such as parking, restrooms, picnic areas, hiking trails and a launch ramp.

Cost: Access is free.

Who to contact: Phone Santa Clara County Parks and Recreation at (408) 358-3741, or the park headquarters at (408) 867-3654.

About Stevens Creek Reservoir: When full, Stevens Creek is quite pretty, covering 95 acres. It can fill quickly during a series of heavy rains, and when that happens, Fish and Game always stocks it with rainbow trout. It is rarely scheduled in advance, but when it happens, it can turn this lake into a respectable prospect. Keep your tabs on it in late winter and early spring.

In the summer, the place can just about go dry. It has the possibility of holding bass, sunfish and catfish, but fluctuations in water levels for several years has reduced spawning success and shrunk the population down to just about zilch.

---

67. VASONA LAKE

Reference: In Los Gatos; map E1 grid i7.

How to get there: Take Highway 17 in Los Gatos to the Lark Avenue exit and follow signs to entrance.

Facilities: This lake is located in a county park, so full facilities are provided, such as parking, restrooms, picnic areas, fishing pier and a launching area.

Cost: Day-use fee is $3 per vehicle.

Who to contact: Phone the Santa Clara County Parks and Recreation at (408) 358-3741, or the park headquarters at (408) 356-2729.

About Vasona Lake: This is the kind of place you would go for a Sunday picnic, maybe play some softball or volleyball, perhaps try sailing around in a dinghy, or paddling a canoe. While visiting here, occasionally someone pulls out a fishing rod, hooks a nightcrawler, and tosses in their bait. They might catch a catfish or bluegill, but more likely, they will not.

According to legend, there is at least one fish in this lake. Oh yeah? Where?

---

68. CAMPBELL PERCOLATION PONDS

Reference: In Campbell; map E1 grid i7.

How to get there: Take Highway 17 in Campbell to the Camden Avenue Interchange. Follow west on Camden to Winchester. Go south on Winchester to Dell Avenue. Go left and follow to park entrance.

Facilities: Restrooms, water and parking are available, as well as lawn area for picnics.

Cost: Day-use fee is $3 per vehicle daily from Memorial Day to Labor Day. During the off-season, this fee applies only on weekends.

Who to contact: Phone the Santa Clara County Parks and Recreation at (408) 358-3741; Department of Fish and Game at (707) 944-5500.

About Campbell Percolation Ponds: This little spot, just five acres in all, a veritable dot of water, can provide some surprisingly good trout fishing during the winter and spring. The fish aren't big, but stocks from the DFG are decent, providing opportunity for shoreliners.

It becomes critical to track the DFG stocking operations for this lake. Because the lake is so small, it reacts quickly and strongly to any trout stocks.

---

69. CUNNINGHAM LAKE

Reference: In San Jose; map E1 grid i9.

How to get there: In San Jose, drive south on US 101 to the Tully Road East exit. Follow the signs to the lake.

Facilities: This is a regional park and has full facilities, including restrooms, water and parking.

Cost: Day-use fee is $1.50 per vehicle daily in the summer months. During the off-season, this fee applies only on weekends.

Who to contact: Phone the City of San Jose Parks Department at (408) 277-4661, or phone the park itself at (408) 277-4319.

About Cunningham Lake: Trout fishing in an urban setting? It doesn't get much more urban than this.

Cunningham Lake, covering 50 acres, is located adjacent to the Raging Waters water slide. If you bring kids along and the fish don't bite, you can always keep the water slide in mind as an insurance policy. Because the fishing can go down the tubes, too. However, there are short periods of decent prospects in late winter and spring, when the lake is stocked every other week with rainbow trout.

---

70. COTTONWOOD LAKE

Reference: In San Jose; map E1 grid i9.

How to get there: In San Jose, drive south on US 101 to the Hellyer exit. Follow this exit to Hellyer County Park.

Facilities: This lake is located in a county park and has full facilities, including restrooms, water, parking and picnic areas.

Cost: Day-use fee is $3 per vehicle.

Who to contact: Phone the Santa Clara County Parks and Recreation at (408) 358-3741, or contact the park at (408) 225-0225.

About Cottonwood Lake: The definition of "lake" is stretched here a bit. It's more like a pond, eight acres in all, but a pretty spot in the center of Hellyer Park. Access is quite easy, a short hop off US 101. It is a favorite spot for windsurfing and sailing, and also has good picnic sites, six miles of bike trails, and is stocked a few times with rainbow trout during the cool months. Right, the fishing is almost an afterthought. Regardless, a chance is a chance.

---

71.   LOCH LOMOND RESERVOIR

Reference: Near Ben Lomond in the Santa Cruz Mountains; map E1 grid j4.

How to get there: From the Peninsula or Santa Cruz take Highway 9 west into Ben Lomond, then turn east at the intersection with the sign for Loch Lomond Reservoir and drive to the lake.

A more complicated, detailed route from San Jose: From San Jose, take Highway 17 south. Take the Mount Hermon Road exit west for about three miles to Graham Hill Road. Turn left and head south on Graham Hill Road for about .8 of a mile. At Zayante Road turn left and travel about five miles until you reach Lompico Road. Turn left and continue for about five miles until you reach West Drive. Turn left on West Drive and drive until you reach Sequoia. Turn right and continue into the park. Sequoia dead ends at the park. Most of this route is well marked.

Facilities: Restrooms, parking, picnic tables, a tackle shop, boat rentals, and a boat launch are available. Electric motors only are allowed—no power or sailboats permitted. The park is open from sunrise to sunset seven days a week. Day use only.

Cost: Day-use fee is $2.50 per vehicle. There is a fee for boat launching.

Who to contact: Phone the reservoir at (408) 335-7424.

About Loch Lomond Reservoir: Just add water and this is one of the prettiest places in the greater Bay Area. Ah, but water is the catch. The lake is apt to be closed if there isn't enough water in it to allow trout plants, boating and recreation.

The lake, created from a dam on Newell Creek, sits in a long, narrow canyon. Boating and trout fishing can be excellent at Loch Lomond, and with the surrounding forest in the Santa Cruz Mountains, can provide one of the great one-day destinations for Bay Area anglers. The one thing it lacks is trophy-size trout. Trolling is often quite good at Loch Lomond, keeping your boat about 30 yards offshore, adjacent to the shoreline. I remember a day when Dave "Hank" Zimmer and his dad, Ed, caught a few trout, then landed the boat along the shore and barbecued them right then and there. It was practically like being in the Sierra Nevada.

72. LEXINGTON RESERVOIR

Reference: Near Los Gatos in the Santa Cruz Foothills; map E1 grid j7.

How to get there: In Los Gatos, drive south on Highway 17 and take the Alma Bridge Road exit. Follow to the reservoir.

Facilities: Parking, picnic areas and a boat ramp are available.

Cost: Day-use fee is $3 per vehicle.

Who to contact: Phone the Santa Clara County Parks and Recreation at (408) 358-3741, or contact the park at (408) 356-2729.

About Lexington Reservoir: Instead of Lexington Reservoir, maybe this lake should be renamed the Lexington Dust Bowl. It seems to be empty most years, and then even when it fills up, creating a big, beautiful lake that covers 450 acres, the local water agency just drains it on purpose about every three years. They say it is necessary in order to clear silt from the outlet hole, but there has to be a way it can be accomplished without draining the lake. The place has so much potential, though. When it is full, the survival rates of planted rainbow trout are very high, making for good trolling (often near the dam) and shoreline fishing (in the coves). The DFG makes regular stocks of 500 adult large mouth bass throughout the spring when water conditions permit it to give spawning a boost.

Lexington is also big enough to handle power boats, but they aren't allowed to dominate the place day after day. That is because boats with motors over 10 horsepower are permitted only on even numbered days.

73. GUADALUPE RESERVOIR

Reference: Near Los Gatos; map E1 grid j7.

How to get there: In San Jose, drive south on Almaden Expressway. Turn right at Coleman Road and continue for three miles to Camden Avenue. Turn right onto Camden Avenue, then immediately left onto Hicks Road. Continue to the reservoir (about four miles from Camden Avenue).

Facilities: No facilities are available. This reservoir adjoins the Almaden Quicksilver County Park.

Cost: Access is free.

Who to contact: Phone the Santa Clara County Parks and Recreation at (408) 358-3741.

About Guadalupe Reservoir: If only looking good beat doing good. Guadalupe Reservoir covers 75 acres in the foothills of the Sierra Azul Range just southeast of Los Gatos. It looks so good that in the spring, anglers new to the area can start chomping at the bit after just a quick glance.

But then when you actually start fishing, you discover all the problems. The bass and other fish here are contaminated with mercury, courtesy of runoff from the nearby mine that has since been closed down. In fact, that it why the surrounding parkland was named Quicksilver.

The populations of fish don't seem very good, either. You see, doing good beats looking good, every time.

---

74.   ALMADEN RESERVOIR

Reference: Near San Jose; map E1 grid j7.

How to get there: From San Jose, drive south on Almaden Expressway for about five miles to the reservoir. Note: The Almaden Expressway becomes Almaden Road as you near the reservoir.

Facilities: No facilities are available. No boats permitted.

Cost: Access is free.

Who to contact: Phone Santa Clara County Parks and Recreation at (408) 358-3741.

About Almaden Reservoir: The best thing going for Almaden is that a lot of folks bypass it, making it a good picnic site, particularly on weekdays. It covers 62 acres, and like Guadalupe and Calero, is set near some abandoned mines where mercury runoff has made all fish dangerous to eat.

Some shoreline baitdunkers catch-and-release a few small bass and panfish at this lake, but for the most part, it is ignored by fishermen.

---

75.   CALERO RESERVOIR

Reference: Near Coyote; map E1 grid j8.

How to get there: From San Jose, drive south on US 101 and take the Burnel Road exit. Travel west to the Monterey Highway exit. Take this exit and head south to Bailey Avenue and make a right. Follow Bailey Avenue to McKean Road. Turn right and continue to the reservoir entrance (about one-half mile).

Facilities: Portable restrooms, picnic tables, parking, and a boat ramp are available.

Cost: Day-use fee is $3 per vehicle. There is a boat launching fee.

Who to contact: Phone Santa Clara County Parks and Recreation at (408) 358-3741, or contact the park at (408) 268-3883. Reservations are required on the weekend. Phone (408) 927-9144 for reservation information. For fishing tips, phone Coyote Bait & Tackle at (408) 463-0711.

About Calero Reservoir: The value of catch-and-release fishing for bass and crappie is seen here, because both fish populations and fishing success are quite good. Nobody keeps anything, because the fish are contaminated with mercury and cannot be eaten. Picky, picky, picky.

That aside, Calero is the one lake in the foothills of Santa Clara County that is often full to the brim, even when other lakes are nearly dry from extended droughts. That makes it very popular for boating, fishing, and all lakeside recreation. On weekends, waterskiers can be a pain in the rear end.

But it is a big lake, covering 333 acres. Over the past 10 years, it has provided the most consistent fishing for bass and crappie of any lake in the Bay Area. Just keep throwing them back and it will stay that way.

---

76. PARKWAY LAKE

Reference: In Coyote; map E1 grid j9.
How to get there: From San Jose, drive south on US 101 and take the Bernel Avenue exit. Continue to Highway 82 (Old Monterey Road). Turn left and travel two miles to Metcalf Avenue, then turn left and cross the bridge. You will see the lake on your left.
Facilities: A small tackle shop, refreshments and snacks, restrooms, and boat rentals are available. No private boats or gas engines are permitted.
Cost: Access is $10 per person.
Who to contact: Phone Parkway Lake at (408) 629-9111 (recording), or Coyote Discount Bait & Tackle at (408) 463-0711.
About Parkway Lake: Your search for trout is over. Instead of traveling across the state in search of fish, you have the fish brought to you at 40-acre Parkway Lake.

The scenery isn't the greatest, and there are times on weekends when your fellow anglers here aren't exactly polite, but the rainbow trout are large (to 15 pounds) and abundant (averaging 3 fish per rod). From fall through spring, the most consistent stocks of large trout anywhere in California are made here. No trout is under a foot, one out of three is over 16 inches, and there are many bonus fish in the 5 to 12-pound class, rarely even bigger.

In the summer, the lake is converted over to sturgeon and catfish, but catch rates are inconsistent. Not so for trout. The expensive access fee goes to purchase the big fish, and a lot of them. A typical allotment is about 15,000 trout per month, which is equivalent to what Bon Tempe Lake (a decent place) in Marin gets all year.

The best technique is to use a Woolly worm, half a nightcrawler or Power Bait, casting it behind an Adjust-a-Bubble, using a hesitating retrieve. Spinners such as the Mepps Lightning, Panther Martin and gold Kastmaster can go through binges as well.

If you want to get a kid hooked on angling, try a Thursday when the crowds are down. You will be able to demonstrate that fishing also includes some catching, even a lot of catching.

---

77. CHESBRO RESERVOIR

Reference: Near Morgan Hill; map E1 grid j9.

How to get there: From San Jose, drive south on US 101 to the Burnel Road exit. Travel west to the Monterey Highway exit. Take this exit and head south to Bailey Avenue. Turn right. Continue on Bailey Avenue to McKean Road and turn left. Follow this road, which becomes Uvas Road, for about five miles to Oak Glen Avenue and then turn left. This road will lead you right into the reservoir.

Facilities: A boat ramp is available. No other facilities are provided.

Cost: Access is free. If boat ramp is in use there is a launch fee.

Who to contact: Phone Santa Clara County Parks and Recreation at (408) 358-3741.

About Chesbro Reservoir: This can be a frustrating lake for bass fishermen, but is certainly worth a look during the spring.

The bass tend to be very, very small, or absolutely giant with a case of lock-jaw, so you end up catching midgets and perhaps seeing a monster. Visiting anglers often leave in wonderment of a fish they saw, but not a fish that they caught. Although its official name is Chesbro Reservoir, locals refer to the lake as "Chesbro Dam." When full, it covers 300 acres, and also provides some good-size crappie prospects during the spring. In low water years, the crappie fishing goes down the tube.

---

78. UVAS RESERVOIR

Reference: Near Morgan Hill; map E1 grid j9.

How to get there: From San Jose, drive south on US 101 to the Burnel Road exit. Travel west to the Monterey Highway exit. Take this exit and head south to Bailey Avenue. Turn right. Continue on Bailey Avenue to McKean Road and turn left. Follow this road, which becomes Uvas Road, for about eight miles to the reservoir.

Facilities: A boat ramp is available. No other facilities are provided.

Cost: Access is free. If boat ramp is in use, there is a launch fee.

Who to contact: Phone the Santa Clara County Parks and Recreation at (408) 358-3741.

About Uvas Reservoir: There was a time in the mid-1980s when Uvas was the best bass lake in the Bay Area. It was full to the brim with water, and largemouth bass could be located in the coves, then caught with a purple plastic worm or small Countdown Rapala. It was good both by boat and shoreline, and I remember how exciting it was sneaking up on the coves on a cool spring morning.

In the 1990s, it is no more. Low water and manipulation of water levels year after year, have reduced the population of bass here to infinitesimal size. Hope abounds, however. Once full of water, the elements that made this lake once great can make it great again. When it rains a lot in the winter, keep your tabs on it for the next two springs.

When Uvas is full, Fish and Game also adds to the bounty by stocking rainbow trout twice per month, from late winter through spring. Some say the big bass in Uvas like to eat those hatchery-raised trout, making the big bass even bigger.

---

79. LAKE ANDERSON

Reference: Near Morgan Hill; map E1 grid j9.

How to get there: From San Jose, drive south on US 101 toward Morgan Hill. As you come into Morgan Hill take the Cochran Road East exit and follow to the base of the dam (about one and a half miles).

Facilities: Picnic areas, parking, restrooms, and launch ramps are available.

Cost: Day-use fee is $3 per vehicle. There is a boat launching fee.

Who to contact: Phone the Santa Clara County Parks and Recreation at (408) 358-3741, or phone the park at (408) 779-3634. For fishing information, phone Coyote Discount Bait & Tackle) (408) 463-0711.

About Lake Anderson: Anderson is the boating capital of Santa Clara County, a big lake covering nearly 1,000 acres, set among the oak woodlands and foothills of the Gavilan Mountains. However, a five-mph speed limit on the southern half of the lake provides quiet water for fishermen.

This lake needs a lot of water to be filled, and it only provides good boating and fishing when water levels are high. The area near the dam can be especially good for crappie and bass, particularly in the morning. When the lake is full of water, the best prospects are at the extreme south end of the lake, from the Dunne Bridge on south. This can be very good for bass, bluegill and crappie in the early spring before too many anglers have hit it, which has a way of smartening up the fish.

When I was a mere lad of 12, my dad and I were fishing along the shore, when a boat pulled up on the opposite side, and two young women proceeded to lay down towels and sunbathe in the nude all afternoon long. No matter how hard we squinted, however, they were out of clear visibility range. Meanwhile, while our attention was diverted, a turtle snuck up and ate all the fish off our stringer.

80.   COYOTE RESERVOIR

Reference: Near Gilroy; map E1 grid j9.

How to get there: From San Jose, drive south on US 101 toward Gilroy. Take the Leavsley Road exit east and drive for about three miles. Turn left on New Avenue and drive to Roop Road. Turn right on Roop Road (Roop Road will become Gilroy Hot Springs Road). Drive up over the hill and drop down onto Coyote Lake Road. Continue to the reservoir.

Facilities: Parking, picnic areas, restrooms, and a boat launch are available.

Cost: Day-use fee is $3 per vehicle. There is a boat launching fee.

Who to contact: Phone the Santa Clara County Parks and Recreation at (408) 358-3741, or phone the park at (408) 842-7800. For fishing information, phone Coyote Bait & Tackle at (408) 463-0711.

About Coyote Reservoir: Coyote has been another victim of low rainfall and curious water politics in Santa Clara County. In fact, one of the things that prevents the Department of Fish and Game from setting up fishery management plans at Coyote, Anderson, Uvas, Lexington, and Stevens Creek reservoirs are the weird water fluctuations. For instance, Coyote was full of water in 1984 and 1985, and began to provide some outstanding fishing for largemouth bass. There were both size and numbers, and the spring of '85 was a time to be remembered when Coyote became the best bass lake in the Bay Area. Then, they drained the lake completely in the fall of '85. Goodbye bass. In 1986, though, the lake filled up again, and by 1988, the bass fishery was just starting to come back, and to get anglers interested. The DFG even stocked some trout in the spring. But then the lake was drained again, and as the 90s opened, it was completely empty save for a little puddle at the north end.

If this full/empty pattern continues through the 1990s, this lake will never realize its potential as a first-class bass lake. When full, the lake fills a canyon located about five miles upstream (south) of Lake Anderson. It covers 688 acres and is stocked in the spring with trout, and then when warm weather moves in, the bass take over. When water conditions are suitable the DFG stocks the lake with 500 adult large mouth bass each year in order to give spawning a boost.

Except that most years it looks more like Craters of the Moon National Monument.

81.

Reference: South of San Jose in Coyote Creek County Park; map E1 grid j9.

How to get there: From San Jose, drive south on US 101 for six miles to the town of Coyote. Take the Cochran Road exit and head east to the base of Anderson Dam. Coyote Creek runs downstream of Anderson Dam.

Facilities: Picnic tables are available in Coyote Creek County Park. Tackle and fishing information are available nearby in Coyote.

Cost: Access is free.

Who to contact: Phone Coyote Discount Bait & Tackle at (510) 463-0711.

About Coyote Creek: Like Alameda Creek, many people have no idea of the possibilities here. Coyote Creek gets its water from Lake Anderson, with dam releases decent enough in the summer months to provide suitable habitat for planted trout from the DFG.

The fishing at Coyote Creek always comes in binges, with short periods of limit fishing and long periods of slow hopes. The best stretch of water is about a mile downstream from Anderson Dam, with most of the trout being taken on bait.

MAP E2

9 LISTINGS
PAGES 466-477

NOR-CAL MAP . see page 120
adjoining maps
NORTH (D2) ...... see page 340
EAST (E3) .... see page 478
SOUTH (F2) .... see page 554
WEST (E1) .... see page 414

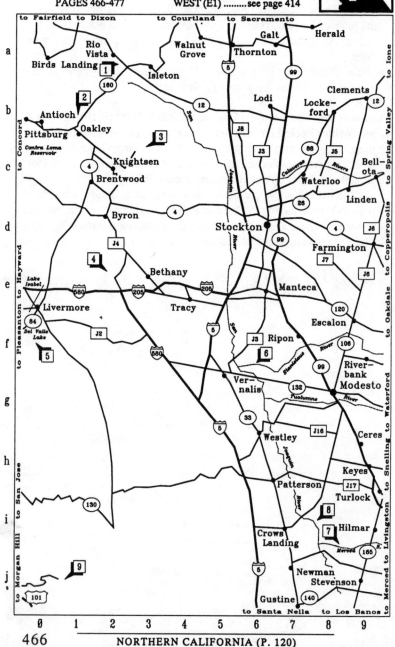

to Fairfield to Dixon   to Courtland   to Sacramento

a   Rio Vista   Walnut Grove   Galt   Herald
   Birds Landing   [1]   Thornton
   160   Isleton   99   to Ione

b   Antioch   12   Lodi   Clements
   Pittsburg   Oakley   Lockeford   12
   Contra Loma   [3]   J8   88   J5   Bell-
   Reservoir   J3   Calaveras River   ota

c   to Concord   Knightsen   Waterloo
   4   Brentwood   Linden

d   Byron   4   26
         Stockton   4   Farmington   J6
   J4   99   J7

e   [4]   Bethany   Manteca   J6
   580   205   205   120
   Livermore   Tracy   Escalon
   Lake Isabel

f   84   J2   J3   Ripon   106
   Del Valle Lake   5   [6]   River   Riverbank
   [5]   580   99   Modesto

g   Vernalis   132   Tuolumne River
         33

h   5   Westley   J16   Ceres
         Keyes

i   130   Patterson   J17   Turlock
         [8]
   Crows Landing   [7]   Hilmar
         Merced R.   165

j   [9]   Newman
   101   Stevenson
   to Morgan Hill to San Jose   Gustine   140
   to Santa Nella   to Los Banos

0   1   2   3   4   5   6   7   8   9

1.   SACRAMENTO RIVER DELTA

Reference: Near Rio Vista; map E2 grid a2.

How to get there from Sacramento: Take Interstate 5 south of Sacramento for about 35 miles, then turn west on Highway 12 and drive to Rio Vista. Just after crossing the Rio Vista Bridge, turn left and drive to Main Street. The boat ramp is on your left, Hap's Bait is on your right.

How to get there from the Bay Area: Take Interstate 80 east to Fairfield, then turn east on Highway 12 and drive to Rio Vista. As you enter town, The Trap will be on your left side.

Boat ramps: Boat ramps are available in Rio Vista at the end of Main Street (adjacent to Hap's Bait); in Isleton, on Highway 160 (across from Bill's Bait Shop); in Walnut Grove at New Hope Landing, off Walnut Grove Road; at Brannan Island State Recreation Area (south of Rio Vista), off Highway 160.

Facilities: Campgrounds are available at Brannan Island State Recreation Area. Lodging, full-service marinas, bait, tackle, and supplies are available near the boat ramps.

Cost: Most river access is free. There is a $5 entrance fee at Brannan Island State Recreation Area, as well as a boat launching fee.

Who to contact: Phone The Trap, (707) 374-5554 or Hap's Bait, (707) 374-2372, both in Rio Vista; guide Barry Canevaro in Isleton, (916) 777-6498; Bill's Bait Shop in Isleton; The Brannan Island State Recreation Area, (916) 777-6671.

About Sacramento River Delta: A lot of insiders were curious when guide Barry Canevaro shifted his base of operations from Bethel Island in the San Joaquin Delta over to Rio Vista on the Sacramento River. Why the switch?

"Because there's a lot more fish over here, that's why," Canevaro said. "I keep close track of my fish counts and in my first winter here, my customers caught 1,300 stripers (releasing many). That's up more than 600 fish from what we were doing on the San Joaquin side."

I book a trip with Canevaro every year, and have fished the Delta in rental boats, and then my own boat for much of my life. The Delta is an extraordinary place, with some 1,000 miles of navigable waterways, a mosaic of rivers, sloughs and lakes. When I fly over it, I have always felt that it looks like intricate masonry work. When I fish it, it looks more like paradise.

Right off, though, you must check the water temperature. If it is 56 degrees or over, then troll for stripers, using the big Rebels or Bombers. If it is 55 degrees or under, then forget trolling. You must anchor and baitfish, using either fresh shad or mudsuckers.

The striped bass start arriving in mid-September in decent numbers to the Sacramento River, and through mid-April, different schools will arrive at different times. For instance, the biggest Delta stripers of the year often are caught the week before Christmas, when it is very cold and foggy. Then in early April, there is usually a short-lived but wide-open trolling bite, which then turns off completely, a total zilch so sudden you'd swear the fish disappeared. During summer months, a few resident stripers hang around the area, but for the most part, waterskiers take over.

Some of the best spots for striped bass are quite near the boat ramp at Rio Vista. Good prospects include: the Rio Vista Bridge, Isleton Bridge, Steamboat Slough upstream of Rio Vista, the southern tip of Decker Island downstream of Rio Vista, "The Towers" (actually power lines) downstream of Decker Island, and the deep holes in Montezuma Slough.

Options are sturgeon and salmon, and sometimes they are more than options—they're by far the fish of choice. Some huge sturgeon have been caught on the Sacramento River Delta in this area, including several in the 250 to 300-pound class. One November day, Bill Stratton was on his first trip on a new boat with a new rod, fishing for striped bass when he hooked a monster sturgeon here by accident. He had to hop aboard another boat to fight the fish, and after several hours, landed a 390-pound sturgeon that stands as the world record for 30-pound line. The better sturgeon spots are downstream, especially in the vicinity of the southern tip of Decker Island, holes in Montezuma Slough, and downstream in the center of the channel adjacent to the Pittsburg PG&E Plant. The number of sturgeon attracted to these areas is linked directly to rainfall. In high rain years, a lot of sturgeon move in. In low rain years, not too many.

Salmon have also become a viable option to striped bass, especially from late August through September when the salmon pass through this area en route to their upstream spawning areas. The better results have come trolling in the area adjacent to the Rio Vista boat ramp.

If you are new to the game, then book a trip with Canevaro and learn the ropes. He can be as much a teacher as a guide. In one four-hour spree with Barry, I caught and released 12 striped bass up to 23 pounds. It is a reminder of what is possible when everything is right.

---

2. SAN JOAQUIN DELTA

Reference: Near Antioch; map E2 grid b1.
How to get there from Sacramento: From Interstate 5 south of Sacramento, take the Highway 12 exit and travel west to Highway 160, then turn south and continue, driving over the Antioch Bridge to Antioch.
How to get there from the Bay Area: Take Interstate 80 east to the Hercules/Rodeo area and turn east on Highway 4. Drive east on

Highway 4 to Antioch.

Boat ramps: Boat ramps are available at Eddo's Boat Harbor, off Sherman Island-Levee Road (northeast of Antioch); Bethel Island (east of Antioch), at Hennis Marina; Franks Tract Lake (adjacent to Bethel Island) at Beacon Harbor and Russo's Marina & Trailer Park.

Facilities: Campgrounds are available in the Bethel Island area, at Eddo's Boat Harbor, and at several places near Stockton. Lodging, boat rentals, bait, tackle, and supplies are available in adjacent towns.

Cost: River access is free.

Who to contact: Phone Panfili's in Antioch, (510) 757-4970; Eddo's Boat Harbor, north of Antioch, (510) 757-5314.

About San Joaquin Delta: The old green San Joaquin still provides a viable fishery, but it is slipping away like a wooden bridge, coming apart board by board from years of neglect and punishment.

Striped bass still arrive in late September, although in modest numbers. Come winter, so do the sturgeon. They provide a fair chance for skilled anglers with boats, but it takes time and persistence to get a bite—and when you do, you had better not blow the set.

Much of the life of the San Joaquin has been eroded away year by year by the terrible water pumping near Tracy, pumping so strong that tides are reversed, and fish are sent with the water right down the hole. Ever since the pumps started cranking full blast in 1968, the San Joaquin fisheries have declined a bit most every year, until now in the 90s, only a scant resemblance of what was remains.

But one of the advantages to fishing the San Joaquin, as opposed to the Sacramento River side of the Delta, is the wide variety and number of hopeful spots. Some of the better spots are just west of the Antioch Bridge (good trolling from Mayberry Slough to Antioch PG&E Powerplant), Big Break, Blind Point (at the mouth of Dutch Slough, upriver from Buoy 17), the mouth of False River (near Buoy 25), and Santa Clara and San Andreas Shoals (good trolling in fall and spring).

This a great playground for a boat owner, with calm water and hundreds of options. I love to scan a map and dream of where to visit next. You could fish every weekend of the year and not see the entire Delta in your lifetime. There is just too much of it.

That factor causes it to be inundated with boats in the summer, particularly waterskiers in unbelievable numbers. The place gets wild, with very heavy drinking, bikini contests at marinas, and so many people having trouble launching and loading their boats that some marinas set up football stands so people can sit and watch.

In low rain years, that can be more entertaining than the fishing. The amount of striped bass, sturgeon and salmon that choose to swim up the San Joaquin has been factored out to be nearly equivalent to the

---

amount of freshwater flowing through the San Joaquin. When rain and snowmelt runoff is low, the pumps continue to gorge themselves 24 hours per day, and the fish have very little reason to choose to swim here.

Maybe there will come a day when the pumps get shut down for the spring spawn, and once again allow the rivers to take their natural courses westward through the Delta, bays, and out to sea. The day that happens is the day the fisheries will start their recovery.

---

3.   BACK DELTA

Reference: Near Stockton; map E2 grid c3.

How to get there from Sacramento: From Interstate 5 south of Sacramento, take the Highway 12 exit and travel west to Highway 160, then turn south and continue, driving over the Antioch Bridge to Antioch. Turn east on Highway 4 and drive through Oakley, then turn north on Bethel Island Road and drive north for about four miles. Turn east on Harbor Road and drive one mile to Frank's Tract Recreation Area. A boat launch is located a mile to the south along Willow Road.

How to get there from the Bay Area: Take Interstate 80 east to the Hercules/Rodeo area and turn east on Highway 4. Drive east on Highway 4 through Antioch and Oakley, then turn north on Bethel Island Road and drive north for about four miles. Turn east on Harbor Road and drive one mile to Frank's Tract Recreation Area. A boat launch is located about a mile to the south along Willow Road.

Boat ramps: Boat ramps are in Stockton, off Webber Street (downtown) and at Buckley Cove (next to Ladd's Marina); in Discovery Bay (off Highway 4) at Discovery Bay Yacht Harbor ($22 fee for non-association members); at the junction of Interstate 5 and Highway 120 (south of Lathrop) at both Mossdale Trailer Park and Mossdale Crossing (there is a double ramp at Mossdale Crossing).

Facilities: Campgrounds, lodging, boat rentals, bait, tackle, and supplies are available in the Stockton area.

Cost: River access is free.

Who to contact: Phone Ladd's Stockton Marina, (209) 477-9521; Delta Harbor in Bethel Island, (510) 684-2260; Del's Harbor near Clifton Court Forebay, (209) 835-8365; Tony's Tackle in Livermore, (510) 443-9191; Discovery Bay Yacht Harbor, (510) 634-5928.

About Back Delta: Question: Of the dozens and dozens of lakes and reservoirs that offer fishing for largemouth bass, which do you think provides the most consistent catches? Answer: None of them. That is because it is the back or eastern Delta that now provides it. There's some irony to this. Water flows have become minimal because reduced amounts of water are allowed to run through the Delta, yet pumping to points south has been increased, so the back Delta now has the qualities of a lake, not a river. Instead of striped bass and salmon, there are largemouth bass and catfish.

The bass fishing, in particular, is quite good in spring, summer and fall. The water gets very cold in the winter, like in the low 40s, and that freezes the bite. The back Delta does not have the giant Florida bass, such as Lake Amador and Clear Lake in Northern California, or Castaic Lake, Casitas Lake, and Lower Otay Lake in Southern California. But it has the numbers, with plenty in the 11 to 15-inch class.

In the summer, because of the high numbers of waterskiers and jet skis careening around, the best bass waters are naturally the quiet, out-of-the-way spots with navigation hazards. Frank's Tract is the top area, particularly on the tules from the short connector slough (which extends to the San Joaquin River) on south to the mouth of Old River. To the west, Fisherman's Cut, which connects False River to the San Joaquin, also has a lot of bass sitting in the tules. It is also a good spot to lay over for the night if you have a houseboat.

Farther back in the Delta, the shoreline along Old River has become a good bass spot, along where it connects to Middle River and farther north in the Stockton River and Disappointment Slough.

There is a lot of water to explore, and it can take all summer just to hit the spots mentioned so far.

As you get deeper into the back Delta, the better fishing is for catfish. West of Stockton, the area around King Island is one of the better spots, particularly in Disappointment Slough and White Slough. Farther north, the Mokelumne River also holds a lot of catfish, with the best spots just inside Sycamore Slough, Hog Slough and Beaver Slough, which you run into in a row while cruising north on the Mokelumne River, north of Terminous.

The areas farther south used to provide excellent fishing for catfish, and striped bass as well, but no more. I remember fishing here, anchored and using anchovies for bait for striped bass or catfish, and needing just a one-ounce sinker to hold my bait on the bottom during an incoming tide. Now, with the pumps running, the tide direction is reversed and even with a five-ounce sinker, it won't hold bottom. The pull is too strong. Areas that suffer the worst are the San Joaquin, just north of Clifton Court, and just southeast of Clifton Court, at Old River and Grant Line Canal. At one time, this was the heart of the Delta. But Clifton Court and the giant water pumps have cut the heart right out.

4. BETHANY RESERVOIR

Reference: Near Livermore in Bethany Reservoir State Recreation Area; map E2 grid e2.

How to get there: From Interstate 580 at Livermore, travel east and take the Altamont Pass exit. Turn right on Altamont Pass Road and travel to Kelso-Christianson Road. Turn right and continue to the park entrance.

Facilities: Picnic areas, portable toilets and a boat ramp are available.

Cost: Day-use fee is $5 per vehicle. There is a fee for boat launching.

Who to contact: Phone California State Parks and Recreation, Diablo District at (510) 687-1800.

About Bethany Reservoir: A veritable smorgasbord of fish are available at Bethany Reservoir, but it definitely isn't "all you can eat." Bethany has rainbow trout, largemouth bass, striped bass, catfish, bluegill and crappie living in it. Catching them is another matter.

This reservoir, 162 acres, is similar to Contra Loma Reservoir to the north in that it gets its water via the California Aqueduct. That is why striped bass are in the lake; they're sucked out of the Delta and pumped here. The better fishing is on the southwest side of the lake, across from the boat ramp, which has a series of coves.

Though all boats are allowed on the lake, a 5-mph speed limit keeps the water quiet. The exception is in the spring, when the winds can howl through this area. A bonus is that a good bike trail is routed through the park.

---

5. DEL VALLE RESERVOIR

Reference: Southeast of Livermore in Lake Del Valle State Recreation Area; map E2 grid fØ.

How to get there: Eastbound on Interstate 580, take the North Livermore Avenue exit. Turn south and travel on North/South Livermore Road (this will turn into Tesla Road) to Mines Road. Turn right and drive about three miles south on Mines Road to Del Valle Road. Turn right and continue for four miles to the lake entrance.

Facilities: A campground is available. Picnic areas, a full-service marina, a boat launch, boat rental, a concession stand, and paved walking and bike trails are provided. The facilities are handicapped accessible.

Cost: Parking fee is $3 per vehicle. A fishing permit is required to fish at the lake; the fee is $2 per person. Campsite fee is $10 per night; reservations are recommended in the summer months.

Who to contact: Phone East Bay Regional Parks at (510) 531-9300; Del Valle Regional Park at (510) 443-4110; Del Valle Boathouse at (510)

443-5201.

About Del Valle Reservoir: Here is one of the Bay Area's top adventure lands for fishing, camping, boating and hiking.

The lake sits in a long, narrow canyon in Alameda County's foothill country, covering 750 acres with 16 miles of shoreline. It provides a setting for the newcomer or expert, with very good trout stocks during winter and spring, and a good resident population of bluegill. They are joined by more elusive smallmouth bass, catfish and a few rare, but big, striped bass. It is one of the few lakes in the Bay Area that also provides for camping, rental boats, and a good ramp for power boats. The trailhead for the Ohlone Wilderness Trail is also available.

As long as water clarity is decent in the winter months, trout fishing is most often excellent. Swallow Bay and the Narrows are the best spots, but the boat launch and inlet areas also are often quite good. Most of the trout are in the 10 to 12-inch class, but range to eight pounds. The bigger ones are usually caught by accident, by folks baitfishing with Power Bait and nightcrawlers on separate hooks.

The striped bass provide a unique longshot. The best bet is casting deep-diving plugs at the dam, right at sunrise. The biggest I know of is a 28-pounder caught by my friend Keith Rogers.

In the summer, the fishing slows, with catfish and bluegill offering the best of it until October. Then, with the water cool, the trout plants resume by the Department of Fish and Game, with bonus fish contributed by the Regional Park District

---

6.   STANISLAUS RIVER

Reference: Near Stockton; map E2 grid f6.

How to get there: Excellent access is available in Caswell Memorial State Park. From Stockton, drive south on Highway 99 to Manteca. Continue south for about two more miles to the Austin Road exit. Turn south and continue for five miles to the park. Another public access spot is located just outside of the town of Ripon, where Highway 99 crosses the river.

Facilities: A campground and picnic areas are provided at the park. Supplies are available in Stockton and Manteca.

Cost: Day-use fee at Caswell Memorial State Park is $5 per vehicle; campsite fees are $12-$14 per night.

Who to contact: Phone the park at (209) 599-3810.

About Stanislaus River: Caswell Park provides a good access point to the Stanislaus River. It also offers surrounding parkland covering 250 acres, a visitor center and nature trail.

This section of the Stanislaus is a green, slow-flowing waterway, much of it bordered by varied deciduous trees. Even in the worst years, it provides a suitable habitat for catfish. Most folks show up at the park on a summer evening, toss their line out with a chicken liver, cut a chunk of sardine or anchovy for bait and wait for a catfish to come along.

In its best years, when good waterflows are running from the mountains to the Delta, this river can still attract salmon and striped bass as far upriver as Caswell Park and beyond. There haven't been too many of those years lately, however.

---

7.   MERCED RIVER

Reference: Near Newman in George J. Hatfield State Recreation Area; map E2 grid i8

How to get there: The only fishing access to the Merced River in this zone is in George J. Hatfield State Recreation Area, near the town of Newman. From Interstate 5 south of Stockton, take the Newman exit. Drive east on Stuhr Road to Newman, then turn right on Highway 33 and drive about one mile to Hills Ferry Road. Turn left and travel east to the park entrance.

Facilities: A campground and picnic areas are provided. Supplies are available in Newman.

Cost: Day-use fee is $6 per vehicle; phone the park for campsite fees.

Who to contact: Phone Four Rivers district office at (209) 826-1196.

About Merced River: Numbers just don't speak with forked tongue.

In 1986, when high rain and snowpack resulted in high flows for the Merced River, something like 15,000 salmon made the journey up the Merced, and for the entire San Joaquin River system, the count was 70,000. By 1991, with little water allowed to flow from reservoirs to the sea, less than a hundred salmon returned to the Merced and only 600 returned to the San Joaquin system.

The connection has become so clear: High river flows equal high fish counts. It is about that simple.

What's left on the Merced are some catfish that survived the years of low flows. Some say the catfish are so loaded with pesticides, which are washed from farmers' fields into the river, that if you eat them, you will glow in the dark for several days. Regardless, the catfish are the best thing going these days, especially in the areas that are best accessible, such as Hatfield Park. Folks show up in the evenings, toss out their bait, maybe sip at a refreshment and nibble at some fried chicken, and hope a catfish gets interested in their bait.

The bottom line is that until decent river flows return to the Merced for several consecutive years, this stream offers a tale of woe and little else.

8.   SAN JOAQUIN RIVER

Reference: Near Stockton; map E2 grid i8.

How to get there: From Interstate 5 at Stockton, drive south to Highway 132. Turn east and travel to County Road J3. Turn left and continue north to Durham Ferry State Recreation Area. Direct fishing access is available in the park. Access is also available out of a private campground called Fisherman's Bend River Campground, and in George J. Hatfield State Recreation Area. Both are located off Interstate 5 near Newman. Take the Newman exit and travel east on Stuhr Road to Hills Ferry Road. Turn right and continue northeast to the park, or turn north on River Road to reach the campground.

Facilities: Camping is available at all of the areas mentioned. Supplies are available in adjacent towns.

Cost: Day-use fee at Durham State Recreation Area is $3 per vehicle on weekends; $2 on weekdays. Day-use fee at George J. Hatfield State Recreation Area is $6 per vehicle.

Who to contact: Phone Durham Ferry State Recreation Area, (209) 953-8800; George J. Hatfield State Recreation Area, (209) 826-1196; Fisherman's Bend River Campground, (209) 862-3731.

About San Joaquin River: Striped bass still make the ol' push up the San Joaquin River, and if they get by the pumping plant at Clifton Court, they will swim up past Stockton, then south past Mossdale and perhaps even make it all the way to the mouth of the Stanislaus River.

In the process, they provide short periods of good fishing and long periods of bad fishing. The best of it comes when a pod of fish arrives in the Stockton Turning Basin, right at the Port of Stockton, but again, this can last for just a short period, then be over. If you have a boat, if you hear about the run, if you are on the spot, if you get bit . . . a lot of ifs.

As you move south (upstream), the San Joaquin becomes less of a river and more of a slough, providing better habitat for catfish and a sprinkling of largemouth bass than for anadromous fish such as striped bass, salmon and sturgeon. This is certainly the case at the park areas listed, which provide opportunity for catfish. Access can be tough on any river, particularly one such as this section of the San Joaquin which flows through so much private, diked-off farmland, but at least Durham Ferry Park offers a spot to toss out a line.

---

9.   HENRY COE STATE PARK

Reference: Southeast of San Jose; map E2 grid j1.

How to get there: From San Jose, drive south on US 101 for seven miles

---

to Morgan Hill. Take the East Dunne Avenue exit and drive east past Morgan Hill, over Lake Anderson for 15 miles to the park.

Facilities: Developed campsites and primitive hike-in sites are available. Piped water, pit toilets, fireplaces and picnic tables are provided. Supplies are available in Coyote.

Cost: Day-use fee is $6 per vehicle. Camp fee is $7-$9 per night.

Who to contact: Phone state park rangers at Coe State Park at (408) 779-2728. For a map, send $2 to Henry Coe State Park, P.O. Box 846, Morgan Hill, CA 95038.

About Henry Coe State Park: This is the Bay Area's backyard wilderness, some 70,000 acres of wildlands with 74 lakes and ponds, more than half of which support fisheries. Great pond fishing for small bass and bluegill is available, but to get it requires a killer hike, at least ten miles one-way to the better lakes. Most people are not prepared physically, mentally or with enough equipment (backpacker stove and water purifier required) to make the trip, or don't allow enough time (three days, not a weekend). As a result, they end up having a terrible time.

The best lakes are Coit Lake, Hoover Lake and Paradise Lake, where it is possible to average a bass per cast on a warm spring evening. Other good lakes are Kelly Lake, Hartman Reservoir and Bass Lake. As recent as 1987, Mississippi Lake had a rare population of large, native rainbow trout, but low water prevented spawning through 1991, devastating the population.

Henry Coe State Park is one of my favorite places in California. The park contains more than 100 square miles of wildlands, a place for someone who wants solitude and quality fishing in the same package, and isn't adverse to rugged hiking to find it.

Most of the bass are in the 10 to 13-inch class, but most of the little lakes have a pond king in the five-pound range. One time, a ranger told me that I could catch a fish per cast at Coit Lake. He was wrong. I actually caught two bass on the same Rapala lure, hooking a bass on each of the two treble hooks. This is California catch-and-release pond fishing at its finest.

But what happens with most folks is that they get up Saturday morning, make the drive (longer and more twisty than they expect), and finally start hiking off at noon when the heat is worst. They come to little Frog Lake, the first pond on the route out, stop and make a cast, don't catch anything, and declare the trip a bust. If only they knew.

MAP E3

15 LISTINGS
PAGES 478-491

NOR-CAL MAP . see page 120
adjoining maps
NORTH (D3) ...... see page 348
EAST (E4) .... see page 492
SOUTH (F3) .... see page 560
WEST (E2) .... see page 466

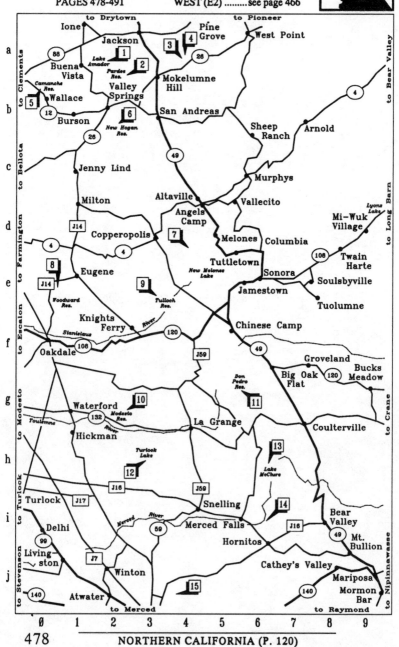

1.   LAKE AMADOR

Reference: Northeast of Stockton; map E3 grid a1.

How to get there: From Stockton, drive 35 miles east on Highway 88. Turn right on Jackson Valley Road and travel four miles to Lake Amador Drive. Continue to the lake.

Facilities: A campground, picnic areas, a boat ramp, boat rentals, bait and groceries are available at the lake.

Cost: Day-use fee is $5 per vehicle (two person maximum, $1 for each additional person). A fishing permit is required to fish in the lake; the fee is $2 per person, per day. Campsite fees range from $12-$18 per night. A charge also is assessed for boat launching.

Who to contact: Phone the Lake Amador Marina at (209) 274-4739.

About Lake Amador: Imagine a fish factory that turned out giant bass and numbers of trout like they were being made on an assembly line. At times, Lake Amador is like that fictional fish factory.

Amador is famous for producing giant largemouth bass, such as the record two-man limit of 10 fish that weighed 80 pounds, and the lake record that weighed 15 pounds, 13 ounces. In late March, it seems more bass that weigh five to 12 pounds are caught here than at any lake in Northern California.

So, that means everybody is fishing for the big bass, right? Wrong. The catch rates for rainbow trout have become so good from late winter through early summer that it is the trout that now attract most of the fishing pressure.

Amador is set in the foothill country east of Stockton at 485 feet elevation, covering 425 acres with 13 miles of shoreline. The lake is perfect for fishing, with several extended coves—Carson Creek Arm, Cat Cove, Big Bay, Jackson Creek Arm, Rock Creek Cove, and Mountain Springs—and a law that prohibits waterskiing and jet skiing.

In the spring, the best bet for getting one of those big bass is using live crawdads for bait (for technique, see Secrets of the Masters in the front of this book) up the Jackson Creek, Mountain Spring or Carson arms of the lake. If you can't get crawdads, casting plastic worms right along the shoreline also can work. The skill and light touch required for both of these techniques can take a lot of time to develop, however. That is why the trout fishing has become so popular at Amador. With weekly stocks, it takes no time at all to figure out how to do it. The lake opens either the last Friday of January or first Friday of February, and it is the trout fishing that provides the best hopes. As the weather warms, there are days when everyone on the lake limits. The Jackson Creek area is my favorite spot for trout.

The only time this lake really frustrates is in late summer, when week after week of warm temperatures put the trout deep and makes the bass wary. That is when a number of people switch to catfish in Big Bay and Cat Cove.

Add it all up, and you just about do have a fish factory.

---

2. PARDEE LAKE

Reference: Northeast of Stockton; map E3 grid a2.

How to get there: From Stockton, drive 24 miles east on Highway 88 to the town of Clements. Look for the sign for Pardee Lake and turn right on Highway 12. Continue east, following the signs to the reservoir.

Facilities: A campground, a boat ramp, boat rentals, boat storage, and groceries are available.

Cost: Day-use fee is $4 per vehicle. A permit is required to fish at the reservoir; the fee is $2 per person, per day. Campsite fees range from $9-$14 per night.

Who to contact: Phone Pardee Recreation Area at (209) 772-1472.

About Pardee Reservoir: Pardee is the prettiest of the lakes in the Mother Lode country, covering more than 2,000 acres with 43 miles of shoreline. It is most beautiful in early spring, when the lake is full, the hills are green, and the wildflowers are blooming. And one other thing: The trout also are biting.

The lake opens each year in mid-February, and is set up exclusively for fishermen, with no waterskiing or jet skis permitted. Most anglers use boats, get on the water early, and troll from the boat launch right down the North Arm.

Start in the center of the lake, then work along the east side, turning east down the long Channel Arm of the lake. Most of the trout are in the foot-long class.

As summer arrives, anglers must be on the water very early, or fish quite deep. Some anglers get their trout limit and are done by 9 a.m. One of the easiest ways is to just troll a Needlefish lure five to 15 feet deep, although many rely on the traditional flashers followed by a nightcrawler.

Shoreliners don't try anything fancy either, using Power Bait and a nightcrawler on separate hooks.

Another possibility is trolling for kokanee salmon, using flashers followed by a No. 10 Wedding Spinner made by Luhr Jensen. The kokanee also seem to be a morning bite.

Because of its nearby proximity to the other Mother Lode lakes, one option is to connect on the trout at Pardee in the morning, then to skip over to Amador in the evening for the bass. It's a great combination offer, an offer too good to refuse.

3. MOKELUMNE RIVER

Reference: Northeast of Stockton; map E3 grid a4.

How to get there: From Stockton, drive 24 miles east on Highway 88 past the town of Clements, continue on Highway 88 past Camanche Reservoir and Pardee Lake. At Martel, turn south on Highway 49-88 and drive through Jackson and continue to Electra Road. Turn east on Electra Road and drive east. The river is accessible off this road for four miles upstream to that powerhouse at Electra.

Facilities: No facilities are provided.

Cost: Access is free.

Who to contact: Phone Delta Angler in Stockton at (209) 474-8216.

About Mokelumne River: Much of the Mokelumne River has been devastated by low flows, toxic runoff, and channelization by the East Bay Municipal Utility District, but this short three-mile stretch provides a window to the way the entire river once was.

From the powerhouse here on downstream, the Mokelumne has many riffles, dropoffs and pools that hold trout. It provides an opportunity during summer evenings for skilled flyfishers or spinfishers making quiet approaches and precise casts. This section of water is also good for kayaking.

But there is a major problem. The river is a prisoner of water releases, which means that flows can fluctuate wildly according to the whims of the water master, and not rainfall or snowmelt. If the flows are suddenly lowered, it always kills the bite.

---

4. LAKE TABEAUD

Reference: Near Jackson; map E3 grid a4.

How to get there: From Stockton, drive approximately 45 miles east on Highway 88 to the town of Jackson. Turn south on Highway 49 and drive one-half mile, then turn left on Clinton Road. Drive five miles east, then turn right on Pine Grove-Tabeaud Road and continue two miles to the lake.

Facilities: A picnic area is provided by PG&E. Supplies are available in Jackson. No gasoline motors are permitted on the lake.

Cost: Access is free.

Who to contact: Phone the PG&E regional office at (209) 263-5230, or Jackson Family Sporting Goods at (209) 223-3890.

About Lake Tabeaud: It is always funny to hear people try to pronounce the name of this lake on their first visit. My pal Foonsky, who commonly mangles names, called it Lake "Tay-Be-A-Ud."

It's pronounced "Tah-Bow." Nice and simple. So is the fishing. It is stocked with 6,000 rainbow trout each year in the nine to 11-inch class, offering decent prospects, best in the spring.

The lake is set at 2,000 feet, an hour's drive east of Stockton, just high enough elevation to keep the water cool into early summer. Tabeaud (how do you pronounce it?) provides quiet water and a chance to catch trout in a small lake that is often overlooked by the masses.

---

5. CAMANCHE LAKE

Reference: Northeast of Stockton; map E3 grid bØ.

How to get there: From Stockton, drive 24 miles east on Highway 88-12 to the town of Clements. Drive six miles east on Highway 12 to reach the south shore, or continue for two miles past Clements and turn east on Liberty Road to reach the north shore.

Facilities: Campgrounds, picnic areas, boat ramps, boat rentals, groceries, and bait are available.

Cost: Day-use fees are $5 per vehicle. There is a charge for boat launching.

Who to contact: Phone the north shore at (209) 763-5121, or the south shore at (209) 763-5170.

About Camanche Lake: Come the first warm days of spring, and some of the best lake fishing in California can be had at Camanche Lake. There is a wide variety of fish—bass, trout, crappie, bluegill, catfish—and on a spring or early-summer weekend, it is possible to catch all of them.

Alas, there is always a catch. It's called summertime. That is when the place gets inundated by waterskiers and jet skis, and if those goofs hit the coves, the best spots get spooked. But before the surface temperature heats up, you can have the lake to yourself, poking around the series of excellent coves on the north shore, just west of the North Shore Resort.

Camanche is probably the most misspelled lake name in California. Writers are always calling it "Comanche." But by any name, it is a large, multi-faceted facility that covers 7,700 acres and has 53 miles of shoreline. It is set in the foothills east of Lodi at 325 feet elevation.

The bass tend not to be huge at Camanche, but they often have abundant population levels for boaters working the shoreline, casting lures as they go. Most of the bass are in the 12 to 14-inch class, with a sprinkling of 15 and 16-inchers, and just rarely a monster. They provide excellent sport.

But if you want fish, then Camanche will give you crappie. There are times in the spring when the crappie fishing at Camanche can be the best thing going in the state. One trick is to fish at night, bringing one of those bright "minnow lights." The light sits in the water and attracts both gnats and minnows, and in turn, crappie show up to eat both. If you toss a live minnow or white crappie jig their way, you can have periods of a fish per cast.

The one concern at Camanche is always the water level. This lake can get very low, particularly during the late summer and fall. If you are considering making the trip out here following a poor snowmelt, always call ahead before finalizing your plans.

---

6. NEW HOGAN RESERVOIR

Reference: Northeast of Stockton; map E3 grid b2.

How to get there: From Stockton, drive about 35 miles east on Highway 26 to Valley Springs. Turn southeast on Hogan Dam Road and continue to the reservoir.

Facilities: Two campgrounds are provided. Picnic areas, a marina, a four-lane boat ramp, bait, tackle and groceries are available.

Cost: Campsite fees are $6-$15, depending on the season and number of vehicles.

Who to contact: Phone New Hogan Reservoir at (209) 772-1462.

About New Hogan Reservoir: Since New Hogan sits less than 10 miles upstream of Camanche Lake, it always provides a good option if the fishing suddenly goes belly-up at Camanche.

But that alone says it all. It is most always a second choice to any of the other lakes in the immediate area, not a first choice.

The blame for that is the opinion that when the Department of Fish and Game introduced striped bass to this lake in the early 1980s, it condemned it to a life of mediocrity. The voracious stripers not only eat their share of other sportfish, but also eat a lot of the minnows in the lake. By doing so, they leave fewer for the other fish, reducing overall survival rates.

Regardless, New Hogan still offers a viable option. It is a big lake, covering 4,000 acres with 50 miles of shoreline, and offers many good spots along the eastern shore near Deer Flat for boat-in camping. The latter makes a tremendous vacation spot for boaters/campers/anglers.

Despite the presence of striped bass, which are rarely caught most of the year, there remain decent largemouth bass and trout fisheries. In fact, there are some huge Florida bass in the lake (Coyote Point is a good spot), well over the 10-pound mark, and trolling for trout can be exceptional in the spring. The one time the striped bass come to life is in September and early October, boiling on the surface as they chase baitfish. Approach the boil with a boat, then cast out a Rebel Pop-R or a Zara Spook, work it so it chugs back and forth on the surface, and you can catch some nice stripers.

During the summer, you have to fight the waterskiing traffic here, but there are still some excellent spots with quiet water up the lake

---

arms. The best areas are to the far north end of the lake up the Calaveras River arm, and to the far south end of the lake, up the Bear Creek and Whisky Creek arms.

This lake is not the place most folks choose for a one-day hit-or-miss deal. It is rather a place for an overnighter, camping along the lake, searching the lake arms for the most productive area and fishery.

---

7.   NEW MELONES LAKE

Reference: Near Sonora; map E3 grid d4.

How to get there: From the San Francisco Bay Area, drive east on Interstate 580 past Livermore, then continue east on Interstate 205 until it bisects with Interstate 5, and drive north on I-5 for two miles. Then turn east on Highway 120, continue through Manteca and Oakdale (where it becomes Highway 120/108) and to Sonora (some small roads west connect to the lake). At Sonora, turn north on Highway 49 and drive north to the lake. This route will get you to the boat ramp at the north end of the lake, where the better fishing is.

Facilities: Two campgrounds are provided. A marina, boat ramps, boat rentals, and picnic areas are available. Supplies can be obtained in Sonora.

Cost: Campsite fee is $10 per night.

Who to contact: Phone the U.S. Bureau of Reclamation, New Melones Lake, at (209) 984-5248.

About New Melones Lake: When the dam was raised at New Melones in the early 1980s, a lot of people figured this lake would soon be the number one bass lake in California. After all, went the thinking, there will be 100 miles of shoreline with submerged trees, an absolutely perfect bass habitat for a young, growing and vibrant fishery.

Well, it hasn't worked out that way. The dramatic fluctuations in lake levels have greatly reduced spawning success and the amount of threadfin shad minnows in the lake that bass (and trout) need to grow big in a reservoir like this. Some say planting salmon also hurts the lake by putting additional pressure on the supply of fish food.

Whatever the reason, what you get at New Melones are a lot of dink-size bass, and the DF&G stocks 73,000 rainbow trout each year. Some bluegill and catfish also are available.

It is a big lake, almost giant when full, but my advice is to avoid the main lake body to the south, and instead focus on the northern arms. This upper section is the new part of the lake, the part created by the rising water from the higher dam, and it is here where you will find the best aquatic habitat for bass, bluegill and trout.

The bass bite can be good in the spring, probing the protected coves and casting around the submerged trees. If you approach the area quietly, and then make precise, soft-landing casts, you can catch bass to 15 or 16 inches. My preference is for Shad Raps, Rattletraps and similar crankbaits, working the early-morning and late-evening bites. If you find yourself wading through the dinks, then it's time to move to another spot.

On a trip with Ed "The Dunk" Dunckel, I had a real beauty on that managed to get around a submerged tree and break my line. When we moved the boat closer, though, we discovered the bass was still hooked and fighting away—and the line was still wrapped around the tree limb. The Dunk managed to grab the bass, then unhooked it and let it go. The fish deserved it, we agreed. An option here is heading your boat well up the lake arms, as far as is possible right into the current, then anchor and let a nightcrawler drift downstream of the boat. It's a system that can take some beautiful native rainbow trout.

But most folks just troll the main lake body, content to pick up a fish now and then. In the summer, trollers in the main lake must go quite deep.

New Melones is still getting established as a recreational facility, with the campgrounds still new, and more on the drawing board. While they're making a blueprint for the future, they might also try keeping the water levels somewhat stable.

---

8.   WOODWARD RESERVOIR

Reference: Near Oakdale in Woodward Reservoir County Park; map E3 grid eØ.

How to get there: From Stockton, drive south on Highway 99 to Manteca. Turn east on Highway 120 and travel about 20 miles to County Road J14 (Six Mile Road). Turn north and drive five miles north to the reservoir.

Facilities: A campground and picnic areas are provided. A marina, boat ramps, boat rentals, bait, tackle, and groceries are available.

Cost: Day-use fee is $5 per vehicle. Campsite fees are $10-$12 per night. There is a fee for boat launching.

Who to contact: Phone the park at (209) 847-3304.

About Woodward Reservoir: The only solution to the waterskier versus fisherman conflict is to separate them. At Woodward Reservoir, that is exactly what is done. May each go thine separate way and live in peace and happiness.

The two large coves on the south and east ends of the lake, respectively, as well as behind Whale Island, are for low-speed boats only. No waterskiing, no jet skis. It is an ideal choice, for this is where the fishing is best. Meanwhile, the jet boats can have the main lake and all the fun they want.

Woodward is a large reservoir covering 2,900 acres with 23 miles of shoreline, set in the rolling foothills just north of Oakdale at 210 feet elevation.

The fishing is fair for bass and catfish, with bass best during the early summer, and catfish during summer evenings. There are plenty of little coves along the shoreline to stick casts for bass. Most of the bass are not big, and they aren't necessarily easy to come by, either. But what the hell, a chance is a chance.

---

9. TULLOCH RESERVOIR

Reference: Near Jamestown; map E3 grid e3.

How to get there: From Stockton, drive south on Highway 99 to Manteca. Turn east on Highway 120 and travel 35 miles. Turn left on Tulloch Road to get to the south shore, or continue for ten more miles on Highway 120-108 to Byrnes Ferry Road and turn left to reach the north shore.

Facilities: Several campsites (most are semi-primitive, with no hookups), picnic areas, marinas, boat ramps, boat rentals, and groceries are available at the lake. Lodging, a restaurant and a bar are available on the north shore.

Cost: Day-use fee is $3 per vehicle. There is a fee for boat launching.

Who to contact: Phone the Lake Tulloch Marina at (209) 881-3335.

About Tulloch Reservoir: The first time I flew an airplane over Tulloch Reservoir, I couldn't believe how different it looked by air than from a boat. It resembled a giant "X" more than a lake. After landing at the strip in Columbia and making the trip to the lake, I understood why.

The reservoir is set in two canyons that criss-cross each other, and by boat, you never see the other canyon. The lake is actually the "afterbay" for New Melones Reservoir, with the water to fill Tulloch coming from the New Melones Dam on the northeastern end of the "X." With such extended lake arms, there are 55 miles of shoreline.

Fishing? It can be like a yo-yo, sometimes like a yo-yo without the string. The best thing going is the chance for smallmouth bass. It is one of the better spots in the Central Valley for smallmouth, but not quite in the class of Trinity Lake. Smallmouth are different than their largemouth counterparts in that they start feeding earlier in the season. It can still be very cold in early March, and the smallmouth can go on the bite. The smallmouth like to hang out around submerged rock piles and shoreline points, often suspended about 15 to 20 feet deep. Diving plugs, grubs and Gits-Its all work the best, and it is much more difficult to get them to strike a surface lure or plastic worm.

Tulloch also has a fair trout fishery, but that, too, goes up and down. The DF&G stocks 12,800 catchable-size rainbow trout each year. Most of the trout are caught by vacationing fishermen in summer, trolling with lead-core line and flashers/minnows, going deep during the warmer months.

10.   MODESTO RESERVOIR

Reference: Near Modesto; map E3 grid g2.

How to get there: From Modesto, drive 16 miles east on Highway 132, past Waterford. Turn left (north) on Reservoir Road and continue to the reservoir.

Facilities: A campground, picnic areas, a full-service marina, boat ramps, boat rentals, gas, bait, tackle, and groceries are available.

Cost: Day-use fee is $5 per vehicle. Campsite fees are $10-$12 per night.

Who to contact: Phone Modesto Reservoir at (209) 874-9540.

About Modesto Reservoir: Here lies one of California's quality yet relatively undiscovered bass lakes.

The southern shoreline of the lake is loaded with submerged trees, coves, inlets — and protected with a 5-mph speed limit to keep the water quiet. It adds up to good prospects for bass fishing, although many of the fish are small. That keeps it from being listed among the great bass lakes of California. Modesto Reservoir is a big lake, covering 2,700 acres with 31 miles of shoreline. It is set in the hot foothill country, just east of guess where?

A key here is the boat-in camping opportunities in many coves at the southern end of the lake. A good idea is to bring a shovel in order to dig out a flat spot to sleep, something which is often necessary when boat-in camping at a reservoir.

That done, get on the lake early for the largemouth bass, casting Rattletraps along the stick-ups. After awhile, the lure will land practically right on top of a bass, and it will seem as if the lure is whacked almost as soon as it hits the water. The overwhelming majority of fish range nine to 13 inches. Maybe in future years, they will get bigger.

11.   DON PEDRO RESERVOIR

Reference: Northeast of Modesto; map E3 grid g5.

How to get there from the Bay Area: From the San Francisco Bay Area, drive east on Interstate 580 past Livermore, then continue east on Interstate 205 until it bisects with Interstate 5, and drive north on I-5 for two miles. Then turn east on Highway 120, continue through Manteca and Oakdale (where it becomes Highway 120-108). Turn east on Highway 120 and drive to the town of Chinese Camp. To reach the boat launch at Moccasin Point at the upper end of the lake, continue east on Highway 49-120 for five miles, then turn left to Moccasin

Point. To reach the boat launch near the dam at the southern end of the lake, turn south from Chinese Camp and take Redhill Sims Road-La Grange Road, then veer east on Bond Flat Road and drive to the dam.

How to get there from Modesto: From Modesto, drive approximately 32 miles east on Highway 132 to the town of La Grange. Turn north on County Road J59 (La Grange Road) and travel to the Don Pedro Dam.

How to get there from Sonora: If approaching from Sonora, drive east on Highway 108-49, then turn east at Highway 49 and drive to the town of Chinese Camp. To reach the boat launch at Moccasin Point at the upper end of the lake, continue east on Highway 49-120 for five miles, then turn left to Moccasin Point. To reach the boat launch near the dam at the southern end of the lake, turn south from Chinese Camp and take Redhill Sims Road-La Grange Road, then veer east on Bond Flat Road and drive to the dam.

Facilities: Several campgrounds, boat ramps, full-service marinas, boat rentals, bait, tackle, gas, and groceries are available at the reservoir. Some facilities are wheelchair accessible.

Cost: Day-use fee is $4. Campsite fees range from $12-$16 per night.

Who to contact: Phone Don Pedro Recreation Agency, (209) 852-2396; Moccasin Point Marina, (209) 989-2383; Fleming Point Marina, (209) 852-2479.

About Don Pedro Reservoir: This is the second best salmon lake in California.

Now wait just a minute. Salmon? In a lake? Is that a misprint? No, that is exactly what we're talking about. Other than number one Lake Almanor, there is no other lake where the experimental salmon stocks in the early 1980s have worked out better.

Don Pedro is a giant lake with many extended lake arms, providing 160 miles of shoreline and nearly 13,000 surface acres when full. It is in the foothill country at 800 feet, and many see the lake when they take the Highway 49 route to Yosemite National Park.

What makes Don Pedro number two when it comes to salmon, however, is that the salmon are usually 50 to 70 feet deep, and to get there requires special techniques. The most successful anglers use downriggers with a separate reel of wire line, which the fishing line is clipped to. They rig with dodgers and either frozen shad or silver lures that will imitate a shad minnow. With that set-up, the best area is from the Highway 49 Bridge on south down the middle channel. The reason is that the bottom here is loaded with rocks, and the minnows and salmon congregate here until mid-summer.

Bass fishing is also good at Don Pedro. My pal Clyde "The Wrench" Gibbs has hooked some monster bass in this lake. He exclusively fishes well up the lake arms, where there is plenty of cover available, and then gently casts a nightcrawler or live minnow out under the cover. In the process, he not only gets bass, but also some nice bluegill. The DF&G also stocks 60,000 catchable-size rainbow trout each year.

Don Pedro's natural production of largemouth bass is given a big bonus plant of 75,000 fingerling-sized largemouth bass. Because of the large amount of aquatic food in the lake, survival rates are high and the fish grow quite quickly.

Boat-in campers should always bring a shovel and a light tarp with some poles. The shovel is to dig out flat spots in the shoreline for sleeping areas, and the tarp and poles are to create a sunblock. Because the water can recede quickly here, the spot you fished three weeks ago can be high and dry for the coming weekend.

Regardless, this lake offers outstanding opportunity for boaters, campers and anglers. You might even catch a salmon.

---

12.   TURLOCK LAKE

Reference: East of Modesto in Turlock Lake State Recreation Area; map E3 grid h3.

How to get there: From Modesto, drive about 20 miles east on Highway132, past Waterford, to Roberts Ferry Road on the right. Turn south and drive one mile, then turn left on Lake Road and travel three miles east to the lake entrance. The boat ramp is located on the northwest shore, about one mile east of the Lake Road turnoff.

Facilities: A campground, a full-service marina, boat rentals, a boat ramp, bait, tackle, gas, and groceries are available at the lake. Some facilities are handicapped accessible.

Cost: Day-use fee is $6 per vehicle. Campsite fees are $12-$14 per night.

Who to contact: Phone the park at (209) 874-2008.

About Turlock Lake: The Tuolumne River feeds Turlock Lake with cold, fresh water in the spring. Despite its low (250 foot) elevation in the Modesto foothills, that cool water in combination with trout stocks from the Department of Fish and Game creates one of the few trout fisheries in the Central Valley.

It lasts for as long as the water is cool, with the better prospects trolling on the western end of the lake, across from the boat launch and near a series of small islands.

When full, Turlock Lake covers 3,500 acres and has 26 miles of shoreline. In the summer, the water heats up like a big bathtub and the place is converted to one of the waterskier capitals of the western world. Those skiers would be wise to break out a fishing rod and try casting around the islands (on the eastern section of the lake as well as the western) for bass, which provide a decent morning/evening bite, or tossing out a bait at night for the catfish.

---

13. LAKE MᶜCLURE

Reference: East of Modesto; map E3 grid h6.

How to get there: From Modesto, drive 32 miles east on Highway 132 to the town of La Grange. Continue for 11 miles east to Merced Falls Road. Turn right (south) and drive three miles to the entrance at Barrett Cove, or continue south to Lake McClure Road and head east to McClure Point. If approaching from Highway 49, access is available south of Coulterville at Bagby Recreation Area. Boat ramps are located near all main entrances.

Facilities: Campgrounds and picnic areas are provided around the lake. A marina, multi-lane boat ramps, boat rentals, bait, and groceries are available.

Cost: Day-use fee is $4 per vehicle. Campsite fees are $10-$13 per night.

Who to contact: Phone Barret Cove Marina at (209) 378-2441.

About Lake McClure: Some people think that Lake McClure and adjoining Lake McSwain are the same lake. That will teach them to think. While they are connected by the Merced River, they are two separate lakes with separate identities.

McClure is the giant of the two, with 82 miles of shoreline, warmer water and more water activity, including skiing and houseboating. It is shaped like a giant "H." Its primary fisheries are warmwater species, including bass, crappie, bluegill and catfish. In the cool months of late winter, however, it receives a few bonus stocks of rainbow trout from Fish and Game. The DF&G stocks 42,000 catchable-size rainbow trout each year.

The best area for bass are the two major coves in the southeastern end (the left half of the "H") of the lake, where both Cotton Creek and Temperance Creek enter the lake. Since they are located directly across from the dam, they are not affected by water drawdowns as much as the northern arm of the lake up Piney Creek.

In late winter, the upriver half of McClure (the right half of the "H") is best for trout. There is a boat launch just east of where Highway 49 crosses the lake, providing access to the upper Merced River arm. Here, you can get a mix of wild trout and recently stocked rainbows.

14. LAKE MᶜSWAIN

Reference: East of Modesto; map E3 grid i6.

How to get there: From Modesto, drive 32 miles east on Highway 132 to the town of La Grange. Continue for 11 miles east to Merced Falls Road. Turn right (south) and drive 13 miles to Lake McClure Road. Turn right and head east to the entrance at McClure Point.

Facilities: A campground is provided. A marina, a double boat ramp, boat rentals, gas, bait, and groceries are available.

Cost: Day-use fee is $4 per vehicle. Campsite fees are $10-$13 per night.

Who to contact: Phone Lake McSwain Marina at (209) 378-2534.

About Lake McSwain: If you find Lake McClure just too big with too many big boats, then little Lake McSwain provides a perfect nearby option. It's small and waterskiing is prohibited. The water is much colder than at McClure to the east, and the trout fishing is better.

McSwain is like a small puddle compared to McClure, but the water level is usually near full at McSwain. That gives it a more attractive appearance, especially in low water years where McClure can almost look barren by late fall. Since McSwain is small, the DFG gets a lot more mileage out of its trout stocks. DFG stocks 36,000 catchable-size rainbow trout each year. The big problem at Lake McSwain comes in mid-summer, when its surface waters begin to heat up significantly. The trout go deep to never-never land, and fishing success often falls right off the table.

---

15.   YOSEMITE LAKE

Reference: North of Merced in Lake Yosemite Park; map E3 grid j4.

How to get there: From Merced on Highway 99, turn north on Highway 59 and travel four miles to Bellevue Road. Turn right and drive five miles east to Lake Road, then turn left and continue to the lake.

Facilities: Picnic areas and restrooms are provided. A marina, a boat ramp, and boat rentals are available. Group picnic areas and buildings are available for reservation. Lodging and supplies are available in Merced.

Cost: Day-use fee is $2 per vehicle. There is a fee for boat launching.

Who to contact: Phone Merced County Parks and Recreation at (209) 385-7426.

About Yosemite Lake: Now don't get confused. Yosemite Lake is not in Yosemite National Park. It has nothing to do with Yosemite National Park, which is in adjoining Zone E4.

This Yosemite Lake is on the outskirts of east Merced, a little 25-acre lake that provides backyard opportunity for local residents. It is stocked with 47,200 small rainbow trout during early spring, but then the sun takes over, and it is goodbye trout. You see, it gets hot here, with 95 to 105-degree temperatures common all summer, and that turns Yosemite Lake into a hot tub-like playground for swimming and boating. Fishing? The lake has a sprinkling of resident bass, bluegill and catfish, most of which refuse to bite during the daytime. There is a late-afternoon chance for bluegill, a short binge for bass at dusk, and then only at night do the catfish go on the prowl here.

MAP E4

27 LISTINGS
PAGES 492-515

NOR-CAL MAP. see page 120
adjoining maps
NORTH (D4) ...... see page 382
EAST (E5) .... see page 516
SOUTH (F4) .... see page 566
WEST (E3) .... see page 478

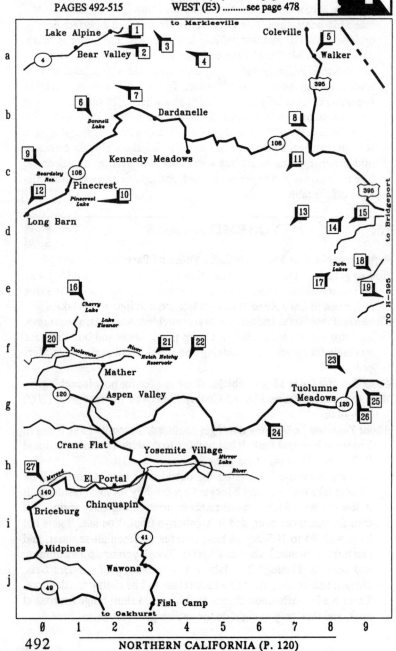

Lake Alpine   1   to Markleeville   Coleville   5

Bear Valley   2   3   Walker

a   4   395

4

7

6   Dardanelle   8

Donnell
Lake   108

Kennedy Meadows   11

9

Beardsley
Res.   108   395

12   Pinecrest   10

Pinecrest
Lake   13   15

14

Long Barn   18

Twin
Lakes

17   19

16

Cherry   TO H-395
Lake

Lake
Eleanor

20   Tuolumne   River   21   22

Hetch Hetchy
Reservoir   23

Mather

120   Aspen Valley   Tuolumne
Meadows   120   25

24   26

Crane Flat

Yosemite Village   Mirror
Lake

27   El Portal   River

Merced

140

Briceburg

Chinquapin

Midpines   41

Wawona

49   Fish Camp

to Oakhurst

1. LAKE ALPINE

Reference: Northeast of Arnold in Stanislaus National Forest; map E4 grid a2.

How to get there: From Highway 99 at Stockton, turn east on Highway 4 and drive east to Ang Highway 4 and drive east to Angels Camp at the junction of Highways 4 and 49. Continue east on Highway 4 for approximately 51 miles east to the lake. Turn right at the entrance road across from Alpine Resort to reach the boat ramp.

Facilities: Campgrounds, picnic areas, a boat ramp, boat rentals, groceries, bait, and tackle are available nearby.

Cost: Campsite fees are $8 per night.

Who to contact: Phone the Stanislaus National Forest District Office at (209) 795-1381.

About Lake Alpine: Damn, this lake is pretty. The first time I saw it was in the early 1970s, when I was taking the long way home over the Sierra Nevada via Ebbetts Pass on Highway 4 during a cross-country motorcycle/camping/fishing trip. I arrived at little Lake Alpine at about 7 p.m., when there wasn't a hint of breeze on the surface, just little pools from hatching bugs and rising trout. I parked my bike, turned the key and let the giant engine rumble to silence. I had my six-piece pack rod together and rigged in minutes.

On my first cast, I got a strike, missed the set, but knew I was on to something special. Next cast got him, a frisky 11-incher that shortly thereafter ended up in my small frying pan at a beautiful little camp set near the lake.

Too good to be true? Well, in a way it was. In the time since that episode, quite a few other people have discovered Alpine Lake, its camp and easy access off Highway 4, and spent a vacation here every year. You no longer get the solitude, the absolute Sierra quiet, but you still do get good camping and decent fishing in a beautiful setting.

Lake Alpine is set at 7,320 feet in the Sierra Nevada, just above where the snowplows stop in winter. It usually becomes accessible sometime in April. Because of the good access and increased number of vacationers, Fish and Game has made it a priority for stocking, and plunks 25,000 rainbow trout in here every summer. It's a good idea to get here in May, prior to the summer rush.

---

2. UNION RESERVOIR

Reference: Northeast of Arnold in Stanislaus National Forest; map E4 grid a2.

How to get there:to get there: From Highway 99 at Stockton, turn east on Highway 4 and drive east to Angels Camp at the junction of

Highways 4 and 49. Continue for approximately 32 miles east on Highway 4 to Forest Service Road 7N01 (Spicer Reservoir Road). Turn right and travel about ten miles east, then turn left on Forest Service Road 7N75 and travel four miles to the reservoir.

Facilities: No campsites are provided at the lake, but there is one available on Spicer Reservoir Road. Supplies are available off Highway 4 in Tamarack.

Cost: Access is free.

Who to contact: Phone the Stanislaus National Forest District Office at (209) 795-1381. For a map, send $2 to Office of Information, U.S. Forest Service, 630 Sansome Street, San Francisco, CA 94111.

About Union Reservoir: For some, just getting here is far enough "out there." But you can get a lot farther "out there" if you want.

Union and adjoining Utica Reservoirs are set in Sierra granite at 6,850 feet. It is Union that provides the better fishing, being stocked with 6,000 rainbow trout each summer while Utica gets none. The best of it comes for visitors with car-top boats who can carry them down to the water, then hand-launch them. The north end of the lake has some shallow spots, with some small islands poking through, but the south end is quite deep.

There is another option. There is a trailhead with an adjacent parking area at Union Reservoir, with the trail routed deep into the Carson-Iceberg Wilderness. Several lakes are within little more than a mile's hike, including Summit Lake, and Mud Lake. Further east, the trail runs alongside Highland Creek and near Iceberg Peak.

---

3.   CARSON-ICEBERG WILDERNESS

Reference: North of Yosemite National Park in Stanislaus National Forest; map E4 grid a3.

How to get there: Trailheads are located off Highway 4 east of Lake Alpine, and off Highway 108 in the Dardanelle area.

Facilities: No facilities are available. Campgrounds and supplies are available in and near adjacent towns.

Cost: Access is free.

Who to contact: Write to the Stanislaus National Forest Headquarters at 19777 Greenly Road, Sonora, CA 95370, or phone (209) 532-3671. For a map, send $2 to Office of Information, Forest Service, 630 Sansome Street, San Francisco, CA 94111.

About Carson-Iceberg Wilderness: Hiker-extraordinaires always cast a knowing, smiling nod when people start talking about the Carson-Iceberg Wilderness. Despite being set in the heart of the Sierra Nevada, it is one of the more overlooked wilderness areas, especially when compared to Desolation Wilderness to the northwest of Tahoe and

Emigrant Wilderness to the south, just north of the Yosemite border.

The Carson-Iceberg Wilderness is a place where hiking and mountaineering come first and fishing comes second. The Pacific Crest Trail passes through this High Sierra country, providing access to numerous small streams, including the headwaters of the Carson river. The whole area is stark and pristine, and hikers should be cautious whenever crossing rivers. During an early summer day, a river that is low and easily crossed during the morning can become high in the afternoon due to increases in snowmelt.

Compared to other wilderness areas, there are few lakes that provide decent fishing. Then once you reach them, you will discover that most of the fish are dinkers. The following lakes are stocked by air by the Department of Fish and Game: Rock Lake (rainbow trout), Bull Run Lake (brook trout), Lost Lake (rainbow trout), and Sword Lake (brook trout).

Regardless, it is a place with a special sense of history, beauty and quiet. For a backpacker on vacation, that is what really counts, not the size of fish and number of lakes.

4.　　　　HIGHLAND LAKES

Reference: Near Ebbetts Pass in Stanislaus National Forest; map E4 grid a4.

How to get there: From Highway 99 at Stockton, turn east on Highway 4 and drive east to Angels Camp at the junction of Highways 4 and 49. Continue for approximately 64 miles east on Highway 4, past Lake Alpine, to Forest Service Road 8N01 (Highland Lakes Road). Turn right and travel five miles to the lake. If approaching from US 395, proceed as follows: From the junction of US 395 and Highway 89 (just south of Topaz Lake on the Nevada/California border), turn east on Highway 89 and drive about 15 miles to the Highway 4 junction. Turn south and travel 15 miles to Ebbetts Pass. Continue west for one mile and turn left at Forest Service Road 8N01 (Highland Lakes Road). Proceed to the lake.

Facilities: A campground is provided, but there is no piped water. Supplies are available at Lake Alpine Resort on Highway 4.

Cost: Access is free.

Who to contact: Phone the Stanislaus National Forest District Office at (209) 795-1381. For a map, send $2 to Office of Information, U.S. Forest Service, 630 Sansome Street, San Francisco, CA 94111.

About Highland Lakes: This is an ideal jump-off spot for a backpack trip into the Carson-Iceberg Wilderness. Because it is located at 8,600 feet, just below Ebbetts Pass, you don't have to start your trip by hiking up, up and up, because you're already about as far up as you can get in

---

this area.

After hiking all over this planet, I have learned my lesson the hard way about how to select trailheads. Most trails start at the bottom of canyons along rivers, and that means your first day in is always a steep killer, when you are in the worst shape and your pack is the heaviest. This provides a preferable alternative to the norm.

If you drive here and decide to make a camp for the night before heading out, you will discover a small, primitive camp, and two small lakes. Both have little brook trout in the classic dinker size, and not exactly astounding numbers, either. They bite readily enough, but be careful. If you reel them in too fast, you might drown them.

---

5. WEST WALKER RIVER

Reference: Northwest of Bridgeport in Toiyabe National Forest; map E4 grid a8.

How to get there: From US 395 at the town of Bridgeport, continue northwest. Excellent roadside access is available on US 395 north of Sonora Junction, as well as off of Highway 108 going west.

Facilities: Several campgrounds are available off US 395 and Highway 108. Supplies are available in Bridgeport.

Cost: River access is free.

Who to contact: Phone the Toiyabe National Forest District Office at (619) 932-7070, or Ken's Sporting Goods in Bridgeport at (619) 932-7707.

About West Walker River: The West Walker River is for the angler who is not the specialist, the camper who wants an easy-to-reach stream where chances are good he'll catch a trout or two for dinner. It is a good place to bring a kid for his first stream fishing experience. After high flows from the spring snowmelt, regular plants and improved fishing starts from late June on through summer. West Walker River receives plants of 61,000 rainbow trout each year.

Several campgrounds are positioned along the West Walker right off US 395, providing fishing for brook trout and camping access. Brook trout are stocked near the campgrounds, as well as at accessible locations from the bridge (downstream a good spot) to just below Mountain Gate Lodge.

Once summer arrives, this stream runs quite clear and mid-day prospects can be terrible. By evening, insects start hatching, shade is on the water, and you have prospects to rip the lips off a few brookies.

6.   DONNELLS RESERVOIR

Reference: Near Strawberry in Stanislaus National Forest; map E4 grid
  b1.

How to get there: From the junction of Highways 49 and 108 in Sonora,
  drive 29 miles east on Highway 108 (a winding two-laner) to the town
  of Strawberry. Continue northwest for four more miles to Beardsley
  Road. Turn left and proceed for a short ways, then turn right on Hells
  Half Acre Road (Forest Service Road 5N06), drive four miles, then
  turn right again on the access road to Donnells Reservoir.

Special note: A heavy-duty 4-wheel drive is required to get near the lake,
  followed by a difficult hike over boulders. Light-duty 4-wheel drive
  vehicles can be damaged on the access road.

Facilities: No facilities are provided.

Cost: Access is free.

Who to contact: Phone the Stanislaus National Forest District Office at
  (209) 586-3234.

About Donnells Reservoir: Only the deranged need apply. But sometimes
  being a little crazy can keep you from going insane.

   Donnells Reservoir, set in the Stanislaus River canyon at 4,921
feet, is one of the toughest lakes to reach in California. Because of its
steep sides, there is no way to fish it effectively from the shoreline.
Ah, but with a boat, the insanity ends. This lake has big beautiful trout,
but it'll practically kill ya to try and catch them.

   So the first question is: How do you get a boat in? Answer: Only
by dragging it for a considerable length over boulders down to the dam
at the western end of the lake. And once you do that, it is "Goodbye
boat." You might somehow get a boat in, but it is damn near impossible
to get it out, making the climb out of the canyon over boulders.

   But believe it or not, there are a couple of boats here. Permanently.
There is no way to get them out of the lake. They are beat up, sure,
and they are chained up, too, but they are boats. What people do is
bring along bolt cutters, cut them free, use them to catch fish, then
re-chain them. Yeah, it's crazy. The water is clear and deep, but drifting
with the spring afternoon wind, letting a set of flashers flutter lightly,
trailing a nightcrawler, is the way to get these big trout to bite.

   Now don't go jumping off on this trip without a good look in the
mirror and a long talk with yourself. If you go anyway, I have one
thing to say: "Don't blame me. I warned you."

7.   SPICER MEADOW RESERVOIR

Reference: In Stanislaus National Forest northeast of Arnold; map E4 grid b2.

How to get there: From Highway 99 at Stockton, turn east on Highway 4 and drive east to Angels Camp at the junction of Highways 4 and 49. Continue for approximately 32 miles east on Highway 4 to Forest Service Road 7N01 (Spicer Reservoir Road). Turn right and travel about ten miles, then turn right (south) on Forest Service Road 7N75 and continue to the lake.

Facilities: No facilities are available on-site. A campground, called Stanislaus River, is available on Spicer Reservoir Road.

Cost: Access to the reservoir is free.

Who to contact: Phone the Stanislaus National Forest District Office at (209) 795-1381. For a map, send $2 to Office of Information, U.S. Forest Service, 630 Sansome Street, San Francisco, CA 94111.

About Spicer Meadow Reservoir: This is one of the older reservoirs in the high central Sierra Nevada. Spicer Meadow was established in 1929 when a dam was built in the canyon on Highland Creek, creating a short, narrow lake. It was closed for a few years in the late 1980's, and as the 90's evolve, it seems that the average size of trout is much larger here than at many other lakes in the area.

It isn't a big lake by reservoir standards, covering 227 acres, but it is quite pretty from a boat, surrounded by canyon walls at 6,418 feet. The best fishing is using standard trolling techniques for stocked rainbow trout.

At one time long ago, there were many giant brown trout in this lake. The stories I have heard about them put Spicer Meadow Reservoir in the "legend" class. But the DFG poisoned the lake to get rid of bullheads, and in the process, all the giant browns were killed. While a few nice browns are in the mix of rainbows at this lake, it is nothing like the dreams of the good old days.

---

8.   KIRMAN LAKE

Reference: Near Bridgeport; map E4 grid b7.

How to get there: From Bridgeport, drive 20 miles northwest on US 395 to its intersection with Highway 108. Turn west on Highway 108 and drive one-half mile, then turn left on a dirt road. Parking is available past the cattle guard on the road. From the parking area, walk the three-mile trail to the lake.

Facilities: No facilities are available on-site. Campgrounds are available nearby. Supplies can be obtained in Bridgeport.

Cost: Access is free.

Who to contact: Phone Ken's Sporting Goods in Bridgeport at (619) 932-7707.

About Kirman Lake: Once all but unknown, little Kirman Lake has become known as a unique and quality fishery. You get an intimate setting, specialized angling, and large cutthroat trout at little Kirman Lake.

It is a small lake, but the fish are huge. Lahontan cutthroat are common in the 18 to 20-inch class, and there are also giant brook trout, with a four-pound, six-ounce brookie documented. It stands to stay that way. The rules mandate special restrictions (always check the DFG rulebook before fishing anywhere), including mandatory use of lures or flies with a single barbless hook. You should release what you catch to insure a trophy fishery here.

The trail in is three miles, including an easy hop over a fence, and that stops some anglers from bringing much gear. But this is where a light float tube is really essential for best access and being able to reach the key areas outside the shallows.

The best fly patterns are leeches, Zug bugs, and Matukas, and the best lure is the 1/16-ounce Panther Martin, black body with yellow spots. Another pattern that works great is a 1/16-ounce Dardevle that has one side painted flat black, then has five small red dots on it. This was developed by Ed Dunckel, and we appropriately call it "The Mr. Dunckel Special."

An average day here is to catch one of these cutthroats, maybe a brook trout, too. But among those fish is the chance for a 20-incher.

9.　　　　BEARDSLEY RESERVOIR

Reference: Near Strawberry in Stanislaus National Forest; map E4 grid cØ.

How to get there: From the junction of Highways 49 and 108 in Sonora, drive 29 miles east on Highway 108 (a winding two-laner) to the town of Strawberry. Continue northwest for four more miles to Beardsley Road. Turn left and proceed west to Beardsley Reservoir.

Facilities: A picnic area and a boat launch are provided. Campgrounds and supplies are available in Strawberry.

Cost: Access is free.

Who to contact: Phone the Stanislaus National Forest District Office at (209) 586-3234; Rich & Sal's Sporting Goods, Pinecrest, (209) 965-3637.

About Beardsley Reservoir: Beardsley Reservoir has two faces. For anglers, she offers the classic paradox of a love/hate relationship.

Most folks show up in the summer and learn quickly to hate her.

The lake is subject to severe drawdowns, making it look like the Grand Canyon made out of dirt. As it is, the lake is set deep in the Stanislaus River canyon with an eight-mile access road off Highway 108 that drops about 2,000 feet. There's a primitive flat camping area for a car or two on the left side of the access road, but there's no real campground available.

When the lake is low, you have to drive down on the dry lake bed to hand-launch your boat, then as a reward, you catch primarily pan-size rainbow trout during a short evening snap. It requires very slow trolling, or heading east to the powerhouse, and then anchoring or tying up along the shoreline and using nightcrawlers, Power Bait or salmon eggs for bait. This is the lake you learn to hate.

But in the spring, during a short period in April, this lake can become your secret weekend lover. In the late afternoon, the wind blows just right, and you turn off your engine and let the wind push you along. It is the perfect speed to drift with a set of flashers trailed by a half of a nightcrawler for limits of trout, both foot-long rainbow and brown trout, with the chance of a trophy-size brownie.

On a trip here with The Dunk, we kept getting our nightcrawlers bit off right behind the hook. So we added a trailer hook, a "stinger" that is, and that got 'em. We limited in about two hours, a hell of a trip, even though I lost about a 19-inch brown at the boat, right before The Dunk could get him in the net.

Because the access road is steep, it is often closed by the Forest Service during the beginning of this key period in the spring. The reason is that if the road gets iced up, it is easy to get stuck down at the lake. So the key is to pay attention when the gate is open, then flat jump on it until the DFG stocks all the little planters and the weather warms. The DFG stocks 32,600 catchable-size rainbow trout each year.

This lake, you see, is like a chameleon.

---

10.   PINECREST LAKE

Reference: Near Strawberry in Stanislaus National Forest; map E4 grid c1.

How to get there: From the junction of Highways 49 and 108 in Sonora, drive 29 miles east on Highway 108 (a winding two-laner) to Dodge Ridge Road (one mile south of the town of Strawberry). Turn and continue to the lake.

Facilities: Campgrounds, lodging, a boat ramp, picnic area, groceries, bait, and tackle are available at the lake.

Cost: Campsite fees are around $10 per night.

Who to contact: Phone the Stanislaus National Forest District Office at (209) 965-3434, or Pinecrest Lake Resort at (209) 965-3411.

About Pinecrest Lake: No secrets here. The word is out about Pinecrest Lake, a family-oriented vacation center that provides the most consistent catch rates for pansize rainbow trout in the region.

It is located near the Dodge Ridge Ski Resort, and Pinecrest Lake provides in summer what Dodge Ridge provides in winter: a fun spot with full amenities. It is pretty with decent fishing, but the quiet wilderness it is not. The campground usually has plenty of takers.

Pinecrest Lake is set at 5,621 feet, covering 300 acres, and gets regular stocks of rainbow trout to join a resident population of brown trout. Every now and then, someone catches a big brown which causes quite a stir, but it is usually by accident and not design. Most of the fishing is done by trolling the flasher/nightcrawler combination, or baitdunking.

---

11.   TWIN LAKES

Reference: Near Bridgeport in Toiyabe National Forest; map E4 grid c1.
How to get there: From Bridgeport on US 395 at the north end of the town, drive 12 miles southwest on Twin Lakes Road. Boat ramps are located at the far east end of the lower lake and the far west end of the upper lake.
Facilities: Several campgrounds are available near the lakes. Lodging, a marina, boat rentals, two boat launches, picnic areas, and groceries are available. Fishing is permitted from one hour before sunrise to one hour after sunset.
Cost: Campsite fees are in the vicinity of $8 per night.
Who to contact: Phone the Toiyabe National Forest District Office at (619) 932-7070; Doc & Al's Resort, (619) 932-7051; Ken's Sporting Goods in Bridgeport, (619) 932-7707.
About Twin Lakes: More big brown trout are caught at Twin Lakes than any other water in California, but it is hardly an assembly line.

The two biggest brown trout in California history were caught here, the state-record 26 1/2-pounder caught by Danny Stearman in 1987, and the previous record, 26-6, landed by John Minami in 1983. One of the wildest catches I've ever heard of was in 1991, when 11-year-old Micah Beirle of Bakersfield caught a trout that weighed 20 1/2 pounds. In addition, there are browns in the five to 10-pound class caught nearly every week.

But what most people catch are not the giant browns, but the planted rainbow trout in the nine to 11-inch class, and if they're lucky, maybe a three-pounder or a frying pan full of kokanee salmon. The dream is a giant brown, and occasionally, it happens. The reality is usually something smaller.

The Twin Lakes are actually two lakes, of course, connected by a

---

short stream (no fishing here), set high in the eastern Sierra at 7,000 feet elevation. Twin Lakes Resort is set near Lower Twin, and Mono Village Resort is set on Upper Twin. Waterskiing is permitted at Upper Twin. If there are too many people around for you, a trailhead is available nearby for a route into the Hoover Wilderness, where there are many small but quality trout waters.

Most of the big browns are not caught by accident; the lake gets too much fishing pressure for that to happen. Instead, they are taken by specialists trolling Rapalas. The No. 18 Rapala is probably the best lure ever designed for these big browns. But it takes a lot of time on the water, and some anglers work at it all summer and never get one of the big ones.

At Lower Twin, the better spots include the shallows near Marti's Marina, where trolled woolly worms are productive early and late in the day for rainbow trout. At Upper Twin, the kokanees usually go on their best bite of the year when the weather cools off in September.

The preponderance of big brown trout are caught when the weather is cold, often windy. That is because in warm, calm weather, they are more easily spooked and more apt to hide under deep ledges until nightfall. So if you want a real try at a big brown, show up during the cold, miserable weather of early May, and troll until you're so cold that you feel like petrified wood.

---

12.   EMIGRANT WILDERNESS

Reference: North of Yosemite National Park in Stanislaus National Forest; map E4 grid c7.

How to get there: Forest Service Roads that lead to trailheads are available off Highway 108.

Facilities: No facilities are available. Campgrounds and supplies are available in and near the towns of Pinecrest and Dardanelle.

Cost: Access is free.

Who to contact: Write to the Stanislaus National Forest Headquarters at 19777 Greenly Road, Sonora, CA 95370, or phone (209) 532-3671. For a map, send $2 to Office of Information, Forest Service, 630 Sansome Street, San Francisco, CA 94111.

About Emigrant Wilderness: What if you flipped a coin and it landed on its side?

That is what it can be like trying to choose a destination in the Emigrant Wilderness. There are more than 100 lakes to choose from, with elevations ranging from 4,500 feet (trailhead at Cherry Lake) to peaks over 9,000 feet. The most popular trailhead is at Kennedy Meadows, located along Highway 108. From there, you can hike south past Relief Reservoir and on to the Emigrant Lake area. It is at the latter where you will discover dozens and dozens of lakes situated fairly close together.

Of all the lakes, however, a special note is that golden trout are available in a few places: Black Hawk Lake, Blue Canyon Lake, Iceland Lake, Red Bug Lake, Ridge Lake, Sardella Lake, and Wilson Meadow Lake. Many of these are located off-trail, accessible for those willing to first hike the Pacific Crest Trail, and then head off on their own chosen route to these lesser-known lakes.

Many other lakes provide decent fishing for small rainbow and brook trout. The following are the lakes in Emigrant Wilderness stocked by airplane by the Department of Fish and Game: Bear Lake, Big Lake, Bigelow Lake, Black Bear Lake, Buck Lakes, Camp Lake, Upper Chain Lake, Chewing Gum Lake, Coyote Lake, Dutch Lake, High Emigrant Lake, Estella Lake, Fisher Lake, Fraser Lake, Frog Lake, Gem Lake, Granite Lake, Grizzly Peak Lakes, Grouse Lake, Hyatt Lake, Jewelry Lake, Karls Lake, Kole Lake, Leighton Lake, Leopold Lake, Lertora Lake, Lewis Lakes, Long Lake, Maxine Lakes, Mercer Lake, Mosquito Lake, Olive Lake, Pingree Lake, Pinto Lake, Powell Lake, Pruitt Lake, Red Can Lake, Relief Lakes, Rosasco Lake, Shallow Lake, Snow Lake, Starr Jordan Lake, Yellowhammer Lake, Toejam Lake, Waterhouse Lake, Wire Lakes, "W" Lake.

The wilderness also has good populations of wildlife. Hikers who explore the high country near the Sierra ridgeline will discover good numbers of deer, including some bucks with very impressive racks.

---

13. SOUTH FORK STANISLAUS RIVER

Reference: Near Strawberry in Stanislaus National Forest; map E4 grid d0 .

How to get there: From the junction of Highways 49 and 108 in Sonora, drive approximately 25 miles east on Highway 108 (a winding two-laner) to the access road for Fraser Flat Campground on the left (Forest Service Road 4N01). Access is available at the campground itself, an off-the-trail that parallels the river west of Fraser Flat. Another dirt access road, Forest Service Road 4N13, is available out of Strawberry, about five miles farther north on Highway 108.

Facilities: Camping is available at Fraser Flat. Supplies can be obtained in Strawberry.

Cost: River access is free.

Who to contact: Phone the Stanislaus National Forest District Office at (209) 586-3234. For a map, send $2 to Office of Information, Forest Service, 630 Sansome Street, San Francisco, CA 94111.

About South Fork Stanislaus: The mountain symphony is the sound of rushing stream water pouring over rocks, into pools, and that is the

---

music you hear on the South Fork Stanislaus River.

This is a beautiful river, one that often gets underestimated only because it only rarely produces large trout. Like many of the streams on the western flank of the Sierra Nevada, this river doesn't seem to grow big trout. But once the mosquitos and caddis start hatching during the evening, it doesn't much seem to matter. The rush of the water, the sneak up to the hole, a short cast and bingo, you've got one.

The reaches accessible by car are stocked with 18,400 rainbow trout in the nine to 11-inch class, and if you hike onward up the stream, you will get into areas habitated only by natives. Most of these are just five to seven-inchers, and will take a No. 16 mosquito pattern tossed lightly at the head of a pool.

---

14.   HOOVER WILDERNESS

Reference: East of Stockton in Toiyabe/Inyo National Forests; map E4 grid d7.

How to get there: Trailheads that lead into the wilderness are available off Forest Service Roads that junction with US 395 and Highway 108.

Facilities: No facilities are available. Campgrounds and supplies are available off US 395 in the Bridgeport area and off Highway 108.

Cost: Access is free.

Who to contact: Phone Toiyabe National Forest Headquarters at (619) 932-7070, or Inyo National Forest Headquarters at (619) 873-5841. For maps, send $2 for each one to Office of Information, Forest Service, 630 Sansome Street, San Francisco, CA 94111.

About Hoover Wilderness: Nine trailheads offer access to the remote interior of the Hoover Wilderness, with many lakes within range of one-day hikes. Among the best trailheads to reach lakes quickly are those out of the Virginia Lakes, Lundy Lake, and Saddlebag Lake. The latter, set at 10,087 feet, is the highest lake you can reach by car in California, and makes an outstanding trailhead.

The best of the wilderness is the Sawtooth Ridge and Matterhorn Peak areas, which look like the Swiss Alps and make for fantastic lookouts and off-trail clambering. Most of the back-country provides good fishing in early summer, with Green Lake, East Lake, Barney Lake, Crown Lake and Peeler Lakes the best of the lot.

Including those, the following are stocked by air by Fish and Game: Anna Lake, Barney Lake, Bergona Lake, Cascade Lake, Cooney Lake, Crown Lake, East Lake, Frog Lake, Gilman Lake, Glacier Lake, Green Lake, Hoover Lakes, Oneida Lake, Odell Lake, Peeler Lake, Shamrock Lake, Steelhead Lake, Summit Lake, West Lake.

This is a special area and with such easy one-day access, it has become quite popular for hikers. Those who go beyond the one-day range, however, and explore the interior and high wilderness ridge will discover a place that is difficult to improve. After all, it is difficult to improve on perfection.

---

15. BUCKEYE CREEK

Reference: East of Bridgeport in Toiyabe National Forest; map E4 grid d8.

How to get there: From the town of Bridgeport on US 395, drive seven miles southwest on Twin Lakes Road to Doc & Al's Resort, then turn north on Buckeye Creek Road (dirt) and continue to the creek.

Facilities: A campground is available near the creek, off Buckeye Creek Road. Primitive campgrounds also are located on the creek itself. Supplies can be obtained in Bridgeport.

Cost: Creek access is free.

Who to contact: Phone the Toiyabe National Forest District Office at (619) 932-7070; Doc & Al's Resort, (619) 932-7051; Ken's Sporting Goods in Bridgeport, (619) 932-7707. For a map, send $2 to Office of Information, 630 Sansome Street, San Francisco, CA 94111.

About Buckeye Creek: Buckeye Creek, like nearby Robinson Creek, is known for its brush-free, grassy banks (no tangled casts), with occasional deep pools and cut bank. It takes a cautious wader to fish this right, with large brown trout often laying right under the cut banks. This is where Chief Lone Wolf became famous by catching big trout with his bare hands, laying on his side along the shoreline and then scooping them right out from under the bank.

If you want something easier, brook trout are planted at the Buckeye Camp where Buckeye Creek Road crosses the creek. Try from there on upstream a bit.

If you want more of a challenge and a chance for some big fish, hike up to the upper stretches of Buckeye Creek, where you will discover some brush-filled beaver dams. They create some deep holes where a mix of brown trout and rainbow trout will hang out. Toss out a nightcrawler, no bait, keeping your reel on free spool, and you can catch some beauties in this area.

Buckeye Creek receives plants of 3,800 rainbow trout each year.

---

16. ROBINSON CREEK

Reference: Near Bridgeport; map E4 grid d8.

How to get there: From the town of Bridgeport on US 395, turn on Twin Lakes Road and travel about seven miles south. Direct access is available from the road and at the campgrounds.

Facilities: Several campgrounds are available in the vicinity. Supplies can be obtained in Bridgeport.

Cost: Creek access is free.

Who to contact: Phone the Toiyabe National Forest District Office at (619) 932-7070; Doc & Al's Resort, (619) 932-7051; Ken's Sporting Goods in Bridgeport, (619) 932-7707. For a map, send $2 to Office of Information, 630 Sansome Street, San Francisco, CA 94111.

About Robinson Creek: Robinson Creek has a mix of wild brown trout, including a rare lunker, along with brook trout and 50,600 planted rainbow trout.

The best bet for newcomers is to start fishing at the bridge adjacent to Doc & Al's Resort, on downstream a bit, and also near campgrounds set along Twin Lakes Road. Why? Because this is where the DFG plunks in their hatchery trout.

Only rarely are the big brown trout caught out of Robinson Creek. Consider that there are a series of camps here, with fishermen working the water near all of them. By early summer, those big browns have been well-schooled, getting fishing lessons every day.

But even those browns have to eat now and then, and the best bet is trying for them early in the season, before the summer vacationers arrive. Offer a nightcrawler in front of a big brown in mid-May or late October, drifting it past with no weight, and it will likely be an offer he can't refuse.

---

17. CHERRY LAKE

Reference: Northwest of Yosemite National Park in Stanislaus National Forest; map E4 grid e1.

To get there from US 395: From the junction of US 395 and Highway 120 (just south of Mono Lake), drive approximately 80 miles west on Highway 120, through Yosemite National Park, to Cherry Valley Road on the right (the road is located four miles east of Buck Meadows). Highway 120 is narrow and very twisty. Turn north and drive 24 miles to the lake. Take the signed turnoff on the right to reach the boat ramp.

To get there from the Bay Area: Drive east on Interstate 580 past Livermore, then continue east on Interstate 205 until it bisects with Interstate 5, and drive north on I-5 for two miles. Turn east on Highway 120 and proceed to Manteca. Continue east on Highway 120 for approximately 80 miles to Buck Meadows. The road is very narrow and twisty as you head into the mountains. Continue east for four miles to Cherry Valley Road on the left. Turn north and drive 24 miles to the lake. Take the signed turnoff on the right to reach the boat ramp.

Facilities: A campground and a boat ramp are available.

Cost: Campsite fees are $8-$16 per night.

Who to contact: Phone the Stanislaus National Forest District Office at

(209) 962-7825. For a map, send $2 to Office of Information, Forest Service, 630 Sansome Street, San Francisco, CA 94111.

About Cherry Lake: Considering the circuitous route to reach Cherry Lake, many newcomers are surprised to see other people here. But don't get spooked, they are here for a variety of reasons.

Fishing is just one of them. Cherry Lake provides a base of operations for many activities. It is set at 4,700 feet, just northwest of Yosemite National Park, and that right there is the key. At the dam at Cherry Lake is a trail that is routed north into the Emigrant Wilderness, or to the east to Lake Eleanor and further into Yosemite National Park. Between the two wilderness areas, there are literally dozens and dozens of backcountry lakes.

If you don't want to leave, that isn't such a bad decision. The trout fishing at Cherry Lake is better than most any of the lakes in nearby Yosemite Park. Cherry Lake is a good-size lake, about three miles long, and is stocked regularly with 33,400 rainbow trout in the nine to 11-inch class, joining larger holdovers.

Fishing is best in May and early June here, although the weather can be quite nasty during late spring. Pick one of the nice days, troll adjacent to the shoreline, and you should pick up fish. If you show up instead at mid-summer and try fishing from shore, you may be out of luck.

---

18. GREEN CREEK

Reference: Near Bridgeport in Toiyabe National Forest; map E4 grid e9.

How to get there: From the town of Bridgeport on US 395, drive six miles south on US 395. Turn west on Green Creek Road (a rough dirt road) and drive for eight miles to Dymano Pond. Continue four more miles to the Green Creek Campground. Access is available at the campground and at several access points on the road in.

Facilities: A campground is provided. Supplies are available in Bridgeport.

Cost: Campsite fee is $5 per night.

Who to contact: Phone the Toiyabe National Forest District Office at (619) 932-7070, or Ken's Sporting Goods in Bridgeport at (619) 932-7707. For a map, send $2 to Office of Information, U.S. Forest Service, 630 Sansome Street, San Francisco, CA 94111.

About Green Creek: Most people don't come to Green Creek to fish. They come here to hike.

The access road leads to a nice, little camp at streamside, with an adjacent trailhead for backpackers. The trail is routed past Green Lake and then into the magnificent Hoover Wilderness. Visitors will often arrive here in the afternoon after a long drive, then overnight it and plan to start their backpack trip the next morning, rested and ready.

In the meantime, they should get out their fishing rods. Because Green Creek is stocked with 6,400 rainbow trout at the campground, as well as at several obvious access points along Green Creek Road. Most people don't know that. Now you do.

---

19. VIRGINIA LAKES

Reference: Near Lee Vining; map E4 grid e9.

How to get there: From the town of Lee Vining on US 395, drive north to the top of Conway Summit. Turn left and travel west on Virginia Lakes Road. The leads to Lower Virginia Lake.

Facilities: A campground is available nearby on Virginia Creek. Lodging is available at Virginia Lakes Lodge. Rentals for horsepack trips are also available. Supplies can be obtained in Lee Vining.

Cost: Access is free.

Who to contact: Phone Ken's Sporting Goods in Bridgeport at (619) 932-7707.

About Virginia Lakes: Virginia Lakes are the gateway to a beautiful high-mountain basin where there are eight small alpine lakes within a two-mile circle. The best fishing is at the larger of the Virginia Lakes and also at little Trumbull Lake (first lake on the north side on Virginia Lakes Road). It is set at 9,600 feet, between mountain peaks that reach 12,000 feet.

Both Virginia and Trumbull offer decent fishing for small trout, but excellent shoreline access. Rarely, Virginia is planted with brood fish. The upper Virginia Lakes are stocked by the DFG with 3,600 dink-size brown trout and 12,200 catchable-size rainbow trout each year. The lower Virginia Lakes get 3,600 dink-size brown trout and 11,200 catchable-size rainbow trout. The area has great value for anglers who like to test different waters. The Virginia Lakes are the gateway to many lakes, including Red Lake, Blue Lake, Moat Lake and Frog Lakes. The latter form almost a triangle.

In addition, a trail is available that is routed just north of Blue Lake, located inside the boundary for the Hoover Wilderness, then leads west to Frog Lake, Summit Lake and beyond into a remote area of Yosemite National Park. The entire area has great natural beauty, but is best seen on foot, exploring the different lakes as you go.

---

20. TUOLUMNE RIVER

Reference: East of Yosemite National Park in Stanislaus National Forest; map E4 grid fØ.

How to get there: From Stockton on Highway 99, drive south on 99 to

Manteca. Turn east on Highway 120 and drive approximately 70 miles to the small town of Groveland. Continue east on Highway 120 for about eight miles, then turn left (the turnoff is located about a mile past the turnoff for County Road J20) and travel one mile north. Turn right on Forest Service Road 1N01 and continue east. Access is available along the road and at campgrounds set on the river. Another access point is located farther north: Continue east on Highway 120 to Forest Service Road 1N07. Turn north and continue to where the road crosses the river.

Facilities: Several campgrounds are available and near the river, but they offer no piped water.

Cost: River access is free.

Who to contact: Phone the Stanislaus National Forest District Office at (209) 962-7825. For a map, send $2 to Office of Information, U.S. Forest Service, 630 Sansome Street, San Francisco, CA 94111.

About Tuolumne River: The Tuolumne is not the greatest stream you've ever seen, but it isn't the worst either.

For starters, you must have a Forest Service map in hand before trying to figure out the best access points, then follow the above directions. That will get you to the more promising spots where 16,000 rainbow trout are stocked by the Department of Fish and Game.

For finishers, if you are more ambitious and want to chase wild trout, you will need to scan the Forest Service map to make sure you are not trespassing on private property. This country is "checkerboarded," that is, parcels are owned by private individuals and Forest Service in a checkerboard pattern. If a sign says "No trespassing," you'd best believe it.

The hard-to-reach sections of the Tuolumne don't offer large fish, a frustration considering the effort required to reach it. I think my biggest here was a 11-incher, and most have been in the five to seven-inch class.

Regardless, it is a small, pretty stream. This is where Ed "The Dunk" Dunckel lives with his wife, Ruth, in a wilderness cabin without electricity or telephone. Says The Dunk: "Sometimes I just like to watch the water go by."

---

21.   HETCH-HETCHY RESERVOIR

Reference: In Yosemite National Park; map E4 grid f3.

How to get there: On Highway 120, drive to Evergreen Road, located one mile west of the Big Oak Flat entrance at the far west border of the park. Turn north on Evergreen Road and continue to Hetch-Hetchy Reservoir.

Facilities: A campground, a picnic area and parking are available. No

---

private boats are permitted on the lake.

Cost: Park entrance fee is $5 per vehicle.

Who to contact: Phone Yosemite National Park Headquarters at (209) 372-0302.

About Hetch-Hetchy Reservoir: The Grand Canyon of the Tuolumne was one of the great natural wonders of the world, similar in qualities to the legendary Yosemite Valley. The difference, however, was that a dam was built across the canyon to store water for the City of San Francisco, and the canyon was destroyed, flooded by water to create a lake.

What is there now is a granite-edged water hole where no boats are permitted, no trout stocks are made, and the fishing is regularly horrible. The lake is huge, covering 2,000 acres, set at 4,000 feet in the northwest corner of Yosemite Park. The lake has brook trout, rainbow trout, and a few large brown trout, but they are almost never caught.

It was a tragedy for John Muir when this canyon was filled with water, and then became a nightmare when the fluctuating water levels began leaving water lines on the canyon walls. For those of us who would like to see it drained, we hope the ghost of Muir haunts members of Congress every night.

---

22.   YOSEMITE NATIONAL PARK

Reference: East of Stockton; map E4 grid f5.

How to get there: Trailheads leading into the park can be reached via Forest Service Roads that junction with Highways 99, 140, 41, 120, and US 395. The following routes lead to major park entrances:

From Stockton: Drive south on Highway 99, then turn east on Highway 120 and drive 75 miles.

From Merced: Drive 55 miles northeast on Highway 140.

From Fresno: Drive 65 miles north on Highway 41.

From US 395: Drive north to the town of Lee Vining and turn west, then continue for about ten miles to the park.

Facilities: Campgrounds, lodging, and supplies are available in the park. Horse, bike, and raft rentals can also be obtained. Non-motorized boats are permitted in a limited number of lakes; check with park officials for current restrictions.

Cost: Park entrance fee is $5 per vehicle. Campsite fees vary within the park. Be sure to make campsite reservations far in advance.

Who to contact: Write to Yosemite National Park, Wilderness Office, P.O. Box 577, Yosemite National Park, CA 95389, or phone (209) 372-0285. Or, phone Park Headquarters at (209) 372-0302.

About Yosemite National Park: Many people don't realize that just 150 years ago, there were no fish at all in 95 percent of the thousands of lakes in the Sierra Nevada range. That includes the high country of Yosemite National Park, where the lakes are barren rock bowls, filled with pure water, with little nutrients to provide for aquatic life.

The only lakes that had any fish were the few that had inlets to large streams, where the trout were able to live in the lake in summer, then swim upstream to spawn in the winter and spring.

But as time passed, trout were stocked in the high Sierra lakes, with golden trout, rainbow trout, brook trout, and rarely, brown trout and even cutthroats planted. Well, while aerial plantings have continued into the '90s at lakes in national forests, they have stopped at Yosemite Park. There are no plants and those high mountains lakes are again returning to their natural state as barren rock bowls.

Of the 318 lakes in Yosemite National Park, only 127 have ever had fish. Of those 127, only a handful now provide viable prospects. And despite 3.5 million visitors to Yosemite each year, the Park Service does not even have a fisheries management plan. They are more interested in socking it to the public and cashing out, than providing what should be a required service. The following provide the better fishing: Benson Lake, Bernice Lake, Doe Lake, Lower Edna Lake, Edyth Lake, Harriet Lakes, Ireland Lake, Matthes Lake, Mattie Lake, Minnow Lake, Rodgers Lake, Shepherd Lake, Skelton Lakes, Smedberg Lake, Tallulah Lake, Tilden Lake, Twin Lakes, Virginia Lake, Washburn Lake, Wilmer Lake, Young Lakes.

Cathedral Lake is a good example of what can happen without stocks—and also without natural production and rules mandating catch-and-release fishing. Because of the unique rock spire near the lake, its natural beauty, and small, pristine camps set at lakeside, Cathedral has always been a favored destination. It is also a perfect layover spot for hikers on the John Muir Trail. In the 1970s, Cathedral Lake even provided very good fishing despite getting hit every day by anglers. Well, with no more stocks, no natural spawning, no catch-and-release fishing, Cathedral Lake is now virtually fished out. This same scenario has played itself out at many lakes in Yosemite.

Regardless, Yosemite is God's Country, one of the most beautiful places on earth, and I have hiked most of it. You get the classic glacial-sculpted domes, cirques, moraines, and canyons, with some of the best vista points available anywhere. But when I sit on a mountain peak and scan this remote country and its hundreds of lakes, I always imagine what is possible, and then wonder why Park Service bureaucrats have such restricted vision and imagination when it comes to fisheries.

---

23. **SADDLEBAG LAKE**

Reference: West of Lee Vining in Inyo National Forest; map E4 grid f8.
How to get there: From US 395 at the town of Lee Vining, drive a short
 distance south and turn west on Highway 120. Drive 16 miles, then
 turn north on Saddlebag Lake Road and continue 2.5 miles to the lake
 and the boat ramp. The entrance road is steep; trailers are not advised.
Facilities: A campground, a boat ramp and a grocery store are available.
Cost: Campsite fees are $7 per night.
Who to contact: Phone the Inyo National Forest District Office at (619)
 647-6525.
About Saddlebag Lake: If you want to feel like you are standing on top
 of the world, just try this trip. Your vehicle will lag as it makes the
 climb, gasping for breath, but when you finally make it, you will be
 at the highest lake in California accessible by car—Saddlebag Lake at
 10,087 feet.

It is an outstanding destination, either to camp, boat and fish for a
while, or to use as a jump-off point for a wilderness backpacking trip.

Saddlebag Lake is by far the biggest lake in the region, which is
set off by stark, pristine granite, well above treeline. The fishing is
especially good on summer evenings. The water is clear and pure, and
the fishing is best by boat during the evening bite. Like all high
mountain lakes, the trout get a case of lockjaw during still, blue-sky
afternoons. Saddlebag Lake receives plants of 11,200 rainbow trout
from the Department of Fish and Game.

A bonus here is the trail that loops around the eastern side of lake,
then heads north and splits into two wilderness routes. It's a take-your-
pick deal. At the fork, head right to go up Lundy Pass and reach Odell
Lake and Shamrock Lake, or left to Greenstone, Wasco, and Steelhead
Lakes. These are all close enough to reach on an afternoon day hike,
a fantastic way to spend a day.

---

24. **TENAYA LAKE**

Reference: West of Lee Vining in Yosemite National Park; map E4 grid
 g6.
How to get there: From US 395 at the town of Lee Vining, drive a short
 distance south and turn west on Highway 120. Proceed 11 miles west
 to the Yosemite National Park entrance and continue for 15 miles to
 the lake.
Facilities: Walk-in campsites are available at the lake. More campsites
 are available nearby at Tuolumne Meadows (reserve far in advance).
 Picnic areas and nature trails are provided. No motorized boats are

permitted on the lake. Supplies are available in Lee Vining and in the park.

Cost: Park entrance fee is $5 per vehicle. Campsite fees vary within the park.

Who to contact: Phone Yosemite National Park Headquarters at (209) 372-0302.

About Tenaya Lake: There may be no prettier lake on earth than Tenaya Lake on a warm, windless evening. The lake is set in a natural rock basin in the pristine, high granite country of Yosemite, and it is one of the few places anywhere that provides a sense of "feeling" just by looking at it. It is set at 8,141 feet, and covers 150 acres. It feels almost sacred, like a mountain temple. The lake was named after Chief Tenaya of the Ahwahneechee Indian Tribe, who was Yosemite's last Indian chief and caretaker before the entire tribe was deported to a reservation by an army troop.

Perhaps that is why the fishing is so terrible. I've always called it "Tenaya's Revenge." There are no stocks, natural reproduction is very poor, and only a sprinkling of small brook trout and rainbow trout have managed to survive. You might as well fish in an empty bucket.

No matter. To spend a day just looking at this place is plenty.

25.　　　ELLERY LAKE　　

Reference: West of Lee Vining in Inyo National Forest; map E4 grid g9.

How to get there: From US 395 at the town of Lee Vining, drive a short distance south and turn west on Highway 120. Continue nine miles west to the lake.

Facilities: A campground is provided on the west side of the lake. Supplies can be obtained in Lee Vining.

Cost: Campsite fee is $7 per night.

Who to contact: Phone the Inyo National Forest District Office at (619) 647-6525.

About Ellery Lake: Congress blew the deal when they set the borders for Yosemite National Park by not including Tioga and Ellery lakes within park boundaries. Both are set just two miles outside the Highway 120 entrance on the eastern side of the park and are Yosemite-like in all ways but one. The fishing. It's good, not bad like so many places in Yosemite.

The lakes offer spectacular deep blue waters set in rock in the 9,500-foot range. It looks like Yosemite, feels like Yosemite, but is not Yosemite. While all plants have been suspended in Yosemite Park, turning the lakes into barren water bowls, Ellery gets stocked with 15,400 rainbow trout. They join a fair population of rainbow and brook trout.

While shoreline prospects are decent during the evening bite, anglers with car-top boats do best on the far southwest side. Options? Nearby Saddlebag Lake provides them.

26.   TIOGA LAKE

Reference: West of Lee Vining in Inyo National Forest; map E4 grid g9.

How to get there: From US 395 at the town of Lee Vining, drive a short distance south and turn west on Highway 120. Continue ten miles west to the lake.

Facilities: A small campground is provided. More campgrounds are available within Yosemite National Park. Supplies can be obtained in Lee Vining.

Cost: Campsite fee is $7 per night.

Who to contact: Phone the Inyo National Forest District Office at (619) 647-6525.

About Tioga Lake: Some rare golden trout can be found in Tioga Lake, one of the rare drive-to lakes where you have any chance at all at a golden. Just don't plan on it. The few golden trout join more abundant numbers of rainbows and brookies, the latter two being planted occasionally by the Department of Fish and Game. Tioga, like nearby Ellery, is a gorgeous spot located just outside the borders of Yosemite National Park, set at 9,700 feet elevation. If the park boundaries had been drawn to include Tioga, it would get no stocks and provide about the same results as near fish-less Tenaya Lake.

The four major lakes in this region, Tioga, Ellery, Tenaya and Saddleback, are usually locked up by snow and ice until late May. The 15 hike-to lakes in the vicinity don't usually become accessible until mid-June, with a high-mountain spring arriving in July.

27.   MERCED RIVER

Reference: West of Yosemite National Park in Sierra National Forest; map E4 grid h0.

How to get there: From Merced on Highway 99, drive approximately 45 miles northeast on Highway 140 to the town of Briceburg. Continue north; the road parallels the river, and direct access is available.

Facilities: A campground, called Indian Flat, is located on Highway 140, four miles south of El Portal. Other camps are located along the river west of the park entrance near El Portal. Supplies are available in El Portal.

Cost: River access is free.

Who to contact: Phone the Sierra National Forest District Office at (209) 683-4665. For a map, send $2 to Office of Information, U.S. Forest

Service, 630 Sansome Street, San Francisco, CA 94111.

About Merced River: Here is the stream that so many vacationers drive right by in their scramble to get to Yosemite National Park. The irony is that as they pass the Merced River, they are passing better fishing water than can be found anywhere in the park. There are also several campgrounds along the Merced that have fewer people in them compared to the camps in Yosemite.

In the summer, it is an ideal river to jump into during the day time, with many deep holes and rocks situated perfectly for jumping platforms (always check the depth of the hole before jumping in and never dive head first into a river, of course). Then, as the day cools off and shade falls on the river, it becomes better for fishing, not swimming, with a good evening bite for rainbow trout in the nine to 12-inch class, some smaller, very few bigger.

In the summer, all the spots near campgrounds are stocked with 10,000 subcatchable trout by the Department of Fish and Game. It is a pretty river, set in a canyon, that too many people rush by in their panic-stricken attempt to get in line for a camp in Yosemite. The fishing is best from June through July, then starts to wane a bit in August as temperatures climb and water flows drop.

MAP E5

26 LISTINGS
PAGES 516-538

NOR-CAL MAP . see page 120
adjoining maps
NORTH..........................no map
EAST ....no map
SOUTH (F5) .... see page 578
WEST (E4) .... see page 492

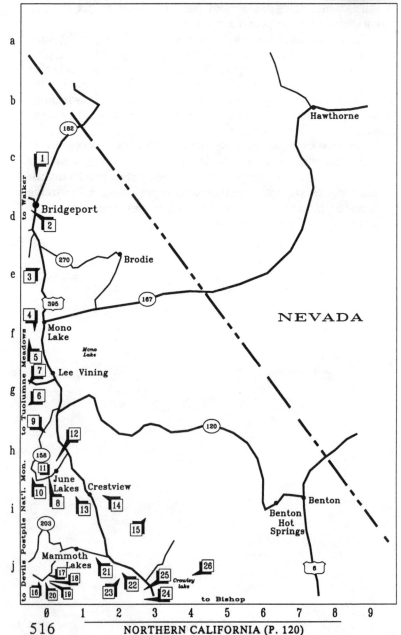

NORTHERN CALIFORNIA (P. 120)

1.   BRIDGEPORT RESERVOIR

Reference: Near Bridgeport; map E5 grid cØ.

How to get there from Southern California: Take US 395 to Bishop and onward to Bridgeport. At Bridgeport, turn north on Highway 182 and continue for three miles to the lake. The boat ramps are located directly off the highway.

How to get there from Northern California: From Sacramento, take Highway 50 east to Echo Summit (near South Lake Tahoe), and turn south on Highway 89 and drive to its junction with US 395. Turn south on US 395 and drive through Bridgeport, then turn north on Highway 182 and continue three miles to the lake.

Facilities: Three boat ramps and a picnic area are provided along the eastern shore of the lake. Many campgrounds are available in the area. Boat rentals are also available. Supplies can be obtained in Bridgeport.

Cost: Access is free.

Who to contact: Phone Ken's Sporting Goods in Bridgeport at (619) 932-7707.

About Bridgeport Reservoir: Some waters just seem to grow large fish, others just small ones. Despite numerous shenanigans pulled on Bridgeport Lake by the county water authority in nearby Nevada, this is one of the lakes that grows big fish. Just leave the water in the lake alone for a few years and just like that, big brown trout and rainbow trout start showing up.

The lake is shallow in the northern end so it warms up, receives abundant nutrients from the feeder streams, and together that results in a tremendous aquatic food chain. Because of those factors, there can be an algae bloom problem late in the summer during years that are quite warm. The bigger fish always are caught in early summer and early fall, when it is cold and the big browns are active.

Bridgeport Reservoir attracted national attention late in the summer of 1989 when it was completely drained to provide water to some hay farmers in Nevada who wanted to get an extra crop in at the end of the year. In the process, they again ruined this lake, as well as the East Walker River (see details later in this zone).

But this lake has been dried up before and it has always come back as a premiere water. When full, it covers 3,000 surface acres, and is quite pretty, with the bright blue water contrasting with the stark surrounding countryside of the eastern Sierra. It is set in a valley at 6,500 feet elevation.

You need a boat to fish it right, both for the regular stocks of 33,800 rainbow trout in the 10 to 12-inch class, as well as for the 71,000 subcatchable big browns. Even though the lake has 25 miles of shoreline, and has been emptied several times, it also seems to respond at a few key spots: Rainbow Point (the one obvious point on the western shore), as well as near the outlets of Buckeye, Robinson and Virginia Creeks at the southern end of the lake.

2. EAST WALKER RIVER

Reference: North of Bridgeport; map E5 grid cØ.

How to get there: From Bridgeport, take Highway 182 and drive north along Bridgeport Reservoir, then continue past the dam. The road runs right aside the river, providing direct access. Always check with DFG for current fishing regulations.

Facilities: Campgrounds and supplies are available in the Bridgeport area.

Cost: Access is free.

Who to contact: Phone Ken's Sporting Goods in Bridgeport at (619) 932-7707.

About East Walker River: Year after year, the East Walker River was the No. 1 brown trout stream in California, and one of the best flyfishing streams as well in the Western U.S. Then overnight, it was murdered.

A Nevada watermaster's fingerprints were all over the evidence, though. The water bully boy decided he would release all the water out of Bridgeport Reservoir, allowing it to flow eastward down the East Walker River and into Nevada where ranchers could grow an extra hay crop at the end of summer. In the process, unknown thousands of tons of silt from the lake bottom poured into the river, suffocating the fish and burying the gravel stream bed.

After a successful lawsuit pressed by the organization California Trout, such a scenario will never be allowed again. In the meantime, restoration efforts have started.

If you are in the area, you should drive by and give this river its due respect and hope restoration efforts return it to its former supreme qualities.

3. VIRGINIA CREEK

Reference: South of Bridgeport; map E5 grid eØ.

How to get there: From the town of Bridgeport on US 395, drive south. The highway parallels the creek, and direct access is available. Some access points require a short hike to reach.

Facilities: Campgrounds are available off US 395. Supplies are available in Bridgeport.

Cost: Access is free.

Who to contact: Phone Ken's Sporting Goods in Bridgeport at (619) 932-7707.

About Virginia Creek: This is a snaggy creek, made even more confounding by the large but elusive brown trout that live here. When you finally hook one, you can get wrapped around a branch so fast you'll wonder if you even actually hooked the trout.

Of course, there is an easier way to fish it. From Creekhouse Resort on upstream for two miles, Virginia Creek is stocked with 11,000 rainbow trout by the Department of Fish and Game. There are several spots along this stretch of water that are easy to fish.

But for the more challenging affair with a bigger potential award, it is the browns you must pursue. The best habitat for these brownies is around the pools created by beaver dams. The best areas are south of Bridgeport to the top of Conway Summit. While requiring some hiking to reach, you won't have the competition from all the Highway 395 baitdunkers, and maybe, just maybe, it will be your turn to tangle with a trophy.

---

4. MILL CREEK

Reference: North of Lee Vining near Lundy Lake; map E5 grid fØ.

How to get there: From the town of Lee Vining on US 395, drive six miles north and turn left (west) on Lundy Lake Road. The road parallels the creek, and direct access is available.

Facilities: A campground is available on Lundy Lake Road. Supplies are available in Lee Vining.

Cost: Creek access is free.

Who to contact: Phone the Inyo National Forest District Office at (619) 647-652, or Ernie's Tackle in June Lake at (619) 648-7756.

About Mill Creek: Hit-and-run isn't against the law when it comes to fishing. In fact, when it comes to fishing a stream like Mill Creek, it is the exact approach you need.

That is because Mill Creek is bordered by Lundy Lake Road, the stream pouring from the dam at Lundy Lake on downstream (eastward) until it eventually runs into the west end of Mono Lake. The strategy should be to hit a good spot on Mill Creek along the road, parking and making the quick stick, and then return to your vehicle, heading to the next spot. Hit-and-run. The sections of river below Lundy Lake are stocked with 2,000 rainbow trout. For smaller, wild trout, an option is hiking the river above Lundy Lake.

---

5. LUNDY LAKE

Reference: Near Lee Vining; map E5 grid fØ.

How to get there: From the town of Lee Vining on US 395, drive six miles north and turn left (west) on Lundy Lake Road. Continue to the lake at the end of the road.

Facilities: Lodging and boat rentals are available at Lundy Lake Resort. A picnic area is provided. A few primitive campsites are available at Mill Creek on Lundy Lake Road. Campgrounds are also available at Virginia Creek to the north and Saddlebag Lake to the south. Supplies can be obtained in Lee Vining.

Cost: Access is free.

Who to contact: Phone Ken's Sporting Goods in Bridgeport at (619) 932-7707.

About Lundy Lake: Lundy Lake is set in a high mountain valley in the stark eastern Sierra just a short drive from US 395, providing good fishing, a campground, and a jump-off point for hikes. Yet it is often overlooked as a destination site by so many highway cruisers.

Why? Because as they cruise 395, they become fascinated with the giant Mono Lake, located just to the east of the highway. The area is something of a moonscape, with this giant saline lake as a centerpiece. It is the nesting site for nearly all of the species of gulls in California. If you ever have seen seagulls in the mountains and wondered what they are doing there, Mono Lake provides the answer. As vacationers stare at the lake, though, they don't even see the adjacent turnoff marked "Lundy Lake Road."

If they did, they might take a quick look at Lundy Lake and end up trying it on for size. It is a long, narrow lake, set at 7,800 feet elevation, that provides good fishing for stocked trout, with a big brown trout caught every now and then. A bonus is that in the 1990s, the Department of Fish and Game has started planting 30,000 rainbow trout in the two to five-pound class and 3,600 subcatchable brown trout here. You need a boat to do it right, with most fish caught trolling. There are also several options for non-boaters, however. Mill Creek is located just below the outlet at the dam and is a good spot, with several primitive camps available here. In addition, a trail is available near the west end of the lake that is routed along upper Mill Creek and into the Hoover Wilderness. With two cars and a shuttle, a great, short trip is possible by hiking from Lundy Lake, up over Lundy Pass, and over to Saddlebag Lake.

---

6.   ANSEL ADAMS WILDERNESS

Reference: East of Yosemite National Park in Inyo National Forest; map E5 grid gØ.

How to get there: Trailheads and roads that lead to trailheads are available off the following highways: Highway 120; US 395 between Lee Vining and Mammoth Lakes; Highway 158 (June Lakes Loop); Highway 203 (Mammoth Lakes Road).

Facilities: No facilities are available. Numerous campgrounds are available near trailheads. Supplies can be obtained in Lee Vining, June Lake and Mammoth Lakes.

Cost: Access is free.

Who to contact: Write to Inyo National Forest, 873 Main Street, Bishop, CA 93514, or phone (619) 873-5841. For a map, send $2 to Office of Information, U.S. Forest Service, 630 Sansome Street, San Francisco, CA 94111.

About Ansel Adams Wilderness: This is one of the prettiest backpacking areas in the world. It is where John Muir and Ansel Adams counseled with heaven, with Banner, Garnet and Ritter Peaks and the rest of the Minarets providing the backdrop for some of nature's finest architecture. Dozens and dozens of small lakes speckle this high mountain country, all of them created by glacial action and then filled by the melting drops of snow. The John Muir Trail is routed right through this wilderness, and only hikers who get in deep into its interior will discover its greatest rewards. The best approach is connecting to the JMT, then taking sidetrips (off-trail if necessary) to reach remote, pristine lakes.

That approach also provides for better fishing. Any lake within a day's hike of a trailhead often provides poor to fair fishing. Get in deeper, two or three days from pavement, however, and you will have the opportunity to cast a line in crystal pure waters where fish have seen few lures.

The lakes are stocked with fingerlings by airplane, and while the trout are not big, they do provide good sport and evening campground fish fries. The deeper lakes have high survival rates from year to year, however, and have last year's holdovers (a bit larger) joining this year's recruits.

Here is the complete list of lakes in the Ansel Adams Wilderness stocked by airplane: Dana Lake, Kidney Lake, Gibbs Lake, Sardine Lakes, Parker Lake, Alger Lakes, Gem Lake, Waugh Lake, Lost Lakes, Marie Lakes, Rodgers Lake, Davis Lakes, Thousand Island Lake, Ruby Lake, Garnet Lake, Emerald Lake, Altha Lake, Shadow Lake, Nydiver Lake, Rosalie Lake, Ediza Lake, Iceberg Lake, Cecile Lake, Minaret Lake, Beck Lakes, Holcomb Lake, Trinity Lakes, Anne Lake, Cora Lakes, Frying Pan Lake, Joe Crane Lake, Lost Lake, McClure Lake, McGee Lake, Porphury Lake, Post Lakes, Rockbound Lake, Rutherford Lake, Sadler Lake, Slab Lakes, Twin Island Lakes, Ward Lakes, Blackie Lake, Fernandez Lakes, Flat Lake, Gale Lake, Lillian Lake, Lady Lake, Vandenburg Lake, Monument Lake, Rainbow Lake, Ruth Lake, Shirley Lake, Staniford Lakes and Lower Twin Lake.

The trail system in the wilderness is very extensive, with more than 250 miles in the Minarets alone, and connects to even more trails on the Inyo side of the wilderness. Elevations range from trailheads at

7,200 feet to the peak at Mt. Ritter at 13,157 feet. For views alone, the vista from Thousand Island Lakes of Banner and Ritter is the kind of scene where you could just sit there and stare for hours, letting it all sink in.

One of the better fishing/hiking routes for newcomers is the Lillian Lake Loop. The trout are not small and abundant at Staniford, Vandenburg, and Lillian Lake, and the trip provides a glimpse into one of the rare, special places on this planet.

---

7.   LEE VINING CREEK

Reference: East of Lee Vining in Inyo National Forest; map E5 grid gØ.
How to get there: From the town of Lee Vining, drive a short distance south on US 395 to Highway 120. Turn west and travel 3.5 miles, then turn left on Poole Power Plant Road (it parallels the creek) and continue west. Direct access is available.
Facilities: A campground, called Big Bend, is available on Poole Power Plant Road.
Cost: Campsite fee is $6 per night.
Who to contact: Phone the Inyo National Forest District Office at (619) 647-6525.
About Lee Vining Creek: When worst comes to worst, there is always Lee Vining Creek to throw a line in.

The jinx got ya? Been ki-boshed all week? Want to turn your rod into firewood kindling? Then try an evening here. This section of stream is often overlooked, but 36,800 hatchery-planted rainbow trout are available along Poole Power Plant Road, from the bridge to where the road crosses the creek. Look for the obvious access points—that is where the fish are.

The trout aren't big. The trout aren't wild. But if you haven't caught anything for a while, a trout is still a trout.

---

8.   REVERSE CREEK

Reference: Near Lee Vining in Inyo National Forest; map E5 grid hØ.
How to get there: From the town of Bishop on US 395, drive north for 54 miles to the Highway 158/June Lake Loop Road turnoff. Turn southwest on Highway 158 and drive past June Lake and Gull Lake to where the creek crosses the road. Access is available here and from nearby access roads near the creek.
Facilities: Campgrounds, lodging, and supplies are available nearby.
Cost: Creek access is free.
Who to contact: Phone the Inyo National Forest District Office at (619) 647-6525; Reverse Creek Lodge at (619) 648-7535; Ernie's Tackle in

June Lake at (619) 648-7756.

About Reverse Creek: It is no secret how Reverse Creek was named. It is the only stream in the region that flows towards the mountains, not away. Reverse Creek is a small, tree-lined stream that provides a quiet option to the nearby lakes in the June Loop Lakes.

The creek starts quite small, but builds to a respectable size by the time it reaches past Fern Creek Lodge. It is stocked with 400 rainbow trout just east of Carson Peak Inn and continuing to Dream Mountain Resort. Small lures, such as the 1/16-ounce Panther Martin, and small baits do the job just fine during the evening bite. Wading is advised, and hip-waders work well.

You will notice that there are several vacation cabins in the area, and some may even have the inevitable "no trespassing" sign posted. If so, you should alert the Forest Service's district office because the sign may be illegally posted on public land. The land bordering the stream is owned by the Forest Service, and the adjoining private property owners legally cannot prevent you from walking down the stream.

---

9. GRANT LAKE

Reference: Near Lee Vining in Inyo National Forest; map E5 grid hØ.

How to get there: From the town of Bishop on US 395, drive north for 60 miles (five miles past the first exit for Highway 158 and June Lake). Then turn southwest on Highway 158 (June Lake Loop Road) and continue for approximately five miles to the marina.

Facilities: A boat ramp is provided. Boat rentals are available. A marina, trailer park and campground are available. Supplies can be obtained in Lee Vining.

Cost: Access is free.

Who to contact: Phone the Inyo National Forest District Office at (619) 647-6525, or Ernie's Tackle in June Lake at (619) 648-7756.

About Grant Lake: Dramatic panorama sunsets and good fly-and-bubble fishing make Grant Lake a special place, the largest of the waters among the June Loop Lakes. The lake is set at 7,600 feet elevation and covers 1,100 surface acres, shaped like an hour glass.

What is available here are a series of quality waters accessible by car in a loop road off US 395, including Grant Lake, Silver Lake, Bull Lake, and June Lake, as well as a fishable section of Rush Creek between Silver Lake and Grant Lake. There are a series of hike-to lakes nearby—one of my most favorites areas in California.

Grant Lake provides good trolling in the morning and good fly-and-bubble prospects in the evening. The better spots for shorefishing are at the lake narrows (when the lake is full), at the peninsula, and

---

also where Park Creek enters the lake near the dam. It is stocked regularly with 58,000 rainbow trout and 7,100 subcatchable brown trout.

But Grant Lake does not come problem-free. It is the only lake in the June Loop that allows waterskiing, and that drives a lot of anglers elsewhere to more quiet waters. The lake is also subject to drawdowns courtesy of the Los Angeles Department of Water & Power, those lovely folks for whom fish just get in the way of their raid on the mountains' water.

---

10.   SILVER LAKE

Reference: Near Lee Vining in Inyo National Forest; map E5 grid hØ.

How to get there: From the town of Bishop on US 395, drive north for 54 miles to the Highway 158/June Lake Loop Road turnoff. Turn southwest on Highway 158 and drive past June Lake, Gull Lake and continue for another three miles to Silver Lake. The boat ramp is at the south end of the lake.

How to get there: From the town of Lee Vining on US 395, drive 11 miles south to June Lake Junction. Turn south on Highway 158 (June Lake Loop Road) and drive six miles to the boat ramp at the south end of the lake.

Facilities: A campground, a full-facility resort, a boat ramp, boat rentals, bait, groceries, and gas are available.

Cost: Campsite fees are $8 per night.

Who to contact: Phone Silver Lake Resort at (619) 648-7469; Inyo National Forest District Office at (619) 647-6525; Ernie's Tackle in June Lake at (619) 648-7756.

About Silver Lake: Silver Lake is the most hidden of the waters in the June Lake Loop. It is a small, intimate lake, covering just 80 acres at 7,600 feet. Yet all services are provided, and an outstanding trailhead is available that is routed up the beautiful Rush Creek drainage.

It is stocked weekly with rainbow trout, providing good evening fishing for both trollers and shorecasters tossing the fly-and-bubble combination. Occasional plants of trophy-size rainbow trout also are made, joining a small population of quality browns. The lake receives plants of 45,600 rainbow trout annually.

Unlike Grant Lake, Silver Lake doesn't seem to have nearly the problems of lake drawdowns. It is filled with snowmelt in spring and glacial water in summer, creating a pure setting that is easily accessible.

The wilderness, it is not. But that is not far away, either. A trail is routed west from Silver Lake along the Rush Creek drainage and runs past Agnew Lake, Gem Lake and Waugh Lake into the Ansel Adams Wilderness. One of the great hikes available in California is to take this trail all the way up to the ridge, where it connects to the Pacific Crest Trail, then head north over Donohue Pass into Yosemite, and out down Lyell Fork and to Tuolumne Meadows. You need two cars for this trip, using the shuttle system, parking one at Silver Lake and the other at Tuolumne Meadows.

---

11. GULL LAKE

Reference: Near Lee Vining in Inyo National Forest; map E5 grid hØ.

How to get there: From the town of Bishop on US 395, drive north for 54 miles to the Highway 158/June Lake Loop Road turnoff. Turn southwest on Highway 158 and drive past June Lake and continue another mile to Gull Lake.

Facilities: A campground, a boat ramp, boat rentals, and a full-service marina are available. Groceries can be obtained nearby.

Cost: Campsite fee is $8 per night.

Who to contact: Phone Gull Lake Boat Landing at (619) 648-7539; Inyo National Forest District Office at (619) 647-6525; or Ernie's Tackle in June Lake at (619) 648-7756.

About Gull Lake: Little Gull Lake is the smallest of the June Loop Lakes, covering just 64 acres. It is intimate and dramatic, in the eastern Sierra, small at 64 acres, but beautiful, set in a rock bowl below the peaks of the eastern Sierra.

Just because it is the smallest of the lakes in the immediate area, don't sell it short. The lake is stocked with 36,800 rainbow trout that range five to eight pounds, joined by the 10 to 12-inchers courtesy of the Department of Fish and Game. They provide opportunity for shoreline baitdunkers, trollers, and evening flyfishers.

---

12. JUNE LAKE

Reference: Near Lee Vining in Inyo National Forest; map E5 grid hØ.

How to get there: From the town of Bishop on US 395, drive north for 54 miles to the Highway 158/June Lake Loop Road turnoff. Turn southwest on Highway 158 and drive three miles to June Lake.

Facilities: Two campgrounds are provided. A marina, a boat ramp, boat rental, bait, tackle, and groceries are available nearby.

Cost: Campsite fee is $8 per night.

Who to contact: Phone June Lake Marina at (619) 648-7726; Inyo National Forest District Office at (619) 647-6525; Ernie's Tackle in June Lake at (619) 648-7756.

About June Lake: Even though it is a long drive to reach June Lake, that doesn't mean you will find a lake with few people around. The opposite is true. This lake gets as intense fishing pressure as any in California.

It is a fully developed resort area. It has everything going for it except solitude. Beauty? It's a 160-acre mountain lake set at 7,600 feet below snow-capped peaks. Good fishing? Weekly stocks make sure of it. Accommodations? If you need something, you can get it here.

Catch rates are high here for boaters, poor to fair for shoreliners. The lake is clear and deep, and the trout are sensitive to light and temperatures, especially with so many people fishing. The lake seems particularly vulnerable to full moon-itis, when the trout will feed at night, then disappear during the day, so always arrange your vacations during new moons.

That done, you will have a chance for trout in the five to eight-pound class, along with the more typical sized rainbows that range 10 to 12 inches. The lake receives plants of 81,000 rainbow trout each year.

---

13. GLASS CREEK

Reference: Near Crestview in Inyo National Forest; map E5 grid i1.

How to get there: From the town of Bishop on US 395, drive north for 47 miles to Crestview. Turn right on Glass Creek Road (across from the Crestview Maintenance Station) and drive west to the campground. Access is available where the road crosses the stream and along the trail that parallels it.

Facilities: A free, primitive campground is provided at the creek. There is no piped water. Supplies can be obtained in Lee Vining.

Cost: Access is free.

Who to contact: Phone the Inyo National Forest District Office at (619) 647-6525, or Ernie's Tackle in June Lake at (619) 648-7756.

About Glass Creek: The guy that drives the DFG hatchery truck doesn't need any smart pills. Now, where do you think he plants the 1,400 rainbow trout on Glass Creek? Why, right near the campground, of course.

A lot of folks forget that, particularly on an obscure little water like Glass Creek. On one trip, a fairly experienced angler walked a lot of river to catch only a dink-sized wild trout. Then a little kid, plunking out some bait near the campground, got a couple of brookies for dinner on Power Bait, courtesy of the hatchery trout.

I remember this well because I was the one with the dinkers.

---

14. DEADMAN CREEK

Reference: Near the Mammoth Lakes in Inyo National Forest; map E5 grid i2.

How to get there: From the town of Bishop on US 395, drive north for 47 miles to Crestview. Continue for one-half mile and turn right on White

Wing Camp Road (improved dirt). Continue west to the campground. Access is available from the campground west.

Facilities: A free, primitive campground is provided. There is no piped water. Supplies can be obtained in Lee Vining or Mammoth Lakes.

Cost: Access is free.

Who to contact: Phone the Inyo National Forest District Office at (619) 647-6525, or Kittredge Sports in Mammoth Lakes at (619) 934-7566.

About Deadman Creek: Here is another oft-missed little stream, similar in quality and not far geographically from Glass Creek. Actually, Glass Creek is a tributary of Deadman Creek, with separate roads providing access to each.

As at Glass Creek, pan-size brook trout are planted near the campground (2,200 to be exact), with the rest of the stream providing access to small natives. If you are cruising US 395, the best bet is to make quick hits on both streams, Deadman and Glass creeks, sticking the water near the camps, then moving onward on your trip.

---

15. OWENS RIVER

Reference: East of Mammoth Lakes; map E5 grid i3.

How to get there: From the town of Bishop on US 395, drive approximately 46 miles north to Owens River Road. Turn left and travel two miles east, then turn north on Big Springs Road and travel to the campground, where the river's headwaters are located. Public access is available from the campground downstream about a mile. Beware of crossing onto private property. Access is available through Alper's Owens River Ranch and Arcularius Ranch for their guests only. Other public access is available via Benton Crossing Road, located approximately 13 miles south of the Owens River Road turnoff off US 395. Turn east and continue to the bridge. The area between the Arcularius Ranch and Crowley Lake is accessible to the public.

Facilities: A campground is available at Big Springs. Supplies are available in Lee Vining, Mammoth Lakes and Tom's Place.

Cost: River access is free.

Who to contact: Phone Sierra Bright Dot in Mammoth Lakes at (619) 934-5514, or Kittredge Sports in Mammoth Lakes at (619) 934-7566.

Note: Always check DFG regulations for laws governing the Owens River.

About Owens River: Comparing the Owens River to most other trout streams in California is like comparing the North Pole and South Pole. Owens River is a world apart.

The Owens is a "spring creek," a meandering stream whose quiet flows pretzel their way through meadows for 30 miles before entering Crowley Lake. The water is very clear, sometimes deep, full of a huge assortment of aquatic life, and loaded with large, fast-growing trout

---

that you can often see cruising along. Loaded with them? Loaded. It is an amazing phenomenon.

But before you throw your gear in your car and make a dash for the Owens Valley, put on the brakes and read on. Why? Because it is my opinion that while the Owens Rivers can conjure up visions of greatness in the mind of most any angler, the reality is that it produces few trout on the end of a fishing line. There are two reasons. One is so much of the river is bordered by private property that access is largely a pain in the ass. For all the 30 miles of river, the one decent public accessible spot is at Big Springs (see directions). This stretch of water, as well as that bordering the private resorts, gets fished so hard that it takes absolute preeminent skills to get bit.

The fish spook very easily. I watched my brother, Rambob, sneak up on his hands and knees, yet the fish still spooked downriver. That kills it right there for most anglers. Strike One. The presentation must be perfect, very soft, and the fly can't skid across the water, but drift downstream as if no line was attached. Strike Two. The water is so clear and so slow flowing that the trout have all day to inspect the fly, and then decide not to bite. I've seen five-pound browns swim right up to my Hare's Ear, just to sluff it off. Strike Three, and you're out.

There are few resident fish in the Owens River. The big guys tend to live in Crowley Lake, then enter the river to spawn, the big browns doing so in the fall, the rainbows in the spring. Those are the best times to fish, the obvious window of opportunity when the monster-sized fish are in the river.

In the summer, the river gets hit hard every day, catch rates are low, and only very rarely is a true trophy-size rainbow or brown trout actually caught.

So what's all the hoo-ha about?

Simply this: The Owens River demands the best out of the best flyfishers in America—and it is always a challenge that the best find most compelling.

---

16.   HORSESHOE LAKE

Reference: Near Mammoth Lakes in Inyo National Forest; map E5 grid jØ.

How to get there: From the town of Bishop on US 395, drive north for 39 miles to Mammoth Junction. Turn west on Highway 203 (Minaret Summit Road) and drive four miles, then turn left onto Lake Mary Road and drive seven miles west to the lake.

Facilities: A group campground is available; reservations are required. Supplies can be obtained in Mammoth Lakes and Lake Mary.

Cost: Group campsites are $20-$45 per night.

Who to contact: Phone the Inyo National Forest District Office at (619) 934-2505, or Kittredge Sports in Mammoth Lakes at (619) 934-7566.

About Horseshoe Lake: The Mammoth Lakes Basin is often compared to the June Loop Lakes to the nearby north, but is not nearly as traveled nor developed as the June Loop Lakes.

Horseshoe Lake is a good example. It is set at 8,900 feet and equals the natural beauty of any lake in the eastern Sierra. There is no resort here, no boat rentals, no boat ramp, but alas, no trout stocks either. A light population of brook trout and rainbow trout is available, however. For fishing alone, the other lakes near Mammoth are better prospects.

But what makes this lake special is the trailhead at the northern side of the lake. The trail heads west up to Mammoth Pass and then connects shortly with the Pacific Crest Trail. I have hiked all of this, and the best bet is to head south into the John Muir Wilderness and take cutoff trails along Deer Creek to Deer Lake, or continue another five miles south on the PCT and head to Duck Lake or Purple Lake.

---

17. TWIN LAKES

Reference: Near Mammoth Lakes in Inyo National Forest; map E5 grid jØ.

How to get there: From the town of Bishop on US 395, drive north for 39 miles to Mammoth Junction. Turn west on Highway 203 (Minaret Summit Road) and drive four miles, then turn left onto Lake Mary Road and drive three miles to the lake.

Facilities: A campground is provided. Supplies are available nearby.

Cost: Campsite fee is $7 per night.

Who to contact: Phone the Inyo National Forest District Office at (619) 934-2505, or Kittredge Sports in Mammoth Lakes at (619) 934-7566.

About Twin Lakes: Don't get this Twin Lakes confused with the Twin Lakes located farther north, just west of Bridgeport. They are two different animals.

The Twin Lakes west of Bridgeport are a large set of lakes in a well-developed area, stocked weekly with rainbow trout, and where more big brown trout are caught than any lake in California. For information, see Zone-E4.

This Twin Lakes is set west of Mammoth, a pair of small lakes on little Mammoth Creek, high in Inyo National Forest, 8,700 feet elevation. It is stocked by the Department of Fish and Game with 18,200 rainbow trout in the nine to 11-inch class, but receives no bonus large fish. The lakes are absolutely beautiful, set amid the Sierra granite country and ringed by old stands of pines.

It's the kind of place where an angler with a car-top boat would arrive for an evening of flyfishing. This is not the place to get ambitious. After all, you are on vacation. Leave your ambitions behind.

18. LAKE MAMIE

Reference: Near Mammoth Lakes in Inyo National Forest; map E5 grid jØ.

How to get there: From the town of Bishop, drive north for 39 miles to Mammoth Junction. Turn west on Highway 203 (Minaret Summit Road) and drive four miles, then turn left onto Lake Mary Road and drive five miles to the lake.

Facilities: Rental cabins, bike and boat rentals, and groceries are available at Wildyrie Lodge. A boat ramp is also available; no motors are permitted on the lake. Campgrounds are available at nearby lakes.

Cost: Access is free. There is a fee for boat launching.

Who to contact: Phone the Inyo National Forest District Office at (619) 934-2505; Wildyrie Lodge at (619) 934-2444; Kittredge Sports in Mammoth Lakes at (619) 934-7566.

About Lake Mamie: Of the waters in the Mammoth Lakes Basin, Lake Mamie is one of the few that is stocked by the Department of Fish and Game. The others are Twin Lakes, Lake Mary and Lake George.

It is little Mamie, however, that often provides the best fishing. The lake is small and narrow, easily fished by boat or bank, with a variety of methods working, including good ol' shoreline baitdunking, trolling, and the fly-and-bubble technique, which is traditional during the evening at all lakes in the eastern Sierra. In addition, the DFG has come to stocking Lake Mamie with 12,400 brood-stock rainbow trout, trout that range to five pounds.

One key at Lake Mamie is using light line. The water is quite clear, and line heavier than six-pound test can be detected and avoided by the larger fish. My suggestion is to use three-pound Fenwick line, which is designed for micro-spinning reels.

19. LAKE MARY

Reference: Near Mammoth Lakes in Inyo National Forest; map E5 grid jØ.

How to get there: From the town of Bishop on US 395, drive north for 39 miles to Mammoth Junction. Turn west on Highway 203 (Minaret Summit Road) and drive four miles, then turn left onto Lake Mary Road and drive three miles to the lake.

Facilities: A campground, a boat ramp, boat rentals, and groceries are available. Lodging is also available at the lake.

Cost: Access is free. There is a fee for boat launching.

Who to contact: Phone the Inyo National Forest District Office at (619) 934-2505; Crystal Crag Lodge at (619) 934-2436; Kittredge Sports in Mammoth Lakes at (619) 934-7566.

About Lake Mary: This is headquarters for the Mammoth Lakes area. Of the 11 lakes in the immediate vicinity, Lake Mary is the largest lake, provides a resort, launch and boat rentals, and is the most heavily stocked of the lot. The plants include 30,600 trout of all sizes, big as in up to 10 pounds, and small as in dinkers, and lots ranging in-between.

It only takes one look, and you see why this lake is so popular: The natural beauty is astounding. The lake is set high in the mountains, 8,900 feet elevation, among some of nature's most perfect artwork.

Standard fishing techniques work just fine here, either trolling (best), casting a bubble and fly (OK), and fishing from shore with bait (fair). A trip to Lake Mary isn't exactly roughing it, but you get decent fishing and great natural beauty, anyway.

If there are too many people for you, an excellent trailhead for backpackers is available on the east side of the lake. The trail is routed south along Mammoth Creek to Arrowhead Lake, Skeleton Lake, Barney Lake then finally to big Duck Lake. The latter is larger than Lake Mary and set just a mile from the junction with the Pacific Crest Trail.

---

20. LAKE GEORGE

Reference: Near Mammoth Lakes in Inyo National Forest; map E5 grid jØ.

How to get there: From the town of Bishop on US 395, drive north for 39 miles to Mammoth Junction. Turn west on Highway 203 (Minaret Summit Road) and drive four miles, then turn left onto Lake Mary Road and drive four miles, past Lake Mary, to Lake George.

Facilities: A campground, a boat ramp, boat rentals, bait, and tackle are available. Lodging is available at Woods Lodge.

Cost: Access is free. There is a fee for boat launching.

Who to contact: Phone the Inyo National Forest District Office at (619) 934-2505; Kittredge Sports in Mammoth Lakes at (619) 934-7566; Woods Lodge at (619) 934-2261 (summer) or (619) 934-2342 (winter).

About Lake George: You get a two-for-one offer at Lake George. You can camp and fish here, with decent prospects for rainbow trout and brook trout to 12 inches, or you can strap on a backpack and hoof it down the trail. Either way, it is tough to go wrong.

Lake George is set at the 9,000-foot range, a small, round lake fed by creeks coming from both Crystal Lake and TJ Lake, both just a mile away. It is set just west of Lake Mary, yet doesn't get nearly the number of people. That makes it attractive, along with decent fishing for trout

---

up to a foot, rarely larger. A sprinkling of 21,800 rainbow trout to five pounds are planted every year.

Another option, however, is to lace up your hiking boots and go for broke. The trail that starts at the northwest end of the lake is routed past Crystal Lake, a beautiful little lake set below giant Crystal Crag, and then up, up, up to the Mammoth Crest and on south a few miles to the little Deer Lakes. The latter provide quiet, seclusion and great natural beauty.

21.   MAMMOTH CREEK

Reference: Near Mammoth Lakes in Inyo National Forest; map E5 grid j1.

How to get there: From the town of Bishop on US 395, drive north for 39 miles to Mammoth Junction. Turn west on Highway 203 (Minaret Summit Road) and drive to the town of Mammoth Lakes. Turn left on Old Mammoth Road and continue to the road located just before the bridge. Turn left and continue west.

Facilities: Campgrounds are available at nearby lakes. Supplies can be obtained in Mammoth Lakes.

Cost: Creek access is free.

Who to contact: Phone the Inyo National Forest District Office at (619) 647-6525, or Kittredge Sports in Mammoth Lakes at (619) 934-7566.

About Mammoth Creek: Little Mammoth Creek flows downstream (east) from Twin Lakes and provides an option amid the Mammoth area known mostly for a series of small, productive lakes.

Always start your day here at the bridge on Old Mammoth Road. From there, you will find access points to the creek along the road to US 395. That's it. This stretch of water is stocked with 11,000 rainbow trout and provides decent public access.

As the river flows east past US 395, it runs into the Hot Creek geyser and forms Hot Creek, where less than a mile of the stream is open to the public.

22.   CONVICT CREEK

Reference: North of Bishop in Inyo National Forest; map E5 grid j2.

How to get there: From the town of Bishop on US 395, drive 35 miles north on US 395 to Convict Lake Road on the left. Turn south and travel toward Convict Lake. Direct access is available off the road.

Facilities: A campground is available at Convict Lake. Supplies are available in Bishop and Mammoth Lakes.

Cost: Creek access is free.

Who to contact: Phone the Inyo National Forest District Office at (619)

647-6525; Kittredge Sports in Mammoth Lakes at (619) 934-7566; Culver's Sporting Goods in Bishop at (619) 872-8361.

About Convict Creek: If you get zilched at Convict Lake, this small stream provides a viable option. 15,400 catchable trout are planted from the dam on the east end of the lake on downstream toward US 395, with access right along Convict Lake Road.

Convict Lake is one of the prettiest places anywhere, and also offers a multitude of recreational choices. Of them all, fishing below the dam on Convict Creek is the most overlooked.

---

23. CONVICT LAKE

Reference: North of Bishop in Inyo National Forest; map E5 grid j2.

How to get there: From the town of Bishop on US 395, drive 35 miles north on US 395 to Convict Lake Road on the left. Turn south and travel two miles to the boat ramp.

Facilities: A campground and a picnic area provided. A boat ramp, boat rentals, bait, tackle, and groceries are available at the lake. Lodging is available at Convict Lake Resort.

Cost: Access is free. There is a fee for boat launching.

Who to contact: Phone the Inyo National Forest District Office at (619) 934-2505; Convict Lake Resort at (619) 934-3803 or (619) 934-3800; Culver's Sporting Goods in Bishop at (619) 872-8361.

About Convict Lake: The first time I saw Convict Lake, my mouth dropped like an egg from a long-legged chicken. It is a mountain shrine, a place where people who love untouched, natural beauty can practice their religion. The lake is framed by a back wall of wilderness mountain peaks, and fronted by a conifer-lined shore. All this is set at 7,583 feet, bordered by the John Muir Wilderness to the west, yet with very easy access off US 395 to the east.

The fishing is damn good, too. Time your trip when the moon is dark, and the lake surface has become ice free, and you will get excellent trolling results. Most of the summer catches are rainbow trout and brook trout, but in the early summer and early fall, when the weather is cold and fishing pressure is low, some huge brown trout are always caught.

If you want more, you can get more. The trail on the north side of the lake is routed west along the lake, and then up through a canyon alongside Convict Creek. In the space of five miles, it leads into the John Muir Wilderness and a series of nine lakes, including large Bighorn Lake, which is bigger than Convict Lake. Another option is fishing for the planters stocked in Convict Creek just downstream of the dam along Convict Lake Road.

When you put it all together, this is a great place to spend a week—beauty, quality fish, and hiking options.

---

24. MCGEE CREEK

Reference: North of Bishop in Inyo National Forest; map E5 grid j3.

How to get there: From the town of Bishop on US 395, drive 28 miles north (past the southern end of Crowley Lake) and turn west on McGee Road (just past the McGee Lodge). Continue one-quarter mile south on Old Highway 395 to McGee Pack Station Road. Turn south and continue. Direct access is available off the road.

Facilities: A campground is provided on the creek. Supplies are available in Bishop.

Cost: Creek access is free.

Who to contact: Phone the Inyo National Forest District Office at (619) 647-6525, or Culver's Sporting Goods in Bishop at (619) 872-8361.

About McGee Creek: When the wind is blowing a gale at Crowley Lake, little McGee Creek provides the answer to a fisherman's prayer.

The wind can really howl at Crowley, particularly during the afternoon in the early summer. It drives everybody off the lake looking for cover. Only a few folks who know little spots like McGee Creek keep looking for trout.

McGee Creek is located just southwest of Crowley Lake, flowing eastward until it joins up with Convict Creek and enters the big lake. The section between Old Highway 395 and the Upper Campground are stocked here with 9,200 rainbow trout. Not big trout, but trout just the same, and when a hurricane is blowing at Crowley, any trout is a good trout.

Another option at McGee Creek is using the end of the road as a trailhead for a wilderness adventure. The trail is routed west into the John Muir Wilderness, passing Horsetail Falls and then up to the high country, where you discover dozens of lakes. One of the better destinations is the source of McGee Creek, Big McGee and Little McGee lakes, set amid the stunning, high granite country of the Silver Divide.

---

25. HOT CREEK

Reference: Near Mammoth Lakes; map E5 grid j3.

How to get there: From the town of Lee Vining, turn south on US 395 and drive about 30 miles to the Hot Creek Hatchery. Turn left on Owens Road and look for the sign indicating public access. Continue straight to the dirt parking areas and hike down to the creek.

Facilities: No facilities are available on-site. Campgrounds, lodging, and supplies are available in the Mammoth Lakes area.

Cost: Access is free.

Who to contact: Phone Sierra Bright Dot in Mammoth Lakes at (619) 934-5514; Hot Creek Ranch at (619) 935-4214.

About Hot Creek: So many trout are caught and released at Hot Creek that through the process of natural selection, they soon might start being born with grommets in the sides of their mouth. It is the most popular catch-and-release fishery in California, with each trout being caught an average of five or six times a month. Crazy? Not so crazy. What will drive you crazy is when you spot several 22-inch, 4-pound native rainbow trout and then try to catch them.

Hot Creek is the classic meandering spring creek, wandering through a meadow in the eastern Sierra like a pretzel. Only two small pieces of it are accessible, totaling just three miles. Below the Hot Creek Hatchery, there are two miles of stream that are bordered by private land, with access limited to flyfishers booking one of the nine cabins at Hot Creek Ranch. Downstream of that section is another piece of water just under a mile long that is public accessible. The best time to fish is from the season opener on the last Saturday in April through early July. After that, weed growth becomes a problem.

The Hot Creek Ranch section of river is something of a legend, where the big trout have names, and where some of the most expert flyfishers in the world will come to practice their art. All wear polarized sunglasses so they can see the trout in the river. Almost never will the trout actually smack the fly, but more often will simply stop it. The know-hows, seeing this through their special glasses, will then set the hook. Newcomers to the game, without polarized glasses, will just keep waiting for the bite that never comes. All fish are released on this stretch of river. The best fly patterns are the standards for spring creeks. They include caddis, duns and parachutes.

The free-to-the-public stretch of water is one of the most intensely fished streams in the world. There is an 18-inch minimum size limit, and gear type is restricted to flies and lures with single barbless hooks. There are a lot of big fish here, and only rarely does anyone take one to eat. It is considered sacrilege.

The stream is called Hot Creek because just below the public-accessible stretch of water, hot water pours into the stream, way too hot to support trout. So there you have it, a tiny piece of water just three miles long from the hatchery to hot spring, where there are not only a lot of big, native rainbow trout—but where you can actually see them. It comprises a one-of-a-kind fishery that every flyfisher should sample at some time.

---

26. CROWLEY LAKE

Reference: North of Bishop; map E5 grid j4.

How to get there: From the town of Bishop on US 395, drive 29 miles north on US 395 to the well-signed lake entrance on the right.

Facilities: Campgrounds, boat ramps, boat rentals, bait, tackle, and groceries are available.

Cost: Phone ahead for current entrance and camping fees.

Who to contact: Phone the Mono County Water & Power Department at (619) 872-1101, or Culver's Sporting Goods in Bishop at (619) 872-8361.

About Crowley Lake: At some point, every fisherman should experience a trout opener at Crowley Lake. It is a wild-ass scenario that can make weak men drink and strong men cry.

In the big years, some 50,000 anglers will arrive here on the Friday evening prior to the annual opener, the last Saturday in April every year, and convert the little nearby town of Tom's Place into an all-night cowboy rocker. The idea of "trout, trout, trout" mixed with favorite elixirs whips the place into a frenzy. Before dawn, there can be so many anglers on the northwestern and southern shore of Crowley Lake that the DFG will sometimes even put up a rope barricade to keep people from fishing too early. When the legal opening time arrives, the DFG fires off a flare into the morning sky to signify the start of the trout season.

Then comes the reward. By 9 a.m., there are usually many limits, including good numbers of large rainbow trout in the three and four-pound class, rarely even bigger, and maybe a few monster brown trout. Then by early afternoon, everybody has either passed out or gone to sleep from exhaustion.

Crowley Lake is not exactly a pretty sight. In fact, it's kind of like an ugly dog you learn to love. It is bordered by high desert country, sparse and dry looking, with 45 miles of shoreline at 6,720 feet. In addition, the winds out of the west can be nasty, particularly on early summer afternoons. When it blows a gale, an option is fishing McGee Creek, Convict Creek, or Mammoth Creek, located off US 395 to the west.

In recent years, the lake has had problems with water levels, poor services and fishing results. A number of those problems will be solved by a return to more normal snow pack and rainfall during winter, a new concessionaire operation now in place, new facilities and, of course, the traditional giant plants of 100,000 rainbow trout (and another 100,000 subcatchable Eagle Lake trout and rainbow trout) in April before the lake is opened. Crowley Lake is L.A.'s payback for ripping off the water out of the Owens River Valley for so many years, and the public will demand and inevitably get a quality operation here.

The lake is fed from the north by the Owens River, Convict Creek to the west, and between those two inlets is the best shorefishing on the lake. By boat, many fish are caught trolling, but another technique is straight-line jigging with small, purple or white crappie jigs with a small worm trailer. You might catch more than trout with that method, too. You also might get Sacramento perch, which have a large population in the lake. Or you might get a big brown trout, which reach the 15-pound class, sometimes bigger. For several years, the state record brown was one taken from Crowley, a fish that weighed 25 pounds, 11 ounces. It has been beaten twice by browns landed at Twin Lakes (see Zone E4). Because of the high amount of aquatic life in the lake, trout can grow as fast as an inch per month during the summer months.

A trick for big browns at Crowley is to troll a Rapala or drift a whole nightcrawler well up the Owens River arm of the lake. In the fall, most of the lake's population of browns will head up in this area to spawn, the one time the big ones are vulnerable. All it takes is to hook one, and you will be back. After all, only those who see the invisible can do the impossible.

CENTRAL
CALIFORNIA

RATING SYSTEM

POOR————————————FAIR————————————GREAT

CENTRAL CALIFORNIA MAP SECTIONS

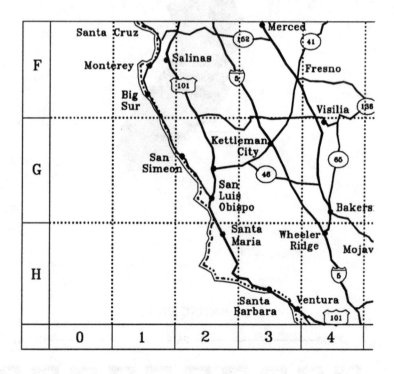

Laguna L. 11) Hartford Fishing Pier 12) San Luis Obispo Bay Deep Sea 13) Lopez L.

G3 (1 listing)..page 606
1) California Aqueduct

G4 (6 listings)..page 608
1) Bravo L. 2) L. Kaweah 3) L. Success 4) Tule R. 5) L. Woollomes 6) L. Ming

G5 (10 listings)..page 614
1) Sequoia Nat'l. Park 2) Tuttle Cr. 3) Diaz L. 4) Golden Trout Wilderness 5) Cottonwood Cr. 6) Middle Fork Tule R. 7) South Cr. 8) Kern R. 9) Isabella L. 10) Erskine Cr.

G6 (no listings)

G7 (no listings)

H2 (2 listings)..page 622
1) Oso Flaco Ls. 2) Gaviota St. Park

H3 (10 listings)..page 626
1) Manzana Cr. 2) Davy Brown Cr. 3) L. Cachuma 4) Santa Ynez R. 5) Goleta Beach County Park 6) Stearns Wharf 7) Santa Barbara Deep Sea 8) L. Casitas 9) Ventura Deep Sea 10) Ventura Pier

H4 (12 listings)..page 638
1) Buena Vista Aquatic Recreation Area 2) Brite Valley L. 3) Reyes Cr. 4) Sespe Cr. 5) Pyramid L. 6) Elizabeth L. 7) California Aqueduct 8) N. Fork Ventura R. 9) L. Castaic 10) Santa Paula Cr. 11) L. Piru 12) Bouquet Canyon Cr.

H5 (3 listings)..page 648
1) California Aqueduct 2) Little Rock Cr. 3) Little Rock Res.

H6 (no listings)

H7 (no listings)

H8 (no listings)

H9 (1 listing)..page 652
1) Colorado R.

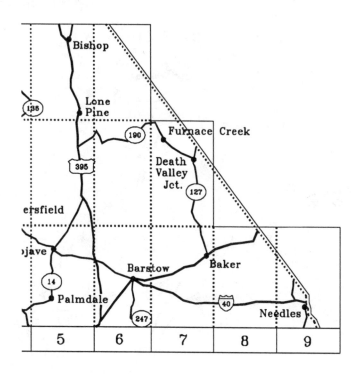

MAP F1

14 LISTINGS
PAGES 542-553

CEN-CAL MAP . see page 540
adjoining maps
NORTH (E1)....... see page 414
EAST (F2)............see page 554
SOUTH ....no map
WEST ....no map

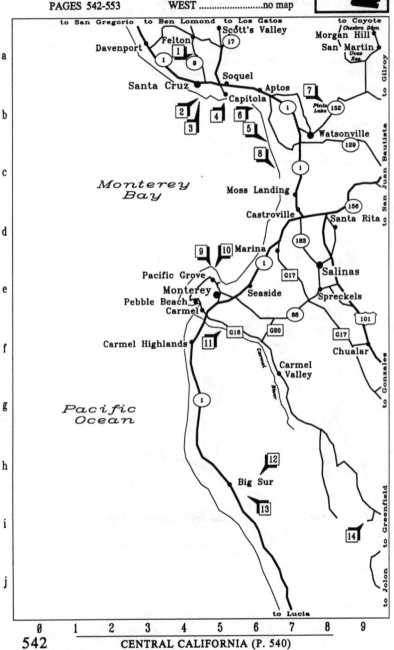

1. SAN LORENZO RIVER

Reference: In Santa Cruz; map F1 grid a4.

How to get there: Access to the river is available at many pullouts along Highway 9. However, a campground and access point is available upstream at Henry Cowell State Park. To reach the park from Santa Cruz, drive three niles north on Highway 17. Take the Mount Herman Road exit, then travel west over the freeway and continue for 3.5 miles to the end of the road. Turn right on Graham Hill Road and travel 0.3 miles to the stoplight in Felton. Turn left on Highway 9 and continue a short distance south to the park entrance on the left.

Special note: Anglers can take a train ride along the river, get dropped off at their chosen spot, and be retrieved later in the day. For information, phone the Roaring Camp Train, (408) 335-4484.

Facilities: Henry Cowell State Park provides a campground and fishing access.

Cost: River access is free, but there is a $5 entrance fee at Henry Cowell State Park.

Who to contact: Phone Henry Cowell State Park or Roaring Camp Train for more information.

About San Lorenzo River: This is a wild card for local steelhead anglers who don't want to make the long drive north to more promising waters.

Fishing has improved quite a bit in recent years, due to conservation work and a private hatchery provided by a volunteer fishing organization in Santa Cruz. Steelhead leave the ocean to enter the river in winter months when high stream flows correspond with high tides.

The best fishing is right after one of these periods, bankfishing in the lagoon just upstream from the mouth of the river, or hitting upriver spots along Highway 9 up to Felton. If you want a special treat in the spring, you can actually see large steelhead spawn. This is possible by exploring the headwaters in the Santa Cruz Mountains, located farther east along Highway 9 near San Lorenzo Park.

As with all small steelhead streams, a key is having a good phone contact to learn exactly when the fish are moving through.

2. SANTA CRUZ DEEP SEA

Reference: South of San Francisco at Santa Cruz Wharf; map F1 grid b4.

How to get there: From the San Francisco Bay Area, drive south on Highway 1. Take the Ocean Street exit and follow the signs to the Municipal Wharf. Boat launches are located at Santa Cruz Small Craft Harbor and farther south off Highway 1, at Moss Landing. A hoist is available in Capitola.

Facilities: Party boat charters, boat ramps, a boat hoist, and boat rentals are available in the area. Lodging, campgrounds and supplies are available in Santa Cruz. Rod rentals, bait and tackle can be obtained at the wharf.

Cost: Party boat fees range from $24-$35 per person.

Who to contact: Phone Stagnaro's Charters at (408) 425-7003; Shamrock Charters, (408) 476-2648.

Party boat list: Stagnaro, Cottardo Stagnaro, reservations through Stagnaro's Charters, (408) 425-7003; *New Holiday, Sea Dancer;* reservations through Shamrock Charters, (408) 476-2648.

About Santa Cruz Deep Sea: It would be nice to have a crystal ball to be able to predict where the best places to fish will be in the next ten years. But when it comes to Santa Cruz, no crystal ball is needed. This is one place that shouldn't be missed.

Good marine habitat, abundant levels of baitfish, plenty of young fish being recruited into the adult population, and most importantly, no gillnetting, all insure a promising future. Gillnetting had just about wiped out rockfish at inshore reefs in the late 1980s, especially the larger fish, the older, slower-growing red rockfish and lingcod. With no gillnetting, numbers of adult fish are rising each year, and so is spawning success. That can only mean good things for the future.

Fishing access is also good, with charters, boat launches and boat rentals all available. The opportunity available to rent a boat and motor is what gives this rating a slight edge over Monterey.

Santa Cruz is a beautiful area, set on the northwestern tip of Monterey Bay, with a rejuvenated boardwalk, a pretty beach, and nearby redwood forests among the highlights. The fishing is just as varied. Rockfish are available year-round, with chilipepper, black and blue rockfish the most abundant species.

Special trips for large lingcod are offered from late August through October, and in the spring and early summer, migrating salmon march through the area in a procession of schools. In addition, there is a sprinkling of halibut, and more rarely white sea bass, but always huge numbers of kingfish (white croaker) in the area.

The day-in, day-out fishery, though, is for rockfish. The best spots are the edge of the Monterey Canyon, roughly 240 to 280 feet deep, and northward just offshore Ano Nuevo Island, where the larger rockfish are available. At the inshore reefs, which provide an easy shot on the small rental skiffs, the rockfish tend to be small, and if you get over a sandy bottom, the kingfish will drive you crazy.

Most of the rockfish are not large, averaging in the three to five-pound class, sometimes smaller. Because the big red rockfish, the six to 12-pounders, are 20 to 25 years old, it will take several more years before they are recruited back into the fishery, a reminder of the devastation of the gillnets. For bigger fish, party boats offer special trips north to Ano Nuevo Island, the best lingcod habitat in the area. This trip is most popular in the fall, when the big lings move inshore at Ano Nuevo and also when the north winds are lightest, making the ride "uphill" an easy one.

Another option in the fall is fishing for blue sharks, which roam off Santa Cruz in large numbers in September and early October. They can get big, six to nine feet, and will readily take a large bait, such as a rockfish, several squid or a big hunk of shark meat on a hook.

Wind is always a key when fishing the ocean, but the Santa Cruz area often gets lighter winds than farther north on the California coast. In the spring months, when the salmon move through, fishing is a lot more enjoyable. Salmon start arriving in small pods in March, then build in numbers throughout the month. The best spots in the early season are usually adjacent to the Cement Ship, or farther south off Moss Landing, mooching very deep. By April 7 or 8, however, a big school of salmon always schools up just a mile offshore in an area known as "Three Trees." This area, which is named for three large cypress trees that sit in a group on an otherwise stark coastal bluff, is just north of Santa Cruz and provides the best salmon fishing of the year. The logbook rarely lies.

When you add it up, it makes a very attractive picture. It is one of the few places anywhere on the Pacific Coast where boat rentals are available (nearby Capitola is another), and also where fisheries are on a definite upswing.

---

3. SANTA CRUZ MUNICIPAL PIER

Reference: At Santa Cruz; map F1 grid b4.

How to get there: From the San Francisco Bay Area, drive south on Highway 1 to Santa Cruz. Take the Ocean Street exit and follow the signs to the Municipal Wharf.

Facilities: Restrooms, benches and fish-cleaning tables are provided. Rod rentals, bait, tackle, a boat launch, and boat rentals are available. Several shops and restaurants are located in the vicinity.

Cost: Access is free.

Who to contact: Phone the Municipal Wharf at (408) 429-3628.

About Santa Cruz Pier: At most piers, folks are content to catch a fish, any fish. At Santa Cruz Pier, you can do better than that from late summer through fall. Mackerel are particularly abundant, large jack-smelt also can arrive in large numbers, and between them you can fill your bucket. The rest of the year? You always have kingfish to keep you company.

---

4.   CAPITOLA PIER

Reference: South of Santa Cruz at Capitola Fishing Wharf; map F1 grid b5.

How to get there: From Santa Cruz, drive south on Highway 1. Take the 41st Avenue exit and turn right, then turn left on Capitola Road. Go through three stop signs and continue west to the wharf. Parking lots are available nearby.

Facilities: Restrooms, fish-cleaning tables, benches, and picnic tables are provided. Rod rentals, bait, tackle, a boat hoist, and boat rentals are available. Several shops and restaurants are located nearby.

Cost: Access is free.

Who to contact: Phone Boat & Bait at (408) 462-2208.

About Capitola Pier: When I look at Capitola Pier, it seems that 30 years has flashed by in a day or two.

It was back in 1962 when my dad, Bob Stienstra, Sr., first took my brother, Rambobby, and I to Capitola. While fishing, we'd listen to the baseball game on the radio, and while Willie Mays made basket catches, we'd catch small rockfish like crazy on the inshore reefs and edge of the kelp beds.

Spots such as Adams Reef, Surfers Reef, Soquel Reef, and South Rock still hold good populations of small rockfish. You still can rent a boat here. And just like in 1962, if a sea lion shows up around a kelp bed, the fish still stop biting; if you get over a sand bottom, all you get are kingfish; and in the fall, large blue sharks can still be enticed with a hunk of a smelly, bloody bait.

The Capitola Pier itself provides a decent fishery in the fall months, when jacksmelt and mackerel can move in hordes into the area, and the inevitable kingfish always will nibble at your bait.

I still occasionally return to Capitola and walk the pier. One day my dad and I even rented a skiff, and went out and caught a few small rockfish. It felt like standing in a time machine.

5.   MONTEREY BAY SHORELINE

Reference: Along Monterey Bay; map F1 grid b6.

How to get there: From the San Francisco Bay Area, drive south on Highways 1 or 17 to Santa Cruz and continue south on the coast. Fishing access is available at several state beaches off Highway 1, including Moss Landing State Beach, Natural Bridges State Beach, Sunset State Beach, New Brighton State Beach, Salinas River State Beach, Sea Cliff State Beach, Zmudowski State Beach, Carmel River State Beach, Marina State Beach, and Monterey State Beach South.

Facilities: Camping is available at some state beach campgrounds. Lodging and supplies are available in Santa Cruz, Capitola, Moss Landing and Monterey.

Cost: A day-use fee is charged at state beaches.

Who to contact: For general information and a free travel packet, phone the Santa Cruz Chamber of Commerce at (408) 423-1111; Monterey Peninsula Chamber of Commerce at (408) 649-1770; Carmel Visitor Bureau at (408) 624-2522. For fishing information, phone Stagnaro's Charters in Santa Cruz at (408) 462-2208; Sam's Sportsfishing in Monterey at (408) 372-0577.

About Monterey Bay shoreline: Anybody who has scuba dived in Monterey Bay understands why the fishing from the beach is often so poor: marine habitat.

The most abundant fish in Monterey Bay are rockfish, but they demand a kelp forest, reef or underwater canyon for habitat. The beach areas and shoreline areas don't provide that. Instead, nature provides long stretches of beach with only a gentle curve to them. There is little habitat anywhere along the shoreline to attract fish. So what you get is a sprinkling of surf perch, and not many at that, best just after a low tide has bottomed out and the incoming tide starts.

The best thing about surf fishing the beach in Monterey Bay is the view. On a calm, blue-sky day, the water just kind of laps at the shore. It looks almost like Hawaii. Bring a sand spike for your rod, and some eats and drinks, and enjoy yourself.

---

6.   SEACLIFF STATE BEACH

Reference: Near Capitola at the Cement Ship; map F1 grid b6.

How to get there: From Santa Cruz, drive about six miles south on Highway 1 and take the Seacliff State Beach exit. Turn right and continue west to the beach, the pier and the "cement ship."

Facilities: Campsites are available by reservation only. Restrooms are provided. Supplies are available nearby.

Cost: Entrance fee is $6; phone ahead for campsite fees.

Who to contact: Phone Seacliff State Beach at (408) 688-3222.

About Seacliff State Beach: The beaches of Monterey provide poor to fair fishing most of the year, but the one exception is the old cement ship, located at Seacliff State Beach.

The cement ship provides not only a fishing platform, but an underwater structure in an area otherwise devoid of it. Perch and kingfish are most common year around; rarely there will be halibut and striped bass in the summer. In the fall, mackerel and jacksmelt can arrive here in large schools during high tides.

On one trip to Monterey Bay, my old buddy Chuck Hildebrand

---

told me, "If you want guacamole, then you'd better have an avocado." In other words, if you want to catch fish, you'd best be throwing your line where some fish are waiting. The cement ship is one of the few spots along the beaches of Monterey Bay where you can do that.

---

7.   PINTO LAKE

Reference: Near Watsonville; map F1 grid b8.

How to get there: From Santa Cruz, drive south on Highway 1 to the Highway 152 turnoff. Head east to Green Valley Road, then turn left and continue north to Pinto Lake.

Facilities: A campground, picnic areas and a boat ramp are available. Boat rentals also are available.

Cost: Day-use fee on weekends is $2 per vehicle; weekday access is free.

Who to contact: Phone Pinto Lake County Park at (408) 722-8129.

About Pinto Lake: The first time I saw Pinto Lake was when I was making an approach in an airplane at Watsonville Airport. I looked down and saw this horseshoe-shaped lake, bordered by a park-like setting, and said to myself, "There's got to be fish in there." Well, after landing the plane, I decided to find out for myself. There were.

Trout are stocked from late fall through early summer. Then when the water heats up, a fair population of crappie, bluegill and catfish take over. Trout are the mainstay, however, being planted with 38,000 trout, a little over 4,000 trout per month. It isn't stocked from August through October. That is when the focus shifts to warmwater species. In the mid-1980s, the crappie fishing was fantastic, but crappie populations always seem to cycle up and down with little regard to anything, Now in the '90s, it won't exactly get you panting.

The lake is one of the few in the area that offers camping, and with all the state beach campgrounds jammed with motor homes, Pinto provides an excellent option. The trout fishing isn't too shabby either.

---

8.   ELKHORN SLOUGH

Reference: At Moss Landing; map F1 grid c7.

How to get there: From Santa Cruz, drive 20 miles south on Highway 1 to Moss Landing. Turn west on Moss Landing Road and continue to the boat ramp.

Facilities: Campgrounds and lodging are available in the vicinity. A boat ramp, bait, and tackle are available nearby.

Cost: Access is free.

Who to contact: Phone the U.S. Department of Fish & Game at (408) 649-2870.

About Elkhorn Slough: OK, OK, so the fishing is lousy. If you have come to Elkhorn Slough, it shouldn't be the fishing you are interested in but the clams.

Elkhorn Slough is something of a legend for its Horseneck and Washington clams. You should be out during a minus low tide, scanning the tidal flats, searching for the little siphon hole. The hole is actually the neck hole for the clams, through which they feed. Should you spot a bubbling hole, dig, and dig fast. The clam will withdraw its long neck, leaving no sign of its whereabouts. That is why clammers use a long, slender tool called the Clammer's Shovel, which is engineered to dig a narrow, yet deep, hole in the fastest amount of time possible.

The clams get big, and their meat requires an extensive beating with a mallet to soften up. After cooking them, which can be as simple as frying in a butter/lemon/garlic sauce, you quickly will find out why clamming is so popular.

---

9. MONTEREY DEEP SEA

Reference: South of San Francisco at Monterey Wharf; map F1 grid e5.

How to get there: From the San Francisco Bay Area, drive south on Highway 1 to Monterey and take the Pacific Grove-Del Monte Avenue exit. Travel about one mile to Figuaro Street, then turn right and continue west to Wharf #1. Boat ramps are located at the wharf and at the Coast Guard Headquarters.

Facilities: Party boat charters, boat ramps, lodging, campgrounds, and supplies are available in the vicinity. Rod rentals, bait and tackle can be obtained at the wharf.

Cost: Party boat fees range from $24-$35 per person.

Who to contact: Phone Chris' Sportfishing, (408) 375-5951; Randy's Sportfishing, (408) 372-7440; Sam's Sportfishing, (408) 372-0577; Monterey Sportfishing, (408) 372-2203.

Party boat list: Holiday, New Holiday; reservations through Chris' Sportfishing, (408) 375-5951. *Captain Randy, Sir Randy, Randy I, Randy II;* reservations through Randy's Sportfishing, (408) 372-7440. *Point Sur Clipper, Star of Monterey, Miss Monterey*; reservations through Sam's Sportfishing, (408) 372-0577. *Top Gun, Optimist Star;* reservations through Monterey Sportfishing, (408) 372-2203.

About Monterey Deep Sea: Monterey stands apart from the rest of California. It has the best of both worlds: Southern California's weather and Northern California's beauty. To get a picture of the fishing available, all you have to do is stroll through the Monterey Aquarium, where the giant tanks are like giant houses, allowing an inside view of the multiple levels of marine life in Monterey Bay.

The key for marine life in Monterey Bay is the 5,000-foot deep canyon that generates nutrient-rich water from upwelling that sets off one of the West Coast's most diverse marine systems.

Fishing season starts in March, when salmon begin migrating through the area. About 70 percent of the salmon caught in Monterey Bay are taken between Moss Landing and Fort Ord, best from late March through April. There is a larger percentage of big fish in Monterey's spring run than anywhere else on the coast, with occasional trips where a 15-pound salmon is average, with a number of 20 to 25-pounders as well.

As summer arrives, most of the salmon head north, and the focus at Monterey turns to rockfish, which have become rejuvenated in recent years due to the ban on gillnetting. The better spots are the edge of Monterey Canyon, and also "around the corner" off Cypress Point, Point Lobos, and Carmel Bay.

Longer trips south to the Big Sur area can be fantastic, especially in the shallow reef areas, using light tackle and casting three-ounce split-tail Scampi jigs.

One unique element here in the deep sea trips for rockfish is the opportunity to catch live squid for bait. It is quite a sight: The squid spurt a stream of sea water when taken, then make a perfect live bait for the larger rockfish and lingcod. If squid are not available, the traditional squid-baited shrimpfly is used near the bottom in the deep areas, 200 to 300 feet down.

If you have your own boat, Monterey Bay is an excellent destination. Because the wind is much calmer here than at points north, especially in the late summer and early fall, the big bay can get so flat that it looks like a big frog pond.

If there is a drawback, it is the expense of lodging and difficulty in getting a campsite at one of the state beaches. Monterey is a world-class destination, after all, and other people want to go there too. Another problem can be getting reliable fishing reports, especially if albacore make a rare appearance in the fall.

But that aside, Monterey is a beautiful area with a returning abundance of all marine life. It will always be a favorite.

---

10.   MONTEREY MUNICIPAL PIER

Reference: At Monterey Municipal Wharf; map F1 grid e5.

How to get there: From Santa Cruz, drive south on Highway 1 to Monterey and take the Pacific Grove-Del Monte Avenue exit. Travel about one mile to Figuaro Street, then turn right and continue to Wharf No. 2. Pier fishing is permitted only at Wharf No. 2.

Facilities: Restrooms and benches are provided. Rod rentals, bait and tackle are available at the wharf. Several restaurants and shops are available in the vicinity.

Cost: Access is free.

Who to contact: Phone the Monterey Harbormaster at (408) 646-3950.

About Monterey Pier: Watching the sea lions beg for handouts becomes more popular than fishing at Monterey Pier.

But no matter how cute they may appear, don't give them anything, not even that dried-up piece of anchovy on your bait board. For one thing, it is now a federal crime to feed a sea lion, punishable by a $5,000 fine. For another, once you feed a sea lion, they never leave. And as long as sea lions are hanging around, fish will vacate the premises.

The fishing has never been so hot at Monterey Pier anyway. Kingfish and perch are most common, with mackerel and sardines showing in September and October. Add in a colony of sea lions and you might as well try to find a polar bear in the desert.

---

11. CARMEL RIVER

Reference: Near Carmel; map F1 grid f5.

How to get there: From Monterey, drive about four miles south on Highway 1 to Carmel. Turn east on County Road G16. Access is available from the mouth of the river up to Robles Bridge on Wednesdays and weekends.

Facilities: Campgrounds, lodging and supplies are available in the vicinity.

Cost: Access is free.

Who to contact: Phone the U.S. Department of Fish & Game at (408) 649-2870.

About Carmel River: The five-year drought from 1987-91 just about killed this river.

In fact, for many winter months, the river ceased to exist. Its mouth consisted of a giant sand bar, and instead of water flowing, there were kids on bicycles riding right down the dry river bed.

In the early 1980s, this river was the best small steelhead stream in California, with so many fish that poaching had become a problem upstream near Robles Bridge. Now, as the 1990s evolve, we wonder if any steelhead are even left. In March of '91, there finally came enough rain for water to again flow to sea, and there were a few undocumented reports of steelhead trying to get upstream to spawn.

If so, this river will have a chance to come back. But only with good rainfall—every winter for many several consecutive years. Fish and Game is considering closing this river to fishing in order to protect what few steelhead remain. Always check DFG regulations before fishing anywhere.

12. VENTANA WILDERNESS

Reference: Southeast of Monterey in Los Padres National Forest; map F1 grid h6.

How to get there: Access to trailheads is available off several roads that junction with Highway 1. See a Forest Service map for details.

Facilities: No facilities are available.

Cost: Access is free.

Who to contact: Phone Los Padres National Forest at (408) 385-5434. For a map, send $2 to Office of Information, 630 Sansome Street, San Francisco, CA 94111.

About Ventana Wilderness: The Ventana Wilderness is a rugged coastal environment that is often little-traveled.

It can be hot and dry, with severe fire danger in the summer and fall, when just finding drinking water can be difficult. But spring arrives here early, often in March, and by the time the trout season opens on the last Saturday in April, the wilderness provides a quiet, beautiful setting, and a few secret spots for hikers who fish.

The best prospects are on the headwaters of the Carmel River, Big Sur River and Little Sur River. Upper Carmel River is the best, with trout as large as 10 or 11 inches. No trout are stocked in the Ventana Wilderness; all waters contain only native trout, mostly rainbows, with a few scarce brown trout mixed in.

The rivers still provide viable fisheries, but it is only a shadow of the former glory here before the Marble Cone Fire in the 1970s. After that fire, heavy rains caused erosion damage, where silt was washed in the streams and covered some spawning gravels. That, in turn, lowered spawning success, which explains the general population decline.

It is something that only time will heal, but as the soils stabilize and spring rains scour the river, this fishery will again rebound.

13. BIG SUR RIVER

Reference: Near Big Sur in Los Padres National Forest; map F1 grid i6.

How to get there: From Monterey, drive approximately 30 miles south on Highway 1 to Big Sur. Limited access is available off the highway; access is excellent at Pfeiffer-Big Sur State Park.

Facilities: Campgrounds, picnic areas and supplies are available at Pfeiffer-Big Sur State Park.

Cost: Day-use fee at the park is $5 per vehicle; walk-in access is free.

Who to contact: Phone Pfeiffer-Big Sur State Park at (408) 667-2315.

About Big Sur River: This stream is set amid the southernmost stand of redwoods, a pretty spot known primarily as a summer vacation site, not as a winter destination for steelhead fishermen.

Regardless, from January through early March, it attracts anglers from the Monterey area. It takes the combination of rain and high tides for the steelhead to feel compelled to leave the ocean and swim upstream. When that combination occurs, anglers should be on the stream.

Catch rates are quite low, with long periods of nothing interspersed by short periods when the steelhead move through. If you are like most people, you show up and come to the conclusion that there are no fish here. Wrong. They are. But it takes perfect timing to find them.

---

14.   THE LAKES

Reference: Near Greenfield in Los Padres National Forest; map F1 grid i9.

How to get there from Northern California: From Salinas, drive approximately 25 miles south on US 101 to County Road G17 (Arroyo Seco Road). Turn south and continue southwest for 21 miles to the lakes.

How to get there from Southern California: From San Luis Obispo, drive abut 90 miles north on US 101 to the town of Greenfield. Turn left on County Road G16 (Elm Avenue) and drive six miles west, until the road joins Arroyo Seco Road. Continue ten miles west on Arroyo Seco Road to the lakes. The road runs right aside the northernmost of the two lakes, with a short hike required to the smaller lake to the south.

Facilities: A campground and a picnic area are provided.

Cost: Lake access is free.

Who to contact: Phone Los Padres National Forest at (408) 385-5434. For a map, send $2 to Office of Information, 630 Sansome Street, San Francisco, CA 94111.

About The Lakes: With a name like "The Lakes," you might expect a lot more than you get here.

They are just two little reservoirs in the Los Padres foothills, more like ponds, the kind of place where on a hot summer day with nobody around, you'd get buck naked and take a quick dunk.

Then, during the evening, maybe you'd toss out a line and see if there are any fish in the lakes. Alas, it is not the kind of fishing that will get you chomping at the bit. Just some bluegill, with poor catch rates at that, and nothing else. At least you had a swim and found a quiet little spot that is virtually unknown.

CEN-CAL MAP . see page 540
adjoining maps
NORTH (E2).......see page 466
EAST (F3)...........see page 560
SOUTH (G2).......see page 594
WEST (F1)..........see page 542

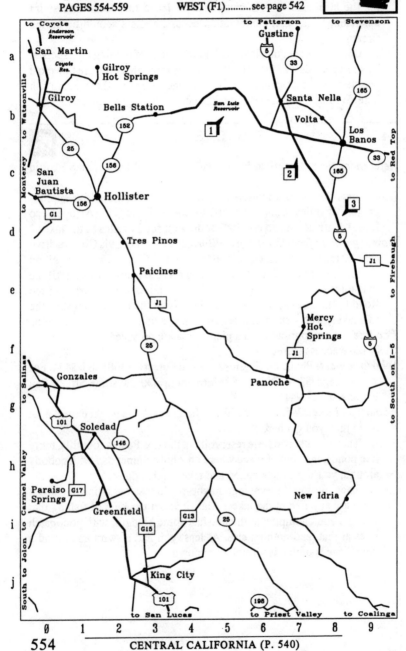

1.   SAN LUIS RESERVOIR

Reference: Near Gilroy in San Luis Reservoir State Recreation Area; map F2 grid b5.

How to get there: From the San Francisco Bay Area, drive south on US 101 to Gilroy. Turn east on Highway 152 and continue approximately 23 miles to the reservoir. A boat ramp is located at the end of Dinosaur Point Road. If approaching from Interstate 5, take the Highway 152 exit. Turn west and drive ten miles to the park entrance. Access to a boat ramp is available off the park entrance road.

Facilities: Campgrounds, picnic areas and boat ramps are available. Supplies can be obtained in Gilroy or Los Banos.

Cost: Day-use fee is $6 per vehicle, $11 if entering with a boat. The fee includes boat-launching privileges.

Who to contact: Phone San Luis Reservoir State Recreation Area at (209) 826-1196.

About San Luis Reservoir: With every striped bass caught at San Luis Reservoir and the adjacent O'Neill Forebay comes a degree of irony, for every striped bass in this lake has been sucked right out of the Delta by the California Aqueduct pumps and then delivered via the canal.

After pumping fish and water since 1968, the lake is full of both of them. It is a huge, squarish man-made lake set in otherwise desolate country, covering nearly 14,000 acres with 65 miles of shoreline. Whenever I fly through the area, heading to or from Monterey Bay, I always use the giant lake as a checkpoint, and maybe do a circle to scan for boats.

Most of the stripers here are in the 10 to 15-inch class; after all, most of the fish are pumped in when they are quite small, but there is also a sprinkling of 25 to 40-pounders, some even bigger. In fact, a 66-pound striped bass was caught on June 29, 1988, in the O'Neill Forebay by Ted Furnish. That striper is the largest caught in California history, and also the world record for landlocked striped bass. There have been several other records set here, most by flyfishing specialist Al Whitehurst. He has caught fly rod world records with stripers weighing 27 pounds (eight-pound tippet), 40 pounds, four ounces (12-pound tippet), and 54 pounds, 8 ounces (16-pound tippet). One other world record for landlocked striped bass has been set here by Fred Brand Junior, with a 55-pounder on a 12-pound line.

Come fall, and suddenly this reservoir, as ugly as it is with the annual drawdowns to send water south, suddenly comes to life with all matter of birds, bait and bass. You don't even need a boat, though it can help plenty.

Remember this: Birds never lie. When you see birds cruising, you know they are on the move, looking for food. When they circle, hover or dive, you know they have found it. At San Luis Reservoir, schools of striped bass will corral large schools of shad, which send the baitfish near the surface, and, in turn, cause the birds to feed in divebomb raids. The angler, seeing this, then cruises to the scene, stops short of surface boil, and casts to the fish.

It can be done by boat or bank. By boat is simplest, of course, although there can be a tremendous amount of water to cover. By bank, you scan shoreline waters for diving birds, then when spotting them, drive around the lake to the spot, jump out and make long casts—just like surf fishing for stripers off Pacifica.

In the spring and early summer, the wind can howl through here, particularly in the afternoon, and a warning light is posted at Romero Overlook to warn of gales exceeding 30 mph. It is also in the spring and early summer when the striped bass are most difficult to catch, tending to head deep, scatter and roam the wide open expanses of the lake in the search of baitfish. Few are caught by deepwater trolling techniques using large diving plugs.

My first visit here was a memorable one. I was cruising through the area, didn't have a boat with me, and decided to stop and walk some of the shoreline, casting a Rattletrap plug as I went. In an hour, I caught two small striped bass, about eight inches long, and tossed them back.

Then I came upon a fellow who was really excited.

"Man, they're really hitting today, aren't they?" he said. "I already got three, and I had a big one on but it got away."

He then retrieved his stringer from the water and held up his fish. They were all about eight or nine inches long.

It turned out the "big one," you see, was all of about 14 inches long.

---

2.   LOS BANOS RESERVOIR

Reference: Near Los Banos; map F2 grid c7.

How to get there: From Interstate 5, turn east on Highway 152 and travel three miles to Volta Road. Turn right and drive one mile south, then turn left on Pioneer Road and drive one mile east. Turn right on Canyon Road and continue south for five miles to the reservoir.

Facilities: A campground and picnic areas are provided. Two unimproved boat ramps are available.

Cost: Access is free.

Who to contact: Phone California Parks & Recreation Department, Four Rivers Area at (209) 826-1196.

About Los Banos Reservoir: This is catfish country, the kind of place where some of the locals will stay up through the night during the summer, sitting on a lawn chair along the bank, waiting for a catfish to nibble their baits. It can be worth the wait, with some big catfish roaming these waters.

In the spring, there is a fair bass fishery as well, though the fish rarely reach large sizes. The better spots are along the Los Banos Creek arm and in Salt Springs Cove. The reservoir also is stocked with 13,000 rainbow trout when the water is cool enough to support them in winter and early spring.

During typical summer days, it really can get hot at Los Banos Reservoir. It is set in a long, narrow valley, with the surrounding hills often baked brown by late May. The lake covers 410 acres, has 12 miles of shoreline, and has a 5-mph speed limit.

Like nearby San Luis Reservoir, the wind can howl through this country in the early summer. That is why the number one activity here has become windsurfing (where the speed limit is often exceeded) and sailing. This is not exactly paradise, but for anybody making the long cruise up or down nearby Interstate 5, it is an excellent spot to overnight or take a quick fishing hit as a respite from the grinding drive.

---

3.   CALIFORNIA AQUEDUCT

Reference: East of Fresno; map F2 grid d8.

How to get to the Mervel Avenue site: From Interstate 5 south of Los Banos, take the Mervel Avenue exit. Turn east and continue to the access site.

How to get to the Fairfax site: From Interstate 5 about 60 miles north of Kettleman City, take the Panoche Road exit. Turn east and travel about three miles to Fairfax Road. Turn left and drive three miles north to the fishing site.

Facilities: Parking areas and toilets are provided.

Cost: Access is free.

Who to contact: Phone the Department of Water Resources in Los Banos at (209) 826-0718.

About California Aqueduct: The Department of Water Resources likes to call the California Aqueduct the "World's Longest Fishing Hole." What it really is, however, is the "damndest fish trap in the world," according to former Fish and Game Director Charles Fullerton.

All the fish in the aqueduct have been sucked right out of the Delta by the giant pumping station at Clifton Court Forebay, then sent south with the water. Striped bass and catfish are the primary victims, and have the highest survival rates in the aqueduct, feeding on the latest crop of baby fish pulled out of the Delta. The stripers and catfish are of all sizes, from the tiny juveniles recently arriving from the Delta, or stripers in the 40-pound class and catfish to 20 pounds. The chance of hooking one of the latter is what gets people out here trying.

There are several fishing access points, where folks can sit along the cement-lined canal, toss in their bait, and hope a striped bass or catfish isn't too full from eating all the newly-arrived baby fish, and will consider taking a nibble. There is no "structure" or habitat in the aqueduct. It is just a canal, steeply-lined at that, so don't fall in. There is no great strategy, or any particularly good spots. You just toss out your bait and wait, and spend your time watching all that water go by.

MAP F3

6 LISTINGS
PAGES 560-565

CEN-CAL MAP . see page 540
adjoining maps
NORTH (E3)........see page 478
EAST (F4)...........see page 566
SOUTH (G3).......see page 606
WEST (F2)...........see page 554

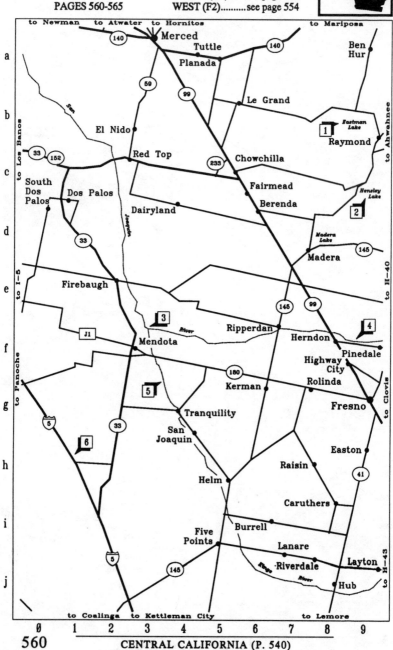

1. EASTMAN LAKE

Reference: Southeast of Merced; map F3 grid b9.

How to get there: From Merced, drive 15 miles south on Highway 99 to the town of Chowchilla. Take the Avenue 26 exit and turn east. Continue east for 17 miles, then turn north on County Road 29 and drive eight miles to the lake.

Facilities: Campgrounds, picnic areas, and a boat ramp are available at the lake. Supplies can be obtained in Chowchilla.

Cost: Lake access is free.

Who to contact: Phone the U.S. Corps of Engineers, Eastman Lake, at (209) 689-3255.

About Eastman Lake: This can seem like the weediest lake on planet earth, often plugged up with the water plant hydrilla, and can make fishing for bass, bluegill and catfish impossible. In early 1992, the lake was even closed to all water-contact activities while government officials tried to figure out what do to clear the lake.

Before the lake was opened to the public in 1978, many brush piles were anchored along the lake bottom to provide aquatic habitat in what would otherwise be a barren water hole. Well, it has worked. But unfortunately, with the rampant weed growth from 1989 through 1991, nobody has caught much of anything.

If you happen to be roaming about Madera County, it is a good idea to make a call to check on the weed conditions. If it is not a serious problem and boating is permitted, then make an evening hit for the bass here. The northern arm of the lake provides the best bass fishing during the spring.

In summer, decent catfishing is often available near the campgrounds on the southeastern shore of the lake. But beware of blowtorch heat during the summer, which makes the weeds grow like crazy, and puts the bass and catfish off the bite until dusk arrives.

2. HENSLEY LAKE

Reference: North of Fresno; map F3 grid c9.

How to get there: From Fresno, drive 20 miles north on Highway 99 to Madera. Take the Highway 145 exit and turn east. Travel about six miles, then bear left on County Road 400 and drive ten miles north to the lake.

Facilities: Campgrounds and boat ramps are provided. Supplies can be obtained in Madera.

Cost: Lake access is free.

Who to contact: Phone the U.S. Corps of Engineers, Hensley Lake, at (209) 673-5151.

About Hensley Lake: What makes a reservoir good for largemouth bass? This is what: Plenty of shoreline coves, lots of points and sheltered bays. Most reservoirs do not provide that, but Hensley is an exception. That is what makes it the best fishing bet in the immediate region.

It is set at 540 feet in the Central Valley foothills northeast of Fresno, a good-sized lake covering 1,540 acres and with 24 miles of shoreline when full. Spring comes early here and so does the bass fishing, often starting up in early March and continuing at a good clip until late May. At that point, the better bass fishing becomes a dawn or dusk proposition. There are also catfish, sunfish and bluegill in the lake.

The northern shore is best for bass, and also offers a semblance of protection from the spring winds. If it is windy, another good spot is the cove east of the dam, which is protected by a stubby peninsula. The lake is ideal for bass boats with foot-controlled electric motors, gliding adjacent to the shoreline, fanning the shallows with casts.

Hensley is also stocked with rainbow trout by the Department of Fish and Game. It gets 12,000 trout each year, spaced out over the cool months. Once water warms up during late spring, waterskiers take over during the day, and they just love "hitting the coves." The resulting wakes slap against the shore and spook the bass. If the skiers would just stay in the vicinity of the dam, they wouldn't hurt the fishing, but they don't.

The solution is to take advantage of the Central Valley's warm weather in early spring. That is not only before the waterskiers arrive, but also when the bass start waking up at Hensley, far earlier in the year than at lakes farther north.

---

3. MENDOTA POOL

Reference: Near Mendota; map F3 grid f3.

How to get there from Highway 99: From Fresno, drive about 32 miles west on Highway 180 to the town of Mendota. Turn north on Bass Avenue and drive two miles to the park entrance.

How to get there from Interstate 5: In Fresno County, take the exit for County Road J1 and head east to Mendota. The road has several 90-degree turns. In Mendota, turn north on Bass Avenue and drive two miles to park entrance.

Facilities: A boat ramp, restrooms, picnic areas, a softball field, and barbeque pits are provided. Supplies are available in Mendota.

Cost: Entrance fee is $3 per vehicle.

Who to contact: Phone Fresno County Department of Parks & Recreation at (209) 488-3004.

About Mendota Pool: Mendota Pool is actually just the northern access point to Fresno Slough, the centerpiece for surrounding county parkland.

Most fishermen will launch their boats here, then cruise south about a mile where the slough has a deep bend on both sides, as well as a small island on the eastern side. Here they will anchor and fish for catfish, the main attraction. A few striped bass are available, but they are caught only when available. For a second option, bring a small spinning rod, hook, bobber, and tub of worms, and you may catch some panfish, which hold in the same areas as the catfish.

One word of caution: In the hot summer months, waterskiers will sometimes also launch their boats at Mendota Pool, then hurtle up and down the slough to the Highway 180 overpass. No waterskiing is permitted south of the highway.

---

4.   SAN JOAQUIN RIVER

Reference: Near Fresno; map F3 grid f9.

How to get there: From Highway 41 at the north end of Fresno, take the Friant Road exit and drive north on Friant Road. Access is available at Lost Lake Park and at the "broken bridge" located about a mile past the park in Friant. Access is also available at Fort Washington Beach Park: From Friant Road, travel one mile to Rice Road. Turn left and continue until the road forks, then bear left and proceed to the park. The river can also be accessed northwest of Fresno, where Highway 99 crosses the river.

Facilities: A campground is available at Fort Washington Beach Park. Full facilities are available in Fresno.

Cost: Entrance fee at Lost Lake Park is $3; day-use fee at Fort Washington State Beach Park is $2.

Who to contact: For general information, phone the Fresno Visitors Bureau at (800) 543-8488. For fishing information, phone Herb Bauer Sporting Goods in Fresno, (209) 435-8600; Fort Washington Beach Park, (209) 434-9600; guide Jeff Boghosian, (209) 229-5640.

About San Joaquin River: From its headwaters in the Sierra Nevada to its outlet into the Delta, the San Joaquin River takes on more characteristics and changing appearances than a chameleon.

In this stretch of water, it is a gentle stream that rolls its way slowly through the San Joaquin Valley, skirting just north of Fresno. The best areas to fish are at Lost Lake Park and "Broken Bridges," where access is good and rainbow trout are planted in good numbers in the spring and early summer months. Another good access point is at the Highway 99 crossing, where catfish provide hope. This relatively short stretch of river is very heavily planted, getting 50,000 rainbow trout per year. The stocks are made virtually weekly as long as the river is cool enough to support them.

Note that there is no public access by shore between Fresno at the Highway 99 crossing on east all the way up to Lost Lake Park. Except, that is, at "Fort Washington Beach Park." The reality is that this is not really a park at all, just some riverside property owned by a friendly old gent who is looking to make a buck or two by offering an access point and a spot to camp.

---

5.   FRESNO SLOUGH

Reference: West of Fresno in Mendota Wildlife Refuge; map F3 grid g3.

How to get there: From Fresno, turn west on Highway 180 (White Bridges Road) and drive about 30 miles, through the town of Kerman, to where the road crosses the slough. The entrance to the wildlife area is directly across from Jack's Resort. If approaching from Interstate 5, take the exit for County Road J1 and drive east to Mendota, then turn south on Highway 180 and continue to the slough. Boats can be launched at Jack's Resort.

Facilities: A boat launch, rowboat rentals, bait, and tackle are available at Jack's Resort. A campground also is available nearby.

Cost: There is a boat launching fee; fishing access at the wildlife refuge is free.

Who to contact: Phone the Mendota Wildlife Refuge at (209) 655-4645; Jack's Resort at (209) 655-3349 or (209) 655-3778 (for camping information).

About Fresno Slough: If you visit here, try always to get here before dawn so you can see the surrounding marsh wake up with the rising sun. It is one of the highlights of the San Joaquin Valley, watching all matter of waterfowl waking up, lifting off and flying past in huge flocks while the morning sun casts an orange hue to everything.

The Fresno Slough is the water source for the surrounding Mendota Wildlife Refuge, and offers a quiet spot to fish for catfish amid a wetland vibrant with life. Striped bass and perch are also in these waters, but caught just rarely.

Most anglers will launch off the Highway 180 access point, then cruise south for three miles to the first major cove on the east side. This is the best catfish area in the slough. It is also adjacent to prime wetland habitat where lots of waterfowl take up residence.

Another bonus to fishing the southern part of Fresno Slough as opposed to the Mendota Pool is that no waterskiing is permitted south of the Highway 180 overpass to keep the ducks from being disturbed. The obvious side benefit is that fishermen are not disturbed either.

6.   CALIFORNIA AQUEDUCT

Reference: Southeast of Fresno; map F3 grid h2.

How to get there: From Interstate 5, take the Highway 33-Mendota exit and turn north on Highway 33-Derrick Avenue. Continue for about five miles to Three Rocks. Turn right on Clarkson Avenue and drive east to the fishing access sign.

Facilities: Parking areas and toilets are provided. No other facilities are available.

Cost: Access is free.

Who to contact: Phone the Department of Water Resources at (209) 826-0718.

About California Aqueduct: For people cruising the endless monotony of Interstate 5, the California Aqueduct can provides a rare respite. Along with the water pumped out of the Delta comes striped bass and catfish, and they provide poor to fair fishing at special access sites. It is nothing complicated, with two options. You might try what I do when I make the long drive in the San Joaquin Valley. I'll bring along a spinning rod for the trip, with a Rattletrap lure tied on, and then when I need a break from the driving, I will stop at these Aqueduct access spots. I can hardly wait to reach the water and then make five or 10 casts. Sometimes a striped bass will be wandering by right where you are casting. The other option is to take it more seriously, sitting on your fanny and tossing out your bait, and then waiting for a striper or catfish to come cruising down the aqueduct. The best hope is in the early evening and into the night, with anchovies the preferred entreaty.

MAP F4

CEN-CAL MAP . see page 540
adjoining maps
NORTH (E4).......see page 492
EAST (F5)...........see page 578
SOUTH (G4).......see page 608
WEST (F3)..........see page 560

14 LISTINGS
PAGES 566-577

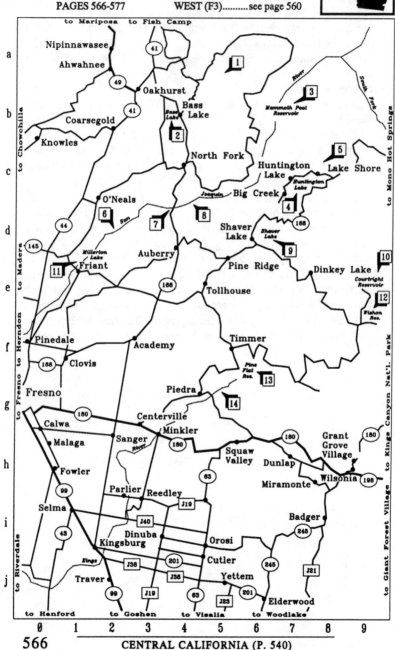

to Mariposa   to Fish Camp

Nipinnawasee
Ahwahnee

a

49

Oakhurst

41

1

River

South Fork

3

to Chowchilla

b

41

Coarsegold

Bass
Lake

Bass Lake

Mammoth Pool
Reservoir

to Mono Hot Springs

Knowles

2

North Fork

5

Lake Shore

c

O'Neals

Huntington
Lake

Big Creek

Huntington
Lake

4

Joaquin

6

San

7

8

Shaver
Lake

Shaver
Lake

9

168

44

d

145

Millerton
Lake

Friant

Auberry

Pine Ridge

Dinkey Lake

10

11

168

Tollhouse

Courtright
Reservoir

12

e

Fishon
Res.

Pinedale

Academy

Timmer

to Fresno   to Herndon   to Madera

168

Clovis

Pine
Flat Res.

13

f

Fresno

180

Piedra

14

Calwa

Centerville

Grant
Grove
Village

g

Malaga

Sanger

Minkler

River

180

180

Fowler

180

Squaw
Valley

Dunlap

Wilsonia

198

to Riverdale

99

Parlier

Reedley

Miramonte

to Kings Canyon Nat'l. Park

h

Selma

63

Badger

to Giant Forest Village

43

J19

i

J40

Dinuba
Kingsburg

Orosi

245

Kings

201

Cutler

245

J21

j

J38

J38

Yettem

Traver

99

J19

63

J23

201

Elderwood

to Hanford   to Goshen   to Visalia   to Woodlake

1.   SIERRA NATIONAL FOREST

Reference: Northeast of Fresno in Sierra National Forest; map F4 grid a5.

How to get there: Access to roads and trailheads is available off Highways 168, 41, 49, and 140 east of Fresno.

Facilities: Full facilities are available within the forest. Supplies are available in adjacent towns.

Cost: Access is free.

Who to contact: Write to Sierra National Forest Headquarters at 1600 Tollhouse Road, Clovis, CA 93612, or phone (209) 487-5155. For a map, send $2 to Office of Information, U.S. Forest Service, 630 Sansome Street, San Francisco, CA 94111.

About Sierra National Forest: You could spend many years exploring the Sierra National Forest and never tire of it. A vast, beautiful area, it borders several wilderness areas and provides an opportunity for a backpacker to spend many days in paradise.

But let's get one thing straight: The trout are not big. But that's OK. Just bring a small lightweight frying pan, and they'll look bigger at dinner time. They do bite readily and can often provide an antidote to those suffering from a serious fishing jinx. Get a Forest Service map, scan the following lakes, then route your trip, and plan at least three or four days in the back country.

The following hike-to lakes are stocked by airplane with finger-ling-sized brook trout: Beryl Lake, Brewer Lake, Deer Lake, Dinkey Lakes, Doris Lake, Eastern Brook Lake, Ershim Lake, Hidden Lake, Mirror Lake, Mystery Lake, Red Lake, South Lake, Swamp Lake, Swede Lake, Tocher Lake, Tule Lake, West Lake, Jackass Lakes, Upper Star Lake. None receive rainbow trout or golden trout.

One of the best destinations is along Dinkey Creek, located north-west of Courtright Reservoir and southwest of Florence Lake. The trail is routed to First Dinkey Lake, the centerpiece of the area, but there is also Mystery Lake, South Lake, Rock Lake and Cliff Lake all within a few miles. It has everything but big fish.

---

2.   BASS LAKE

Reference: Northeast of Fresno in Sierra National Forest; map F4 grid b4.

How to get there: From Fresno, drive about 25 miles north on Highway 41 to North Fork Road (County Road 200). Turn right and travel 13 miles east, then turn left on County Road 222 and drive north to the lake. Several boat ramps are available off Road 222. The lake can be accessed farther north as well: Drive 25 miles farther on Highway 41 to Yosemite Forks, then turn right on County Road 222 and drive six miles east to the lake.

Facilities: Several campgrounds, boat ramps, a marina, boat rentals, bait, tackle, and groceries are available at the lake.

Cost: Lake access is free. There may be a fee for boat launching.

Who to contact: Phone the Sierra National Forest District Office at (209) 683-4665; Pines Marina, (209) 642-3565. For a map, send $2 to Office of Information, U.S Forest Service, 630 Sansome Street, San Francisco, CA 94111.

About Bass Lake: The first time I visited Bass Lake, it seemed like the Hells Angels National Monument. Turned out they make a run here once a year, and despite some apprehension by family campers around the lake, the bikers kept the peace, didn't litter, and won over a lot of doubters before roaring off down Highway 41, one after another, like bullets coming out of a machine gun. I had a bigger problem with a yahoo on a jet ski who plowed into a cove where I was fishing out of my canoe.

By now, you should have figured that Bass Lake is popular with a huge diversity of people. That makes sense. It is a long, beautiful lake, set in a canyon at 3,400 feet and surrounded by National Forest. It covers nearly 1,200 acres when full, and has five campgrounds, four resorts, and two boat launches.

The lake also has 13 different species of fish, making it a take-your-pick deal. In the winter and spring, Fish and Game stocks it with rainbow trout in the 10 to 12-inch class, which provide a good troll fishery through May. The lake is stocked with 19,000 rainbow trout each year during this period. By June, though, the weather really heats up, and nature converts the lake to a warmwater special, with bass (not as good as the lake's name implies), bluegill, crappie and catfish all coming to life.

It helps plenty to have a boat here, with the better spots along the southeastern shore from the point south of Pines Village on toward the dam. There you will find one deep cove, and a series of smaller ones, where the warmwater species will hold during the summer months.

---

3.   MAMMOTH POOL RESERVOIR

Reference: Northeast of Fresno in Sierra National Forest; map F4 grid b7.

How to get there: From Fresno, drive about 25 miles north on Highway 41 to North Fork Road (County Road 200). Turn right and drive 18 miles northeast to the town of North Fork. Turn right on County Road 225 (Mammoth Pool Road) and travel east and south to Forest Service Road 4S01 (Minarets Road). Turn left and continue north to the reservoir. The boat ramp is located on the north shore of the lake. The total distance from North Fork is 42 miles on a narrow, twisty road.

Facilities: Campgrounds, a boat ramp, bait, tackle, and a grocery store are available.

Cost: Lake access is free. There may be a fee for boat launching.

Who to contact: Phone the Sierra National Forest District or the Mammoth Pool Reservoir Boat Ramp, at the same number (209) 877-2218. For a map, send $2 to Office of Information, 630 Sansome Street, San Francisco, CA 94111.

About Mammoth Pool Reservoir: This lake was created by a dam in the San Joaquin River gorge, a steep canyon that drops nearly 3,000 feet, creating a long, narrow lake with steep, high walls. Mammoth Pool always seems to be much higher in elevation than its listed 3,330 feet. That is because of the surrounding high ridges.

The access road is blocked by snow each winter, but as soon as it is plowed, often in early April, the lake is stocked with 8,000 trout in the 10 to 12-inch class by the Department of Fish and Game. It also gets 20,000 dinkers, which are supposed to some day grow up and become real trout. The best fishing in spring and early summer is usually located just east of the boat launch, trolling adjacent to the shoreline on up to the narrows.

Later in the summer, especially when there is a significant snow-melt, the better fishing is well up the San Joaquin arm. A boat-in camp is available at China Bar, located in a cove on the northwest side of the San Joaquin arm, set in a perfect location for a boating/fishing vacation.

One word of caution: If visiting from late August through November, always call ahead and ask for lake levels. Since the water is used to generate hydro-electric power at the dam, water levels can drop significantly late in the season.

---

4.   HUNTINGTON LAKE

Reference: Northeast of Fresno in Sierra National Forest; map F4 grid c7.

How to get there: From Fresno, drive 68 miles northeast on Highway 168 (a narrow, winding two-laner). Boat ramps are located on the north shore of the lake.

Facilities: Campgrounds, lodging, picnic areas, boat ramps, a marina, boat rentals, bait, tackle, and groceries are available at the lake.

Cost: Lake access is free.

Who to contact: Phone the Sierra National Forest District Office at (209) 841-3311; Huntington Lake Resort Marina, (209) 893-6750.

About Huntington Lake: Boy Scouts fantasize about spending a week or two here, and now and then, they actually get the chance at specially-arranged camp-outs. The fact that they like it means that you will probably like it too.

Huntington Lake is set at 7,000 feet in the Sierra Nevada, a big

---

lake surrounded by National Forest. The lake is four miles long, a half-mile wide, and has 14 miles of shoreline, five campgrounds, five resorts, and a jump-off point for a backpack trip into the nearby Kaiser Wilderness.

The lake is planted with rainbow trout as soon as snowplows start rolling and the access road is cleared. The stocks continue regularly through summer, providing good catch rates for trollers, with a good evening bite. We're talking bigtime plants, with 50,000 rainbow trout planted each year. The best camps for anglers are the Deer Creek and College camps, located on the northeastern shore, and the Lower Billy Creek Camp, located on the northwest shore. Boat launches are available near both of them.

A Wilderness Permit is required for hikers entering the Kaiser Wilderness, but a Forest Service office is available at the upper end of the lake, just off the loop road east of Highway 168.

---

5. KAISER WILDERNESS

Reference: Northeast of Fresno in Sierra National Forest; map F4 grid c8.
How to get there: Access to trailheads is available off Highway 168 east of Fresno, and off Forest Service Roads that junction with Highway 168 near Huntington Lake.
Facilities: No facilities are available in the wilderness area. Campgrounds are located at Huntington Lake and at some trailheads.
Cost: Access is free.
Who to contact: Phone the Sierra National Forest District Office at (209) 841-3311. For a map, send $2 to Office of Information, U.S. Forest Service, 630 Sansome Street, San Francisco, CA 94111.
About Kaiser Wilderness: Many of the wilderness areas in the southern Sierra Nevada include huge portions above tree line, comprised of stark granite country and lakes set in rock bowls. The Kaiser Wilderness, however, is an exception.

The area is mostly wooded, though Kaiser Peak is bare and provides a great lookout. The best jump-off spot is at Huntington Lake, 8,000 feet elevation, where there are two trailheads available: **1.** A popular loop hike starts near Lakeshore and heads north to Kaiser Peak, then loops back around to Nellie Lake and south along Home Camp Creek to the west end of Huntington Lake. **2.** From the trailhead at Lakeshore, hike about a mile, turn right at the fork and the trail will lead to Lower Twin Lake and Upper Twin Lake. Both are stocked with trout.

The following hike-to lakes are stocked by airplane in the Kaiser Wilderness: Bobby Lake, Bonnie Lake, Campfire Lake, Idaho Lake, Long Lake, Nellie Lake, Upper Twin Lake, Walling Lake. They receive fingerling rainbow trout, no brook trout or golden trout.

Compared to many wilderness areas, it is not heavily traveled nor spectacularly beautiful. But what it does provide is a series of small remote lakes, decent prospects for small trout, and lakeside camps that can seem near perfect in their quiet and untouched state.

6. SAN JOAQUIN RIVER

Reference: Northeast of Fresno in Sierra National Forest; map F4 grid d2.

How to get there: River access is limited to campgrounds on the river. From Fresno, drive north on Highway 41 and take the Friant Road exit. Drive north on Friant Road to the town of Friant, then turn east on Millerton Road and continue past Millerton Lake. Look for entrance signs to campgrounds between Millerton Lake and Auberry.

Facilities: Campgrounds are located along the river. Supplies are available in Friant and Auberry.

Cost: Campgrounds may charge a fee.

Who to contact: Phone the Bureau of Land Management at (408) 637-8183.

About San Joaquin River: The San Joaquin is the chameleon of California rivers, with different looks and appearances according to which stretch you choose to take a close look at. In this area, the only stretch planted with trout by the DFG is below Millerton Lake, downstream of Friant; for information, see Zone F-3. Upstream of Millerton Lake, the best stretch of river is in adjacent Zone F5, near the Devil's Postpile National Monument.

So what you get here are a few accessible spots located near the campgrounds, spots that get picked over year after year. The fish tend to be small and are not particularly amenable to donating themselves to your frying pan. The river also has dramatic changes in water flows, even during the summer, due to unpredictable releases from dams at Kerckhoff and Redinger lakes, and Mammoth Pool Reservoir.

As for me, maybe I'll sample it for an hour, but before long, I'll be back in my rig, heading up the mountain.

7. KERCKHOFF RESERVOIR

Reference: Northeast of Fresno in Sierra National Forest; map F4 grid d4.

How to get there: From Fresno, drive north on Highway 99 to Madera. Turn east on Highway 145 and drive 19 miles. Turn right on Road 206 and drive south to the town of Friant. From Friant, drive 19 miles northeast on Millerton and Auberry Roads to the town of Auberry. Turn north on Powerhouse Road and drive seven miles to the reservoir.

Facilities: A picnic area and small campground are provided by PG&E. Supplies are available in Auberry or North Fork.

Cost: Lake access is free.

Who to contact: Phone PG&E at (209) 263-5234.

About Kerckhoff Reservoir: Well, you can't win 'em all, and when it comes to Kerckhoff, it can be difficult to win ever. The lake is something of a dud, with no trout and virtually no largemouth bass, but it does present a chance for striped bass.

It is not an easy chance, however. The fishery goes up and down faster than the lake levels; hit it wrong and you will swear there isn't a single fish in the entire lake. Hit it right and you will feel like you have discovered a secret spot everybody else ignores. The stripers tend to be deep most of the year, requiring specialized trolling with diving, deepwater plugs, with just short spurts in the fall when the show moves up on the surface. It takes a boat to chase them, but only those with car-top boats need apply, since there are no boat launching facilities available. Nearby Redinger Lake five miles to the east provides an option and has a boat launch available.

Kerckhoff is set in the foothill country east of Fresno, and it can seem hotter than the interior of Mt. Vesuvius. If you camp here, be sure to bring a plastic tarp and some poles so you can rig a makeshift roof to provide a shelter from the sun.

---

8.   REDINGER LAKE

Reference: Northeast of Fresno in Sierra National Forest; map F4 grid d4.

How to get there: From Fresno, drive north on Highway 99 to Madera. Turn east on Highway 145 and drive 19 miles. Turn right on Road 206 and drive south to the town of Friant. From Friant, drive 19 miles northeast on Millerton and Auberry Roads to the town of Auberry. Turn north on Powerhouse Road and drive eight miles to Kerckhoff Reservoir. Turn right on Road 235 and drive six miles to Redinger Lake.

Facilities: A primitive campground, a picnic area, and a boat ramp are available. Supplies can be obtained in Auberry.

Cost: Lake access is free.

Who to contact: Phone the Sierra National Forest District Office at (209) 877-2218.

About Redinger Lake: Redinger Lake is on the DFG's thumbs-down list. That is the list of waters that get nothing, as in no stocked trout, no bass, no catfish, no fishery management of any kind, and no pressure for water level management. No nuthin'.

They might as well just turn it over to the waterskiers. There can be plenty of the latter, being located about an hour's drive from Fresno, set at 1,400 feet in the hot Sierra foothills. The lake is three miles long, a quarter-mile wide, and the 35-mph speed limit is tested by every jet boat launched.

The best option for fishermen/boaters is to head well up the San Joaquin arm, where there are primitive boat-in camps along the north shore. In the spring, there can be fair trout fishing at the headwaters of the lake, almost always on nightcrawlers for bait.

---

9. SHAVER LAKE

Reference: Northeast of Fresno in Sierra National Forest; map F4 grid d6.

How to get there: From Fresno, turn north on Highway 168 and drive 63 miles to Shaver Lake. The marina and boat ramp are located seven miles north of the town of Shaver Lake on Highway 168.

Facilities: Campgrounds, picnic areas, boat ramps, boat rentals, a marina, bait, tackle, and groceries are available.

Cost: Lake access is free. There may be a fee for boat launching.

Who to contact: Phone the Sierra National Forest District Office at (209) 877-2218; Sierra Marina, (209) 841-3324.

About Shaver Lake: You have to pass by Shaver Lake if you are heading to Huntington Lake, and a lot of folks can't stand the tease. They stop and check it out.

Though Shaver is not as high in elevation as Huntington, Shaver being set at 5,370 feet while Huntington is at 7,000 feet, it is very pretty and a good lake for early summer trout fishing. By summer, waterskiing is very popular, and it becomes time for fishermen to head to higher country.

The DFG stocks Shaver with "catchable" trout from late spring through mid-summer, providing good fishing for trollers and baitdunkers alike. It gets 50,000 rainbow trout each year. There are a series of coves on the southern shoreline that provide good prospects for both. Avoid the main lake area. An option is to try for bass. It's best when the surface of the lake starts to warm up from the heat of summer. The last two hours of daylight provide the best summer topwater action.

---

10. COURTRIGHT RESERVOIR

Reference: Northeast of Fresno in Sierra National Forest; map F4 grid d9.

How to get there: From Fresno, drive 63 miles northeast to the town of Shaver Lake. Turn east on Dinkey Creek Road and drive 12 miles, then turn right on McKinley Grove Road and drive 14 miles east. When the road forks, bear left on Courtright Reservoir Road and drive ten miles north to the lake.

Facilities: Campgrounds, picnic areas and a boat ramp are available. Supplies can be obtained in Fresno or Shaver Lake.

Cost: Lake access is free.

Who to contact: Phone PG&E at (209) 263-5234 or the Sierra National Forest District Office at (209) 855-8321.

About Courtright Reservoir: Courtright Reservoir provides a two-for-one offer, and for many it's an offer they can't refuse. You have the option to camp, boat and fish, or you can park at the trailhead at Voyager Rock Campground (northeast side of the lake) and head off into the John Muir Wilderness.

Courtright is set in the high Sierra at 8,200 feet elevation, and if you plan to stick around, is best visited in the early summer. That is when the lake level is the highest by far (it can drop quickly from mid-August on through fall). Stocks of rainbow trout are made regularly, and cool but warming water temperature keep the trout biting. The DFG stocks Courtright with 24,000 rainbow trout each year. A 15-mph speed limit guarantees zero waterskiing, and in turn, calm water. The boat launch is located just west of the dam.

Backpackers have several options. The best is to head east from the trailhead at Voyager Rock Campground and into the high granite country of the LeConte Divide and poke around the Red Mountain Basin. There are six lakes in the basin: Disappointment Lake, Devil's Punchbowl, Blackrock Lake, Hell For Sure Lake, Horseshoe Lake and Arctic Lake. If you would prefer a loop hike, you can start at the same trailhead, but instead turn north at the junction two miles in and spend the first night at Hobler Lake, continue north and camp at Thompson Lake the second night, then return by heading over Hot Springs Pass and down Helms Creek, which will return you to Courtright Reservoir.

---

11. MILLERTON LAKE

Reference: North of Fresno in Millerton Lake State Recreation Area; map F4 grid e1.

How to get there: From Fresno, drive north on Highway 41 to the Friant Road exit. Drive north on Friant Road for about 15 miles, then turn right (east) on Millerton Road and continue to the lake entrance. Boat ramps are located on the south shore near the park entrance.

Facilities: Campgrounds, picnic areas, boat ramps, a marina, boat rentals, and bait are available at the lake. Supplies can be obtained in Friant.

Cost: Day-use fee is $6 per vehicle; an additional $5 is charged for entering with a boat. The entrance fee includes boat launching privileges.

Who to contact: Phone Millerton Lake State Recreation area at (209) 822-2332.

About Millerton Lake: Millerton Lake may seem like the perfect setting for a bass bonanza. Sometimes, it actually is.

At 578 feet elevation in the foothills of the San Joaquin Valley,

Millerton gets good weather for bass providing a nine-month growing season, although it's very hot during mid-summer. The lake also has a lot of shoreline bass habitat, with 43 miles of shoreline in all, including many little coves on the San Joaquin arm. The lake seems to have lots of bass in the nine to 13-inch class. The bigger ones are in there—my pals in Fresno swear to it even though I have never caught one, and I'll take their word for it.

One major problem here is that this lake seems to be a perennial victim to low water levels, with drawdowns lessening the natural beauty of the area, and at the same time often leaving the spring bass spawn high and dry on the mud flats.

Regardless, Millerton gets a lot of traffic because of its nearby proximity to Fresno and Madera. The shape of the lake, large lake body and a long narrow inlet, seems to naturally separate waterskiers from anglers.

Millerton is not on the stocking list of the Department of Fish and Game, but an experimental plan starting in 1992 will try planting catchable-size rainbow trout during the winter months. If the public responds, the experiment will become an annual winter event. What you get at Millerton is a good base lake where the catch rates actually approach some resemblance to what people say they are catching.

12.   WISHON RESERVOIR

Reference: Northeast of Fresno in Sierra National Forest; map F4 grid e9.
How to get there: From Fresno, drive 63 miles northeast to the town of Shaver Lake. Turn east on Dinkey Creek Road and drive 12 miles, then turn right on McKinley Grove Road and drive 14 miles east. When the road forks, bear right and continue for about three miles to the boat ramp on the southeast shore.
Facilities: Campgrounds, a picnic area, a boat ramp, boat rentals, bait, and groceries are available.
Cost: Lake access is free.
Who to contact: Phone PG&E at (209) 263-5238; Sierra National Forest District Office, (209) 855-8321; Wishon Village, (209) 841-5361.
About Wishon Reservoir: At Wishon you never get stuck if you don't like scenery.

Not that you will want to leave. It is an attractive lake when full, set at 6,500 feet, surrounded by National Forest, filled with snowmelt poured from the North Fork Kings River. It's just that Wishon doesn't ever seem to be full. The interminable fluctuations in water levels can hurt the trout trolling. When it is stable, the fishing is good, courtesy of stocks of 10 to 12-inch rainbow trout from the DFG, plus a few lunker browns that rarely show. The lake receives 18,000 rainbow trout per year from the DFG. A 15-mph speed limit keeps the lake quiet.

An option, however, is the five-mile hike that starts at the trailhead at Woodchuck Creek, then is routed east into "Woodchuck Country" and into the John Muir Wilderness. Woodchuck Country has three lakes, Woodchuck Lake, Marsh Lake, and Chimney Lake, that provide good spots for a quick overnight backpack. If you have more time, you can extend the trip to Half Moon Lake, over Scepter Pass and beyond into the Blackcap Basin, where there are more than a dozen high mountain lakes in pristine granite country.

---

13.   PINE FLAT LAKE

Reference: East of Fresno; map F4 grid f6.

How to get there: From Fresno, turn east on Highway 180 and drive 15.5 miles to Centerville. Turn left on Trimmer Springs Road and drive eight miles to the lake. Boat ramps are located on the north shore off Trimmer Springs Road and on the south shore off Sunnyslope Road.

Facilities: Several campgrounds, boat ramps, picnic areas, a marina, boat rentals, bait, tackle, and groceries are available.

Cost: Lake access is free.

Who to contact: Phone the U.S. Corps of Engineers at (209) 787-2589; Lakeridge Marina, (209) 787-2506.

About Pine Flat Lake: Spotted bass provide good catch rates for anglers throughout most of the year at Pine Flat Lake, despite how little water is in the place.

Think it might be a little low? You ain't lyin'. Pine Flat is commonly kept 80 to 90 percent empty, with much of the water being given at subsidized rates by the government to farmers to grow cotton, who then sell the cotton to the government via another subsidy. It's called a double subsidy, and has been one of the big pork barrel rip-offs and water wastes in America, and it is my prediction that it will be found out and ordered stopped by Congress.

When Pine Flat is full, courtesy of monsoon-level snowstorms in the Sierra and the ensuing meltoff, the lake becomes quite pretty. It is set in the foothills east of Fresno at 961 feet elevation, 21 miles long with 67 miles of shoreline.

Spotted bass are the mainstay of the lake, but there are also largemouth bass, bluegill, catfish, and crappie, and a lot of trout planted. When water levels are high enough and cold enough in the spring, the DFG plunks in 56,000 rainbow trout in the nine to 12-inch class. Until the hot weather arrives, the trout fishing is quite good using standard trolling techniques, as well as baitfishing from the shore near the boat ramp. The best bet, however, is always fishing for the spotted bass up the main lake arm, where there are two major coves where the fish hold. As spring gives way to summer, Millerton always comes alive. If only they could keep the water in the lake, instead of being funneled to the cotton fields, this place would be something great.

---

14. KINGS RIVER

Reference: Northeast of Fresno; map F4 grid g5.

South of Pine Flat Lake: From Fresno, turn east on Highway 180 and drive 15.5 miles to Centerville. Turn left (north) on Trimmer Springs Road, which parallels the west side of the river, or continue east to Minkler and turn left (north) on Piedra Road, which borders the east side of the river. Access is available upstream to the bridge at Piedra.

North of Pine Flat Lake: From Fresno, turn east on Highway 180 and drive 15.5 miles to Centerville. Turn left on Trimmer Springs Road and drive 26 miles north, past Pine Flat Lake. Continue east on Trimmer Springs Road for seven miles to Garnet Dike Camp. Access is available off the road and off unimproved roads that parallel both sides of the river.

Facilities: Several campgrounds are available on the river. Supplies can be obtained in Piedra.

Cost: River access is free.

Who to contact: Phone the Sequoia National Forest District Office at (209) 338-2251; Herb Bauer Sporting Goods in Fresno at (209) 435-8600.

About Kings River: This section of the Kings River is not exactly awe-inspiring. However, the nearby section in Zone F5 does border the awesome, and also provides very high catch rates, so don't give up on this river just yet.

In this area, the Kings River is stocked with rainbow trout downstream of the dam at Pine Flat Lake. It gets 46,000 trout per year in this section of river. That's not too shabby. Upstream of the lake, you get a chance for wild rainbow trout, including some elusive giants, in a section of the Kings better known for providing some of the best rafting and kayaking water in California. Because rafting is so popular in the early summer, it is better to fish here during the evening rather than from morning to mid-day.

The best bet for this stretch of river is driving all the way to Garnet Dike Camp, surveying the river as you go, then fishing your way back downstream to Pine Flat Lake, driving, parking, then making quick hits several times.

MAP F5

20 LISTINGS
PAGES 578-593

CEN-CAL MAP ..see page540
adjoining maps
NORTH (E5).......see page 516
EAST ....no map
SOUTH (G5).......see page 614
WEST (F4)..........see page 566

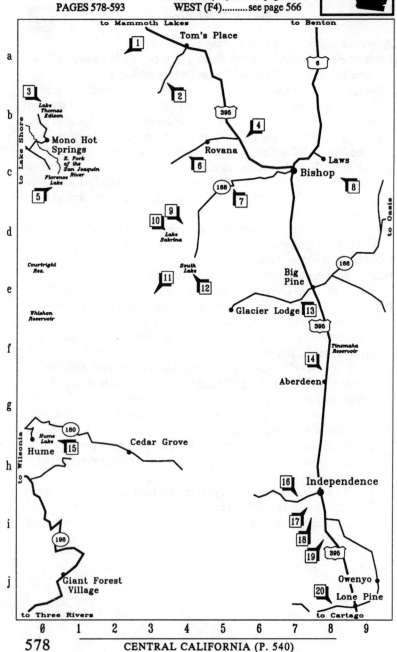

1. JOHN MUIR WILDERNESS

Reference: East of Fresno in Sierra National Forest; map F5 grid a2.

How to get there: Access to trailheads is available off roads that junction with Highway 395 to the east and Highway 168 to the west.

Facilities: No facilities are available in the wilderness area. Campgrounds are available at many trailheads.

Cost: Access is free.

Who to contact: Phone Sierra National Forest Headquarters at (209) 487-4155. For a map, send $2 to Office of Information, U.S. Forest Service, 630 Sansome Street, San Francisco, CA 94111.

About John Muir Wilderness: Trails reaching as high as 12,000 feet, mountaintops poking holes into the heavens, and hundreds of pristine lakes set in granite bowls make for paradise in the John Muir Wilderness. It is the kind of place where a hiker can get religion without making a single donation in an offering plate. I'll tell you the kind of impact it had on me: Visiting it is such a transcendent experience that it has made me stay in good physical condition, with the idea in the back of my mind that I could return at any time, any day.

There are many trailheads and access points. The best are at Edison Lake, Florence Lake or at the end of Highway 180 in Kings Canyon National Park. I suggest that you scan the trip notes for other waters within this grid zone for jump-off points and suggested routes.

Usually when you plan on eating trout for dinner when backpacking, it guarantees that you will get skunked. The John Muir Wilderness might be the exception to that, but bring plenty of jerky anyway. My brother Rambob and I have never failed to limit on trout every evening we have ever spent in the John Muir Wilderness. The trout are not large, only very rarely over eight inches, but they include the rare golden trout, California's state fish. Most of the lakes have lots of small brook trout and some rainbow trout, the kind that practically jump into your frying pan come the evening rise.

The following hike-in lakes are stocked with golden trout by the DFG's flying tanker: Apollo Lake, Aweetasal Lake, Bearpaw Lake, Beartrap Lake, Big Bear Lake, Bighorn Lake, Black Bear Lake, Brown Bear Lake, Chapel Lake, Claw Lake, Coronet Lake, Den Lake, Hooper Lake, Island Lake, Neil Lake, Upper Nelson Lake, Orchid Lake, Pemmican Lake, Rose Lake, Rosebud Lake, Silver Pass Lake, Spearpoint Lake, Teddy Bear Lake, Three Island Lake, Toe Lake, Tooth Lake, Ursa Lake, Vee Lake, Virginia Lake, White Bear Lake.

Meanwhile, these lakes are stocked with rainbow trout and brook trout: Blue Jay #2 Lake, Minnie Lake, Vermillion Lake, Anne Lake, Chimney Lake, Cirque Lake, Coyote Lake, Crown Lake, Davis Lake,

Frog Lake, Geraldine Lakes, Maxon Lake, Pearl Lake, Rae Lake, Rainbow Lake, Scepter Lake.

Many visitors to the John Muir Wilderness hike primarily on the John Muir Trail, partially in reverence for the master. In the process, however, they miss many of the more hidden and lesser-visited lakes. Remember, when Muir hiked from Mt. Whitney to Yosemite Valley, there was no trail, but rather a general route. Much of it was cross-country, and on the way, he was apt to explore any lake, any mountain. That is the best approach to make. Once in the high country, head off the trail, clambering your way to lakes that are like mountain temples, where mankind is only a temporary visitor, and where Muir's ghost still may watch over.

---

2. ROCK CREEK LAKE

Reference: Northeast of Bishop in Inyo National Forest; map F5 grid a3.
How to get there: From the town of Bishop, drive 30 miles north on US 395 to Tom's Place. Turn west on Rock Creek Road and drive eight miles to Rock Creek Lake.
Facilities: Lodging, a campground, a picnic area, a boat ramp, boat rentals, bait, and groceries are available.
Cost: Access is free.
Who to contact: Phone the Inyo National Forest District Office at (619) 873-4207; Rock Creek Lake Resort, (619) 935-4311.
About Rock Creek Lake: Most natural lakes are prettier and smaller than reservoirs, and Rock Creek Lake in the high Sierra is a perfect example of that. The lake and surrounding area has great natural beauty, set in the Little Lakes Valley in the high country, 9,682 feet, just north of the boundary to the John Muir Wilderness.

A five-mph speed limit guarantees quiet water. While there is no similar guarantee to the fishing, it is decent enough. Rainbow trout are stocked during the summer, with the plants starting as soon as the ice melts and the access road is plowed (usually some time in May). Rock Creek Lake is stocked with 33,200 rainbow trout, most ranging nine to 11 inches. That is more than many lakes in the area, and those rainbows join a light sprinkling of brown trout. Shoreline baitdunkers will find the best prospects by far near the outlet of the lake.

It is an excellent destination for a camping/hiking vacation, with some 35 other lakes nearby, many within range for a one-day round trip. The hike out west to Mono Pass gets quite steep, but you can stop on the way at Ruby Lake, named for its gem-like qualities.

3.   EDISON LAKE

Reference: Northeast of Fresno in Sierra National Forest; map F5 grid b∅.

How to get there: From Fresno, drive 68 miles northeast on Highway 168 (a narrow, winding two-laner) to Huntington Lake. Continue northeast on Kaiser Pass Road for 21 miles to Edison Lake. The boat ramp is located on the west shore; the road leads directly to it.

Facilities: Lodging, a campground, a picnic area, a boat ramp, boat rentals, bait, and groceries are available at the lake.

Cost: Lake access is free.

Who to contact: Phone the Sierra National Forest District Office at (209) 841-3311; Vermillion Valley Resort, (213) 697-0312.

About Edison Lake: Here is one of the great family camping destinations in California. Edison Lake offers four lakeside camps, a resort, boat launch, boat rentals, horseback riding rentals, a nearby trailhead to the Pacific Crest Trail . . . and good fishing. A 15-mph speed limit keeps the nuts off, and a ferry service is available that runs across the lake twice a day.

Edison Lake is set at 7,650 feet elevation, fed by Mono Creek, a cold, pure and pristine trout stream. Fishing is fair by boat or shoreline, with stocks of rainbow trout in the 10 to 12-inch class. Sometimes it doesn't seem like there are enough to go around here, however. Most boaters use standard trolling techniques and do well enough on rainbow trout, with occasional brook trout and big brown trout. Shoreliners who are willing to hike fare no worse. You should take the trail on the north side of the lake and hike up toward the inlet of the lake. The fishing in Mono Creek is also good, especially during the evening.

If you like hiking, Edison Lake provides one of the better jump-off points available. The trail along the north side of the lake is routed along Mono Creek and then connects to the Pacific Crest Trail (where a bridge crosses the stream). From there, if you don't mind a steep climb, head south up Bear Mountain. It takes about a 40-minute hike to reach an absolutely wondrous aspen grove that is pretty any time of the year. The first time I saw it, I just sat down, leaned against one of the trees, and soaked in the lush beauty.

4.   PLEASANT VALLEY RESERVOIR

Reference: Near Bishop; map F5 grid b6.

How to get there: From Bishop, drive seven miles north on US 395 to the signed turnoff for the reservoir. Turn north and continue for 1.5 miles to the barrier across the road. Park and walk to the dam.

Facilities: No facilities are available on-site. Campgrounds and supplies are available in Bishop.

Cost: Access is free.

Who to contact: Phone Culver's Sporting Goods in Bishop at (619) 872-8361.

About Pleasant Valley Reservoir: Well, at least the name makes it sound nice. But you would want to go here for more reasons than just the name. The DFG provides 32,000 reasons, all of them rainbow trout in the 10 to 12-inch class, which join a fair population of native brown trout, some of them huge.

It is a long, narrow reservoir, created from a small dam on the Owens River. It is not particularly pretty, set at 4,200 feet bordering the Volcanic Tableland to the immediate east. You have to hike about 15 minutes from the campground to reach the lake, meaning only the hardy few willing to portage a canoe on their shoulders will have the advantage of fishing from a boat.

Timing is critical. The trout fishing can be decent from late winter through early June, and then again in the fall from mid-September until snow shuts off access in November. In the latter, there is a chance for some big browns in the uppermost stretches of the lake. In the summer? Fair, with evenings decent. A trail is routed along the eastern side of the lake.

---

5.   FLORENCE LAKE

Reference: Northeast of Fresno in Sierra National Forest; map F5 grid cØ.

How to get there: From Fresno, drive 68 miles northeast on Highway 168 (a narrow, winding two-laner) to Huntington Lake. Continue northeast on Kaiser Pass Road to Florence Lake Road (two miles south of Mono Hot Springs). Turn south and continue to the lake.

Facilities: A campground, a picnic area, a boat ramp, boat rentals, bait, and groceries are available at the lake.

Cost: Access is free.

Who to contact: Phone the Sierra National Forest District Office at (209) 841-3311; Florence Lake Resort, (209) 966-3195.

About Florence Lake: Like nearby Edison Lake to the north, Florence Lake is a good vacation destination. It has everything but large numbers of trout, with mountain beauty, excellent hiking options and fair trout fishing. The lake is set at 7,327 feet elevation, smaller than Edison, but just as pretty with the awesome Glacier Divide country providing a backdrop to the east. A 15-mph speed limit maintains the sanity of the place.

The lake usually opens around the beginning of June and remains open through late September, rarely later. In the process, it is stocked with rainbow trout the same days as Edison Lake (so there is no big advantage in jumping from lake to lake). Boaters should start trolling immediately upon launching, then head along the western shore on up to the inlet, where the South Fork of the San Joaquin River enters the lake. Shoreliners will discover a trail available along the western side of the lake, with the better prospects both near the dam and near the inlet, only fair in between.

If you like hiking, then strap on a backpack and just keep on going. From the inlet, the trail is routed up the South Fork to the Pacific Crest Trail (about five miles in). From there, you can continue southeast along the San Joaquin, turning into Evolution Valley, one of the prettiest meadow/woodlands in the entire high Sierra.

---

6. PINE CREEK

Reference: North of Bishop in Inyo National Forest; map F5 grid c4.

How to get there: From Bishop, drive 15 miles north on US 395 to Pine Creek Road on the left. Turn and drive west to where the road crosses the creek. Access is available west of this point.

Facilities: No facilities are available on-site. Campgrounds and supplies are available in Bishop.

Cost: Access is free.

Who to contact: Phone the Inyo National Forest District Office at (619) 873-4207; Culver's Sporting Goods in Bishop at (619) 872-8361.

About Pine Creek: The relatively few people who have even seen this little stream usually just keep on going. Most visitors taking the Pine Creek Road exit are heading for the wilderness, using the trailhead at the end of the road to hike off to Pine Lake, Upper Pine Lake, Honeymoon Lake and beyond into the high country of the John Muir Wilderness.

The irony is that there are often bigger trout in the stream right along the access road. It is stocked with trout from where Pine Creek Road first crosses the stream on upstream to where the road crosses the stream again near the Union Carbide storage area. The plants are usually made right from both bridges, the DFG plunking in 2,000 rainbow trout per year. Put that in your cash register and add it up. It is worth the quick hit.

---

7. BISHOP CREEK

Reference: Near Bishop in Inyo National Forest; map F5 grid c5.

How to get there: From Bishop on US 395, turn west on Highway 168 and drive southeast. Direct access is available along the highway and off Bishop Creek Road, which parallels the highway to the south.

Facilities: Several campgrounds are available on the road in. Supplies are available in Bishop.

Cost: Access is free.

Who to contact: Phone the Inyo National Forest District Office at (619) 873-4207; Culver's Sporting Goods in Bishop at (619) 872-8361.

About Bishop Creek: Access is easy, with turnouts right along Bishop Creek Road, but most folks just sail on by on their way up to Lake Sabrina, or nearby North Lake and South Lake. But if they stop, they will discover good evening trout fishing. Bishop Creek receives very large numbers of stocks from the DFG, and can provide very good fishing if you know where to hit.

So read this closely: The stream is stocked in four key areas: 1. Upstream from Bullpit Park to Powerline Road (stocked with 2,200 rainbow trout). 2. From Intake II to Cardinal Lodge (stocked with 19,000 rainbow trout). 3. Downstream of Lake Sabrina (44,000 rainbow trout). 4. South Fork from South Lake to Highway 168 (44,000 rainbow trout). Got it?

---

8. OWENS RIVER

Reference: From Bishop to Big Pine; map F5 grid c8.

How to get there: From Bishop on US 395, turn east on Highway 6, East Line Street, Warm Springs Road, or Collins Road. Access is available where these roads cross the river and off roads that junction with them. From Big Pine on US 395, turn east on Steward Lane or Westgard Pass Road. Direct access is available.

Facilities: Campgrounds and supplies are available in the Bishop and Big Pine areas.

Cost: Access is free.

Who to contact: Phone the City of Los Angeles at (213) 485-4853; Culver's Sporting Goods in Bishop at (619) 872-8361.

About Owens River: You want trout? The DFG answers your request with huge numbers of stocked rainbow trout here, 67,000 in all plunked on a regular basis throughout the summer. It is stocked in the Bishop area from Laws Bridge on Highway 6 on downstream to Collins Road, with the stocks usually made at those two key access points. South near the town of Big Pine area, the stream is stocked at Westgard Pass Road and Steward Lane.

This section of the Owens River is at the mercy of water releases from Crowley Lake, and further downstream, Pleasant Valley Reservoir. But the water spigot is generally turned up enough to keep this river like a little trout factory in the desolate Owens Valley. The saving grace are the trout plants.

The Owens River has been dammed, diverted, pumped, tunneled, and sometimes run just about dry. The piece of water between Bishop and Big Pine provides just a glimpse of what once was.

---

9.   NORTH LAKE

Reference: Southwest of Bishop in Inyo National Forest; map F5 grid d4.
How to get there: From Bishop on US 395, turn west on Highway 168 and drive 17 miles to the North Lake turnoff on the right. Turn west and continue to the lake.
Facilities: A campground is available nearby, on Bishop Creek. Supplies can be obtained in Bishop.
Cost: Access is free.
Who to contact: Phone the Inyo National Forest District Office at (619) 873-4207; Culver's Sporting Goods, (619) 872-8361.
About North Lake: Little North Lake is a tiny, intimate setting in the high country, with decent shoreline prospects for a mix of brook trout and rainbow trout. The lake is just 13 acres, more the size of a high mountain pond than a lake, located at 9,500 feet elevation. Some bring car-top boats for improved access, but the lake is too small and too shallow for good trolling prospects. The better fishing is with a fly-and-bubble combination. It is stocked each year with 11,000 rainbow trout, and only rarely in recent years with brook trout, too.

It makes for a good layover before heading off on a backpacking expedition. Just west of the lake is a trailhead for a route that follows the North Fork of Bishop Creek up to a remarkable granite basin loaded with similar small mountain lakes. Loch Leven and Piute Lake are just a three-mile hike distant, and if you head over the pass into Humphreys Basin, you can venture cross-country to your choice of 25 lakes, many with golden trout.

If you don't want to hike, nearby Sabrina Lake or South Lake provide better prospects.

10. SABRINA LAKE

Reference: Southwest of Bishop in Inyo National Forest; map F5 grid d4.
How to get there: From Bishop on US 395, turn west on Highway 168 and drive 18.5 miles southwest to the lake.
Facilities: A campground is available nearby. A boat ramp and boat rentals are also available. Supplies can be obtained in Bishop.
Cost: Access is free.
Who to contact: Phone the Inyo National Forest District Office at (619) 873-4207; Culver's Sporting Goods, (619) 872-8361.
About Lake Sabrina: This is the largest of the four lakes in the immediate vicinity in the Bishop Creek drainage. It is also the most popular. It is set at 9,130 feet, covering nearly 200 acres, yet is only a 20-mile ride out of Bishop.

Sound good? It is. Sabrina has consistent fishing, provides a good boat ramp, has a 15-mph speed limit to guarantee quiet water, and yet still has good hiking options with two lakes within a 2.5-mile hike of the lake. It really helps to have a boat here. The only good shorefishing is usually at the south end, near the inlets. By boat, you can fish the northwest shore, either trolling or casting a fly-and-bubble. The evening bite is often a good one during the summer months. It is stocked regularly with 10 to 12-inch rainbow trout, and because of the lake's depth, holdover survival is good. The DFG stocks Sabrina with 30,000 rainbow trout each year, a pretty good number considering the size of the lake.

If you want to get off by yourself, the trail on the southeast side of the lake provides it. Shortly after leaving the lake's shore, it forks—head to the left, and you can hike to George Lake, head to the right, and you will hit Blue Lake, and then Donkey and Baboon Lakes. All are excellent day-hike destinations.

11. KINGS CANYON NATIONAL PARK

Reference: East of Fresno in Sequoia National Forest; map F5 grid e3.
How to get there: From Fresno, drive east on Highway 180 to the Big Stump Grove, then turn north on Highway 180 and continue east past Boyden Cave. The best fishing is along South Fork Kings River between Boyden Cave and Cedar Grove. For back-country access, continue on Highway 180 along the South Fork Kings until it deadends (28 miles from the park entrance) at the wilderness trailhead.
Facilities: Campgrounds, lodging and supplies are available in the park.
Cost: Entrance fee is $5 per vehicle.
Who to contact: Phone Kings Canyon National Park at (209) 565-3341.

About Kings Canyon National Park: Let's get right to the point: Kings Canyon is the best national park in California for anglers. There just flat out are more fish. They may not be big—few are over 12 inches anywhere in the park—but they are plentiful, both brook trout and rainbow trout.

The park has remarkable variety, with 800 miles of streams and 500 lakes. The centerpiece is the South Fork Kings River, which provides outstanding catch rates despite the number of visitors to the park and the easy access along Highway 180. The river sits at the bottom of the deepest canyon in America, a 8,350 foot drop from the top of Spanish Mountain down to the river. It is common for flyfishers to catch 20 or 25 trout from late afternoon to dusk on the South Fork Kings, with the good fishing starting at Boyden's Cave on upstream. It is here where you have the best chance in the park of catching a large native rainbow trout. The big ones come only rarely, but they do come. Guide Jeff Boghosian specializes in this stretch of water.

Even the drive-to areas are spectacular in natural beauty. From lookouts along the highway, you can see the Sierra crest, with a long series of peaks over 11,000 feet elevation and higher, as well as the awesome Kings Canyon and the river below.

Those who get such a glimpse of the back-country wilderness may want to take a week or more and explore it. One of the best loop hikes in America is available starting at the trailhead where Highway 180 deadends. The trail from here routes up into the high country along Bubbs Creek, circles the awesome Sixty Lakes Basin, then returns via Woods Creek. Included in this hike is the climb over Glen Pass, 11,978 feet elevation, and a one-night camp at Rae Lakes in the John Muir Wilderness.

Rae Lakes is the spot where Rambob and I caught limits of brook trout on a bare hook, catching nearly a fish per cast, right in the middle of the day. We would have caught a trout on every cast except they kept hitting the split-shot sinker we had for weight rather than the bare hook. When we finally put a lure on and pinched down the barbs, we each caught and released 70 or 80 trout before finally turning our backs on them. Rae Lakes is set near a fragile meadow area, and camping is limited to one-night only; back-country rangers make sure you abide.

No problem, not with so many other spectacular areas. One of the most breathtaking is the Kearsage Lakes, set just below the Kearsage Pinnacles. They are pristine, sapphire blue, bordered by granite, and overlooked by mountain peaks. The hike in takes you past Bullfrog Lake, which has good fishing.

Another great pleasure are the short, intense thunderstorms during hot summer afternoons. During hot, blue-sky days, the sky can suddenly cloud up with giant cumulonimbus over the peaks, then cut loose by hurtling lightning bolts on the mountain rims and giant thunder claps down the canyons. The rain is intense, then suddenly, as fast as it started, it ends. The sky clears, and the trout start their evening bite.

If it sounds like Kings Canyon National Park is a great place, it's because it is.

---

12. SOUTH LAKE

Reference: Southwest of Bishop in Inyo National Forest; map F5 grid e4.

How to get there: From Bishop on US 395, turn west on Highway 168 and drive 15 miles southwest to South Lake Road on the left. Turn and drive seven miles south to the lake.

Facilities: Several campgrounds are available on South Lake Road. A boat ramp, boat rentals, a picnic area, lodging, bait, and groceries are available at the lake.

Cost: Access is free.

Who to contact: Phone the Inyo National Forest District Office at (619) 873-4207; Parcher's South Lake Landing, (619) 873-4177.

About South Lake: This is the high country, where visitors get a unique mix of glacial-carved granite, lakes the color of gems, and good evening fishing for rainbow trout ranging to 11 or 12 inches, rarely a big brown. The DFG stocks South Lake with 25,000 rainbow trout each year starting at ice-out in early summer.

South Lake is set at 9,755 feet elevation, covering 166 acres, created by a small dam on the South Fork of Bishop Creek. A good boat ramp is available, popular among owners of trailered aluminum boats, who can launch easily and then troll adjacent to the lakes shore. A 15-mph speed limit is in effect.

It is stocked regularly through the summer, soon after ice-out when the access road gets plowed. While boaters do quite well here, shoreline prospects only seem to be fair. No problem. A trail routed along the southeast part of the lake forks off, providing trails to two different series of lakes. If you head to the right, you will reach the Treasury Lakes, about a two-mile hike, a good day trip. If you head to the left, you will be on the trail that is routed up to Bishop Pass, in the process passing Bull Lake, Long Lake, Saddlerock Lake, and Bishop Lake. If you cross over the top of the pass, you will then drop into the Dusy Basin, a wonderful, pristine environment; one of my favorite camps.

13. BIG PINE CREEK

Reference: South of Bishop in Inyo National Forest; map F5 grid e7.

How to get there: From the town of Big Pine on US 395 (16 miles south of Bishop), turn west at the Chevron station onto Glacier Lodge Road. Continue west; direct access is available.

Facilities: Campgrounds are available on the creek. Supplies can be obtained in Big Pine.

Cost: Access is free.

Who to contact: Phone the Inyo National Forest District Office at (619) 873-4207.

About Big Pine Creek: Big Pine Creek is often bypassed in the excitement to get somewhere else, just like so many streams that border two-lane access roads to wilderness areas. The road along Big Pine Creek is routed westward to one of the best trailheads for the John Muir Wilderness. If you hike up the trail along the North Fork of Big Pine Creek, it takes only four miles of walking to hit a short loop trail that is routed along seven different lakes.

That is why folks just keep on driving. But Big Pine Creek is stocked with trout from the Sage Flat Campground to Glacier Lodge. Just upstream from the campground is a good area, particularly in the vicinity of where a little feeder stream enters on the north side of the creek. Now here is the surprise: This little stream is stocked with 38,200 rainbow trout each summer. That should blow your mind.

14. TABOOSE CREEK

Reference: South of Big Pine; map F5 grid f8.

How to get there: From the town of Big Pine on US 395, drive 11 miles south on US 395 to the Taboose Creek Campground turnoff. Turn west and drive a short distance, then turn left at the first road past Old Highway 395 and continue to the creek.

Facilities: A campground is available on the creek. Supplies can be obtained in Big Pine or Independence.

Cost: Access is free.

Who to contact: Phone the County Parks Department at (619) 878-2411, ext. 2272.

About Taboose Creek: Not many people know about Taboose Creek and the adjacent campground. That is because it is operated by the county, not the state or federal agencies, so it gets relatively few visitors other than a few locals. Yet access is easy, the campground is decent, and the fishing good if you stick to the stretch of water from Old Highway

395 on upstream for one mile. That is where the trout stocks are
concentrated, getting 16,000 rainbow trout per year.

15.　　　　　　　HUME LAKE

Reference: East of Fresno in Sequoia National Forest; map F5 grid hØ.

How to get there: From Fresno, turn east on Highway 180 and drive
approximately 55 miles east on the winding two-laner to the town of
Wilsonia in King's Canyon National Park. Continue north on Highway
180 for six miles to the Hume Lake Road Junction. Turn right and
drive three miles south to the lake.

Facilities: A campground is available at the lake. Groceries can be
obtained nearby.

Cost: Access is free.

Who to contact: Phone the Sequoia National Forest District Office at (209)
338-2251.

About Hume Lake: When you first see Hume Lake, you may figure that
there are a lot of dinkers but actually very few large trout in the lake.
After all, a highly-developed camp center is located just a mile away,
and you may deduce that the lake gets hammered by vacationers day
after day, all summer long.

　　Not so. First off, the camp is a Christian retreat, and the participants
seem more interested in prayer and bible study than trout fishing.
Secondly, the trout that are stocked here are not the little Slim Jims,
but good-size rainbow trout, often 12 to 14 inches. Even though the
lake is small, it receives 32,000 rainbow trout per year. That's a
tremendous amount considering the size of the lake and that most of
the religious retreaters do not fish.

　　But it is a good lake for shorefishing, with the best spot on the
southern corner of the dam, using the magic Power Bait. The lake is
set in the vicinity of Kings Canyon National Park, where the deepest
canyon in the world can be seen, making for an excellent tour (and
trout fishing, too, in the Kings River).

　　If some of the religious retreaters pull you aside, it usually is not
necessary to ask them to pray for the trout to start biting.

16.　　　　INDEPENDENCE CREEK

Reference: Near Independence in Inyo National Forest; map F5 grid i7.

How to get there: From the town of Independence on US 395, turn west
on the road just north of the Independence Post Office. Access is
available off the road.

Facilities: Campgrounds are available on the creek. Supplies can be
obtained in Independence.

Cost: Access is free.

Who to contact: Phone the Inyo National Forest District Office at (619) 876-5542.

About Independence Creek: The lower stretches of Independence Creek are hardly surrounded by much natural beauty. It is fairly desolate, with most visitors heading right on westward to the Onion Valley trailhead, which puts them on the Pacific Crest Trail and near several lakes (Bullfrog and Kearsage lakes are the most notable) after a day's hiking. This is the area where a large bear ripped open my brother Rambob's backpack and scored the Tang.

The irony for Independence Creek is that its ugliest section provides the best fishing, often with excellent catch rates. It is stocked at the little Independence Campground, located a half-mile east of Independence, on upstream for seven miles to where the road crosses the stream above Seven Pines Village. In all, it gets 35,000 rainbow trout per year. The better fishing is just upstream of the campground, and between Seven Pines Village and upstream to the bridge. Nearby Symmes Creek provides an option.

---

17. SYMMES CREEK

Reference: Near Independence; map F5 grid i7.

How to get there: From the town of Independence of US 395, turn west on the road just north of the Independence Post Office. Continue for about five miles (along Independence Creek) to Foothill Road, then turn left and continue south to the Symmes Creek Campground. Access is available at the campground and off nearby trails.

Facilities: A campground is available on the creek. Supplies can be obtained in Independence.

Cost: Access is free.

Who to contact: Phone the Bureau of Land Management at (619) 872-4881.

About Symmes Creek: Little Symmes Creek is not going to make anybody's list of the California's great trout waters. But it might make the list of places you can reach by car that are very quiet, with few people, and where you might catch a trout, too. When nearby Independence Creek to the north is stocked, the DFG driver usually makes a quick hit at Symmes Creek, dropping a load right at the campground. If the water is too low, it is bypassed. The access road, by the way, heads up to a little-used trailhead that routes backpackers up over Shepherd Pass, just north of Mt. Tyndall.

---

18.   SHEPHERD CREEK

Reference: Near Independence; map F5 grid i7.

How to get there: From the town of Independence on US 395, drive five
miles south, and look on the east side for the road with a cattle guard.
Turn east on that road and continue until it ends at the Los Angeles
Aqueduct. Turn right and continue to the creek.

Facilities: No facilities are available on-site. A campground and supplies
are available in Independence.

Cost: Access is free.

Who to contact: Phone the City of Los Angeles at (213) 485-4853.

About Shepherd Creek: For a place such a short distance off a major
highway, it is hard to believe how remote little Shepherd Creek feels.
This is basically out in the middle of the nowhere land of the Owens
Valley, yet it is easy enough to reach that it gets stocked with trout.
Where? Where? Right near the sand trap where the road meets the
creek. It gets 2,200 rainbow trout per year.

Beautiful? No. Big fish? No. A chance to catch something? Yes.
Well, just about everything has at least one redeeming quality.

19.   GEORGE CREEK

Reference: South of Independence; map F5 grid i8.

How to get there: From the town of Independence on US 395, drive seven
miles south to a road located one-quarter mile northwest of the Los
Angeles Aqueduct crossing. Turn south; direct access is available.

Facilities: No facilities are available on-site. A campground and supplies
are available in Independence.

Cost: Access is free.

Who to contact: Phone the City of Los Angeles at (213) 485-4853.

About George Creek: Don't bring your camera. After all, you don't want
to break the lens. No, it isn't you that's ugly, it's the desert, which
doesn't have high inspirational value for visitors who prefer woods
and water. In fact, it is amazing how ugly this area is considering how
beautiful the mountains are just 10 miles to the west. So why show up
here at all? Because it is stocked with trout at the sand trap, the main
access point for the DFG tanker truck. How many? Just 2,200 per year,
providing a quick hit option if you're cruising through the area.

Reference: Near Lone Pine; map F5 grid j8.

How to get there: From the town of Lone Pine on US 395, turn west at the traffic light in the center of town onto Whitney Portal Road. Continue west; direct access is available.

Facilities: Campgrounds are available on Whitney Portal Road. Supplies can be obtained in Lone Pine.

Cost: Access is free.

Who to contact: Phone the Bureau of Land Management at (619) 872-4881.

About Lone Pine Creek: The first time we drove the road along Lone Pine Creek, Rambob, Foonsky and Mr. Furnai all thought something was wrong with the engine. No power. By the time we reached Whitney Portal, it sounded like it was throbbing its last breath. A dead engine? Nope, just high altitude and a steep grade, with the road climbing from 3,000 feet to 8,361 feet in just 10 miles.

In the process of making this trip, visitors will discover Lone Pine Creek is set adjacent to the road for most of the ride up to the Whitney Portal Camp. It is stocked with trout in the lower stretches just west of Lone Pine, between the Los Angeles Aqueduct and Lone Pine Campground. It is stocked at the other camps along the creek, as well as at the little pond near the Whitney Portal Store. On the road, you may not think the stream has much promise. Guess again. It is stocked with 45,400 rainbow trout every year, and for the people who take the time to try the stream out, they rarely have an empty frying pan come dinner time.

This spot is best known, of course, as the jump-off for climbing Mt. Whitney, at 14,495 feet, the highest point in the Lower 48. From the trailhead at Whitney Portal, the trail climbs more than 6,000 feet to the Whitney Summit, including 100 switchbacks to get above Wotan's Throne. That journey can completely overshadow the fishing at Independence Creek. Regardless, check it out.

MAP G2

13 LISTINGS
PAGES 594-605

CEN-CAL MAP . see page 540
adjoining maps
NORTH (F2).......see page 554
EAST (G3)..........see page 606
SOUTH (H2).......see page 622
WEST ....no map

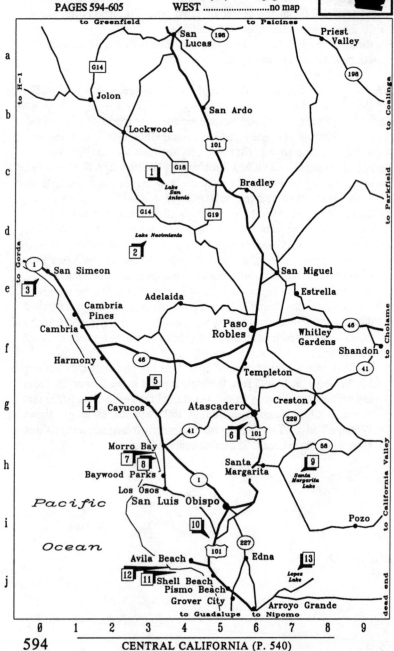

1.   LAKE SAN ANTONIO

Reference: North of San Luis Obispo; map G2 grid c3.

How to get there: From San Luis Obispo, drive approximately 47 miles north on US 101. Turn west on County Road G18 (Jolon Road) to reach the north shore, or County Road G19 (Nacimiento Road) to reach the south shore. Follow the signs to the boat ramps on the north and south shores.

Facilities: Campgrounds, picnic areas, boat ramps, boat rentals, bait, tackle, and groceries are available.

Cost: Day-use fee is $5 per vehicle; additional $3.50 if entering with a boat. Entrance fee includes boat launching privileges.

Who to contact: Phone the lake at (805) 472-2311.

About Lake San Antonio: The changing faces of Lake San Antonio make the timing of your trip critical. Fishing? You'd best show up in the fall, from late September through mid-October, when the striped bass emerge from the depths and roam near the surface, corralling schools of baitfish. Stripers can also be caught the early summer to mid-June by trolling or casting diving plugs. The rest of the year they can be quite difficult to catch.

In some years, this lake also provides good fishing for trout and largemouth bass. Low water in the early 1990s has hurt it a bit. When the good fishing happens, it is always best early in the year, from March through early May. The lake has two lake arms on the southwest part of the lake, and another on the northwest side. These are the best spots during the spring bass bite. No trout stocks are made here.

By summer, the water skiers take over, this being the most popular water ski lake in the region. In the winter, eagle tours are the main attraction, with the excellent chance of seeing both bald and golden eagles by boat.

San Antonio is a big lake, but long and narrow, with about 60 miles of shoreline, three boat ramps and several campgrounds. It is set at 900 feet in the dry, hilly grassland country. If you make the trip, keep an eye out to the skies. At this lake, you never know when a bald eagle might be watching.

2.   LAKE NACIMIENTO

Reference: North of San Luis Obispo; map G2 grid d3.

How to get there: From San Luis Obispo, drive 25 miles north on US 101 to Paso Robles. Turn west on County Road G14 (Nacimiento Lake Drive) and continue west to the dam. Or, continue north on US 101 to the turnoff for County Road G19, then turn west and continue to the lake. Boat ramps are located on the north and east shores of the lake.

Facilities: A campground, lodging, boat ramps, boat rentals, bait, tackle, and groceries are available.

Cost: Day use fee is $4 per vehicle.

Who to contact: Phone the lake at (805) 472-2456.

About Lake Nacimiento: Just add water and Nacimiento provides the highest bass-per-cast rate in California. A simple recipe? Sounds like it, but nature does not always provide the required ingredients. With low water, this lake was closed to fishing, boating and recreation in April of 1990, and remained closed through 1991. It will re-open as soon as nature stirs in some water.

That done, Nacimiento will quickly regain its former status as a place where the sport of "fishing" can be called "catching." For starters, there are white bass, so many that there is not even a limit on them. For finishers, the smallmouth bass action can measure up to that anywhere elsewhere in the state. A fair number of largemouth bass provide the kicker. It is a big lake set in the coastal foothill country, covering more than 5,000 acres with 165 miles of shoreline when full of water, with remarkable numbers of lake arms and coves. By the way, no trout stocks are made here, regardless of water conditions. The DFG instead stocks largemouth bass, about 50,000 fingerlings to help natural spawning.

The key here is to think quantity, not quality. Most of the white bass are like big crappie, but if you use ultra-light tackle and 2-pound line, you can still have all the tussle you can ask for. All you have to do is tie on a lure such as a Roostertail, Mepps, or Kastmaster and start casting. The best spots are the narrows of the Nacimiento River, Las Tablas Creek, and Town Creeks.

The white bass go on wild feeds just after they move into one of the several tributaries of the lake to spawn. It usually happens the first time the water temperature hits 58 degrees, usually after the first week of good warm weather in the spring.

Of course, that's assuming there was some rain over the winter. Rain? What's that? When it arrives at Nacimiento, so do the fish.

---

3.   SAN SIMEON LANDING

Reference: North of San Luis Obispo at San Simeon Bay; map G2 grid eØ.

How to get there: From San Luis Obispo, drive 41 miles north on Highway 1 to the beach entrance.

Facilities: A pier, restrooms, bait, tackle, a sink for cleaning fish, benches, and picnic tables are provided at the park. A campground is available south on Highway 1 at San Simeon State Beach.

Cost: Day-use fee is $5 per vehicle.

Who to contact: Phone San Simeon Landing at (800) 347-9717, or San Simeon Chamber of Commerce at (805) 927-3500.

Party boat list: Predator, Patriot, Holiday II, Sportsfisher; charters available through San Simeon Landing at (800) 347-9717.

About San Simeon Landing: The most dramatic stretch of California coast is becoming one of the best inshore fisheries as well. It is one of the most beautiful areas in the world, with giant cliffs, sheer drop-offs, and shallows strewn with rocks and kelp beds. It is a sanctuary for otters, and therein lies the beauty. Commercial netting is outlawed between Point Sur Rock and San Simeon in order to protect the otters, and the byproduct of the ban on nets is some of the best shallow water rockfishing in the state.

Much of the fishing is in just 35 to 60 feet of water on the edge of the kelp beds, where there is a wide variety of rockfish. Big fish bonuses come in the form of halibut in the spring and early summer, and lingcod in the fall. Most fishermen use very light line for the ocean, just 6 to 12-pound test, and have a wild time casting light jigs for the rockfish. Three state records were set here in the summer of 1991, for vermillion, goldeneye and yellowtail rockfish.

A key to the marine abundance is the undersea habitat. Just two miles offshore, the bottom of the ocean drops off to 1,500 to 2,000 feet deep. Because of it, the ocean has a dramatic upwelling here, kicking up nutrient-rich water and with it all matter of baitfish to the shoal area, about 120 to 190 feet deep. If a heavy ocean swell ever prevents boaters from fishing the shallow areas around the kelp beds, they can instead fish the shoal.

Between the protected marine otter sanctuary and the San Simeon Shoal, anglers have a unique two-for-one offer; it is never necessary to fish 300 or 400 feet deep as is necessary in other areas. Sound good? It is.

---

4. CAYUCOS BEACH PIER

Reference: North of San Luis Obispo; map G2 grid g2.

How to get there: From San Luis Obispo, drive 14 miles north on Highway 1 to the beach entrance.

Facilities: A pier, restrooms, benches, fish-cleaning tables, showers, and picnic areas are provided.

Cost: Access is free.

Who to contact: Phone Bill's Sporting Goods at the pier at (805) 995-1703.

About Cayucos Beach Pier: Cayucos is one of the more productive piers on the California coast. It juts well out into the ocean, providing a chance for a variety of species. The best bets are in the summer for mackerel, and in the fall for smelt. However, perch, bocaccio, rarely

---

halibut and even salmon are sometimes caught here. The folks at the tackle shop located at the pier are quite friendly and will provide any how-to info you may need.

5. WHALE ROCK RESERVOIR

Reference: Near Cayucos; map G2 grid g3.

How to get there: From San Luis Obispo, drive north on Highway 1 to Morro Bay. Continue north for about five miles (just south of the town of Cayucos) to Cypress Mountain Road.

Facilities: No facilities are available on-site. A campground is available at Morro Bay. Supplies can be obtained in Morro Bay or Cayucos. No boating is permitted at the reservoir.

Cost: Access is free.

Who to contact: Phone Virg's Landing in Morro Bay at (805) 772-2216.

About Whale Rock Reservoir: No boaters need apply. Nobody wanting an easy go at it either. This is a unique place with an equally unique fishery.

At one time, Whale Rock Reservoir flowed to sea. The lake now covers nearly 600 acres, and is set just a mile from the Pacific Ocean. When the dam was built, apparently some steelhead were trapped in the lake, steelhead that still spawn in the feeder streams when flows are sufficient in winter. That makes this lake one of the few in California that have landlocked steelhead. No rainbow trout are stocked at this lake.

The fishing does not come easy, nor access. Not only is no boating allowed, but most of the lake's shoreline is off limits. Fishing pressure is light, and so are the catches.

6. ATASCADERO LAKE

Reference: North of San Luis Obispo in Atascadero Memorial Park; map G2 grid g6.

How to get there: From San Luis Obispo, drive north on US 101 to Atascadero. Turn left on Highway 41 and drive two miles west to the park entrance on the left.

Facilities: Restrooms, a concession stand, a boat ramp, and paddleboat rentals are available. No gas motors are permitted on the lake.

Cost: Access is free.

Who to contact: Phone Parks & Recreation Department (805) 461-5000.

About Atascadero Lake: This 30-acre lake is the centerpiece for a nice city park that provides a variety of activities. The DFG makes sure that fishing is one of them by stocking rainbow trout from mid-November through early April. It is stocked with 15,000 rainbow trout, about

2,000 trout per month, but that is subject to decent water conditions. The DFG also stocks 50 adult largemouth bass each year to help provide some brood stock. Most folks do just fine baitdunking from the shoreline. In summer months, the lake has some small bass and bluegill. No boat launch, no gas motors, so get your ambitions in focus: This is a nice little park, not angler's paradise.

---

7. MORRO BAY CITY T-PIER

Reference: North of San Luis Obispo; map G2 grid h3.

How to get there: From San Luis Obispo, drive 13 miles north on Highway 1 to Morro Bay. Take the Main Street exit and turn right. Continue up the grade, under the freeway, to Beach Street. Turn right and continue to the Embarcadero, then turn right and continue to the pier.

Facilities: Restrooms are provided. A bait shop is located nearby.

Cost: Access is free.

Who to contact: Phone the Morro Bay Harbor Master's Office at (805) 772-6254; Virg's Landing, (805) 772-2216.

About Morro Bay City T-Pier: There are just plain a lot of fish caught at this pier, making it an ideal spot for mom and dad to take the kids fishing. The best of it is in the late summer and fall. In the summer, parents and kids catch lots of small red snapper, some baby bocaccios, take them home and have a pan fry. In the fall, the jacksmelt arrive in good numbers, along with fair numbers of perch. For a wild card, in the spring and summer, try using a live anchovy for bait (available at Virg's) and keep it right on the bottom for halibut.

---

8. MORRO BAY DEEP SEA

Reference: At Morro Bay; map G2 grid h3.

How to get there: From San Luis Obispo, drive 13 miles north on Highway 1 to Morro Bay. Take the Main Street exit and turn right. Continue up the grade, under the freeway, to Beach Street. Turn right and continue to the Embarcadero, then turn right and continue to the facilities at the bay.

Facilities: Party boat charters, boat rentals, boat ramps, bait, tackle, and supplies are available at the bay. Lodging, restaurants, and shops are located in the town of Morro Bay.

Cost: Party boat fees are $25-$28 per person.

Who to contact: For general information and a free travel packet, phone the Morro Bay Chamber of Commerce at (805) 772-4467. For fishing information, phone Virg's Landing, (805) 772-2216; Bob's Sportsfishing, (805) 772-3340; Morro Bay Harbor Patrol, (805) 772-1214;

Party boat list: *Big Mama, Lota Fun, Mallard, Harbor Pathfinder, Princess, Admiral;* reservations through Virg's Landing at (805) 772-2216. *Shir-Lee,* reservations through Bob's Sportsfishing at (805)772-3340.

About Morro Bay Deep Sea: The drive here along Highway 1 can be worth the trip by itself, coming from either the south or the north. It is an ideal way to shake the cobwebs free, cruising the great coastal highway, regardless of what time of year you plan your visit. The party boats have a wide range of trips available, including for salmon in March and April, for albacore in September and October, and for rockfish and lingcod year-round.

It is the rockfishing that provides day-in, day-out meat on the table. Limits are common, along with good numbers of lingcod, the latter peaking in the fall months. The party boats focus at four key areas for rockfish: straight west at Church Rock, south off Point Buchon, and north off Point Estero and at Radar Dome. The boats leave early and the anglers aboard start catching fish almost as soon as they are over the reefs. It is about the closest thing to a guarantee in the world of fishing.

The salmon and albacore are wild cards, the results fluctuating wildly year to year, but can really add some sizzle when schools move into the area.

When the salmon move in here, it is often within very close range. One of the best areas is often the vicinity of the red buoy called the "Red Light," which is located about three miles south of the breakwater at Morro Bay. When the salmon move in this close, you can catch them trolling as shallow as 15 or 20 feet deep at daybreak, and as deep as 80 feet down at mid-day. Salmon charters often head south "around the corner" of Point Buchon where salmon may congregate as well in the spring. As the season progresses, salmon go very deep here, sometimes as deep as 300 feet down, requiring trollers to use a downrigger. As a migratory fish, salmon will migrate to where the conditions best suit them: 52 to 58-degree water, heavy plankton (green water with low clarity), and high numbers of baitfish.

Albacore are far less predictable. Some years they don't even show. Other years, well, it's like the fish are on a mission from hell. Albacore like the clear, blue water that is 62 to 66 degrees, and will roam anywhere from 25 to 150 miles off the coast in order to find it. On most trips, you practically troll your little petunia off in the search for them, ripping along at 10 or 11 knots, with feather jigs trailing behind the boat. When there is a strike, the boat stops, deckhands chum, and anglers rush to the rail, using live anchovies for bait. A good albacore bite is one of the wildest affairs available, but it can be like a slow boat to China trying to find them.

Morro Bay is an excellent vacation site, a good fishing town, and has an improving charter operation. The area is pretty and less populated than many good coastal areas. When you put it all together, it makes a good headquarters for a saltwater angler.

---

9. SANTA MARGARITA LAKE

Reference: East of San Luis Obispo; map G2 grid h7.

How to get there: From San Luis Obispo, drive eight miles north on US 101. Take the Highway 58 exit and drive four miles east, past Santa Margarita, to Pozo Road. Turn right and drive seven miles southeast, then turn north on Santa Margarita Lake Road and continue to the lake. The boat ramp is located on the southwest shore.

Facilities: Picnic areas, a marina, a boat ramp, boat rentals, bait, a campground, and groceries are available at the lake.

Cost: Day-use fee is $3 per vehicle; an additional $2.50 if entering with a boat. Entrance fee includes boat launching privileges.

Who to contact: Phone the Santa Margarita Lake Marina at (805) 438-5485.

About Santa Margarita Lake: When anglers go to fishing heaven, it is assumed there will be no waterskiers there. Well, Santa Margarita Lake brings a little bit of heaven down to earth by not allowing waterskiing or any water contact sport. There is no camping, either, but what the heck, it's a good trade.

The lake has a fair fishery for a variety of species. Rainbow trout are stocked by the Department of Fish and Game during winter and spring. Some 40,000 rainbow trout are stocked, about 5,000 trout per month, which provides a decent fishery over the winter. As the lake warms up in early summer, trout stocks are stopped, and the fishing is converted over for largemouth bass, bluegill, catfish and crappie. A very light sprinkling of striped bass are also in the lake, and every once in awhile, someone hooks a big one and loses all their line. Whoo-ya!

The lake covers nearly 800 acres, most of it long and narrow, set in a dammed-up valley in the foothill country, 1,300 feet elevation, five miles southeast of the town of Santa Margarita.

---

10. LAGUNA LAKE

Reference: Near San Luis Obispo; map G2 grid i5.

How to get there: From San Luis Obispo, drive two miles south on US 101 to Madonna Road. Turn west and continue to the park entrance.

Facilities: Restrooms, a boat ramp and boat rentals are available. No gas motors are permitted on the lake.

Cost: Access is free.

Who to contact: Phone Parks & Recreation Department at (805) 781-7300.

About Laguna Lake: It is good that places like Laguna Lake are available. They provide a close-to-home urban fishing opportunity where otherwise nothing would exist.

Laguna Lake, a 60-acre lake, comes complete with a small park and trout stocks, similar to Atascadero Lake to the nearby north. In fact, Atascadero is usually stocked on the same days as Laguna with the same amounts of trout. However, Laguna's closer proximity to the coast keeps water temperatures cooler and better for trout, especially if the Los Osos Valley to the west gets fogged in. It usually is stocked with 15,000 rainbow trout per year, November through April, 2,000 trout per month, but that can be canceled due to low or warm water levels. The DFG also stocks 50 largemouth bass to give spawning a boost.

In the summer, you can poke around during evenings, casting for bass, or dunking a worm under a bobber for a bluegill. The lake is not large, but still has three coves that provide the best fishing results.

---

11.   HARTFORD FISHING PIER

Reference: South of San Luis Obispo at Avila Beach; map G2 grid j4.

How to get there: From San Luis Obispo, drive south on US 101 to the San Luis Drive exit. Turn west and continue until you reach Avila Drive. Turn right and continue west to the parking area at the end of the street. Fishing is permitted off the third pier.

Facilities: A bait shop, a concession stand, a fish-cleaning area, a restaurant, and a bar are available at the pier.

Cost: Access is free.

Who to contact: Phone Port San Luis Harbor at (805) 595-5400; Paradise Sportsfishing, (805) 595-7200.

About Hartford Fishing Pier: There may be no better pier in California to try for halibut than right here. It is statistically proven: The halibut like this harbor. Use a live anchovy for bait; get it on the bottom. It takes persistence with spirit, and even then, you can still blow it on the set. Regardless, it is worth the effort with halibut in the 10 to 15-pound class, rarely bigger. For less of a wait, fall months bring good jacksmelt numbers. Other options in summer months are perch (fair), small rockfish, and sometimes mackerel.

---

12.   SAN LUIS OBISPO BAY DEEP SEA

Reference: South of San Luis Obispo at Port San Luis; map G2 grid j4.

How to get there: From San Luis Obispo, drive south on US 101 to the San Luis Drive exit. Turn west and continue until you reach Avila

Drive. Turn right and continue west to the parking area at the end of the street. Party boats operate from the third pier.

Facilities: Party boat charters, a pier, a boat ramp and hoist, boat rentals, picnic areas, bait, tackle and supplies are available at the harbor.

Cost: Party boat fees are $28 per person.

Who to contact: For general information and a free travel packet, phone the San Luis Obispo Chamber of Commerce at (805) 543-1323. For fishing information, phone Paradise Sportsfishing at (805) 595-7200; Port San Luis Harbor District, (805) 595-5400.

Party boat list: Diablo, Cheyenne, Eclipse, Marauder; reservations through Paradise Sportsfishing at (805) 595-7200.

About San Luis Obispo Deep Sea: The day starts early at Avila Beach, and it isn't difficult to wake up in the middle of the night if it means going fishing out of Port San Luis. Calm water equals good fishing, and since the sea breezes are often light here, prospects are usually worth setting your alarm for.

The best and most predictable fishing here is for rockfish, lingcod, and calico bass. The better spots for rockfish include a reef just offshore Point Sal to the south, and also Diablo Canyon and the Santa Rosa Reef. Skippers also choose to sometimes head north off Point Buchon, providing the north wind is down and it makes for an easy trip "uphill." An option is renting a boat and fishing for small calico bass and sand bass.

In the late winter and spring, from March to early April, salmon provide a longshot. But longshots can come in, especially when it comes to salmon. They often show up anywhere from Avila Beach to Pismo Beach, and right on down to the mouth of the Santa Maria River. In good years for salmon, they often school outside the latter in mid-March.

In the fall, there is a friendly competition with charter operations in Morro Bay to the nearby north for albacore. Come September and the albacore are apt to be anywhere in that warm, crystal blue water 25 to 150 miles offshore. Albacore can provide the best fishing of the year when the water is warm and the schools of fish move within range of small boats, 20 to 30 miles out, but that seems to happen only two or three years a decade.

Avila Beach is a favorite destination for a cult of L.A.-area anglers. The drive up is a pretty one, the road working its way along the coast around the Sierra Padre Mountains. In the process, they leave behind the crowds, the traffic and the stop lights, and instead look forward to the open sea and a day of good fishing.

13.   LOPEZ LAKE

Reference: East of San Luis Obispo; map G2 grid j7.

How to get there: From San Luis Obispo, drive 16 miles south on US 101 to Arroyo Grande. Turn east on Lopez Drive and continue ten miles to the lake. The boat ramp is located on Lopez Drive.

Facilities: A campground, a marina, a boat ramp, boat rentals, bait, and groceries are available.

Cost: Day-use fee is $3 per vehicle; an additional $3.50 if entering with a boat. Entrance fee includes boat-launching privileges.

Who to contact: Phone the Lopez Lake Marina at (805) 489-1006; Lopez Lake main office, (805) 489-1122.

About Lopez Lake: This isn't the lake to bring a canoe to, or for that matter, any boat that can't handle wind. Why? You guessed it: The springs are very windy here, especially in the afternoon, making it great for windsurfers and sailboaters, but lousy for fishing.

But it is a decent-sized lake, 940 acres when full, and there are plenty of times when the wind is down and the fishing is up. When the water is cool, the DFG stocks it with rainbow trout, 40,000 trout in all and 5,000 trout per month. That is equal to the amount stocked in Santa Margarita Lake. Another bonus is Lopez Lake's proximity to the coast, which keeps the lake colder than reservoirs farther inland. That also provides conditions for smallmouth bass, which also prefer the cooler water.

But when summer arrives, this lake gets hot, too. That is when the largemouth bass, bluegill, crappie and catfish get active. The lake has three major lake arms: Arroyo Grande Creek Arm, Wittenberg Creek Arm and Little Fish Creek Arm. All are worth exploring for bass and crappie. Especially bass. It provides one of the more consistent fisheries in central California. The best areas are up the two main creek arms, where shad and crawdads get the bass feeding. Summer evenings are quite good, often with surface bites in the coves along the lake arms.

MAP G3

1 LISTING
PAGES 606-607

CEN-CAL MAP . see page 540
adjoining maps
NORTH (F3).......see page 560
EAST (G4)..........see page 608
SOUTH (H3).......see page 626
WEST (G2)..........see page 594

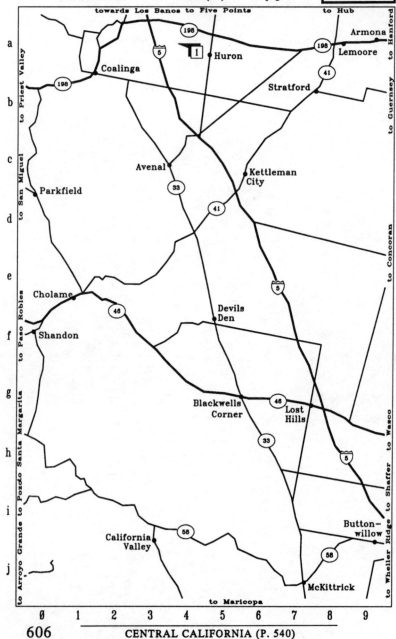

1.   CALIFORNIA AQUEDUCT

Reference: From Huron to Kettleman City; map G3 grid a4.

How to get to the Huron site: From Kettleman City, drive 24 miles north on Interstate 5 to the Highway 198 exit. Turn east and continue on Highway 198-Dorris Avenue to the fishing site at the junction with Siskiyou Avenue.

How to get to the Avenal Cutoff site: From Kettleman City, drive ten miles north to the Highway 269 exit. Loop around under the freeway and turn northeast on Avenal Cutoff Road. Continue for three miles until the road crosses the California Aqueduct.

How to get to the Kettleman City site: From the north end of Kettleman City, turn west on Milham Avenue and continue to the access site at the aqueduct crossing.

Facilities: Toilets are provided at all access sites. Supplies are available in Kettleman City.

Cost: Access is free.

Who to contact: Phone the Department of Water Resources in Coalinga at (209) 884-2405.

About California Aqueduct: This may be the ugliest fishing spot on planet Earth. The California Aqueduct is an engineer's dream, endless and straight, with beveled edges made of concrete. The surrounding area is hot, flat and desolate, a paragon of nothingness. But for people cruising Interstate 5, it provides a rare respite. Along with the water pumped out of the Delta comes striped bass and catfish, and they provide poor to fair fishing at these California Aqueduct Fishing Access sites. It is nothing complicated. You sit on your fanny and toss out your bait, with anchovies the preferred entreaty, and wait for a striper or catfish to come cruising down the aqueduct. The best fishing is in the early evening on into the night. For highway cruisers who want to break the monotony of I-5, a longshot is making a quick hit at these access points, casting Rattletrap lures out. Who knows, maybe a striped bass is wandering by. On the other hand, maybe not.

MAP G4

6 LISTINGS
PAGES 608-613

CEN-CAL MAP . see page 540
adjoining maps
NORTH (F4).......see page 566
EAST (G5)..........see page 614
SOUTH (H4).......see page 638
WEST (G3).........see page 606

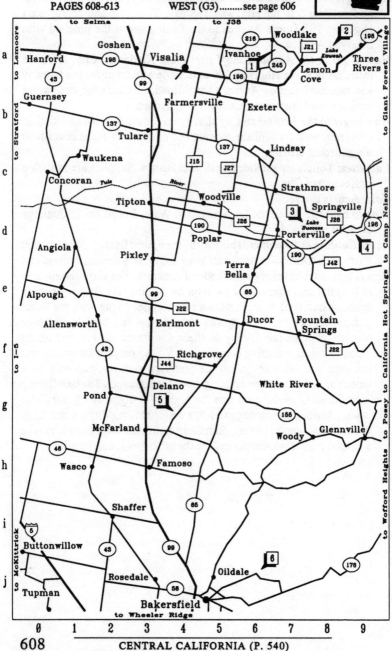

1. BRAVO LAKE

Reference: In Woodlake; map G4 grid a7.

How to get there: From Visalia, drive northeast on Highway 216 to the town of Woodlake. Continue east on Highway 216, which becomes Naranjo Avenue, to the lake.

Facilities: Walking trails are provided around the lake. No boating is permitted.

Cost: You must have a permit to fish at the lake; fee is 50 cents per day, $3 per year, or $5 for a family per year. Permits can be obtained at City Hall or at the local market.

Who to contact: Phone the City of Woodlake at (209) 564-8055, or Boa's Minnow Farm, (209) 564-8563.

About Bravo Lake: You have to wonder how this lake was named. Bravo? Bravo for whom? Not the fishermen, that's for sure. What you get at Bravo Lake are fish that have trickled down from Lake Kaweah, a lot of carp more than anything else. The number of catfish in the lake seems decent enough (clams are the best bait), but no night fishing (or access) is permitted for them. A few crappie and bass provide options. The lake is primarily used as a place where locals can jog on the paths around the lake.

---

2. LAKE KAWEAH

Reference: East of Visalia; map G4 grid a8.

How to get there: From Visalia, drive 20 miles east on Highway 198 to the lake. The boat ramp is located on the south shore.

Facilities: A campground, a marina, a boat ramp, boat rentals, a picnic area, bait, a concession stand, and groceries are available at the lake.

Cost: Access is free.

Who to contact: Phone the U.S. Army Corps of Engineers, Lake Kaweah, at (209) 597-2301; Kaweah Marina, (209) 597-2526.

About Lake Kaweah: If you visit Kaweah in late March, April or early May, you will discover a big reservoir set in the foothill country, where the prospects for trout (late winter) and bass (spring) seem pretty good. When the lake is full, it covers nearly 2,000 acres with 22 miles of shoreline. But if you visit Kaweah in late summer or fall, you will be greeted by a pit of a water hole and weather so hot, you may think that the lake will start boiling any minute.

Don't blow the deal and show up at the wrong time. Many people do, thinking the late summer heat is the perfect time to "head to the lake" to cool off. Wrong. The annual water drawdown here shrinks the lake down and makes it looks like a dust bowl. The fish don't like the drawdown either, nor the hot weather.

In late winter, the action starts when the Department of Fish and Game stocks rainbow trout. Kaweah receives 37,000 rainbow trout from the Department of Fish and Game, enough to provide decent fishing when the water is cool. That is followed by rising water levels in spring, and then good bass fishing as the water warms up. Because the lake is drawn down, a lot of vegetation grows on the lake bottom every year, vegetation that provides good cover for bass when the lake starts filling. The Horse Creek area is one of the best for this reason.

As the 90s evolve, this lake could turn into one of the better bass fisheries in the state. It was poisoned in the fall of 1987 to kill off the white bass, then restocked with Florida bass and spotted bass. Habitat improvement work was also conducted. Those Floridas should start getting giant-sized by the mid-90s.

3.   LAKE SUCCESS

Reference: Near Porterville; map G4 grid d8.

How to get there: From Bakersfield on Highway 99, take the Highway 65 turnoff and drive 44 miles north to the junction with Highway 190 south of Porterville. Turn right and drive east on Highway 190 for seven miles to the lake. Boat ramps are located on the east and west shores of the lake.

Facilities: A campground, a marina, boat ramps, boat rentals, picnic areas, bait, and groceries are available.

Cost: Access is free.

Who to contact: Phone the U.S. Army Corps of Engineers, Lake Success, (209) 784-0215; Success Marina, (209) 781-2078.

About Lake Success: If only this lake fills up in the spring...then greatness is possible. Lake Success is one of the fast-rising quality bass lakes in California, with very high catch rates in late winter and spring. "Just add water" is the magic recipe.

Like Lake Kaweah (see previous listing), Lake Success was poisoned out, the DFG having done so in 1988—killing 600,000 pounds of carp in the process. With the carp out, the water has cleared, survival rates of small bass seem higher, and in turn, catch rates are quite good for bass in the 9 to 13-inch class. If the lake levels stay high enough, keeping aquatic food levels high, some monster-sized bass could be produced in the 1990s. The South Fork is a favorite area for bassers, with submerged trees and vegetation that provides cover for fish.

It is a big lake with a series of major lake arms. When full, Success covers nearly 2,500 acres with 30 miles of shoreline, yet is much shallower than most reservoirs. It is set in bare foothill country at 650 feet elevation.

By summer, the bass become difficult to catch except during short periods at dawn and dusk, and there are often a lot of waterskiers to contend with too. Bluegill, crappie and catfish provide an option in the summer months. In the cool months it is stocked with 18,000 rainbow trout.

---

4. TULE RIVER

Reference: Northeast of Bakersfield; map G4 grid d9.

How to get there: From Bakersfield on Highway 99, take the Highway 65 turnoff and drive 44 miles north to the junction with Highway 190 south of Porterville. Turn right and drive east on Highway 190, past Lake Success. Access is available off the highway.

Facilities: Campgrounds are available at Lake Success. Supplies can be obtained in Porterville.

Cost: Access is free.

Who to contact: Phone the Sequoia National Forest District Office at (209) 565-3341.

About Tule River: The Tule River runs out of Sequoia National Forest, winding its way down the western slopes of the southern Sierra. The best stretch of river in this grid zone is well upstream of Lake Success along Highway 190, from Springville on upriver. It is stocked with rainbow trout by the Department of Fish and Game, receiving 7,000 trout, most during the early summer. You can cruise the highway, making quick stops at the turnouts, and hit many spots while heading east into the mountains. See adjacent Zone G5 for more information.

---

5. LAKE WOOLLOMES

Reference: Near Delano; map G4 grid g4.

How to get there: From Bakersfield, drive 25 miles north on Highway 99 to Delano. Turn east on Highway 155 and drive one mile, then turn south on Mast Avenue. Drive one mile, then turn east on Woollomes Avenue and continue to the lake.

Facilities: A boat ramp, boat rentals, a concession stand, a picnic area, bait, tackle, and groceries are available. No motorized boats are permitted.

Cost: An annual permit is required to fish at the lake; phone Kern County Parks and Recreation for fee.

Who to contact: Phone the Kern County Parks & Recreation Department at (805) 861-2345.

About Lake Woollomes: It's hard to believe there is much of anything out in this country. It is dry, hot and flat. Little Lake Woollomes provides a respite from that, set in a small park, the kind with lawns and a few

---

picnic spots. Angler's paradise it is not, with some bluegill, catfish, rarely a bass. In the late winter, it gets 7,000 rainbow trout from the Department of Fish and Game. Some folks will spend evenings here, having a picnic along the shore, tossing out their bait and waiting for a nibble. Woollomes does cover about 300 acres, and in the barren south valley, any lake, even this one, is considered something special. Well, almost any lake.

---

6. LAKE MING

Reference: Near Bakersfield; map G4 grid j6.

How to get there: From Bakersfield, drive 11 miles northeast on Alfred Harrell Highway to Kern River County Park.

Facilities: A campground, a boat ramp, a concession stand, a picnic area, bait, and groceries are available.

Cost: An annual permit is required to fish at the lake; phone Kern County Parks Department for fee.

Who to contact: Phone the Kern County Parks Department at (805) 861-2345.

About Lake Ming: This lake has a natural calendar. The only fishing is from late fall through spring, from October to March. The summer is zilch time, with no fishing and the little lake taken over by power boaters. It is stocked by the Department of Fish and Game with rainbow trout in the winter months, 5,000 rainbow trout in all, and has a sprinkling of bluegill, catfish, crappie and bass. Ming Lake is set near the Kern River, 450 feet elevation, and covers just 100 acres. If you squint your eyes just right in February, when things have greened up a bit, it can almost look pretty. Almost.

MAP G5

10 LISTINGS
PAGES 614-621

CEN-CAL MAP . see page 540
adjoining maps
NORTH (F5).......see page 578
EAST ....no map
SOUTH (H5).......see page 648
WEST (G4).........see page 608

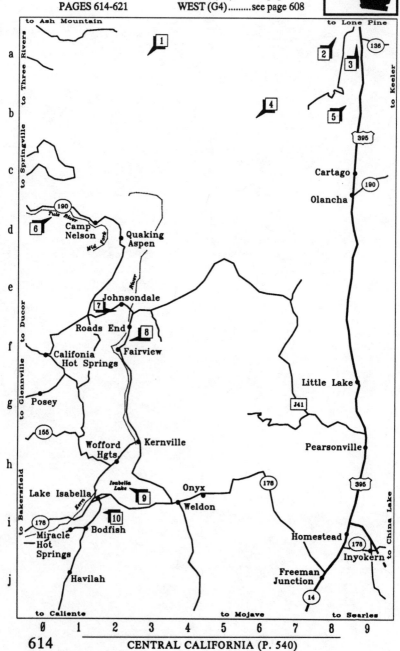

CENTRAL CALIFORNIA (P. 540)

1.   SEQUOIA NATIONAL PARK

Reference: East of Visalia; map G5 grid a3.

How to get there: From Visalia, drive 20 miles east on Highway 198 to Lake Kaweah. Continue northeast to the park entrances.

Facilities: Campgrounds, lodging, and picnic areas are available.

Cost: Entrance fee is $5 per vehicle.

Who to contact: Phone Sequoia National Park at (209) 565-3341.

About Sequoia National Park: Sequoia Gigantea, the massive mountain redwood, is the world's largest tree, with an awesome diameter that can take 30 people joining hands to ring one. The General Sherman Tree, the largest of living trees in the world, is 101 feet in circumference, 3,500 years old, and the most famous of its species for which the park is named.

Sequoia National Park is connected to Kings Canyon National Park to the north, together comprising 850,000 acres and 65 consecutive miles of national parkland. It is Kings Canyon National Park that provides the better fishing of the two parks, but after admiring the groves of giant redwoods, there are still many excellent waters that can be explored that include the native habitat of golden trout.

The best of the fishing is at the headwaters of the Kern River, set in the high country of Kern Canyon (see text for Golden Trout Wilderness). The Kaweah River is more accessible, set along the southern access road, Highway 198, and provides poor to fair fishing.

As at so many national parks, it is anglers who are willing to backpack who will experience the best fishing. Stocks are not made in national parks, and without catch-and-release fishing rules in effect, heavy angler pressure results in poor fishing populations. What is left in easily accessed waters that are not stocked are small trout (the largest ones are always kept) that have taken daily smart lessons from visiting anglers from all over America.

Those who explore the interior of Sequoia National Park will find a far different world. Instead of big trees, you will find scarcely any trees at all. Much of the high country of the Great Western Divide is above tree line, with bare glacial-cut granite ridges, canyons and bowls. It is the canyons that have the streams, the bowls that have the small lakes. Among the better destinations are the Nine Lakes Basin (set just below Kaweah Peaks Ridge), where a series of lakes are untouched and beautiful, including a series of stream-connected lakes that can be reached by off-trail hiking.

The fishing comes in second at Sequoia National Park. A visit here will verify that being first isn't always so important.

2.   TUTTLE CREEK

Reference: Near Lone Pine; map G5 grid a8.

How to get there: At the town of Lone Pine on US 395, turn west at the stoplight in the center of town onto Whitney Portal Road. Drive west for about three miles, then turn left on Horseshoe Meadow Road and drive for two miles to the Tuttle Creek Campground. Access is available at and near the campground.

Facilities: A campground is available, but there is no piped water. Supplies are available in Lone Pine.

Cost: Access is free.

Who to contact: Phone the Bureau of Land Management at (619) 872-4881.

About Tuttle Creek: The trout in Tuttle Creek can provide some evening entertainment for campers. The camp here, set at 5,100 feet elevation, is a good spot for folks looking for a layover while cruising US 395, or getting ready for the hike up Mt. Whitney, with the trailhead at nearby Whitney Portal. Nearby Lone Pine Creek provides an option for both camping and fishing (see Zone F5). Tuttle Creek is stocked with rainbow trout adjacent to the campground, the plants totaling 6,400 rainbow trout over the summer. You could roll in on an early summer afternoon, set up camp, fish for a few hours during the evening, then have a trout fry. There may be no better way to fortify yourself before climbing Mt. Whitney.

---

3.   DIAZ LAKE

Reference: South of Lone Pine; map G5 grid a9.

How to get there: From the town of Lone Pine on US 395, drive three miles south to the lake.

Facilities: A campground, a boat ramp, a picnic area, and a restaurant are available. Supplies can be obtained in Lone Pine. Boats over 22 feet are prohibited.

Cost: Access is free. There is a fee for boat launching.

Who to contact: Phone the Diaz Lake Campground at (619) 876-5656; County Parks Department, (619) 878-2411.

About Diaz Lake: Little Diaz Lake is set at 3,650 feet in the Owens Valley, where it gets overshadowed by nearby Mt. Whitney and the Sierra range to the west. The lake has three campgrounds along the western shore, making it a decent spot for camper/boaters. In the summer months, waterskiing is popular and fishing becomes just a sidelight for a few bass, bluegill and catfish. From late winter through April, the lake is stocked with rainbow trout and a 15-mph speed limit is in effect (November through April). It receives 13,200 rainbow trout per year. After stocks, results can be good both for shorefishing with bait near the campgrounds, and also for trollers in the vicinity of the boat launch.

---

4. GOLDEN TROUT WILDERNESS

Reference: East of Cartago in Inyo National Forest; map G5 grid b6.
How to get there: Access to trailheads is available off roads that junction with US 395 near the towns of Cartago and Olancha.
Facilities: No facilities are available in the wilderness area.
Cost: Access is free.
Who to contact: Write to Inyo National Forest at 873 N. Main Street, Bishop, CA, 93514, or phone (619) 873-5841. For a map, send $2 to the Office of Information, 630 Sansome Street, San Francisco, CA 94111.
About Golden Trout Wilderness: Those who start fantasizing about trips into the Golden Trout Wilderness usually dream about one lake after another loaded with giant golden trout. Well, the reality just doesn't work out that way. There are actually relatively few waters available, especially when compared to the back country of the adjacent John Muir Wilderness and Kings Canyon National Park to the immediate north.

The difference, however, is that the waters here have native golden trout, and that the headwaters of the Kern River are rare native habitat for goldens. Four other hike-to waters also have native golden trout: Rocky Basin Lakes, Johnson Lake, Chicken Spring Lake, Golden Trout Creek, and a few other small creeks. These waters are not planted by air with hatchery fish. They are wild fish, native born and bred, descendants of the ages.

Access is best by taking the Pacific Crest Trail, then heading west at the trail junction near Cottonwood Pass and hiking via Big Whitney Meadow up to the Rocky Lakes Basin. From there, it isn't too difficult to roam off trail to Johnson Lake, then north over the Boreal Plateau to Funston Lake. The latter two are rarely visited, set just south of the Siberian Outpost Mountains.

If it sounds stark and forboding, it's because it is. At one time, virtually all of the high Sierra lakes were barren bowls. It is only through the efforts of the DFG airplane stocking program that they have trout in them. Up here in the remote Golden Trout Wilderness, however, is the exception. These trout are the wild fish of your dreams.

It is some of the most quiet country you will ever find, with most hikers exploring the John Muir Wilderness and its hundreds of lakes. Quiet? It's so quiet you can practically hear the tiny wildflowers bloom.

---

5.   COTTONWOOD CREEK

Reference: North of Olancha in Inyo National Forest; map G5 grid b8.

How to get there: From the junction of Highway 190 and US 395 at the town of Olancha, drive 11.5 miles north on US 395 to the Cottonwood Powerhouse turnoff on the left. Turn left and continue west, keeping to the left as you cross the Owens Canal. Direct access is available off the road.

Facilities: A primitive campground is available on Cottonwood Road. Supplies are available in Lone Pine, about ten miles north of the turnoff.

Cost: Access is free.

Who to contact: Phone the Inyo National Forest District Office at (619) 876-5542. For a map, send $2 to the Office of Information, U.S. Forest Service, 630 Sansome Street, San Francisco, CA 94111.

About Cottonwood Creek: If it is angler's paradise you want, this is not the place. But if you don't mind the desolate surroundings and fairly limited fishing opportunity, Cottonwood Creek is the spot for a quick hit. The fact that a campground is adjacent to the creek is a nice bonus. The stream is stocked with rainbow trout from the campground (near the powerhouse intake) to the end of the road. The DFG plunks 2,200 rainbow trout during the summer in this stretch. Stick and move, hit and run, and a few trout will come along for the ride.

---

6.   MIDDLE FORK TULE RIVER

Reference: Northeast of Bakersfield in Sequoia National Forest; map G5 grid dØ.

How to get there: From Bakersfield on Highway 99, take the Highway 65 turnoff and drive 44 miles north to the junction with Porterville. Turn east on Highway 190 and continue east, past Lake Success. Access is available off the highway up to Camp Nelson.

Facilities: Campgrounds are available along the river. Supplies can be obtained in Porterville.

Cost: Access is free.

Who to contact: Phone the Sequoia National Forest District Office at (209) 539-2607. For a map, send $2 to the Office of Information, 630 Sansome Street, San Francisco, CA 94111.

About Middle Fork Tule River: The Tule River is created from the many tiny drops of snowmelt in the high Sierra, then joins in rock fissures, gravity taking it downhill to the west, eventually melding in a canyon to form this stream. It runs through Sequoia National Forest downslope eventually to Lake Success. In the process, it is stocked at several access points along Highway 190. One good spot is in the vicinity of the Wishon Drive turnoff. Another option is to take the Wishon Drive turnoff and take the primitive road, which borders the upper reaches of the river. In all, the river gets 14,000 rainbow trout, most ranging from 9 to 11 inches. The largest trout in the stream are these planters, which are joined by smaller wild trout.

---

7. SOUTH CREEK

Reference: North of Lake Isabella in Sequoia National Forest; map G5 grid e2.

How to get there: From Bakersfield, drive approximately 45 miles east on Highway 178 to Isabella Lake. At the town of Lake Isabella, turn north on Highway 155 and drive 11 miles to Kernville. Turn north on Kern River Highway-Sierra Way and continue for 21 miles to the Limestone Campground. Access is available off Kern River Highway-Sierra Way between the campground and Johnsondale.

Facilities: Campgrounds are available on Kern River Highway-Sierra Way. Supplies are available in Kernville.

Cost: Access is free.

Who to contact: Phone the Sequoia National Forest District Office at (619) 376-3781. For a map, send $2 to the Office of Information, U.S. Forest Service, 630 Sansome Street, San Francisco, CA 94111.

About South Creek: This little stream gets very few fishermen. In fact, most people discover it by accident. This is how it happens: Someone is attracted to the area because the upper Kern River provides first-class whitewater rafting. They arrive early in the evening at South Creek Falls, excited over the next day's rafting adventure, and find they have a few hours to burn. So they get out a fishing rod and head up South Creek. When they start catching trout, they can't believe it. Well, believe it. South Creek, a tributary to the Kern River, is one of the obscure waters stocked by the DFG. It gets only 1,300 trout per year, but few people are aware that it has any fish at all. The best stretch is in the vicinity of where the little bridge crosses the river, located west of Johnsondale. It takes a circuitous route to get this far, but it is unlikely anybody will be here.

---

8. KERN RIVER

Reference: Northeast of Bakersfield in Sequoia National Forest; map G5 grid f2.

How to get there: From Bakersfield, drive approximately 45 miles east on Highway 178 to Isabella Lake. Access to the lower river is available directly off the highway ten miles east of Bakersfield to Kernvale. The upper river can be accessed as follows: At Isabella Lake, turn north

---

on Highway 155 and drive 11 miles to Kernville. Turn north on Kern River Highway-Sierra Way. Direct access is available off the road.

Facilities: Campgrounds are available on Highway 178 and Kern River Highway-Sierra Way, as well as at Isabella Lake. Supplies can be obtained in Bakersfield, Kernville or Kernvale.

Cost: Access is free.

Who to contact: Phone the Sequoia National Forest District Office at (619) 376-3781.

About Kern River: Merle Haggard vows "I'll never swim Kern River again," or at least he says so in his song about it. Why not? Because he lost his "little darlin'" on the Kern when the "swiftness took her life away." Oh yeah? Well, there might be something to that, because the Upper Kern has some of the better stretches of whitewater for rafting, and it can be dangerous for the inexperienced.

Merle knows about this stuff. You see, he's originally from Bakersfield, where in between getting in all kinds of trouble, he occasionally fished and swam the Kern River. If you do the same, you will find a series of four campgrounds along the river between Kernville (just north of Lake Isabella) and the little town of Fairview. The DFG stocks this section of the Kern with rainbow trout at the four campgrounds, 38,000 in all, with the best fishing five to seven miles upstream of Lake Isabella. Afternoon swimming and evening fishing make for a good camping vacation. This is the best place to fish, not up near South Creek Falls, which is where Merle probably lost his little darlin'.

---

9.   ISABELLA LAKE

Reference: East of Bakersfield; map G5 grid h2.

How to get there: From Bakersfield, drive approximately 45 miles east on Highway 178 to the lake.

Facilities: Several campgrounds and picnic areas are provided. Marinas, boat ramps, boat rentals, bait, tackle, and groceries are also available. Boats under 11 feet are prohibited.

Cost: Lake access is free. An annual permit is required to boat on the lake; fee is $20.

Who to contact: Phone the Sequoia Ntional Forest, Isabella Lake Office, at (619) 379-5646; Dean's North Fork Marina, (619) 376-3241.

About Isabella Lake: This is the largest freshwater lake in Southern California, covering 38,400 acres with 38 miles of shoreline when full. It provides good fisheries for both largemouth bass (including some monsters) and rainbow trout, and fair numbers of bluegill, crappie and catfish. The lake is set at 2,600 feet in the foothills east of Bakersfield, the centerpiece for a wide variety of activities, including waterskiing, bird watching, and camping. In addition, the nearby Kern River, which feeds the lake, has a good stretch of whitewater for rafters.

Bass fishing is the best thing going here. The French Gulch dam area commonly produces largemouth bass to five pounds. The North Fork area has a lot of submerged trees where the bass hang out during the summer. The lake record is 18 pounds, 13 ounces, and some locals say a 20-pounder will surely be caught in the 90s. It gets windy here in the spring, and like a lot of big reservoirs, that means the water always gets muddy around shoreline points.

The lake is heavily stocked with rainbow trout by the Department of Fish and Game. The DFG funnels in 33,000 rainbow trout, coming from two different hatcheries. That provides good opportunity for trollers, with the best fishing near the dam, and also plenty of food for the giant bass. Standard trolling techniques are used, varying the depth according to water temperature, with the best of it coming on flashers trailed by a Needlefish lure or half of a nightcrawler. Most of the trout are in the one-pound class, with a sprinkling to 15 or 16 inches.

---

10.   ERSKINE CREEK

Reference: South of Isabella Lake; map G5 grid i1.

How to get there: From Bakersfield, drive approximately 45 miles east on Highway 178 to the town of Kernvale (do not confuse this with Kernville at the north end of Isabella Lake). Turn southeast on Erskine Creek Road. Access is available off the road; be aware of private property lines.

Facilities: Campgrounds and supplies are available near Isabella Lake.

Cost: Access is free.

Who to contact: Phone the Bureau of Land Management at (619) 872-4881.

About Erskine Creek: Nearby Isabella Lake can be packed to the rafters with boaters, campers and anglers, yet little Erskine Creek can be all but completely ignored. Its headwaters start near Inspiration Point in the Paiute Mountains of Sequoia National Forest, then it tumbles northwest downslope about eight miles until it feeds into the Kern River below Kernvale. The fishable section is right along Erskine Creek Road, where it receives light stocks of rainbow trout, 1,200 in all. Without them, it would be like the dead sea of Kern County. Don't make the mistake of crossing private property to reach Erskine Creek. You might end up getting a load of rocksalt in your rear end, and it is unnecessary since the sections of river bordered by private property are not stocked and have few fish of any kind.

MAP H2

2 LISTINGS
PAGES 622-625

CEN-CAL MAP . see page 540
adjoining maps
NORTH (G2) ...... see page 594
EAST (H3) .... see page 626
SOUTH .... no map
WEST .... no map

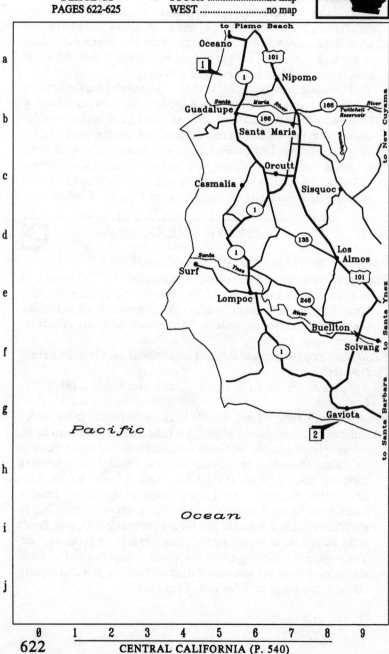

1. OSO FLACO LAKES

Reference: Near Pismo Beach; map H2 grid a5.

How to get there: From Arroyo Grande (about 16 miles south of San Luis Obispo), turn south on Highway 1 and drive 9.5 miles to Oso Flaco Lake Road. Turn west and continue to the parking area. A short hike is required to reach the lakes.

Facilities: No facilities are available on-site. A campground is available nearby at Pismo Beach, and supplies can be obtained in Arroyo Grande.

Cost: Access is free.

Who to contact: Phone The Outdoorsman in Grover City, (805) 473-2484; Guadalupe Department of Parks & Recreation, (805) 343-1340.

About Oso Flaco Lakes: If you have this book in your hands because you want to know easy-to-reach lakes that almost nobody knows about, then Oso Flaco Lakes qualifies to be on your list. These two lakes are set in the middle of sand dunes adjoining Pismo State Beach, and even though they're just a few miles from Highway 101, literally millions of tourists pass right on by with nary a clue to their existence. Only the locals seem to fish here, catching bass from the shore during warmer months of the year. The lakes cover 110 acres, and because they are set within a mile of the ocean, remain fairly cool year-round. No boat launch is available. This is the kind of place where you fish from the shore, hiking around the lakes (a three-mile trip). The fishing is fair, mostly small bass, though remember: Every pond has a king.

2. GAVIOTA STATE PARK

Reference: North of Santa Barbara; map H2 grid g8.

How to get there: From Santa Barbara, drive 33 miles north on US 101 to the park entrance.

Facilities: A pier, a campground and a boat hoist are available. Supplies can be obtained nearby.

Cost: Day-use fee is $6. There is a fee for boat hoisting, and you must provide your own sling. The weight limit is three tons, length limit is 22 feet. Driving on the pier is not permitted, so boat owners must have their own transport dolly if they can't tow it by hand.

Who to contact: Phone Gaviota State Park at (805) 968-3294, or (805) 968-1033 for camping information.

About Gaviota Beach: By beach or boat, this is an outstanding stretch of coast with a wide variety of species available and methods possible.

From Gaviota Beach on east to El Capitan Beach is 10 miles of coast that provides good surf fishing. The biggest fish are halibut, which arrive within range in the spring, and the most abundant are surf perch and barred perch, best in the fall and winter. The rocky areas have kelp bass, sand bass and some rockfish.

If you have a boat, you get access to some really prime territory. There are a series of kelp beds along the inshore coast that attract a number of species of bass, and more rarely, halibut and sometimes even white seabass. If your boat is a fast, stable one, you can roam farther out to San Miguel Island, Santa Cruz Island, north to Point Conception, or even around the corner to Point Arguello. There are also some seamounts in the area identified on ocean charts (always carry a chart) where lingcod and rockfish numbers are quite good.

The one catch if you have a boat is using the hoist. It comes with a hook, but that's it. That means you must supply your own strap. In addition, no driving is permitted on the pier, so boats have to be "walked" to the hoist. That means boats in the 17 to 22-foot class need a transport dolly, and smaller, lighter boats on trailers must be pulled along by hand. That done, let her rip.

MAP H3

10 LISTINGS
PAGES 626-637

CEN-CAL MAP . see page 540
adjoining maps
NORTH (G3) ...... see page 606
EAST (H4) .... see page 638
SOUTH (I3) .... see page 658
WEST (H2) .... see page 622

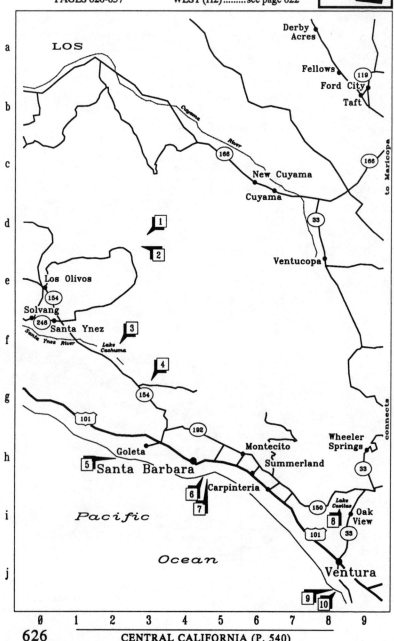

1.   MANZANA CREEK

Reference: North of Santa Barbara in Los Padres National Forest; map H3 grid d3.

How to get there: From US 101 at the north end of Santa Barbara, turn north on Highway 154 and drive 22 miles (past Lake Cachuma). Turn right on Armour Ranch Road and travel 1.5 miles, then turn right on Happy Canyon Road and drive 11 miles to Cachuma Saddle. Continue north on Sunset Valley-Cachuma Road (Forest Service Road 8N09) for four miles to Davy Brown Campground. Continue northeast for 1.5 miles to Nira Campground. Access is available there and off trails in the San Rafael Wilderness.

Facilities: A campground is available. Supplies can be obtained in Santa Barbara or Santa Ynez.

Cost: Creek access is free.

Who to contact: Phone the Los Padres National Forest District Office at (805) 925-9538. For a map, send $2 to the Office of Information, U.S. Forest Service, 630 Sansome Street, San Francisco, CA 94111.

About Manzana Creek: Little Manzana Creek is set on the edge of the San Rafael Wilderness in Los Padres National Forest, an obscure water that is difficult to reach, but provides decent fishing for rainbow trout in the seven to nine-inch class. Believe it or not, it is stocked with 3,000 trout by the DFG when water flows are suitable in the spring from the Nira Campground to the end of the road. Nearby Davy Brown Creek provides an option, but both are stocked on a same-day basis. Most people who visit this area do so for the wilderness trailhead. The trout fishing has provided another reason all along.

2.   DAVY BROWN CREEK

Reference: North of Santa Barbara in Los Padres National Forest; map H3 grid d3.

How to get there: From US 101 at the north end of Santa Barbara, turn north on Highway 154 and drive 22 miles (past Lake Cachuma). Turn right on Armour Ranch Road and travel 1.5 miles, then turn right on Happy Canyon Road and drive 11 miles to Cachuma Saddle. Continue north on Sunset Valley-Cachuma Road (Forest Service Road 8N09) for four miles to Davy Brown Campground, where access is available.

Facilities: A campground is available, but there is no piped water. Supplies can be obtained in Santa Barbara or Santa Ynez.

Cost: Creek access is free.

Who to contact: Phone the Los Padres National Forest District Office at (805) 925-9538. For a map, send $2 to the Office of Information, U.S. Forest Service, 630 Sansome Street, San Francisco, CA 94111.

About Davy Brown Creek: In the early season, when the Sierra Nevada is locked up by snow and ice, a lot of folks just keep their trout rods packed away. Turns out there is an alternative, however. Davy Brown Creek, which is set near the wilderness boundary of the San Rafael Wilderness, provides a primitive campground and a good chance to catch trout in spring when streamflows are decent. Now get this: It is stocked with trout, some 3,000 seven to nine-inchers, which are plunked in from the Davy Brown Campground on to Manzana Canyon. Nearby Manzana Creek provides an option. When you add it up, this area provides a fairly remote and primitive fishing/camping option, yet without the five-hour drive to the Sierra.

---

3.   LAKE CACHUMA

Reference: North of Santa Barbara; map H3 grid f2.

How to get there: From Santa Barbara, drive about 17 miles north on Highway 154 to the lake. The boat ramp is located on the south shore. Craft under 10 feet are prohibited.

Facilities: A campground, a boat ramp, boat rentals, picnic areas, bait, tackle, and groceries are available.

Cost: Day-use fee is $3.50 per vehicle.

Who to contact: Phone the lake at (805) 688-4658.

About Lake Cachuma: When Lake Cachuma is full, you are apt to think you have come upon a fisherman's paradise. There are several lake arms with protected coves that hold bass, trout plants are abundant, and best of all, no waterskiing or jet skis are permitted. But the problem is that Cachuma is only rarely full of water. In fact, it was all but dry in February of 1991 due to lack of rain and continued use by the city of Santa Barbara. Heavy rains from mid-February through March brought the lake level up, and as the 1990s progress, the fisheries here will be re-established.

Cachuma is set at 780 feet elevation in the foothills east of Santa Ynez. When full it covers 3,200 acres with what appears to be an abundance of bass habitat. All matter of aquatic vegetation, stick-ups, shaded coves, rocky points and dropoffs should make for large numbers of big bass. The lake record largemouth bass here is 16 pounds, 7 ounces, caught in 1988, which shows what is possible. But for the most part a lot of the habitat is unfilled with bass due to the continual problems with water levels. If a desalinization plant is eventually built for Santa Barbara, the water levels at Cachuma should be consistently higher, and should give the fishing a great, needed boost.

Because a lot of good-looking spots don't have bass, you really need to cover a lot of water to be successful. Anglers using bass boats with electric motors have a tremendous advantage in their ability to do that. The best spots to start are around Arrowhead Island, Cachuma Bay, Jackrabbit Flat, and the Narrows, where catch rates are highest. Few of the real big bass are at such spots, however. They prefer to stay down, 15 to 20 feet deep, often suspended next to dropoffs, and require substantial effort in March for anglers to pull one out. Most folks catch a few of the smaller bass, figure they'll do better next time, and only very rarely get one over five pounds. The lake also has a sprinkling of smallmouth bass, though they are always a longshot. The ends of the dam are the best bet.

Cachuma could become a producer of giant bass, if the water would just stay high enough to sustain them. For one thing, the food supply is excellent. The lake is stocked with nearly 50,000 trout per year by the Department of Fish and Game, which are like growing pills for the big Florida strain. Those trout also provide a good alternative fishery. The stocks are made from spring through early summer, then again in the fall, and include 10,000 that range 12 to 14 inches. Shorefishing for trout is decent enough from the campground areas near the boat ramp when the water is cool, and standard trolling techniques do fine, especially in late spring.

All this lake needs to fulfill the hopes of fishermen is water. Unfortunately, that is the one thing that is often in shortest supply.

---

4.   SANTA YNEZ RIVER

Reference: North of Santa Barbara in Los Padres National Forest; map H3 grid g3.

How to get there: From US 101 at the north end of Santa Barbara, turn north on Highway 154 and travel 12 miles. Turn right on Paradise Road and drive east to the ranger station. Access is available off Paradise Road. Note: Paradise Road is sometimes closed due to high water. Phone the ranger station before making your trip: (805) 967-3481.

Facilities: Several campgrounds are located on the river. Supplies can be obtained in Santa Barbara.

Cost: River access is free.

Who to contact: Phone the Los Padres National Forest District Office at (805) 967-3481. For a map, send $2 to the Office of Information, U.S. Forest Service, 630 Sansome Street, San Francisco, CA 94111.

About Santa Ynez River: Hit this river right and you may not want to make the long drive to the Sierra Nevada ever again. Hit it wrong, and well, when does the next bus leave? It is no secret that the Santa Ynez River is easily accessible from the adjacent Paradise Road, and well stocked with rainbow trout as well. We're talking here about the stretch of river between Lake Cachuma and Gibraltar Reservoir, with the best stocked stretch of water being between Red Rock Camp on downstream to the Forest Service ranger station. The DFG stocks nearly 10,000 trout per year here, most going seven to nine inches. This river is at the mercy of water releases out of Lake Cachuma, and in dry years, they can be pretty sparse. In summer, the flow can be reduced to a mere trickle, plants are stopped, and the fishing turns to zilch. Say, when is the bus leaving for Bishop?

---

5.   GOLETA BEACH COUNTY PARK

Reference: North of Santa Barbara; map H3 grid h2.

How to get there: From Santa Barbara, drive north on Highway 101 to Goleta. Turn west on Highway 217 and head toward the University of California. Just before the entrance to the university, turn left onto Sandspit Road and continue to the beach.

Facilities: A pier, picnic areas, boat hoist, a restaurant, and bait are available.

Cost: Beach access is free. There is a charge for the boat hoist, and you must provide your own sling.

Who to contact: Phone the County Parks Department at (805) 568-2461, or the park ranger at (805) 967-1300.

About Goleta Beach County Park: The Goleta Pier and adjacent beach area are symbolic of much of the quality fishing non-boaters can take advantage of in Southern California. This particular stretch of water attracts good numbers of perch, both barred and walleyes, and they can be caught in decent numbers from the Goleta Pier. In addition, in the spring, halibut are rarely caught at the pier, and the chance of hooking one will always be in the back of your mind.

Boaters who use the hoist at the pier can make short trips to inshore kelp beds, then fish on the edge of it. Summers are good here, with rare barracuda, bonito and sometimes even yellowtail and white seabass swimming through and joining the resident populations of rockfish and sheephead. A lot of people take the small rockfish at the kelp beds for granted. Don't. They add a tremendous dimension to the quality of local sportfishing.

---

6.   STEARNS WHARF

Reference: In Santa Barbara; map H3 grid h5.

How to get there: From Ventura, drive north on US 101 to Santa Barbara. Take the Anacapa Street exit and turn left. Continue to Cabrillo Boulevard and turn right. Travel a short distance to State Street, then turn west and continue to the wharf at the end of the street.

Facilities: A pier, restrooms, fish-cleaning tables, sinks, and bait are available. A boat launch and boat rentals are available nearby.

Cost: Access is free.

Who to contact: Phone the wharf at (805) 564-5518.

About Stearns Wharf: You watch and you learn. Over the course of time, it is amazing how many different species of fish are caught at Stearns Wharf. Perch? Halibut? Rockfish? Mackerel? They all move through here on a seasonal basis. The best and most consistent fishing is for perch during the winter and early spring. Many species of perch are caught during this period, and when the sea is calm and storms infrequent, the perch seem to move in along the pier pilings in large numbers. In the summer, mackerel can be even more abundant. There is no middle ground: They arrive in hordes or don't show at all. When they do show, anybody with a bait on a hook has a good chance of getting a bucketful of them. When that occurs, they are so common that the entire affair is just taken for granted. Not so with halibut, which provide a longshot in late spring and early summer. They are always treated as the king of the piers. A sprinkling of small rockfish, jacksmelt and croakers are also caught during the summer.

---

7. SANTA BARBARA DEEP SEA

Reference: North of Ventura; map H3 grid h5.

How to get there: From Ventura, drive 28 miles north on US 101 to Santa Barbara. Take the Cabrillo Boulevard exit and at the bottom of the offramp turn left. Drive west towards the beach and continue to Harbor Way, the seventh stop light. The sportfishing operations are located on Harbor Way.

Facilities: Party boat charters, campgrounds, lodging, and supplies are available in the Santa Barbara area.

Cost: Party boat fees range from $23-$63.

Who to contact: For general information, phone the Santa Barbara Chamber of Commerce at (805) 965-3021. For fishing information, phone Sea Landing at (805) 963-3564.

Party boat list: Condor, Hornet, Seahawk; reservations through Sea Landing at (805) 963-3564.

About Santa Barbara Deep Sea: The unique stretch of coast along Santa Barbara is characterized by dense kelp forests, oil platform drilling rigs, and the offshore Channel Islands. Each helps give the area its own distinct identity, along with this stretch of coast's unusual west-to-east geographical alignment.

In particular, the kelp beds provide outstanding marine habitat for a variety of species. The best area is just west of Santa Barbara. It is here where many species can be caught, with rockfish, kelp bass and

---

cabezone the most common. While these fish tend not to be large, they are often abundant. This is why the kelp forests provide an excellent destination, especially for parents who want to introduce their children to marine fishing. My first ocean fishing trips were as a 10-year-old out to the kelp beds, and these trips produced some of the first feelings of real success I can remember. Another advantage to fishing around kelp is the light-tackle techniques that can be employed (see Secrets of the Masters section on rockfish) to get a lot of sizzle out of even rockfish. It is becoming popular to use gear designed for freshwater fishing, casting jigs as if you were fishing for largemouth bass in lakes, but instead catching ocean-tough rockfish.

There are other options as well. The sandy-bottomed areas attract good numbers of halibut along the coast between El Capitan State Beach on westward to the vicinity of Gaviota State Park. In summer, bonito and yellowtail also arrive in the vicinity. As subspecies of tuna, these migratory fish are nomads whose location from year to year cannot be predicted with any degree of precision. Rarely in summer and early fall, white seabass and barracuda are caught west of Santa Barbara.

The most popular trips on party boats are out to the Channel Islands. For information on this area, see Zone-I3.

If you own your own boat or are new to the area, it is advisable to have a Loran to assist in navigation. The reason becomes clear as you head out to sea, particularly if your destination is Santa Cruz Island. You will find yourself heading due south, and you might even think something is wrong with your compass. Nothing is. The reason for this anomaly is that the local coast is nearly on a line, west to east, not north to south as elsewhere along California. What usually happens, however, is that boaters head out on a clear day, not paying any attention to the compass heading. If fog then moves in and reduces visibility, many then "instinctively" head east to return to shore, and then find themselves about 90 degrees off course, cruising straight toward Ventura. In the fog, it will seem right, but it will be wrong. You must instead head north to return, even though it may seem contrary to every feeling in your bones.

For the most part, boaters do not get lost and the Santa Barbara area provides an outstanding fishery.

---

8. LAKE CASITAS

Reference: North of Ventura; map H3 grid i8.
How to get there from Ventura: From the north end of Ventura on US 101, turn north on Highway 33 and drive 12 miles to Highway 150. Turn east and continue for four miles to the lake.

How to get there from Santa Barbara: From Santa Barbara, turn south on US 101 and drive about 11 miles to Highway 150 on the left. Turn east and continue for four miles to the lake.

Facilities: A campground, picnic areas, a boat ramp, a boat hoist, a full-service marina, boat rentals, bait, tackle, and groceries are available. Craft under 11 or over 25 feet are prohibited.

Cost: Day-use fee is $3 per vehicle; additional $3.50 if entering with a boat.

Who to contact: Phone the lake at (805) 649-2233.

About Lake Casitas: It was Lake Casitas where Ray Easley caught the 21-pound, 3-ounce largemouth bass that first attracted world attention to the bass lakes in Southern California. It was also Casitas where a crawdad I planned to use to catch an even bigger bass clamped onto one of my fingers. I had one response to that: "Yeeeeeeeeow."

Most of the shockwaves here are caused from fish, however, not from finger-grabbing crawdads. But without the crawdads, you wouldn't get the shockwaves because Casitas has always been loaded with crawdads, perfect for growing big bass, and perfect as well for bait.

Casitas is located north of Ventura, at 285 feet elevation in the foothill country bordering Los Padres National Forest. The lake has 32 miles of shorelines with a remarkable number of sheltered coves, and when full of water, covers 2,700 acres. A bonus for anglers is that no waterskiing, jet skis or any water contact sports are permitted. A lot of people figured it would be Casitas that would dominate the world's line-class bass records, but it hasn't worked out that way; Lake Castaic has that honor. Regardless, lots of big bass are caught at Casitas, so many that it takes a 10-pounder to raise any eyebrows. Casitas also has big redear sunfish and catfish. It was a former state record-holder for catfish and bass, and still holds the record for redear sunfish (3 pounds, 7 ounces).

With all the available bass habitat, you can be confused as to where to start your search. Simplify your mission by starting along the eastern shore, the lake's most productive stretch of water. If you want big bass, crawdads are a must, and so is a lot of time on the water with plenty of dud days. If you want a higher catch rate but smaller fish, then wait until the water has warmed up to 63, 64 degrees, when shad move into the shallows, then fan the shoreline with casts with shad-patterned plugs. In addition, low visibility, six-pound line is a must, with both clear water and a lot of fishing pressure the rule. Anything heavier can spook the bass. Like all lakes, the bass here change their temperament, depth and feed patterns according to time of year and water temperature. You must follow accordingly.

One bonus at Casitas, as at many lakes in Southern California, are the large stocks of rainbow trout. They not only provide an alternative fishery, but also provide food to help the bass grow to giant sizes. Casitas is stocked with 13,000 trout averaging three-to-the-pound, 25,000 averaging two-to-the-pound, and 10,000 averaging a pound. Shoreline baitdunking is good right near the campgrounds for the trout, especially in the early summer before the water has heated up too much.

Because of the trout, rumors surface here that fishermen are using them illegally for bait for the big bass. One bizarre story was that Mr. Enraged Angler believed that two gents in a boat were doing just that in order to catch a huge stringer of bass. Mr. Enraged pulled up suddenly in his boat, pulled a gun, and demanded to see what bait the two fellows were using. Shocked and frightened, they managed to reel in their lines, whereupon Mr. Enraged saw their bait: crawdads. "Sorry about that," he mumbled. Shortly thereafter, Mr. Enraged was arrested, and the judge, not being a fisherman, thought that Mr. Enraged was making up the tale about the suspected trout for bait, and added a week in the clink for the "outrageous story."

It could have been worse. Mr. Enraged could have been sentenced to an experience that I went through. Anybody who has had a crawdad try to pinch off one of their fingers knows exactly what I'm talking about.

---

9.   VENTURA DEEP SEA

Reference: At Ventura Harbor north of Los Angeles; map H3 grid j8.

How to get there: From Los Angeles, drive north on US 101 to Ventura. Take the Seaward exit and turn left. Continue to Harbor Boulevard, turn left, and drive 1.5 miles to Schooner Street. Turn right and continue until the street dead ends at Anchors Way. Turn right and continue a short distance to the harbor on the left.

Facilities: Party boat charters, bait, tackle, a full-service marina, campgrounds, lodging, and supplies are available in and near Ventura. A launch ramp is available at the harbor.

Cost: Party boat fees range from $25-$67 per person, depending on length of trip.

Who to contact: For general information, phone the Ventura Chamber of Commerce at (805) 648-2875. For fishing information, phone Ventura Sportfishing at (805) 644-7363, or (805) 650-1255.

Party boat list: Ellie-M, Shar-D, Coroloma, Sea Hunt; reservations through Ventura Sportfishing at (805) 644-7363.

About Ventura Deep Sea: From land, the sea looks just like a broad, flat expanse of nothingness, something nice for the sun to set into each evening. But from the undersea view of a fish, the coast offshore of Ventura is one of the most distinctive in Southern California. Directly offshore of Port Hueneme in Oxnard is the Hueneme Canyon, a massive underwater gorge that drops quickly to never-never land (see Zone-I3). Yet just north of the canyon, just offshore of Ventura, is the Ventura Flats, and just 15 miles west are the tops of an undersea mountain range, the Anacapa Islands (also see Zone-I3).

The Ventura Flats are featured for attracting halibut in the summer, and rarely salmon in the spring. The sea bottom here is a sand-and-mud mix, perfect for halibut. One problem has been commercial netting, which tends to crop the larger halibut out of the picture. As inshore net bans are implemented, this is one area that stands to make prominent gains. It is not fished as heavily as many other areas of the Southern California coast, primarily because locating large concentrations of halibut over such an expansive area can be difficult. But those who keep tuned in to the week-to-week movements of halibut can do well here. Some years, bonito even move through the Ventura Flats in the summer, and even more rarely, barracuda and white seabass.

The salmon are another story. They offer a sport similar to the old shell game. It is often a question of whether any are even out there, but when they do arrive, they can create quite a stir. When salmon do migrate this far south, they usually swim first through Hueneme Canyon to the south, then start migrating north via the Ventura Flats. When it happens, it is always between mid-March and early April, and provides a rare opportunity for Southern California saltwater anglers.

Kelp forests in a few inshore areas north of Ventura also provide an option, holding a variety of small rockfish and kelp bass. They are located just south of Point Pitas, offshore Seacliff (Punta Gorda), and south of Point Rincon.

Whenever you fish the ocean, remember to look at the sea as if you are a fish, not a person. You don't need to sprout a set of gills, but you will certainly have better prospects.

---

10.   VENTURA PIER

Reference: In Ventura at San Buenaventura State Beach; map H3 grid j8.
How to get there: From US 101 at Ventura, take the California Street exit. Turn left on California and continue to the intersection. Turn left on Harbor Boulevard and continue past the pier to the park entrance station and parking area.
Facilities: Restrooms and fish-cleaning sinks are provided. Bait, tackle and picnic areas are available nearby.
Cost: Day-use fee is $5 per vehicle.
Who to contact: Phone San Buenaventura State Park at (805) 654-4611.

MAP H4

CEN-CAL MAP . see page 540
adjoining maps
NORTH (G4) ...... see page 608
EAST (H5) .... see page 648
SOUTH (I4) .... see page 662
WEST (H3) .... see page 626

12 LISTINGS
PAGES 638-647

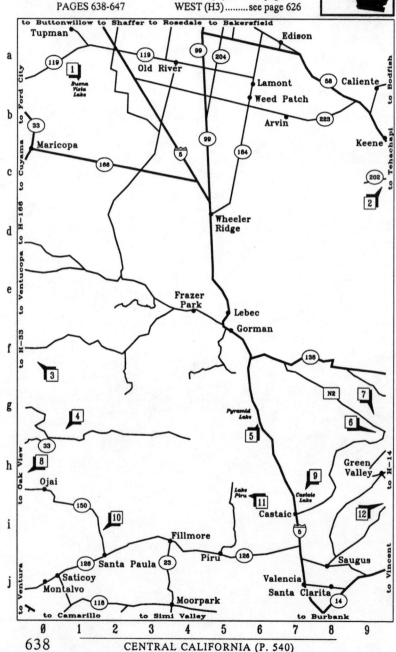

CENTRAL CALIFORNIA (P. 540)

1. BUENA VISTA AQUATIC REC. AREA

Reference: Near Bakersfield; map H4 grid a1.

How to get there: From Interstate 5 east of Bakersfield, turn west on Highway 119 and drive two miles. Turn south on Enos Lane and continue to the park entrance.

Facilities: A campground, boat ramps, picnic areas, bait, tackle, and groceries are available. Power boats under 11 feet are prohibited—that's right, no jet skis.

Cost: Day-use fee is $3 per vehicle. There is a charge for boat launching.

Who to contact: Phone the park at (805) 763-1526.

About Buena Vista Aquatic Recreation Area: It may not resemble your idea of paradise, but in the desolate western San Joaquin Valley, any water body is something of a haven. Buena Vista is actually two connected lakes fed by the West Side Canal, little Lake Evans to the west and larger Lake Webb to the east. It is critical that you know the difference. Lake Webb is open to all boating (except the hated jet skis), and jet boats towing skiers are a common sight all summer long. Lake Evans, on the other hand, is small and quiet with a 5-mph speed limit. Neither lake is stocked with trout. Rather, they provide fair fisheries for bass, bluegill, catfish and crappie. The bass and crappie are best in the spring, before the west valley gets fried by the blow-torch heat of summer. By then, the fishing is decent only at dusk for bass and into the night for catfish.

2. BRITE VALLEY LAKE

Reference: Near Tehachapi at Brite Valley Recreation Area; map H4 grid c9.

How to get there: From Bakersfield, turn east on Highway 58 and drive 40 miles toward the town of Tehachapi. Take the Highway 202 exit and drive west for three miles to Banducci Road. Turn left and continue south to the park.

Facilities: A campground, picnic areas, an unimproved boat ramp, and a fish-cleaning station are available. No gasoline motors are permitted on the lake. Bait and tackle can be purchased in the Bakersfield area. Groceries are available nearby.

Cost: Day-use fee is $3 per vehicle; additional $2 if entering with a boat.

Who to contact: Phone the park at (805) 822-3228.

About Brite Valley Lake: Here's a hidden spot that gets overlooked by the out-of-towners every time. Little Brite Valley Lake is a dot of a water hole in the northern flanks of the Tehachapi Mountains. From winter through spring, it is stocked with about 15,000 rainbow trout, which provide good shoreline prospects for baitdunkers. In the hot summer months, fishing for resident warmwater species is only fair. Although gas engines are prohibited, it is a good lake for hand-powered craft, such as canoes or rafts. You get a little-known spot, quiet water, and in the cool months, decent trout fishing.

3.   REYES CREEK

Reference: North of Ventura in Los Padres National Forest; map H4 grid fØ.

How to get there: From Ventura, turn north on Highway 33 and drive approximately 50 miles to the Ozena Guard Station. Turn east on Lockwood Road. Drive 3.5 miles east, then turn south on Forest Service Road 7N11 and continue to the campground.

Facilities: A campground is available. Supplies can be obtained in Ojai.

Cost: Access is free.

Who to contact: Phone the Los Padres National Forest District Office at (805) 646-4348. For a map, send $2 to the Office of Information, U.S. Forest Service, 630 Sansome Street, San Francisco, CA 94111.

About Reyes Creek: This is the kind of trout stream that gets ignored, yet if you keep your anticipation in focus, it can provide a good weekend adventure. Reyes Creek is in the remote Pine Mountain area of Los Padres National Forest, a small creek that is overlooked by all but the few people who know the area. It is stocked with small rainbow trout, 3,600 per year in the seven and eight-inch class, from the campground on upstream. The stream is reduced to a trickle in the summer and fall, so if you come to fish, plan your trip for spring and early summer. There are several trails in the area, providing side-trip options. Sespe Creek and North Fork Ventura River to the south along Highway 33 provide nearby options, but get far more attention.

4.   SESPE CREEK

Reference: North of Ventura in Los Padres National Forest; map H4 grid g1.

How to get there: From Ventura, drive north on Highway 33 to Ojai. Continue north on Highway 33 for about six miles to Wheeler Gorge Campground. Turn east on Forest Service Road 6N31 and continue for about six miles to Lion Campground. Access is available from the campground on east. Or, continue north on Highway 33 to Sespe Gorge Campground. Fishing access is available directly off the highway.

Facilities: Several campgrounds are available in the vicinity. Supplies can be obtained in Ojai.

Cost: Access is free.

Who to contact: Phone the Los Padres National Forest District Office at (805) 646-4348. For a map, send $2 to the Office of Information, U.S. Forest Service, 630 Sansome Street, San Francisco, CA 94111.

About Sespe Creek: Los Padres National Forest has a network of small streams and creeks, and it is Sespe Creek that is the largest, best-known, and provides the most consistent water conditions and trout fishing. It also gets large numbers of trout stocks, receiving nearly 30,000 trout in the seven and eight-inch class. The best stretch of water is at Lion Campground, and also along Highway 33 between Beaver and Sespe Gorge campgrounds. It is nowhere as remote as nearby Reyes Creek to the north, but catch rates are higher and the range of time for fishable water flow levels is longer.

---

5. PYRAMID LAKE

Reference: North of Los Angeles in Angeles National Forest; map H4 grid g6.

How to get there: From Los Angeles, drive about 60 miles north on Interstate 5. Take the Hungry Valley Road exit (about eight miles south of Gorman) and turn west. Continue to the lake.

Facilities: A campground, picnic areas, boat ramps, boat rentals, a concession stand, bait, and groceries are available.

Cost: Parking fee is $4 per vehicle.

Who to contact: Phone Pyramid Boat Rentals at (805) 257-2892.

About Pyramid Lake: This is one of the cornerstones of California's Central Valley Project, Pyramid Lake being a major storage facility for water as it is moved from north to south. Since the pumps in the Delta take fish as well as water, Pyramid Lake is frequently pumped full to the brim with both. It provides a decent fishery for striped bass as well as for rainbow trout.

Pyramid Lake is located at 2,600 feet, and although surrounded by Angeles National Forest, Interstate 5 is routed right past several lake arms. This makes it one of the more easily accessed waters in California, and as a showpiece, the water boys tend to keep it more full than other lakes on line with the California Aqueduct. The lake is a favorite for power boaters, especially water skiers (35-mph speed limit enforced), and the main lake often should be avoided to get away from the water plows. The saving grace is the lake arms. A five-mph speed limit is in effect at four of the five major lake arms; the Snowy Creek arm, Carlos Canyon arm, Gorman Creek, and Liebre Gulch.

The lake is stocked with decent numbers of trout, but it is also heavily fished. The DFG stocks 60,000 trout in the 10 and 11-inch class, along with another 10,000 in the 12 and 13-inch class. They join holdovers from previous years, some in the 15 to 20-inch class.

Because of the lake's steep banks, shorefishing access is poor. The best hopes for shoreliners are in the main lake arm south of the marina, just down from the beach.

The best prospects are for trollers. After launching, start trolling immediately, keeping off the western shore. Many boaters rush through this area to reach the main lake and bypass some good water. Trout fishing is decent until summer, when they go deep, and most anglers troll right over the top of the fish.

Striped bass provide a bonus, with fish occasionally caught in the 20-pound class, with most smaller. The stripers can be difficult to catch most of the year, although there are a few periods when they are vulnerable. One is in the spring, when trout plants are regularly made at the head of the lake. The stripers often are attracted to feed on the trout, and if you are on the spot during such activity, you can cast a Rattletrap or Hair Raiser jig and have a chance of a quick hookup. Another time is first thing in the morning, prior to sunrise, when the stripers often feed in the vicinity of the dam and Chumash Island, and can rarely be enticed with deep-running plugs. Finally, in the fall, the stripers occasionally will emerge from the depths and chase their feed near the surface.

Pyramid is one of the more heavily used recreation lakes in California. Always keep that in mind and your expectations have a better chance of being fulfilled.

---

6. ELIZABETH LAKE

Reference: West of Lancaster in Angeles National Forest; map H4 grid g9.

How to get there: From Los Angeles, drive about 40 miles north on Interstate 5 to Castaic. Turn north on Lake Hughes Road and continue to Elizabeth Lake Road. Turn right and drive about three miles east, past Lake Hughes and Munz Lake to Elizabeth Lake.

Facilities: Picnic areas and an unimproved launch ramp are available.

Cost: Access is free.

Who to contact: Phone the Angeles National Forest District Office at (805) 296-9710.

Special note: The eastern half of Elizabeth Lake is private, off-limits to the public.

About Elizabeth Lake: They might want to import some Mi-Wok Medicine Men to conduct a rain dance here every winter because Elizabeth Lake is often extremely low. It is a prisoner of rainfall; so is nearby Hughes Lake to the west, which dried up in 1991. Elizabeth is set at 3,300 feet in the northern outskirts of Angeles National Forest below Portal Ridge. It's a small lake that provides fair trout fishing in the cool months and bass fishing in the spring and summer. When the water is cool enough and high enough to support trout, it is stocked each year with 9,000 rainbow trout in the eight-inch class and another 16,000 in the 10 to 12-inch class. Standard trolling and shoreline baitfishing techniques do fine here, and in late spring, the water is warm enough to swim in during the day, yet cool enough to catch trout in the evening. One note is that an exceptional side trip is available nearby to the Antelope Valley California Poppy State Reserve, located a few miles to the north. In the spring, it is wall-to-wall blooming poppies, about nine square miles of them, a fantastic sight.

7.   CALIFORNIA AQUEDUCT

Reference: Near Elizabeth Lake; map H4 grid g9.

How to get there: From Los Angeles, drive about 40 miles north on Interstate 5 to Castaic. Turn north on Lake Hughes Road and continue to Elizabeth Lake Road. Turn right and drive about three miles east, past Lake Hughes and Munz Lake, to Elizabeth Lake. Turn north on Munz Ranch Road and continue to the fishing site at the aqueduct crossing.

Facilities: A parking area and toilets are provided.

Cost: Access is free.

Who to contact: Phone the Department of Water Resources in Castaic at (805) 257-3610.

About California Aqueduct: At least it provides a place to toss a line, and in the south valley, that's saying something. This access point on the California Aqueduct is located just a mile from Quartz Hill and a short hop west from both Palmdale and Lancaster. You bring your bait and your bucket, bait up, toss out your line, and hope a wandering striped bass or catfish roams past and decides to take a bite. You might bring some reading material, a quick read between bites, something like *War and Peace.*

8.   NORTH FORK VENTURA RIVER

Reference: North of Ventura in Los Padres National Forest; map H4 grid hØ.

How to get there: From Ventura, drive north on Highway 33 to Ojai. Continue north on Highway 33; direct access is available off the road and at Wheeler Gorge Campground.

Facilities: A campground is available at Wheeler Gorge. Supplies can be obtained in Ojai.

Cost: Access is free.

Who to contact: Phone the Los Padres National Forest District Office at (805) 646-4348. For a map, send $2 to the Office of Information, U.S. Forest Service, 630 Sansome Street, San Francisco, CA 94111.

About Ventura River: Here is a stream that is worth exploring on your way north into Los Padres National Forest, one of three waters where you can play hit-and-run. Driving south to north on Highway 33, this is the first stream you come to. Stop and give it a try between Matilija Canyon Road and Wheeler Gorge Campground; it is stocked with 21,000 trout per year in the seven and eight-inch class. The Sespe River and Reyes Creek to the north provide nearby options.

---

9. LAKE CASTAIC

Reference: North of Los Angeles; map H4 grid h7.

How to get there: From Los Angeles, drive about 40 miles north on Interstate 5 to Castaic. Turn north on Hughes Road and continue to the lake entrance.

Facilities: Picnic areas, boat ramps and boat rentals are available at both the lake and the lagoon. Bait and groceries are available at the lake. Motorized boats are prohibited on the lagoon. No boats under eight feet are permitted on the lake.

Cost: Day-use fee is $5 per vehicle. There is a charge for boat launching.

Who to contact: Phone Castaic Boat Rentals at (805) 257-2049; Lagoon Launch Ramp, (805) 257-4050.

Lake Castaic: It is almost certain that a world record largemouth bass is swimming around at Lake Castaic. This is the place where Bob Crupi caught a 22-pounder in 1991, the largest ever photographed in the world and just four ounces shy of the most legendary of all world records. Yet Crupi released that fish, and by now, it has probably grown a bit more, perhaps to world record proportions. As you read this, it is probably out there, looking for its next meal.

Because of that vision, anglers from all over the world are heading to Castaic. They want to be the one who lands it. In the meantime, however, a series of giant bass have been caught, world records for several different line classes. Crupi is responsible for four of them.

Castaic is easy to reach, just a short hop from the junction of Interstate 5 and Highway 126. It is set at 1,500 feet elevation in the foothills adjoining Angeles National Forest to the north, shaped like a giant "V" covering nearly 9,000 acres when full. It's a big lake, gets fantastic stocks of rainbow trout and intense fishing pressure by experienced bass anglers.

Because of all the people out to set a world record, the bass really have smartened up here. Line weight has become critical; too heavy a test will spook the fish, and you'll rarely get a nibble. Because of that, most bassers use six to 12-pound line, never heavier, and then pray that if they hook the world record, the fish won't break them off. Unlike a lot of lakes, the bass are deep almost all year (except when spawning), and it takes a lot of persistence and skill to work jigs slowly over structure 25 to 40 feet deep. The best bet is to carefully graph areas, then fish the deepwater structure. Always start at the upper lake areas.

If you get the idea that catch rates are not high, you are right. But at Castaic, there is an option: trout. Standard trolling techniques result in good catches ,providing anglers adjust for depth according to water temperatures. The lake is stocked with 108,000 trout in the eight-inch class, 130,000 trout in the 10 and 11-inch class, and a bonus of 10,000 going 12 inches and up. That is nearly 250,000 trout in all, tremendous annual numbers.

Waterskiing is also popular at Castaic (35-mph speed limit), and the bassers do their share of jetting around as well. If that bugs you, and you prefer quiet water, the nearby Castaic Lagoon located less than a mile to the south is the answer. No motors are permitted on the lagoon, yet the trout fishing is often excellent for anglers with canoes, rowboats, or fishing with bait from shore. It is stocked with 87,000 trout per year, a large amount for such a small water, just 180 acres.

Many newcomers to Castaic arrive with tremendous exuberance over the chance at a world record. Then, the lack of action makes them feel like the 'ol jinx has them by the throat. "All these giant bass are here and I can't even get a bite," they start thinking. Finally, they either switch over to trout, slink quietly away to more familiar territory, or grit their teeth and renew the effort, realizing it takes remarkable persistence and skill to entice a trophy. After all, few things worth remembering come easy.

---

10.   SANTA PAULA CREEK

Reference: North of Ventura; map H4 grid i2

How to get there: From Ventura, drive northeast on Highway 126 to Santa Paula. Turn north on Highway 150. Access is available in Steckel Park and off the highway.

Facilities: Full facilities are available in Ventura. Supplies can be obtained in Santa Paula.

Cost: Access is free.

Who to contact: Phone the County Parks & Recreation Department at (805) 654-3951.

About Santa Paula Creek: Talk about a backyard fishing hole . . . The residents of Santa Paula may not realize how good they have it. This stream is just a few miles north of Santa Paula, and gets stocked with

---

20,000 rainbow trout per year, mostly seven and eight-inchers. The best stretch of water is from Steckel Park upstream to Ferndale Ranch. You'll see the pullouts along the road.

While some local residents don't take advantage of Santa Paula Creek, one old gent definitely does. You see, there's this one fellow who gets tipped off on what day the DFG will stock the creek, then will wait in his car for the DFG tanker truck to come through town. Then he'll follow it out and be the first one on the creek after a plant. But during one such episode, the DFG truck did not stop at the creek. It kept driving on, heading well into Los Padres National Forest, off on dirt roads up to a remote ridge line. The truck chaser kept pace, eating dust the entire way, figuring he was about to learn a new secret spot. Well, the DFG driver got out of the truck, and then dumped an entire tanker load of water on the road. "No trout today." Heh, heh, heh.

---

11.   LAKE PIRU

Reference: Northwest of Los Angeles; map H4 grid i5.
How to get there: From Los Angeles, drive about 35 miles north on Interstate 5 to the Highway 126 exit. Turn west and drive 12 miles to the Piru Canyon Road exit. Turn north and drive six miles northeast to the lake entrance. You may also park at the dam or along the road and walk in for free.
Facilities: A campground, picnic areas, a boat ramp, a marina, boat rentals, bait, tackle, and groceries are available. Boats under 12 feet are prohibited.
Cost: Day-use fee is $4 per vehicle; additional $4 if entering with a boat. Entrance fee includes boat-launching privileges.
Who to contact: Phone the Piru Lake Recreation Area at (805) 521-1500; Lake Piru Marina, (805) 521-1231.
About Lake Piru: Here is a wildcard of lakes. It may be just the place to shuffle your cards and deal them face up. Piru often is overlooked because of its proximity to Lake Casitas to the west and Lake Castaic to the east, lakes where many believe a world-record bass will be caught. Piru may not produce the immense bass like Casitas and Castaic, but the catch rates are much higher. In addition, trout fishing is also good at Piru.

The lake covers 1,200 acres when full, set at 1,055 feet elevation in Los Padres National Forest. It is a popular waterskiing lake, and the best advice is to stay away from the area anywhere south of the boat ramp at all times, and to get off the lake in the summer as soon as the sun warms up and the jet boats start ripping up the place. Unlike so many reservoirs, there are no areas off-limits to waterskiers.

But like so many lakes with bass and trout, the prime time is in March, April and May. The difference here is that catch rates are excellent, especially during very strong morning and evening bites. The three principal cove areas, one on the west side of the lake and two on the east side, are natural spots for the bass at Piru. In the spring, it is common to catch five or more in a few hours, most in the 11 to 13-inch class, rarely to 15 or 16 inches. To get anything bigger, it helps plenty to use crawdads for bait. The lake has lots of crawdads and rainbow trout, and the big bass here take a pass on anything smaller.

Trout? Piru has plenty of them. The lake is stocked with 62,000 trout in the eight-inch class, 57,000 in the 10 or 11-inch class, and an additional 15,000 going about a foot. They join holdovers from previous years, providing both a consistent fishery for trollers as well as feed for the few elusive monster-sized bass here. The best areas to troll for trout are the cove just north of the boat ramp, up the main lake arm, and then late in the summer, in the deep water along the dam. Shoreliners do best just north of the boat ramp, and along the cove around the corner from the ramp. Piru may not get the ink that Castaic and Casitas do, but it often produces more fish.

12.　　BOUQUET CANYON CREEK　

Reference: East of Lancaster in Angeles National Forest; map H4 grid i9.

How to get there: From Los Angeles, drive about 35 miles north on Interstate 5 to the Magic Mountain Parkway exit. Drive east to Valencia Boulevard, then turn left and drive two miles to Bouquet Canyon Road. Turn left and continue north; access is available off the road.

Facilities: Several campgrounds are available on Bouquet Canyon Road, but they offer no piped water. Supplies can be obtained nearby.

Cost: Access is free.

Who to contact: Phone the Angeles National Forest District Office at (805) 296-9710. For a map, send $2 to the Office of Information, U.S. Forest Service, 630 Sansome Street, San Francisco, CA 94111.

About Bouquet Canyon Creek: Unlike the streams in Los Padres National Forest, Bouquet Canyon Creek has the benefit of a reservoir to insure fishable water releases for much of the year. It is not a famous stream, but the water conditions are suitable enough for the DFG to stock it with more trout than any stream or creek in the region. It receives 45,000 rainbow trout per year, most ranging seven to eight inches. The key area is along Bouquet Canyon Road, where the stream is stocked from Bouquet Reservoir on downstream nine miles to Texas Canyon. It is the most productive water for anglers living in the vicinity of the Lancaster/south valley area.

MAP H5

3 LISTINGS
PAGES 648-651

CEN-CAL MAP . see page 540
adjoining maps
NORTH (G5) ...... see page 614
EAST ....no map
SOUTH (I5) ....see page 668
WEST (H4).........see page 638

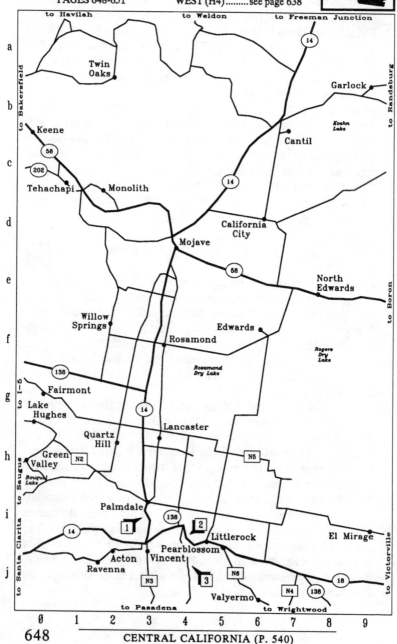

CENTRAL CALIFORNIA (P. 540)

1. CALIFORNIA AQUEDUCT

Reference: From Quartz Hill to Pearblossom; map H5 grid i3.

How to get to the 70th Street West site: From Los Angeles, drive north on Interstate 5 to the Highway 14-Palmdale exit. Turn east and continue past Palmdale to the Avenue N exit. Take the exit and turn west. Continue on Avenue N to 70th Street West, then turn left and travel a short distance south to the fishing site.

How to get to the Avenue S site: From Los Angeles, drive north on Interstate 5 to the Highway 14-Palmdale exit. Turn east and continue to the Avenue S exit (about two miles south of Palmdale). Turn west and continue to the fishing site just past Tierre Subida Avenue.

How to get to the 77th Street East site: From Los Angeles, drive north on Interstate 5 to the Highway 14-Palmdale exit. Turn east and continue to the Palmdale-Highway 138 exit. Turn east on Highway 138 and drive southeast to Littlerock. Turn right at 77th Street East and drive south to Avenue V, then turn right and continue to the fishing site.

How to get to the Longview Road site: From Los Angeles, drive north on Interstate 5 to the Highway 14-Palmdale exit. Turn east and continue to the Palmdale-Highway 138 exit. Turn east on Highway 138 and drive southeast to Pearblossom. Turn right on 121st Street East and go to East Avenue West. Turn left and drive until you reach Longview Road, then turn right and travel south to the fishing site.

Facilities: Parking areas are provided at all sites; most offer toilets as well. Supplies can be obtained in Palmdale.

Cost: Access is free.

Who to contact: Phone the Department of Water Resources in Palmdale at (805) 947-4111.

About California Aqueduct: The longest fishing hole in the world? The California Aqueduct qualifies, stretching from the Delta on south for hundreds of miles. In this stretch are four different access points that look remarkably like all the other ones: Concrete beveled edges, always full of water, an adjacent parking area and a little outhouse. This area of the California Aqueduct has fewer striped bass than at the access points farther north; after all, they have to survive being pumped several hundred miles, through a series of lakes, and over the Tehachapi Mountains. However, there are catfish, and also rarely trout and bass that are pumped out of Lake Pyramid.

    The benefit of the fishing access points is for people who want to make a quick hit, or those ready for an all-night stand. The quick hit comes for people cruising through the area who need a break from the driving, who park and cast lures for five or 10 minutes, then drive on. The all-nighters bring a lawn chair along, cast out their bait, and wait for a fish to wander by. What the heck, it beats taking sleeping pills.

2. LITTLE ROCK CREEK

Reference: Near Palmdale in Angeles National Forest; map H5 grid i4.

How to get there: From Los Angeles, drive north on Interstate 5 to the Highway 14-Palmdale exit. Turn east and continue to Palmdale, then turn east on Highway 138 and drive through the stoplight at the intersection. Turn right on Cheseboro Road; access is available off the road down to the dam at Little Rock Reservoir. Limited access is available off the trail south of Little Rock Reservoir.

Facilities: Campgrounds are available on the creek and at Little Rock Reservoir. Supplies are available in Palmdale or at the resort on the reservoir.

Cost: Access is free.

Who to contact: Phone the Angeles National Forest District Office at (805) 944-2187.

About Little Rock Creek: This stream starts as the drops of melting snow up near Kratka Ridge and Mt. Waterman, joins to form two feeder streams, which then join again to form Little Rock Creek. As long as snow is melting up "on top," this river has decent flows and is stocked with trout. The DFG stocks 13,500 rainbow trout in the seven to eight-inch class over a two-month period each spring. The best stretch of river to fish is from the headwaters of Little Rock Reservoir on up about five miles. The best advice here is start upstream, then fish your way down toward the lake. During years when there is a low snowpack up at Kratka, you can find this river reduced to a trickle by early summer. What to do? Head to nearby Bouquet Canyon Creek in Zone H4, which has more consistent flows and is stocked with far more trout.

3. LITTLE ROCK RESERVOIR

Reference: Near Palmdale in Angeles National Forest; map H5 grid j4.

How to get there: From Los Angeles, drive north on Interstate 5 to the Highway 14-Palmdale exit. Turn east and continue to Palmdale, then turn east on Highway 138 and drive through the stoplight at the intersection. Turn right on Cheseboro Road and continue for four miles to the reservoir.

Facilities: A campground, picnic areas, an unimproved boat ramp, boat rentals, bait, tackle, and groceries are available.

Cost: Access is free.

Who to contact: Phone the Angeles National Forest District Office at (805) 944-2187; Little Rock Lake Resort, (805) 944-1923.

About Little Rock Reservoir: Timing is always critical when it comes to fishing, but at Little Rock Reservoir if you don't time it right, you might as well go for a walk on the moon. For starters, get here in the spring and early summer. The water levels are highest then and rainbow trout are stocked on a regular basis. The Department of Fish and Game stocks 43,000 rainbow trout in the 8 to 11-inch class in this small lake, providing for decent catch rates if not large fish. Fair shoreline access is available on the west side of this narrow reservoir, but boaters who troll adjacent to the shoreline have the best catches.

The lake is set at 3,258 feet elevation in Angeles National Forest, but covers just 150 acres. When it starts to be drained down the Palmdale Ditch and into the California Aqueduct to the north, it can go from being a pretty mountain lake to a miniature grand canyon in just a few months. By then, you might as well see when the next spaceship leaves for the moon.

CEN-CAL MAP . see page 540
adjoining maps
NORTH ....no map
EAST ....no map
SOUTH (I9) ....see page 700
WEST ....no map

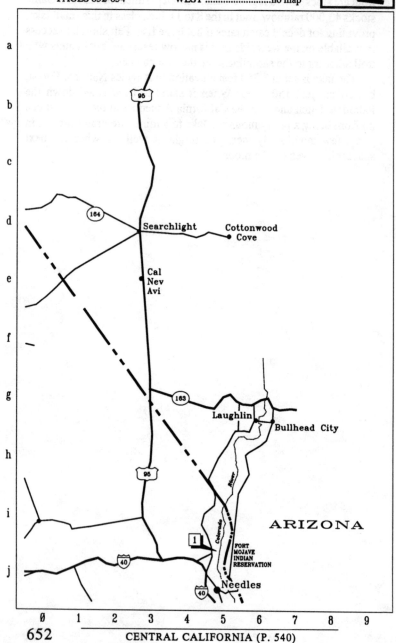

CENTRAL CALIFORNIA (P. 540)

1. ## COLORADO RIVER

Reference: From Nevada border to Needles; map H9 grid j5.

How to get there from Southern California: Take Interstate 15 north to Interstate 40 at Barstow and drive approximately 150 miles east to Needles.

How to get there from Northern California: Drive south on US 395 to Highway 58 at Kramer Junction, then cross over on Interstate 15 to Interstate 40. Proceed approximately 150 miles east to Needles.

Facilities: Campgrounds, full-service marinas, boat rentals, boat ramps, picnic areas, restaurants, bait, tackle, and groceries are available in the Needles area.

Cost: A nominal day-use and/or boat-launching fee is charged at most parks and marinas in the area.

Who to contact: Phone Park Moabi Marina, (619) 326-4777; Rainbow Beach Marina, (619) 326-3101; Needles Marina Park, (619) 326-2197.

About Colorado River: Bring your suntan lotion and a big towel. This section of the Colorado River is a big tourist spot where the body oil and beer can flow faster than the river. There are a lot of hot bodies and hot boats, with waterskiing the dominant activity in the summer. That doesn't mean there is no fishing. Just the opposite is true, nearly year around. Because the river is big, deep and flows about six miles per hour, you really need a boat to do it right.

The fishing starts from late winter through spring when the Department of Fish and Game stocks 54,000 rainbow trout in the stretch of river between Topock Bridge upstream to Needles. Most of the trout are not large; they are seven to 10-inchers with a sprinkling of bigger fellows. As summer approaches, the trout bite wanes and striped bass, largemouth bass and catfish start taking over. In May, an annual striped bass derby sponsored by the Bullhead City Chamber of Commerce is quite a deal, with big prizes and intense competition. Following that weekend, however, the most serious competition has more to do with suntans and fast boats.

SOUTHERN
CALIFORNIA

RATING SYSTEM

POOR————————————————FAIR————————————————GREAT

SOUTHERN CALIFORNIA MAP SECTIONS

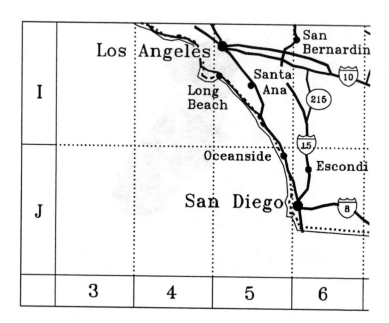

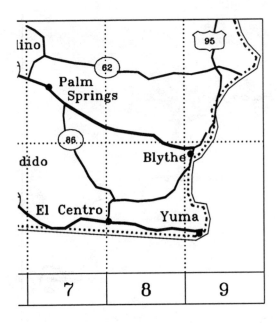

MAP I3

2 LISTINGS
PAGES 658-661

SO-CAL MAP ....see page 656
adjoining maps
NORTH (H3) ......see page 626
EAST (I4) ....see page 662
SOUTH ....no map
WEST ....no map

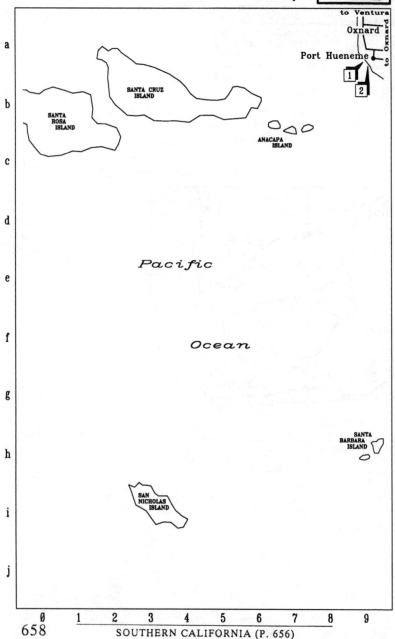

to Ventura

Oxnard

to Oxnard

Port Hueneme

1

2

a

b

SANTA CRUZ
ISLAND

SANTA
ROSA
ISLAND

ANACAPA
ISLAND

c

d

Pacific

e

f

Ocean

g

SANTA
BARBARA
ISLAND

h

SAN
NICHOLAS
ISLAND

i

j

Ø   1   2   3   4   5   6   7   8   9

SOUTHERN CALIFORNIA (P. 656)

1. CHANNEL ISLANDS DEEP SEA

Reference: Offshore of Oxnard; map I3 grid a9.

How to get there: From Santa Barbara, drive south on US 101 to the Highway 1 turnoff to Oxnard. Turn south and follow the signs to Channel Islands and Port Hueneme Harbors. Party boats that run excursions to the islands are available out of these harbors, as well as out of Ventura and Santa Barbara (see Zone H3).

Facilities: Party boat charters, bait and tackle are available at both harbors. A boat ramp, a boat hoist and boat rentals are available at Channel Islands Harbor. Full facilities are available in Ventura and Oxnard.

Cost: Party boat fees range from $20-$62 per person.

Who to contact: Phone Channel Islands Sportfishing at (800) 322-FISH; Port Hueneme Sportfishing, (805) 488-4715.

Party boat list: China Clipper, Explorer II, Sea Watch, Speed Twin, Pacific Clipper, Morning Star, Vanguard; reservations through Channel Islands Sportfishing at (800) 322-FISH. *Pacific Eagle, Mirage, Genie, Erna-B, Sea Angler;* reservations through Port Hueneme Sportfishing at (805) 488-4715.

About Channel Islands Deep Sea: The wide-open sea is the savior for Southern California residents, and in many ways it is the Channel Islands that are the savior for anglers. The islands are far enough offshore to provide a complete separation from mass urbanity, yet also provide the marine habitat to support a tremendous and varied fishery.

Four islands lie in a row here. From west to east, they are San Miguel, Santa Rosa, Santa Cruz and Anacapa. Each offers a distinctive habitat and fishery and receives different levels of fishing pressure. Santa Cruz and Anacapa are fished the most extensively because of their closer proximity to ports, as well as more severe weather conditions which affect San Miguel and Santa Rosa islands. Here is a capsule listing:

—San Miguel Island: This is the westernmost of the four islands, ranging seven miles long and 3 miles wide, and a long grind of a trip to reach by boat. It gets far less fishing pressure than any of the other islands. It is primarily a rocky setting, with major shoals on both the west and north sides. The most consistent fishing is for a variety of rockfish and lingcod, best at the reefs on the southern and northwestern side. An option is just east of Harris Point at Cuyler Harbor, where kelp bass, more rarely halibut and rockfish can be located. If you are visiting for the first time, a good side trip is to visit the beach on the west end of the island near Point Bennett, where there is a huge population of sea lions, so many that it can look as if it is paved in black. One note: It is often foggy out here in summer months.

—Santa Rosa Island: This is not only a big island, but it requires a long trip to reach it. This combination means that anglers must have a clear plan of attack. What do you want? Halibut? Rockfish? Maybe a chance at tuna in the late summer? Each significant fishing area offers something a little different. The northwest end between Sandy Point and Brockway Point is a good example of that, where the shoreline and sea bottom are quite rocky and hold large numbers of rockfish, lingcod, sheephead, and more rarely, white seabass. The southwest end in the vicinity of Bee Rock is similar, with large numbers of rockfish and some kelp bass. If you want halibut, there are several excellent spots: the north side of the island just off Carrington Point, as well as nearby in the southeast side of Bechers Bay. These are among the better spots for halibut anywhere in the Channel Islands. Another good halibut spot is on the southeastern side of the island, just west of East Point. When varieties of tuna start roaming in the area, they often use the Santa Cruz Channel around the southeastern side of the island as a gateway.

—Santa Cruz Island: This is the biggest of the four Channel Islands, and its closer proximity to the coast makes it a much more popular destination than San Miguel or Santa Rosa Islands. When the wind is down, there is good rockfishing nearly all along its northern shore, best in the vicinity of Double Point and Arch Rock, and the reefs located between those island points. When the wind is up, boaters instead duck to the southeast side to get protection from the north wind, and also get decent rockfishing. The bonus appeal here is for bonito, yellowtail and rarely larger tuna, which some years will roam in schools both on the southeast side of the island, as well as in the Santa Cruz Channel near Santa Rosa Island to the west. Some years the tuna show, some years they don't. Keep tuned in, and when they show, don't miss out.

—Anacapa Island: Anacapa really gets hammered by fishermen, but that is what you would expect. After all, it is just a short cruise out here during a calm sea, and there are decent numbers of a large variety of fish. The best fishing tends to be at either end of the islands on the southern, leeward side. The southwest end is a longer trip out but has better fishing, with kelp bass, sheephead, rockfish, and more rarely in the summer months, barracuda, and if the gods are smiling, yellowtail. Don't count on the latter, though. If you pull up at Arch Rock, the first land you come to on the eastern side, small rockfish hold on the bottom. That is not enough to put the brakes on. What is, however, is when barracuda and yellowtail roam through this area. It can happen.

2.   PORT HUENEME PIER

Reference: Near Oxnard at Port Hueneme Beach Park; map I3 grid a9.

How to get there: From Ventura, drive south on Highway 1 to Oxnard and turn right on Hueneme Road. Continue west to Ventura Road and follow the signs to the beach.

Facilities: Restrooms and a concession stand are available.

Cost: Parking fee is 50 cents per hour or $4 per day.

Who to contact: Phone Port Hueneme Beach Park at (805) 986-6555.

About Port Hueneme Pier: Start with something simple. Whatever you do, do not pronounce Hueneme as "Hoo-Neh-Mee." Do that and locals will clam up so fast that you will need a Jaws of Life to pry out any fishing information. So get it right, pronouncing it "Wah-Nee-Mee." It makes a difference when you want to get tipped off, and the fishing fluctuates so much here that tips are just what you need. Most of the fish come and go with the seasons, with perch best in the winter, halibut in the late winter and spring, and lingcod and sharks in the fall and early winter. The summer season is only fair, with some resident kelp bass in the area. Results can be decent during two and three-week periods, then can be a complete dud. The telephone, then, is your most important piece of fishing equipment—that and pronouncing "Hueneme" right.

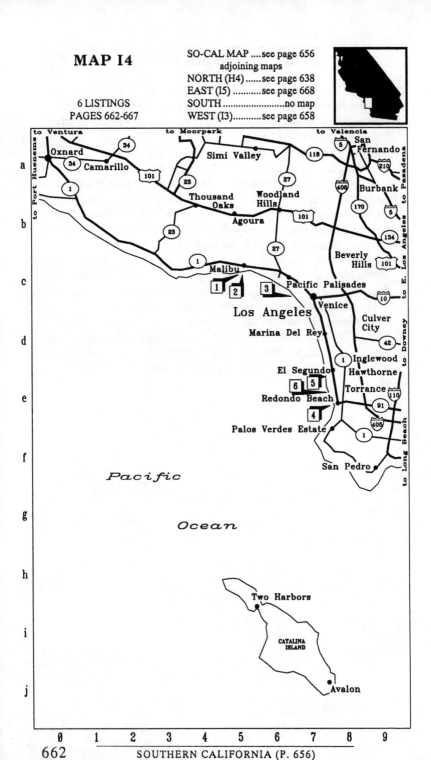

MAP I4

6 LISTINGS
PAGES 662-667

SO-CAL MAP ....see page 656
adjoining maps
NORTH (H4) ......see page 638
EAST (I5) ....see page 668
SOUTH ....no map
WEST (I3)...........see page 658

to Ventura

to Moorpark

to Valencia

Oxnard

Camarillo

Simi Valley

San Fernando

Burbank

to Pasadena

to Port Hueneme

Thousand Oaks

Woodland Hills

Agoura

Beverly Hills

to E. Los Angeles

Malibu

Pacific Palisades

Los Angeles

Venice

Culver City

Marina Del Rey

to Downey

Inglewood

El Segundo

Hawthorne

Torrance

Redondo Beach

Palos Verdes Estate

to Long Beach

San Pedro

Pacific

Ocean

Two Harbors

CATALINA ISLAND

Avalon

1. SANTA MONICA REDONDO DEEP SEA

Reference: From Malibu to Redondo Beach; map I4 grid c5.

How to get to Malibu Pier: From Los Angeles, turn west on the Santa Monica Freeway (Interstate 10) and continue until it turns into Highway 1. Continue about 12 miles northwest to Alice's Restaurant in Malibu; Malibu Sportfishing is located at the end of Malibu Pier, directly off the highway.

How to get to Redondo Harbor: From Los Angeles, drive south on Interstate 110. Take the 190th Street exit and turn right. Continue west until the street deadends at the beach on Harbor Drive. Turn left and continue one-quarter mile to Redondo Sportfishing at 233 North Harbor Drive.

Facilities: Party boat charters, bait and tackle are available at sportfishing operations. Lodging, restaurants and shops are available in towns along the coast. A paved boat ramp and a hand-launching area are located at the Marina del Rey Small Craft Harbor.

Cost: Party boat fees range from $16-$55 per person.

Who to contact: For information, phone the Malibu Chamber of Commerce, (310) 456-9025; Malibu Sportfishing, (310) 456-8030; Santa Monica Chamber of Commerce, (310) 393-9825; Redondo Beach Chamber of Commerce, (310) 376-6911; Redondo Sportfishing, (310) 372-2111.

Party boat list: Aquarius; reservations through Malibu Sportfishing at (310) 456-8030. *Isle of Redondo* (open-water fishing barge), *Blackjack, Seaspray, City of Redondo, Redondo Special;* reservations through Redondo Sportfishing at (310) 372-2111.

Special note: Albacore runs are always unpredictable. A good phone contact is Paul Poesche (Po-shay) at Redondo Sportfishing, (310) 372-2111.

About Santa Monica/Redondo Deep Sea: This stretch of coast is among the most popular in the world for saltwater anglers. It sits adjacent to the most densely populated area of California, yet the fisheries largely have been able to keep up with the demand for them. When gillnet bans take effect, it will get even better. The most consistent fishery is for rockfish, but there are seasonal options with halibut in the spring, and often bonito and yellowtail in the summer.

Santa Monica Bay is fairly shallow, but is cut by the Redondo and Santa Monica Canyons, and it is the rocky edges of these canyons where the rockfishing is best. Most of the local sportfishing boats will work along the southern edge of Redondo Canyon. Here, you will find a wide variety of rockfish, including bocaccio, vermillion, gopher, chilipepper and canary rockfish. In the spring and early summer, halibut often move into the flats of Santa Monica Bay. My ol' pal Bill

Beebe, a columnist with *Western Outdoor News*, won the halibut derby here one year and donated his entire $1,000 cash prize to United Anglers of California. It paid off big, because UAC was instrumental in helping to pass the state proposition to ban gillnets.

Another good area for rockfish and kelp bass is the kelp beds offshore of Zuma Beach, north of Malibu. The fish tend not to be large, but can provide light-tackle saltwater action, and can be a lot of fun. It is an excellent opportunity for anglers who want to try freshwater-style techniques yet catch saltwater-strength fish.

Several other options exist as well. Redondo Sportfishing operates the only open-water fishing barge on the Pacific Coast. In addition, bonito often move into Redondo Harbor, and can be caught from small boats using light tackle and live anchovies. My longtime buddy Clyde "The Wrench" Gibbs specializes here, using spinning tackle, four-pound line, and small gold hooks, hooking bonito like crazy. The key is the light line. The fish get so much angling pressure that anything heavier is too visible and will spook the fish.

Albacore and yellowtail are always the wildcard option here. A good albacore bite is like nothing else in California fishing, especially when the fish are chummed to the surface in a frenzy. Occasionally, large tuna may be in the mix. Albacore alone are something else, but when a big tuna grabs your bait, you can look down at your reel and say, "Goodbye fishing line." They are line burners.

But with albacore and yellowtail, there is a high level of unpredictability that can practically make strong men cry. When will they show? How far out? Can they be chummed to the surface? The answers change every year. But usually they start arriving sometime in August, anywhere from 30 to 120 miles offshore. If the skipper has luck on his side, he'll be able to circle the school of fish after getting a strike on a trolled jig, allowing deckhands to chum the fish up.

When it happens, it is among the most exciting moments in California fishing. When it doesn't, it is a dry piece of life.

---

2.   **MALIBU PIER**

Reference: West of Los Angeles in Malibu; map I4 grid c5.
How to get there: From Los Angeles, turn west on the Santa Monica Freeway (Interstate 10) and continue until it turns into Highway 1. Continue west to Alice's Restaurant at Malibu; the pier is directly off the highway.
Facilities: Benches, a tackle shop, a concession stand, tackle rentals, benches, and fish-cleaning tables are available.
Cost: Access is free.
Who to contact: Phone the Malibu Pier at (310) 456-8030.

About Malibu Pier: This area is known more for its beach-house residents, who turn out to be a definitive list of the rich and famous. For many visitors, that tends to overshadow the Malibu Pier, but for anglers without boats, it is the fishing that is attractive, not the chance of seeing a superstar jogging down the beach. Over the course of a year, Malibu Pier gets a huge variety of fish, and all sizes too. The biggest are sharks (many species), halibut and white seabass, and though rare, they provide a chance at a top prize. More abundant are perch, bass, corvina and sargo. In the summer, schools of mackerel can move in and anyone with a line in the water can hook up. The best prospects are in late spring and early summer, when the ocean has calmed down and baitfish are roaming the area. That starts attracting the larger species in the vicinity of the pier.

---

3. SANTA MONICA MUNICIPAL PIER

Reference: In Santa Monica; map I4 grid c6.
How to get there: From Los Angeles, drive west on the Santa Monica Freeway (Interstate 10). Take Lincoln Boulevard exit. Turn right on Lincoln and continue to Colorado. Turn left and continue to the pier.
Facilities: Restrooms, benches and fish-cleaning sinks are provided. Limited bait and tackle is available on the pier. Numerous shops and restaurants are located nearby.
Cost: A fee is charged for parking.
Who to contact: Phone the pier office at (310) 458-8689.
About Santa Monica Municipal Pier: The marine habitat in any coastal area determines the variety of fish available. Off Santa Monica, it is primarily a sand bottom, and that, in turn, dictates what fish you might catch. For the most part, anglers at this pier catch opaleye, surfperch, kelp bass and sargo. It's not great. It's not bad. It is a fair year-round fishery that produces a few fish as long as the ocean surge is not too great.

---

4. REDONDO BEACH PIER

Reference: Southwest of Los Angeles at Redondo Beach; map I4 grid e7.
How to get there: From Los Angeles, drive south on Interstate 110. Take the 190th Street exit and continue west until the street deadends at the beach on Harbor Drive. Turn left on Harbor Drive and continue to the pier.
Facilities: Restrooms, benches, fish-cleaning tables, a tackle shop, a restaurant and bait and tackle are available.
Cost: Access is free.
Who to contact: Phone Redondo Beach Sportfishing at (310) 372-2111.

About Redondo Beach Pier: When the bonito are in, Redondo provides one of the great inshore fisheries on the Pacific coast. Schools of them will roam the harbor, searching for anchovies, and the angler that has the opportunity to offer them one can have some exciting hookups. They are most abundant in the summer months. In the spring and early summer, halibut provide another quality fishery, though it can take time, persistence and skill to get a keeper. One wildcard at Redondo are the sharks and rays. Don't overlook them. The bat rays in particular get quite large, have tremendous strength and initial runs, and provide a good longshot during the winter months.

5. MANHATTAN BEACH MUNICIPAL PIER

Reference: Southwest of Los Angeles at Manhattan Beach; map 14 grid e7.

How to get there: From Interstate 405 near Manhattan Beach, take the Inglewood Avenue exit. Turn south and continue to Manhattan Beach Boulevard, then turn west and continue to the pier at the end of the street.

Facilities: Restrooms, benches and fish-cleaning sinks are provided. A bait shop is available.

Cost: There is a fee charged for parking.

Who to contact: Phone the Manhattan Beach City Department of Parks and Recreation at (310) 545-5621, ext. 550.

About Manhattan Beach Municipal Pier: This is the newest fishing pier on the South Coast, opening in early '92, and anglers are discovering a series of seasonal fisheries available. In the spring and early summer, halibut roam this area, providing a rare hope. In the summer, there are larger numbers of mackerel and shark in the area, the best prospects of the year. In the winter, perch and rare-but-large bat rays are the best prospects. Because the fisheries are in a perpetual cycle here, fishing success has great fluctuations. When it's good, you'll wonder, "Why didn't they build this pier long ago?" When it's bad, you'll counter, "Why did they built it at all?"

6. HERMOSA BEACH MUNICIPAL PIER

Reference: North of Redondo Beach at Hermosa Beach; map I4 grid e7.

How to get there: From Interstate 405 south of Los Angeles, take the Artesia Boulevard exit. Turn west and continue to Highway 1. Turn south and drive a short distance to Pier Avenue. Turn right and travel west to the pier.

Facilities: Restrooms, benches and fish-cleaning tables are provided. A bait shop is located nearby.

Cost: Access is free.

Who to contact: Phone (310) 376-0951.

About Hermosa Beach Municipal Pier: At Hermosa Beach Pier, you get a chance for something big, and a chance for something small. Big? Sharks, bat rays, halibut, even a rare white sea bass roam this area. Small? Surfperch, mackerel and bonito can arrive in large numbers. Most people arrive with modest expectations, hoping to catch a few perch, but always ready for something better. It is most likely to happen in the summer, when bonito and sharks are most abundant in the area. Wild cards? Bat rays and halibut. In the winter and spring, respectively, keep the chance of hooking one in the back of your mind.

MAP I5

SO-CAL MAP ....see page 656
adjoining maps
NORTH (H5) ......see page 648
EAST (I6) ....see page 684
SOUTH (J5) ....see page 706
WEST (I4)...........see page 662

23 LISTINGS
PAGES 668-683

SOUTHERN CALIFORNIA (P. 656)

1. BIG TUJUNGA CREEK

Reference: North of Los Angeles in Angeles National Forest; map I5 grid a1.

How to get there: From Interstate 5, turn east on Interstate 210. Take the Foothill Boulevard exit and drive to Sunland. Turn north on Sunland Boulevard and drive to Mount Gleason Avenue. Creek access is available directly off Mount Gleason Avenue. To reach the upper section of the creek, continue east on Interstate 210 to the Highway 2-Angeles Crest Highway exit. Turn north and travel to Clear Creek Station. Bear left and drive north on Angeles Forest Highway. Continue past Monte Cristo Station and look for the signed turnoff on the right for Upper Big Tujunga Canyon Road. Turn south and continue to the creek.

Facilities: Several campgrounds are available in the vicinity. Supplies can be obtained in surrounding towns.

Cost: Access is free.

Who to contact: Phone the Angeles National Forest District Office at (818) 899-1900. For a map, send $2 to the Office of Information, U.S. Forest Service, 630 Sansome Street, San Francisco, CA 94111.

About Big Tujunga Creek: If you can't wait for the Sierra Nevada deep freeze to defrost in the springtime, Angeles National Forest provides several possibilities for camper/anglers. One of the best is Big Tujunga Creek, which is located near the L.A. Basin, yet provides decent trout fishing and camping. It is stocked with rainbow trout in several sections, with most of the fish in the seven to eight-inch range. The lower section of Big Tujunga receives 8,400 trout, being planted at public access points along Mount Gleason Avenue, north of Sunland. The upper section of the creek gets 2,100 trout, planted along Upper Big Tujunga Creek Road, from a half-mile above old Wickiup Camp to one mile above Alder Creek. Got it? OK, then give the stream a try from spring to early summer, when it is planted. By summer, the flows have dropped to a trickle, plants are discontinued, and by then, you can make that trip to the Sierra.

2. BIG ROCK CREEK

Reference: Northeast of Los Angeles in Angeles National Forest; map I5 grid a7.

How to get there: From Los Angeles, drive north on Interstate 5 to the Highway 14 exit. Turn east and continue northeast to Palmdale. Take the Highway 138 exit and turn east. Continue for 15 miles to Pearblossom. Turn south on Longview Road and drive a short distance to Valyermo Road. Turn east and drive about six miles, passing through

Valyermo, to Big Rock Creek Road. Turn right and drive south up the canyon. Direct access is available off the road.

Facilities: Campgrounds are available on Big Rock Creek Road. Supplies are available in Pearblossom.

Cost: Access is free.

Who to contact: Phone the Angeles National Forest District Office at (805) 944-2187. For a map, send $2 to the Office of Information, U.S. Forest Service, 630 Sansome Street, San Francisco, CA 94111.

About Big Rock Creek: Is the ground shaking? Yes? Well, it's not likely to be from the mass celebration over the fishing. This stream is located in the San Andreas Rift Zone on the northern flank of the San Gabriel Mountains, where a little give-and-take along the fault line comes with the territory. So does a chance for stream trout fishing during the spring months when river flows are decent. That is when 8,400 rainbow trout are stocked in Big Rock Creek, most in the seven to eight-inch class. Where? Where? This is where: From the border of Angeles National Forest on upstream about two miles. Get it right.

---

3. ARROYO SECO CREEK

Reference: North of Pasadena in Angeles National Forest; map I5 grid b1.

How to get there: From Interstate 210 north of Pasadena, take the Highway 2-Angeles Crest Highway exit. Turn north and drive to the Switzer Forest Service Station. Access is available at the campground.

Facilities: A campground is available. Supplies can be obtained in surrounding towns.

Cost: Access is free.

Who to contact: Phone the Angeles National Forest District Office at (818) 790-1151.

About Arroyo Seco Creek: I discovered this little stream by accident. After giving a seminar, I got lost in Pasadena (What? Me get lost?), felt overwhelmed by the traffic, and decided to hell with everything. I just headed straight toward the mountains. It wasn't long before the traffic was left behind, and instead this little stream flowed alongside the road. I parked at the little camp near the Forest Service station, just to watch the water roll by and get my bearings. Suddenly, I saw a trout roll. I couldn't believe it. Believe it. I quickly retrieved my rod, then caught a few of them, which provided a nice boost after such a frustrating day. Later, I found out that Arroyo Seco Creek is stocked with 3,330 trout averaging seven to eight inches every spring, with the plants being made right at the campground. After looking at a map, I also realized that when driving through Pasadena, I had been going in exactly the wrong direction. I've never been lost, just a little confused.

4. NORTH FORK SAN GABRIEL RIVER

Reference: North of Azusa in Angeles National Forest; map I5 grid b5.

How to get there: From Interstate 210 near Azusa, take the Azusa Canyon exit and drive north on Highway 39 (San Gabriel Canyon Road). Continue north past San Gabriel Reservoir. Direct access is available off the highway.

Facilities: A campground is available 18 miles north of Azusa. Supplies can be obtained in Azusa.

Cost: Access is free.

Who to contact: Phone the Angeles National Forest District Office at (818) 335-1251.

About North Fork San Gabriel River: The San Gabriel River is the most famous trout stream in Angeles National Forest, but the North Fork is the least known and least fished section of it. (The East Fork gets most of the fishing pressure). The best section of water here is three miles upstream from its confluence with the West Fork San Gabriel (see listing). This spot is stocked with 6,000 trout in the seven to eight-inch class when river flows are decent in the spring. Access is easy here, and little Crystal Lake to the north provides a nearby option.

---

5. WEST FORK SAN GABRIEL RIVER

Reference: Northeast of Los Angeles in Angeles National Forest; map I5 grid b5.

How to get there: From Interstate 210 near Azusa, take the Azusa Canyon exit and turn north on Highway 39 (San Gabriel Canyon Road). Continue north, past the Rincon Guard Station. You can park at the mouth of the West Fork and fish upstream.

Facilities: No facilities are available on the river. Supplies and lodging are available in Azusa and surrounding towns.

Cost: Access is free.

Who to contact: Phone the Angeles National Forest District Office at (818) 335-1251.

About West Fork San Gabriel River: Of the three forks of the San Gabriel River, this is the place to come if you like to hike and have the option for catch-and-release fishing for wild trout. After parking, the best strategy is to hike upstream. The first piece of water, from the mouth of the West Fork on upstream to the second bridge, is stocked with rainbow trout. The DFG plunks in 15,000 trout per year here, with the fish in the seven to eight-inch class. Once you pass the second bridge, however, it is time to change your focus and your methods. From the second bridge on up 4.5 miles to Cogswell Reservoir, this is a designated wild trout stream with catch-and-release fishing. The best of both worlds? Not quite, but considering it is in the Angeles National Forest, it is plenty good enough.

6. CRYSTAL LAKE

Reference: Northeast of Los Angeles in Angeles National Forest; map I5 grid b6.

How to get there: From Los Angeles, take Interstate 210 east to the Highway 39 offramp at West Covina. Or, from Interstate 210, take the Azusa Canyon exit. Turn north on Highway 39 (San Gabriel Canyon Road) and drive about 20 miles north to the signed turnoff for Crystal Lake on the right.

Facilities: A campground, picnic areas, a grocery store, and a visitor information center are available. No motors are permitted on the lake.

Cost: Access is free.

Who to contact: Phone the Angeles National Forest District Office at (818) 335-1251.

About Crystal Lake: Little Crystal Lake is more of a pond than a lake, a little dot of water set deep in the San Gabriel Mountains. But it provides a chance at trout fishing during the cool months. When the lake fills from rains in the late winter, the Department of Fish and Game responds by stocking it with rainbow trout. It receives 3,000 trout averaging six and seven inches, 8,000 averaging nine and ten inches, and a bonus allotment of 2,000 more in the foot-long class. As long as water conditions are suitable, they will continue the plants. This is not the place to bring a boat, but a spot to fish from shore using standard baitdunking techniques, or a place to plop a small raft in and paddle about.

7. EAST FORK SAN GABRIEL

Reference: North of Azusa in Angeles National Forest; map I5 grid b6.

How to get there: From Interstate 210 near Azusa, take the Azusa Canyon exit and turn north on Highway 39 (San Gabriel Canyon Road). Continue to the north end of San Gabriel Reservoir and turn right on East Fork Road. Drive east; direct access is available along the road.

Facilities: No facilities are available on the river.

Cost: Access is free.

Who to contact: Phone the Angeles National Forest District Office at (818) 335-1251.

About East Fork San Gabriel River: Most anglers from the L.A. area who want mountain-style trout fishing without a long drive make the direct connection to the East Fork of the San Gabriel River. Why?

Because access is easy, and the trout are often willing and abundant. The river is stocked with 33,000 rainbow trout per year, with the trout in the seven to eight-inch class. All of these fish are planted in a relatively short section of stream: From the mouth of the West Fork on upstream three miles to the Cattle Canyon Guard Station. As you drive along the road, the best access points are obvious. This is an ideal place to make a quick hit, catch a trout, drive a little, then hit again.

8.   PECK ROAD PARK LAKE

Reference: East of Los Angeles in Arcadia; map I5 grid c3.

How to get there: From Los Angeles, drive east on Interstate 10 to the Peck Road exit. Turn north on Peck Road and drive 2.5 miles to Peck Road Park on the left. Watch for the signed turnoff.

Facilities: A parking lot, restrooms and picnic areas are provided. No boating is permitted on the lake.

Cost: There is an entrance fee at the park.

Who to contact: Phone the park at (818) 448-7317, or the Los Angeles County Department of Parks and Recreation District Office at (818) 444-1872.

About Peck Road Park Lake: This lake is a good example of how large stocks of rainbow trout can turn an urban water hole into a viable fishery. And stocks it gets. As soon as the weather turns cool enough in the fall, the plants start. It receives 20,000 rainbow trout in the 10-inch class, another 6,000 a little smaller and another 2,000 a little bigger. That adds up to 28,000 trout—fair numbers for a small lake. Santa Fe Reservoir to the nearby east provides another option, and is a more popular destination because it provides for boating. When the weather heats up the water temperature in the spring, the plants stop at Peck Lake, and this lake reverts to a skunk hole.

9.   SANTA FE RESERVOIR

Reference: East of Los Angeles in Irwindale; map I5 grid c4.

How to get there: From Los Angeles, drive east on Interstate 10 to Interstate 605. Turn north and travel to the Live Oak exit. Turn right and follow the signs to the park.

Facilities: A picnic area, a boat ramp, rowboat rentals, a concession stand and bait are available. No gasoline motors are permitted. Boats under eight or over 16 feet are prohibited.

Cost: Entrance fee is $5 per vehicle. There is a charge for boat launching.

Who to contact: Phone the Santa Fe Dam Recreational Area at (818) 334-1065. For fishing information, phone (818) 334-0713.

About Santa Fe Reservoir: This lake was built as a flood control area for the San Gabriel River. Flood? What's a flood? Nobody around has ever heard that word. Given a fair shot of rainfall in the San Gabriel Mountains, then decent water releases from San Gabriel and Monis reservoirs, and the Santa Fe Dam has enough water to provide a viable urban trout fishery. It is stocked from late fall through early spring with 36,000 rainbow trout. The breakdown is 24,000 in the seven to eight-inch class, and another 10,000 in the 10 to 11-inch range. Since the lake has a boat ramp, it is more desirable to many than nearby Peck Lake to the west.

---

10. LEGG LAKES

Reference: South of El Monte at Whittier Narrows Recreation Area; map I5 grid d2.

How to get there: From Interstate 605, take the Highway 60 exit and head west. Take the Santa Anita Avenue exit and continue south to the park.

Facilities: A boat ramp, boat rentals, bait, and a concession stand are available. The concession stand is available on weekends only. No private boats are permitted.

Cost: Entrance fee is $2 per vehicle on weekends; free on weekdays.

Who to contact: Phone Whittier Narrows Recreation Area at (818) 444-9305.

About Legg Lakes: The little Legg Lakes are actually three connected ponds, built as a flood-control area, set in the middle of mass urbanity—surrounded by Montebello, Pico Rivera, Whittier and South El Monte. The lakes are similar in fishing quality to the other urban lakes set along the San Gabriel River (Peck Lake and Santa Fe Lake). They are stocked with rainbow trout as long as the water temperature is cool enough to provide suitable conditions. From fall through spring, the lake gets 27,000 trout in the seven to eight-inch class, along with another 12,000 ranging to 11 inches. No swimming is permitted here, not that you are in danger of getting pulled into the water by one of these planted behemoths.

---

11. PUDDINGSTONE LAKE

Reference: In San Dimas at Frank G. Bonnelli Regional County Park; map I5 grid d6

How to get there: From Pomona, drive five miles west on Interstate 10 to the Fairplex exit. Turn north and continue to Via Verde, then turn left. Travel to the first stop sign and turn right to enter the park.

Facilities: A campground, picnic areas, a boat ramp, boat rentals, a concession stand, bait, tackle, and groceries are available. Non-motorized boats under eight feet and motorized boats under 12 feet are prohibited.

Cost: Day-use fee is $5 per vehicle.

Who to contact: Phone the park at (714) 599-8411; Puddingstone Boat Rentals, (714) 599-2667; guide Gregg Silks, (714) 987-7721.

About Puddingstone Lake: The "old mud puddle" provides a good chance to catch bass and trout during the morning and evening and waterski during the day. That's not too shabby considering the lake is located within such short proximity of millions of people. It is set just south of Raging Waters in San Dimas, bordered on its southern side by Bonnelli Regional Park.

When full, the lake covers 250 acres, and is an excellent destination during the winter and spring months. As soon as the weather turns cold, the general public abandons the place—the waterskiers included. Yet that is when the trout plants start up, and they are generous: the lake gets 64,000 rainbow trout from fall through spring. The breakdown is 36,000 trout in the eight-inch class, 28,000 to 11 inches. They provide good catch rates for shoreliners and trollers alike.

As the warm weather begins to arrive, usually in late February here, the bass fishing gets quite good. The water is still too cool for waterskiers, but not too cool for the bass to bite. The best areas are around the docks, and the underwater dropoffs, as deep as 40 to 50 feet deep in the winter, 15 to 20 feet deep in the early spring, then quite shallow from mid-March through early April. The lake record bass weighed 14 pounds, 12 ounces, but most are in the 10 to 13-inch class.

By May this lake begins to turn into a hell hole. From May through early September, folks suddenly remember how much fun it is to go boating and nearby Puddingstone provides an easy-to-reach outlet for it. Even though the lake is small, waterskiing is allowed and the skiers dominate the place. The lake is managed as a park and the rules permit waterskiing between 10 a.m. and 5 p.m., so know-hows fish from dawn to 10 a.m., then from 5 p.m. to sunset.

The nickname of the lake, as mentioned, is the "old mud puddle." That is because after particularly intense rains, runoff from the southern slopes of the San Gabriel Mountains muddies up the lake significantly. When that occurs, the fishing turns off. But how often does it rain that much around here for that to be a factor? Not too often. The ideal situation is a moderate rain, which clears the air, allowing anglers an excellent view of the mountains to the north, and freshens the lake. During the summer, it gets so smoggy in this area that the mountains are often not even visible. When that happens, no problem—just leave the lake to the waterskiers. After all, from fall through spring is the prime time here for anglers.

12. PRADO PARK LAKE

Reference: Near Corona in Prado Regional Park; map I5 grid e7.

How to get there: From Highway 91, take the Highway 71 exit north. Drive 4 miles to Euclid Avenue, then turn west and continue to the park.

Facilities: A campground, a picnic area, a boat ramp, and boat rentals are available. No gasoline motors or inflatables are permitted.

Cost: Day-use fee is $4 per vehicle. There is a charge for boat launching.

Who to contact: Phone Prado Regional Park at (714) 597-4260.

About Prado Park Lake: This little lake is a backyard fishing hole for folks in Corona and Norco. It doesn't look like much in the summer, and it doesn't produce much either. But in the early winter, it undergoes a complete transformation. A little rain, cold temperatures, and the water becomes oxygenated and cool. The Department of Fish and Game steps in and starts planting rainbow trout, and keeps at it until hot weather closes the door in April. Prado receives 12,000 trout in the eight-inch class and 11,000 in the 11-inch class, fair numbers for such a small lake. By boat or bank, most folks here have the best luck by baitfishing.

---

13. LOS ANGELES DEEP SEA

Reference: From San Pedro to San Clemente; map I5 grid fØ.

How to get to San Pedro Harbor: From Los Angeles, drive south on Interstate 110-Harbor Freeway to San Pedro. Turn left on Gaffey Street and travel to 22nd Street. Continue for 4.5 blocks to 22nd Street Landing. To reach L.A. Harbor Sportfishing, drive south on Harbor Freeway until it deadends, then exit at Harbor Boulevard. Continue to #79 in the Port O'Call Village.

How to get to Long Beach Harbor: From Los Angeles, drive south on Interstate 405 to Long Beach. Exit at Seal Beach Boulevard and turn west. Continue to Seal Beach Sportfishing at the end of the pier. Belmont Pier Sportfishing is located one pier over. To reach Long Beach Sportfishing, drive south on the Long Beach Freeway. Bear right at the sign for Long Beach Port-Queen Mary and take the Pico Avenue exit. Continue to Long Beach Sportfishing at 555 Pico Avenue.

How to get to Newport Harbor: From Los Angeles, take Interstate 405 to Highway 55. Drive south to Newport Beach, where the highway becomes Newport Boulevard. Continue past Highway 1. About one-quarter mile past the bridge, Newport Boulevard becomes Balboa Boulevard. Travel one mile on Balboa to Adams Street, then turn and continue to Newport Landing Sportfishing at 309 Palm Street. To reach

Davey's Locker, proceed as above to Balboa Boulevard and continue to Main Street. Turn west and continue to 400 Main Street.

How to get to Dana Point Harbor: From Los Angeles, drive south on Interstate 5. Continue through Mission Viejo and San Juan Capistrano, then take the Pacific Coast Highway-Dana Point Harbor offramp. Continue to Del Obispo and turn left. Continue through two more signals, then turn left again; the street will lead you directly to Dana Wharf Sportfishing.

Facilities: Lodging, campgrounds, piers, restaurants, shops, bait, tackle, and groceries are available all along the coast. Boat ramps are at the following locations: In San Pedro, at Cabrillo Beach, (310) 548-7738; in Long Beach, at Golden Shores, Marine Stadium and Davies Launch Ramp, phone (310) 437-0375; in Seal Beach, at Sunset Aquatic Marina, (310) 592-2833; in Newport Beach, at the Newport Dunes Marina, (714) 729-1100; in Dana Point, at Embarcadero Marina, (714) 496-6177. Embarcadero Marina offers a sling hoist and boat rentals as well. Motorboat rentals are also available at Davey's Locker in Newport Beach, (714) 673-1434.

Cost: Party boat fees range from $20-$75 per person. Parking and/or boat launching fees are charged at most marinas and launch ramps.

Who to contact: For general information, phone the San Pedro Chamber of Commerce, (310) 832-7272; Long Beach Visitors Bureau, (800) 452-7829; Newport Beach Visitors Bureau, (714) 644-1190; Dana Point Chamber of Commerce, (714) 496-1555. For fishing information, phone any of the sportfishing operations listed below.

San Pedro boats: Shogun, Outer Limit, First String, Sport King, Matt Walsh, Top Gun, Pacifica; reservations through L.A. Harbor Sportfishing, (310) 547-9916. *New Image, Islander, Monte Carlo, Grande, Freedom;* reservations through 22nd Street Landing, (310) 832-8304.

Long Beach boats: Enterprise, City of Seal Beach; reservations through Seal Beach Pier Sportfishing, (310) 598-8677. *Eldorado, G.W., Sundown;* reservations through Belmont Pier Sportfishing, (310) 434-6781. *Southern Cal, Tornado, Aztec, Real Special, Phantom, Sharpshooter, Victory;* reservations through Long Beach Sportfishing, (310) 432-8993.

Newport boats: Amigo, Nautilus, Patriot; reservations through Newport Landing, (714) 675-0550. *Thunderbird, Freelance, Western Pride, California Dawn, Bongo, Andele;* reservations through Davey's Locker, (714) 673-1434.

Dana Point boats: Sea Horse, Clemente, Sum Fun, Reel Fun; reservations through Dana Wharf Sportfishing, (714) 496-5794.

About Los Angeles Deep Sea: The closest thing to freedom in Southern California is on the open ocean, cruising across the smooth briny green to a favorite fishing spot. No traffic jams, no stoplights, no concrete, no angry people and no problems. Just the open sea, the friendly hum of the boat engine and a clean wake as you leave your troubles behind back on the mainland.

This stretch of coast not only offers the opportunity for peace of mind, but a varied and sometimes excellent fishery as well. The variety is tremendous: Inshore kelp beds, mud/sand bottoms, bays, shallow and deepwater reefs, underwater canyons, and along the mainland and several piers set in the path of passing fish. Four major sportfishing centers are located at San Pedro, Long Beach, Newport and Dana Point. Between them, dozens of sportfishing charters are available, offering trips covering the complete spectrum of Southern California saltwater angling.

It is marine habitat, of course, that determines the species of fish available. In turn, the diversity of habitat here means that a huge variety of fish are available. It makes it a take-your-pick kind of deal. Here is a capsule listing:

—Inshore kelp beds: Taking a boat out and fishing around kelp beds can provide good action for a large number of species. The areas where kelp beds are located include just off Point Vicente, just off Royal Palms State Beach, south of Newport, and northwest of Laguna Beach. Another kelp bed is just south of Los Angeles Harbor, yet is virtually submerged, making it more difficult to locate. Several more kelp beds are located along the inshore coast south of Dana Point, both between San Clemente and Dana Harbor, and also between San Clemente and San Mateo Point. While most of the fish are not large, they are usually abundant, and can be caught on light tackle and jigs. In the summer months there is always the chance of a bonus, of catching one of the larger species. The most common species are kelp bass, sand bass, and many kinds of rockfish including olive, grass and vermillion rockfish. Sheephead are also a resident fish of these areas. In the summer, barracuda, and even more rarely, white seabass are caught. If you have the luck of hooking one of the latter while fishing for the former, believe me, you will have your hands full.

—Mud and sand bottom: Halibut arrive in large numbers every spring and can provide good fishing through the summer where the sea bottom is flat and made of mud or sand. While halibut were hammered in shallow areas by netters in the 1980s, there is a real opportunity for population increases as the netters are moved out to deeper water in the 1990s. Some of the better spots for halibut are just offshore Huntington Beach, just off Point Fermin and also in San Pedro Bay.

—Inshore bays: Anglers who own their own boats have the opportunity to fish a number of bays that attract primarily sharks, rays, some perch, and sometimes in the summer, mackerel and bonito. In the best of years during the spring and early summer, halibut fishing is the top prize, such as in San Pedro Bay, and a bonus of a variety of saltwater bass make Newport Bay attractive. Other good areas are at Alamitos and Seal Beach.

—Shallow and deepwater reefs: The problem is not with the number of rockfish at the reefs, it is their depth. Sometimes it is necessary to fish very deep to catch quality rockfish and lingcod at the reefs in this area, too deep to make it much fun. The best spots are at the Lasuen Seamount, better known as the 14-Mile Bank, located about 20 miles southwest of Newport Beach, the 50-fathom line west of Huntington Beach, and also in the deep water off Laguna Beach. The largest area of rockfish habitat is between the 50 and 100 fathom lines west of Huntington Beach, with the larger and more desirable red rockfish in the deeper water here.

—Underwater canyons: A series of underwater canyons provide occasional migratory routes for a variety of somewhat rare but alluring species. The most famous is the Newport Submarine Canyon, located directly southwest of the pier at Newport Beach, and to the north is the Santa Monica Canyon in the center of Santa Monica Bay, Redondo Canyon directly west of Redondo Beach Pier, and also Hueneme Canyon located directly west of Port Hueneme off Oxnard (see Zone-I3). During years when the ocean temperatures are cool, schools of salmon roam up through these canyons in March and early April. During years when the ocean temperatures are warm, the prized striped marlin and even schools of tuna cruise through in late summer. If either occurs, do not miss out; it is a rare opportunity.

---

14.   BELMONT PIER

Reference: In Long Beach; map I5 grid fØ.

How to get there: From Interstate 405 at Long Beach, take the 7th Street exit. Loop around and drive about three miles to Terminal Avenue. Turn left and continue to the pier at the end of the street.

Facilities: Restrooms, a bait shop, a concession stand, picnic tables, and fish-cleaning sinks are available.

Cost: Access is free.

Who to contact: Phone Belmont Pier Sportfishing at (310) 434-6781.

About Belmont Pier: The pier gets a variety of small fish, the most common being kingfish, perch, and in the late winter and spring, jacksmelt.

15.   SEAL BEACH PIER

Reference: At Seal Beach; map I5 grid g1.

How to get there: From Huntington Beach, drive north on Highway 1 to Seal Beach. Turn left on Main Street and drive about two blocks to the pier at the end of the street.

Facilities: Restrooms, a restaurant, benches, and fish-cleaning areas are available. Bait can be obtained nearby.

Cost: Access is free.

Who to contact: Phone Seal Beach Pier Sportfishing at (310) 598-8677.

About Seal Beach Pier: Anglers have a longshot for a halibut at this pier, with the nearshore area one of the better areas for halibut along the coast. Perch, kingfish, jacksmelt, and sharks are more common.

16.   IRVINE LAKE

Reference: Southeast of Los Angeles; map I5 grid g5.

How to get there: From Interstate 5 east of Los Angeles, take the Highway 91 exit east. Drive about nine miles to Highway 55. Turn south and drive four miles to Chapman Avenue, then turn east and travel nine miles. Chapman Avenue will become Santiago Canyon Road. The lake is on the left.

Facilities: A boat ramp, boat rentals, and picnic tables are available.

Cost: Fishing fee is $10 per person. There is a fee for boat launching.

Who to contact: Phone the lake at (714) 649-2991.

About Irvine Lake: Instead of searching across miles and miles of country to catch a fish, at Irvine Lake, you get the opposite approach: They bring the fish to you. At Irvine Lake, a $10 access fee is charged, which is turned around and used in part to purchase stocks of huge trout in the winter and huge catfish in the summer. How big? Well, it is kind of mind-boggling, with rainbow trout in the 10-pound class and a lake-record catfish of 59 pounds. Bluegill, crappie and largemouth bass are also in the lake.

It's not the prettiest place in the world, but when the big fish start biting, that can be overlooked. The chosen species is dependent on water temperature, with the trout plants going in from mid-November through March when the water is cool, and the big catfish the rest of the year when the water is warm. Almost never is a trout under a foot stocked in the lake; they leave the dinkers to the DFG. Most of the fish are caught on bait.

It is the ultimate put-and-take fishery, with the fish often so big that it can be a real mind-bender. On a trip to Alaska's famed Kulik River, I ran into world-class flyfisher Ed Rice, and it wasn't long before we started discussing the size of Alaska's rainbow trout. Then he smiled and said, "You want to know where the biggest trout in the world are? They aren't in Alaska. They're at that Irvine Lake in Los Angeles." We both laughed. After all, he was right.

17. HUNTINGTON PIER

Reference: At Huntington Beach; map I5 grid h2.

How to get there: From Laguna Beach, drive north on Highway 1 to Huntington Beach. The pier is located at the intersection of Highway 1 and Main Street, about one mile north of Beach Boulevard.

Facilities: A bait shop, restrooms, benches, and fish-cleaning areas are available.

Cost: Access is free.

Who to contact: Phone the Huntington Beach Visitors Bureau, Beach Division, at (714) 536-5511.

About Huntington Pier: This pier was rebuilt, opening in summer of 1992. It is set in an area that has both good numbers of halibut in the spring, and resident populations of sand bass. If you get lonely, kingfish are usually around to keep you company.

18. NEWPORT PIER

Reference: At Newport Beach; map I5 grid h2.

How to get there: From Highway 1 at Newport Beach, turn west on Newport Boulevard and continue to the pier.

Facilities: Restrooms, fish-cleaning sinks and picnic areas are available. Supplies can be obtained in Newport Beach.

Cost: Access is free.

Who to contact: Phone the Newport Marine Department at (714) 644-3044.

About Newport Pier: This spot is set just on the edge of the Newport Canyon, providing a chance for a wider variety of fish to roam within casting range than at many piers. In addition to the typical parade of kingfish, perch, jacksmelt and sharks, there is also a chance for opaleye and a variety of rockfish. Pray a bit, maybe you'll get one.

19. BALBOA PIER

Reference: At Newport Beach; map I5 grid h2.

How to get there: From Highway 1 at Newport Beach, turn west on Newport Boulevard and continue to Balboa Pier, located about two miles south of Newport Pier.

Facilities: Restrooms and picnic areas are available. Supplies can be obtained in Newport Beach.

Cost: Access is free.

Who to contact: Phone the Newport Marine Department at (714) 644-3044.

About Balboa Pier: Balboa Pier gets less fishing pressure than at the nearby Newport Pier to the north. The primary species available are kingfish and perch, with some binges of jacksmelt in the spring, and rarely a large bat ray or shark.

---

20.   TRABUCO CREEK

Reference: East of Mission Viejo; map I5 grid h8.

How to get there: From Interstate 5 at El Toro, take the El Toro Road exit. Turn north and drive seven miles to Live Oak Canyon Road. Bear right and drive four miles to Trabuco Canyon Road. Turn left and drive east. Access is available upstream of O'Neill Park.

Facilities: A campground and limited supplies are available nearby at O'Neill Regional Park.

Cost: Access is free.

Who to contact: Phone the County Department of Parks and Recreation at (714) 854-2491; O'Neill Regional Park at (714) 858-9365.

About Trabuco Creek: A lot of folks overlook little Trabuco Creek. After all, most anglers from the L.A. area think the only nearby stream fishing is in the Los Angeles or San Bernardino national forests. Not so, not with Trabuco Creek flowing down the slopes of lesser-used Cleveland National Forest. The stream is decent only in the spring months, when flows can support planted trout. The DFG responds by stocking 4,500 trout in the seven to eight-inch class, and I will tell you where: They go in about 2.5 miles above O'Neill Park, with Trabuco Creek Road providing easy access.

---

21.   ALISO PIER

Reference: In South Laguna at Aliso Beach; map I5 grid i4.

How to get there: From Highway 1, drive to the south end of the town of Laguna Beach. The pier is directly off the highway.

Facilities: A concession stand, fish-cleaning sinks and bait are available on the pier. Picnic areas are nearby on the beach.

Cost: Access is free.

Who to contact: Phone Dana Point Harbor at (714) 661-7013.

About Aliso Pier: The Aliso Pier juts into the ocean in an area that has a sandy bottom. That attracts primarily perch, many species of them, as well as some sand bass and jacksmelt. Rarely some lucky fellow catches a halibut here.

22.   LAGUNA NIGUEL LAKE

Reference: In South Laguna; map I5 grid i6.

How to get there: From Interstate 5 near Mission Viejo, take the La Paz exit and turn south on La Paz Road. Continue for four miles to the park entrance.

Facilities: Picnic areas and a concession stand are available. No boating is permitted.

Cost: Entrance fee is $2 per vehicle.

Who to contact: Phone Laguna Niguel Regional Park at (714) 831-2791.

About Laguna Niguel Lake: In the spring, Laguna Niguel is a very pretty lake, being set in a canyon in the coastal foothills south of the L.A. Basin. It is the centerpiece for a regional park, a nice spot for picnics, walks, and folks who might want to toss out a fishing line and see what bites. It is a baitdunker's paradise, with no competition for boats. It is stocked with 25,000 rainbow trout from fall through spring; the breakdown is 15,000 in the eight-inch class, and 10,000 in the 11-inch class.

23.   SAN CLEMENTE PIER

Reference: South of San Juan Capistrano; map I5 grid j6.

How to get there: From Interstate 5 at San Clemente, take the Avenida Palazada exit. Turn right and continue to El Camino Real. Turn left and drive to Avenida del Mar, then turn right and continue to the parking lot at the beach. Walk across to the pier.

Facilities: Restrooms, a bait and tackle shop, a restaurant, and fish-cleaning sinks are available.

Cost: Parking fee is 75 cents per hour.

Who to contact: Phone the City of San Clemente, Marine Safety, at (714) 361-8200.

About San Clemente Pier: The stretch of shore surrounding San Clemente Pier is the classic sandy beach. As long as the inshore surge of the surf is light, a large variety of perch hold in the area. They are joined by the inevitable kingfish, some sharks, and rarely the prize of them all, halibut.

SO-CAL MAP ....see page 656
adjoining maps
NORTH.......................no map
EAST (I7) ....see page 698
SOUTH (J6)........see page 712
WEST (I5)...........see page 668

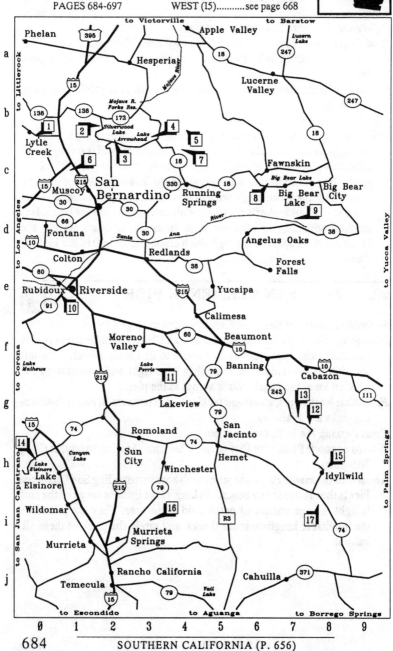

1.   LYTLE CREEK

Reference: Northwest of San Bernardino in San Bernardino National Forest; map I6 grid bØ.

How to get there: From San Bernardino, drive west on Highway 66 to Fontana. Turn north on Sierra Avenue and drive five miles, then continue north on Lytle Creek Road. Drive past the Lytle Creek Ranger Station to Forest Service Road 2N48. Turn left; access is available off the road. You may also continue north on Lytle Creek Road; the creek runs parallel to the road. Access is available in the vicinity of Apple White Campground.

Facilities: A campground is available. Supplies can be obtained in the San Bernardino area.

Cost: Access is free.

Who to contact: Phone the San Bernardino National Forest District Office at (714) 887-2576. For a map, send $2 to Office of Information, U.S. Forest Service, 630 Sansome Street, San Francisco, CA 94111.

About Lytle Creek: Most flat don't have a clue about this spot. One time I gave a seminar at the REI store in San Dimas, and out in the parking lot, somebody spotted the fishing rod in my rig, all ready to go. "What's that for?" he asked. I just smiled. The answer was Lytle Creek, a nice little stream that provides easy access, a feeling of separation from the mass of humanity in the valley below, and a chance to catch small rainbow trout.

   Nothing like a little inside knowledge. The stream is stocked at two key spots: 1) 2,700 rainbow trout (averaging seven to eight inches) along Forest Service Road 2N48, from the turnoff on upstream a mile or so. 2) 2,700 rainbow trout at Apple White Campground to the stream's juncture with the Middle Fork.

2.   SILVERWOOD LAKE

Reference: North of San Bernardino at Silverwood State Recreation Area; map I6 grid b2.

How to get there: From San Bernardino, drive north on Interstates 215 and 15 to the Silverwood Lake exit at Cajon Junction. Turn east on Highway 138 and continue for 12 miles to the lake. The boat ramp is located on the south shore of the lake.

Facilities: Campgrounds, a marina, a boat ramp, boat rentals, picnic areas, and bait are available at the lake. Supplies can be obtained in Cajon Junction or Crestline.

Cost: Day-use fee is $6; additional $5 if entering with a boat. There is a charge for boat launching.

Who to contact: Phone Silverwood Lake State Recreation Area, (619) 389-2303; Silverwood Lake Marina, (619) 389-2320.

About Silverwood Lake: Someone must have taken some smart pills when they made the boating rules at Silverwood Lake. All of the significant coves that provide good fishing have 5-mph speed limits and that is just what the doctor ordered to keep the waterskiers and anglers separated and happy.

Silverwood is set at 3,378 feet elevation, and when full to the brim, covers 1,000 acres with 13 miles of shoreline. Bordered by San Bernardino National Forest to the south and the high desert to the north, its proximity to San Bernardino to the south makes it very popular for boaters, especially during hot summers.

The best fishing is in the cooler months, when waterskiers are few and trout are plentiful. In the summer, that quotient is reversed. This lake does get large numbers of trout stocks, being planted with 83,000 trout per year; 54,000 averaging seven or eight inches, and 28,000 running larger to 11 inches. Survival and growth rates are high, since the water is imported from the Delta and is rich in aquatic food. From February through early June, the catch rates are similarly high. If it is a significant snow year, that schedule can be delayed by a month.

Silverwood not only has good trout fishing, but a decent population of largemouth bass and a sprinkling of bluegill, crappie and catfish, and a few striped bass. Most of the largemouth bass feed on shad minnows, and know-hows often will look for diving birds in the area before picking their spots. Water temperatures have huge swings here from winter through summer, and they have a large effect on the bass. The best fishing is usually in late March when the water temperature is climbing from 56 to 63 degrees during warm weather, and the bass start moving into the shallow areas, often in the backs of coves.

In addition to the five-mph speed limits in all of the major coves, several other boating rules keep the place relatively sane. The main lake area south of the dam is where waterskiing takes place, with a 35-mph speed limit. From October 1 through March 31, the lake is closed to boating from 7 p.m. to 7 a.m. From April 1 through September 30, it is closed to boating from 9 p.m. to 6 a.m. In other words, no night action.

---

3.   LAKE GREGORY

Reference: North of San Bernardino at Lake Gregory Regional Park; map I6 grid b2.

How to get there: From San Bernardino, drive north on Highway 18 to the town of Crestline. Turn northeast on Highway 138 and drive a short distance, then turn right on Lake Drive and continue east to the lake.

Facilities: A campground, a picnic area, rowboat rentals, a snack bar, a restaurant, groceries, and bait are available. No private boats may be launched; boating is restricted to rentals only.

Cost: Day-use fee is $2 per person.

Who to contact: Phone Lake Gregory Regional Park at (714) 338-2233.

About Lake Gregory: Little Lake Gregory is like the personal backyard fishing hole for a group of the lucky few who own vacation homes around the lake. The lake is set at 4,520 feet elevation, located just a short drive north of San Bernardino on the edge of San Bernardino National Forest. Silverwood Lake to the northwest and Lake Arrowhead to the east are larger lakes and provide nearby options.

Despite its relatively small size, Lake Gregory provides a viable brown trout fishery, one of the better in the region. The fishing is best for the browns trolling in the late winter and early spring. Once the hot weather shows up, they become very difficult to catch. To make up for that lapse, Fish and Game comes to the rescue with consistent trout plants of catchable-sized rainbow trout. The DFG stocks 36,000 rainbow trout averaging seven to eight inches, another 14,000 to 11 inches, and usually in the fall, plunk in 21,300 fingerling-sized brown trout.

This is a popular lake, one of the relatively few in California where you can buy lakeside property. The drive is a nice one, too, on Rim of the World Drive, a slow but pretty road, that adds a bit of suspense before your arrival.

---

4. LAKE ARROWHEAD

Reference: North of San Bernardino; map I6 grid b3.

How to get there: From San Bernardino, turn north on Highway 18 and drive 15 miles northeast to the town of Lake Arrowhead. Turn north on Daley Canyon Road and drive a short distance, then turn right on Highway 173 and continue east to the lake.

Facilities: Campgrounds are available near the lake. Lodging, a marina, boat rentals, tackle rentals, groceries, a snack bar, and bait are available at the lake. No public boat launching is permitted.

Cost: Access is free.

Who to contact: Phone Lake Arrowhead Marina at (714) 337-8451.

About Lake Arrowhead: For such a large, beautiful lake, it is amazing that the public does not demand better access. It is managed pretty much as a private reserve for members of the golf club and home association in the area. If you show up with a trailered boat, you will be told to turn around and go back home. Boat rentals to non-members, as well as camping access, is permitted.

Lake Arrowhead is set at 5,114 feet elevation, surrounded by a large grid of private land within San Bernardino National Forest. Waterskiing and sailing are the primary activities. Because it is a privately-managed facility, the DFG refuses to stock trout here—a smart move. As a result the lake has a sprinkling of a wide variety of species; some trout, kokanee salmon, bass, bluegill, crappie and even catfish. What to fish for? Because of the tremendous water temperature changes here during the year, each is a seasonal fishery: trout in the winter and early spring, bass from spring to early summer, then bluegill, crappie, and catfish in the summer and early fall.

---

5. HOLCOMB CREEK

Reference: Northeast of San Bernardino in San Bernardino National Forest; map I6 grid b4.

How to get there: From San Bernardino, turn north on Highway 18. Drive 15 miles to the Arrowhead Ranger Station. Continue 12 miles east to the town of Arrowhead Lake, then turn north on Green Valley Lake Road (Forest Service Road 3N16) and continue north to the creek crossing. A dirt road parallels the creek to the east.

Facilities: Campgrounds are available near the creek. Supplies can be obtained in Running Springs.

Cost: Access is free.

Who to contact: Phone the San Bernardino National Forest District Office at (714) 337-2444. For a map, send $2 to Office of Information, U.S. Forest Service, 630 Sansome Street, San Francisco, CA 94111.

About Holcomb Creek: Little Holcomb Creek may be the least-known fishing spot in this area. It starts deep in San Bernardino National Forest and tumbles its way downslope, actually crossing the Pacific Crest Trail at one point. You don't have to hike much, however, to fish the best stretch of water. It is stocked with 2,700 rainbow trout, mainly seven and eight-inchers, with plants made along Forest Service Road 3N16. The best area is at Crab Creek Crossing; sometimes plants are made where beaver ponds have dammed up small sections of river.

---

6. GLEN HELEN PARK LAKE

Reference: Northwest of San Bernardino at Glen Helen Regional Park; map I6 grid c1.

How to get there: From San Bernardino, turn north on Interstate 215 and drive north to the Devore exit at the intersection of Interstates 15 and 215. Turn left at the top of the ramp and continue to the stop sign. Proceed until you cross the railroad tracks, then turn on Devore Road and drive one mile to the park.

Facilities: A campground is located across the freeway. Restrooms and picnic areas are provided. Supplies can be obtained in San Bernardino. No boating is permitted on the lake.

Cost: Entrance fee is $4 per vehicle; fishing fee is $3-$4 per person.

Who to contact: Phone the park at (714) 880-2554 or (714) 880-2556.

About Glen Helen Park Lake: This tiny lake is a little baitdunker's haven, so small it is overlooked by most out-of-towners, yet it gets decent plants during the cool months. It is a veritable dot, with easy access, set little over a mile from the intersection of Interstates 15 and 215.

No boating is permitted, but no problem, because the lake is too small for that anyway. Instead, you show up with your bait and your bucket, take a seat and wait for a nibble. The nibbles are forthcoming after stocks of trout, which are made by both the local park district as well as the DFG. The state plunks in 15,000 trout averaging eight inches, and another 9,000 averaging 11 inches. A campground adds a new bonus option here, having been constructed in early 1992.

---

7. GREEN VALLEY LAKE

Reference: North of San Bernardino; map I6 grid c5.

How to get there: From San Bernardino, turn north on Highway 18. Drive 15 miles to the Arrowhead Ranger Station. Continue 12 miles east to the town of Arrowhead Lake, then turn north on Green Valley Lake Road and continue to the lake.

Facilities: A campground is available nearby. Picnic areas, a boat ramp, rowboat rentals, a snack bar, groceries, and bait are available at the lake. All motorized craft prohibited on the lake.

Cost: Fishing fee is $3 per person.

Who to contact: Phone the lake at (714) 867-7757.

About Green Valley Lake: This lake is small, pretty, and other than the regulars who either own property north of the lake or who just keep coming back, it is pretty much overlooked as well. It is located at 6,854 feet elevation in San Bernardino National Forest, and because of its proximity to nearby Lake Arrowhead to the west and Big Bear Lake to the east, many folks just don't get around to making the trip.

It's quiet and intimate, ideal for canoes and rowboats, as well as for shoreline baitdunkers. It is stocked by the Department of Fish and Game with 23,000 trout each year, most coming from spring through early summer. The breakdown is 15,000 in the seven to eight-inch class, and 8,000 averaging 10 or 11 inches. The lake also has some catfish which are sometimes caught by accident during the summer by trout fishermen using nightcrawlers for bait.

Reference: Northeast of San Bernardino in San Bernardino National Forest; map I6 grid c7.

How to get there: From San Bernardino, turn north on Highway 18. Drive 15 miles to the Arrowhead Ranger Station. Continue east for about 15 more miles to Big Bear Lake.

Facilities: Campgrounds, picnic areas, full-service marinas, a boat hoist, boat ramps, boat rentals, bait, tackle, and groceries are available. Boats under eight feet or over 26 feet are prohibited.

Cost: A boating permit, available at most marinas, must be obtained for all private boats; fee is $10 per day. There may be a fee for boat launching.

Who to contact: Phone Big Bear Marina at (714) 866-3218; Gray's Landing, (714) 866-2443.

About Big Bear Lake: Here is a lake that has it all: It is big and beautiful, has good trout fishing, quality boating opportunities, many campgrounds and a few resorts, and is located near the highest regions of San Bernardino National Forest. Alas, it also can have a lot of people. Like I said, it has it all.

It is set at 6,738 feet, with the Pacific Crest Trail passing just a few miles north of the lake, with easy trailhead access available. So if you want to bust away, you can.

The lake has unmatched beauty among the waters in the region, particularly in the spring when the snow is melting. The deep blue waters make a striking contrast with the surrounding white mountain tops. The lake covers over 3,000 acres, has 22 miles of shoreline, and is a faithful vacation destination, something like the Lake Tahoe of Southern California.

Trout fishing? It is often very good. Big Bear gets huge numbers of rainbow trout courtesy of Fish and Game: 75,000 averaging seven or eight inches, 44,000 averaging 10 or 11 inches, and 150,000 fingerlings. They join a good population of holdover fish from previous years' stocks, with survival rates quite good. The best results are slow trolling adjacent to the shoreline. In the summer, the fishery can become primarily an early morning/late evening affair, with the lake becoming the domain of waterskiers during mid-day. There are also a sprinkling of bass, bluegill, rarely a salmon, but few people focus on them.

Fish, boat, camp and hike, you can do it all here. Just don't expect to have the place to yourself.

9. SANTA ANA RIVER

Reference: East of Redlands in San Bernardino National Forest; map I6 grid d7.

How to get there: From Interstate 10 at Redlands, take the Highway 38 exit and turn east. Drive past Angeles Oaks to Seven Oaks Road and turn left; access is available off the road.

Facilities: Campgrounds are located off Highway 38. Supplies can be obtained in Redlands.

Cost: Access is free.

Who to contact: Phone the San Bernardino National Forest District Office at (714) 794-1123.

About Santa Ana River: This plumb ain't no secret. The Santa Ana River provides a trout stream alternative to the heavily-used Big Bear Lake to the nearby north, and a lot of people take advantage of it. Access is easy, trout stocks are quite high, and catch rates are decent enough.

How many trout are stocked? Get this: 36,000 in all, mostly seven and eight-inchers, week after week as long as water conditions are suitable to allow it. Where? From Seven Oaks on upstream about seven miles to the South Fork Bridge on Highway 38. Several turnouts provide direct access to the better spots.

---

10. LAKE EVANS

Reference: In Riverside in Fairmount Park; map I6 grid eØ.

How to get there: From Highway 60 at the north end of Riverside, take the Market Street exit. Turn left; the park will be directly on your right.

Facilities: Restrooms and picnic areas are provided. No motorized boats or inflatables are permitted. Boats under eight feet or over 15 feet are prohibited, with the exception of canoes. A free boating permit must be obtained at the park. Supplies are available in Riverside.

Cost: Access is free.

Who to contact: Phone the Riverside City Department of Parks and Recreation at (714) 782-5301; The Bass Connection in Riverside, (714) 785-7336.

About Lake Evans: The Department of Fish and Game's urban fishing program searches out little water holes, then by stocking trout, creates fisheries where otherwise none would exist. Lake Evans is a classic case, a tiny lake on the northern flank of Riverside, which would be barren without the plants. It receives 9,000 trout averaging eight inches, and another 4,000 in the 11-inch class.

Evans is a good spot to bring a small rowboat or canoe, then anchor and baitfish for trout. Shoreliners do decent enough during the cool

---

months. If there is a catch, it's monitoring water temperatures. This area gets smoking hot for weeks in the summer and fall, and during that time, you might as well fish in an empty bucket. The lake is small enough that it is kind of like fishing in a bucket anyway, but at least in late winter and spring, there are fish in that bucket.

---

11.   LAKE PERRIS

Reference: Southeast of Riverside at Lake Perris State Recreation Area; map I6 grid f3.

How to get there: From Riverside, turn south on Interstate 215 and drive about 11 miles. Take the Ramona Expressway exit and turn east. Continue to Lake Perris Drive, then turn left and continue to the park. Boat ramps are located on the north shore of the lake.

Facilities: A campground, picnic areas, a marina, boat ramps, boat rentals, a snack bar, bait, tackle, and groceries are available at the lake.

Cost: Day-use fee is $4 per vehicle.

Who to contact: Phone Lake Perris State Recreation Area at (714) 657-9000; Lake Perris Marina, (714) 657-2179; The Bass Connection, (714) 785-7336.

About Lake Perris: Legends can throw newcomers off the track, and the legend of Lake Perris as the No. 1 spotted bass lake in the world throws many anglers on a wild goose chase on their first adventure here.

Perris dominates the line-class world records kept by the International Game Fish Association (see listings in the Secrets of the Masters section) for spotted bass like no other water in the world for any species. But the big spotties are not as easy to catch as many think, and in their attempt to track down a monster, they overlook outstanding surface fishing for largemouth bass, and solid trout fishing.

The largemouth bass fishing here is much better than that for spotted bass, world records aside. It is an ideal place to learn how to fish the surface, either casting a floating Rapala, Zara Spook, Jitterbug or Chugger, or even flyfishing with a popper or mouse. As long as the water isn't too cold, the popping and plugging can produce excellent catch rates. In the warm months, get on the water early or late, and leave it to the waterskiers between 10:30 a.m. and 5 p.m.

I remember the first time I gave up on the spotted bass here and instead tried for largemouth one early summer morning. I caught and released nearly a dozen, and figured I'd really done something special. But back at the launch ramp at 11 a.m., it turned out nearly everyone was catching 10 to 15 apiece, some anglers even more. It completely changed my focus.

The irony is that there are, of course, huge spotted bass at Perris. The world records prove it. The better fishing for spotted bass is not with surface lures, but with Gits-Its or grubs, fishing them 20 to 25 feet deep. The top spots for spotties are in breaks between submerged structure that is bottomed out by rocks. It can take a lot of searching.

What does not take a lot of searching are the trout. The DFG stocks large numbers of rainbow trout, nearly 70,000 per year, including 24,000 in the 11-inch range. In the cooler months when the bass are sluggish, the rainbow trout provide good catch rates for both trollers and bait fishermen.

It also does not take much searching to find the waterskiers during the summer. The weather out here can be like a firepit in the summer and fall, and that makes waterskiing very popular.

The lake is set in Moreno Valley at 1,500 feet elevation, just southwest of The Badlands foothills. It is a roundish lake, covering 2,200 acres, with an island that provides a nice picnic site.

---

12.   FULLER-MILL CREEK

Reference: South of Banning in San Bernardino National Forest; map I6 grid g7.

How to get there: From Interstate 10 at Banning, turn south on Highway 243 and drive about 17 miles (two miles past the Fulmor Lake turnoff) to the creek crossing. Access is available at the picnic area.

Facilities: A picnic area is provided. Campgrounds are available nearby. Supplies are available in Banning.

Cost: Access is free.

Who to contact: Phone the San Bernardino National Forest District Office at (714) 659-2117.

About Fuller-Mill Creek: There's a little picnic area out here. Folks just kind of watch the water go by as they're nibbling on a piece of chicken, then maybe they suddenly see a trout swim past. Whoa! What's that? Why, it's a rainbow trout, about an eight-incher. That is what this obscure little stream offers, being stocked with 2,100 of them in the spring. The top spot is right at the picnic area, at the creek crossing.

---

13.   LAKE FULMOR

Reference: Near Banning in San Bernardino National Forest; map I6 grid g7.

How to get there: From Interstate 10 at Banning, turn south on Highway 243. Drive about 15 miles south to the entrance on the left.

Facilities: Campgrounds are available north and south of the lake, off Highway 243. A picnic area is provided at the lake. Supplies can be obtained in Banning.

Cost: Access is free.

Who to contact: Phone the San Bernardino National Forest District Office at (714) 659-2117.

About Fulmor Lake: Wanted: A lake not everyone knows about. Provided: Fulmor Lake.

Little Fulmor Lake is a tiny sliver set at 5,300 feet on the western slopes of the San Jacinto Mountains near the Black Mountain National Scenic Area. It is small, obscure and often discovered only by accident by folks heading to nearby Mount San Jacinto State Park, or hikers heading into the adjacent wilderness area to the east.

The lake is a good spot for shoreline fishing. Just pick a spot, cast out, and wait for a trout to wander by. The best prospects are in the spring, of course, when water conditions are ideal. The DFG stocks Fulmor with 4,500 trout averaging seven or eight inches, and another 4,000 in the 11-inch class.

A sidetrip option is continuing on the road past the lake, which leads to a trailhead. The trail is routed east up to the ridgeline, intersects with the Pacific Crest Trail, and provides a route to Fuller Ridge, Castle Rocks or south to San Jacinto Peak.

---

14.   LAKE ELSINORE

Reference: South of Riverside at Lake Elsinore State Recreation Area; map I6 grid hØ.

How to get there: From Riverside, drive south on Highway 91 to Interstate 15. Turn south and drive about 20 miles on Interstate 15 to the town of Lake Elsinore. Turn west on Highway 74 and drive three miles to the park entrance. Boat ramps are located on the north and west shores.

Facilities: Campgrounds, a marina, boat ramps, rowboat rentals, picnic areas, a snack bar, bait, and groceries are available at the lake.

Cost: Day-use fee is $4 per vehicle, up to 2 people; 50 cents for each additional person. A fee of $10 is charged if entering with a boat. Boat fee includes a lake permit and launching privileges.

Who to contact: Phone Lake Elsinore State Recreation Area at (714) 674-3177; Elsinore West Marina, (714) 678-1300.

About Lake Elsinore: Whoosh! Whoosh! What's faster than a speeding bullet? Whoosh! Whoosh! If it is at Lake Elsinore, then the answer is a jet-boat propelled waterskier. The place is loaded with them. You can't blame them though, not with day-after-day of barnburner weather all summer and into fall, and few fishermen in their way.

The lake is set at 1,239 feet, and by now you have probably figured this lake isn't exactly God's Gift to Fishing. Correct. It gets no trout stocks, bass fishing is poor, and light numbers of bluegill, crappie and catfish provide a longshot. Instead, the squarish Elsinore is best known for waterskiing dominance. If many fishermen were out there, they would just get used as markers in a slalom course.

15. STRAWBERRY CREEK

Reference: In Idyllwild; map I6 grid h8.

How to get there: From Interstate 215 at Perris, turn east on Highway 74 and drive to the town of Hemet. Continue east for about 20 miles to the Highway 243-Idyllwild turnoff. Turn north and continue to where the creek crosses the road just south of the town of Idyllwild; direct access is available.

Facilities: Campgrounds are available north of Idyllwild at Idyllwild County Park or Mount San Jacinto State Park. Supplies can be obtained in Idyllwild.

Cost: Access is free.

Who to contact: Phone the San Bernardino National Forest District Office at (714) 659-2117.

About Strawberry Creek: In this particular area, it is Lake Hemet to the south that gets most of the attention, Lake Fulmor to the north that gets the hikers. But in between is Strawberry Creek, which flows right through the center of Strawberry Valley, and provides a backyard fishing hole for folks who live in the Idyllwild area. Out of towners miss it every time. No longer. In the spring, it is stocked with 2,100 rainbow trout, mostly seven and eight-inchers, right where Highway 243 crosses the stream. Park your car, hike a little, cast a little, maybe you'll catch a few—and add another little fishing spot to your list of previously unheard of successes.

16. LAKE SKINNER

Reference: Near Temecula at Lake Skinner County Park; map I6 grid i3.

How to get there: From Interstate 15 at Temecula, take the Rancho California exit and drive nine miles northeast on Rancho California Avenue to the park.

Facilities: A campground, a picnic area, a marina, a boat ramp, boat rentals, bait, and groceries are available at the lake. Boats under 10 feet, canoes, kayaks, and all inflatables are prohibited. A 10-mph speed limit is enforced.

Cost: Day-use fee is $4 per vehicle. Fishing fee is $3.50. There is a charge for boat launching.

Who to contact: Phone Lake Skinner County Park at (714) 926-1541.

About Lake Skinner: You no like waterskiers? You no like jet skis? You no like fast boats of any kind? Well, you came to the right place.

As Lake Elsinore to the nearby west is dominated by waterskiers, Skinner is dominated by anglers. And they are rewarded with tremendous numbers of trout plants, considering the size of the lake, and good bass fishing as well.

Skinner is set within a county park, located at 1,479 feet in sparse foothill country, and covers 1,200 surface acres when full. It receives 75,000 trout per year from the DFG; 48,000 in the eight-inch class, another 28,000 to 11 inches. They provide good prospects for trollers, with the northeast cove and northern shore a good stretch of water. Shoreline anglers have their best hopes in the southeast arm of the lake, within walking distance of the parking area and campgrounds. The lake also has bass, crappie, perch and catfish.

No body-contact water sports are permitted at the lake, and you know what that means. Right: No waterskiers.

---

17. LAKE HEMET

Reference: East of Hemet in San Bernardino National Forest; map I6 grid i8.

How to get there: From the junction of Interstate 10 and Highway 79 south of Riverside, turn south on Highway 79 and drive to the town of Hemet. Turn south on Highway 74 and drive 23 miles southeast to the lake entrance on the right.

Facilities: A campground, picnic areas, a boat ramp, boat rentals, bait, and some groceries are available at the lake. Additional supplies can be obtained in Hemet. Boats under 10 feet, canoes, sailboats, and all inflatables are prohibited.

Cost: Day-use fee is $7 per vehicle, up to two people; $2 for each additional person. A fee of $4 is charged if entering with a boat. Fee includes boat launching privileges.

Who to contact: Phone Lake Hemet Campground at (714) 659-2680.

About Lake Hemet: At just 420 surface acres, Lake Hemet is not about to be mistaken for Big Bear Lake. At the same time, however, that can be one of the best things about little Hemet. Because of its small size, some folks just pass on by, never really allowing the lake to enter into their consciousness. But it provides a good camping/fishing destination, especially when the water is cool and the lake receives large stocks of trout.

Lake Hemet is set at 4,335 feet elevation, located just west of Garner Valley in San Bernardino National Forest. It has a campground, boat ramp and a 10-mph speed limit that keeps the place quiet and fairly intimate. Best of all, it receives nearly 70,000 rainbow trout per year from the DFG, a large number for the size of the lake. If catch rates weren't good, the fish would have to be planted vertically in order to fit.

The lake also has some bass and catfish, which provide an option during the summer months. But it is the spring-through-summer transition period, then again in early winter, when Hemet really shines. The weather is cooler, the trout plants abundant, and the catches are good.

MAP I7

1 LISTING
PAGES 698-699

SO-CAL MAP ....see page 656
adjoining maps
NORTH.......................no map
EAST ....no map
SOUTH (J7).........see page 728
WEST (I6)...........see page 684

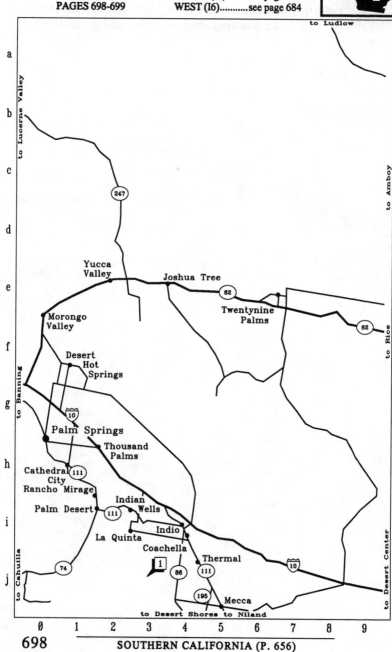

to Ludlow

a

to Lucerne Valley

b

c

247

d

Yucca
Valley

e

Joshua Tree

62

Twentynine
Palms

Morongo
Valley

62

to Rice

f

Desert
Hot
Springs

to Banning

g

10

Palm Springs

Thousand
Palms

h

Cathedral 111
City
Rancho Mirage

Indian
Wells

Palm Desert 111

i

Indio

La Quinta

Coachella

1

Thermal

to Cahuilla

74

86

111

10

to Desert Center

j

195

Mecca

to Desert Shores   to Niland

0   1   2   3   4   5   6   7   8   9

1.　　　　　LAKE CAHUILLA

Reference: Near Indio at Lake Cahuilla County Park; map I7 grid j3.

How to get there: From the Los Angeles area, drive east on Interstate 10 to the town of Indio. Turn south on Washington Street and drive three miles, then turn west on Highway 111 and drive about two miles to Jefferson Street. Turn south on Jefferson and continue for five miles to the park.

Facilities: A campground and picnic areas are available. Supplies can be obtained in Indio. No gasoline motors are permitted on the lake.

Cost: Day-use fee is $3 per vehicle.

Who to contact: Phone Lake Cahuilla County Park at (619) 564-4712.

About Lake Cahuilla: What a place. If it wasn't for this little patch of water, there are times when you could put up a sign on Highway 10 that says, you are now entering hell.

Lake Cahuilla covers just 135 acres, but those 135 acres are the most important in the entire region. Temperatures are commonly in the 100-degree range, and the desert winds can blow a gale. In fact, a little boat ramp used to be at the lake, but it was destroyed by high winds.

The best time to fish this lake is during the cool months, all three of them, when trout are stocked at a good clip. The lake receives 18,000 in the seven to eight-inch class and another 10,000 ranging to 11 inches. They join a few resident catfish. They provide the one beacon of hope in a large region of otherwise impenetrable darkness. If you find yourself out this way during the winter, a good side trip is to Joshua Tree National Monument to the northeast. God help you if you are here at any other time.

SO-CAL MAP ....see page 656
adjoining maps
NORTH (H9) ......see page 652
EAST ....no map
SOUTH (J9)........see page 736
WEST ....no map

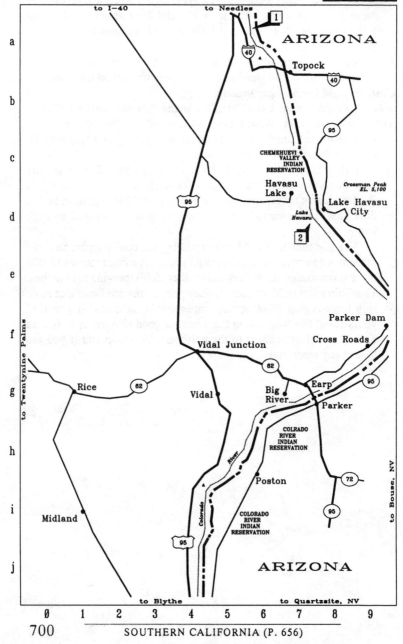

Reference: From Parker Dam to Palo Verde Dam on California/Arizona Border; map I9 grid a6.

How to get there from Southern California: Take Interstate 10 east to Blythe and turn north on US 95. Or, take Highway 62 east to Vidal Junction at the intersection of US 95 and Highway 62 and turn south on US 95. There are numerous access points off US 95 between Blythe and Vidal Junction in the Parker Valley area. To reach the Parker Dam section of the river, drive about 20 miles east of Vidal Junction on Highway 62 to the town of Parker. From Parker, turn north on either Highway 95 or Parker Dam Road. Numerous access points are available off these roads.

How to get there from Northern California: Drive south on US 395 to Interstate 10. Proceed east on Interstate 10 all the way to Blythe, then turn north on US 95. Or, turn north off Interstate 10 on Highway 62 near Palm Springs and continue northeast to Vidal Junction at the intersection of US 95 and Highway 62. Turn south on US 95. There are numerous access points off US 95 between Blythe and Vidal Junction in the Parker Valley area. To reach the Parker Dam section of the river, drive about 20 miles east of Vidal Junction on Highway 62 to the town of Parker. From Parker, turn north on either Highway 95 or Parker Dam Road. Numerous access points are available off these roads.

Special note: The Parker Valley portion of the river is part of the Colorado River Indian Reservation, and the tribe requires that all anglers obtain a permit. Permits are available at the Department of Fish and Game in Parker. Phone (602) 669-9285 for information.

Facilities: Campgrounds, resorts, marinas, boat ramps, boat rentals, bait, tackle, and supplies are available off Highway 95 near Parker, Palo Verde and Blythe.

Cost: A nominal fee is charged at most resorts for day-use and/or boat launching.

Who to contact: Phone the Imperial County Department of Parks and Recreation, (619) 339-4381; Big River RV Park near Parker, (619) 665-9359; Oxbow Marina near Palo Verde, (602) 726-6300.

About Colorado River: Whoa, look at all the waterskiers. On hot summer days, the Colorado River is about the only thing liquid around these parts that isn't in a can or bottle. One way or another, the natural response is to get in the water: boat, waterski, swim, float around on an intertube, anything, just get on the river. If this sounds like a primary place for water recreation, you are right.

For fishing, the best stretch of water in this area is in the upper stretch of Parker Valley. Because an access permit is required by the tribal office, waterskiers tend to bypass it. This piece of water provides good fishing for bass, bluegill, catfish and sometimes crappie, and is a good duck hunting area during the early winter.

2. LAKE HAVASU

Reference: From Topock to Parker Dam on Colorado River; map I9 grid d7.

How to get there from Southern California: Take Interstate 10 east to Blythe and turn north on US 95. Continue to Vidal Junction at the intersection of US 95 and Highway 62. Or, take Highway 62 directly east to Vidal Junction. To access the west side of the lake, turn north on US 95 and drive about 28 miles to Havasu Lake Road. Turn east and continue to the lake. To reach the east side of the lake, drive east on Highway 62 to Parker, then turn north on Highway 95 or Parker Dam Road and drive to Parker Dam. Continue north on Highway 95 to Lake Havasu City.

How to get there from Northern California: Drive south on US 395 to Interstate 10. Proceed east on Interstate 10 all the way to Blythe, then turn north on US 95 and continue to Vidal Junction at the intersection of US 95 and Highway 62. Or, turn north off Interstate 10 onto Highway 62 near Palm Springs and continue northeast to Vidal Junction. To access the west side of the lake, turn north on US 95 and drive about 28 miles to Havasu Lake Road. Turn east and continue to the lake. To reach the east side of the lake, drive east on Highway 62 to Parker, then turn north on Highway 95 and drive to Parker Dam. Continue north on Highway 95 or to Lake Havasu City.

Facilities: Campgrounds, resorts, marinas, boat ramps, boat rentals, bait, tackle, and supplies are available off Highway 95 in the vicinity of Lake Havasu City. There are 40 shoreline miles of boat access camping on the Arizona side of the lake between the dam and Lake Havasu City.

Cost: A nominal fee is charged at most resorts and marinas for day-use and/or boat launching.

Who to contact: Phone the Lake Havasu City Chamber of Commerce, (602) 855-4115; Fisherman's Bait and Tackle in Lake Havasu City, (602) 855-FISH; Havasu Landing Resort at Havasu Lake, (619) 858-4593; Lake Havasu Marina in Lake Havasu City, (602) 855-2159; Black Meadow Landing near Parker Dam, (619) 663-4901.

About Lake Havasu: Giant Lake Havasu is like a lone sapphire in a vast field of coal. Only the Colorado River breaks up a measureless expanse of desert. With the Parker Dam set across the river, Havasu is created, 45 miles long and one of the most popular boating areas in the southwestern U.S.

You really need a boat to do it right at Havasu (with one exception to be noted). It is virtually impossible to fish, get a secluded camping spot, and enjoy the area to the maximum without one. With a boat, you can cover the largest amount of water in the search for fish, pick a do-it-yourself boat-in campsite along the Arizona side of the lake, and see the varied shoreline habitat and scenic beauty.

The best fishing here is for striped bass, but the results come with tremendous swings in catch rates, areas fished and techniques. Large catfish are also available, and some bluegill and crappie. But the star of the show is the striped bass, and because the striper is a migratory fish, you have to track them according to time of year. Your telephone is the most important piece of fishing tackle you could ask for at Havasu, so you can make a phone call to learn up-to-the minute tendencies just prior to your trip. It can save a busted weekend.

The best striper fishing is the spring, March, April and May, and a big striper derby is held to commemorate it. In the winter, before the first warm weather starts arriving, most of the stripers are down near Parker Dam. Nearby Havasu Springs Resort is a good headquarters for fishermen early in the year. But believe me, the stripers are not easy to catch during this period. They tend to be deep, and if the water is very cold, they don't much like hitting lures, and with bait are quite subtle on the bite. This all begins to change quickly as March arrives, and with it, the first warm weather of the year.

From late March through April and into May, the striped bass are on the move, on the prowl, and provide the best fishing of the year. Most people fish for them as if they were fishing for largemouth bass, using large jigs that simulate baitfish. Some of the best patterns are the Hair Raiser, Striper Razor and Worm-Tail jig.

The fish start migrating upstream, past Lake Havasu City and beyond. The best spots in Lake Havasu for striped bass during this migratory period are just north of the vicinity of Havasu City, including Grass Island and Skier's Island. Eventually the bass will keep going all the way up to Davis Dam, adjacent to Bullhead City. In this area, Havasu isn't so much a lake as it resembles the once-mighty Colorado River. This is also the one time when you don't necessarily need a boat to catch stripers. From the shore at the Davis Dam area, you can use gear styled for surf-casting and reach the migrating fish with long casts. This can be a lot of work, and if you aren't in shape, you will be after a weekend of shore casting. Fishing deep-running Rapalas is best by boat here, Hair Raisers by shore.

Once summer arrives, the stripers scatter all over creation, and for the folks willing to work at it, provide fair trolling results. The best luck comes for those out at daybreak, with the best bite at dawn just after a night with a dark moon. After that, the stripers tend to be deep, and you can troll your little petunia off looking for one. The exception is late in the summer and early fall, when stripers can corral schools of baitfish near the surface, complete with diving gulls, just like in the ocean. If you are lucky enough to see such an affair, circle it with your boat and cast Hair Raisers in the direction of the birds. While waiting for a surface boil, a good idea is to drift, using anchovies for bait 30 feet down, and hope to pick up a stray or two.

By summer, there are a lot of sideshows. There are waterskiers galore, lots of hot, oiled-down bodies, and the beer flows faster than the river. Some anglers will just bait up for catfish, toss out their fishing line, and watch all the passing action. Some giant catfish roam this area, by the way, and every once in awhile someone catches an absolute monster with a head the size of a salad bowl.

There is one option at Havasu that is often overlooked. In the winter months, when the place is virtually abandoned, there is decent fishing for trout and crappie, respectively. The trout are way upstream near Bullhead City, in the stretch of water below Davis Dam. The crappie can be good in Topock Bay, which is located just upstream of the Highway 140 Bridge. Another good area is just downstream of the Highway 140 Bridge.

With Lake Havasu you have a tremendous amount of water to pick from and a series of fisheries that provide wildly varying results depending on the time of year. What to do? Enjoy yourself. Get a boat, pick out a spot along the shore for a boat-in camp, and enjoy the water—a jewel in the desert.

SO-CAL MAP ....see page 656
adjoining maps
NORTH (I5)........see page 668
EAST (J6) ....see page 712
SOUTH ....no map
WEST ....no map

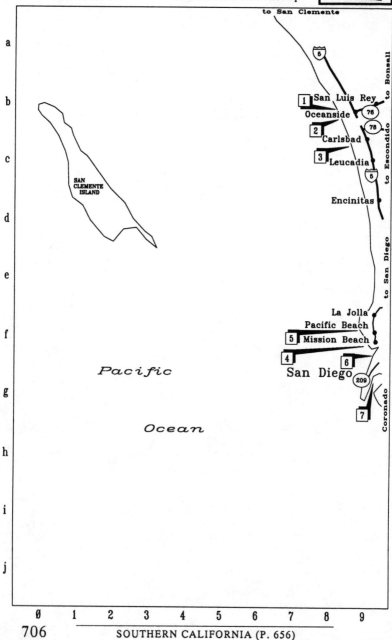

to San Clemente

a

b   1 San Luis Rey
         Oceanside   76

c   2   78
           Carlsbad

         3
           Leucadia

d
           Encinitas

e

         La Jolla
         Pacific Beach
f   5 Mission Beach

         4   6
                San Diego
g   209

         7

h

Pacific

i

Ocean

j

       0   1   2   3   4   5   6   7   8   9

       SOUTHERN CALIFORNIA (P. 656)

SAN
CLEMENTE
ISLAND

to Bonsall

to Escondido

to San Diego

Coronado

1.   OCEANSIDE DEEP SEA

Reference: North of San Diego; map J5 grid b8.

How to get there: From Interstate 5 at Oceanside, take the Oceanside-Harbor Drive exit. Turn west and continue to the harbor.

Facilities: Party boat charters, a boat ramp, a picnic area and bait and tackle are available at the harbor. Lodging, campgrounds and supplies are available in Oceanside.

Cost: Party boat fees range from $20-$35 per person.

Who to contact: Phone the Oceanside Chamber of Commerce at (619) 722-1534; Helgren's Sportfishing, (619) 722-2133.

Party boat list: Oceanside 95, Electra, Sea Trek, Sea Star, Tortuga, Advance, Laura J, Sea Adventure, Top Producer, Mako; reservations through Helgren's Sportfishing, (619) 722-2133.

About Oceanside Deep Sea: More and more people are just discovering Oceanside as a quality fishing port, and old-timers always just smile and say, "We've been here all along."

The place is an ideal headquarters for anglers who own their own boats, as well as for those who board the big sportfishing vessels. Access to several good fishing areas requires just a 20- to 40-minute run, rarely longer. The engine gets a fair run at it, you have a chance to get the sea breeze in your face, and the final reward is an array of different fisheries.

The marine habitat provides two attractive settings: inshore kelp beds and deep water shelves. Take your pick. The kelp forests are widespread and abundant north of Oceanside both off Camp Pendleton and farther north off the San Onofre power plant outfall, as well as along the inshore coast from Carlsbad on south. This habitat is ideal for kelp bass and all matter of rockfish, and rarely sheephead, barracuda and yellowtail (you can always pray). The lush undersea forests give an angler a chance to use light saltwater tackle, casting jigs along the kelp almost as if you were in a lake casting jigs for largemouth bass.

For larger fish, however, you need to go deeper. The deep undersea shelves are made for a wide variety of bottom-dwelling rockfish, the most common being chilipepper and canary rockfish, with some large, ugly bocaccio. I mean, hey, they don't make fish any uglier, right? These fish hang along the ledges between 280 feet and 600 feet deep, located both northwest and southwest of the harbor. The bonus here is that the bottom of the ocean drops off to never-never land quite quickly, just two, three miles offshore. Instead of a long, boat-thumping grind to reach the fishing grounds, it is a short trip.

The charter boat operation out of Oceanside offers all kinds of trips, with both local and offshore focuses. In the best of years, when warm water and abundant baitfish populations move in along the coast, trips for all matter of blue-water fish can be arranged. This can include even striped marlin and tuna, although the spotlight always starts with albacore. Then as summer progresses into fall, the "whatever happens" approach follows. This is one place where "whatever happens" is often worth getting in on.

2. OCEANSIDE PIER

Reference: In Oceanside; map J5 grid b8.

How to get there: From Interstate 5 in Oceanside, take the Mission Boulevard exit and turn west. Go as far as you can and turn right, then immediately left, and continue to the pier.

Facilities: Restrooms, fish-cleaning tables, a bait shop, a restaurant, and benches are available.

Cost: Access is free.

Who to contact: Phone The California Tackle Box at (619) 724-0121.

About Oceanside Pier: Habitat always determines what species are available. At Oceanside Pier, the sandy bottom means you get a chance at halibut in the spring and early summer, along with steady numbers of kingfish, perch and sand bass. There are occasional runs of jack-smelt, and at best, bonito and even barracuda can roam within casting range in the summer.

3. AGUA HEDIONDA LAGOON

Reference: Near Carlsbad; map J5 grid c9.

How to get there: From Oceanside, drive south on Interstate 5 to Tamarack Street. Turn left and travel to Adams Street, then turn right and follow to Chiquapin. Continue to Harrison Street, then follow Harrison Street to the lagoon.

Facilities: A boat ramp, a picnic area, and a snack bar are available. You must obtain a permit through the city of Carlsbad before boating on the lagoon. Camping is available at Carlsbad State Beach; reservations are required in advance.

Cost: There is a fee for boat launching. Parking fee is $3.

Who to contact: Phone Snug Harbor Marina at (619) 434-3089.

About Agua Hedionda Lagoon: Boaters must show "proof of insurance" with a coverage of $300,000 minimum before they are allowed on this saltwater lagoon, and that should tell you everything you need to know about this place. What you have is a spot where jet boats towing waterskiers up to 50 mph (no kidding) roar around, and then every once in awhile, plow into a shoal for a spectacular crash. You have the windsurfers, who damn near fly across the place when the north wind is ripping. An outlet to the ocean, however, allows halibut, seabass and maybe an occasional perch to sneak in.

---

4. MISSION BAY

Reference: Northwest of San Diego; map J5 grid f9.

How to get there: From Interstate 5 north of San Diego, take the Sea World Drive exit. Turn west and travel to Mission Bay Drive. Continue west to the sportfishing operations on the bay. Boat ramps are located throughout the bay.

Boat ramps: Dana Landing Ramp, De Anza Cove Ramp, Santa Clara Point Ramp, Ski Beach Ramp; all managed by the San Diego Coastal Division, (619) 221-8901. Both a ramp and a sling hoist are available at Campland on The Bay, (619) 581-4200. A sling hoist is also available at Sea World Marina, (619) 226-3915.

Facilities: Party boat charters, a campground, boat ramps, boat hoists, boat rentals, bait, tackle, groceries, and various restaurants are available at the bay.

Cost: There may be a fee for boat launching. Party boat fees range from $20-$40 per person. A Mexican fishing license is required for some deep sea sportfishing trips; they can be obtained at the sportfishing operations, and the cost is usually included in the price of the party boat fee.

Who to contact: Phone Seaforth Sportfishing, (619) 224-3383; Islandia Sportfishing, (619) 222-1164; Campland on the Bay, (619) 581-4200.

Party boat list: Mission Belle, New Seaforth, San Diego, Phoenix; reservations through Seaforth Sportfishing at (619) 224-3383. *Dolphin, Sea Biscuit, America II;* reservations through Islandia Sportfishing at (619) 222-1164.

About Mission Bay: California's South Coast is a wondrous place with excellent fishing opportunities, and one of the reasons for that is Mission Bay and its nearby coast.

The nearby coastal fishing grounds provide outstanding fisheries for just about any warmwater ocean species. Yet if you don't want to venture out to sea, you can catch a variety of smaller species right in the sheltered confines of the bay itself. Just match the habitat:

—Kelp forests: A series of easy-to-reach huge kelp forests provide havens for a large variety of species. One large expanse of kelp is located between Point La Jolla on south past Bird Rock, and another is set to the south, spanning from offshore Ocean Beach to Point Loma. The bottom ranges from 60 to 140 feet deep here, with most catches being kelp bass, rockfish and sheephead, but in the summer there are sometimes even yellowtail, barracuda, white seabass, and rarely even bonito roaming in the area.

—Deepwater shelves: A deep, underwater dropoff is located directly west of Point Loma, where the bottom of the ocean drops off from 280 feet to 600 feet deep in the matter of a few miles. This is an excellent spot for big cowcod, lingcod and rockfish. It's about a seven-mile run (hopefully, by boat) out of Mission Bay.

—Bluewater: Come summer, and the best of the best often arrive— marlin, tuna, albacore and yellowtail. Often you don't have to venture far for yellowtail and bonito, which move through just off Point La Jolla, along the southern edge of La Jolla Canyon. Marlin, tuna and albacore are another matter. From year to year, you never know how close to shore they will come. In the lucky years when they move in close during September and October, they can be located about 10 miles offshore, almost never any closer.

—Flat sea bottom: A bonus at Mission Bay is that between the La Jolla kelp and Point Loma kelp is a flat-bottomed area located directly west of Mission Bay, within quick reach of owners of small boats. In the spring, halibut move right in along this area, a once-a-year chance that offers a nice change of pace.

—Mission Bay: If the sea is rough, or you desire a quiet water option, Mission Bay itself has a variety of fisheries. The most abundant are kingfish, smelt and perch, but sometimes even halibut, bonito and barracuda will enter the bay. Mission Bay is used more often as a private parkland, like a big lake. It has 27 miles of shoreline, with waterskiing and sailboarding popular. Note, however, that strict boat noise limits are in effect; a 5-mph speed limit is in effect from 11 a.m. to 5 p.m. on the northwest bay, and also on the entire bay from sunset to sunrise.

---

5. CRYSTAL PIER

Reference: North of San Diego in Pacific Beach; map J5 grid f9.

How to get there: From Interstate 5 north of San Diego, take the Balboa exit. Turn right onto Garnet Avenue at the second light. Continue to the end of Garnet; you will see the pier as you cross Mission Boulevard.

Facilities: Restrooms, a bait shop, a hotel, a restaurant, benches, and fish-cleaning areas are available on the pier.

Cost: Access is free.

Who to contact: Phone Dana Marina Bait & Tackle, (619) 225-0440.

About Crystal Pier: Renovation of Crystal Pier was completed in late 1991, and it is open only during daylight hours. In addition to kingfish, perch, jacksmelt and sharks, the rocky shoreline just south of the pier provides an opportunity for opaleye, kelp bass, and rarely, cabezone.

6. OCEAN BEACH PIER

Reference: Northwest of San Diego; map J5 grid f9.

How to get there: From Interstate 5 at the west end of San Diego, take the Sea World drive exit. Turn west and drive until you cross a bridge, then bear right on Sunset Cliffs Boulevard. Continue to Newport Avenue, then turn right and continue to the pier.

Facilities: Restrooms, benches, fish-cleaning areas, picnic tables, and limited bait are available.

Cost: Access is free.

Who to contact: Phone the Ocean Beach Town Council at (619) 225-1080.

About Ocean Beach Pier: Here is one of the top spots on the coast for anglers who like their feet on something solid when they do their fishing. The Ocean Beach Pier is set within close range of several ideal habitats that cause a large variety of fish to be taken through the year. The top prize is halibut, and this is one of the best piers in California to get the longshot opportunity to hook one. Kingfish, perch and sharks are more common, of course (of course!). Just to the south of the pier is a rock-strewn shore that provides a chance for bass and rockfish.

---

7. SHELTER ISLAND PIER

Reference: South of San Diego; map J5 grid g9.

How to get there: From Interstate 5 at the west end of San Diego, take the Rosecrans exit. Turn west and follow to Shelter Island Drive, then turn left. Stay to the right and continue to the pier on the left.

Facilities: Restrooms, fish-cleaning tables, benches, and a bait shop are available.

Cost: Access is free.

Who to contact: Phone Shelter Island Marina at (619) 222-0561.

About Shelter Island Pier: This is the major shoreline access point in San Diego Bay, located near the entrance to the bay in the migration path of a Heinz 57 variety of fish. The most consistent results are for perch, many species of them, along with smelt, sand bass, sharks and rays. The lucky few even intercept halibut (in the spring) or bonito (in the summer) when they sneak through the mouth of the bay.

SO-CAL MAP ....see page 656
adjoining maps
NORTH (I6)........see page 684
EAST (J7) ....see page 728
SOUTH ....no map
WEST (J5) ....see page 706

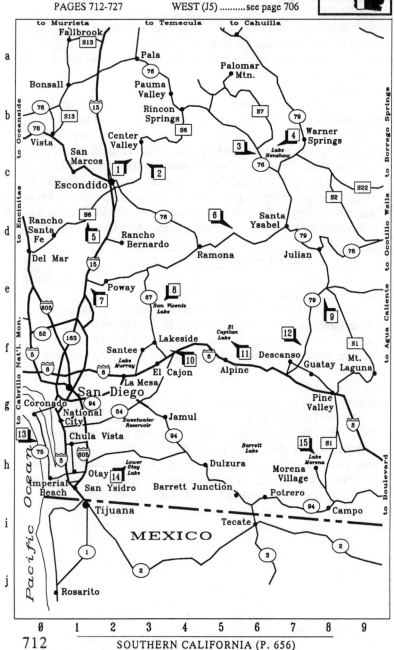

SOUTHERN CALIFORNIA (P. 656)

1.   DIXON LAKE

Reference: Near Escondido at Dixon Lake Recreation Area; map J6 grid
   c2.

How to get there: From Escondido, take El Norte Parkway east to La
   Honda Drive. Turn left and drive north to the park entrance.

Facilities: A campground, picnic areas, a fishing pier, boat rentals, a snack
   bar and bait are available. Supplies can be obtained in Escondido. No
   private boats are permitted; boating is restricted to rentals only.

Cost: Entrance fee is $1 on weekends; free on weekdays.

Who to contact: Phone Dixon Lake Recreation Area at (619) 741-4680.

About Dixon Lake: Little Dixon Lake is the centerpiece for a regional
   park set in the San Diego foothills, 1,405 feet elevation. The fishing
   is just fair, with a sprinkling of bass and catfish, and rarely, private
   stocks of trout add to hopes during the cool winter months. Nearby
   Lake Wohlford to the east provides a preferred alternative. No private
   boats are permitted on Dixon Lake, a downer, but a 5-mph speed limit
   for the rentals keeps the small lake quiet. The fishing is rarely anything
   to shout about either.

2.   LAKE WOHLFORD

Reference: East of Escondido; map J6 grid c3.

How to get there: From Escondido on Interstate 15, turn east on County
   Road S6 and drive five miles to Lake Wohlford Road. Turn right and
   continue about two miles to the lake. The boat ramp is located on the
   north shore.

Facilities: A boat ramp, boat rentals, picnic areas, bait, a snack bar and
   some supplies are available. A campground is available nearby. No
   canoes, inflatables or sailboats are permitted. Boats under 10 feet or
   over 18 feet are prohibited.

Cost: Fishing fee is $4 per person.

Who to contact: Phone the Lake Wohlford Boat Ramp at (619) 749-2661.

Special note: Open daily from January through August.

About Lake Wohlford: San Diego County has several of California's top
   bass lakes, but Lake Wohlford is not one of them. Believe it or not,
   that can be a plus because it gets a lot less pressure than the more
   famous waters. Wohlford does provide decent prospects from winter
   through early summer, and a 5-mph speed limit keeps the lake quiet.
   The lake sometimes provides fair trout fishing early in the year, but
   by late February or early March the warm-water species take over.
   We're talking bass, bluegill and catfish, with some crappie on the side.
   The results are decent enough, but there is a key period here when the
   water warms up from 58 to 63 degrees, about a two to three-week zone.

When that happens, the bass move up to just five to ten feet deep, and provide a good bite for anglers casting towards the shore from boats.

---

3. SAN LUIS REY RIVER

Reference: East of Escondido in Cleveland National Forest; map J6 grid c6.

How to get there: From Escondido, turn north on Interstate 15 and drive about 15 miles. Take the Highway 76 exit and head east; the highway parallels the river. Access is available from the Lake Henshaw Dam about three miles upstream, to the public campground.

Facilities: A campground is available on Highway 76.

Cost: River access is free.

Who to contact: Phone the Cleveland National Forest District Office at (619) 745-2421.

About San Luis Rey River: A trout stream in San Diego County? That is what the San Luis Rey River offers. You get easy access, with pullouts right along Highway 76, fair fishing for small rainbow trout, and even a small campground.

The best stretch of water is from Lake Henshaw Dam on downstream three miles to the campground. This is where the DFG stocks the stream with 4,500 rainbow trout, with the fish in the seven, eight-inch class. Of course, stream flows must be high enough and cool enough to provide decent habitat to allow stocking, but releases out of Henshaw assure that in the early summer.

---

4. LAKE HENSHAW

Reference: East of Escondido; map J6 grid c6.

How to get there: From Escondido, turn north on Interstate 15 and drive about 15 miles to the Highway 76 exit. Turn east and drive 30 miles to the lake entrance on the left. The access road will take you to the boat launch.

Facilities: A campground, an unpaved boat launch, boat rentals, picnic areas, a snack bar, groceries, a restaurant, and supplies are available. No canoes, inflatables, or craft under 10 feet permitted.

Cost: Fishing fee is $4 per person.

Who to contact: Phone Lake Henshaw Resort at (619) 782-3501.

About Lake Henshaw: When a once-promising fishery goes into the grave, it takes some active, professional management to hope for any kind of rebirth. Henshaw, set at 2,727 feet near Cleveland National Forest, needs exactly that. In the early 1990s, it has been a terrible skunkhole for bass, and the best fishing is for catfish instead, with crappie as a sidelight.

Hey, there have been more carp caught in recent years than bass. Too bad, because at one time Henshaw had some real hope, even producing a lake record that weighed 14 pounds, 4 ounces. It needs to start over, revitalized with fresh stocks, then be managed to produce the maximum number of spawners.

The lake covers 1,140 acres. No swimming is permitted, and a 10-mph speed limit is in effect.

---

5.   LAKE HODGES

Reference: South of Escondido; map J6 grid d1.

How to get there: From Interstate 15 at Escondido, turn southwest on County Road S6 (via Rancho Parkway) and drive five miles to the lake entrance road.

Facilities: A boat ramp, boat rentals, picnic areas, a snack bar, and some bait are available. Full facilities are available in Escondido to the north or San Diego to the south.

Cost: Fishing fee is $3.50-$4 per person. There is a fee for boat launching.

Who to contact: Phone San Diego Water Utilities, Lake Department, at (619) 465-4500; Lake Hotline, (619) 443-2510.

Special note: Open Wednesdays, Thursdays and weekends, March through October.

About Lake Hodges: How you feel about Lake Hodges all depends upon your perspective. You might feel like it's the best lake you have ever fished, where you have a better chance of catching a 10-pound bass than any place in America. Or you might feel like it's the aquatic version of the San Diego Zoo, too many people in too small a place, ridiculous lines at the boat ramp at dawn, and no such thing as a secret spot.

Hodges is both of those outlooks. It is a fantastic producer of big bass, and in fact, is one of the few lakes ever to produce a 20-pounder. The lake record weighed 20 pounds, 4 ounces. But the place is very heavily fished and has a lot of negatives because of it.

Lake Hodges is set at 314 feet elevation, located in the coastal foothills just west of I-15. It is a long, narrow snake-like reservoir that is shaped like an inverted V. Since the lake is closed three days per week, the fish get a regular, needed rest. During these closures, some anglers will park their trucks and trailered boats in line at the boat ramp, actually paying college kids to "car sit" for as long as it takes in order to have one of the first places in line. It gets worse. Once on the water, it's every man for himself, with anglers often moving in right on top of each other if they even believe there is the remotest possibility of a hook-up.

Why do people put up with it? Because of the bass, that's why. They come big at Hodges, and in the spring, they are also abundant during the first few hours after an opener. There are no secret spots at Hodges; at one time or another, everybody fishes the same areas: Both corners of the dam, the Bernardo Arm (early in the year), the Narrows (just west of Felicita Bay), and anyplace where you see stick-ups. The big bass, the 10-pounders and up, tend to be 15 to 20 feet deep.

Because of the amount of fishing pressure, and the fact that catch-and-release is growing in popularity, the bass in Hodges are quite smartened up. Newcomers with little experience can have a lot of problems getting anything, particularly if they show up after 10 a.m.; by then every good spot in the lake has already been hit. Know-hows, on the other hand, who get on the lake early, then fish plastic worms, spinnerbaits, and crankbaits with a delicate enough touch to discern the most subtle bites, may come up with a fish approaching the world record.

6.   LAKE SUTHERLAND

Reference: Near Ramona; map J6 grid d5.

How to get there: From Interstate 15 at Escondido, turn east on Highway 78 and drive about 30 miles to Sutherland Dam Road (located about eight miles past Ramona). Turn left and drive north to the lake. The boat ramp is located on the west shore.

Facilities: A boat ramp, boat rentals, picnic areas, a snack bar, bait and tackle are available at the lake. Other supplies can be obtained in Ramona. Campgrounds are located near the lake. Boats under 10 feet are prohibited.

Cost: Fishing fee is $4 per person. There is a fee for boat launching.

Who to contact: Phone San Diego Water Utilities, Lake Department, at (619) 465-4500; Lake Hotline, (619) 443-2510.

Special note: Open Fridays through Sundays, March through October.

About Lake Sutherland: The intense angler numbers that hammer away at Hodges, El Capitan, San Vicente and Otay just don't seem to make it out here. The lake is just distant enough from the San Diego metropolitan area, and just small enough (only 560 acres) that many of the go-getters do their go-getting somewhere else. In addition, the bass have four days off each week to relax, then four months off each year to think about it. All that adds up to good news for the anglers who visit Lake Sutherland.

The lake is set at 2,058 feet elevation, created from the dammed flows of Santa Ysabel Creek and Bloomdale Creek in the foothills near Cleveland National Forest. In a five-year period at Sutherland, the bass population went from an estimated 10,000 fish to 40,000 fish. Included in that was a lake record that weighed 15 pounds, 8 ounces. There are also some big channel catfish in the lake, along with bluegill and crappie.

The lake is small enough that in a day or two, you can fish nearly all of it. After a while, particularly with the use of electronics, you can get to know the lake as well as your own home with the lights off. The trends here are usually pretty typical. After early-rising anglers get in on the dawn bite, the know-hows then settle in and fish the ledges, 12 to 15 feet down, with bait, for a chance at the big ones.

---

7.   LAKE MIRAMAR

Reference: North of San Diego; map J6 grid e1.

How to get there: From San Diego, turn north on Interstate 15 and drive about ten miles to Mira Mesa. Take the Mira Mesa Boulevard exit and turn east. Continue to Scripps Lake Drive and turn south; proceed to the lake.

Facilities: A boat ramp, boat rentals, a picnic area, a snack bar, bait, and tackle are available at the lake. Other supplies can be obtained in Mira Mesa. Full facilities are available in San Diego.

Cost: Fishing fee is $4 per person. There is a fee for boat launching.

Who to contact: Phone San Diego Water Utilities, Lake Department, at (619) 465-4500; Lake Hotline, (619) 443-2510.

Special note: Open Saturday through Tuesday, open 11 months of the year, closed in October.

About Lake Miramar: The stories just don't get any more outlandish than at Miramar. This is the lake where a 21-pound, 10-ounce bass was caught that was discovered to have a lead diving weight in its stomach—and also the place where a 20-pound, 15-ounce is alleged to have been floating, dead of old age, and then scooped up and presented as a record catch.

Regardless, Miramar is something of a miniaturized factory for making big bass. It is a tiny lake, just 180 acres, with an estimated population of 5,000 bass. But they get huge. Stocked trout are like growing pills, and good numbers of threadfin shad are available as well, prime forage. Fishermen casting shad-patterned crankbaits can have a lot of success during the early summer. Another technique that can work at Miramar is split-shotting worms just above the grass-weed-muck covered bottom.

But for the most part, that is often where it ends. Because Miramar is such a small lake, really more like a large pond, the entire shoreline gets picked over again and again, often many times the same day. The lake has little structure and the water is quite clear, adding to the difficulty. Sometimes anglers with kids will give up on the bass after

---

mid-morning and try for bluegill along the tules. You can't blame them.

After a while, you even feel like putting a few lead weights in a fish. Just don't claim the fish as a new state record.

8.   SAN VICENTE LAKE

Reference: Northeast of San Diego; map J6 grid e3.

How to get there: From San Diego, turn east on Interstate 8 and drive to El Cajon. Turn north on Highway 67 and drive about ten miles to Morena Drive. Turn left and continue to the lake.

Facilities: A boat ramp, boat rentals, a picnic area, a snack bar, and bait are available at the lake. Other supplies can be obtained in Lakeside. Campgrounds are available near the lake. Boats under 9 feet are prohibited.

Cost: Fishing fee is $3.50-$4 per person. There is a fee for boat launching.

Who to contact: Phone San Diego Water Utilities, Lake Department, at (619) 465-4500; Lake Hotline, (619) 465-3474.

Special note: Open Thursdays and weekends, November through May.

About San Vicente Lake: The inside word is that a world record bass is in San Vicente, that this fish has been documented in a survey by the Department of Fish and Game, and then released.

You may not catch that world record bass, but you do have a good chance of getting one in the three to six-pound class. The bass grow fast at San Vicente. An average of 500 are documented each year that weigh five pounds or better, with the average about three pounds. It is a good lake and getting better, with an aerator now pumping oxygen into the lake, adding to the amount of quality habitat—rather than a thin-banded thermocline.

San Vicente is located in arid foothills, 659 feet elevation, covering 1,070 acres when full, complete with island. Waterskiing is permitted only June through October (when it is closed to fishing), so there are no conflicts between the user groups.

That is a good thing, because when a serious basser thinks he's about to catch a 20-pounder, you'd best not shower him with waterski spray. The big bass tend to hang deep in San Vicente, hunkering down in the holes and off ledges. Because the lake has large amounts of feed, including trout, crawdads and shad minnows, you need to use bait in order to entice the big bass. Large Rapalas and plastic worms are popular at here for higher catch rates without sacrificing the chance at that world record.

The lake has a different look than a lot of the other lakes in the San Diego area. The shoreline includes some steep, rocky banks. These are the best areas by far, where the marine food chain gets a good start, from the creation of zooplankton, to insects, to minnows, to trout, to bass.

---

9. LAKE CUYAMACA

Reference: Near Cuyamaca Rancho State Park in the Northeast of San Diego; map J6 grid e8.

How to get there: From Interstate 15 at Escondido, turn east on Highway 78 and drive about 45 miles to the town of Julian. Turn south on Highway 79 and continue nine miles to the lake. The boat ramp is located on the west shore of the lake.

Facilities: A boat ramp, boat rentals, a snack bar, picnic areas, a restaurant, bait, and limited groceries are available at the lake. Campgrounds are available to the south at Cuyamaca Rancho State Park. Boats under 10 or over 22 feet are prohibited. No sailboats or rafts are permitted on the lake.

Cost: Fishing fee is $4 per person. There is a fee for boat launching.

Who to contact: Phone Lake Cuyamaca at (619) 765-0515.

About Lake Cuyamaca: This lake is just far enough away from the San Diego area to make a trip here something special. Anglers are usually rewarded appropriately.

Lake Cuyamaca is set at 4,620 feet on the eastern slopes of the Cuyamaca Mountains. It provides solid prospects for a number of species, with good trout fishing in the cool months, good bass and crappie fishing in the spring and summer, and also prospects for catfish and bluegill in summer and fall.

Most of the attention in this zone is on bass, not trout, but Cuyamaca is an exception, with the best trout fishing by far in the area. Because it is set at a much higher elevation than the other area lakes, the water stays cooler longer. In turn, the Department of Fish and Game rewards it with consistent stocks, plunking in 50,000 rainbow trout per year. The lake receives 30,000 trout averaging seven or eight inches, another 20,000 up to 11 inches, and they join larger holdovers from previous years.

By early summer, the bass and crappie take over. Cuyamaca does not have many large bass, but it has fair numbers in the two and three-pound class. The lake record weighed 10 pounds, 5 ounces. A bonus here is a 10-mph speed limit, which makes the lake ideal for boaters sneaking up on quiet coves, to cast surface lures along the shoreline.

Cuyamaca is a good choice for the boater/camper/angler. There may not be 10-pound bass roaming the place, but with the lake's other positive qualities, it doesn't seem so important.

---

10.   LAKE JENNINGS

Reference: Northeast of El Cajon at Lake Jennings County Park; map J6 grid f4.

How to get there: From San Diego, turn east on Interstate 8 and drive 16 miles to Lake Jennings Park Road. Turn north and continue one mile to the lake.

Facilities: A campground, a boat ramp, boat rentals, a snack bar, picnic areas, bait, tackle, and limited groceries are available at the lake. Full facilities are available in the San Diego area. Canoes, inflatables and sailboats are prohibited. No operation of gas motors is permitted after 7 p.m.

Cost: Fishing fee is $4.25 per person. There is a fee for boat launching.

Who to contact: Phone the County Irrigation District at (619) 466-0585; Jennings Launch Ramp, (619) 443-9503; Lake Hotline, (619) 443-2510.

Special note: Open Fridays through Sundays, year-round.

About Lake Jennings: This lake is of no relation to my friend Waylon, but he wouldn't disown it if it was. Lake Jennings is a nice little backyard fishing hole and recreation area set just outside of Johnstown at 700 feet elevation. It is your basic catfish hole, being stocked every other week with 1,000 pounds of channel catfish.

This is the kind of place where you would come for an evening weekend picnic to enjoy yourself, maybe toss out a fishing line. Bluegill and sunfish can be caught from shore. More serious anglers can try to track down the lake's bass, but for the most part, this lake doesn't try to compete with the bass factories. Nearby San Vicente to the north and El Capitan to the east provide that.

11.   EL CAPITAN LAKE

Reference: Northeast of San Diego; map J6 grid f5.

How to get there: From San Diego, turn east on Interstate 8 and drive 16 miles to Jennings Park Road. Turn north and drive about two miles to the town of Lakeside. Turn right on El Monte Road and continue east to the lake. The boat ramp is located on the south shore.

Facilities: A boat ramp, boat rentals, picnic areas, a snack bar, and bait are available at the lake. Full facilities and supplies are available in the San Diego area. Boats under 10 or over 20 feet are prohibited.

Cost: Fishing fee is $3.50-$4 per person. There is a fee for boat launching.

Who to contact: Phone San Diego Water Utilities, Lake Department, at (619) 465-4500; Lake Hotline, (619) 443-2510.

Special note: Open Fridays, Saturdays and Sundays, from February through September.

About El Capitan Lake: The bassers call this place "El Cap" and rarely without a bit of reverence. While you hear the stories about bass at other lakes, it is El Cap that more often produces them. It is the biggest of the lakes managed by the City of San Diego, covering 1,575 acres when full, and produces the most consistent results for bass anglers. It is set in a long canyon, 750 feet elevation, and within easy reach for many fishermen.

A 10-mph speed limit and no swimming keeps the water quiet, and four off days per week keeps the fish from being stressed. I have always had my best luck here using large spinnerbaits, Shad Raps or Rattletraps. To do it right, you really need a boat with an electric motor, then you need to pepper the shoreline with casts, and try different depths. The magic number is 58, as in 58 degrees. When the lake is warmer than 58, the bass emerge from the depths and will cruise five to ten feet deep, looking for shad minnows. When it is colder, they are deep: 15 to 20 or sometimes 30 to 35 feet deep.

The water clarity is usually only fair at El Capitan, especially in early spring, so the fish are less spooky than at most lakes. That makes this a good lake to break in newcomers to bass fishing. If wind bothers you, get on the lake early and get it done early, because the wind shoots right down the canyon that this lake sits in, especially during the prime spring months. A little wind is good, though, because it keeps water clarity down, allowing the bass to come up in the top 10 feet of water.

The best area on the lake is the Conejos Creek Arm, but this is no secret, and if you don't have an early spot in the line at the boat ramp, someone else will be certain to fish it first. No problem, just keep on the move, casting spinnerbaits in the spring, crankbaits in the early summer. You'll get 'em. The lake has too many bass and too good of conditions to miss.

---

12.   SWEETWATER RIVER

Reference: East of San Diego at Cuyamaca State Park; map J6 grid f7.
How to get there: From San Diego, drive about 35 miles east on Interstate 8 to Highway 79. Turn north and drive to the Green Valley Falls Campground in Cuyamaca State Park. Access is available there as well as north, off Highway 79 between the camp and the town of Julian.
Facilities: Campgrounds are available in the park. Supplies can be obtained in Julian. Full facilities are available in the San Diego area.
Cost: Parking at day-use areas is $5 per vehicle; if you park at the turnouts along the highway, access is free.
Who to contact: Phone Cuyamaca State Park at (619) 765-0755.

About Sweetwater River: Here's a little stream that a lot of folks don't have a clue about. The Sweetwater River runs out of the Cuyamaca Mountains, and two short stretches of it are stocked with rainbow trout during the spring. The fish are not large, just seven inchers, maybe eight if you stretch it, and they are not abundant either, the stream getting just 2,700 per year. But when streamflows are decent, boom— they go in, and provide a unique opportunity for the area. The river is stocked in the vicinity of the Green Valley Falls Campground, and also in the Green Valley Area, located between Descanso and Julian just off Highway 79. Greatness? No. But when you consider how nearby the desert is, it still can be hard to believe you can catch trout in a stream around these parts.

---

13.   SAN DIEGO DEEP SEA

Reference: At San Diego Bay; map J6 grid hØ.

How to get there: From Interstate 5 in San Diego, take the Hawthorne Street/Airport exit. Turn west on Harbor Drive and continue to the sportfishing operations.

Facilities: Party boat charters, boat ramps, full-service marinas, restaurants, lodging, bait, tackle, and supplies are available at the bay. Boat ramps are available at the bay in Chula Vista and National City. Boat rentals are available in Coronado.

Cost: Party boat fees range from $24-$145 per person.

Who to contact: For general information, phone the San Diego Visitor's Bureau at (619) 232-3101. For fishing information, phone H & M Landing, (619) 222-1144; Fisherman's Landing, (619) 222-0391; Point Loma Sportfishing, (916) 223-1627.

Party boat list: Alicia, Challenger, Daiwa Pacific, Fortune, Gallilean, Horizon, Imagination, Indian, Lydia Lee, Mustang, Patriot, Predator, Reel Champion, Sunrise, Big Game, Spirit of Adventure, Qualifier 105, Cherokee Geisha, Producer, Mascot VI, Malihini, Fisherman's III; reservations through H & M Landing, (619) 222-1144. *Prowler, Pacific Queen, Searcher;* reservations through Fisherman's Landing, (619) 222-0391. *Daily Double, La Jollan, Jackie, New Loan, Holiday, Morning Star, Pegasus, Charger, Coral Sea, American Angler, Vagabond, Red Rooster III, New Hustler II, Pacifica, Aztec;* reservations through Point Loma Sportfishing, (619) 223-1627.

About San Diego Deep Sea: The term "Hot Rail" was invented for the boats out of San Diego. That is what happens when there are multiple hookups on a boat. The anglers must chase along the railing, following the fish, often in different directions. You duck under poles, over the top of other lines, and when there are enough hookups simultaneously, it is bedlam, some of the most exciting fishing anywhere in the world.

How good is it? Consider this. As an outdoors writer, I travel throughout the western hemisphere, and in the process, will often connect with other outdoors writers. What do they always ask? This: "Has Rolla retired yet?" Rolla is Rolla Williams, the legendary outdoors writer who has been with the San Diego Union going on 43 years now, who many feel has the best year-round writing job in the country. The answer is no, he is not ready to retire and create a job opening, not as long as the fish keep biting. And they aren't apt to stop any time soon.

The San Diego sportfishing fleet offers a wide variety of trips, but the best of them are often for albacore at Coronado Island and for yellowtail at San Clemente Island, or even longer trips spanning a week to 10 days all the way south of Cabo San Lucas to Clarion Island. Hot rail? It can get so hot you can't touch the thing.

More locally-oriented trips also are also available. One of the favorites and most consistent is the short trip "around the corner" north of Point Loma to the vast kelp forest located there. The Point Loma kelp is home for many resident species, including kelp bass, rockfish and sheephead, and also attracts yellowtail and barracuda. Sometimes bonito even roam the area during the summer. Another option is right along the world-famous Coronado Beach, where halibut arrive during the spring and early summer.

There are also several deepwater rockfish and lingcod areas. The closest is just eight miles offshore, where the bottomfish are abundant along the undersea ledge as it drops from 280 feet to 600 feet deep. Another good rockfish spot is in the Coronado Canyon, same depth, located just northwest of the Islas Los Coronados.

There's more. Marlin and tuna are always a wild card here. Warm ocean temperatures and large amounts of baitfish can compel marlin to migrate north from their typical waters off Baja, and they sometimes can show during the fall just 10 to 15 miles offshore. All it takes for this phenomenon to occur is for Rolla to start thinking about retiring— the marlin and tuna instantly show up and he immediately figures the job is worth another ten years.

San Diego is the home port of several world-known skippers, including Frank LoPreste, a pioneer for long-range trips. These are the fellows who are the top public fish catchers anywhere, who guide their customers across miles of ocean in search of the best saltwater angling on the Pacific Coast. Very often, they find it.

14.   LOWER OTAY LAKE

Reference: Southeast of San Diego; map J6 grid h2.

How to get there: From San Diego, drive south on Interstate 805 to Chula Vista. Turn east on Telegraph Canyon Road and drive five miles to Otay Lakes Road. Turn right and travel two miles east, then turn south on Wueste Road. The boat ramp is located off Wueste Road on the west shore.

Facilities: A boat ramp, boat rentals, picnic areas, a snack bar, and bait and tackle are available at the lake. A campground is located at Otay County Park at the south end of the lake.

Cost: Fishing fee is $3.50-$4 per person. There is a fee for boat launching.

Who to contact: Phone San Diego Water Utilities, Lake Department, at (619) 465-4500; Lake Hotline, (619) 443-2510.

Special note: Open Wednesdays, Saturdays and Sundays from mid-January through mid-October.

About Lower Otay Lake: Imagine a five-bass limit that weighed 53 pounds, 12 ounces . . . such an image might make your brain gears squeak. This is the record limit that Jack Neu caught at Otay, part of a great success story. It is detailed in the Secrets of the Masters section on bass fishing. I fished with Jack on that legendary March day, when there were 35 bass that weighed eight pounds or better weighed in over a two-hour span. The lake record weighed 18 pounds, 12 ounces.

From hearing that, you may think all you have to do is show up and you'll catch a 10-pounder. Unfortunately, it rarely works that way. Otay has long periods of very slow results despite intense fishing, then short periods of unbelievable snaps with giant fish.

Otay is set at 490 feet elevation in the foothills near Chula Vista, just north of the California/Mexico border. When full, the lake covers 1,265 acres and has a variety of habitat, including submerged trees, tules, and underwater holes and ledges. Shad, crawdads and primary levels of aquatic life are abundant, so the bass have plenty of food and grow quite fast.

The key are the shad. When the bass start rounding up the shad, the entire lake seems to come alive. Most anglers will use golden shiners, crawdads or cast large Countdown Rapalas, Shad Raps or Rattletraps. By the way, Jack Neu caught his limit with crawdads.

After launching, the best bet is to head up one of the two major lake arms, and not go down toward the dam area. One of the phenomenons at Otay is that early in the year, the Otay arm always has warmer water compared to the Harvey arm. That can make a big difference in February and early March, when the bass can be in the top 10 to 15 feet of water in the Otay arm, but still 25 to 35 feet deep in the Harvey arm.

A few other notes about Otay: An aeration system should help during the summer months, allowing the fish to have a wider vertical habitat zone, rather than a very thin thermocline. That should make for higher bass populations. Another note is that in the fall, catch rates can be very good for know-hows casting plastic worms around the tules, though newcomers can feel like ramming their heads against a wall.

Finally, between those short periods with wide-open bites, the best fortune comes to anglers who use precision graphs to find groups of fish, toss out a buoy to mark the spot, then cast shiners or crawdads toward the buoy. That is how Jack Neu did it, and you can't argue with the only 50-pound limit caught in history.

---

15.   LAKE MORENA

Reference: East of San Diego at Lake Morena County Park; map J6 grid h8.

How to get there: From San Diego, drive approximately 53 miles east on Interstate 8. Take the County Road S1 (Buckman Springs Road) exit and drive five miles south to Oak Drive. Turn right and follow the signs to the park.

Facilities: A campground, a boat ramp, boat rentals, picnic areas, a snack bar, bait, tackle, and groceries are available at the lake. Boats under nine or over 18 feet are prohibited.

Cost: Fishing fee is $3.50 per person. There is a fee for boat launching.

Who to contact: Phone Lake Morena County Park at (619) 565-3600.

About Lake Morena: You want fish? You get fish. Lake Morena may be the most consistent producer of bass in California, an easy winner, providing a few details are taken into consideration. It's located out in the boondocks, but it is worth the trip. If you like bass, make it.

The key here is the elevation. The lake is set at 3,200 feet elevation just south of Cleveland National Forest, and only seven or eight miles from the California/Mexico border. Because of the altitude, everything gets going a little later in the season than at lakes set at lower elevations and closer to San Diego. Some folks show up in early March, find the bass deep and sluggish, and wonder, "What's all the fuss about Morena?" Show up a month later, however, and you'll find out.

From April through July, Morena consistently produces bass: small ones, big ones, medium ones. It's just flat a fish-catching place. The lake has a lot of brush-lined shore, a lot of rocks, and the bass will hang amid these areas. One of the top spots includes Goat Island, particularly on the back side; but with Morena at 1,000 surface acres when full, a boat and electric motor helps you cover all the good spots in a weekend.

Before the fish move into the shallows, the fishing is best on plastic worms. Then, just like that, when the fish move into the top five, ten feet of water, it's a great lake for casting surface lures. It is exciting fishing, with the strikes coming right on top. Try the Rebel Pop-R, Jitterbug, Zara Spook, floating Rapala, or Chugger. If you have a fly rod, bring it along and lay small poppers along the surface. Bass? There are plenty.

The lake is also stocked with trout, and they provide a fair alternative. The DFG stocks 12,000 rainbow trout in the seven, eight-inch class and another 4,000 to 11 inches. They are more like bass-growing pills, however, and the lake record proves it. It weighed 19 pounds, 2 ounces. Morena also has catfish, bluegill and crappie.

If you haven't fished Lake Morena in several years, then you may just laugh and say, "I know that lake, it's the one with all the dinks." That's right, Morena used to be loaded with small bass. But the evolution of this lake has continued onward since those days. Now, there are bass of all sizes, and they are biters.

MAP J7

1 LISTING
PAGES 728-731

SO-CAL MAP ....see page 656
adjoining maps
NORTH (I7)........see page 698
EAST (J8) ....see page 732
SOUTH ....no map
WEST (J6) ....see page 712

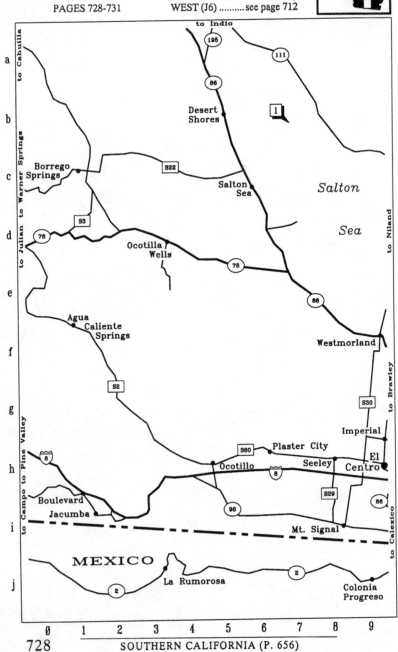

to Indio

195

111

86

Desert
Shores

1

to Cahuilla

Borrego
Springs

S22

Salton
Sea

Salton

to Warner Springs

S3

Sea

78

Ocotilla
Wells

78

86

to Julian to

to Niland

Agua
Caliente
Springs

Westmorland

S2

to Brawley

S30

Imperial

to Pine Valley

S80

Plaster City

8

Ocotillo

Seeley

El

8

Centro

S29

86

Boulevard

98

Jacumba

to Campo

to Calexico

Mt. Signal

MEXICO

to Colexico

2

La Rumorosa

2

Colonia
Progreso

2

1. SALTON SEA

Reference: East of San Diego; map J7 grid b7.

How to get there: From the Los Angeles area, turn east on Interstate 10. Drive east to Indio, then turn south on Highway 111. To reach the east shore of the lake, continue south on Highway 111. To access the west shore, drive about five miles south on Highway 111, then turn south on Highway 86 and continue to the lake. Boat ramps are available at the following locations: Bombay Beach Marina (east shore), Bob's Riveria (east shore), Chris & Al's (east shore), Salton Sea Beach Marina (west shore), Salton Sea State Recreation Area (west shore).

Facilities: Campgrounds, full-service marinas, boat ramps, picnic areas, lodging, restaurants, bait, tackle and groceries are available at various locations around the lake.

Cost: A nominal fee is charged at most marinas and resorts for day-use and/or boat launching.

Who to contact: Phone Salton Sea State Recreation Area, (619) 393-3052; Bombay Beach Marina, (619) 354-4049.

About Salton Sea: Some people pray for rain. Some people pray for riches. At the Salton Sea, you pray for the wind not to blow.

When this huge but shallow saltwater lake calms down, the fish immediately responds, with outstanding corvina action quickly following. The fish often range from a foot to 15 pounds, sometimes bigger, and during a good bite, you can catch plenty of them. It is exciting fishing, too, casting lures in shallow water.

When you first see the Salton Sea, it appears to be a desolate, god-forbidden wasteland. The lake is 35 miles long but with an average depth of just 10 feet, and is surrounded by nothingness for miles in all directions. When the wind blows, nothing slows it down, and it can howl across the water, whipping up large waves that are dangerous to boaters. To help warn newcomers of the arrival of hazardous winds, local authorities have posted a flashing red light on the northeast shore to warn boaters to get off the lake.

But when it calms, this lake can provide some of the best catch rates in California. All you need is a boat and a little luck in the weather, then you can start exploring. And away you go, casting a 3 1/2-inch Thinfin Silver Shad, the one with the gray-scale fish, sinking variety. Tie the lure directly to your line without a swivel, and after casting, use an erratic, hesitating retrieve. If you don't care to catch high numbers of corvina, but would rather try for just the big ones, use live bait, with a croaker the preferred entreaty. It is advisable to use 16 to 20-pound line in order to keep from getting too many serious nicks from underwater barnacles and all matter of structure from old fences, trees, even signs that are now submerged.

In the winter and early spring, the first area of the lake that comes to life is the southeastern end, but any backwater bay where the water temperature is warm enough to get the fish active is worth exploring. The best bet during the cool months is waiting for a period when the wind is down and the temperature is at least 70 degrees for three straight days. That's when the corvina come to life and go on the bite, often in the shallows. In the summer, you need to take a different approach. Day after day of 100-degree temperatures heats up the shallows and depletes the backwater bays of oxygen, so you need to fish deeper, 10 to 15 feet down, and sometimes as deep as 20 feet down.

In recent years, the introduction of tilapia have provided an option, and with abundant numbers of corvina, this lake can provide one of the state's unique and great fisheries. It's a good thing, too, because the place is ugly, maybe the ugliest fishing spot on Planet Earth. It is right up there with the California Aqueduct west of Bakersfield for sheer ugliness. But for fishermen who know how good the corvina fishing can be, they know well that doing good beats looking good.

MAP J8

2 LISTINGS
PAGES 732-735

SO-CAL MAP ....see page 656
adjoining maps
NORTH.......................no map
EAST (J9) ....see page 736
SOUTH ....no map
WEST (J7) ....see page 728

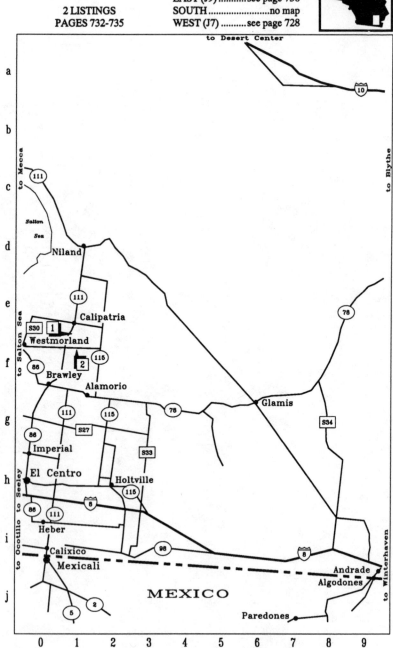

to Desert Center

a

b

to Mecca
(111)
c

Salton Sea

d   Niland

(111)
e   Calipatria

to Salton Sea   S30 [1]
Westmorland

f   (86)   [2] (115)
Brawley
Alamorio

(111)   (115)
g   S27   (78)   Glamis
(86)   S34
Imperial   S33

h   El Centro   Holtville
(8)   (115)

to Ocotillo to Seeley   (86)
(111)
i   Heber
Calixico   (98)   (8)   to Winterhaven
Mexicali   Andrade
Algodones

j   MEXICO
(2)
(5)   Paredones

to Blythe
(10)
(78)

| 0 | 1 | 2 | 3 | 4 | 5 | 6 | 7 | 8 | 9 |

1. RAMER LAKE

Reference: In Imperial Wildlife Area near Calipatria; map J8 grid f1.

How to get there: From the Los Angeles area, turn east on Interstate 10. Drive east to Indio, then turn south on Highway 111 and drive about 70 miles. As you leave Calipatria, look for the sign for Ramer Lake. Turn left and continue to the lake.

Facilities: Vault toilets and a boat launch are provided. A campground is available to the south at Weist Lake.

Cost: Access is free.

Who to contact: Phone Imperial Wildlife Area at (619) 348-2493 or (619) 359-0577.

About Ramer Lake: Almost nobody knows about little Ramer Lake, that is, except for a few duck hunters. It is located in the Imperial Wildlife Area, which provides waterfowl habitat and duck hunting grounds during the winter. The rest of the year it is largely ignored, except for a handful of folks who fish the lake for bass, catfish, and that world-favorite, carp.

It is set in the Imperial Valley, surrounded by farmland, with the massive Salton Sea to the nearby north overshadowing it. One requirement at Ramer Lake is that you must register at the entrance station to the wildlife area, then leave a written record of anything you've caught. That way they can keep track of the carp.

2. WEIST LAKE

Reference: In Weist Lake County Park south of Calipatria; map J8 grid f1.

How to get there: From the Los Angeles area, turn east on Interstate 10. Drive east to Indio, then turn south on Highway 111 and drive about 75 miles to Rutherford Road (about five miles south of Calipatria). Turn left and continue east to the park.

Facilities: A campground, a boat ramp, picnic areas, and a snack bar are available. Supplies are available in Calipatria.

Cost: Day-use fee is around $2 per vehicle; rates may change from season to season. Entrance fee includes boat-launching privileges.

Who to contact: Phone Weist Lake County Park at (619) 344-3712.

About Weist Lake: If you think nobody knows about the previously-listed Ramer Lake, then imagine the brain gap for Weist Lake. This is just a large pond, actually, filled by the Alamo River, but what the heck, it gets stocked with rainbow trout, decent ones at that. It gets 6,000 a year courtesy of Fish and Game, and these aren't dinkers, but average in the 11-inch class, a few bigger and smaller. The trout fishing is in the winter, of course, when the temperatures are habitable. In the spring and summer, this place really heats up and the trout fishing goes kaput. But fair prospects for bass and catfish, with a sprinkling of bluegill as well, come to the rescue. The Imperial Valley is something of a wasteland, but little Weist Lake provides a nice little spot that only locals know about.

MAP J9

1 LISTING
PAGES 736-738

SO-CAL MAP ....see page 656
adjoining maps
NORTH (I9)........see page 700
EAST ....no map
SOUTH ....no map
WEST (J8) ....see page 732

COLORADO RIVER

Reference: From Blythe to Yuma; map J9 grid a4.

How to get to the Blythe-Palo Verde area: From the Los Angeles area, turn east on Interstate 10 and travel to Blythe, located about three miles west of the California-Arizona border. Numerous resorts, marinas and access points are available in Blythe, as well as in Palo Verde farther south. The Palo Verde area may be reached by driving south on Highway 78 to the town of Palo Verde.

How to get to the Yuma-Winterhaven area: From San Diego, turn east on Interstate 8 and drive east to Winterhaven on the California-Arizona border. Turn north on either County Road S24 or Picacho Road and continue to signed access spots.

Facilities: Campgrounds, lodging, picnic areas, full-service marinas, boat ramps, bait, tackle and groceries are available in Blythe, Palo Verde, Picacho State Recreation Area, Senator Wash Recreation Area, Yuma, and Winterhaven.

Cost: Most resorts and marinas charge a nominal fee for day-use and/or boat launching.

Who to contact: Phone the Bureau of Land Management, (602) 726-6300; McIntyre Park in Blythe, (619) 922-5350; Palo Verde County Park, (619) 339-4384; Picacho State Recreation Area (north of Winterhaven), (619) 393-3052; Imperial Oasis (north of Yuma), (602) 783-4171.

Special note: Waterskiing is prohibited below Imperial Dam and in the Imperial Wildlife Refuge, with the exception of the Picacho State Recreation Area.

About Colorado River: When most people think of the Colorado River, they picture parties and speedboats. Not this stretch of river. For the parties, head upstream (see Zones I9 and H9). For fishing in the spring and summer, and duck hunting in the fall, well, you came to the right place. Actually, this section has two major stretches of water, the Palo Verde area and the Yuma area. For more information on technique, see the details in Zone H9.

—Palo Verde Area: This span of water is flanked by agricultural areas, although several developed recreation areas and county parks are on the California side of the river near Palo Verde. Most visitor accommodations are in the Blythe area. The fishing is fair with striped bass, largemouth bass, bluegill, crappie and catfish roaming the area. It's not great; it's not terrible. It's fair.

—Yuma area: This stretch of river is located farther south, of course, and is less developed than the Palo Verde area. That is another way of saying there's damn near nothing out here, other than some recreation opportunities located near Imperial Dam. Some areas are marshy, and these areas provide an opportunity for duck hunting in the fall. For anglers, there are some big catfish roaming this area, along with small largemouth bass and a sprinkling of bluegill.

There are also many side-trip options in the area, from rockhunting in the Palo Verde Mountains to visiting several lakes on the Arizona side of the river, with Martinez Lake and Senator Wash Reservoir the best of the lot.

REFERENCE

ANGLING RECORDS

———— 🐟 ————

Pounds and ounces

■ FRESHWATER

RAINBOW TROUT (incl. steelhead) * 27-4
Smith River (Dec. 22, 1976)................Robert Halley

GOLDEN TROUT * 9-8
Virginia Lake (Aug. 18, 1952)...........O.A. Benefield

BROWN TROUT * 26-8
Upper Twin Lake (April 30, 1987).. Danny Stearman

CUTTHROAT TROUT * 31-8
Lake Tahoe (1911) .... William Pomin

BROOK TROUT * 9-12
Silver Lake (Sept. 9, 1932)................... Texas Haynes

MACKINAW TROUT * 37-6
Lake Tahoe (June 21, 1974).............Robert Aronsen

ARCTIC GRAYLING * 1-12
Lobdell Lake (Aug. 27, 1974)............ Don Acton, Jr.

KOKANEE SALMON * 4-13
Lake Tahoe (Aug. 1, 1973) .... Dick Bournique

KING SALMON * 88-0
Sacramento River (Nov. 21, 1979)....Lindy Lindberg

SILVER SALMON * 22-0
Lagunitas Creek (Jan. 3, 1959)............... Milton Hain

LARGEMOUTH BASS * 22-0
Lake Castaic (March 15, 1991) .... Bob Crupi

SMALLMOUTH BASS * 9-1
Trinity Lake (March 20, 1976)...................Tim Brady

SPOTTED BASS * 9-1
Lake Perris (Feb. 5, 1984) .... Jeff Matthews

STRIPED BASS * 66-0
O'Neill Forebay (June 29, 1988).............Ted Furnish

WHITE BASS * 5-5
Colorado River (May 8, 1972) ....Milton Mize

STURGEON * 468-0
San Pablo Bay (July 9, 1983) ....Joey Pallotta

WHITE CRAPPIE * 4-8
Clear Lake (April 26, 1971) .... Carol Carlton

BLACK CRAPPIE * 4-1
New Hogan Lake (March 29, 1975).... Wilma Honey

BLUEGILL * 3-8
Lower Otay Lake (July 10, 1991)...Davis Buckhanon

REDEAR SUNFISH * 3-7
Lake Casitas (Aug. 5, 1976)............. Nels Gorgensen

SACRAMENTO PERCH * 3-10
Crowley Lake (May 22, 1979)...............Jack Johnson

CHANNEL CATFISH * 48-8
Irvine Lake (June 14, 1987) ....Bobby Calhoun

WHITE CATFISH * 17-7
Lake Success (Nov. 10, 1981).................. Chuck Idell

BLUE CATFISH * 59-4
Irvine Lake (June 14, 1987) ... H. Pravongviengkham

BULLHEAD * 2-11
Hensley Lake (Jan. 11, 1991)...........Donald Templer

FLATHEAD CATFISH * 55-0
Colorado River (April, 1980) ....Herbert Caldwell

AMERICAN SHAD * 7-5
Feather River (May 9, 1985) ....Craig Stillwell

CORVINA * 37-0
Salton Sea (July 15, 1988)...................Dick Van Dam

SARGO * 4-1
Salton Sea (1972) ....Mike Leonte

CARP * 52-0
Lake Nacimiento (April, 1968) ....Lee Fryant

■ SALTWATER

ALBACORE * 79-0
Catalina Island (Oct. 19, 1985)................. Jim Martin

BARRACUDA * 15-15
San Onofre (Aug. 24, 1957) .....................C.O. Taylor

BOCACCIO * 17-8
Pt. St. George Reef (Oct. 25, 1987)........... Sam Strait

BONITO * 22-3
Malibu Cove (July 30, 1978)..................Gini Piccolo

CABEZON * 23-4
Los Angeles (April 20, 1958)..................Bruce Kuhn

DORADO * 66-0
209 Spot (Sept. 9, 1990)...........................Kim Carson

HALIBUT * 53-8
Santa Rosa Island (May 28, 1975) ....Henre Kelemen

LINGCOD * 53-0
Trinidad (1969).................................... Steve Hedglin

JACK MACKEREL * 5-8
Huntington Beach (Sept. 1, 1988)............Joe Bairian

BLUE MARLIN * 672-0 Balboa (Aug. 18, 1931)...........................A. Hamann	**THRESHER SHARK * 527-0** San Diego (Oct. 4, 1980)...............Kenneth Schilling
STRIPED MARLIN * 339-0 Catalina Island (July 4, 1985)..................Gary Jasper	**BLUE SHARK * 231-0** Santa Cruz Island (Aug. 9, 1974)....Robert L. Ballew
OPALEYE * 6-4 Los Flores Creek (May 13, 1956)........Leonard Itkoff	**SHEEPHEAD * 28-14** Paradise Cove (Dec. 6, 1978).........Tibor Molnar, Jr.
BAT RAY * 181-0 Huntington Beach (July 24, 1978).........Bradley Dew	**SWORDFISH * 337-12** San Clemente Island (July 6, 1958).......Keith Grover
BLACK ROCKFISH * 9-2 S. F. Mile Light (Sept. 3, 1988).............Trent Wilcox	**BLUEFIN TUNA * 243-11** 277 Spot (Sept. 8, 1990)................Karl Schmidbauer
COPPER ROCKFISH * 8-3 Pigeon Point (Aug. 18, 1985)...................Kenny Aab	**BIGEYE TUNA * 240-0** Butterfly Bank (Aug. 1, 1987).......Steve Hutchinson
SILVER SALMON * 33-8 Newport Beach (Sept. 9, 1970) .... Harry Bouchard	**YELLOWFIN TUNA * 239-0** Catalina Island (Nov. 4, 1984).........Ronald Howarth
KING SALMON * Open Minimum weight of 35 pounds required for entry.	**SKIPJACK TUNA * 26-0** San Diego (Aug. 28, 1970)....................William Hall
WHITE SEABASS * 77-4 San Diego (April 8, 1950).....................H.P. Bledsoe	**WHITEFISH * 13-12** Cortes Bank (April 23, 1988)...............Bob Schwenk
MAKO SHARK * 298-0 Anacapa Island (July 20, 1970)...............Jack Cleric	**YELLOWTAIL * 62-0** La Jolla (June 6, 1953) ....George Willett

IGFA WORLD RECORDS SET IN CALIFORNIA

■ **FRESHWATER**

LARGEMOUTH BASS
* 16-14; Lake Castaic (2-lb. line)............... Bob Crupi
* 17-1; Lake Castaic (4-lb. line) .... Bob Crupi
* 21-3; Lake Casitas (8-lb. line) ....Ray Easley
* 22-0; Lake Castaic (12-lb. line) .... Bob Crupi
* 19-1; Lake Castaic (20-lb. line)............Dan Kadota

SPOTTED BASS
* 6-5; Lake Perris (2-lb. line) .... Gilbert Rowe
* 7-5; Lake Perris (4-lb. line) .... Gilbert Rowe
* 9-4; Lake Perris (8-lb. line) ....Steven West
* 9-4; Lake Perris (8-lb. line) .... Gilbert Rowe
* 8-11; Lake Perris (12-lb. line) .... Gilbert Rowe
* 9-3; Lake Perris (16-lb. line) ....Barry Hill
* 9-3; Lake Perris (16-lb. line) .... Gilbert Rowe

STRIPED BASS (landlocked)
* 55-0; O'Neill Forebay(12-lb. line) .. Fred Brand, Jr.
* 66-0; O'Neill Forebay (16-lb. line) ......Ted Furnish

BLUEGILL
* 1-10; Lake Perris (2-lb. line) .... Gary Smith

BLUE CATFISH
* 11-8; Dixon Lake (2-lb. line)...... Kevin Woodward
* 58-8; Irvine Lake (8-lb. line)..................Glenn Bell

WHITE CATFISH
* 17-7; Success Lake (16-lb. line) .... Chuck Idell

STURGEON
* 36-0; Lower Delta (2-lb. line) ....Walt Peterson
* 82-0; S. F. Bay (8-lb. line)..................Ron Johnson
* 179-12; Suisun Bay (16-lb. line) ..... Ron Bernhardt

* 237-0; Lower Delta (20-lb. line) ....Alvin Threet
* 390-0; Lower Delta (30-lb. line) ....Bill Stratton
* 322-4; Lower Delta (50-lb. line) ......Pete Anderson
* 468-0; San Pablo Bay (80-lb. line)......Joey Pallotta

BROOK TROUT
* 7-12; Gull Lake (16-lb. line) ....Eric Petersen

■ **SALTWATER**

ALBACORE
* 68-12; Port San Luis (12-lb. line)........ Kevin Crow
* 71-12; Catalina Channel (16-lb. line).......Roy Ludt

STRIPED BASS (non-landlocked)
* 18-6; Suisun Bay (2-lb. line) .... Sandy Ballard

PACIFIC BONITO
* 13-2; La Jolla (8-lb. line).................. Tom Edmunds
* 13-7; Balboa (16-lb. line) ....Bill Seiler
* 21-3; Malibu (20-lb. line)...................Gini Picciolo

CALIFORNIA HALIBUT
* 14-13; Santa Monica (4-lb. line) .... Chris Hart
* 31-12; Oceanside Harbor (8-lb. line)... Steve Mares
* 45-0; Santa Cruz Island (12-lb. line) . Jack Meserve
* 45-1; Redondo Beach (16-lb. line) .... Mike Rogalla
* 53-4; Santa Rosa Is. (20-lb. line) ... Russell Harmon
* 48-8; Cortez Bank (30-lb. line) .... Ron Crawford

WHITE SEABASS
* 56-0; La Jolla Trench (16-lb. line) .... Josh Clark
* 77-4; San Diego (50-lb. line)..............H.P. Bledsoe
* 74-0; Catalina Island (80-lb. line) . Allan Tromblay

MAKO SHARK
* 31-12; Catalina Channel (2-lb. line)....Robert Levy

ANGLING RECORDS   **741**

THRESHER SHARK
* 36-0; Santa Monica Bay (4-lb. line)....Robert Levy
* 91-8; Santa Monica Bay (8-lb. line)....James Olson
* 159-8; Santa Monica Bay
    (12-lb. line)................... Donald McPherson, Jr.
* 215-0; Santa Monica Bay
    (16-lb. line).................... Donald McPherson, Jr.
* 207-0; Catalina Channel (20-lb. line)........ Leo Dee
* 329-0; Newport Beach (30-lb. line)... Michael Welt

PACIFIC BIGEYE TUNA
* 83-0; San Diego (8-lb. line)................Robert Kurz
* 143-8; Santa Cruz Is. (12-lb. line) . David Denholm
* 157-12; San Clemente Is.
    (16-lb. test) ....Jerry Wells, Sr.
* 137-0; San Diego (20-lb. test) .... Gary Graham

CALIFORNIA YELLOWTAIL
* 41-8; Catalina Island (12-lb. line) Charles Beckhart
* 56-14; Catalina Island
    (16-lb. line)..............................Ronald Howarth
* 59-0; La Jolla (20-lb. line)......... Stephen Whybrew

IGFA FLY ROD RECORDS SET IN CALIFORNIA

LARGEMOUTH BASS
* 13-9; Lake Morena (8-lb. tippet) .... Ned Sewell

STRIPED BASS (landlocked)
* 27-0; San Luis Res. (8-lb. tippet) ..... Al Whitehurst
* 40-4; O'Neill Forebay
    (12-lb. tippet)..............................Al Whitehurst
* 54-8; O'Neill Forebay
    (16-lb. tippet)..............................Al Whitehurst

STRIPED BASS (non-landlocked)
* 42-0; Sacramento River(8-lb. tippet).. Ron Hayashi

BROWN BULLHEAD
* 1-1; Lake Arrowhead (2-lb. tippet).Jim Lindsay, Jr.

AMERICAN SHAD
* 7-4; Feather River (2-lb. tippet).......... Rod Neubert
* 6-7; Yuba River (8-lb. tippet)... Eugene Schweitzer
* 6-12; Feather R. (12-lb. tippet).... James Humphrey

ALBACORE
* 26-2; San Diego (12-lb. tippet)...........Les Eichhorn

PACIFIC BONITO
* 3-13; Santa Monica Bay
    (2-lb. tippet)..................................Terry Greene
* 3-10; Santa Monica Bay
    (4-lb. tippet)..................................Terry Greene
* 15-8; Monterey Bay (12-lb. tippet) .... Bob Edgley
* 1-2; San Diego (16-lb. tippet). Robert Woodard, Jr.

WHITE SEABASS
* 12-6; Santa Cruz Island (12-lb. tippet) Roy Lawson

BLUE SHARK
* 140-0; Anacapa Island (16-lb. tippet).... Steve Abel

SKIPJACK TUNA
* 14-12; Santa Barbara (8-lb. tippet).... Patt Wardlaw
* 15-0; Santa Barbara (12-lb. tippet).... Patt Wardlaw

YELLOWTAIL
* 6-2; Santa Monica Bay (4-lb. tippet)...Roy Lawson
* 17-10; Anacapa Island (8-lb. tippet)....Roy Lawson

IGFA ALL-TACKLE WORLD RECORDS
State or country noted unless set in California

ALBACORE
* 88-2; Canary Island
    (Nov. 19, 1977) .... Siegfried Dickemann

BARRED SAND BASS
* 13-3; Huntington Beach
    (Aug. 29, 1988) ....Robert Halal

LARGEMOUTH BASS
* 22-4; Georgia (June 2, 1932)..............George Perry

SAND BASS
* 8-11; Oceanside (July 1, 1989).............Dave Bruce

SMALLMOUTH BASS
* 11-15; Kentucky (July 9, 1955).......... David Hayes

SPOTTED BASS
* 9-4; Perris Lake
    (Jan., April, 1987) .... Steve West, Gilbert Rowe

BLUEGILL
* 4-12; Alabama (April 9, 1959) .............T.S. Hudson

BONITO
* 23-8; Seychelles (Feb. 19, 1975)......Anne Cochain

CHANNEL CATFISH
* 58-0; South Carolina (July 7, 1964) .. W.B. Whaley

WHITE CATFISH
* 17-7; Lake Success (Nov. 15, 1981) .... Chuck Idell

BLACK CRAPPIE
* 4-8; Virginia (March 1, 1981) ....Carl Herring, Jr.

WHITE CRAPPIE
* 5-3; Mississippi (July 31, 1957)............Fred Bright

CALIFORNIA HALIBUT
* 53-4; Santa Rosa Is. (July 7, 1988).... Russ Harmon

PACIFIC HALIBUT
* 356-8; Alaska (Nov. 8, 1986)................Greg Olsen

KOKANEE SALMON
* 9-6; British Columbia (June 18, 1988).Norm Kuhn

LINGCOD
* 64-0; Alaska (Aug. 2, 1988) ....David Bauer

STRIPED MARLIN
* 494-0; New Zealand (Jan. 16, 1986) ..Bill Boniface

BLUE MARLIN
* 1376-0; Hawaii (May 31, 1982).....Jay deBeaubien

YELLOW PERCH
* 4-3; New Jersey (May, 1865) ................C.C. Abbot

PACIFIC SAILFISH
* 221-0; Ecuador (Feb. 12, 1947)......... C.W. Stewart

KING SALMON
* 97-4; Alaska (May 17, 1985).............Les Anderson

SILVER SALMON
* 33-4; New York (Sept. 27, 1989) ....Jerry Lifton

WHITE SEABASS
* 83-12; Mexico
     (March 31, 1953)..................L.C. Baumgardner

AMERICAN SHAD
* 11-4; Massachusetts (May 19, 1986)..Bob Thibodo

BLUE SHARK
* 437-0; Australia (Oct. 2, 1976).............. Peter Hyde

LEOPARD SHARK
* 18-5; Ventura (April 12, 1989)............ Paul Bodtke

HAMMERHEAD SHARK
* 991; Florida (May 30, 1982) .... Allen Ogle

GREAT WHITE SHARK
* 2,664; Australia (April 21, 1959) .... Alfred Dean

SKATE
* 144-0; Scotland (Nov. 16, 1984) ..Brian Swinbanks

STRIPED BASS (landlocked)
* 66-0; O'Neill Forebay
(June 29, 1988)......................................Ted Furnish

STRIPED BASS (non-landlocked)
* 78-8; New Jersey (Sept. 21, 1982) .Al McReynolds

STURGEON
* 468; San Pablo Bay (July 9, 1983) ......Joey Pallotta

REDEAR SUNFISH
* 4-12; Florida (March 13, 1986)............. Joey Floyd

BROOK TROUT
* 14-8; Canada (July, 1916) ......................W.J. Cook

BROWN TROUT
* 35-15; Argentina
     (Ded. 16, 1952) ....Eugenio Cavaglia

CUTTHROAT TROUT
* 41-0; Pyramid Lake, Nevada
     (Dec., 1925)..........................John Skimmerhorn

GOLDEN TROUT
* 11-0; Wyoming (Aug. 5, 1948).........Charles Reed

MACKINAW TROUT
* 65-0; Northwest Territories
     (Aug. 8, 1970) ....Larry Daunis

RAINBOW TROUT (steelhead)
* 42-2; Alaska (June 22, 1970) ....David White

BIGEYE TUNA
* 435-0; Peru (April 17, 1957) .... Russell Lee

YELLOWFIN TUNA
* 388-12; Mexico (April 1, 1977) .Curt Wiesenhutter

WAHOO
* 155-8; Bahamas (April 3, 1990).... William Bourne

YELLOWTAIL
* 78-0; Baja (June 27, 1987) ....Richard Cresswell

Note: For information about world records,
write the International Game Fish Association, 3000 E. Las Olas Boulevard, Fort Lau-
derdale, FL 33316-1616, or phone at (305)
467-0161. For information about California
state records, write the Department of Fish
and Game, Inland Fisheries, 1416 Ninth
Street, Sacramento, CA 95814, or phone at
(916) 653-6420.

INDEX

750

---

764   REFERENCE

White Slough: 471
white-water rafting: 328
Whitehurst, Al: 555
Whitney Portal Camp: 593, 616
Whitney Portal Store: 593
Whittier: 674
Whittier Narrows Recreation Area: 674
Wohlford Lake: 713
Wickiup Camp: 669
Wild Lake: 144
Wildyrie Lodge: 530
Williams, Rolla: 723
Willits: 249-250
Willits Chamber of Commerce: 251
WILLOW CREEK: 161, 279, 306
Willow Glen Creek: 349
WILLOW LAKE: 279-280
Willow Springs: 282
Willows: 259
Wilmer Lake: 511
WILSON LAKE: 282
Wilson Meadow Lake: 503
Wilsonia: 590
Winifred Lake: 392-393
Winnemucca Lake: 402
Winterhaven: 737
Winters: 334
Wire Lakes: 503
Wishon Village: 575

WISHON RESERVOIR: 575
Wittenberg Creek: 604
Wohler Bridge: 318
Wolf Creek: 326
Wolverine Lake: 144
Woodchuck Country: 576
Woodchuck Creek: 576
Woodchuck Lake: 576
Woodfords: 399, 406
Woodlake: 609
Woods Creek: 402, 587
WOODS LAKE: 350, 394, 401-402
Woods Lodge: 531
Woodside: 248
Woodson Bridge State Park: 267
WOODWARD RESERVOIR: 485
Woody's Sportfishing: 389
Wooley Creek: 144
Wooley Lake: 144
WOOLLOMES LAKE: 611
Wotan's Throne: 593
Wright Lakes: 144
WRIGHTS LAKE: 394-395
Wyandotte: 295

— Y —

Yellow Bluff: 435
YELLOW CREEK: 288
yellow perch: 13-14, 148
yellow rockfish: 412

Yellowhammer Lake: 503
yellowtail rockfish: 74, 98, 597, 632, 660, 663-664, 707, 709, 723
yellowtail seabass: 630
Yolla Bollies: 259
Yolla-Bolly Lake: 194, 257
YOLLA-BOLLY MIDDLE EEL WILDERNESS: 257
YOLLA-BOLLY WILDERNESS: 194, 257
Yosemite: 525
Yosemite Forks: 567
YOSEMITE LAKE: 491
Yosemite National Park: 488, 494, 502, 506, 508-510, 512-514, 520
Young Lakes: 511
Young's Corral Springs: 262
Yreka: 142, 147-148
Yuba City: 342, 343
Yuba County: 349
Yuba Gap: 362
Yuba River: 276, 342
Yuba River Canyon: 359
Yuma: 737

— Z —

Zimmer, Dave "Hank": 431, 458
Zimmer, Ed: 458
Zmudowski State Beach: 546
Zuma Beach: 664

ABOUT THE AUTHOR

Tom Stienstra is the outdoors editor of the
San Francisco Examiner, the camping editor
of *Western Outdoor Magazine*, and was
named **Outdoor Writer of the Year** in 1990.
He has been an angler all his life, traveling
throughout California in search of secret
places to camp and catch fish.

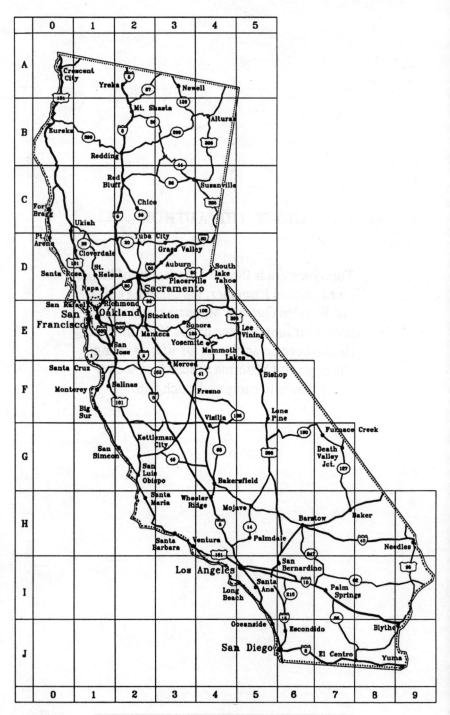